The *NEW*
MURDERERS'
Who's Who

'Gentlemen, I'll tell you the plain truth.
Every day of the year we take up a paper,
we read the opening of a murder.'

THOMAS DE QUINCEY

The *NEW* MURDERERS' Who's Who

J. H. H. Gaute and Robin Odell

Forewords by

Colin Wilson and Richard Whittington-Egan

DORSET PRESS
New York

For our wives
FRANCES GAUTE and JOAN ODELL
with love and a huge 'thank-you' for
their unstinting help and patience while
this volume was being prepared

This edition published by Dorset Press,
a division of Marboro Books Corporation,
by arrangement with W. H. Allen & Co. Plc
1991 Dorset Press

ISBN 0-88029-582-1

Printed in the United States of America
M 9 8 7 6 5 4 3 2 1

Contents

Foreword
by Colin Wilson

It must have been in the year 1881 that John H. Watson, M.D., made a list of the educational qualifications of his newly acquired flat-mate which included the comment: 'Knowledge of Sensational Literature—Immense. He appears to know every detail of every horror perpetrated in the century.' The flat-mate was, of course, Sherlock Holmes, and his creator, Conan Doyle, showed remarkable prescience in endowing him with this encyclopaedic knowledge of crime; for in the year 1881 the science we now know as criminology was virtually non-existent. In the previous chapter of *A Study in Scarlet* Doyle displayed another piece of inspired foresight. As Watson and Stamford approach Holmes in the laboratory at Bart's, Holmes introduces himself with the words 'I've found it! I've found it!' What he has found is an infallible test for bloodstains—a test that was not to be discovered in actuality for another twenty years, when Paul Uhlenhuth performed some classic experiments with rabbit-blood serum.

It would be interesting to know what passed through Conan Doyle's mind when he first sketched the character of Holmes. We know that the model for Holmes was Dr Joseph Bell, the surgeon at the Edinburgh Infirmary, who had a remarkable capacity for inferring the professions of his patients from their clothes or manners. It seems clear that what fascinated Doyle about Sherlock Holmes was that Holmes is in his way *a man of genius*—and one whose genius is exercised in the peculiar sphere of crime. Such a thing had never been known—or at least, Doyle himself could not have known about it. For the only man of genius—or near-genius—who had at that time exercised his intellectual powers in the sphere of crime was the Italian 'alienist' (the nineteenth-century term for a mind-doctor) Cesare Lombroso. 'Lombroso was one of the group of great thinkers of the nineteenth century who had the courage and the wisdom to apply the positive, inductive method of modern science to the study of human and social phenomena,' says Dr Maurice Parmelee in his introduction to Lombroso's *Crime: Its Causes and Remedies* (1911). And this, it would seem, is what Holmes had in mind, when he explains the advantages of his blood test: 'I could name a score of cases in which it would have been decisive.'

Now, the interesting point is that not only was there no science of criminology in 1881—Lombroso's *L'Uomo Delinquente* was not published until 1899—but that Holmes would have been unable to obtain accounts of these cases he mentions from books. The Victorian tabloid *Illustrated Police News* might have provided him with the outline of a few cases as far off as Germany or America, but Holmes would certainly have found it too sensational and unreliable—certainly not sufficiently detailed to satisfy his own passion for precision. In fact, Holmes would have had considerable difficulty in studying the history of crime in his own century. The last great compilation of criminal cases had been *The Newgate Calendar* of 1774, reissued in 1825 with a sprinkling of nineteenth-century cases. And when, many years before Holmes met Watson, a barrister named Camden Pelham edited a two-volume compilation with the promising title *Chronicles of Crime, or the New Newgate Calendar* it turned out to be basically a reissue of the old *Newgate Calendar* with a few later additions.

What it seems to amount to, then, is that for some odd reason the British public in the nineteenth century had no desire to purchase books on crime. Why should this be so? I can only imagine that it was because the book-buying public of the nineteenth century was basically middle class, and the Victorian bourgeoisie were too high-minded to show a morbid interest in the crimes of their own century. The only comprehensive history that Holmes might have possessed was Luke Owen Pike's bulky *History of Crime in England* (1876), which is really a history of criminal law. The Victorians felt that crime was simply a disagreeable footnote to history, and preferred to read novels and volumes of sermons.

One has to admit that they had a point. The reasons that led the Elizabethans or Jacobeans to purchase pamphlets about the execution of notorious criminals were the same as those that guarantee the sales of our more sensational newspapers—morbidity and prurience. Yet no one could accuse Holmes of a fascination with the gruesome for its own sake. Neither was it simply the pleasure of hunting down the criminal—a kind of glorified sportsmanship. Its precise nature become clear in the early story *A Case of Identity*, first published in 1891:

> 'My dear fellow,' said Sherlock Holmes, as we sat on either side of the fire in his lodgings at Baker Street, 'life is infinitely stranger than anything that the mind of man could invent. We would not dare to conceive the things which are really mere commonplaces of existence. If we could fly out of that window hand in hand, hover over this great city, gently remove the roofs, and peep in at the queer things which are going on, the strange coincidences, the plannings, the cross-purposes, the wonderful chain of events, working through generations, and leading to the most *outré* results, it would make all fiction with its conventionalities and foreseen conclusions most stale and unprofitable.'

You could express the point crudely by saying that crime has touched Holmes's poetic imagination; but that tells us little. What Holmes is really trying to say is that as he looks down on London, and thinks about all the crimes that are taking place, he has a sense of contemplating vast and interesting *patterns*. The first work of which he might have approved appeared in 1898—*Mysteries of Police and Crime* by Major Arthur Griffiths. This makes some attempt to offer a history of the police force, and to classify crimes under various headings. Then with the new century came the flood—dozens, hundreds of books on crime, with titles like *Crimes of Passion, Sidelights on Criminal Matters, Twenty Years at the Yard*, and so on. There was a new reading public, which had been created by universal education, and it revelled in accounts of famous criminal cases—the more gruesome the better.

At which point I have to speak of my own small part in this story of the literature of crime. I must have been about ten years old when my father borrowed from a friend a compilation called *The Fifty Most Amazing Crimes of the Last Hundred Years*. I read it from end to end. I found the subject fascinating, and graduated to reading issues of the American *True Detective* magazines. When at the age of eighteen I began to write my first novel, *Ritual in the Dark* (based loosely on the Jack the Ripper murders), I spent weeks in the British Museum reading-room, studying the original accounts of the Ripper in *The Times* for 1888. I came across Karl Berg's book on the 'Düsseldorf Ripper' Peter Kürten, *The Sadist*, and was fascinated by the light it threw on the Ripper case. My interest in the history of crime—which had lapsed during my teens—suddenly revived, and I began to study parallel cases—Vacher, Grossmann, Denke, Haarmann, Fish, Pommerencke. After my first book, *The Outsider*, appeared in 1956, I made a habit of picking up books on crime whenever I saw them in second-hand shops. By the time *Ritual in the Dark* finally appeared in 1960, I had five hundred or so. (The number has since doubled.) It was in this year that the novelist John Braine introduced me to the journalist Robert Pitman and his wife Pat. To my delight, Pat also proved to be a student of crime, and it suddenly struck me that she would be an ideal collaborator on an encyclopaedia of murder. I met the publisher George Weidenfeld at a literary party and suggested the idea of an *Encyclopaedia of Murder*, and he agreed; the book appeared in the following year.

Now my idea in suggesting *An Encyclopaedia of Murder* was simply that it was frustrating to try to recall a detail of some interesting murder case, and to have to spend an hour and a half searching through dozens of volumes with titles like *Dramas of the Law* or *The Black Maria*. Most of these volumes do not even have indexes. Mr Leonard Gribble has written about two dozen volumes on crime—an invaluable crime library in itself—yet the task of locating any specific case is made irksome by his habit of giving his chapters titles like 'A Touch of Arsenic', 'The Killer Who Came Back', 'The Floating Corpse'.

I was not the first person to think of the idea of an encyclopaedia of murder. Mr E. Spencer Shew beat me to it by producing *A Companion to Murder* in 1960, while Pat Pitman and I were still compiling our volume. This is a dictionary of death by poison, shooting, drowning and so on, and was followed in 1961 by *A Second Companion to Murder*; but both these volumes covered only British cases in the first half of the present century. And at the same time that our book appeared, Sir Harold Scott, former chief of Scotland Yard, edited a *Concise Enclyclopaedia of Crime and Criminals*. This kind of coincidence is enough to make one believe in the real existence of that interesting abstraction, the 'spirit of the age'.

But then, I have to admit that none of these volumes are very satisfactory, the reason being simply that the field is far too vast to be covered by any single volume—or, in fact, by anything less than an encyclopaedia the size of *Britannica*. However, an interesting possibility presented itself. A firm of part-work publishers (magazines intended to be bound up into volumes—cookery books and suchlike) approached me and asked if I would be willing to help to edit a comprehensive series on crime, running to perhaps a hundred issues. I accepted with pleasure. Besides, it gave me an opportunity to work with an old friend and a fellow-specialist in crime, Joe Gaute. I met Joe soon after the publication of the *Encyclopaedia*—he and his wife Frances called to see me at my home in Cornwall, and I instantly recognized a fellow-spirit. Joe had been working for the publisher Harraps since 1935, and had been responsible for the publication of many volumes on the subject of crime, including the standard biography of Sir Bernard Spilsbury. His collection of books on crime was far larger than my own—some 2,500 volumes. It was clear to me that he would be an invaluable addition to the editorial board of our part-work on crime; the result was that during 1972 we saw one another regularly at the board-room table of Phoebus Publications, and spent a long weekend sketching out a detailed plan for the whole work. When another old friend, Angus Hall, was appointed editor of the project we started work in earnest; the result was the 96-part series *Crimes and Punishment*. My task was to write the introductory article to each issue of the part-work. It was a fascinating, if exhausting, experience. The result still strikes me as being far from ideal; it is true that in its 2,500 pages the work deals with almost every notable crime known to history, and that an index in the last volume makes all this material reasonably accessible. Yet it is still a popular survey, and Holmes would undoubtedly have had harsh things to say about it.

So Holmes's ideal remains unrealized—a survey of criminality that should be far more than a mere list of crimes and criminals, yet which should also be more human in its essence than that rather academic branch of social science known as criminology. What seems to have fascinated Holmes is the feeling that there must be *underlying patterns* that have been so far unrecognized. And such patterns must obviously lie in the mind of the murderer, as well as in his social environment. But how does one go about recognizing them? The answer, I think, is that each individual connoisseur of crime must begin from the angle that most interests him. My own interest, for example, centres around the notion of the criminal as a rebel against various kinds of frustration. My 'outsider' feels himself lost among the overwhelming number of people who make up modern society; he feels himself a 'person of no account', yet he feels he has a *right* to be of some account. It is easy to imagine that Jack the Ripper was such a person, and that the sensation created by his murders gave him enormous satisfaction. In July 1888 he is a nonentity; by late August everybody in the country is discussing him. . . . His crimes could be regarded as a twisted form of self-expression, like the books of the Marquis de Sade. But there is one paradoxical disadvantage—that in spite of his 'fame', he himself should remain unrecognized. Moreover, there is the knowledge that even if he *were* recognized—by being brought to trial—he would be hated and rejected by his fellow human beings. His triumph contains the seeds of his own destruction, and the result is almost bound to be suicide or mental disintegration.

This, then, strikes me as an example of the kind of underlying pattern that fascinated Holmes. But it is by no means the only kind. If I open any of the books of the late William Roughead, I realize immediately that he would have found my approach abstract and rather baffling. Roughead prefers the murder that takes place against a commonplace domestic background. You get the feeling that what fascinates him is the way that perfectly ordinary people can be driven—or tempted—to commit a crime as irreversible as murder. It produces in him the same feeling that people in the Middle Ages had about tales of men who sold themselves to the devil—a mixture of horror and morbid interest. The American Edmund Pearson had roughly the same approach. The short-lived William Bolitho, on the other hand, seemed to regard crime with an amused, ironic eye—as typified in the chapter heading 'The Self-Help of G. J. Smith' (the Brides in the Bath murderer). His title *Murder for Profit* suggests that the book is also a critique of a greedy and materialistic society, and that the 'self-help of G. J. Smith' and 'the philanthropy of Fritz Haarmann' are distorted expressions of the commercial ethic. Again, the comment strikes me as valid if not profound. Yet Holmes's dream remains as distant as ever.

It seems to me that the authors of the present book *are* groping towards something closer to the Holmes ideal, and that this *Murderers' Who's Who* is a valuable step in the right direction. Both Joe Gaute and Robin Odell are 'amateurs' of crime in the best sense of the word. That is to say, both of them are fascinated by the subject for reasons that have nothing to do with making a living. It is true that Joe Gaute has been responsible for the publication of many books on murder; but since he is a publisher, he would have made just as good a living if he had specialized in books on gardening or cookery (better, perhaps). Robin Odell has written two books on murder, one on Jack the Ripper, the other on Major Armstrong; but since both took several years to research, and neither came near achieving best-sellerdom, he could hardly be accused of making a living from crime. (He is, in fact, also a publisher, but in the field of technical publications.) So here, then, we have two men who are true representatives of the Holmesian spirit. Robin Odell's interest in murder, like my own, grew from a youthful fascination with the case of Jack the Ripper. In the late 1950s 'Ripperology'—which had been marking time for a decade or so—received a new stimulus from Dan Farson's discovery of the identity of Sir Melville Macnaghten's three suspects—described but not named in Macnaghten's autobiography *Days of My Years* (1914). The chief suspect turned out to be an unsuccessful barrister turned schoolmaster named M. J. Druitt. In the same year that Dan Farson presented his television programme on the Ripper, Donald McCormick came out with his own theory that the Ripper was a Russian psychopath named Pedachenko. Stimulated by this flood of new information, Robin Odell undertook to summarize all the major theories of the Ripper's identity, including William Stewart's curious notion that the killer was a midwife. Joe Gaute heard of the projected book, and encouraged Robin Odell to go ahead. *Jack the Ripper in Fact and Fiction* appeared in 1965, and included Robin's own theory that the killer was a Jewish *shochet*, or ritual slaughterman. His theory has never been high on my own list of probabilities, but I think there can be no doubt that his book is the most wide-ranging and comprehensive that had been published until that time. My own well-thumbed copy bears witness to how many times I have read it.

Like Robin Odell's, Joe Gaute's interest in crime dates back to his childhood—

specifically, to the year 1913, when he was nine years old. On the morning of December 11, a bargeman who tried to open a lock gate in Liverpool found it blocked by some obstruction; it proved to be the battered corpse of a 40-year-old woman in a sack. She was identified as Christina Bradfield, the manageress of a shop. An 18-year-old shopboy named Elltoft was arrested, but it seemed clear that he was only an accessory; the man the police wanted to interview was a 22-year-old assistant named George Ball, who had disappeared. For the next nine days the newspapers were full of details of the murder, and the hunt for Ball. Joe Gaute recalls the photograph on the front page of the *Daily Mirror*, showing the amulet worn by the victim, with three monkeys on it. On the 20th of December Ball was arrested in a lodging-house. Joe recalls the newspaper photographs of the murderer, and the statement that he had confessed. The crime is now forgotten, but for a few weeks in that December of 1913 it was as widely discussed as the Ripper murders had been in 1888. It stuck in young Gaute's mind, so that when he could afford it he began to collect volumes of the Notable British Trials series. Fifteen years later, as a young novice in a publishing house, he achieved a certain indirect contact with the world of crime when he handled books of memoirs by detectives, police surgeons and others. (By this time the British public had developed a ravenous appetite for such works.) In the mid-1930s he approached the great pathologist Sir Bernard Spilsbury with a request to write his memoirs; but Spilsbury seemed to feel it would be unethical to use his experience as a pathologist to make money. Twelve years later, in 1947, Spilsbury committed suicide, and Joe immediately commissioned Douglas Browne and E. V. Tullett to write the biography that has since become a classic of criminology; it is probably one of the most important books for which he has been directly responsible. I would enjoy discussing his interest in specific cases, like the Croydon poisoning mystery, or the classic Wallace murder—both still unsolved (although in the latter case, Joe, like many other criminologists, is convinced that the murderer is still alive). But then, the readers of *The Murderers' Who's Who* have a convenient summary of his collection in their hands. For this book is conceived on an interesting plan, that makes it perhaps the most valuable single volume ever published on murder.

In a word, the chief problem for the student of crime is that his subject is still unmapped territory. The other day I came across a reference to Arthur Rottman. I knew I'd seen it somewhere in my collection, but had no idea where. With a thousand volumes to look through, it took me most of a morning to locate. With a copy of *The Murderers' Who's Who* on my shelf, I could have found it in five minutes. For the authors not only give a brief account of almost every famous case of the past hundred and fifty years, but also mention the books in which it can be found.

In short, the authors have created a basic mapping system to cover the enormous history of crime that has accumulated over the past century—particularly during the last fifty years. Their system has, in fact, already been anticipated by the new edition of *Encyclopaedia Britannica*, whose twenty-nine volumes are supplemented by a one-volume 'propaedia' which attempts to arrange all human knowledge under a number of headings, then to detail precisely where any item can be found.

The Gaute-Odell Propaedia will of course be useful to everyone who is interested in reading about crime, providing them with a comprehensive list of books that they can order through the library inter-loan system. But I see it rather as a blueprint for some future criminologist who, like Holmes, is in search of basic patterns. When I, for example, began to read about murder I was less interested in the Crippens and Armstrongs and Madeleine Smiths than in the type of killer that I called an 'assassin'—the man who deliberately sets out to kill, like a sportsman setting out on a day's shooting or fishing. In the nineteenth century, Lacenaire and Ravachol belonged to this type; so did Jack the Ripper. All habitual sex murderers belong to it. So, in our own time, do Brady and Manson and the uncaught 'Zodiac killer' of San Francisco, and David Berkowitz, who became known as 'Son of Sam'. But when I wanted to write about Whiteway, the Teddington Towpath rapist, in the *Encyclopaedia of Murder*, I had to rely on one sensational book by a journalist, and on the newspaper accounts of the time. With the aid of *The Murderers' Who's Who* I could now locate five different accounts of the case. And most of these volumes refer to other cases of sex killers, which would be equally easy to track down. If my interest had been in 'domestic murders', or medical murderers or poisoners, this book could again be used virtually as a study guide. In short, it is basically an index to the trackless waste of my crime collection, and a model for some future Macropaedia of Crime.

It will also, I trust, bring pleasure to that select band of cheerfully morbid souls who regard the 'horrors of the century' as a more civilized entertainment than watching sport on television.

C.W.

Foreword
to the Second Edition
by Richard Whittington-Egan

There is a venerable saw to the effect that nothing and nobody is indispensable, and like many such potted, and potty, maxims of homespun pseudo-sagacity, it presents a highly question-able proposition. Certainly you would be hard put to find anyone interested in what the late William Roughead, Scottish crime chronicler superlative, beguilingly described as 'the criminous' who would agree to the suggestion that Joe Gaute and Robin Odell's *New Murderers' Who's Who* is dispensable.

The plain, indisputable fact of indispensability is that since its original publication, a decade ago now, *The Murderers' Who's Who* has become a universally recognized classic work of reference. What is unique about it is that not only does it provide a thorough and reliable summary of the surrounding circumstances and salient points of the murders of which it treats, but additionally it supplies a comprehensive guide to the seminal literature; that is to say, those printed sources wherein to seek for, as lawyers express it, further and better particulars. More than a thousand titles are listed in the Bibliography, and since every entry in *The Murderers' Who's Who* is based upon the existence of a book or books in which is set forth the full account of the case under consideration, a simple numerical cross-reference system links each individual case with the appropriate authorities.

The Murderers' Who's Who differs from its unbloodied social namesake in that it is a volume to be entered only by achievement; there is no birthright — a deathright, perhaps! — to inclusion in its columns. The men and women herein enrolled and celebrated are all achievers; they have by hook, crook, instrument blunt, sharp or explosive, rope, poison or unique device of devilish ingenuity, contrived the erasure of a fellow-human from the state of being. They are here purely as result and reward of their own endeavours. Smilesian self-help.

That said, it must in fairness be acknowledged that all human liquidators are not of equal merit and interest. Consequently, problems of equitable selection arise. In these latter days particularly, when murder seems, for whatever reason, to have proliferated amok, the task of keeping an encyclopaedic work of this kind up to date is a most daunting undertaking. In the good — or bad, according to where you notionally stand and whether or not you have been personally affected by murder — old days of hanging, the matter of selecting suitable cases for treatment was a relatively simple one. Your Creams, Crippens, Seddons, Smiths, Christies, Heaths and Haighs left you in no doubt as to the rightness of their claims. But nowadays the bestowal of the murderous Order of Merit — or 'Dismerit' — is much more difficult to determine. Those upper-echelon murderers, those aristocrats of the blood as it were, who earned the distinction of entry to the 'Red Book' — that is, a place in the serried ranks of the *Notable British Trials*, a kind of serial (William) Burke's landed (on the scaffold) gentry — presented certain qualities, which, like good, old-fashioned manners, seem to have vanished from our grave new world.

Against all the manifold temptations Messrs Gaute and Odell have most magnificently held out in the putting together of this decennial second edition. They are to be congratulated, not only upon what they have included, but, even more importantly, upon what they have *ex*cluded. Shoddy knife-work, poor marksmanship, careless ministerings of unhealthy pills and potions, inept strangulations, are accorded no portion here. Not just any cut-throat, pistol-popper, or gun-slinger can carve or blast his way into these select and selective pages, slay his way to the top.

With all the Americas — and Canada, Australia, New Zealand, Japan, Burma, India, indeed where'er you will on this benighted globe — to plunder to the villainies, the masterworks of the practitioners of the Art of Cain, the coming to final decisions as to where to award the scarlet plumes must have been worrisome and taxing. However . . . just as — according to another of those aged saws — the proof of the pudding is in the eating, so here a sample tasting testifies to the excellence of the mixture. The tentative insertions of my thumb have pulled out a number of very satisfying plums.

Here, at random, is a butcher's dozen.

David Berkowitz, the sorry Son of Sam, whose voices told him to go forth and multiply, in an orgy of slaughter, his *mordlust* killings of New York's loving couples . . . Smiling Ken Bianchi, Los Angeles' sado-psychopathic Hillside Strangler, whose Jekyll-and-Hyde 'alibi', acted out under hypnosis, was multiple personality . . . Bible John, the holy ghost slayer of Glasgow, who tripped the light fantastic through his Barrowland Ballroom parish and danced his partners to their deaths . . . Ted Bundy, plausible, intelligent, ruthless law student and accredited killer of a possible forty women in four years in five American states . . . The horrendous Cleveland Butcher, an invisible monster who beheaded and sexually mutilated those men who had the bad fortune to encounter him on the derelict wasteland of the Kingsbury Run . . . Ronald De Feo, flesh-and-blood slayer in Amityville's poltergeist House of Horrors . . . Craig Crimmins — no relative of child-killer Alice — stage-hand convicted of a real-life Phantom-of-the-Opera homicide at the Met. in New York . . . The Killer Clown, John Wayne Gacy, who just loved the young — to death . . . All-American boy, Doc Jeff MacDonald, physician and Green Beret, whose fatal lack of vision turned his success story to ashes with his conviction for mass murder . . . The mysterious death of Hilda Murrell, the anti-nuclear rose-grower of Shrewsbury . . . The curious and murderous relationship between school-teachers Dr Jay Smith and Ezra Pound buff William Bradfield, terminating in the callous extermination of a young schoolmistress and her two children . . . Wayne Williams, the young black found guilty of committing the long series of Atlanta child murders, over whose actual guilt a gigantic question-mark has been erected . . . Charles Yukl, crazed sex killer, known as the Piano Teacher, who, in a re-run in New York of a killing he had committed eight years before, gruesomely snuffed out the life of a young aspiring actress.

Provided too are nourishing morsels of new information, added, like improving seasoning, to a number of the cases which were dealt with in the first edition.

In serious criminology, as in the more academic areas of the law, basic works of reference require to undergo regular updating. The criminal lawyer's hefty 'bible'; Archbold, revised every few years, grows wider still and wider, and mightier yet after each new edition. Similarly, *The Murderers' Who's Who* cannot be permitted to stagnate. It must — and I am glad to affirm can – be said that, like the categories of negligence, these pages are never closed to the really meritorious case.

Authors' Preface

During the ten years that have elapsed since *The Murderers' Who's Who* was first published there has been a steady increase in homicidal violence. This rise has been characterized by two principal features—a higher proportion of mass murders, and the greater use of firearms.

It is evident that the sense of isolation and alienation experienced by some individuals has precipitated a kind of rage against society, and led to spontaneous eruptions of violence. The massacre which occurred in Hungerford, a quiet English town, in August 1987 when Michael Ryan, a gunman dressed in combat clothing, shot dead fourteen persons before killing himself, is an example. Three months later, and a continent away, an ex-USAF Sergeant killed sixteen people in Russellville, Arkansas, because he had been spurned by a woman friend.

Both men nursed grievances against life, and their familiarity with firearms made possible revenge against society on a scale totally out of proportion to the hurt they believed they had suffered. In consequence, thirty innocent human beings were destroyed because two of their fellow-creatures could not master their emotions.

Mass murder is not exactly a rare phenomenon in the history of crime, as is borne out by some of the entries in *The Murderers' Who's Who*. In the last century Mary Ann Cotton claimed fifteen victims in England, and H. H. Holmes killed twenty-seven times in Chicago. In the present age records have been set by Fritz Haarmann, the German sex murderer, with his twenty-seven victims equalled in number by both Marcel Petiot and Dean Corll, and surpassed in 1979 by John Wayne Gacy with his thirty-three victims.

Where mass murder was once a scarce event, it has now become a common occurrence—made possible by the availability of firearms. Mass murderers of old used poison or strangulation as the means of putting their motive into effect. While their *modus operandi* was certainly brutal—as murder always is—at least their actions were on a human scale and, if motivated by lust or gain, were understandable. By contrast, modern mass murder seems to consist of the indiscriminate taking of life for trivial reasons, avoiding contact with the victims by lethal use of firearms. Selected at random and at distance, the victims have no fighting chance save the possibility of bad aiming.

Mass murder of this kind probably began with Charles Whitman, who shot dead sixteen persons at the University of Texas, Austin, in 1966. Since then mass murder has been alarmingly on the increase. Although frequently defined as involving four or more victims, mass murders tend to be more commonly in double figures. Jack the Ripper with his five victims would find it difficult to be included in any modern league table. Indeed, as the numbers of victims have increased, so has the terminology evolved to describe them—mass murder, for example, has become multicide, a modern phenomenon which occurs on average three times a month in the USA.

Recent studies have shown the mass murderer to be an isolated individual with a frustrating, often menial job whose mental balance is liable to be disturbed by some emotional crisis such as the loss of a job or rejection by a loved one. Forty-three passengers aboard a Pacific Southwest Airlines flight were killed in December 1987 when the jet crashed on a flight over California. Investigators believe that a disaffected employee, sacked for alleged theft, deliberately destroyed the aircraft by discharging a firearm on board.

Another phenomenon of the last decade has been the advent of the serial murderer, a type personified by Ted Bundy and Ken Bianchi. These are men with the advantages of good looks, outwardly charming personalities and above-average intelligence. They do not share the lonely, dejected world of the mass murderer who unleashes a desperate kind of instantaneous violence—they kill because they enjoy the feeling of power it gives them.

Serial killers usually operate over a long period and use their intelligence to outwit investigators. Thus the Green River Killer, who has murdered thirty-seven women in northern Oregon over a five-year period, remains at liberty. Police are uncertain whether he has abandoned his murder trail, met an anonymous fate or gone into some sinister hibernation. Bundy operated over four years, as did Peter Sutcliffe, the Yorkshire Ripper, and Dennis Nilsen. When Nilsen was finally apprehended he remarked, 'If I had been arrested at sixty-five years of age there might have been thousands of bodies behind me.' This outlook exemplifies the rationale of the serial killer.

Mass murder, multicide and serial killings have become an international trend. Thierry Paulin confessed to killing twenty-one elderly people in Paris's so-called 'Market Murders' between 1984 and 1986. 'Il Mostro'—the Monster—the unidentified killer of eight couples in the Florence area since 1968, has so far escaped capture, although two young men from good families, Wolfgang Abel and Marco Furlan, were convicted in 1987 of the 'Ludwig Murders' (also in Italy), having claimed thirteen victims.

The fact that twenty-five million Americans keep a gun in their homes is not unconnected with the rising tide of multiple homicide. Domestic violence occurs more readily when there is a firearm to hand, and revenge for a personal emotional setback is also more easily perpetrated for the same reason. The lack of control in keeping and maintaining firearms means that juveniles also have access to guns, with the result that non-accidental shooting of young people in the USA has increased by 60 per cent since 1985.

In the city of Detroit, where there are more guns than people, 365 children under the age of sixteen were shot in quarrels during 1986. Forty-three of these died, adding their quota to the city's total of over 600 murders a year. Most of these shootings resulted from arguments over trivial insults—schoolboy bullying takes on a whole new dimension when guns are substituted for fist fights!

Feuds between rival gangs in Los Angeles have created the 'drive-by shooting' whereby the victims of a vendetta are shot from a passing car. The city's police force counted it a success when on a hot Saturday night during the summer of 1987 there were only three drive-by killings recorded in their district. Los Angeles suffered 817 murders in 1987; an LAPD officer described the situation as 'worse than Beirut'.

If ready access to firearms makes murder an easier option, the availability of drugs which blot out reality helps to take away any remaining distinction between what is right and wrong. It is a combination which adds a new dimension to *mens rea*, the intent to kill, which is such an important element in proving murder. Serious crime is on the increase in cities around the world, and much of it is drug-induced. Over 300 of New York City's 1987 total of 1672 murders were thought to have been drug-related.

The USA is almost alone among western nations in exercising the death penalty. Recent polls show that 80 per cent of the American public favour capital punishment, and in 1987 the US Supreme Court ruled that accessories to murder, if they acted with 'reckless disregard for human life', could be given the death sentence. With many juveniles convicted of murder, and eligibility for execution as low as twelve years of age in the state of Montana and thirteen in Mississippi, there has been much soul-searching in the media. 'Psychotic acting out' is the description given by some psychiatrists to murder committed by juveniles. The majority of teenagers on Death Row are of low IQ and have a history of being sexually and physically abused as young children. Most were under the influence of either drugs or alcohol when they committed serious acts of crime. Some of the murders carried out by juveniles have been horrendous in their brutality, and in some states have led to demands for lowering the age of criminal responsibility.

And what of the victims? Public interest is usually concentrated on the persona of the murderer, who is frequently turned into a folk hero while his victims are quietly forgotten. The classic murders of decades past were as much about the victims as the murderers; there was a human scale to the crime incident in which a relationship existed between people and events. The eighties has been an era of drugs and bullets, of killing at random for no tangible motive, with a forensic process perhaps too willing to explain and excuse.

The last decade has been a dreadful litany of violence, and there is every indication that it will continue more or less unabated. The authorities for law-enforcement find it increasingly difficult in a free society to stem the tide, despite all the resources that a modern state can provide. There is no answer that a reasonable person can give to a teenager who believes that fulfilment comes out of the barrel of a gun. Nor is there satisfactory punishment save extinction by judicial process.

The Murderers' Who's Who does not seek to glorify its subject but rather to bring together in one reference source the principal exponents of murder. The aim is to provide an objective compendium which meets the interests of readers who find in accounts of true crime the flavour of reality that is absent from crime fiction. We have also tried to relate the entries to the ever-expanding literature of crime in order that students and professionals may pursue particular cases in greater depth.

There are many new entries in this second edition which exemplify current trends in murder. While no solution is offered to the problem of crime in society, these cases do perhaps tell us a great deal about the infinite variety of violent behaviour of which human beings are capable, and of the range of responses that society makes.

(It must be emphasized again that *all* the cases described in these pages have subsequently featured in a book or in part of a book, and *only* such cases are included. All these works are on the shelves of Joe Gaute's private library.)

Acknowledgments

The authors wish to express their thanks to Richard Whittington-Egan and Jonathan Goodman, two well-known criminologists and authors, who drew on their comprehensive knowledge of murder to advise on the selection of cases in this book. A similar debt of gratitude is due to Hale Lamont Havers, an American crime devotee and author, whose unstinting help in finding books made it possible to cover the US crime scene so fully.

We should also like to thank crime booksellers everywhere and especially Jack Hammond and Clifford and Marie Elmer, whose pursuit of the criminous both in and out of print has contributed many volumes to our crime libraries which have formed the basis of our research. Numerous friends have also hunted out books on our behalf, and we should particularly like to record our appreciation of the efforts made by Richard Floyd and Susan Fennell. Grateful thanks are also extended to Minna Fryman for preparing the typescript, and to Roy Minton for valuable advice during the editing process.

For writing a foreword and, more importantly, for showing the way, we acknowledge the inspiration of Colin Wilson. A special appreciation is given to Richard Whittington-Egan for his willingness to provide information and check facts, and for writing the foreword to this revised edition.

We are grateful to the following who have granted permission to use copyright illustrations: Associated Press, Associated Newspapers, Desmond O'Neill Features, John Fairfax UK, Lanny Budd, Lawrence D. Klausner, London Express News and Features Service and Stephen Vaughan. We apologize for any instances where it has not been possible to trace copyright-holders.

The Cases

Notes

Murders are listed under the surname of the perpetrator unless they are better known by a popular name such as the BOSTON STRANGLER or MOORS MURDERS.

An entry is referred to as a CASE when a murder trial has resulted in a lesser verdict or an acquittal. Unsolved murders and convictions quashed on appeal are also listed in this form. Thus an account of the shooting of Prince Ali Kamel Fahmy is to be found under FAHMY CASE. A Not Proven verdict is regarded for the purposes of this book as Guilty. In many instances the listing is under the name of the victim—e.g., the FOSTER CASE. Where it has been the practice in the literature to use the full name in reference to a case—e.g., the NAN PATTERSON CASE—the listing appears under the initial letter of the first name.

Within some of the case descriptions there has been reference on occasion (by the use of italic) to other cases occurring in this book, where it has seemed to the authors that similarity of the modus operandi, or of any other aspect, is of interest. At the foot of each case, again in italic, the reader will find numbers. These refer to the comprehensive numbered bibliography towards the end of the book (pp. 331 et seq.). Those interested can pursue their favourite case further through the books in this list.

A

ABBOTT, Burton W. A 27-year-old student at the University of California in Berkeley, executed for kidnapping and murdering a schoolgirl.

On 28 April 1955, 14-year-old Stephanie Bryan failed to return home after school. Apart from finding a school textbook in a field close to the town, the police had little to go on.

On 15 July the police received a call from near-by Almeda. Mrs Georgia Abbott reported that she had found some of Stephanie Bryan's personal effects in the basement of her house. Mrs Abbott explained that she had been in the basement looking for items suitable for a theatrical production when she came across a purse and an identification card bearing Stephanie's name. In her excitement she rushed upstairs and blurted out the news of her discovery to her husband and their dinner guests.

The police made extensive searches at the Abbotts' home. They found some of Stephanie's school books, her brassiere and her spectacles. Georgia and Burton Abbott were unable to explain how the items came to be there. The Abbotts had a week-end cabin some 300 miles away in the Trinity Mountains. In a shallow grave near-by was found the badly decomposed body of the missing girl—bludgeoned to death. Burton Abbott was arrested and indicted for kidnapping and murdering the girl.

Abbott was a disabled veteran with only one lung, as a result of surgery for tuberculosis. At his trial, which began in Oakland in November 1955, the prosecution established him to be a constitutional psychopath and a sexual deviant. Abbott's alibi that he was out of town when the girl was kidnapped failed under questioning. The prosecution had difficulty establishing a link between the accused and the missing girl, but a criminologist testified that hairs and fibres on Abbott's car matched those from the girl's head and clothing.

The jury was out for 7 days reaching its verdict. They found Abbott guilty of first-degree murder

and of kidnapping. He was sentenced to death on both counts. Amid a hubbub of publicity about stays of execution, Burton Abbott went into the gas chamber at San Quentin on 15 March 1957.
[*108, 216, 224, 619, 983*]

ABBOTT, Jack Henry. Convicted bank-robber and murderer whose cause was championed by Norman Mailer, the best-selling American writer. Abbott wrote to Mailer from prison and so impressed him with his talent that Mailer persuaded a major publishing house to produce a selection of letters in a book with the title *In the Belly of the Beast*.

Abbott, aged 37, had spent more than 20 years of his life in prison, 14 of them in solitary confinement. In 1966 he stabbed a fellow-prisoner to death and was sentenced to 14 years' imprisonment. He spent his time educating himself and reading the works of the great scholars. Norman Mailer described Abbott as an important writer and facilitated his release on parole. The ex-convict worked for a while as Mailer's research assistant, but found it difficult to adjust to life outside prison.

On 18 July 1981 Abbott became involved in an argument with a waiter in a New York restaurant and stabbed the man to death. After two months on the run he was eventually located in Louisiana, and in due course was convicted of murder. On this occasion he received a sentence of 15 years which he began in 1982 in the maximum security prison at Marion, Illinois.

In the Belly of the Beast has been described as a credo for the outlaw. Ironically, in view of his conviction for murder, the author described in graphic terms the ease with which killing with a knife could be achieved. 'It is like cutting into hot butter, no resistance at all,' he wrote.

Jack Abbott continued to be a celebrity criminal, and in 1983 his book was adapted into a widely acclaimed play staged in Chicago. The director said he had attempted to interpret a foreign culture and to penetrate the mystery of a man like Abbott, who

talked of the natural leaning that people had towards violence.
[6, 996]

ACID BATH MURDER. See HAIGH, John

JOHN BODKIN ADAMS CASE. Memorable murder trial in the 1950s of an Eastbourne doctor, several of whose patients died in suspicious circumstances after leaving him substantial legacies.

One of Dr Adams's patients was Gertrude Hullett, widow of a Lloyds underwriter, whom he was treating for a nervous breakdown. His treatment consisted chiefly of prescribing barbiturate drugs to the extent that the patient became addicted. In July 1956 Mrs Hullett became seriously ill, and while she lay unconscious Dr Adams made it his priority to telephone the coroner about a 'very peculiar case' and to make arrangements for a private post-mortem for a patient not yet dead. The coroner was shocked, and later accused Adams of an 'extraordinary degree of careless treatment'.

Mrs Hullett died on 23 July 1956, and Dr Adams certified death as due to cerebral haemorrhage. Dr Francis Camps, the Home Office pathologist, disagreed with this finding and suggested barbiturate poisoning. The dead woman's friends had voiced concern over the medical treatment she had been receiving, and their anxiety was increased when it was discovered that she had bequeathed her Rolls-Royce to the doctor. The inquest on Mrs Hullett found that she had committed suicide, and Dr Adams was reprimanded by the coroner.

Scotland Yard had been alerted regarding the doctor : during his career as a medical practitioner Adams had been a beneficiary in over a hundred wills, and had acquired two Rolls-Royces and other bequests of antiques and jewellery. The trail of suspicious deaths among the doctor's patients stretched back to 1946, when a widow he was treating died suddenly, leaving him £5,000 in her will. It was whispered around Eastbourne that when he went on his rounds he carried a blank will form in one hand and a bottle of morphine in the other.

One of Dr Adams's patients whom he had attended over a long period was Mrs Edith Alice Morrell, widow of a wealthy food-importer. She had suffered a heart attack, and was ill from partial paralysis and severe arthritis; she moved to Eastbourne in 1949, where she came under his medical supervision. He prescribed regular doses of heroin and morphine to control her irritability and pain. During 1950 she was cared for in her Eastbourne

Adams Case: The doctor

home by private nurses, and became increasingly dependent on Dr Adams's visits.

Mrs Morrell made several wills, one of which left the entire residue of her estate to the doctor, but in a subsequent will he received no mention. In March 1950 Dr Adams made representations to Mrs Morrell's solicitor about promises she had made to leave him her Rolls-Royce and a box of silver. The doctor wanted a codicil drawn up to that effect, but the solicitor declined to accede to his request. On 24 August 1950 Mrs Morrell made a will bequeathing a chest of silver to her doctor, but three weeks later made a final codicil completely cutting him out of her bequests. On 13 November 1950 Mrs Morrell died of cerebral thrombosis according to Dr Adams who, despite the provisions of the will, was allowed to receive the chest of silver, the Rolls-Royce and an antique cupboard.

After carrying out extensive inquiries the police decided on 1 October 1956 to confront Dr Adams on the matter of the bequests and his declaration on the form consigning Mrs Morrell's body for cremation that he was not a beneficiary under her will. During a subsequent interview with the police the doctor referred to Mrs Morrell's death as follows: 'Easing the passing of a dying person is not all that wicked. She wanted to die—that cannot be murder. It is impossible to accuse a doctor.' Impossible or not, Dr Adams was arrested and charged with murder. In March 1957 he was tried at the Old Bailey before Mr Justice Devlin, and pleaded not guilty.

The outcome of the trial was generally regarded as a triumph for Geoffrey Lawrence QC, defence counsel, who exploited weaknesses in the prosecution's case. Crucial evidence was given by the nurses who had attended Mrs Morrell, and recollections from memory proved to be at variance with the nursing log books. This allowed the defence to show that Dr Adams had made fewer visits and administered less morphine than was supposed. The doctor did not take the witness stand and thus any evidence relating to cases other than that of Mrs Morrell was not permitted. Hence it was not possible for the nurse involved with one of his previous patients to repeat what she said when the patient died, 'You realize, Doctor, that you have killed her.'

On 10 April 1957 Dr Adams was found not guilty. He resigned from the National Health Service, and in July was fined following conviction on charges of forging medical prescriptions. Later in the year he was struck off the Medical Register although he continued to treat a few private patients in Eastbourne, where he remained despite his disgrace. To the annoyance of the police, the Director of Public Prosecutions declined to proceed against the doctor with other murder accusations. It was firmly believed that he had killed 8 or 9 other persons during his 35 years as a practitioner in Eastbourne.

Dr Adams was reinstated by the General Medical Council in 1961, and he resumed his practice in Eastbourne, where he died in 1983 aged 84. His estate was valued at over £400,000. In 1984 many of his personal effects were sold at auction, raising £12,500. A number of books have been published on the case, including a full account of the trial by the judge, Lord Devlin. Many observers believe Dr Adams committed murder for gain, while more charitable commentators have suggested he merely practised euthanasia.

The story of Dr Adams featured in a successful television programme.

[59, 229, 404, 453, 504, 857]

AGRA DOUBLE MURDER. A lover's conspiracy in Agra, India, in 1911 which resulted in 2 murders, a hanging and a life sentence.

Henry Lovell William Clark, a 42-year-old doctor in the Indian Subordinate Medical Service, unhappily married with 4 children, fell in love with another man's wife. Augusta Fairfield Fullam, aged 35, was the wife of Edward Fullam, a military accounts examiner.

Clark and his paramour decided to do away with Edward Fullam. Mrs Fullam proposed a poison which would simulate the effects of heat-stroke. Dr Clark selected arsenic, then a favourite poison in India and easily obtainable, for the task, and he sent quantities of it to Mrs Fullam to administer to her husband. After treatment for 'heat-stroke', and an injection given by Clark of gelsemine, Fullam died on 10 October 1911. Dr Clark signed his death certificate, and he was duly buried.

Now the pair decided to eliminate Mrs Clark. Poison proved too subtle a method, and more violent means were resorted to. On 17 November 1912, 4 assassins, hired by Clark for 100 rupees, attacked Mrs Clark in her home and struck her down with a sword.

Clark acted foolishly by drawing police attention to Mrs Fullam, with whom he admitted dining on the evening of the murder. Officers interviewed Mrs Fullam, and her bungalow was searched. Underneath the bed the police found a tin box which Mrs Fullam said was Clark's dispatch box. The box contained some 400 letters neatly tied up in bundles of 50. Most of them were love-letters written by Mrs Fullam to Clark, and initialled by him. Their contents virtually provided the prosecution case against the murderous lovers. 'Please send me the powder one day next week,' Mrs Fullam wrote in one letter. In a letter to his wife Clark wrote, 'I am fed up with your low disgusting ways' and ended his abuse with, 'Trusting this will find you quite well, as it leaves me the same, with fond love and kisses to self.'

Edward Fullam's body was exhumed nearly 14 months after he died—it contained arsenic. Clark and Mrs Fullam were tried twice at the Allahabad High Court. Once for murdering Fullam, and again, with the 4 hired assassins, for Mrs Clark's murder. Mrs Fullam, who was pregnant with Clark's child, turned 'King's Evidence', and Clark made a confession from the dock. Their guilt was unquestionable. Clark, sentenced to death, was executed on 26 March 1913. Mrs Fullam, whose pregnancy prevented her execution, served 15 months of a life sentence before dying (ironically, of heat-stroke) on 29 May 1914.

[253, 380, 558, 732, 954]

Allaway: The fatal telegram

ALLAWAY, Thomas Henry. A 36-year-old chauffeur and ex-soldier hanged at Winchester Prison on 19 August 1922 for murdering a young woman at Bournemouth.

On 22 December 1921 Irene Wilkins, the unmarried daughter of a London lawyer, had an advertisement published in the *Morning Post*. She sought a position as a school cook, and stated her experience and desired salary. On the same day she received a telegram from Bournemouth asking her to come at once by train, and offering to meet her with a car.

The following day Irene Wilkins's body was found in a field on the outskirts of Bournemouth. She had been killed by blows to the head inflicted by a heavy instrument. Her clothing was disarranged, but she had not been raped. The police quickly noted a valuable clue—car-tyre tracks in the road near the body.

It was soon discovered that in addition to the telegram sent to Miss Wilkins, 2 others in the same handwriting had been sent from post-offices in the Bournemouth area. All three contained spelling errors, and seemed to be aimed at decoying women to Bournemouth.

The tyre tracks had been made by a car fitted with Dunlop Magnums. The police began a round-up of all cars in the district, and questioned every driver and chauffeur. Among those questioned was Thomas Henry Allaway, who was a chauffeur to a business-man for whom he drove a Mercedes fitted with three Dunlop Magnums and one Michelin tyre. What was needed was a specimen of the man's handwriting. Allaway 4 months later attempted to pass cheques on which he had forged his employer's signature. He vanished from Bournemouth and was arrested in Reading; betting slips found in his pocket bore writing matching that on the telegrams. Post-cards and letters written by her husband and provided by Mrs Allaway clinched the identity of the telegram handwriting. A Post Office employee also identified Allaway by his voice.

Allaway was tried at Winchester in July 1922. His defence was built on an alibi. It failed to convince, and the jury returned a guilty verdict. He confessed his guilt to the Prison Governor the night before he was executed. The case is significant for the apparent absence of motive. Robbery was ruled out, and sexual lust has been

assumed. But why fetch a woman from 100 miles away when with a Mercedes car a pick-up on Bournemouth front would be simple?
[*2, 128, 281, 343, 354, 365, 462, 492, 555, 558, 592, 606, 846, 1010*]

ALLEN, Margaret. A 42-year-old lesbian hanged at Strangeways Prison on 12 January 1949, the first woman for 12 years to be executed in Britain.

Margaret Allen was born into a large family at Rawtenstall. She was short and sturdily built, had her hair cut short, and dressed in male clothing. She preferred to be called 'Bill' Allen.

During the Second World War she worked as a bus conductress. Her mother died in 1943, and Margaret took her bereavement badly. She lived alone, smoked heavily and denied herself proper meals. She had medical treatment in 1945 for attacks of dizziness, and quickly slipped into a physically unkempt and mentally depressed condition.

On 29 August 1948 an elderly widow, Nancy Ellen Chadwick, was found dead in the street outside Margaret Allen's house. The old woman, a local eccentric, had been battered to death.

Margaret Allen was visited by the police. They noticed bloodstains on the wall inside the front door. Margaret Allen readily confessed to murdering Mrs Chadwick. She said, 'I was in one of my funny moods'. The old woman got on her nerves, and she silenced her with blows on the head from a hammer.

Margaret Allen appeared at her trial dressed in men's clothing. The proceedings were short, lasting only 5 hours. The accused did not testify, and her defence was based on insanity. However, she had virtually convicted herself by the confession she made to the police. It took only 15 minutes for the jury to find her guilty.
[*460, 1001*]

ALLEN and EVANS. Peter Anthony Allen and Gwynne Owen Evans, both in their twenties, were the last two to be hanged in Britain.

A 53-year-old laundry-van driver, John Alan West, who had worked for the same firm for over 25 years, was found dead in his Workington house on 7 April 1964. West, who lived alone, had returned as usual on 6 April, and was seen by a neighbour in the evening working on his car. That night, at about 3.00 a.m., his immediate neighbour was awakened by thuds next door. He looked out of the window and saw a car disappearing down the street.

The police were called, and West was found dead from severe head injuries and a stab wound in the chest. In the house was found a raincoat with various items in the pockets. There was a medallion inscribed 'G.O. Evans, July, 1961', and an Army Memo Form with the name 'Norma O'Brien' on it, and a Liverpool address. Miss O'Brien was a 17-year-old Liverpool factory worker who told police that in 1963, when she was staying with her sister and brother-in-law at Preston, she met a man called 'Ginger' Owen Evans. She confirmed that the medallion was the one she had seen Ginger Evans wearing around his neck.

Forty-eight hours after the murder 2 men were arrested and charged. Gwynne Owen Evans (real name John Robson Welby) had a watch inscribed to John West in his pocket. Evans lodged with Peter Allen and his wife in Preston. They were below average intelligence, and had been in trouble with the police before.

Evans told police, 'I never hit Jack, it was Peter that did all the hitting', but he admitted stealing West's watch, and it was clear that he masterminded the whole incident. Allen said that they had stolen the car in Preston to drive to West's house so that Evans could borrow some money from his onetime work-mate. Mrs Allen and the children went along for the ride.

Allen and Evans were tried at Manchester Crown Court in June 1964, when the judge posed the question of whether it was Allen or Evans who committed the murder—or both? The jury decided it was both, and found the pair guilty of capital murder. Their appeal was turned down, and the perpetrators of this sordid murder were hanged on 13 August 1964, Allen at Liverpool and Evans at Manchester.
[*505*]

ANTIQUIS MURDER. Alec de Antiquis was shot dead in Charlotte Street, in London's West End, on 29 April 1947, while trying to frustrate the escape of 3 armed robbers from a jeweller's shop.

Masked gunmen raided the shop in broad daylight, the firm's director was beaten about the head with a revolver, and his attackers ran into the street after firing a shot. Alec de Antiquis, on his motor-cycle, drove his machine into the path of the raiders. One of them shot him through the head,

Antiquis: Passers-by comfort the dying man

leaving him dying in the street, while they disappeared into the busy traffic.

Superintendent Robert Fabian ('Fabian of the Yard') was quickly on the scene. There was not much to go on—several widely differing eye-witness's descriptions of the raiders with a stolen car. A taxi-driver reported seeing 2 masked men disappear into Brook House, Tottenham Court Road, just after the murder. A search of the building produced a discarded raincoat and a scarf folded into a triangle to make a mask. The raincoat was traced to 23-year-old Charles Henry Jenkins, who had a criminal record for assault.

The murder gun had been found by a schoolboy lying on the muddy foreshore of the river Thames. It was loaded, and one chamber had been fired. Ballistics tests proved it to be the weapon which had killed Alec de Antiquis.

Witnesses to the shooting failed to pick out Jenkins when he was put on an identity parade. But the police had rounded up 2 of his friends, Christopher James Geraghty, aged 21, and Terence Peter Rolt, aged 17. Geraghty confessed first, and then Rolt, implicating Jenkins. All were charged with murder. Rolt, too young for the death penalty, was ordered to be detained during His Majesty's pleasure; Jenkins and Geraghty were hanged at Pentonville Prison on 19 September 1947.

The Antiquis case was significant for the way it highlighted the arguments about the death penalty. There was a public outcry concerning the execution of Jenkins and Geraghty, but scant recognition was paid to the father of 6 who forfeited his life carrying out his citizen's duty. But the gang to which the murderers belonged disbanded, and many guns were discarded.
[*133, 269, 282, 420, 486, 585, 813, 851, 961*]

ARCHER-GILLIGAN, Amy. Proprietress of the Archer Home for Elderly People in Windsor, Connecticut, whose nursing records showed that 48 residents died in a 5-year period. The high death rate led to rumours.

The home was founded in 1907 by James H. Archer and his wife, and appeared to be prospering when Archer died suddenly in 1910, leaving his widow to run the Home on her own. Amy remarried in 1913, but her new husband, Michael W. Gilligan, died after a short illness. On 30 May 1914 death again visited the Home when Franklin R. Andrews, apparently in good health, complained of feeling unwell after dinner and expired during the night. The doctor gave cause of death as gastric ulcers, and supported Amy in the face of mounting criticism.

The community in Windsor felt considerable unease about the home for the elderly in their midst and voiced certain suspicions to the editor of the local newspaper. Discreet police inquiries were begun into Amy Archer-Gilligan's affairs. Her terms for accepting residents were that each client paid a fee of up to $1,500 depending on their age and financial background, in return for which they received care for life. In view of the home's death rate (which was six times higher than the average in the region), life for many of the residents was not very long. When two of the deaths at the home were investigated, including that of the late Mr Gilligan, and exhumation led to the discovery of arsenic in their bodies, the game was up for Amy.

In June 1917 Amy Archer-Gilligan was tried on 5 counts of murder at Hartford. The circumstantial evidence levelled against her was overwhelming, especially the fact that she had bought huge quantities of arsenic from a local druggist, ostensibly for poisoning rats. Amy denied everything, claiming to be a devoted nurse and regular worker for the Church. This won little sympathy from the judge, who instructed the jury that wilful poisoning was premeditated murder in the first degree. Amy was duly found guilty, but an appeal won her a retrial in June 1919. In the end she confessed and was imprisoned for life at Wethersfield. She died in 1928 at the age of 59.
[862]

ARMSTRONG, Herbert Rowse. Small-town solicitor and retired British Army major executed in 1922 for the murder of his wife by arsenic.

Armstrong practised as a solicitor in the Welsh border town of Hay-on-Wye. Mild-mannered and small of stature, he had the misfortune to marry a hypochondriac and a nagger. He found refuge from her hen-pecking as a part-time officer in the Territorial Army, eventually rising to the rank of major.

In July 1920 Katharine Armstrong became ill, and was certified insane. After several months in an asylum she returned home only to die of an agonizing illness. The major noted laconically in his diary, on the 22 February—'K died'. Cause of death was given as gastritis, and Mrs Armstrong was duly buried. Free of his nagging wife, the Major went on a long recuperative holiday which was notable for his philandering.

In 1921 Armstrong found himself in dispute over a professional matter with rival Hay solicitor Oswald Martin. Armstrong invited Martin to his house for tea, during which he handed him a scone with the apology, 'Excuse fingers'. On returning home Martin was violently ill with sickness and diarrhoea. His father-in-law, the town's chemist, was suspicious of Armstrong on account of purchases he had made of arsenic. The local doctor was called in, and after being acquainted with the chemist's suspicions agreed to send a sample of Martin's urine for analysis. It proved to contain arsenic.

The authorities were notified, and the accusation against Armstrong was investigated by the police. Unaware that he was suspected, Armstrong made further invitations to Martin to take tea with him. On 31 December 1921 Major Armstrong was arrested in his office at Hay, charged with the attempted murder of Martin. Mrs Armstrong's body was now exhumed, and Bernard Spilsbury carried out the post-mortem. Her body was full of arsenic.

Armstrong was tried at Hereford for his wife's murder. The proceedings developed into a contest of the medical experts, with Spilsbury lending his weight to the prosecution. The judge gave Armstrong a bad time in the witness-box. What proved damning for the Major was that he could not satisfactorily explain why he had a packet of arsenic in his pocket on the day he was arrested, or why he had tried to conceal it from the police. Armstrong's moral reputation had already suffered badly from evidence given by his doctor in court that he was being treated for a venereal disease.

Found guilty of murder, Major Armstrong was hanged at Gloucester Prison on 31 May 1922.

The case, a classic, is often compared with that of *Harold Greenwood*, another solicitor with a practice in Wales. He too was tried for poisoning his wife with arsenic, but he gained an acquittal.

Gloucester   Prison

30 May   1922

My dear Matthews.

My heart was too full today to say all I wished. Thank you, my friend, for all you have done for me. No one could have done more. Please convey also to all your Staff my gratitude for the unsparing work they put in. No team could have worked more loyally or with more devotion to duty

Ever yours gratefully friend

H Rowse Armstrong

No. 24

(8252—20-4-00)

Armstrong, H. R.: The last letter

Armstrong, H. R.: The major leaves after the death sentence

[*1, 47, 104, 133, 204, 332, 347, 357, 386, 398, 449, 485, 607, 687, 706, 757, 794, 846, 873, 964, 982*]

ARMSTRONG, John. A 25-year-old Royal Navy Sick Berth Attendant convicted in 1956 for poisoning his infant son with Seconal.

On 22 July 1955 Terence, the 5-month-old son of John and Janet Armstrong, died in their home at Gosport, near Portsmouth. It was supposed that the boy had eaten poisonous berries from the garden given him innocently by his 3-year-old sister. The little girl had also eaten some berries, and was sick. A post-mortem was carried out, and red skins, presumed to be from the poisonous berries, were found in the child's stomach and windpipe.

Baby Terence was duly buried, but the police were not wholly satisfied, and called in Scotland Yard's Forensic Laboratory to report on the stomach contents of the child. It was soon discovered that the red skins were not from a natural berry but were the gelatine capsules of the drug Seconal. The baby was exhumed, and the presence of Seconal was confirmed.

The Armstrongs were questioned further by the police; they denied having had any Seconal in the house. Meanwhile, police inquiries at the naval hospital where Armstrong worked revealed that several months previously a dangerous-drugs cupboard had been broken into, and that among the drugs stolen were some Seconal capsules.

The Coroner's Inquest on the dead child recorded an open verdict, and there the matter rested until July 1956. That month, Mrs Armstrong, now separated from her husband, made a statement to the police about the death of her son. She said that there had been Seconal in the house, which her husband had been taking to help him sleep. After the police had questioned them about the drug, her husband told her to dispose of the capsules, which she did. Mrs Armstrong agreed to give evidence if any further action was taken against her husband.

On 1 September 1956, over a year after the death of the baby, both John and Janet Armstrong were arrested and charged with the murder. They were tried at Winchester. John Armstrong denied all knowledge of how his son was poisoned. Janet Armstrong said that her husband had the opportunity, when he returned home for lunch on the fatal day, to be alone with the baby. She also confirmed that there had been Seconal in the house at the time.

John Armstrong was pronounced guilty, Janet was acquitted. Armstrong was reprieved, and in a final sensational development a month later Mrs Armstrong admitted giving the baby a capsule of Seconal to help him sleep.

[37, 309, 509, 851, 857]

AXE-MAN OF NEW ORLEANS. Unsolved series of violent killings between 1911 and 1919. The Axeman's method was to gain entry to his victim's home by breaking in through a door panel and then wreaking death and destruction with an axe. The murder weapon (frequently the property of the victim) was invariably left at the scene of the crime. Robbery did not appear to be the motive.

The series of murders was accompanied by sensational press reports, and panic reactions by the public were reminiscent of *Jack the Ripper*. An extraordinary aspect of the murders was the accusations and lies of some of the victims who survived.

On 28 June 1918 Louis Besumer, a grocer, and Harriet Lowe, with whom he was living, were attacked by the axeman. A panel in the rear door of the shop had been forced, and Besumer's own axe was found in the bathroom. Mrs Lowe died in hospital, but not before she had accused Besumer of attacking her. Besumer was arrested, but on the same night the Axeman struck again.

On 10 March 1919 the Cortimiglia family were visited by the Axeman. Charles and Rosie sustained head injuries, but their daughter Mary was killed. The usual signs were present—the forced door panel and the bloodied axe left behind. When Rosie Cortimiglia recovered she accused Iorlando and Frank Jordano, the neighbours who had found them, of murdering her child. The Jordanos were sent for trial, and both were found guilty, Frank being sentenced to death and Iorlando to life imprisonment.

Meanwhile the Axeman struck again, once in September and again in October when Mike Pepitone was murdered. This turned out to be the last axe murder in New Orleans.

In December 1920 Rosie Cortimiglia turned up at a New Orleans newspaper office and admitted that she had falsely accused the Jordanos. They were both freed. A few days earlier on a Los Angeles street Mike Pepitone's widow had killed Joseph Mumfre with a revolver. She said he was the Axeman, and her husband's murderer. The police checked on Mumfre, who had a prison record. His periods of imprisonment were such that he was free when the axe murders were committed. But there was no proof, only coincidence.

The axe murders remain unsolved. Various theories have been expounded; that they were Mafia killings, and that there was not one but several murderers. Like Jack the Ripper, the Axeman's identity remains a mystery.

[898]

A6 MURDERER. See HANRATTY, James

A34 CHILD MURDERER. See MORRIS, Raymond Leslie

B

BALL, Edward. Remarkable Irish murder case in which a conviction was brought for matricide, although the victim's body was never found.

A man delivering morning newspapers in Shankill, County Dublin, on 18 February 1936 noticed a car parked at an odd angle in a road facing the sea. The driver's door was partially open, but there were no occupants. Inside he saw a bloodstained towel, and drops of blood on the back seat.

The car belonged to Mrs Vera Ball, wife of a well-known Dublin physician. Police officers visited the Ball home at Booterstown, a Dublin suburb, where they were received by 19-year-old Edward, the Balls' youngest son. Doctor and Mrs Ball had separated, and 55-year-old Vera Ball continued to live at the Booterstown house with her son.

Edward said he had last seen his mother at about 7.45 p.m. on the previous evening, when she left alone in her car. He suggested she might be staying with friends. The house was searched, and Mrs Ball's bedroom was found to be locked. Unbeknown to Edward, officers had already found a bundle of bloodstained linen wrapped in wet newspaper in his room. It was decided to force the door of Mrs Ball's room. The bed was made but it had not been slept in, and a large, wet stain on the carpet was being dried out by an electric fire.

Wet, muddy and bloodstained clothing was found in Ball's room for which he gave no explanation, and a check on his movements showed that he had left a suitcase with a friend, saying he would call for it later. It contained bed-linen, towels, woman's clothing and 2 shirts, all badly bloodstained.

Extensive land and sea searches failed to locate the missing woman, but Edward Ball was nevertheless sent for trial. He had told the police that his mother was depressed, and in the privacy of her own room cut her throat with a razor blade. When he found her dead he decided to dispose of her body at sea. He carried the body to the car and

drove to Shankill. There he waited until darkness would conceal his movements, and in order to avoid the suspicions of passers-by sat with his arm around the corpse. Under the cloak of darkness, he dragged his mother's body to the water's edge and let the tide take it out to sea.

At Ball's trial, the prosecution contended that the most extensive loss of blood had occurred on the carpet, suggesting that Mrs Ball had died there and not on the bed. Suicide by throat-cutting was a difficult proposition, and it was suggested as far more likely that Ball had struck his mother down with a hatchet, found in the garden in a bloodstained condition.

The defence contended that Ball was suffering from dementia praecox, and made much of his mother's suicidal tendencies. The judge's summing up was sympathetic to Ball, and the jury reached a verdict of guilty but insane. Edward Ball was ordered to be detained during the pleasure of the Governor-General.

[*218*]

BALL, George. A 22-year-old tarpaulin-packer, hanged for the callous murder of his employer. The Liverpool Sack Murder was committed by Ball, who was assisted by an 18-year-old youth, Samuel Angeles Elltoft. They both worked for Bradfield's, a firm of tarpaulin-makers in the city. Their crime was brought home to them largely by chance.

On 10 December 1913 a ship's steward was waiting for his girl-friend in Old Hall Street when a shutter blew down from the window of Bradfield's shop and struck him on the head. Ball appeared from within the shop and offered apologies. A few minutes later the man saw a boy emerge from the shop pushing a handcart. He was joined by Ball, and the two disappeared down the street with their handcart. Quite by chance, and unknowingly, this bystander had witnessed the disposal of a murder victim's body.

The following day a sack was found obstructing

Ball, G.: The victim's medallion

one of the gates on a lock of the Leeds and Liverpool canal. When the bundle was pulled ashore it was found to contain the battered body of a woman. A medallion around the neck enabled the authorities to identify the body as that of Christina Bradfield, a 40-year-old spinster who ran her brother's Old Hall Street shop.

The police sought Ball (who also called himself Sumner) and Elltoft for questioning. They found Elltoft in bed at his home, but Ball had disappeared. After a manhunt lasting 10 days, Ball was located in a Liverpool lodging-house. He was disguised, and when he was searched the dead woman's watch was found in his pocket.

Elltoft and Ball were tried at Liverpool Assizes in February 1914. Ball alleged that a man had broken into the tarpaulin shop and threatened the staff with a gun. After hitting Miss Bradfield on the head, he snatched the day's takings and escaped. It was a thin story, bearing in mind that Christina Bradfield had been battered with several savage blows and had then been sewn into a sack for disposal. Moreover, incriminating bloodstains were found on Ball's clothing.

The jury found Ball guilty of murder, and Elltoft not guilty of murder but guilty of being an accessory after the fact. Ball was sentenced to death, and Elltoft was given 4 years' penal servitude. The condemned man confessed in the death cell, and, reviled by the whole of Liverpool for his callousness, was hanged on 26 February 1914.

[*345, 1009*]

BALL, Joe. Entrepreneurial Texan and ladies' man who took his own life rather than face the accusation that he had fed his murder victims to alligators.

Ball ran a profitable bootlegging business during the years of prohibition from Elmdorf, an off-beat town in Texas near San Antonio. When prohibition ended he built a roadhouse called The Sociable Inn close to US Highway 181. This proved to be a prosperous enterprise and visitors were attracted by his choice of beautiful waitresses and the novelty of a pool containing five alligators.

The proprietor of The Sociable Inn liked to entertain his customers by demonstrating how readily his alligators disposed of chunks of meat thrown into their pool. His sadistic tastes led to live cats and dogs being used for this entertainment.

In 1937, after a particularly beautiful waitress had disappeared from the Inn, it was remarked that Ball's girls never seemed to stay long. His comment was, 'You know how they are; they come and go.' After his third wife mysteriously disappeared rumours began to circulate, and the police became suspicious of Ball's activities. In September 1938 they paid a visit to mine host at The Sociable Inn and Ball—who usually laughed off sinister suggestions about his disappearing girls—produced a revolver from behind the bar and shot himself. Subsequent inquiries revealed that Ball's third wife was alive and well in San Diego, California. She said she had left Elmendorf because she feared for her life after Ball told her he had killed one of his glamorous waitresses. Ball's handyman at the roadhouse confirmed that two of the girls had been murdered and their bodies buried. One of the bodies was exhumed, and the woman was shown to have been pregnant at the time she met her death. A local rancher came forward when news of Ball's activities featured in the newspapers and related how he had stumbled across Ball one night feeding pieces of a human body to his alligators. The man's life was threatened, and Ball paid him $500 to keep quiet and leave the county.

It was thought that Ball fed at least 5 of his victims to his alligators. The beasts in question were taken to San Diego zoo, where they were viewed with renewed curiosity.

[*751*]

THE BARKERS. One of the bloodiest families in America's criminal history. This notorious gang of outlaws thrived in several mid-Western states in the 1930s, kidnapping, murdering, robbing banks and accumulating a considerable fortune.

The gang's leader was Kate (Ma) Barker, and the principal members were her 4 sons, Lloyd, Arthur (Doc), Fred and Herman. The Barker boys' youthful criminal activities soon blossomed into big-time crime. They were responsible for the deaths of at least 10 people, and committed robberies which brought in some $3 million.

'Doc' Barker was sentenced to life imprisonment at Alcatraz, and was killed in 1939 during an escape attempt. Herman committed suicide in 1927 after killing a policeman, and Lloyd was killed by his wife in 1949, just 2 years after completing a 25-year gaol sentence.

Ma Barker and Fred were traced by the FBI to Florida in 1935. The couple were holed-up in a cabin which was surrounded by agents. After a 45-minute shoot-out Ma and Fred succumbed to the agents' overwhelming fire-power.

George Barker, Ma's husband who had earlier been deserted by the family, collected the bodies and had them buried at Welch, Oklahoma.

[*194, 513, 693*]

BARLOW, Kenneth. A 38-year-old male nurse sentenced to life imprisonment in 1957 for the murder of his wife by insulin.

On 3 May 1957 a doctor was called to the Barlow house in Thornbury Crescent, Bradford, where Kenneth Barlow reported finding his wife drowned in the bath. He said she had been unwell, and after vomiting in bed had decided to take a bath. Barlow had dozed off to sleep, and awoke to find her under the water. He said he tried to revive her by artificial respiration, but to no avail.

The doctor found no marks of violence on the body, and it seemed quite feasible that Mrs Barlow, unwell and slightly weak, had drowned. But the dead woman's widely dilated eyes had not gone unobserved.

A post-mortem was carried out, but no traces of drugs were found, nor were there any visible injection marks. Hypodermic syringes had been found in the house, which Barlow claimed was not unusual in view of his occupation. Police suspicion was aroused by the lack of splashing in the bathroom and the fact that Barlow's pyjamas were quite dry. This did not seem consistent with his story that he had applied artificial respiration. Eventually 2 needle marks were found in one of the dead woman's buttocks. Evidence of an injection having been given, coupled with Barlow's admission that his wife had been vomiting and sweating and her dilated pupils, suggested insulin. Extracts made from the tissues at the injection sites were analysed, and traces of insulin were found. The doctors' view was that Mrs Barlow had been given a large dose of insulin a few hours before she died.

Inquiries about Barlow indicated that he had access to insulin at the hospital in which he worked. A witness came forward relating that Barlow had boasted to a colleague that insulin could be used to commit the perfect murder.

Much of Barlow's trial for his wife's murder was taken up with the forensic evidence, which proved unassailable. A novel defence argument contended that Mrs Barlow slipped under the bathwater, and in reacting to a state of fear, her body discharged a massive dose of insulin into her bloodstream. Prosecution experts replied that to account for the insulin found in Mrs Barlow's body, her natural insulin secretion would have had to reach the unheard-of quantity of 15 000 Units.

In 1984 Kenneth Barlow was released from prison at the age of 65, having served 26 years. At the time he was Britain's second longest serving prisoner (*John Straffen* is the longest serving), and still maintained his innocence of the crime for which he was convicted.

[*310, 451, 795, 917*]

BARN MURDER. George Ince, who was 3 times identified as the Barn murderer and was twice tried for the crime, was vindicated when 2 other men were brought to justice. (See also *James Hanratty*.)

In the early hours of 5 November 1972, two men forced their way into the home of Barn Restaurant owner Bob Patience at Braintree, Essex. When he refused to hand over keys to the safe one of the men shot Patience, his wife Muriel and his daughter Beverley, stole £900 and left.

Within twenty-four hours of Muriel Patience's death police were told that the gunman might be 35-year-old Londoner George Ince, who was known for his criminal activities. Photofit pictures of the gunman were prepared from descriptions given by Bob Patience and his daughter, and Beverley later identified Ince from photographs.

Learning that he was suspected of murder, Ince reported to the police, maintaining his innocence and stating that on the night of the murder he had been with Dolly Gray, ex-wife of Charles Kray who later married Ince. (See *Kray Twins*.) Ince was put on an identification parade and picked out by Beverley Patience.

He was tried for murder at Chelmsford in May 1973. The case was based almost exclusively on identification evidence with no supporting forensic evidence. Ince protested at the judge's handling of the case. The jury failed to reach a verdict, and a retrial took place with a new judge. The identification evidence was repeated, and Dolly Gray testified that Ince had spent the night of 5 November with her. Ince was found not guilty.

On 15 June there was a development. A man reported that at a Lake District hotel a worker there had shown him a gun which he said had been used in the murder. John Brook, who was 30 and fitted the gunman's description, had a criminal record, and the gun, which ballistics tests proved to be the murder weapon, was found sewn into his mattress. Police now checked on all of Brook's acquaintances. They found the name of Nicholas de Clare Johnson, a small-time thief, regularly in Brook's company.

Johnson admitted taking part in the Barn robbery, but he attributed the shooting to Brook. At the third Barn trial, held at Chelmsford in January 1974, Brook was found guilty of murder and attempted murder and sentenced to life imprisonment. Johnson, described as having been 'harnessed to a tiger', was found guilty of manslaughter and received ten years.
[*187, 279*]

BARNEY CASE. Wealthy 27-year-old socialite Elvira Dolores Barney was separated from her husband. She was tried at the Old Bailey in 1932 for the murder of her lover.

On 31 May 1932 Mrs Barney, in an hysterical

Barney Case: Stephen's body leaves the flat

state, telephoned her doctor asking him to come at once to her Knightsbridge home as 'There has been a terrible accident'. The doctor found 24-year-old Michael Scott Stephen lying dead on the stairs of the mews house. He had been shot at close range in the chest. The police were called, and a 5-chambered .32 Smith and Wesson revolver lying close to the body was found to have 2 empty chambers.

Mrs Barney and Stephen had returned to the mews house in a semi-drunken state after a party at the Café de Paris. The neighbours were awakened by a loud quarrel between the couple—apparently rows were fairly common. Mrs Barney was alleged to have shouted out 'I will shoot you', and one or more shots followed.

Mrs Barney's story was that there had been a quarrel when Stephen said he was going to leave her. She had threatened to commit suicide with the revolver which she kept at her bedside. A struggle ensued, with Stephen trying to obtain the gun, which went off accidentally, killing him.

On 3 June Mrs Barney was arrested and charged with murder. She was defended brilliantly by Sir Patrick Hastings who pointed out that the lack of a safety catch on the weapon and an easy trigger pull made it possible for the gun to have been fired accidentally.

Several unsatisfactory points were not explained in court. There was a bullet-hole in the bedroom wall of the mews house, but no bullet was recovered. Witnesses testified to an earlier incident in which Mrs Barney was supposed to have shot at Stephen from the window. And no charge had been pressed for Mrs Barney's illegal possession of a firearm.

The jury was out for 1 hour 50 minutes before finding Mrs Barney not guilty. Outside the court she was cheered by a large crowd. Elvira Barney went to France, and 4 years later was found dead in the bedroom of a Paris hotel.

[4, 133, 318, 473, 474, 791, 938]

BARTLETT CASE. Celebrated Victorian murder drama in which 30-year-old Adelaide Bartlett was tried at the Old Bailey in April 1886 on a charge of murdering her husband with liquid chloroform.

Adelaide came from a French family, and at the age of 19 married Edwin Bartlett, 10 years her senior, and a prosperous family grocer. The Bartletts were a close family, which Adelaide seemed to resent. Within a year of her marriage

Adelaide had an affair with Edwin's brother, and a bitter row with his father.

Edwin's singular attitude to married life appeared to leave Adelaide unsatisfied. She grew bored and unhappy, and in 1885 became friendly with a young Wesleyan minister, the Rev. George Dyson. Edwin fully approved of this liaison, and in the same year made a will leaving everything to Adelaide and naming Dyson as an executor. Dyson wrote poems to her. This is an example:

> Who is it that hath burst the door,
> Unclosed the heart that shut before,
> And set her queen-like on its throne,
> And made its homage all her own—
>   My Birdie.

The Bartletts moved to lodgings in Pimlico in October 1885. Dyson's visits increased as Edwin's contact with his family diminished. Within a few weeks Edwin was ill. The doctor diagnosed sub-acute gastritis. Hitherto a fit man, Edwin was reduced to an invalid, and died on 1 January 1886.

A large quantity of chloroform was found in Edwin's stomach, but there were no traces of it in the mouth or throat. Adelaide and Dyson were both charged with murder, but the case against Dyson was withdrawn. It was revealed in court that Dyson had bought various amounts of chloroform from different chemists. Adelaide admitted to using chloroform sprinkled on a handkerchief to help her husband sleep during his illness, and also to avoid his sexual approaches.

The jury acquitted Adelaide Bartlett, there being insufficient evidence to show how the poison was administered. It remains a mystery how so much of a volatile substance could get into a man's stomach without leaving corrosive traces around the mouth and throat.

A famous surgeon said of the case, that in the interests of science she should now say how she did it!

[1, 21, 54, 87, 122, 254, 395, 507, 608, 611, 670, 676, 781, 783, 795, 850, 907, 908, 942, 950]

BAUER, Gustav. Lainz Zoo in Vienna was the unusual location for a murder in 1928. An ex-army lieutenant was acquitted despite a majority jury verdict in favour of conviction, but he later took his own life.

On 17 July 1928 gardeners working at the zoo heard several shots. On investigation they found the body of a woman in an area of dry grass which had been set on fire. One of the workmen saw a man standing watching them at a distance of about 300 yards, who promptly made off when he was spotted. The victim had been shot 6 times, but it was over a year before she was identified as Katharina Kellner, aged 31. She was separated from her husband, and was regarded as a lady with a large number of men in her life. Her husband was a prime suspect, but he vehemently denied any involvement and openly accused Gustav Bauer.

Bauer, a travelling salesman, had a reputation as a ladies' man and at the time he became a suspect was in Berlin escorting the head of one of the city's fashion houses. Letters from the dead woman were found in his possession, and he also owned a Steyr pistol for which he had bought ammunition prior to the murder. Bauer was identified by a taxi-driver as the fare he picked up outside the opera house on the day in question accompanied by the victim.

Bauer was put on trial in October 1930, and faced conflicting evidence. Two witnesses claimed to have seen him at the zoo at the critical time, whereas he maintained he was visiting his brother in hospital. The judge ordered an identity parade to be carried out at the murder location. One of the witnesses picked out Bauer, but the other identified someone else. The judge decided to adjourn the trial so that new evidence could be brought forward. At the second trial in March 1931 Bauer was acquitted when the jury split 7 for conviction and 5 against. He was freed because Austrian law required 8 votes for conviction in order to obtain a guilty verdict.

Considerable public disquiet resulted, and on 17 July 1932, 4 years to the day after the murder had occurred at Lainz Zoo, Gustav Bauer committed suicide in what was taken to be an expression of guilt.
[396]

BAYLY, William Alfred. Double murder in the 1930s in New Zealand which caused a sensation at the time and became a *cause célèbre*.

On the morning of 16 October 1933, on a farm some 60 miles from Auckland, a woman was found dead in a duck-pond. She was immediately recognized as Mrs Christobel Lakey. Her husband, Samuel Pender Lakey, was missing, and some of his clothes and 2 guns had been taken.

The police established that the Lakeys had been alive the previous afternoon. The owner of the neighbouring farm, William Bayly, suggested that Lakey might have quarrelled with his wife, then killed her and disappeared. Bayly's remarks about the incident took on a new light when police found Lakey's missing guns on his ground.

It became evident that bad blood existed

between Bayly and the Lakeys. Samuel Lakey had bought his farm 15 years previously from Bayly's father. Later Bayly junior became their neighbour, and relations were friendly until a dispute arose over fences and an access road. Thereafter Bayly adopted a hostile attitude, and the Lakeys grew apprehensive about his intentions.

The police intensified their searches of Bayly's ground. They found clear evidence that a human body had been disposed of recently. Human hair and bone, pieces of a denture, blood and clothing fragments pointed to a crime, but the finding of Lakey's watch and cigarette lighter put it beyond doubt that Lakey had been disposed of on his neighbour's farm. Remnants of human ash were also found on a shovel, suggesting that the victim's body has been burned.

Bayly was charged with murder and sent for trial. It was suggested that he had attacked Mrs Lakey and drowned her in the duck-pond. He then ambushed Samuel Lakey, shooting him with a .22 rifle. A cartridge case found on the Lakey farm matched a .22 Spandau rifle belonging to Bayly. It was contended that after killing Lakey, Bayly burned the body in an oil drum and scattered the remains around his orchard and garden. Probably he intended disposing of Mrs Lakey in the same way, but ran out of time.

The trial jury found Bayly guilty of double murder, and he was hanged in Auckland Prison on 20 July 1934.
[*517, 614, 792, 856, 997*]

BEARD, Arthur. An important case in English law. Beard, a nightwatchman, was convicted at Chester Assizes in 1919 of the murder of a young girl and sentenced to death.

Beard was drunk when he suffocated 13-year-old Ivy Lydia Wood while raping her. His plea was heard before the Court of Criminal Appeal, which changed the original finding from one of murder to manslaughter on the grounds that as Beard was drunk at the time of the assault he was not capable of acting with malice aforethought.

The case went to the House of Lords, where judgement was again upset. The Lord Chancellor ruled that while Beard may have been too drunk to form the intention to kill, he was able to form the intention to commit a felony—i.e. rape—in the furtherance of which he used violence. Therefore he was guilty of murder. He was, however, reprieved.
[*709*]

BECK and FERNANDEZ. Martha Beck and Raymond Fernandez were America's Lonely Hearts Killers of the 1940s.

Raymond Fernandez, aged 37, led a more or less normal life until he was badly injured in a shipboard accident, as a result of which he suffered brain damage. Thereafter he developed a belief in his own supernatural powers, claiming that he could hypnotize people at a distance and compel women to fall in love with him. He preyed on women advertising in the lonely hearts magazines, and they seemed to find his charm irresistible.

Martha Beck, aged 31, was a misfit (having been raped at the age of 13 by her brother) who had suffered an unhappy adolescence due also to her great weight—280 pounds! Despite the humiliations caused by her size, she qualified as a nurse, and was modestly successful in her jobs. Her overactive glands stimulated her sexually, and she formed several disastrous relationships before joining the unhappy band of Lonely Hearts Clubs members.

By this means Martha and Ray met in December 1947, and the two misfits established an amorous partnership which quickly developed criminal overtones. They decided to make a business out of Ray's ability to charm women through the Lonely Hearts Clubs, and then to fleece them of their valuables. Ray did the wooing, with Martha close to hand to ensure his fidelity to her, and together they tricked dozens of vulnerable women out of their savings.

In December 1948 greed turned to murder when Martha and Ray killed 66-year-old widow Janet Fay. Ray tricked her into marriage, and she drew out all her savings. During a quarrel at her Albany flat Mrs Fay was killed with a hammer and her body taken in a trunk to New York, where the murderous pair buried it in the cellar of a rented house.

Fernandez and Beck now practised their charm in Michigan, where they shot 41-year-old Delphine Downing and drowned her 20-month-old child. After burying the bodies in the cellar, Martha and Ray went off to the cinema, only to return and find the police waiting for them. Their murder of Mrs Fay had been uncovered in New York, and the Michigan police turned the couple over to their colleagues, who duly charged them with 3 murders and suspicion of 17 others.

The trial of the Lonely Hearts Killers in New York lasted for 44 days, and Martha's account of her intimate life with Ray gave the newspapers sensational headlines. Fernandez and Beck were found guilty of first-degree murder and sentenced to death. Both were electrocuted at Sing Sing Prison on 8 March 1951.
[*130, 399, 789, 812*]

BECKER, Charles. New York police lieutenant involved in graft and corruption.

Herman Rosenthal, a gambling-joint owner, was shot dead outside New York's Hotel Metropole on 15 July 1912 by several gunmen who fled the scene in a car. Earlier Rosenthal had featured in press headlines declaring that he would name a police officer in connection with corrupt practices in the city. The man in question was Lieutenant Charlie Becker, a 42-year-old officer who had used his privileged position to enforce protection rackets, and thus line his own pockets.

Having lost his prime witness, whose testimony would have helped smash police corruption, District Attorney Charles Whitman decided to bring the murder home to Charlie Becker. Whitman offered immunity to anyone who would help him convict Becker. It was not long before underworld character Black Jack Rose named Becker in a 38-page confession as the man who had ordered him to hire Rosenthal's killers.

Becker was tried along with 6 others in October 1912 for Rosenthal's murder. Black Jack Rose's testimony was vital, and it was clear that the District Attorney, committed to purging police graft, had decided that Becker was the man behind the trigger, even though he had not been present at the murder scene. Becker's conviction and sentence of death was hailed in the press with headlines such as 'Defeat of the Underworld'.

Becker appealed, and was granted a second trial in April 1914. Meanwhile Black Jack Rose had taken his immunity, and 4 of the men accused with Becker had been executed. Despite the suggestion that District Attorney Whitman had promised rewards to the prosecution witnesses, Becker was again found guilty. Charles Whitman, now elected State Governor, refused to exercise his prerogative to pardon Becker, and the police lieutenant was electrocuted on 30 July 1915.
[*587, 639, 779, 959*]

BELL CASE. Mary Flora Bell, aged 11, killed 2 small boys in Newcastle in 1968.

On 25 May 1968 4-year-old Martin Brown was found dead in a derelict house in the Scotswood district of Newcastle. Two days later teachers at a near-by nursery school found that classrooms had been broken into. Apart from some vandalism, police found 4 scribbled notes in childish handwriting—one of them referred to the death of Martin Brown.

Eight weeks later another child, Brian Howe, aged 3, was found dead on an area of waste ground in the same district. He had been strangled, and his body was marked with small cuts.

A massive police investigation was mounted, during which 1200 children were questioned. Among a handful of children whose replies were unclear or evasive were 2 girls, 13-year-old Norma Joyce Bell and 11-year-old Mary Flora Bell. The 2 girls were not related, but they were neighbours and close friends. They were questioned several times by the police, and changed their statements twice.

Police suspicions hardened. Further questioning of the girls resulted in each accusing the other of 'squeezing' Brian Howe's throat. Mary stated that Norma had made cuts on the boy's body with a razor blade. The 2 girls were arrested on 5 August 1968 and charged with Brian Howe's murder; Mary said, 'That's all right by me.'

The girls were tried at Newcastle Assizes in December 1968. In court Norma appeared bewildered and child-like, in keeping with her age, but Mary was calm and self-possessed. She showed an adult grasp of the complex proceedings, and demonstrated guile and understanding well beyond her years. The girls admitted writing the notes which they had left behind after breaking into the nursery school. The same day, as her contribution to the Delaval Road Junior School 'Newsbook', Mary Bell had drawn a picture of the outstretched body of a child lying on the floor of a room under a window—the position in which Martin Brown's body was found.

On the ninth day of the trial the jury found Norma Bell not guilty of the charges, and she was acquitted. Mary Bell was found guilty of manslaughter rather than murder, on account of diminished responsibility on both counts. She was sentenced to life detention, and was sent to a special approved school, as no mental hospital could be found to accept her.

In September 1977, Mary Bell, aged 20, absconded from Moor Court open prison for 3 days; she wanted to prove that she could live a normal life. She has since been released.

[599, 831, 1000]

BENNETT, Herbert John. The 20-year-old Yarmouth beach murderer executed for wife-murder.

Bennett was an opportunist who turned his hand to various money-making schemes, including the sale of fake violins. He married in 1897, and his wife helped him in dubious activities; their lives were full of lies and deceit.

In 1900 Bennett became infatuated with a young parlourmaid, Alice Meadows, and even though he was married, with a wife and child, he filled the girl's head with the idea that he would marry her.

In September Bennett arranged for his wife and child to visit Yarmouth, where he joined them. Late on the night of 22 September, a courting couple on Yarmouth beach noticed a man and a woman some 30 yards away. There were sounds of a woman moaning. The following morning a woman's body was found on the beach—she had been strangled with a bootlace.

It was some time before the police identified the body as that of Mrs Bennett. With her usual duplicity, Mrs Bennett had used the name Hood when she booked in at her lodgings. By this time Bennett was back in London and asking Alice Meadows to marry him, but now that the murdered woman had been identified it was a short step to finding her husband. Bennett was arrested in a London street on 6 November.

A gold chain worn by Mrs Bennett as a favourite piece of jewellery played a central part in the investigation. A photograph taken of Mrs Bennett by a beach photographer just prior to her death showed the gold chain, and the Yarmouth landlady said she was wearing it when she left the house. But the chain was missing from the body. A search of Bennett's lodgings, however, produced the damning evidence.

Bennett was defended at his Old Bailey trial by Sir Edward Marshall Hall. The jury convicted him. He made no confession, and was hanged at Norwich gaol on 21 March 1901. As the black flag was hoisted, the flagstaff snapped, which many took as a sign that Bennett was innocent. On 14 July 1912 the murdered body of another woman, Dora May Gray, was found on Yarmouth beach, with a bootlace round the neck. This case was unsolved.

[2, 118, 161, 275, 350, 355, 364, 589, 649, 677, 846, 885, 897]

BENSON, Steven Wayne. On 9 July 1985 two explosions rent the morning air at Quail Creek, an exclusive residential area in Naples, Florida. A car had blown up on the drive of the elegant home belonging to Margaret Benson, killing her and her grandson, Scott, who was at the wheel. Her daughter, Carol Lynn Benson Kendall, was badly injured. When neighbours reached the scene they found Steven Benson, Margaret's son, seated on the porch in a shocked condition. He had been about to ride with the family when he returned to the house to fetch a tape-measure. Seconds later Scott switched on the ignition and the explosion occurred.

On 22 August Steven Benson was arrested and charged with murder. One of the arresting officers described him as the most relaxed person he had ever met; he fell asleep in the back of the police car. The story of the Benson family was a tale of wealth turned to disaster. Margaret Benson's father had made millions out of tobacco, and he had divided his fortune between his two daughters, making Margaret a rich woman. She married Edward Benson, who in due course succeeded his father-in-law as president of the company.

The Bensons spoiled their children with lavish gifts; Carol was given a mink coat while still at school, and both children drove expensive cars. Enviable though the gifts may have been, there were strings attached. The family rule was that if displeasure was incurred the presents would be withdrawn. Margaret in particular was demanding in trivial ways, and, much as her children continued to enjoy

her generosity after they were married, they also had to endure increasingly petty behaviour.

In the 1960s the Benson family lived in style. They owned several houses in the USA and Canada and ran ten cars including a Cadillac and a Jaguar, while Margaret spent a great deal of her time buying new furniture. In 1980 they moved to Florida as part of Edward's retirement plan, but he died within months and Margaret (said to be worth $10 million) turned to Steven for advice on financial matters.

Steven craved success, but all his grand plans to run important business enterprises consumed vast amounts of his mother's money and ended in disaster. She unfailingly bailed him out of financial trouble, a fact of life which inspired him with resentment. Added to the truculence of Steven, Margaret had to put up with the excesses of her grandson, 21-year-old Scott, an aspiring tennis pro who was addicted to drugs, alcohol and wild living. Between them these two were bleeding away Margaret's fortune—Steven alone was supposed to have consumed $2 million.

By the early 1980s Steven, whose skills lay in a certain familiarity with electronics rather than business management, had created a confused tangle of

Benson: The bombed car

companies. In 1985 he used money which his mother believed was going into his business to buy a large new house costing $235,000. Margaret Benson, already concerned that her once considerable wealth was ebbing away, and annoyed at this latest act, called her lawyer down to Florida. She discussed excluding Steven from her will and requiring him to pay back all the money she had loaned him.

Steven heard that his mother intended to stop funding him. On 9 July 1985 he invited her and other members of his family to accompany him to a property he was interested in. As they seated themselves in Scott's Chevrolet Suburban, Steven returned to the house, ostensibly to pick up a tape-measure. There he activated the remote-control device which detonated the two pipe bombs he had planted in the car. Police retrieved from the wreckage two 4 by 12 inch galvanized metal tubes, one of which bore Steven's palm-print.

On 7 August Steven Benson was convicted of murder and received a life sentence. His grandfather, self-made creator of the Bensons' millions, remarked, 'Money can be a bad thing—and that's what happened in the family's case. Money became bad.'
[662, 955]

BENTLEY, Derek. Controversial case in which 2 youths murdered a policeman in London in 1952. *Christopher Craig*, 16, fired the fatal shot, but escaped hanging because he was under age; Derek Bentley, his 19-year-old accomplice, offered no violence, but was hanged.

Craig and Bentley broke into a London warehouse on 2 November 1952. Bentley had a knife, and Craig was armed with a revolver. The 2 youths were seen entering the premises, and the police were called. The would-be robbers went on to the flat roof of the building and hid behind a lift-housing. A detective climbed on to the roof. Craig shouted defiance at him, but Bentley surrendered. At this point Bentley is supposed to have shouted, 'Let him have it, Chris.' Craig fired, and the bullet grazed the officer's shoulder.

Police reinforcements arrived; Craig fired at every movement. Some men were sent up on to the roof. The first policeman to appear in the roof-top doorway was Police Constable Miles—he was shot in the head by Craig. Still shouting defiance but out of ammunition, Craig ran to the edge of the roof and jumped off. He landed 30 feet below, fracturing his spine and left wrist.

Craig and Bentley were tried at the Old Bailey. It was clear from the start that 16-year-old Craig was

Bentley: Craig's knuckleduster lent to Bentley

too young to be hanged, even though he had fired the fatal shot. For Bentley, much depended on the jury's interpretation of his rooftop shout to Craig, apparently inciting him to murder.

The trial opened before Lord Chief Justice Lord Goddard. As the trial progressed what appeared to be an open and shut case for the prosecution faltered on a number of points. The police seemed confused about the number of shots fired on the rooftop, and a ballistics expert threw doubt on whether Craig's gun was the murder weapon. It was suggested that Bentley's remark, 'Let him have it, Chris' was not an incitement to kill but advice to hand the gun over to the police.

In the witness-box Craig admitted his hatred for the police, although he denied intending to kill PC Miles. Bentley, illiterate and educationally subnormal, was ill equipped to answer questions satisfactorily. The jury took 75 minutes to find the 2 youths guilty of murder. Craig was sentenced to be 'detained at Her Majesty's Pleasure'; Bentley was sentenced to death. Various appeals from his family and the public failed to win a reprieve, and he was hanged on 28 January 1953. A storm of protest ensued which was to weigh heavily in the argument leading to the abolition of the death penalty in Great Britain.

Bentley's father died in 1974 after spending many years campaigning for a free pardon for his son. Since the death of Mr Bentley senior, psychic phenomena were reported in the press, including an incident in which the family's vicar went into a trance and spoke in the voice of Derek Bentley.
[1, 79, 116, 318, 389, 721, 859, 1021]

BERG CASE. Alan Berg, outspoken talk-show host on station KAO in Denver, Colorado, was murdered on 18 June 1984. He was shot dead in a hail of bullets as he stepped out of his car at his home. The investigative trail uncovered the activities of a white supremacy group called the Silent

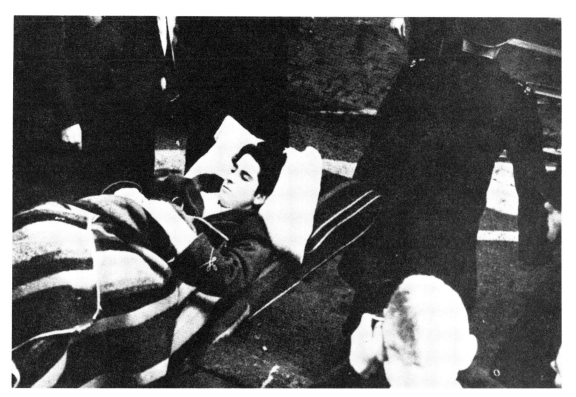

Bentley: Craig is carried from the magistrate's court

Bentley: Bentley goes back to prison

Brotherhood, and although arrests were made, the murder charge in respect of Berg was eventually dropped.

Fifty-year-old Berg had a Jewish background and had trained as a lawyer. He became a controversial figure when he took up radio broadcasting, earning himself the title 'The man you love to hate'. He charmed and offended his interviewees and listeners without warning, and at one time or another had upset practically every section of society. The bullets that killed him had been fired from a .45 MAC–10 machine pistol. Rumours abounded regarding the likely identity of his killers, ranging from assassins sent by Colonel Gaddafi to members of the Ku Klux Klan. Station KAO offered $20,000 reward for information leading to the arrest of his murderer.

In October 1984 FBI agents investigating a series of armed robberies located an arsenal of guns and explosives at a house in Sandpoint, Idaho. In the arms haul was the MAC–10 gun which had been used to kill Berg. In December Robert Jay Mathews, leader of the Silent Brotherhood, was killed in a shoot-out with FBI agents and other members of the Order were arrested.

The Bruders Schweigen, as they called themselves, were a neo-Nazi group of right-wing young men who believed in the use of violence in the pursuance of their aims. Their rules stipulated the weapons with which each unit should be equipped, and the targets of their venom were non-whites, liberals, homosexuals and Jews. Alan Berg's name was on the death list of the Brotherhood's assassination squad.

The largest trial of a white supremacy group to be held in the USA took place in Seattle in September 1985 at a cost of $3 million. Eleven defendants were arraigned on the charges of racketeering and conspiracy. All were found guilty, and received prison sentences varying from forty to a hundred years. When a controversial decision involving plea bargaining—an attempt to entice one of the members to help convict two others of first-degree murder—failed, the Alan Berg case was closed without a conviction being obtained. However, in 1987 two members of the Brotherhood, David Lane and Bruce Pierce, were convicted of killing Berg by a jury in Denver which deliberated for two days before bringing in its verdict. There was no applicable murder statute under Federal law.
[856]

BERKOWITZ, David. New York's Son of Sam killer who subjected the city to a twelve-month

reign of terror in 1976–77. He preyed on young couples sitting in stationary cars during the early hours of Saturdays or Sundays, shooting dead 6 of them and wounding 7 others. In these crimes he used a .44 Bulldog revolver. His territory was the New York boroughs of Brooklyn, the Bronx and Queens, and he inspired the largest murder investigation ever mounted by the NY Police Department. At its peak this employed 300 officers, and received over 200 calls a day from the public on a murder hot-line.

Son of Sam's first killing took place on 29 July 1976 in the Bronx, when he shot a young medical technician in her car and wounded her companion. In October a couple seated in their car in Queens were wounded, and the following month in the same borough a couple were shot and wounded in the street by a man who fired at them without apparent reason. It was proved that the same .44 Bulldog had been used in each incident, and the violent attacks continued during the first half of 1977. The *modus operandi* was invariably the same—the victims were couples seated in their parked cars, and the attacks took place at weekends. The last three crimes were committed on Sundays between 2.30 and 3.00 a.m. No more than 4 shots were fired on each occasion from a .44, adding 3 deaths to the murder toll.

On 17 April 1977, when 2 victims died in the Bronx, one of the police officers at the scene found an envelope addressed to the NYPD. It had been written by the killer, who took the police to task for describing him as a woman-hater, although he admitted, 'I am a monster. I am the Son of Sam.' He also wrote to the New York *Daily News* journalist Jimmy Breslin, who with Dick Schaap wrote a novel about the case in 1978. His last murder was committed on 31 July 1977 when he shot and killed a girl in a stationary car—her companion, though wounded, survived.

Son of Sam was finally tracked down due to a traffic violation. On the night of his last killing he had parked his car next to a fire hydrant and was given a ticket. He was traced to a Yonkers address, where his car was found with a loaded .44 revolver lying on one of the seats. The police waited for him to return to the vehicle, when he was promptly arrested. 'You finally got me' was his rejoinder to the police.

'Son of Sam' was in reality David Berkowitz, a 24-year-old postal worker and former auxiliary policeman, who lived a solitary existence plagued by feelings of rejection and tormented by voices which he called demons. He was kept awake by barking dogs, one of which, a black labrador, was owned by

"I know that I am not well hearing inner voices, having dogs talk to me and being controlled by demons yet, I want to get better.

If I ever get to a mental hospital I want to cooperate with the doctors completely. I don't want to stay behind the walls forever.

I owe my father a chance to receive hope. I owe society a chance to make myself good and repay them"

Berkowitz: Son of Sam's letter from prison

a neighbour whose name was Sam. This seemed to be the origin of the 'Son of Sam' sobriquet. Berkowitz said that voices had been commanding him to kill since 1974, a kind of symbolic transfer of responsibility also used by *Peter Sutcliffe*, the Yorkshire Ripper. The cynics believed that Berkowitz simply used the idea of commanding voices in order to build up a defence of insanity. He was nevertheless judged sane, and fit to face the charges levelled against him.

Berkowitz pleaded guilty to the charge of murder, and in August 1977 was sentenced to 365 years imprisonment. He did not appeal. The building in Pine Street, Yonkers, in which his apartment had been located became a focus for morbid sensation-seekers to such an extent that the owner was obliged to change its number.
[539, 583, 996]

BERTRAND, Louis. Successful dentist aged 35 who lived in one of Sydney's fashionable residental areas and, consumed by jealousy, murdered his lover's husband.

Bertrand and his wife befriended a couple who moved to Sydney from New Zealand in the 1860s. The two families became close, and a passionate affair developed between Bertrand and Ellen Kinder. Not satisfied with cuckolding his friend, Bertrand reached such heights of jealous passion that he decided to eliminate Henry Kinder, because he could not tolerate him as a rival contender for Ellen's affections.

So great was Bertrand's emotion that he tried to involve his young assistant in a murder plot, and said of Kinder, 'I intend to knock his brains out.' In October 1865, in the course of a visit to the Kinder home at St Leonards, a Sydney suburb, Bertrand and Henry Kinder were playing cards after an amiable drink at nearby Dind's Hotel. While they played a hand or two of cards their wives conversed quietly in the parlour. Suddenly the calm was shattered by the noise of a gun-shot and Henry Kinder lay on the floor, bleeding from a head wound, with a pistol beside him. Mrs Bertrand attended the injured man while her husband and Ellen Kinder embraced each other.

It was several days before Henry Kinder died of his wounds, and the delay was sufficient for him to be able to deny Bertrand's charge that he had inflicted the injury on himself. 'What lies to say that I shot myself' he said. At the inquest Bertrand stated that he saw Kinder put the gun to his own head, adding that the dead man had been jealous of his wife. The coroner's jury concluded that Kinder had committed suicide while emotionally disturbed.

The widow moved with her children to her parents' home at Bathurst, where she wrote passionate letters to Bertrand, pouring out her love for him. Like *Madeleine Smith*'s lover, Bertrand kept all her letters, although few of his replies were saved. The scheming dentist was under considerable pressure in addition to the emotional storms created by Ellen Kinder. He was accused by his family of ill-treating his wife, who threatened suicide, and he came to believe that he was being haunted by the late Henry Kinder's ghost.

In due course charges of murder were brought against Louis Bertrand and he was tried in February 1866 by Sir Alfred Stephen at Darlinghurst. The judge was fired by moral indignation at Bertrand's behaviour, but although he made his views plain, the jury was unable to reach a verdict. A second trial was called, and this time the jury brought in a guilty verdict. Judge Stephen vented his spleen against Bertrand, and spoke of the passion eating into the accused man's vitals, before sentencing him to death.

The sentence was contested by Bertrand's uncle and an appeal was carried as far as the Privy Council, which in July 1867 commuted the death sentence to life imprisonment with hard labour. The amorous dentist was released in 1894 after serving 28 years.
[285, 494, 837]

BESSARABO, Hera. Mlle Myrtel was the daughter of a wealthy French business-man. In 1894 she met and married Paul Jacques, a traveller in silk, in Mexico. They had a daughter Paule, and returned to live in Paris.

On 5 March 1914 Paul Jacques was found dead in his room with a revolver at his feet. The verdict was suicide, but it was suggested that his wife had previously tried to poison him.

Widow and daughter went to Mexico to wind up Jacques's affairs. Hera met an elderly, wealthy Rumanian business-man whose real name was Weissmann, but who preferred to call himself Bessarabo. They married and returned to France.

Mme Bessarabo took to drugs and entertaining young men. The Bessarabos quarrelled. On 30 July 1920 Mme Bessarabo shot her husband, and with her daughter's aid put his body into a trunk which ended up at Nancy. The police discovered that he had also been severely battered about the face.

Mother and daughter were arrested. Mme Bessarabo confessed to firing the fatal shot, but under provocation. This confession was later retracted, and there was talk of armed intruders and secret societies. At the trial in February 1921 Paule made a detailed statement implicating her mother and earning an acquittal for herself. Mme Bessarabo was sentenced to 20 years' imprisonment.
[435, 674]

BIANCHI, Kenneth Alessio. Convicted of five killings attributed to the 'Hillside Strangler' which occurred in the Los Angeles area during a 2-year period from 1977 to 1979. The nude body of a strangled 19-year-old Hollywood prostitute was found on a hillside near Forest Lawn Cemetery on 17 October 1977. Wheel-marks near the scene suggested that the girl had ben killed elsewhere and her body dumped where it was found.

Two weeks later another teenage prostitute was found murdered in similar circumstances. She had been raped and strangled, and there was convincing evidence that 2 people had been involved in the crime. In November 4 more women fell victim to the Hillside Strangler. Two of these were teenage girls still at school, and the others were young women with respectable jobs. Although the victims were dumped on hillside locations, their bodies were carefully arranged with legs spread in sexually provocative poses. Part of the *modus operandi* of the crimes was that the victims had at some stage of their abduction been bound. They had also been raped by two different males, one of whom was a non-secretor and hence in a category representing only 14 per cent of the population.

Four more women were to fall prey to the Hillside Stranglers before the police inquiry made a breakthrough. One of these girls worked for a modelling agency which kept a careful note of its employee's assignments in view of the spate of murders. Police checked out her last assignment, and as a matter of routine spoke to a security officer by the name of Ken Bianchi. It was only when Bianchi's name came up again when the killings resumed in January 1979 that suspicion began to harden. Bianchi was security supervisor for the firm which hired 2 girls as house-minders for a residence in Bellingham while the wealthy owners were away. The 2 girls had been strangled and the bodies locked in their car which had been parked in a quiet side street.

Ken Bianchi was questioned by the police and in March 1979 made a full confession implicating his 43-year-old cousin Angelo Buono as the other Hillside Strangler. He admitted to abducting the girls and taking them to Buono's home, where they raped, tortured and strangled them. Following his arrest, Bianchi was interviewed by numerous psychiatric experts and agreed to be questioned under hypnosis. The results proved controversial and raised more questions than they answered. Under deep hypnosis, he answered questions in a different voice which he said was not his but 'Steve's' who emerged as a kind of *alter ego*. 'Steve' said that Ken was another person whom he hated and who had directed Buono to kill.

Doctors talked of multiple personality, while others scoffed at what they regarded as a case of faking. Bianchi was a tall, dark, good-looking man who had been married in 1971 and later came under the influence of his cousin. He had flights of fancy, and set himself up as a psychiatric counsellor using carefully forged certificates to portray his qualifications. At one time he had served on the Sheriff's

Reserve, and was widely regarded as a nice guy.

At a sanity hearing in October 1979 Bianchi wept and expressed sorrow at the killings, although he said he did not commit them. The murders were carried out by the other person within him, 'Steve', while he was really a spectator. Angelo Buono was arrested on the strength of Bianchi's statements given at the hearing. It took five years to arraign Bianchi in court on a charge of murder but in due course he was convicted and given five life sentences. In 1983 Angelo Buono was convicted of one of the ten murders after the longest criminal trial in US history. He was sentenced to life imprisonment.

Controversy over the Hillside Stranglers continued after they had been convicted. In 1984 video tapes made during Bianchi's hypnosis sessions were shown on television. The transition from nice Mr Bianchi to the evil 'Steve' was seen by the public and described by a reviewer as similar to the movie transition of Clark Kent into Superman. Many viewers found it difficult to believe that the man could fake such behaviour. This was borne out by a well-known forensic psychiatrist, Dr Donald Lunde, who described Bianchi as suffering from dissociated reaction, a severe condition bordering on psychosis. This would enable him to commit acts of which he was not aware and of which he would later have no knowledge. Sceptics pointed to the less than spontaneous nature of some of Bianchi's antics such as 'Steve', who turned out to be a living psychiatry graduate whose name and academic records had been stolen. Bianchi had wept throughout his trial and his enigmatic personality was perhaps best described by a journalist as not being able to distinguish 'between really being and pretending to be'.

[583, 704, 824]

BIBLE JOHN. The name given to the anonymous murderer of 3 women in Glasgow in the late 1960s on account of his inclination to quote from the Bible.

The victims were all married women aged between 25 and 32; they were not related by any circumstance except their love of dancing, which directed them to the Barrowland Ballroom where they encountered the mysterious Bible-quoting stranger.

The first victim's body was found in a doorway near Carmichael Place on 22 February 1968; she had been strangled. The second victim was discovered on 16 August 1969 in a derelict building in Mackeith Street—she too had been strangled. Her movements were tracked back to the Barrowland Ball-

room, where she had been seen leaving at around midnight with a male companion described as aged about 35, slim and tall with reddish-coloured hair. An artist's impression created from the description was given wide coverage by television and newspapers in the hope of making an identification.

Police mingled with dancers at the Barrowland Ballroom in the hope of spotting their suspect, but on 30 October 1969 he struck again. Helen Puttock went dancing with a girl-friend and while at the Barrowland they were befriended by two men each of whom was called John. Helen's companion made it fairly clear that he wanted to be alone with her, but the two girls had agreed to stay together. During their time together they conversed about holidays and football and John made a biblical reference. When the dance hall closed the two girls and Bible John took a taxi, the other man went home by bus. Helen's friend was dropped off near her home, and the taxi went on to Earl Road, where Helen and Bible John alighted. Her body was found the next morning behind a tenement block; she had been strangled. Bible John was never seen again.

The dead girl's friend was able to provide the police with a detailed account of their encounter with Bible John, who was naturally regarded as number one murder suspect. The police relentlessly pursued every lead, aided by the newspapers which carried a likeness of Bible John with the question, 'Do You Know This Man?' A forensic psychiatrist drew up a personality profile of the murderer, and Gerard Croiset, the Dutch clairvoyant, lent his psychic powers to the task of murder investigation. Despite all the activity and one of Glasgow's greatest manhunts, Bible John remained uncaptured.

A succession of murders in Scotland in 1977 and 1978 led to suggestions that after eight years Bible John had restarted his murderous activities. There were some similarities, in that the victims were all women and their deaths were unsolved, but no certainty that Bible John was the killer. Apart from occasional theories—such as the suggestion that Bible John and *Peter Sutcliffe*, the Yorkshire Ripper, were the same person or that he was a member of a fundamentalist religious sect—the trail grew cold and the murders remain unsolved.
[889]

BINGHAM POISONING CASE. Three cases of arsenical poisoning in one household over a period of 9 months in 1911 at Lancaster remain unsolved.

James Henry Bingham was appointed to the post of caretaker and official guide at Lancaster

Castle in January 1911. He succeeded his father, William Hodgson Bingham, who died after holding the post for 30 years. The new man took up residence and invited his sister, Margaret Bingham, to join him as housekeeper. This she agreed to do, but within a few days of assuming her duties she died.

Bingham then asked another sister, Edith Agnes Bingham, to be his housekeeper. Within a very short time it became obvious that Edith had pretensions to high living which caused her to neglect her responsibilities. In August Edith's brother engaged another woman to take her place.

On 12 August Bingham was taken ill after eating a meal prepared by Edith. He deteriorated rapidly, and died within a few days. A post-mortem was carried out, and arsenic was found in his body. Suspicion fell on Edith, and questions were asked about the 2 previous deaths at the Castle. The Home Office issued orders for the exhumation of William Hodgson Bingham and Margaret Bingham. Arsenic was found in both cases.

Edith Bingham was arrested and put on trial at Lancaster Assizes—ironically held at the Castle—in October. She was charged with the murder of her father, sister and brother between January and August 1911.

Evidence was given that Edith had quarrelled with her brother over her relationship with her fiancé, and also over money matters. It was suggested that her motive for poisoning her brother was to obtain property which he had inherited from his sister. There was plenty of arsenical weed-killer at the Castle used extensively by the gardeners. But there was no evidence to show that Edith had either possessed or administered arsenic to members of her family.

The judge summed up in favour of Edith Bingham, and after a 20-minute recess the jury found her not guilty.

[492]

BIRCHALL, Reginald. Two farmers walking in fields near Princeton, Ontario, on 21 February 1890 found the frozen body of Frederick Cornwallis Benwell, a young Englishman, with 2 bullets in his brain. Identification was confirmed by another Englishman and his wife, Reginald and Florence Birchall, who came forward after seeing a photograph of the dead man in a newspaper.

Birchall said he met Benwell on board the liner *Britannic*, travelling from Liverpool to New York, but he admitted later a much closer liaison with the dead man. He and Benwell had parted company in

Niagara Falls after discussing plans to enter partnership in a stock farm in Ontario. Suspicion mounted as Birchall was arrested, and numerous revelations followed.

It appeared that Birchall had been seen within a few miles of the murder spot on the day of the murder, and also that he used a false identity. An Englishman, Douglas Pelly, said he had travelled on the *Britannic* with the Birchalls as an emigrant under the farm pupil scheme which was operated to encourage colonization. The system was open to money-grabbing go-betweens such as Birchall, who had sold Pelly a one-fifth share in a farm for £170. He had also sold a partnership to Benwell for £500.

At New York, Birchall and Benwell went off together to look at a prospective farm, leaving Pelly with Mrs Birchall. Birchall returned alone, saying that the farm was no good, and that Benwell had opted out. The Birchalls and Pelly now went to Niagara Falls, where 2 attempts were made on Pelly's life.

Birchall was tried at Woodstock. The prosecution were able to demonstrate Birchall's movements in and around Princeton, and to produce witnesses who had seen him there, and who had heard shots. Birchall was challenged but failed to produce documentary evidence of the negotiations. An impassioned plea for his life was made by his defence counsel, and it was widely thought that he would win an acquittal. But the jury brought in a guilty verdict, and he was sentenced to death. He was hanged on 14 November 1890; the post-mortem on his body revealing that the hangman's insistence on using an unorthodox noose caused death by strangulation rather than by dislocation of the neck.

Mrs Birchall (who had also been arrested, but released without trial) returned to England, where she later remarried.

[370, 558, 581, 815, 953]

BLACK, Edward Ernest. A 36-year-old insurance salesman hanged in 1922 for the murder of his wife by arsenic.

Mrs Annie Black, who was 50, ran the village sweet-shop in Tregonissey, near St Austell, Cornwall. She died on 11 November 1921, seemingly of gastro-enteritis. The doctor was not satisfied with the diagnosis, and a post-mortem was carried out. Analysis of body tissues revealed traces of arsenic.

Annie's husband had left home 3 days before she died. Edward Black sold insurance and made a meagre living. He owed money: and his sudden disappearance won him few friends but many accusers.

Black was traced to a Liverpool hotel on 21 November 1921, and when detectives entered his room he was found with blood pouring from a self-inflicted throat wound. He was present at the Coroner's Inquest on his wife's death. The jury brought in a verdict of poisoning from arsenic administered by her husband. Black made an impassioned speech protesting his innocence, but the damage had already been done by a St Austell chemist's testimony that E. E. Black had signed his poisons register for 2 ounces of arsenic.

Black's trial began at Bodmin on 1 February 1922, and lasted 2 days. The jury took only 40 minutes to find him guilty. His appeal was dismissed, and he was hanged on 24 March 1922.
[118]

BLACK DAHLIA MURDER. This was a brutal murder which produced a rash of confessions but no solution.

A woman's body was found on a plot of waste ground near Los Angeles on 15 January 1947. The corpse had been badly mutilated, having been crudely cut in half at the waist, and the letters BD cut into the flesh of a thigh. The victim was identified from her fingerprints as 22-year-old Elizabeth Short, onetime juvenile delinquent and aspiring film star known as the Black Dahlia on account of her preference for wearing black clothes.

Elizabeth Short suffered a cruel blow when the Serviceman she planned to marry was killed. She went to pieces, and sought refuge in drinking heavily. Her efforts to climb back to a normal life were smashed a second time by the death of her intended husband. She moved to Hollywood and took work as a film extra. It was then that she acquired the name of Black Dahlia. But there was to be no stardom for her; she gave herself up to alcoholism and promiscuity which ended in her violent death.

The discovery of the body produced a spate of false confessions from people acting out their fantasies. In a more serious vein was a note sent to a Los Angeles newspaper prepared from letters cut out of newspapers, reading, 'Here are Dahlia's belongings. Letter to follow.' Enclosed were Elizabeth Short's birth certificate, address book (with one page missing, presumed to bear the sender's name and address) and her social security

card. As her body when found was nude, and her clothing had totally disappeared, it was assumed that the sender of this card must have been associated with the murder. Fingerprints on the card were checked by the FBI, but no matching set was found in the files.

Confessions to the Black Dahlia Murder continued to pour in, and a 29-year-old army corporal who appeared to be very familiar with the details was held on suspicion. He volunteered the information, 'When I get drunk, I get rough with women.' He was thoroughly investigated, and finally dismissed as mentally unbalanced. Black Dahlia's murderer remains unidentified.
[298, 383, 765, 789]

BLACK PANTHER. See NEILSON, Donald

BLOODY BENDERS. Homesteader family of German origin which settled in Cherryvale, Kansas, in 1872. Like the *Barkers*, they were a notorious family of murderers, but less is known about them, and officially they were never brought to justice.

The family consisted of father, aged about 60, mother, aged about 50, a slow-witted son and a daughter called Kate, both in their 20s. Kate had pretensions as a spiritualist, and appeared in several small Kansas shows.

The Benders had a log cabin which consisted of a single room divided by a canvas curtain. They offered meals and hospitality to passing travellers, who were seated with their backs to the canvas curtain. Father or son lurked behind the divide, brandishing a heavy instrument which was used to crush visitors' skulls. The bodies were taken down to a cellar where they were robbed, and later buried in the prairie around the cabin.

In 1873 a Dr William H. York of Fort Scott, Kansas became the Benders' most notable victim. He told his brother Colonel York that he intended staying at the Benders' place, and when he did not return his brother became suspicious. The family denied having seen York, but, having been alerted, promptly disappeared.

Eleven graves were found in the fields around the cabin, including that of Dr York. Numerous searches were made for the Benders, but no official confirmation was made of their capture. One story has it that a posse did find them, and disposed of them in a slaying so brutal that each member swore an oath of secrecy.
[14, 729]

KANSAS HISTORICAL MARKER

THE BLOODY BENDERS

On the high prairie a mile northwest, beyond the nearby Mounds which bear their name, the Bender family -- John, his wife, son, and daughter Kate -- in 1871 built a small house. Partitioned into two rooms by a canvas cloth, it had a table, stove and grocery shelves in front. In back were beds, a sledge hammer, and a trap door above a pit-like cellar. Kate, a self-proclaimed healer and spiritualist, and reported to be a beautiful, voluptuous girl with tigerish grace, was the leading spirit of her murderous family.

The house was located on the main road. Travelers stopping for a meal were seated on a bench, backed tight against the canvas. In the next two years several disappeared. When suspicions were finally aroused, in 1873, the Benders fled. A search of their property disclosed eleven bodies buried in the garden, skulls crushed by hammer blows through the canvas.

The end of the Benders is not known. The earth seemed to swallow them, as it had their victims.

Erected by Kansas Historical Society and State Highway Commission

BOGLE–CHANDLER CASE. Renowned Australian unsolved case involving the deaths in 1963 of Dr Stanley Bogle, a government scientist, and Margaret Chandler. On New Year's Day two youths out walking by Lane Cove River in Sydney stumbled across the body of a man. They were uncertain whether he was drunk or dead, and called the police. When investigators arrived at the scene they identified the man from papers in his wallet and confirmed that he was dead. A short distance away they found the body of a woman, also dead, who was identified later.

Inquiries established that both of the deceased had attended a New Year's party at a house on Sydney's North Shore. Dr Bogle had arrived unaccompanied because his wife was looking after their baby. At the party he met Geoffrey and Margaret Chandler, and when the gathering broke up at about 4.0 a.m. it was agreed that Bogle would escort Margaret home, leaving her husband to make his own way. They drove down to the river and parked the car; their bodies were found about a hundred yards away on a riverside path.

Although he appeared to be dressed when he was discovered, Bogle was in fact naked, but his clothes had been carefully placed over his body. Mrs Chandler was still wearing her dress but it had been bunched up, exposing the lower part of her body and her thighs. Neither body showed any marks of violence nor was there any indication of organic disease; cause of death was given as cardiac failure. What precipitated their deaths was a mystery and strangely—here were two people who had spent several hours at a New Year's party—there was no alcohol in their blood.

One explanation was that the couple, drunk, had sexual intercourse during which one partner became unconscious through asphyxia due to alcoholic intoxication and accidentally suffocated the other. This suggestion left many questions unanswered, and in any case was not consistent with the known facts.

Subsequent speculation focused on the possibility that they were killed by means of an undetectable poison. Despite the fact that analysis showed no traces of poison in their bodies and no tell-tale injection marks, the idea could not be easily dismissed, as the killing in 1978 of the Bulgarian broadcaster Georgi Markov with ricin demonstrated.

At the inquest held in March 1963 experts told the coroner that every technique known to modern

Bogle-Chandler Case: Dr Gilbert Bogle

science had been used to determine the precise cause of death, but to no avail. The inquest concluded that the deaths had resulted from acute circulatory failure of an unknown cause.

The newspapers ran lurid stories about the social life of some of the top scientists working in government laboratories, describing them as Bohemians and a professional élite who rejected normal socializing. Suggestions that Dr Bogle had been working on a secret death ray were discounted, but rumours persisted that he had been killed by enemy agents. It did emerge, though, that he had been due to start a new research programme of military importance to the United States government.

In 1970 it was alleged that the Australian Security Intelligence Organisation was involved in the mysterious deaths, causing questions to be asked in Parliament. At almost the same time the Sydney *Daily Mirror* revealed that Margaret Chandler's husband had received a number of telephone calls from a man who told him that Bogle had been targeted by a group of international conspirators to prevent his departure to the USA, and Mrs Chandler was killed simply because she was in the wrong place at the wrong time.

A simpler theory was that the couple died from an overdose of LSD taken at the New Year's party, but in 1977 a more plausible suggestion was made. This was voiced after the death in London of Margaret Fowler, who had at one time been Bogle's lover, and had turned up at the inquest of his death as a mysterious witness whose testimony the coroner refused to hear. It was suggested that she would have made it known that Bogle used LSD as an aphrodisiac and dosed his and Margaret Chandler's drinks at the party, accidentally using an excess of the drug. Both expired on the river bank, and Margaret Fowler, who had followed them with the aim of jealous confrontation, found them dead. She arranged the bodies in order to minimize the scandal. There speculation on the case ends, except that the murder-by-conspiracy theory is kept alive by the knowledge that the FBI holds a secret file on Dr Bogle.

[*173, 247, 303, 504, 849*]

BOLBER, Dr Morris. Philadelphia doctor who during the Depression of the 1930s took to murder for insurance.

Dr Bolber's patients were mainly poor Italian immigrants, so he decided to swindle insurance companies through his patients.

With an Italian tailor, Paul Petrillo, in 1932 the doctor put his scheme into effect. The plan was for Petrillo to seduce the wife of one of Bolber's patients, then to tell her that her husband was unfaithful and arrange to eliminate him for the insurance. The first victim was a drunken grocer named Tony Giscobbe. One winter's night, on arriving home very late and highly intoxicated, he was stripped of his clothes and put naked on his bed with the windows open. He died of pneumonia. Mrs Giscobbe and Dr Bolber shared the $10 000 insurance money.

The pattern was repeated using Petrillo's actor brother Herman to pose as various named Italian shopkeepers and, without their knowledge, take out large sums of insurance. The first few months' premiums were paid by Bolber, and then the unfortunate policy-holder met with an accident— the insurance companies paid up the double indemnity policies without a murmur.

Dr Bolber now became involved with the infamous Carino Favato, known as the Phila-delphia witch, said to have poisoned 3 of her husbands. She provided the names of the potential victims, and added her experience to that of Bolber's gang. The doctor decided that contriving accidents in order to qualify for the double indemnity was becoming too risky, and he elected to murder his victims by 'natural means'—a canvas bag filled with sand which skilfully used

induced cerebral haemorrhage without leaving a mark.

In 5 years Bolber and his gang dispatched some 30 victims and made a fortune out of the poor Italian community and the insurance companies. But in 1937 Herman Petrillo spoke unguardedly to an ex-convict. The conversation was reported to the police, and the gang was rounded up and sent for trial. Herman Petrillo was identified by doctors who had examined him for insurance applications in other persons' names. He and his brother were found guilty and executed, while Bolber and Favato, also found guilty, received life imprison-ment.

[*524*]

BONNIE AND CLYDE. Bonnie Parker, 23, and Clyde Barrow, 25, America's infamous pair of murdering robbers in the 1930s.

Barrow, from a poor Texas home, teamed up with Bonnie, a Dallas waitress, in March 1932. They embarked on a career of robbing cafés, small banks and filling stations. The pickings were small, but opportunities for aimless killing were many.

They were joined by Clyde's brother and his wife, Blanche. The gang accumulated a consider-able arsenal of weapons with which they liked to pose for photographs. The Barrow gang, driving

Bonnie and Clyde

stolen cars, roared through the south-western states, robbing and killing in a welter of blood and bullets. Their exploits made front page head-lines—Clyde was called 'The Texas Rattlesnake' and Bonnie, 'Suicide Sal'.

After being wounded in several skirmishes with police, Blanche was captured in July 1933, and her husband was shot dead. Bonnie and Clyde escaped, but were kept on the run until they were ambushed the following year. On 23 May a heavily armed police posse shot them dead at a road block near Gibland, Louisiana. Between them Bonnie and Clyde had murdered at least 13 people in their criminal partnership. But Bonnie knew what the end had to be. Her poem, *The Story of Suicide Sal*, ended like this:

> Some day they will go down together,
> And they will bury them side by side.
> To a few it means grief,
> To the law it's relief,
> But it's death to Bonnie and Clyde.

She was wrong about the burial. Clyde went to West Dallas Cemetery, and Bonnie was buried miles away in Fish Trap Cemetery.
[*693*]

BOOST, Werner. Known as the 'Düsseldorf Doubles Killer', and often compared with *Peter Kürten*, this 31-year-old mass murderer was sentenced to life imprisonment in 1959.

Shortly after the Second World War, Boost, illegitimate son of a peasant family, was living just inside the East German border, and making money by escorting parties to the West. In 1950 he moved to Düsseldorf. He was also dishonest, and served 9 months for plundering metal from graveyards.

On 17 January 1953 a lawyer was shot dead in his stationary car in Düsseldorf. Two masked men beat up and robbed the lawyer's companion. The killing shot had entered below the left jaw and exited through the right temple—it was an odd angle.

In November 1955 a young couple disappeared after being seen in one of the city's bars. Later a car containing the missing couple was found in a water-filled gravel pit—their skulls had been badly fractured, and they had been robbed. This was the first 'Doubles Murder'.

The next 'Doubles Murder' was in February 1956, when another young couple were reported missing. They were eventually found in a village outside Düsseldorf. They had been badly burned,

Bonnie and Clyde

and beaten about the head. The man had also been shot in the same manner as the lawyer 3 years previously.

A third 'Doubles Murder' was prevented in May when a courting couple in some woods near Düsseldorf frightened off 2 armed attackers. The following week in the same place a forest ranger patrolling the woods noticed a man shadowing a courting couple. The forester, who was armed, apprehended Werner Boost, who gave up without a struggle.

Months of careful police work were necessary to provide evidence tying Boost in with the 'Doubles

Boost: Marksman and murderer

Borden Case: Pa's body
Borden Case: Ma's body

Murders', but the breakthrough came with the confession of Franz Lorbach, Boost's accomplice. He said he had lived in fear of Boost, who completely dominated him. They played around with pep pills and injections of truth serum. Boost's world was full of fantasies, and he experimented at home with drugs and chemicals. He manufactured liquid cyanide with the intention of releasing cyanide-filled balloons into the interiors of parked cars.

Boost was sexually motivated, and had an urge to attack courting couples. His proficiency with guns allowed him to shoot from the hip, which accounted for the odd angle of entry of the fatal shots in two of his murders. His unhappy accomplice was jailed for 6 years.
[*222*]

BORDEN CASE. Lizzie Borden, 32-year-old spinster, of Fall River, Massachusetts, ranks high in the annals of American crime. She stood trial in 1893 charged with murdering her father and stepmother with an axe, and was acquitted.

Through the efforts of Andrew Borden, his family occupied a prosperous place in Fall River. Borden was noted for his parsimony, except where his daughters, Emma and Lizzie, were concerned. Lizzie adored her father but hated her stepmother, who she thought was trying to extract her father's wealth.

Two drugstores on 3 August of the unusually hot 1892 summer refused to sell Lizzie prussic acid 'for moth-proofing a fur cape', and next day murder struck the Borden household, but not through poison. At a time when all other occupants of the house were out, Lizzie found her father and stepmother dead with their heads brutally smashed in.

An axe-blade, freshly cleaned with wood ash, was found in the house. Lizzie Borden was charged with the murder on the grounds that the killings must have been carried out by someone in the house. A tidal wave of public opinion mounted against her. By the time her trial took place public opinion had swung in her favour, and fainting scenes in court won her sympathy. She was found not guilty.

Lizzie lived out her days in Fall River, where she died in 1927. She was buried alongside her father and stepmother. One theory advanced for the murders was that Lizzie committed them during an epileptic fit which left her with no knowledge of what she had done.

The case is famous for the rhyme

> Lizzie Borden took an ax
> And gave her mother forty whacks
> And when she saw what she had done
> She gave her father forty-one.

Since the Fall River murders were committed, 16 books have been written about the case. In 1984 an account by Frank Spiering argued that Lizzie's elder sister, Emma Borden, was the murderess. The theory was that she decided to protect her inheritance when she learnt that her father planned to cut both daughters out of his will.
[108, 129, 254, 380, 503, 504, 508, 576, 611, 613, 730, 731, 753, 810, 875, 892, 896]

BOSTON STRANGLER. Thirteen women were strangled in Boston, USA, between June 1962 and January 1964. The killer, moved by uncontrollable sexual desires, plausibly talked his way into the confidence of women living alone. Once admitted to their homes, he raped and strangled his victims. His hallmark was to tie the ligature around their necks with a characteristic bow under the chin.

His first victim was 55-year-old divorcée Anna Slesers, who was found by her son in June 1962. Her naked body, with legs spread wide, was sprawled on the floor of her apartment. She had been sexually assaulted, and strangled with her housecoat cord. In some of the murders an attempt

Boston Strangler: Albert DeSalvo

had been made at robbery, but police believed this was a blind—the killer's motive was plainly sex with murder.

As murder followed murder public tension mounted, and Boston's women exiled themselves behind locked doors. Many sexual deviants were questioned and, as is usual, many false confessions made. Then in January 1964 the spate of murders stopped, but on 27 October the Strangler struck again and attacked a young woman in her home, having gained entrance by pretending to be a detective. He pinned her down on the bed and threatened her with a knife—'Not a sound or I'll kill you', he told her. After tying her hand and foot and molesting her, he inexplicably made off, simply saying, 'I'm sorry.'

When she freed herself the girl immediately called the police and gave a full description. He was identified at once as Albert DeSalvo, who had been released from prison in April 1962 following conviction for indecent assault. DeSalvo was interviewed at Cambridge, Mass., and although denying involvement in the murders did admit to housebreaking and rape. When his photograph was published scores of reports came to the police from women, alleging DeSalvo had assaulted them.

DeSalvo was committed to Boston State Hospital, having been judged schizophrenic and not competent to stand trial. There was still no conclusive evidence that he was the Boston Strangler, but while in hospital he confessed to killing 13 women, and described details of both the victoms and their apartments. He described how he killed a 23-year-old graduate student: 'Once I stabbed her once, I couldn't stop . . . I keep hitting her and hitting her with that knife . . . she keep bleeding from the throat . . . I hit her and hit her and hit her. . . .'

Ironically, DeSalvo was never charged with being the Strangler. Instead he was sentenced to life imprisonment in 1967 for sex offences and robberies committed before the crimes.

On 26 November 1973 he was found dead in his prison cell at Walpole State Prison, Massachusetts, stabbed through the heart.
[*42, 135, 136, 294, 755*]

BOTKIN, Cordelia. Murdered her lover's wife and sister-in-law in 1898 with candy poisoned with arsenic.

Cordelia Botkin, a stocky, unbecoming woman

of 44, had deserted her husband and pursued a Bohemian life in San Francisco. There she charmed successful journalist John Presley Dunning into leaving his wife and child and joining her in a seedy life of gambling and whoring.

Dunning lost his job, and in 1896 his wife returned to her parents in Delaware. During the following months Mrs Dunning received a number of anonymous letters warning her against any ideas of rejoining her husband.

In 1898 John Dunning was asked by his old employer to cover the Spanish-American war. He accepted. Frightened that the war would cause her lover to desert her for his wife, Cordelia grew depressed and murderous. She bought a box of candy which she seeded with arsenic and sent with a note to Mrs Dunning.

Two adults and 2 children ate some of the candies. The children survived, but Mrs Dunning and her sister-in-law, Mrs Joshua Deane, both died. The handwriting on the note and in the previous anonymous letters was shown to be Cordelia's.

She was found guilty of murder on 31 December 1898 and sentenced to life imprisonment. She made no confession, and died at San Quentin in 1910.
[*108, 777, 862*]

BOUGRAT, Dr Pierre. A 37-year-old doctor from Marseilles who had a liking for a sleazy and adventurous life far removed from the normal expectations of his respected profession. He married well, but preferred the lure of the red-light district to the niceties of his wife's dinner parties.

In 1924 Bougrat's wife divorced him and he took a prostitute as his companion, having first bought off her protector. His medical practice had been steadily declining due to neglect, and he was heavily in debt. When Jacques Rumebe, an old friend and patient, visited his surgery on 14 March 1925 carrying a bag containing 20,000 francs of his firm's wages money, the doctor saw an escape from his predicament.

Rumebe had syphilis, and was due to have an injection of mercuric chloride. He received a larger dose than normal and was beaten up as well, to the extent that he died in the consulting-room. Bougrat locked his surgery and told his housekeeper on no account to answer the telephone or go into the consulting room. Being curious people, the housekeeper and her husband peeped through the keyhole and saw a person lying on the examination

Bougrat: Practitioner of murder

couch; there was also a brief-case on the floor which did not belong to the doctor.

Mme Rumebe reported her husband missing after talking to Bougrat and confirming that he had treated him. By this time the doctor had hidden his former patient's body in a cupboard in his consulting room which he had pasted over with wallpaper. As the weeks went by and warmer weather arrived an unpleasant smell began to pervade the doctor's premises. Neighbours complained and the City Sanitation Department was called in to spray the place with formalin. Dr Bougrat's explanation was that a rat had died.

At the end of May Bougrat was arrested for issuing fraudulent cheques. While he was in custody the police took the opportunity to search his premises, particularly with a view to establishing the source of the pervasive smell. In due course the papered-over cupboard was located, and out fell the decomposing corpse of Rumebe. Two passports on the doctor's desk indicated his intention to escape with his lady companion from both the smell and the closing net of suspicion.

Bougrat's explanation was that Rumebe had been beaten up on his way to the surgery and robbed. He asked the doctor for help and while the latter was out of the room the distraught man injected himself with a fatal dose of cyanide. Bougrat, fearful that he would be accused of theft, decided to keep Rumebe's death quiet by hiding the body in his surgery until he could dispose of it permanently. Not surprisingly, this account was thought to lack credibility.

Dr Bougrat was tried for murder and sentenced to hard labour for life on Devil's Island. He arrived there in 1927 but escaped to Venezuela, where he was permitted to remain on account of his skills as a doctor. He married and continued to practise medicine until he died in 1962, aged 75.
[*152*]

BOUVIER, Léone. Illiterate French girl of 23 from a village near Cholet found guilty of the murder of her lover.

Léone Bouvier came from a poor family background. Her father was an alcoholic, and her mother was similarly addicted to drink. Léone was something of an ugly duckling, and a simple mind and warm heart made her easy prey for the lads of the village.

She worked in a factory when she left school, and after a number of disappointments found a steady boy-friend in 22-year-old Emile Clenet, a garage mechanic. The couple fell into a routine of regular meetings. Léone cycled to a selected spot every Sunday, where she met Emile before retiring with him to a cheap hotel room.

Léone soon became pregnant, lost the child and her job and endured a bitter row with her parents. The final blow was the lack of understanding shown by Emile, who now began to reject her love.

Without a job or support of any kind, she became a prostitute. In desperation she bought a gun in Nantes which she had with her when she met Emile for what she hoped would be a reconciliation. Emile told her that he was going to work in North Africa, and that their affair was at an end. Léone drew out the .22 automatic, pressed it against her lover's neck and shot him dead.

She fled to the convent where her sister was a nun, and was later arrested there. She stood trial in December 1953 at the Assizes of Maine-sur-Loire at Angers. The prosecution demanded the death penalty. The court showed her scant sympathy, and asked by the judge why she had killed her lover, Léone replied, 'Because I loved him.' The jury did not find premeditation proved, but she was found guilty, and sentenced to life imprisonment.

[341]

BOWERS CASE.

The 42-year-old San Francisco doctor J. Milton Bowers contracted 3 marriages in 15 years, which all ended with the unexpected deaths of his wives. The demise of his third wife in 1885 led to a murder charge.

Bowers appeared grief-stricken at the death of his 29-year-old wife Cecelia, to whom he had been married for 3 years. She had been ill for 2 months, and died of an abscess of the liver. An anonymous letter suggested that Mrs Bowers's death should be investigated. Insurance-company representatives at the inquest demanded an autopsy, and the body, which had been hastily buried, was exhumed and found to contain phosphorus. Dr Bowers was arrested.

The doctor was tried in March 1886, and he was widely suspected of performing abortions. Bowers also came in for heavy criticism from Henry Benhayon, his brother-in-law, regarding his obstructive behaviour during Mrs Bowers's illness. The jury found Bowers guilty of first-degree murder.

While Bowers's appeal was taking its course, an incident occurred which changed the whole case. On 23 October 1887 Henry Benhayon was found dead in a San Francisco rooming-house. A bottle of potassium cyanide was on the table, and there were 3 suicide notes. One of these was addressed to the coroner in the Bowers case, and contained Benhayon's confession that he had poisoned Mrs Bowers. This sensational news appeared to vindicate Dr Bowers, but police were not satisfied that Benhayon's death was suicide. A man called John Dimmig who was known to have visited Bowers in his cell was arrested for complicity in Benhayon's death. Despite his vigorous denials, Dimmig was identified by a druggist as having made a purchase of potassium cyanide.

The evidence was circumstantial, but Dimmig was sent for trial on a charge of murder in December 1887. The jury was deadlocked and the judge ordered a retrial. Dr Bowers still languished in gaol, and his requests for a new trial were rejected. Dimmig's second trial in December 1888 won him an acquittal, and in the following August, after nearly 4 years in prison, Bowers was released.

Dr Bowers resumed his practice, and he married a fourth time. He died in 1904, aged 61. The Bowers case was one of the most protracted in San Francisco's history, and despite 3 trials remains a mystery.

[777, 862]

BOYLE, Tony.

In 1969 the campaign to elect the President of the United States Union of Mine Workers led to the murder of one of the candidates and two members of his family.

Joseph Yablonski, an officer of the UMW, stood for election as President against Tony Boyle, the incumbent. He represented a force for change in the union, but the campaign (which was fought with great bitterness) was won by Boyle. Allegations of vote-rigging and misappropriations followed, and Yablonski alleged that Boyle had used millions of dollars from union funds to finance his election campaign.

On 5 January 1970 Yablonski, his wife and daughter were found dead in their home at Clarksville, Pennsylvania. They had all been shot through the head as they lay in their beds. The killings were viewed against the background of feuding in the union. A routine incident gave the police an early breakthrough in their murder inquiry. On 7 January Aubron Wayne Martin was picked up for a minor offence and proved hostile to questions. A list of telephone numbers which he was carrying contained entries for 'Paul' and 'Claude'.

The numbers led the police to Paul Gilly and Claude Vealey and on 20 January Vealey admitted that with Martin, the three of them had been at Yablonski's house. He gave a full account of the murders which had been planned in the bar five days after Christmas. On 5 January they drove out to the house, waited for a while after the lights had been turned out and then made their entry. The victims were shot with Martin's .38 revolver.

The 3 men were tried separately; Vealey pleaded guilty to all 3 murder charges, saying that a deal was made that 'all three of us would be equally guilty'. Martin, described by the prosecutor as a 'baby-faced killer', was convicted of first-degree murder and Gilly, who recruited the contract killers, was also convicted. The FBI brought separate murder charges against officials of the union for complicity in the killings.

In March 1972 Tony Boyle was convicted on 13 counts of embezzlement and sentenced to 5 years in prison. Later that year Boyle was stripped of the union presidency on the grounds that his win had been fraudulent. Finally, in 1973, he was arrested on a charge of conspiracy to commit murder and, 4 years after the killings, was brought to trial. It was alleged that he had told his close supporters, 'We are in a fight. Yablonski ought to be killed or done away with.' Boyle was convicted of first-degree murder and sentenced to life imprisonment.
[30]

BRADLEY, Stephen Leslie. Kidnapper and murderer whose conviction owed much to forensic botanical evidence. (See also *Hauptmann* and *D'Autrement Brothers*.)

Graeme Thorne, 8, disappeared from his Sydney home on his way to school on 7 July 1960. Mrs Thorne called the police, and while she was talking to a detective she was telephoned by the kidnapper demanding a ransom of £A25 000 for the child by 5 o'clock that day. The Thorne family had recently won £A100 000 in the Sydney lottery.

The Australian police, inexperienced in kidnapping cases, allowed the glare of publicity to fall on the incident and a massive hunt was begun for the missing boy. After a second telephone contact with the Thornes, the kidnapper kept silent.

On 16 August 2 boys playing on waste ground at Seaforth, about 10 miles from the Thorne home, found a bundle wrapped in a carpet—it was the body of Graeme, dead from suffocation and a fractured skull.

The time of death was established by botanical examination of fungus spores found on his clothing. This enabled scientists to state that the body had been there for at least 5 weeks. Plant particles were identified as from 2 species of cypress which it was known only rarely grew together. Detectives scoured the countryside and their determination was rewarded when a house at Clontarf (about a mile from the spot where the body was found) was seen to have both species of tree in its garden.

The present occupants of the house had moved in after the kidnapping, and it was established that the previous tenants had moved out on the morning Graeme Thorne was kidnapped. This couple, Stephen (whose real name was István Baranyay) and Magda Bradley, Hungarian immigrants who had arrived in Australia in 1950, were on board the liner *Himalaya* en route for England. Further evidence linking Bradley to the crime was provided by the carpet in which the dead boy was wrapped—this was identical to one known to have been in Bradley's possession.

Stephen Bradley was taken off the ship at Colombo and returned to Australia. He admitted the kidnapping, but said the boy suffocated in the boot of the car. He was tried at Sydney in March 1961, found guilty and sentenced to life imprisonment.
[*335, 914*]

BRADY, Ian. See MOORS MURDERS

BRAIN, George. A 27-year-old van-driver who picked up a prostitute in Wimbledon late at night. While she was in his van he murdered her and robbed her of 4 shillings.

A motorist driving through Wimbledon on 14 July 1938 spotted a woman's body lying in the road. She appeared to have been the victim of a hit-and-run accident but the police judged from the injuries that she had been killed elsewhere. She was identified as Rose Muriel Atkins, aged 30, known locally as 'Irish Rose'. She had been seen at 11.30 p.m. getting into a green van. Marks on her legs were identified as impressions made by a size of vehicle tyre fitted only on Austin Seven or Morris Minor cars.

On 16 July the sought-after green van was found. A firm of boot-repairers reported one of their drivers, George Brain, for embezzlement and stated that he drove the firm's green Morris van. He had absconded, leaving the vehicle in a work-mate's garage. Bloodstains in the van linked it to the crime, and Rose Atkins's handbag with one of Brain's fingerprints on it were found.

A huge manhunt was mounted to find Brain. On 25 July he was spotted by a schoolboy at Sheerness. He was arrested, and charged with murder. He told the police that he had picked up Rose Atkins, who asked him for money. When he refused she threatened to report him for using his firm's van after hours. He lost his nerve and hit her with the van's starting handle, and later dumped the body at Wimbledon. Brain admitted taking the girl's handbag but could not account for the fact that she had obviously been murdered with a knife which had been found hidden in the van's garage.

He was tried at the Old Bailey. It took the jury just 15 minutes to find him guilty, and he was hanged at Wandsworth Prison on 1 November 1938.

[*175, 815, 853*]

BRAVO CASE. Victorian *cause célèbre* concerning the poisoning by antimony of 30-year-old barrister Charles Delauny Turner Bravo. The case was never solved, although suspicion was cast on Bravo's wife.

Charles Bravo and his wealthy 25-year-old wife Florence lived in style at The Priory, Balham. On 18 April 1876 the Bravos ate dinner in the company of Mrs Jane Cannon Cox, Florence's companion. Florence, who had recently been ill, retired to bed early; she and her husband occupied separate rooms.

About 9.45 p.m. Bravo was heard calling loudly from his room for his wife to fetch hot water. The maid, hearing this urgent request, summoned Mrs Cox, who went to Bravo's room. Bravo was sick, and lapsed into unconsciousness.

Florence was roused from her sleep, and the doctor was summoned. He suspected poisoning but could not identify the agent. Mrs Cox stated that Bravo told her he had taken poison, and when he recovered consciousness he was questioned closely. He said that he might have swallowed some laudanum which he had been rubbing on his gums against neuralgia.

With her husband's life in danger, Florence asked Sir William Gull, the most famous physician in England, to examine him. Gull saw Bravo and told him he was poisoned and asked 'What did you take?' Bravo persisted with the story that he had only taken laudanum. Gull told the family that Bravo was dying of an irritant poison, and he died on 21 April. Post-mortem examination revealed that he had died of antimony poisoning, administered in a single dose of 20 to 30 grains.

The inquest returned an open verdict, and it was widely held that Bravo had committed suicide. It was known that Florence Bravo had an affair with an elderly Doctor Gully, and that Mrs Cox had quarrelled with her mistress's husband.

A second inquest opened in July 1876 which developed more or less into a trial of Florence Bravo and Jane Cox. A verdict of wilful murder was returned, with the rider that there was insufficient evidence to fix guilt upon any person or persons.

Perhaps the case is best summed up by a parody of the time:

> When lovely woman stoops to folly
> And finds her husband in the way,
> What charm can soothe her melancholy
> What art can turn him into clay?
>
> The only means her aim to cover,
> And save herself from prison locks,
> And repossess her ancient lover
> Are Burgundy and Mrs Cox!

[*121, 211, 254, 403, 553, 728, 780, 908, 987*]

BRIGHTON TRUNK CRIMES. Tony Mancini, a 26-year-old waiter and convicted thief, was acquitted of the charge of murder in the sensational Brighton Trunk Case Number Two.

Mancini, whose real name was Cecil Lois England, met 42-year-old ex-dancer Violette Kaye (real name Violet Saunders) in London. The couple moved to Brighton, where they lived in a succession of rented rooms. At first Mancini was content to live off his mistress's immoral earnings, but in May 1933 he took a job in the Skylark Café. On 10 May, following a quarrel at the Skylark (where a semi-drunken Violette had gone to ensure that Mancini was not embroiled with other women), the ex-dancer disappeared.

Inquirers were told by Mancini that she had gone to work in Paris. He decided to move his lodgings, and with the help of a fellow-waiter shifted his belongings, including a heavy trunk which was placed in the corner of his new room. In the days which followed he had to deal with several complaints about the smell in his room, and the landlady observed a dark fluid escaping from the bottom of the trunk. (See *Winnie Ruth Judd.*)

On 17 June the body of a woman, minus head and legs, was found in a trunk at Brighton's Railway Station deposited there 11 days earlier. 'The Brighton Trunk Crime' (Number One) made immediate headlines. The victim's identity was never discovered, but in the course of police inquiries hundreds of persons were interviewed, including Tony Mancini. With his secret knowledge of what lay mouldering in the trunk in his room, he opted for flight, and went to London on 15 July. When police visited Mancini to ask more questions they found Violette Kaye's decomposing body in the trunk at his lodgings.

Mancini was arrested on 17 July. He said, 'Yes, I'm the man. I didn't murder her, though.' He was tried at Lewes Assizes in December, where he pleaded not guilty. He contended that he had found Violette Kaye lying dead on the bed in their lodgings, and in his frightened state of mind decided to hide the body. Asked why he did not call the police, he replied, 'Where the police are concerned, a man who's got convictions never gets a square deal.' Norman Birkett, defending Mancini, brilliantly argued that the man was caught up in a chain reaction of concealment and lies in the wake of his panic at finding the body.

The jury returned a verdict of not guilty, but in a Sunday newspaper in 1976 Mancini stated he was responsible for the woman's death. Trunk Crime Number One was never solved.
[*112, 133, 349, 541, 608, 611, 791, 901, 976*]

Brighton Trunk Crime No. 2: Cupboard in which the trunk stood

Brighton Trunk Crime No. 2: The trunk's contents

BRINKLEY, Richard. Convicted for the murder of 2 persons with prussic acid.

A carpenter by trade, Brinkley cultivated the acquaintance of a 77-year-old widow, Johanna Maria Louisa Blume, who owned a house in Fulham where she lived with her granddaughter.

Brinkley aspired to the old lady's estate. He made out a will whose terms left all her property and savings to him. Folding the paper to obscure its real contents, he told Mrs Blume that he was collecting signatures for a seaside outing. She signed it. In a similar fashion, Brinkley acquired the signatures of two witnesses, Henry Heard and Reginald Parker.

Two days later Mrs Blume died. A certificate of death from natural causes was given. Brinkley now produced the will and claimed ownership of the house at Fulham. Mrs Blume's granddaughter, while recognizing the signature, was not prepared to accept the terms of the will. She consulted a solicitor, who required Brinkley to prove the validity of the will.

Realizing that the witnesses to the document would be questioned, Brinkley set about eliminating them. He began with Parker. Visiting him at his lodgings on the pretext of buying a dog, he produced a bottle of stout to help the bargaining along. This was left on a table while the 2 men went out to inspect the dog. While they were away, Parker's landlord, a Mr Beck, with his wife and daughter came in, saw the bottle and decided to sample it. All three collapsed. Mr and Mrs Beck died, and their daughter recovered after a few days. The stout had been laced with prussic acid.

Brinkley was tried at Guildford Assizes. Mrs Blume's body was exhumed and examined for traces of poison—there were none. The trial was significant for the use made of scientific evidence in regard to the inks used in the signatures on the will. Brinkley was hanged at Wandsworth Prison on 13 August 1907.

[705]

BROWN, Eric. A 19-year-old bank clerk from Rayleigh, near Southend, who killed his father, a wheel-chair invalid, with an army mine.

Archibald Brown, aged 47, had been injured in a motor-cycle accident, and gradually developed paralysis of the spine. By 1942 he was unable to walk without help, and used a wheel-chair. He lived at Rayleigh with his wife and two sons.

On 23 July 1943, Nurse Mitchell went to the air-raid shelter next to the house where the wheel-chair was kept, but found its door bolted from the inside. Eventually Eric emerged from the shelter.

Mr Brown was wheeled out on one of his favourite routes. About a mile from home his nurse stopped, as Mr Brown wanted a cigarette. She lit his cigarette, and while walking round to the back of the chair was thrown violently to the ground by a terrific explosion. Mr Brown was blown to pieces, but, luckily, Nurse Mitchell was unscathed. Police found that an anti-tank device known as a Hawkins No. 75 Grenade Mine had caused the explosion.

When the family was questioned it was revealed that Mr Brown had been an extremely difficult man to live with, even before his accident. He was irrationally strict with his wife and two boys, and had taken a constant bullying attitude towards Eric. Interviewed, Eric told how he had come to resent his father's intolerable treatment of his mother and decided to do away with him. He smuggled the mine into the air-raid shelter, and fitted it under his father's wheel-chair. He had no intention of benefiting from his father's death other than by making a happier life for his mother.

Eric Brown was tried for murder at Chelmsford in November 1943. He was found guilty but insane.

[487, 975]

BROWN, Ernest. A 35-year-old groom who made his employer's wife his mistress, and murdered her husband in a fit of jealousy.

Brown worked for Frederick Ellison Morton, a wealthy cattle factor who lived with his wife and child at Saxton Grange, an isolated Yorkshire farmhouse. Dorothy Morton became Brown's mistress, but their passion was soured by his violent jealousy. Following a disagreement about his duties, Brown left the Morton household, but within days he asked for his old job back. Morton agreed to re-employ him, but far from being grateful, Brown resented his lowly position, and threatened to 'wreck the place'.

Tension reached its peak on 5 September 1933, when Mr Morton went out for the day in one of his cars. Early in the evening an argument occurred when Brown struck Dorothy Morton and she fell to the ground. Thus began a night of terror for Mrs Morton and her companion-help Ann Houseman. Brown fired a shotgun outside the house, saying he was shooting at rats. The 2 women, already aware that the telephone had gone 'dead', locked themselves in upstairs rooms.

At 3.30 a.m. there was a loud explosion, and the garage across the yard was set ablaze. Mrs Morton and her companion rushed terrified from the house and hid in near-by fields. The fire was so fierce that it was not until 9.0 a.m. the following morning that the ruins could be examined. The garage contained the wrecks of Morton's 2 cars, and in one of them lay his charred body. A post-mortem showed that he had been shot in the chest before being burned.

Brown was charged with murder, and sent for trial at Leeds Assizes. The prosecution contended that he had shot Morton and then set fire to the garage. He fuelled the fire with petrol which caused the explosion heard by the 2 women. Brown had taken a knife from the kitchen shortly before the telephone line went 'dead'. Forensic evidence demonstrated that the wires had been cut with this knife.

The jury found Brown guilty, and he was sentenced to death. He was hanged at Armley Prison, Leeds, on 6 February 1934. It has been suggested that Brown might also be the murderer of Evelyn Foster (see *Foster Case*). Asked if he wished to make a confession while on the scaffold, he is alleged to have said either 'ought to burn' or 'Otterburn'.

[58, 920]

BROWN and SMITH.

Case in which two brothers and a third man were thwarted in their first attempt at robbery. At the second attempt one brother dropped out, and later gave evidence against his companions.

Frederick Gosling, 79, kept the shop at Clay Corner, near Chertsey in Surrey. 'Gossy' lived over the shop, and was said to have thousands of pounds hidden.

On 12 January 1951 the old man was found dead from asphyxia in his bedroom. He was bound and gagged, and had been struck hard over one eye. About £60 had been stolen.

The police had been called the previous day, when Mr Gosling had been attacked by 2 men who left when some schoolgirls entered. Within days the police had rounded up Joseph Brown, a 33-year-old general dealer, and his brother Frederick, a 27-year-old labourer, whom they charged with assaulting Mr Gosling on 11 January. A third man, 33-year-old Edward Charles Smith, was also charged.

All three appeared on the charge of assault but this was changed to one of murder, and Frederick Brown was discharged. Brown and Smith were tried at Surrey Assizes in March 1951, when Frederick Brown gave evidence against his brother. He said they drove to the shop at Clay Corner and he stayed with the car while his brother and Smith went into the shop. Their plans to rob the shop-owner were thwarted by the arrival of the schoolgirls. Joseph Brown and Smith returned later. He saw them afterwards, and he was told that they had to tie up the old man but he was all right.

Smith denied smothering the old man, claiming, 'If I had wanted to hurt him I could have hit him or done something.' This was precisely what the medical evidence showed had happened. Both men were found guilty, and executed at Wandsworth Prison on 25 April 1951.

[418]

BROWNE and KENNEDY.

The 47-year-old ex-convict Frederick Guy Browne was found guilty, with his accomplice 36-year-old William Henry Kennedy, of murdering a policeman in Essex in 1927. A singular feature of the murder was that the victim's eyes had been shot out.

On 27 September 1927 the body of PC Gutteridge was found in a country lane between Romford and Ongar. He had been shot 4 times. It was assumed that he had been gunned down while questioning a motorist. A car belonging to a Dr Lovell had been reported stolen in the district early on the day of the murder. This was found abandoned in London. There was blood on the body-work, and an empty cartridge case was found on the floor.

Four months after the murder the police arrested Browne at his garage in Clapham on a charge of stealing a car. Suspicions that he might have been involved in the murder hardened when a Webley revolver was found in Browne's garage. The weapon was loaded with ammunition of the type which had killed the policeman. Meanwhile Browne's accomplice, Kennedy, another ex-convict, was arrested in Liverpool. He admitted being with Browne in the car on the day of the murder. He said Browne fired the gun.

Examination of the cartridge case found in the stolen car revealed distinctive markings made by the weapon which fired it. Ballistics expert Robert Churchill demonstrated that test shots fired from the Webley revolver found in Browne's garage reproduced the markings exactly. The ammunition in Browne's revolver was of two obsolete types used in the early months of the First World War—the bullets removed from the body of the dead policeman were of the same types. Moreover, powder discolouration on the victim's skin matched the black powder used in one of the two ammunition types.

Browne and Kennedy: Browne's armoury

Ballistics evidence produced a triumph for the police and helped to establish forensic ballistics as a science. This was an important step in crime detection, following hard on the heels of the controversial ballistics evidence in the *Sacco and Vanzetti* case.

Browne and Kennedy, charged with murder, appeared at the Old Bailey in April 1928. Both were found guilty. Browne was hanged at Pentonville Prison and Kennedy at Wandsworth Prison on 31 May 1928.

[*1, 32, 81, 131, 239, 420, 462, 463, 555, 558, 559, 624, 814, 819, 826, 846, 916, 958, 964*]

BRUDOS, Jerry. 'I'm really interested in buying encyclopaedias' was the doorstep welcome given by Jerry Brudos to the saleswoman who knocked on the door of his home in Portland, Oregon, in January 1968. Door-to-door encyclopaedia sales representative Linda Slawson was not seen alive again.

Between January 1968 and April 1969 three more young women disappeared without trace in the Portland area. In May 1969 a local fisherman found the body of Linda Salee, one of the missing girls. She had been strangled, and her heavily weighted body thrown into the river. The sexually mutilated body of a second girl was found nearby two days later.

Police inquiries centred on Oregon State University and it was learned that a man, for whom a full description was given, had been in the habit of lurking around the campus, apparently looking for girls to date. Female students were alerted as to their potential danger and asked to inform the police when the man next appeared. On 25 May Jerry Brudos, aged 28, was taken in for questioning. There was insufficient evidence to hold him, and he promptly went to ground. When he was relocated and questioned a second time he told a bizarre story of rape, murder, mutilation and necrophilia. His account was amply supported by a search of his home, which turned up a huge collection of women's shoes and clothing and other paraphernalia of the fetishist.

In the garage, a separate building from the house, Brudos had installed a hook in a ceiling beam from which he suspended the bodies of his victims so that he could toy with them. He dressed his victims in a variety of clothes before photographing them. Boxes of photographic prints were found which testified to his perversions.

Brudos was charged with murder, and at first pleaded insanity. He changed his plea after 7 doctors declared him to be sane, although suffering from severe personality disorders. All his life he had been dominated by his mother, and psychiatrists used this to explain his perverted attitudes to women. He was convicted of murder and sentenced to 3 consecutive terms of life imprisonment. [877]

BRYANT, Charlotte. Illiterate, 33-year-old mother of 5 who poisoned her husband.

Charlotte Bryant was a slovenly woman who neglected her labourer husband and children in pursuit of extra-marital relationships. She developed a strong affection for a man with a gipsy background, Leonard Parsons, who lived in the Bryants' cottage at Coombe, Dorset, as a lodger.

Frederick Bryant did not seem to resent his wife's lodger, who shared their cramped accommodation; indeed, he even shared his razor with the man.

In May 1935 Frederick Bryant was taken ill. The doctor diagnosed gastro-enteritis, and within a few days he returned to work. A few months later, on 11 December, Bryant was again taken ill with violent stomach pains. Again he recovered. On 22 December he suffered further violent stomach disorders and died.

Doctors found 4 grains of arsenic in Bryant's body. On 10 February 1936 Charlotte Bryant was arrested and charged with the murder of her husband. She was tried at Dorchester Assizes in May. A tin which had contained arsenical weedkiller was found on a rubbish tip at the back of the Bryants' cottage, and traces of arsenic were found in the pockets of one of Charlotte's coats.

Neither Charlotte Bryant nor her lover, who was in court, seemed able to follow the proceedings. Indifference was the prevailing feature of the whole case, and it was perhaps her husband's indifference which led Charlotte to eliminate him by poisoning his Oxo drink with arsenical weed-killer.

Charlotte Bryant was hanged at Exeter Prison on 15 July 1936, some 12 weeks after *Dorothea*

Bryant: The lonely cottage where her husband died

Waddingham was executed for poisoning a nursing-home patient.

[*171, 297, 322, 385, 460, 489, 705, 993, 1001*]

BUCHALTER, Louis Lepke. A 47-year-old habitual criminal who graduated to big crime in New York. He was instrumental in setting up a national crime syndicate which netted $50 million annually from racketeering. In 1927 Buchalter took over the tailors and cutters union and manipulated the garment industry. Other unions fell to his criminal empire, and in 1932 he joined with 'Lucky' Luciano, becoming in 1933 chief of the infamous Murder Incorporated.

He served prison sentences for violating anti-trust laws and for narcotics offences. In 1939, while he was in prison, his colleagues implicated him in murder. He was tried in 1941 and sentenced to death, but fought a 3-year legal battle to stave off execution. Finally, on 4 March 1944, Buchalter went to the electric chair with two of his lieutenants, Louis Capone and Mindy Weiss.

[*693, 826*]

BUCHANAN, Dr Robert. Edinburgh-qualified doctor who set up in practice in New York in 1886. He murdered his second wife by giving her morphine, but failed in his attempt to deceive fellow-doctors. (see *Robert Clements*.)

Buchanan enjoyed the seamier side of life, and besides running a successful medical practice took his leisure in clubs and brothels. In 1890 he divorced his first wife and married Anna Sutherland, a brothel-proprietress, having previously persuaded her to make a will in his favour. The doctor soon found that his brothel madame did not go down too well with his patients, who threatened to transfer to another doctor.

In 1892 Buchanan said he was going to Edinburgh by himself but 4 days before he was due to sail, he cancelled his passage because of his wife's sudden illness. She died of cerebral haemorrhage. The doctor quickly collected his $50 000 inheritance.

The *New York World* got hold of the story and it was thereupon discovered that Buchanan had lied about his transatlantic passage. Less than a month after his wife's death he had remarried his first wife.

An exhumation was ordered. Although the post-mortem showed the presence of morphine in the dead woman's body, the infallible indicator—

pin-point pupils—was missing. Nevertheless, Buchanan was arrested. Witnesses stated that the doctor had claimed he could disguise morphine by putting drops of belladonna into the eyes to counteract the pin-pointing. (See *Carlyle Harris*.)

At Buchanan's trial the prosecution killed a cat in court with morphine and dramatically demonstrated that pin-pointing could indeed be prevented with belladonna. The doctor insisted on going into the witness-box, but failed to explain away his lies and boasts. He was found guilty of first-degree murder and, after various appeals, was electrocuted at Sing Sing Prison on 2 July 1895.

[*315, 862*]

BUCKFIELD, Reginald Sidney. Army deserter convicted at the Old Bailey in January 1943 for murdering Ellen Ann Symes. Buckfield wrote a fictionalized account of the murder which helped to convict him.

On 9 October 1942 Ellen Symes, a married woman, was found dead in Brompton Farm Road, Strood. She had been stabbed in the neck. Her 4-year-old son, who was with her, was unharmed. The little boy told the police his mother had been attacked by a soldier.

A soldier in uniform, Gunner Reginald Sidney Buckfield, whose ever-present grin earned him the nickname of 'Smiler', was seen in the area the following day. He was questioned and found to be a deserter. He volunteered information about his movements which placed him near the murder scene at the crucial time.

The civil police handed Buckfield over to the military authorities as a deserter. When he was placed under military escort he handed a bundle of handwritten sheets to a detective. These were the pages of a murder story called 'The Mystery of Brompton Road' by Gunner Buckfield. On 7 November Buckfield was formally charged with the murder of Mrs Symes. Asked about his murder story, he said, 'Oh, that's all fiction. That's how I thought the murder might have been committed.'

Gunner Buckfield was tried at the Old Bailey. Witnesses failed to confirm his alibi, and Buckfield contradicted his own testimony. He was trapped by his murder story, which owed less to fiction than to direct knowledge of Mrs Symes's murder.

Buckfield was found guilty and sentenced to death, but 2 weeks later, having been considered insane, was reprieved and committed to Broadmoor.

[*3, 133*]

BUNDY, Theodore Robert. Ted Bundy, a handsome, well-educated young man, was credited in 1979 with killing up to 40 women in 5 American states over a 4-year period.

Young women students began disappearing in the Seattle area of Washington state in 1974 at a rate of about one a month until mid-1975. During this sequence, in July 1974, a girl picknicking by Lake Sammamich was approached by a handsome man who asked her to help him with his boat. She declined, but heard him make the same request to another girl, to whom he introduced himself as 'Ted'. The bodies of 2 girls were later discovered near the lake; they had been strangled and clubbed to death.

Stories began to accumulate from several students about a man called 'Ted' who had tried to pick them up. The disappearances continued but the action switched to Utah and then to Colorado. On 16 August 1975 Ted Bundy was arrested in Salt Lake City, where he was studying law. Hair found in his car matched that of a girl whose body had been found. He was charged with murder and in 1977 was extradited to Colorado, where he continued to study law in prison while the prosecution case against him was prepared. On 7 June 1977 Bundy escaped only to be recaptured a few days later, but on 30 December he escaped a second time and made his way to Florida.

On 15 January 1978, posing as a student at Florida State University in Tallahassee, he attacked 2 girls in the sorority house, sexually abusing them and killing them by strangulation. Two other girls and a woman in a nearby apartment house survived attacks before he went to ground. Bundy was arrested in February and his reign of terror was ended. He was tried at Miami, where he was sentenced to death after being convicted on 3 counts of murder.

Ted Bundy, the intelligent and good-looking man with a bright future who turned serial murderer, was a criminal who fitted none of the stereotypes. He had told a detective at the time of his arrest, 'Sometimes I feel like a vampire.' He told the authors of one of the books written about him that a malignant force resided within him which gradually took over and induced him to rape and murder.

Bundy pleaded not guilty at his trial and subsequently refused to confess to any of the murders, although he was more than willing to talk about himself. In 1980 Ann Rule, a former policewoman who became a crime reporter, wrote about her association with Bundy over a period of several years when they worked as volunteers at a Seattle

Bundy: Serial murderer

Crisis Clinic. She believed that Bundy fitted no pattern and that there was nothing in his background that could be pointed to as an inevitable cause of his subsequent behaviour. The man was an enigma, and was on a different behavioural wavelength to that of the customary sex murderer, who is usually inadequate as an individual and has a poor image of himself. By contrast, Bundy was intelligent, witty and amusing. He seduced his victims by the power of his personality and confused the analytical sociologists who tried to understand him.

He was executed in Florida on 24 January 1989. [557, 799, 996]

BURDELL CASE. The murder of wealthy New York dentist Dr Harvey Burdell was a major controversy at the time and remains unsolved.

Dr Burdell's consulting-room was on the first floor of the mansion he owned on Bond Street in New York City. He rented out other rooms in the house, and over the years had built up considerable personal wealth and a reputation slightly tarnished by whispers of swindles.

On 29 January 1857 the unmistakeable, tall, bearded figure of Dr Burdell was seen entering the house at about 10.45 p.m. A cry sounding like 'Murd . . .!' was heard shortly afterwards by a neighbour, and also by a passer-by in the street. Next morning Burdell was found lying on the floor of his consulting room. He had been strangled, and

Burdell Case: The murdered dentist

also stabbed several times in the neck and chest. It appeared that he had been caught unawares as he sat working at his desk.

Absence of any signs that the house had been forcibly entered focused suspicion on the other tenants and in particular on Mrs Emma Cunningham. She had an arrangement with Burdell regarding the sub-letting of rooms to occasional boarders. At the time of the murder, there were 2 such boarders, a dealer in hides by the name of John J. Eckel and George Snodgrass, a minister's son.

Despite any lack of supporting evidence, Mrs Cunningham and her two boarders were arrested and charged with murder. Mrs Cunningham immediately made a claim on the dead man's estate, alleging that they had been secretly married. At the ensuing trial she dropped another bombshell by declaring that she was pregnant. She was found not guilty, and the charges against Eckel and Snodgrass were dropped. Mrs Cunningham continued to press her claim to the late dentist's estate, but refused to allow her pregnancy to be confirmed by doctors on the grounds of modesty. She was subsequently charged with fraud when it was discovered that she had bought an infant from an unmarried mother for $1,000. Apparently thriving on the publicity, she allowed circus proprietor P. T. Barnum to display

the child to the paying public as 'The Bogus Burdell Baby'. Her fee for this concession to curiosity was $25 a week.

These lurid sensations distracted attention from the investigation of Dr Burdell's murder, which was later thought to have been perpetrated by one of his creditors. The once wealthy dentist had slid into financial trouble, and his furniture and dental equipment were sold by auction to help pay his debts. The bloodstained carpet from his consulting-room was an especially prized item. Although a man named Lewis—executed in New York for committing another murder—claimed to have killed Burdell, this was never proved, and the case therefore remains unsolved.

[*150, 280, 665, 725, 937, 952*]

BURKE and HARE. Edinburgh's notorious body-snatchers who provided corpses for the city's nineteenth-century medical schools.

William Burke and William Hare, Irish labourers, lived in the West Port area of Edinburgh. In this sleazy district they lodged with Maggie Laird and Nell Macdougal, women of low virtue. Maggie let rooms, and when one of her lodgers died Burke and Hare took the corpse to Dr Knox, whose demand for bodies for dissection exceeded the regular supply. Since they received a handsome price for their corpse, with no questions asked, they decided to go into business.

Nature failing to meet their needs quickly enough, Burke and Hare resorted to murder. In the course of nine months they delivered 16 bodies to the dissection rooms. Their greed led them to murder persons whose disappearance was reported. In due course they were brought to justice. Burke and Nell Macdougal were tried. Hare and Maggie Laird turned King's Evidence. Nell won a verdict of Not Proven, while Burke paid the supreme penalty. He was hanged at Edinburgh on 28 January 1829 before a large crowd.

[*1, 12, 35, 40, 53, 109, 186, 243, 262, 606, 637, 756, 780, 931*]

BURROWS, Albert Edward. Married farm labourer aged 62, who murdered his mistress and her 2 children.

In 1918, 28-year-old Hannah Calladine of Nantwich, Cheshire, mother of a 2½-year-old girl, became the mistress of Edward Burrows. Later that year she had a child by him, and Burrows married her, only to be imprisoned for bigamy.

Burrows failed to pay the child-maintenance order made against him, and Calladine moved into the Burrows home at Glossop, in Derbyshire.

Burrows's life was in a mess. His wife left him and claimed maintenance, his house-rent was in arrears and he had a bastardy order against him. On 11 January 1920 he took Hannah Calladine and his bastard son on to the moors and murdered them. He threw their bodies down the air-shaft of a disused coal-mine where, the following day, he also disposed of Hannah's daughter. Burrows returned to live with his wife, and for 3 years pretended that Hannah was still alive in letters written to her mother.

On 4 March 1923 a 4-year-old boy was reported missing from his home in Glossop. Burrows, who had been seen with the child, was questioned by the police. He took them to a disused coal-mine on Symmondley Moor, where the sexually assaulted body of the boy was found in an airshaft.

Burrows was arrested and the police made a further examination of the air-shaft. There, 8 weeks later, they found the skeletons of Hannah Calladine and her 2 children. Burrows was tried at Manchester Assizes. He did not go into the witness-box, and called no witnesses. It took the jury 11 minutes to find him guilty. He was hanged at Nottingham on 8 August 1923.

[462]

BUSH, Edwin. A 21-year-old Eurasian who murdered a London shop assistant.

On 3 March 1961 Mrs Elsie May Batten, assistant in Louis Meier's Cecil Court antique shop, was found dead. An antique dagger protruded from her chest, and another from her neck.

Neighbouring shop-owners recalled a young coloured man who had been asking about the price of dress swords. The man also tried to sell a sword which was subsequently proved to have been stolen from Meier's shop.

The police took descriptions of this man, and the Identikit system was used in Britain for the first time in a murder investigation. Within 4 days a patrolling policeman recognized the man and took him in for questioning.

Edwin Bush was picked out in an identity parade by 2 Cecil Court shop-owners. Bush made a statement in which he admitted killing Mrs Batten in order to steal the sword. In court he elaborated this by saying he lost his temper when she made an offensive remark about his colour. An Old Bailey

jury found him guilty of murder, and he was executed at Pentonville on 6 July 1961.

[312, 484, 584, 928]

BUTLER, Frank. One of Australia's most notorious murderers, whose adventurous life included service in the Royal Navy, the United States Army and the Canadian North West Mounted Police. He turned up in Australia in 1893, and was soon in trouble with the police on charges of theft. After several short terms in prison he settled down in Sydney and devoted his talents to murder for profit.

Butler placed advertisements in the *Sydney Morning Herald* seeking partners for a gold-prospecting trip. His first client was a Scandinavian recently arrived in Australia with whom he set out in August 1896 bound for the Blue Mountains. Butler returned alone and waited for replies to his next advertisement. A young geology student answered, and the pair set off by train to Emu Plains. Again Butler returned alone and waited for his next respondent. Lee Mellington Weller, a sea captain, took up the offer of a gold-prospecting trip and set off with Butler to Glenbrook. Once again Butler returned alone and began selling the Captain's

Butler: 'Let go! Let go!' he told the hangman

possessions; he also started to masquerade as Captain Weller.

In November 1896 he boarded a vessel bound for San Francisco and sailed for America as reports appeared of Captain Weller's disappearance. On 3 December, while Butler was on the high seas, the party searching for Weller first found the corpse of the missing geology student and later the Captain's body, which had been put in a shallow grave. A warrant was issued for Butler's arrest and the news was imparted to the master of the vessel carrying him to America by a faster New Zealand ship outward-bound from Auckland.

When Butler's ship docked at San Francisco he was taken off and put in prison pending the outcome of extradition proceedings initiated by the Attorney General of New South Wales. He became something of a celebrity and spent his time in custody posing for sketches and selling his autograph. He was extradited from the USA and returned to Australia, where the newspapers had all but convicted him of murder.

He was tried in Sydney's Central Criminal Court in June 1897 and found guilty on largely circumstantial evidence. He made a confession on the eve of his execution and at the drop urged the hangman to perform his duty by shouting, 'Let go! Let go!' [*924*]

BUTTON and BADGE MURDER. See GREENWOOD, David

BYRNE CASE. A 27-year-old Irish construction worker who killed a young woman in Birmingham.

Police were called to investigate a report that a woman had been attacked in a YWCA hostel in the city on 23 December 1959. The 21-year-old girl, Margaret Brown, had been working in the ground-floor laundry room when she was attacked. She screamed, and her attacker ran off.

The grounds were searched and rooms checked. Room 4 in one of the hostel annexes was found to be locked. Police broke into the room, and found the naked, headless body of a woman on the floor, and on the bed a severed head. The occupant of the room, and the victim, was 29-year-old Stephanie Baird.

A full-scale search was mounted for a man whose clothing was presumed to be heavily bloodstained, house-to-house checks were made, and near-by alleys and gardens were searched.

The victim's room contained no significant fingerprints, but there was a note scribbled on an

Byrne Case: His sketch of the crime

envelope. It read, 'This was the thing I Tought would never come'. The girl had first been strangled, and the nature of the mutilations left no doubt that the killing was sexually motivated.

As the weeks passed with no developments, records were double-checked. Some 20 000 men had been interviewed, and so others were now seen. One of these men was Patrick Byrne, an Irishman now in Warrington who worked in Birmingham and had lived near the YWCA hostel.

Byrne was agitated at the routine request to have his fingerprints recorded. Probing questions elicited the confession to the YWCA killing. His handwriting matched that of the scribbled note, and he confirmed other intimate details of the crime known only to the police. Tried at Birmingham Assizes in March 1960, Byrne was found guilty of murder and sentenced to life imprisonment. On appeal a verdict of manslaughter was substituted for the original verdict, but the sentence remained unaffected. [*24, 312, 601*]

BYRON, Kitty. This 23-year-old girl stabbed her lover to death in a London street on Lord Mayor's Day in 1902.

Kitty Byron and Arthur Reginald Baker were unmarried, but lived together in lodgings. Baker drank a great deal, and the couple frequently quarrelled. On the evening of 7 November there was a violent row, and the quarrel persisted well into the night. At one stage Kitty, dressed in her nightgown, was seen on the landing as if taking refuge. The next day the landlady requested them to leave.

Baker was overheard by the maid telling the landlady that Kitty would go if he could keep the room. The landlady refused, and the maid told Kitty what had happened. She was furious; 'I'll kill him before the day is out', she said.

On 10 November, the day of the Lord Mayor's Show, Kitty bought a strong-bladed knife. Just after 1.00 p.m. she sent an express message from Lombard Street post office. It was addressed to Baker at the Stock Exchange where he worked—'Dear Reg. Want you immediate importantly. Kitty.' When Baker turned up an argument ensued; Kitty became very excited, and they walked out to the street, still arguing furiously. Then, witnessed by several bystanders, Kitty produced a knife and stabbed Baker twice. He fell to the ground, and Kitty collapsed over his body, sobbing violently.

Kitty Byron, with public sympathy behind her, was tried in December before Mr Justice Darling. She did not go into the witness-box. Her counsel asked for a verdict of manslaughter, arguing that Kitty had bought the knife to scare Baker by pretending suicide. The judge told the jury that here was a woman who had indisputably committed murder. She was found guilty with a strong recommendation to mercy.

Such was public feeling that a petition of 15 000 signatures was passed to the Home Secretary asking for a reprieve. This was granted, and the sentence was commuted to one of life, but in 1907 this was reduced to 10 years.

[*47, 58, 357, 463, 699*]

BYWATERS, Frederick. See THOMPSON and BYWATERS

C

CAILLAUX CASE. Mme Henriette Caillaux, wife of the French Finance Minister, shot the editor of *Le Figaro*, Gaston Calmette.

Henriette, a society beauty, married Joseph Caillaux after a love affair with scandalous undertones. Caillaux's first wife was given some letters written by her husband to Henriette. She used these as a lever to gain a substantial cash settlement on the break-up of the marriage.

Caillaux was an unpopular politician on account of his pacifism, and he had long been the subject of criticism in *Le Figaro*. As the war clouds gathered over Europe the newspaper's attacks on Caillaux became more bitter. The Minister countered by turning up some unsavoury facts about Gaston Calmette, the paper's editor.

On the morning of 16 March 1914 *Le Figaro* published one of Caillaux's love-letters on its front page. Fearing that her husband intended to confront Calmette, and knowing that he had a revolver, Henriette rushed out to prevent him. Unable to find him, she bought a gun, went to the *Le Figaro* building and to Calmette's office, where she killed the editor with 5 shots.

Henriette Caillaux's trial opened in Paris in July in a climate of prejudice against her and her husband. Caillaux was regarded as a betrayer of his country, while Calmette was praised as a patriot. The tide turned when evidence was produced which implicated Calmette in anti-French propaganda. By a unanimous verdict Mme Caillaux was found not guilty.
[*29, 434, 525, 758, 833*]

CALVERT, Louie. Prostitute, petty thief and murderess aged 33.

In 1925 Louie worked as housekeeper for Arthur Calvert, a nightwatchman with a house in Leeds. After a few months she told Calvert that she was pregnant, and persuaded him to marry her. As the months went by Calvert naturally expected to see obvious signs of child-bearing. But there were none.

After frequent questioning on the subject, Louie said in March 1926 that she was going to stay with her sister in Dewsbury for the confinement. She reassured her husband by sending him an arrival telegram from Dewsbury, but doubled back to Leeds, where she took lodgings with Mrs Lily Waterhouse, an eccentric widow. A teenage unmarried mother with an infant girl agreed to let Louie adopt the child. At the end of March, Louie returned to her husband with the child, which she passed off as their own.

Louie also brought back a suitcase which contained some cutlery and other household items. The police arrived and charged Louie Calvert with the murder of Mrs Waterhouse, who had been found battered to death in her home. Mrs Waterhouse had previously alerted the police to the strange behaviour of her lodger, whom she suspected of stealing from her.

Louie Calvert, who stole worthless items and killed in the process, was convicted at Leeds Assizes. She was executed at Strangeways Prison on 26 June 1926, having confessed to a previous murder, that of John William Frobisher, whose body had been found in a canal, and to whom she had acted as housekeeper under the name of Louisa Jackson.
[*460, 489, 767, 1001*]

CAMB, James. A 31 year-old ship's steward found guilty of the murder at sea of actress Gay Gibson.

In October 1947, Eileen Isabella ('Gay') Gibson was returning to England from South Africa on board the ocean liner *Durban Castle*. On 18 October, when the vessel was off the coast of West Africa, she was reported missing. Assuming that she had accidentally fallen overboard, the captain had the ship turned about, and searches were made without success.

A ship's watchman reported that at 3 a.m. on the morning of 18 October he answered a summons made on the bell-push in Miss Gibson's

Camb: Miss Gibson's Cabin 126

cabin. On reaching the cabin he saw deck steward James Camb in the doorway, who called out to him, 'All right.' When the *Durban Castle* reached Southampton she was boarded by police, who immediately interviewed Camb. He admitted visiting the cabin, claiming that he did so at Miss Gibson's invitation. They had sexual intercourse, during which the woman had a fit and died. He said he tried artificial respiration, but to no avail. Then he panicked and pushed her body out through the porthole.

Camb, charged with murder, was tried at Winchester Assizes in March 1948. Expert witnesses for the prosecution spoke of traces of blood and saliva on the bedclothes, which suggested strangulation. It was alleged that scratches on Camb's wrists had been caused by the fingernails of the woman struggling to defend herself.

Camb stuck to his story, and medical evidence given in his defence contended that the evidence did not rule out the possibility that the woman had died of natural causes, such as heart disease or a fit. What went against Camb was his lack of a satisfactory reason for not seeking help. Moreover, his admission that he pushed her body out of the porthole merely suggested that he thought a murder charge could not be brought without a body as evidence.

James Camb was found guilty on 22 March 1948, but he escaped execution because the Criminal Justice Bill's no-hanging clause was being debated in Parliament. He was sentenced to death and later reprieved.
[*1, 76, 171, 255, 297, 373, 417, 463, 897, 1010*]

CAMDEN TOWN MURDER. Bertram Shaw, a railway dining-car cook, returned to his lodgings in Camden Town about midday on 12 September 1907 to find Emily Jane Dimmock (known as 'Phyllis') with her throat cut. Phyllis was a 23-year-old prostitute with whom he had been living for 9 months.

Death had occurred between 4 and 6 in the morning, but nothing unusual had been heard, and Shaw himself was regarded with suspicion. His alibi was perfect, for he was on the London to Sheffield train. Shaw did not know that Phyllis spent her nights entertaining clients in her Camden Town lodgings. One of her haunts was the Rising Sun public house, where she had met a ship's cook and one of her clients, Robert Percival Roberts.

Roberts said that when he left Phyllis's lodgings 2 letters arrived. One invited her to meet someone signing himself 'Bert' at the Eagle public house in Camden Town that evening. Phyllis showed Roberts a postcard which she took from a chest of drawers—its message, inviting her to meet 'Alice', contained an illustration of a rising sun. Roberts thought both communications were in the same writing. Phyllis then burned the letter but put the postcard back. Charred fragments of the letter were found in the fire-grate, and Shaw discovered the postcard. This 'rising sun' card was publicized by Scotland Yard, and the writing was recognized by 2 persons, but at the time they were asked to keep the information to themselves. The person making the request was a 25-year-old artist, Robert Wood, who explained privately that he had met Phyllis in a pub. She asked him to write 'something nice' on a postcard. At her suggestion he signed it 'Alice', and later posted it to her. Wood had also asked a girl-friend, Ruby Young, to say if asked that he always stayed with her on Monday

Camden Town Murder: Charred fragments of the letter

and Wednesday nights. Miss Young was indiscreet enough to mention this to a journalist friend, who passed the information on to the police.

Wood was questioned by the police, and put on an identity parade. Several women claimed that he

Camden Town Murder: The 'Rising Sun' postcard

was the man seen with Phyllis in the Eagle on the night of the murder. When it became known that Wood had tried to suppress information about his handwriting, he was charged with murder.

He was tried at the Old Bailey in December 1907 with Edward Marshall Hall defending. The prosecution put emphasis on the similarity between fragments of writing on the charred remains of the letter and the rising sun postcard. Marshall Hall dismissed the letter as being trumped up by the man Roberts to divert suspicion from himself, and rejected the evidence of identification as 'the flimsiest and most unsatisfactory . . .' Wood gave evidence on his own behalf, for the first time with a successful outcome since the passing of the Criminal Evidence Act of 1898. The judge summed up in the accused's favour, and the jury found him not guilty. [1, 88, 252, 354, 356, 382, 438, 589, 608, 611, 649, 687, 793, 851, 872, 960]

CAREW, Edith. Walter and Edith Carew lived in a small enclave of expatriates in Yokohama, Japan, where Carew had business interests.

In the autumn of 1896 Walter Carew was suddenly taken ill. Biliousness was diagnosed, but after a brief improvement he relapsed. The doctor's puzzlement was relieved by a diagnosis for his patient's illness provided in a letter sent to him. It read, 'Three bottles of arsenic in one week. Maruya.' But it was too late to save Carew, who died of arsenical poisoning.

At the inquest a Japanese chemist, Maruya, sender of the letter, stated that he had supplied several bottles of arsenic in solution, complying with Mrs Carew's written instructions. Mrs Carew claimed that her husband suffered from a mysterious illness, unbeknown to his doctor, for which he found relief by taking doses of arsenic.

Mrs Carew was arrested, and charged with murdering her husband. Her trial, under the judicial authority of the British Consul in Yokohama, began in January 1897. It was stated that although Mrs Carew appeared to be happily married, she had complained of her husband's ill treatment to a bank clerk who became infatuated with her. Love letters sent to her by this young man were produced in court—expressions of affection were made, and the possibility of separation from her husband was mentioned.

Mrs Carew concocted a story about a fictitious woman who she said had been intimate with her husband. Letters purporting to have been written by this woman to Walter Carew were denounced in court as forgeries made by Mrs Carew.

Edith Carew was found guilty, sentence of death being commuted to penal servitude for life. [498, 1017]

CARIGNAN, Harvey. Sex murderer whose accumulated life sentences amounted to more than a hundred years. He betrayed his violent personality in 1949, when he was serving in Alaska with the US Army. He was convicted of a rape murder, and only narrowly escaped execution. After serving a term in prison he was released on parole in 1960.

Like many murderers before him, Carignan decided to advertise for his victims. In 1973, when he was running a filling station, he placed want-ads in the *Seattle Times*. A 15-year-old girl replied, and she promptly disappeared. Her body was found several weeks later, and Carignan was able to give police satisfactory answers to their questions about his possible involvement.

He moved to Denver and then to Minneapolis, and in 1974 another young girl disappeared after making his acquaintance. There followed a spate of vicious sexual assaults in the Minneapolis area in which girl hitch-hikers were driven down little-used roads to remote fields, where they were subjected to brutal violence. Survivors of these attacks were able to describe the assailant and help the police build up a profile of the man and his methods.

On 24 September 1974 two observant police officers spotted a man answering the sex-attacker's description and arrested him. He proved to be Harvey Carignan, and it was shown that his car had been at the location where one of the murders had occurred. Among his possessions were a number of maps covering the states of Washington, Kansas, Minnesota and others. Red circles marked on the maps in remote countryside areas coincided with the known locations of some of the attacks.

Carignan was known to suffer frequent rages and to spend long periods away from home. He liked to keep on the move, and drove thousands of miles crossing and recrossing state boundaries. He was charged with the attempted murder of a girl assaulted and left for dead in a field near Minneapolis. Although still partially paralysed from her injuries, she was able to testify in court. Questioned about the attack, Carignan said, 'I was sorry I didn't kill her—because I was supposed to.' He claimed that God had instructed him to kill and mutilate 4 women. The jury found him guilty, and several further trials followed.

Like *Peter Sutcliffe* and *David Berkowitz*, Carignan claimed to have been urged to kill by voices. He also claimed that God appeared to him in person, and believed he was an ambassador of murder. He was finally convicted on a variety of charges, including 2 counts of murder, and sentenced to life imprisonment.

[878]

CARITATIVO, Bart. Filipino houseboy found guilty of first-degree murder in California.

Caritativo, 52, and an American citizen, was the houseboy and chauffeur of a wealthy Californian family. In his chauffeuring duties he became acquainted with Camille Malmgren, a rich widow in her forties. Camille discovered that Caritativo, like herself, had literary aspirations. A friendship grew out of this common interest which continued after Camille married Joseph Banks in 1949.

Banks was well disposed towards Caritativo, and did not resent the Filipino's attachment to his wife. After 5 years of marriage Camille divorced Banks because of his heavy drinking, but the couple kept on good terms. In September 1954 Camille decided to sell up and live abroad.

On 17 September Hilda Grunert, a real estate agent, visited Camille to discuss the sale of her property. She saw Joseph Banks sprawled in the living-room, surrounded by empty liquor bottles. In the bedroom she found Camille lying with her head smashed in. When the police arrived they found that Banks was not drunk but dead, with a 14-inch knife in his heart. On the table was a confession note.

Camille's will was found, and in it she left her entire estate to Bart Caritativo. Both the will and an accompanying letter were badly written and contained simple spelling errors. Suspicion was aroused, and Caritativo was questioned. Handwriting experts believed that the documents were forged by the Filipino houseboy. He was charged with double murder, and tried in January 1955.

A doctor testified that Joseph Banks was too drunk to have stabbed himself. This, coupled with the evidence of forgery, convinced the jury of Caritativo's guilt. Sentence of death was carried out at San Quentin on 24 October 1958, and 3 years later the prison psychiatrist claimed that the Filipino confessed.

[108, 224]

CARRAHER, Patrick. A 40-year-old inveterate criminal from Glasgow's slums who was twice tried for murder.

In August 1938 he stabbed a soldier who tried to intervene in a street brawl. Tried by a Scottish court, he was found guilty of culpable homicide, and sentenced to 3 years penal servitude.

On release Carraher continued his criminal life of theft and housebreaking. His reputation as a killer who had done time gave him wide prestige in the underworld. He joined his brother-in-law, Daniel Bonnar—they made a formidable pair, who courted trouble.

In November 1945 Bonnar, who had been drinking heavily, encountered 3 brothers named Gordon. They also had been drinking. A fight ensued, and Bonnar, outnumbered, made off. He and Carraher sought out the rival gang and confronted the Gordons. John died in hospital from a deep knife-wound in the neck. Carraher and other participants in the fight were arrested, and Carraher was charged with murder.

At his second trial for murder in February 1946 Patrick Carraher was shopped by his erstwhile friends, who spoke freely about his boasts of killing. He was found guilty, and hanged at Barlinnie Prison on 6 April 1946.

[1]

CASTAING, Dr Edmé. French doctor who has the infamous claim to fame that he was the first physician to use morphine to commit murder.

The 27-year-old doctor found it difficult to maintain his extravagant life-style due to shortage of money and hit on a plan to improve his finances by murdering 2 of his patients. Hippolyte Ballet was a wealthy man of property who lived at Saint-Cloud near Paris. He had excluded his brother Auguste from his will, and the doctor's plan was to steal the will and destroy it, with the intention that Auguste would inherit on his brother's death. For his part in this plot Castaing would receive a substantial reward. The will was duly disposed of, and Hippolyte died mysteriously from the effects of an unknown poison.

Castaing next turned his attention to Auguste, and on 29 May 1823, while they were supping wine at an inn near Saint-Cloud, Auguste fell ill. With the doctor in constant attendance, the sick man lost consciousness and died. The local doctor who had been called in to assist became suspicious when Castaing disposed of the sick man's vomit, thereby making analysis impossible. A post-mortem indicated that Auguste Ballet had died of morphine poisoning and all eyes turned to Dr Castaing, who was the chief beneficiary under the will.

Castaing was tried for murder in the Paris Assize Court in November 1823. It was brought out in

evidence that while Ballet had been prostrate with sickness the doctor had rushed into Paris to a pharmacy. He bought a quantity of morphine acetate, giving his full name and explaining he needed the substance to kill rats for experimental work. A number of medical men gave evidence regarding the properties of morphine, which at that time was a little-known drug. Castaing was convicted of murder by poisoning, the first but not the last to use morphine for that purpose.
[724]

CHALKPIT MURDER. Thomas John Ley, one-time Minister of Justice in New South Wales, and Lawrence John Smith, a joiner, were found guilty of the murder of John McMain Mudie, a hotel barman.

On 30 November 1946 a man passing a chalkpit near Woldingham in Surrey saw the body of 35-year-old Mudie lying in a trench. Mudie was trussed up with rope, which was fastened around the neck, and had died of asphyxia. He had also been beaten about the head. It was evident that he had been killed elsewhere, and his body disposed of in the chalkpit. Two witnesses reported seeing a man at the chalkpit 2 days previously. He had driven off in a car, part of the registration plate bearing the figures 101.

On 14 December a man named John William Buckingham, who hired cars, reported to the police, and told them how the body came to be in the chalkpit. Thomas Ley, 67, was enamoured of a widow in her sixties, Mrs Maggie Brook. Ley was intensely jealous of this woman, and his insane passion fell on Mudie, who lived at the same lodging-house as Mrs Brook, and who Ley assumed to be involved with her. He conceived a scheme to abduct Mudie from a contrived cocktail party and have him taken to his house, where he was to be forced to sign a confession. To do this Ley needed help. Lawrence Smith, John Buckingham

Chalkpit Murder: Mudie's body

and two others conspired to assist him in a plan which ended in murder.

A Ford car with the registration FGP 101 was traced to Smith, who was the man seen at the chalkpit. Buckingham turned King's Evidence, but Ley and Smith were charged with the murder, and were tried before Lord Goddard at the Old Bailey.

Smith admitted throwing a blanket over Mudie's head and tying him up in Ley's house, but he denied killing him. He was given £200 by Ley for his part in the plan. This statement was broadly in agreement with Buckingham's story. Ley denied everything, and his evidence was a mixture of bluster and rambling irrelevance.

Ley and Smith were both found guilty. Ley told the judge that his summing-up was biased. Both men were sentenced to death, but on 5 May 1947 Ley was reprieved by the Home Secretary and committed to Broadmoor, where he died of a stroke on 24 July 1947. Smith's sentence was reduced to life imprisonment.

[1, 3, 116, 179, 610, 618, 798, 851, 859]

CHANTRELLE, Eugène Marie. A 44-year-old Frenchman who came to England in 1862 after supporting the Communistic cause in France in 1851. He taught French at English schools before settling down to teaching at a private academy in Edinburgh. There he seduced a 15-year-old pupil, Elizabeth Cullen Dyer, and, having made her pregnant, married her in 1868.

The Chantrelles had 4 children, and Elizabeth was a good wife and mother. Her life, however, soon became a misery, as her husband took to ill-treating her. He developed dissolute habits which affected his teaching career; he lost pupils, and his income was reduced. He then began to threaten to kill his wife, boasting that he could do it and defy detection.

In 1877 Chantrelle insured his wife against accident for £1000. Shortly afterwards a servant found Elizabeth Chantrelle unconscious in her bedroom. Chantrelle was summoned, and was left to tend his wife. There was a strong smell of gas in the room afterwards. The doctor was told by Chantrelle that his wife had been overcome by gas escaping from a leaking pipe, but she died.

A post-mortem confirmed that death was not due to coal-gas poisoning, and a narcotic was suspected. Chantrelle was arrested.

Strong circumstantial evidence was put forward. Opium had been found in vomited matter

on Mrs Chantrelle's bed-clothes, and Chantrelle was known to have purchased the drug.

Found guilty of murder, he made no confession, and was hanged on 31 May 1878.

[1, 332, 652, 784]

ANN CHAPMAN CASE. Ann Chapman, a freelance radio journalist, was found dead on 18 October 1971 in a field near the Pine Hill Hotel at Kavouri, a Greek seaside resort. The 25-year-old girl (who had a degree in psychology) had travelled to Greece to record interviews for a holiday tour company. She confided to her family that while in Greece she also planned to follow 'a big story', but did not say what it was.

On the evening of 15 October Chapman left the other members of her party at the Pine Hill Hotel, saying she was taking a bus to Athens to attend a party. She was not seen alive again. Three days later her body was found lying in a field some 200 yards from the hotel and about 20 yards from the main road. She was tied up with wire, and had been strangled.

The murder occurred during the reign of the Colonels in Greece, and the air was thick with political intrigue. Ann Chapman's parents were suspicious about the attitude of the Greek authorities and thought 'the police must be hiding something'. Ten months after the murder, Nikolaos Moundis, a 37-year-old former prison guard with a local reputation as a 'Peeping Tom', was arrested in Kavouri. Moundis had apparently been denounced by his family as the killer of the English girl and confessed as much to the police. He quickly retracted this admission, alleging that it was made under duress, but in April 1973 was put on trial. The court, consisting of 4 judges and 4 jurors, found him guilty of attempted rape and manslaughter.

The legal proceedings under which Moundis was convicted were widely regarded as questionable. The man who found the murder victim's body did not give evidence, and the post-mortem report was not available to the court. When the medical report was made known its findings clearly showed the conviction of Moundis to be wrong. The Greek was left-handed, whereas the autopsy showed the victim had been strangled by 'a right hand compressing the neck'. Wounds inflicted on the head and face with a blunt instrument were also at variance with Moundis's reconstruction of events.

Despite pressure from many quarters, the Greek government refused to reopen the case, and in December 1983 Moundis was released from prison on parole. Moundis had his appeal for retrial twice rejected by the Supreme Court. If there was unease that an innocent man had been made a scapegoat by the authorities, there was considerable disquiet over the possible reasons.

There have been theories that Ann Chapman, an intelligent and enterprising young journalist, stumbled across a big story concerning the underground resistance to the military regime which ruled Greece between 1967 and 1974. She also stumbled into danger, for the story she sought involved the secret intelligence operations of several countries. Word that a London journalist was nosing out a story reached the Colonels' security agents, who decided to rough her up a little and find out exactly what she knew. When she failed to respond to their questions she was beaten up and silenced in a murderous assault staged to look like a sexual attack.

Moundis told a British lawyer that he did see Ann Chapman outside the Pine Hill Hotel and witnessed her abduction by 4 men who took her off in a car. He claimed to have recognized the men as policemen, one of whom was an official at the Ministry of Public Security and Order. While Ann Chapman's death is officially solved as far as the Greek government is concerned, the incidents surrounding her murder remain very much open to question. In 1984 European MP Richard Cottrell took up the case with the European Parliament, which challenged the Greek government with the contention that Ann Chapman was not murdered by Moundis but by agents of the State acting illegally. This led to the Greek's release by presidential edict, although without the benefit of a pardon.
[198, 848]

CHAPMAN, George. His real name was Severin Klosowski, and he was the son of a Polish carpenter. He was aged 38 and poisoned 3 women in London.

Chapman came to England in 1888, and worked as a barber's assistant in London's East End. He married in 1889 and went to America. By 1895 he had parted from his wife, and on returning to England lived with a married woman, Isabella Spink. He used her money to set up as landlord of a public house in City Road. After a few months Mrs Spink became ill with vomiting and abdominal pains. She died in December 1897.

The following year Chapman employed a young woman, Bessie Taylor, as barmaid. She too became ill, and she died in February 1901. The doctors were puzzled but not suspicious.

Soon Chapman took on another barmaid, Maud Marsh. Like her predecessors, she developed abdominal pains and became very ill. Again, the doctors were baffled but Miss Marsh's mother suspected poisoning, and mentioned the possibility to her own doctor. Maud Marsh died on 22 October 1902. Now strongly suspecting poisoning the doctor refused to grant a death certificate. Miss Marsh was found to have died of antimony poisoning, as were the other 2 women when their bodies were exhumed.

Chapman (who was known to have purchased tartar emetic from a local chemist) was charged with the murder of Maud Marsh, and found guilty at his trial at the Old Bailey. He was hanged on 7 April 1903.

Chapman's name is often linked with the murders of *Jack the Ripper*. Chief Inspector Abberline, who investigated the Ripper murders, said to the officer who arrested Chapman, 'You've got Jack the Ripper at last!' It has been suggested that Chapman, motivated by sadism, gave up the Ripper-style murders because of the increased danger of detection, and took to poisoning his victims instead.
[1, 21, 110, 129, 265, 442, 468, 648]

Chapman: Klosowski alias Chapman

CHAPMAN, Gerald. The term 'Public Enemy No. 1' was coined to describe Gerald Chapman, a legendary figure in the American crime world in the 1920s. He teamed up with Dutch Anderson while in prison and, on their release, the pair worked as con-men in Chicago.

They changed their operations to New York City in 1921 and carried out what at the time was America's greatest robbery, stealing over $1 million by holding up a mail truck. Chapman developed a taste for high living, taking a fashionable apartment and earning himself the title 'Count of Gramercy Park'.

He was in and out of prison, and had a reputation as a daring escaper who won public admiration. Cinema audiences cheered when his escapades featured on newsreels, and supporters sent him flowers when he was in prison. The gentleman crook once explained his philosophy by saying that he did not believe it was wrong to rob when speculators made money every day on Wall Street.

In October 1924 he went too far when, during the course of robbing a department store in New Britain, Connecticut, he shot and killed a police officer. Chapman escaped from the scene but his partner in crime named him as an accomplice. He was committed for trial and sentenced to hang. He wrote epigrams while in custody and remarked that 'Death itself isn't dreadful but hanging seems an awkward way of entering the adventure.'

The adventure for Chapman began or ended on 6 April 1926.
[*16*]

CHAPMAN, Mark David. This 25-year-old security guard from Hawaii shot and killed John Lennon, the international singing star, on 8 December 1980. On that evening he approached Lennon and his wife as the couple returned to their apartment in Manhattan. Calling out, 'Hey, John', Chapman fired five shots at Lennon from close range. Mortally wounded, the singer died in hospital while his murderer, clutching a copy of Lennon's album *Double Fantasy*, waited to be arrested.

Chapman was charged with second-degree murder and admitted to hospital for psychiatric examination; his state of mind was the subject of much attention at his trial in June 1981. The murder of such a well-known figure as Lennon on a New York street sent shock-waves around the pop music world. Hundreds of mourners gathered outside the entrance to his apartment in a candle-lit vigil, weeping and singing his songs. As always on such occasions, there were calls for the US Congress to bring in gun-control laws.

Chapman, Gerald: The Count of Gramercy Park

Known to his school friends as a 'Jesus freak', Chapman dropped out of school to devote his energies to good causes. He worked as a counsellor for the YMCA in Beirut in 1976, and was regarded as a sensitive and compassionate person. In 1977 he went to live in Hawaii, where he married a Japanese girl and appeared to settle down. His interests included religion, music, painting and literature, and he was particularly devoted to the Beatles' songs.

J. D. Salinger's book *The Catcher in the Rye* had long been a source of inspiration for Chapman. He had it with him when he killed Lennon, read from it at his trial and kept it by his side while in prison. He apparently took a great deal of the novel literally, and began to identify himself with the central character, an adolescent expressing dissatisfaction with a world which he regarded as phoney.

Chapman's adoration of the Beatles turned into hate-filled resentment which he projected against Lennon, his former idol. He bought a revolver in Hawaii for $169 and flew to New York to confront the singer. He stalked Lennon for several days, and earlier on the day of the murder asked for and was given the singer's autograph.

Chapman's lawyer entered a plea of insanity, but his client changed his plea to guilty when he came up for trial in June 1981. The psychiatrist who had examined *David Berkowitz*, the Son of Sam murderer, testified that at one moment Chapman was an ordinary person but in the next was the type of individual who was hurt by the slightest grievance. His adoration of his future victim was so complete at one stage that he believed he *was* John Lennon. Then the hate set in and he decided the way to self-preservation was to kill his idol. He had prayed to the powers of evil to assist him in carrying out this mission.

If the defence's argument was that the killing was a substitute for Chapman's own suicide, the prosecution took the more straightforward view that his shooting of the singer was intended to bring him fame. Asked if he had anything to tell the court, Chapman quoted from *The Catcher in the Rye*. He talked of standing on 'the edge of some crazy cliff' and said that the book was his statement. Convicted of murder, Mark Chapman was sentenced to 20 years to life imprisonment and was ordered to receive psychiatric treatment.
[*651, 996*]

CHARING CROSS TRUNK MURDER.
See ROBINSON, John

CHESNEY, Ronald. See MERRETT, John Donald

CHEVIS CASE. Unsolved murder case in which Lieutenant Hubert George Chevis, a young artillery officer, died after eating poisoned partridge.

Chevis and his wife had the customary evening meal in their quarters at a camp near Aldershot on 21 June 1931. Partridge was served, but after

Chevis Case: The mysterious telegram

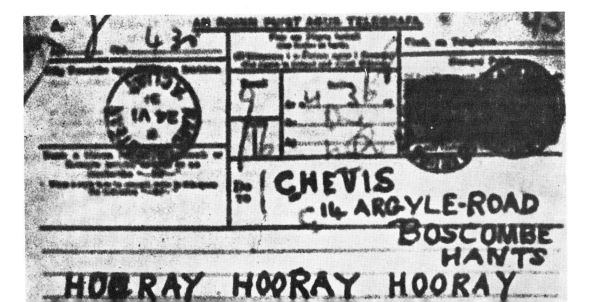

taking a mouthful Chevis declined to eat any more because of its bad taste. Within minutes he was violently ill, and he died an agonizing death the following day. He had been poisoned with strychnine. His wife was ill, but recovered.

The Coroner's Court returned an open verdict, but there was no doubt that Chevis had been murdered. His father, Sir William Chevis, received a telegram on the day of his son's funeral which read simply: 'Hooray, hooray, hooray.' It was sent from Dublin by a 'J. Hartigan'. Later Sir William received another telegram from the same source. It read, 'It is a mystery they will never solve.'

[332]

CHRISTIE, John Reginald Halliday. The 55-year-old mass murderer and sexual psychopath who murdered at least 6 women.

In 1949 Christie lived with his wife in the ground-floor flat at 10 Rillington Place, a grimy house in London's Notting Hill Gate. On the top floor lived *Timothy John Evans*, aged 24, a semi-literate van-driver, with his wife and infant daughter.

On 30 November 1949 Evans walked into a police station in Wales and reported that he had found his wife dead in their London home, and had put her body down a drain. Later the bodies of his wife and year-old child were found in the backyard—they had been strangled. Evans made a statement in which he confessed to the killings, but later he accused Christie. Christie, a witness at

Evans's trial at the Old Bailey in 1950, denied any responsibility. Evans was sentenced to death for the murder of his child, and was hanged on 9 March 1950.

On 24 March 1953 a West Indian tenant of 10 Rillington Place found a papered-over cupboard in Christie's former flat—it contained the bodies

Christie: (above) Where the bodies of Mrs Evans and her child were found; (below) The Evanses' kitchen; (right) Christie's pubic-hair fetish of 3 women. A fourth was found under the floorboards of another room, and the remains of 2 more in the garden. Christie admitted to murdering 4 women, one of them his wife, at 10 Rillington Place. The others, all in their twenties, were prostitutes. He later admitted to murdering the other 2 women in 1943 and 1944. He was then a special constable in the War Reserve Police.

Christie's motives were sexual—he admitted strangling one of his victims during intercourse. Outwardly a respectable but unpopular man, Christie had served prison sentences for theft, and he was known as a habitual liar. In his teens he was known as 'Reggie-no-dick' on account of his sexual inadequacy.

Christie was tried at the Old Bailey for his wife's murder. He related how he had invited women to the house and having got them partly drunk, sat them in a deck-chair, where he rendered them unconscious with coal gas. He then strangled and raped them. His defence plea was based on insanity. Among the various revelations at his trial was his admission that he had also killed Mrs Evans, although he denied having killed the baby. This confession resulted in a legal inquiry as to whether a miscarriage of justice had occurred in the case of Timothy Evans. It was concluded that Evans had been justly sentenced, and that Christie's confession as he said 'The more the merrier' was a device to aid his own defence in some way, but there seems little doubt that Evans was innocent and his confession false. Christie was hanged at Pentonville on 15 July 1953.

[*1, 78, 155, 156, 224, 300, 306, 317, 487, 522, 565, 609, 657, 697, 737, 851, 923, 962*]

CHRISTOFI, Styllou. A 53-year-old illiterate Cypriot who killed her daughter-in-law out of obsessive jealousy, and who had been tried and acquitted in Cyprus in 1925 for the murder of her mother-in-law by ramming a burning torch down her throat.

Stavros Christofi was happily married to a 36-year-old German girl, Hella. They had 3 children and lived in Hampstead. Stavros was a waiter, and Hella worked in a fashion shop.

In July 1953 Stavros's mother arrived from Cyprus. She was a matriarch in the classic mould, she spoke little English and her peasant origins allowed her no understanding of the life her son and daughter-in-law lived.

On the evening of 29 July 1954, after Stavros had left the house, Mrs Christofi stunned Hella with the ash-plate from the stove and strangled her. A neighbour taking his dog into his garden about midnight saw the glow of flames in the Christofis' backyard—Mrs Christofi was attempting to burn her daughter-in-law's body with paraffin-soaked newspaper.

Mrs Christofi herself raised the alarm by stopping a car in the street and shouting, 'Please come. Fire burning. Children sleeping.' The driver saw the corpse in the garden and called the police. Mrs Christofi said she had woken up about 1.0 a.m. smelling smoke and found Hella lying in the yard. Hella's wedding ring was found wrapped in a piece of paper in her mother-in-law's room.

Mrs Christofi was tried at the Old Bailey. She was found guilty and hanged at Holloway Prison on 13 December 1954.

[*487, 1001*]

CHUNG YI MIAO. A 28-year-old Chinese with a doctorate in law who married a wealthy young Chinese girl, 29-year-old Wai Sheung, in New York in 1928 and sailed to Britain for the honeymoon.

Arriving on 18 June, the couple went to Grange, in the Lake District, where they stayed at the Borrowdale Gates Hotel. Miao's wife travelled with jewellery worth nearly £4000, and she was wearing two expensive rings.

The next day the couple went for a walk and Miao returned alone. He made various excuses to the hotel staff concerning his wife's absence, including the explanation that she had gone to Keswick to do some shopping. At 7.30 p.m. her strangled body was found beside a riverside path.

Police informed Miao that his wife had been found dead. He exclaimed, 'It is terrible, my wife assaulted, robbed and murdered.' But none of these possibilities had been mentioned, the bedroom was searched and Miao was duly charged with his wife's murder.

He was tried at Carlisle Assizes in November 1928. The circumstantial evidence, which the judge in his summing-up referred to as 'sometimes better than any other sort of evidence', was strongly against Miao. The ligatures around the dead woman's neck were of the same cord as the hotel blinds, and a diamond solitaire and a wedding ring known to have been worn by the murder victim were found hidden in a film carton among Miao's possessions.

He was found guilty and hanged at Manchester's Strangeways Goal on 6 December 1928.

The motive imputed to Miao was one of thwarted sexual desire, but after he had been executed a newspaper article suggested that he killed his wife in order that he might marry a woman who would give him children.

[*131, 462, 493*]

CLEFT CHIN MURDER. See JONES and HULTEN

CLEMENTS, Dr Robert. A 57-year-old doctor and Fellow of the Royal College of Surgeons who murdered his fourth wife with morphine, and possibly the first three too.

On 26 May 1947 Dr Robert George Clements called in a fellow-physician to attend his wife, who was ill in their Southport home. Mrs Clements was taken to a nursing-home, where she died the following day of an illness diagnosed as mycloid leukaemia.

Doctors carrying out a post-mortem noticed the pin-pointed pupils of the dead woman's eyes. An overdose of morphine was suspected. Inquiries showed that Mrs Clements's health had deteriorated over a long period, during which she had experienced vomiting and lethargy. Friends complained that they could no longer keep in touch with the sick woman because her husband had had the telephone removed. Finally, when it became known that Dr Clements had prescribed morphine for a patient who never received it, Mrs Clements's funeral was stopped and a second post-mortem ordered.

It was clearly established that Mrs Clements had died of morphine poisoning. When the police called on Dr Clements they found him dead—he had taken his own life with an overdose of morphine. Dr James Houston, who first examined the body, also committed suicide, appalled at his wrong diagnosis.

A Coroner's Court found Dr Clements to be the murderer of his wife, whose death would have made him heir to her considerable fortune. His 3 previous wives, all substantially well off, had died of various diseases which Dr Clements had recorded above his signature on their death certificates, and wife No. 3 had been cremated just before the police arrived to claim the body for an autopsy.

Unlike *Dr Robert Buchanan*, Clements had made no attempt to conceal the tell-tale morphine pin-pointing of his victim's eyes.

[*152, 315*]

CLUTTER MURDERS. The brutal murder of 4 members of the Clutter family at Holcomb,

Kansas, on 15 November 1959 was the subject of Truman Capote's *In Cold Blood*.

Herbert Clutter, a wheat-grower and respected citizen of the Kansas community at Holcomb, was found dead with his throat cut and shot through the head in the basement of his home, River Valley Farm. His wife and teenaged son and daughter were also found in the house savagely murdered by shotgun wounds inflicted at close range. The victims had been bound at the wrists and 3 of them gagged. The murderer had collected the empty shell-cases, and had robbed the house.

The key to the murders was provided by an inmate of Kansas State Penitentiary, Floyd Wells. He had once worked for Clutter, and during a previous gaol sentence, had shared a cell with a man named Richard Eugene Hickock. The two men talked about jobs they had done, and Clutter's name was mentioned by Wells. Hickock questioned him intently. Was Clutter wealthy? Did he keep a safe? There was talk that Hickock, aided by one Perry Smith, would rob the Clutter place and silence all the witnesses.

When Wells heard of the murders he told the Prison Warden. Hickock and Smith were found in Las Vegas. On being confronted with footprint evidence placing him at the scene, Hickock said, 'Perry Smith killed the Clutters—I couldn't stop him. He killed them all.' The two men believed that Clutter kept $10 000 in his safe. They only netted between 40 and 50 dollars.

Hickock and Smith were tried at Kansas City in March 1960. Hickock was known to suffer intense headaches following a car crash in 1950, and Smith was considered to be paranoid. In his confession Smith said of Clutter, 'He was a nice gentleman . . . I thought so right up to the moment I cut his throat.' Hickock said Smith shot all 4 victims; Smith said he killed only the women.

Having been reminded by the prosecutor about 'chicken-hearted jurors' who refused to do their duty, the jury found each accused man guilty on all 4 counts of murder. Richard Hickock, aged 33, and Perry Smith, aged 36, were hanged at Lansing, Kansas, in April 1965.

[*162*]

COETZEE, Jacobus Hendrik. Young South African detective whose promising career as a police officer was shattered when he killed a pregnant girl.

The body of a young girl, badly bruised and with torn clothes, was found near the railway line at a spot some 126 miles from Pretoria on 1 February

1935. She also had a .32 calibre bullet in the head. The girl was pregnant, and had gone into labour shortly before death. The infant was born alive, but did not survive.

Railway police sent two detectives to the scene. One of these was Detective Sergeant Coetzee. They found evidence of a violent struggle and picked out tyre-tracks in the grass.

The victim had not been identified, but after a young farm girl disappeared her employer went to the police. He recognized the corpse from photographs as this girl, Gertrina Petrusina Opperman. He showed detectives a letter, dated 29 January, to the dead girl. It read, 'Everything is still arranged. We will talk.' The note was signed 'J. H. Coetzee.' It was revealed that Coetzee had met the girl several times, and had been found in compromising circumstances with her.

On 3 February Coetzee was arrested. He denied the charge of murder, but circumstantial evidence began to build up. Coetzee had in his possession ammunition of the same type as the fatal bullet, and blood was found on a pair of his trousers. The motive suggested was that the girl was about to name Coetzee as the father of her child.

Sergeant Coetzee was tried for murder at Pretoria in May 1935. He was calm in court, and while admitting intimacy with Miss Opperman, denied responsibility for her pregnancy. He said he had received letters making paternity allegations—he disputed these, but offered her financial support.

The prosecution exposed the weaknesses of this defence, and the jury brought in a guilty verdict, adding a recommendation to mercy. The judge acted on this, sentencing Coetzee to life imprisonment.

[65, 76]

COFFIN, Wilbert. Controversial Canadian case in which the accused murderer escaped from custody and voluntarily gave himself up, to face 7 stays of execution before being hanged.

In June 1953 three Americans left their homes in Pennsylvania and headed north for a hunting expedition in a remote area of Canada's Quebec Province. They were reported missing on 5 July, and the Canadian authorities mounted a search. The hunters' truck was found near an abandoned mining camp on the St John River. Wilbert Coffin, a 43-year-old prospector, said he had encountered 3 Americans on 10 June and helped them with their vehicle which had broken down.

One of the bodies was found at a location known

as Camp 24 and the others at Camp 26, some 2 miles away. The corpses had been badly mauled by bears, and moved from the original places where they had been felled by rifle-shots. One of the dead men was known to have had a considerable sum of money with him, and the theory was that he had been robbed and murdered and his companions were then killed because they were witnesses.

Wilbert Coffin, who had admitted meeting the hunters, was arrested and charged with murder. The evidence against him was controversial, and his statement (corroborated by independent witnesses) that he had seen 2 other Americans in the area travelling in a jeep was not followed up. He was convicted of murder and sentenced to death, but after his appeal was turned down he escaped from Quebec City Prison in 1955, bluffing his way past guards with a revolver fashioned from a piece of soap. He consulted his lawyer, who advised him to give himself up. Coffin returned to prison and after numerous stays of execution was hanged on 10 February 1956.

Two years later a man arrested in Miami confessed to murdering the 3 hunters and implicated a second man. Despite this confession and the knowledge that a jeep matching the description given by Coffin had been found abandoned near Bathurst, the Quebec police were disinclined to pursue the matter. The last word lay with Coffin's executioner, who said, 'This man, I swear, was innocent.'
[*429*]

COHEN, Ronald John Vivian. The 41-year-old son of a South African millionaire accused of wife-murder.

Cohen ran a successful business in Cape Town financing building projects. He married a second time in 1963, and his bride, Susan, a beautiful girl half his age, mothered the 2 children of his previous marriage. The Cohens lived in a lavish house in a fashionable district of the city.

On 5 April 1970, about 11.00 p.m., Cohen roused his housekeeper. He had blood on his shirt, and he told her 'Someone has broken in.' Susan Cohen lay sprawled on the floor of the library with her head smashed in. The police were called, and Cohen, bordering on hysteria, stated that he had found his wife struggling with an intruder. He said that he had grabbed a bronze statuette, intending to fight off the attacker, but after that his memory had blacked out. He was examined by a doctor, who noted bruises and scratches on his arms. The police found no disorder in the murder room.

Ronald Cohen was arrested and tried in Cape

Cohen: Court reconstruction of the murder

Town in August 1970. The trial was one of the most dramatic in South Africa's judicial history, chiefly on account of the arguments concerning Cohen's mental state and alleged loss of memory. The judge found it difficult to believe that in such circumstances a man would not have put up the fight of his life to defend his wife and home.

A motive for the killing was lacking, for nothing was stolen from the house and Mrs Cohen had not been sexually assaulted. It was suggested that Cohen killed his wife unintentionally, in a moment of intense rage when he lost all control. This was described as a moment of insanity, not in the legal sense but in 'another sense'.

Ronald Cohen was found guilty as charged by the judge, but was said to have committed the crime in a period of diminished responsibility. He was sentenced to 12 years' imprisonment.
[*71*]

COLLINS, John Norman. A 22-year-old student at Eastern Michigan University whose brutal murder of a co-ed was confirmed by scientific evaluation of trace evidence.

During the period August 1967 to June 1969 6 particularly brutal murders occurred in the Ypsilanti area of Michigan. The victims had been variously shot, strangled, stabbed and bludgeoned with accompanying sexual mutilations. The police were frustrated by a lack of leads, and Dutch 'psychic detective' Peter Hurkos failed to find the killer.

In July 1969 a seventh victim was added to the list when the strangled and sexually assaulted body of 18-year-old Karen Sue Beckemann was found near Ypsilanti. Karen Sue had been seen with a motor-cyclist named as John Collins. Several co-eds spoke of Collins's strange behaviour: he had up-dated the Fifth Commandment, saying, 'If a man had to kill, he killed.' He had also hinted that he was the Michigan co-ed killer.

Collins was apprehended, but released because of insufficient evidence. The breakthrough came when incriminating trace evidence was found in the basement of a relative's house which Collins had used during the owner's absence on holiday. His aunt, Mrs Loucks, found stains which she pointed out to her husband, Ypsilanti police officer Dana Loucks. Collins admitted using the basement, not realizing that the stains were soon to be proved blood of the same group as Karen Sue. Moreover, human hair clippings of male origin found in the basement were matched to similar hairs found on the underclothing of the murdered girl. Mrs Loucks was in the habit of cutting the hair of her 2 boys in the basement, and the traces of her barbering were picked up by the girl's body.

Collins was tried at Ann Arbor in 1970. The proceedings were largely taken up by technical evidence relating to the trace evidence. This was sufficient to convict Collins, who was sentenced to confinement and hard labour for life.
[*527*]

CONEYS, Theodore. Known as the 'Spiderman of Denver', Coneys, a 59-year-old vagrant, committed a bizarre murder in 1941.

Coneys gained access to the house of elderly Philip Peters with the intention of committing theft. Once inside he decided to take up residence in the attic, where he stayed for ten months, making periodic excursions for food when Peters left the house to visit his wife, who was in hospital.

On 17 October 1941 Coneys came down from the attic when he thought the coast was clear but disturbed Philip Peters, who was taking a nap in the kitchen. Seizing a poker, Coneys felled the old man and left him lying in the kitchen while he returned to the attic.

Neighbours eventually found the dead man and shared the vexation of the police confronted by murder in a house where all the doors were securely locked from the inside. When Mrs Coneys returned to the house from hospital she thought she heard noises in the roof. There was talk of ghosts, and she was so disturbed by the occurrence that she left the house and police officers were installed to see if they could solve the mystery. On 30 July 1942 Coneys was spotted disappearing into the roof following one of his periodic sorties. 'The Spiderman of Denver' was brought down from his attic hiding-place and charged with murder. He was sentenced to life imprisonment for killing Philip Peters.

[*773*]

COOK, JONES and NEWALL. Raymond Cook, Eric Jones and Kim Newall were sentenced to life imprisonment in 1967 for a murder which they had rehearsed.

On 2 March 1967 police were called to a car crash near the Oxfordshire village of Nettlebed. A red Mini was found among beech-trees, but little damage had been sustained to it apart from a broken headlamp; the windscreen was still intact, although the interior of the car was heavily bloodstained. The two occupants, Raymond and June Cook, were taken to hospital and it came as a considerable surprise when June Cook died of head injuries.

Raymond Cook said that he and his wife were driving home at about 10.0 p.m. and that because he felt sick he asked his wife to drive. He remembered being dazzled by oncoming lights before the impact of the collision. He thought their speed was between 30 and 40 mph. Forensic investigations at the scene of the crash estimated that the car was travelling at no more than 10 mph when it came to a halt against a tree. Pathologists conducting the post-mortem on the dead woman believed that the severe head injuries she had sustained had been caused by a blunt instrument. There was thus a great discrepancy between the apparent cause of the injuries and the head wounds themselves.

Inquiries revealed that Raymond Cook was overshadowed by his wife, a teacher with a forceful character who earned more than he did. In 1966 Cook took a job as a student nurse at Boroughcourt Mental Hospital near Nettlebed, where he met Kim Newall, a fellow-nurse. Cook and Newall fell for each other, and in due course he left his wife so that he and Newall could live together. In January 1967 June Cook altered her will in the hope of achieving a reconciliation with her husband. Previously their children had been named as beneficiaries, but now it was made out in her husband's favour. By this time Newall was pregnant and Raymond Cook was in financial trouble.

Newall asked a friend, Eric Jones, to arrange an abortion for her, and out of the discussion between the three emerged a plan to concoct a fatal accident for June Cook. The three conspirators rehearsed a scheme involving a riverside car accident which would result in the driver being drowned. This ploy was abandoned in favour of the faked car accident in the beech woods at Nettlebed. On the night in question Jones lay in wait on the quiet road and flagged down Cook with a request to borrow his foot pump to inflate a flat tyre. Cook offered him a lift, and after he got into the car the pair of them attacked June Cook, first with fists and then with a car jack. When she was unconscious they put the car into gear with the intention of staging a substantial impact. In the event, the faked accident failed to convince anyone.

Jones pleaded guilty to the charge and gave evidence for the prosecution at the trial. He related the story of how he was prevented by Cook from implementing the accidental drowning plans because the will had not at that time been changed. Raymond Cook, Eric Jones and Kim Newall were convicted of murder and sentenced to life imprisonment.

[*24, 598*]

COOK, William E. Aged 33, son of a Missouri mine-worker, he was afflicted with a drooping eyelid. Like *Richard Speck*, he was also born to be a hell-raiser—he told his father, 'I'm gonna live by the gun and roam.'

On 30 December 1950 a motorist stopped to pick up a hitch-hiker near Lubbock, Texas. The man said he wanted a lift to Joplin, Missouri, and produced a gun. He forced the driver into the trunk of his own car and drove off. During the journey the trapped man managed to prise the lid open, and when the car slowed he leapt out and ran for it. The gunman drove to Highway 66, where he abandoned the stolen car and set about hitching a lift.

The Mosser family, Carl and Thelma, their 3 children and dog, were driving to New Mexico when a man flagged them down. He then produced a gun, got into the car and ordered Mosser to drive on.

Mosser drove aimlessly following the gunman's directions—to Carlsbad, New Mexico, to El Paso to Houston. They had to stop for petrol at Wichita Falls, and Mosser took the opportunity to jump the gunman, but was thwarted. The gunman ordered Carl Mosser to stop on a deserted road, where he shot and killed all 5 members of the family and their dog. He drove the car containing his victims to some mine workings near Joplin where he disposed of them.

On 3 January 1951 a deputy sheriff spotted the Mossers' bullet-holed, bloodstained car, and the alarm was raised. Their movements were traced, and the service station attendant at Wichita Falls told police what had taken place. The description of the gunman was corroborated by the man who had escaped from his clutches a few days earlier. When his car was returned he found a receipt in it which did not belong to him—it was made out to 'W. E. Cook' for the purchase of a firearm at El Paso.

Cook featured in police records, and was traced to Blythe, California. Incredibly, an officer sent to apprehend him was himself threatened with a gun and made to drive out to the desert. There Cook dumped him unharmed, but later forced himself on a passing motorist, Robert Dewey, whom he killed near Yuma, Arizona. Psychologists thought that Cook's actions were a savage reprisal against a society that did not give him a normal family.

Cook was finally arrested in Mexico, and in due course the bodies of the Mosser family were found. He was tried for the murder of Robert Dewey and convicted. On 12 December 1952 he died in San Quentin's gas chamber.

[693, 883]

COOKE, Eric Edgar. A 32-year-old burglar who took to murder and terrorized Perth with his night-time killings in 1963. Cooke was an ex-Australian Army man who had served in the Korean War. Married with 7 children, he worked as a truck-driver by day and as a burglar by night. After killing a woman in the course of committing robbery in 1969, he developed a liking for violence.

In January 1963 a couple seated in their parked car at Cottesloe were shot and wounded by a gunman who quickly fled to the suburbs. An orgy of violence followed: a young man was shot through the head while he lay sleeping in bed; a retired businessman was shot dead when he answered a knock at his front door; and a student was shot dead in his bed. The man first shot died of his injuries, bringing the toll to 3 fatal killings in one night.

A massive police hunt ensued, and Perth and its environs became a place of fear. For 6 months there was an uneasy lull, but on 10 August the nocturnal gunman struck again and shot dead a student baby-sitting for a family in Crawley. Questions about the murders and the ability of the police to stop them were asked in the Australian Parliament,

Cooke: The murdering cat-burglar

and help was sought from Scotland Yard and the FBI.

The weapon used in the murders was a .22 rifle. While painstakingly testing 60,000 such rifles to see if a weapon could be found which matched the bullets fired at the crime scenes, the police achieved the breakthrough they needed, purely by chance. A couple out walking at Mount Pleasant noticed an object partially hidden by bushes which proved to be a .22 rifle. Forensic tests showed this to be the weapon used to kill the last murder victim. Detectives replaced the rifle in its hiding-place and maintained surveillance. On 1 September 1963 Cooke was arrested when he went to retrieve the gun.

He readily confessed to the 1963 spate of murders, and also admitted the 1959 killing which at that time was still unsolved. He said that his reason for committing the killings was that he wanted to hurt someone. At his trial in November 1963 the defence argued that he was suffering from schizophrenia which caused him to lose control, and destroyed his ability to know right from wrong. Medical evidence for the Crown argued an opposing view, saying that Cooke nursed a grudge against society and would go to any lengths to attract attention to himself. The jury, inclining to the view that Cooke was not subject to any mental disease, found him guilty, and he was sentenced to death.

It was 10 months before the death sentence was carried out, and in that time Cooke confessed to a murder committed at Cottesloe in December 1949 for which another man had been sentenced. He also claimed to have committed other crimes, but his confession to the murder for which Darryl Beamish had been convicted created one of the greatest controversies in Australia's criminal history. Beamish, a 20-year-old deaf-mute, at first admitted the murder but then claimed he had been forced into making the admission. In March 1964 he appealed against the verdict in the knowledge that Cooke had made a confession to the crime. The appeal was dismissed on the grounds that Cooke's admission was prefabricated. On 26 October 1964 Cooke was hanged at Fremantle Gaol, the last but one man to be executed in Australia. The controversy over Beamish continued long after Cooke went to the gallows, and in March 1971 he was released on parole.

[119, 199]

COPPOLINO, Dr Carl. An anaesthiologist in his mid thirties convicted in 1967 of wife-murder. Carmela died suddenly in her Florida home, allegedly after receiving a fatal dose of the drug succinylcholine chloride administered by her husband.

Carl Coppolino was a poor boy who made good. He married Carmela (Musetto), a doctor's daughter, and both husband and wife qualified in medicine. In 1962 Carl became infatuated with Marjorie Farber, 48-year-old wife of a retired army colonel. The following year Colonel Farber died suddenly of coronary thrombosis after being attended by Coppolino.

In 1965 the Coppolinos moved to Florida, where Carl became friendly with 38-year-old divorcée Mary Gibson. When Marjorie Farber became his neighbour jealousy intruded in Carl's life. In September Carmela died of a heart attack, and within 3 weeks Carl married Mary Gibson.

Marjorie Farber contacted the police and accused Coppolino of killing his wife, and further stated that under the doctor's influence she had injected a dose of succinylcholine chloride into her husband, thus contributing to his death.

Succinylcholine chloride is a synthetic muscle relaxant widely used in anaesthiology, and therefore available to Dr Coppolino. Carmela Coppolino was exhumed, and what was presumed to be a needle puncture was found on her body. Colonel Farber's body was also exhumed, and the cricoid cartilage in his throat was found to be broken, a sign of pressure on the throat.

Carl Coppolino was tried for the murder of Colonel Farber, but a New Jersey jury found him not guilty. He was again in court in Florida when tried in April 1967 for the murder of his wife. A great deal of the testimony was scientific, and this first alleged poisoning with the drug worried the forensic experts. Despite defence protestations by F. Lee Bailey that there was no competent evidence regarding the cause of death. Coppolino was found guilty of second-degree murder, and he was imprisoned for life.

[36, 446, 630]

CORDER, William. Perpetrator of the famous Red Barn Murder, a killing which has inspired much legend and melodrama.

Maria Marten, the attractive 25-year-old daughter of a Suffolk farm labourer, lived in the village of Polstead near Bury St Edmunds, where she was highly popular. By contrast, William Corder, four years her junior and a prosperous farmer, was considered shifty and devious.

The couple met in 1826, and when Maria became pregnant Corder promised to marry her. The child died, and the couple quarrelled. Corder was prevailed upon by Maria's parents to marry the girl.

On 18 May 1827 Corder said he would take Maria to Ipswich, where he would marry her. He stressed the need for secrecy, and frightened the girl by telling her that she would be arrested for having bastard children. Corder arranged to take some of Maria's clothes to the Red Barn, a red-roofed building on Corder's land, and the girl was to return to her parents' home and dress in male clothing. Corder would then call for her, and they would cross the fields together without exciting attention. On reaching the Red Barn there would

Corder: The death mask

be a horse and gig waiting to take them to Ipswich. Maria complied with Corder's wishes and bade her parents a tearful farewell. She was not seen alive again.

Corder returned 2 days later, and said Maria was still at Ipswich, because of difficulties in obtaining a marriage licence. On 29 September Corder said he was going to London, where he would meet Maria and marry her. Three weeks later he wrote to the parents saying they were married and living in the Isle of Wight. The uneasy Mrs Marten dreamed that her daughter had been murdered and buried in the Red Barn. Her persistence caused the barn to be searched, and on 19 April 1828 Maria's murdered body was found buried there.

William Corder, who had married a girl in London, was arrested and charged with murder. He pleaded not guilty at his trial at Bury St Edmunds Assizes in August 1828, and made a long statement in which he said that Maria shot herself with a pistol she had taken from his house. He admitted his foolishness in attempting to conceal the body. The jury preferred to believe Maria's younger brother, who stated that he saw Corder leaving the Red Barn with a pickaxe on the day the girl disappeared.

William Corder was found guilty and sentenced to death. He made a written confession of the murder before he was hanged on 11 August 1828 in front of the gaol at Bury St Edmunds, before a huge crowd.

In 1976 a claim was made that Corder had been the victim of a miscarriage of justice. The suggestion was that Maria Marten had been forced into prostitution by acquaintances of her stepmother and that during the meeting in the Red Barn with Corder she staged a mock suicide. She shot herself through the eye and the man whose influence she had come under finished her off with a knife. Corder was too intimidated to tell the truth.

[*2, 31, 254, 327, 354, 627, 947*]

CORLL, Dean. A 33-year-old Houston electrician whose mass murder of boys was brought to light when he was shot dead by an accomplice.

On 8 August 1973 the 18-year-old Wayne Henley told the police that he had killed Corll in his house at Pasadena. Corll, a homosexual with sadistic tastes, had been shot 6 times with a .22 pistol. His house had a torture room in which the furniture consisted of a wooden board with handcuffs fitted at each corner.

Henley told of Corll's dope parties, and how he sodomized boys on his torture board before killing them. Reference to the names of 2 boys known to be missing led the police to a boat-shed rented by Corll in Houston. The bodies of 17 boys were recovered from under the floor of the shed, and 10 more were found at 2 other burial sites. These corpses represented the largest mass murder in America's history.

Henley said that Corll, whom he had known for about 2 years, paid him $200 a head to procure boys for him. Corll loved to play with children; he took them for rides in his van and gave them candy. He was known as 'a real good neighbour and a real good guy'.

Corll arranged children's parties to help him and his accomplices, Henley and another youth, set up prospective victims for his torture toom. He strangled and shot the boys, after indulging in sexual abuse and mutilation. But the murder mill ground to a halt in Pasadena, when Corll lost his domination over his procurers and was shot dead by Henley.

Wayne Henley, who admitted killing some of the victims, was tried for murder in July 1974. Found guilty, he was sentenced to six 99-year terms of imprisonment.

[*394, 400, 714, 762*]

CORONA, Juan Vallejo. Mexican labour contractor charged with 25 counts of murder in the

Superior Court of the State of California in July 1971.

Corona, who was 38, had gone to California in the 1950s as a migrant fruit and vegetable picker. After a period of psychiatric illness, diagnosed as schizophrenia, he went into the labour-contracting business. By the mid 1960s he had built up a successful business in Yuba County, hiring out migrant Mexican workers to Californian growers. His credit rating was good, and he was respected as a hard worker.

In May 1971 police appeared at Corona's home with a search warrant. His house was combed and the Sullivan ranch which he used as a bunkhouse for his labourers was also searched. The bodies of 25 migrant workers were found in shallow graves at the ranch. The victims, all males killed within the previous 5 or 6 weeks, had been hacked and stabbed to death.

Incriminating evidence discovered in Corona's house and car included a machete and rubber boots, both bearing human bloodstains. The most dramatic evidence was provided by a ledger in Corona's handwriting containing the names of some of the victims. There were also dates, and at Corona's trial the prosecution maintained that this ledger was a death list.

Juan Corona pleaded not guilty to the accusations of murder, but a Californian jury, after deliberating for 45 hours, convicted him and he was sentenced to 25 consecutive life terms. Until the Houston murders committed by *Dean Corll* in 1973, Corona had the dubious distinction of being America's greatest mass murderer. In 1973 Corona was stabbed 32 times in his prison cell, losing the sight of one eye. Both the *Boston Strangler* and *Loeb* were killed, showing that some murderers are unacceptable to their fellow-prisoners.

[*200*]

COSTA, Tony. This part-time carpenter from Provincetown, Massachusetts, grew marijuana in his garden—an attraction to the young drug-addicts who frequented the district.

In January 1969 two girls were reported missing from their lodgings in Provincetown. They had last been seen in their blue Volkswagen car accompanied by a man believed to be Tony Costa, a local resident. The car was reported abandoned in nearby woods with a note on the windshield 'Engine trouble, will return'. By the time police arrived at the scene the car had disappeared, but an investigation of the surrounding area produced torn-up

documents bearing the name of one of the missing girls. Fearing that the occupants of the car might have become disoriented in the woods at a time of freezing winter weather, police mounted a large search.

During the course of the search officers located a patch of disturbed soil which on close examination proved to be a shallow grave containing a body. When Costa was questioned he gave the police a number of different accounts of his association with the missing girls. He claimed that they had obtained drugs from him and left without paying. When he saw them in their blue car he offered them a cheap price for the vehicle to offset what he claimed they owed him. During their inquiries detectives learned that Costa kept a marijuana garden in the woods to which he frequently took his girl-friends. This was discovered in a clearing close to the shallow grave found earlier by searchers. The marijuana garden yielded 2 more graves which contained the bodies of the 2 missing girls. Further searches led to the discovery of another grave, making a total of 4 female corpses.

Two of the bodies bore signs of sexual assault, multiple stab injuries and gunshot wounds. In due course all 4 murder victims were identified and Tony Costa (who at first pleaded harassment by the police) made a full confession. He was assessed as legally sane and therefore able to stand trial for murder; the jury convicted him on 2 counts and he was sentenced to life imprisonment. On 12 May 1974 Costa hanged himself in his cell at the age of 29.

[*212*]

COTTINGHAM, Richard Francis. A murderer whose selection of prostitutes as victims in modern New York City earned him comparison with *Jack the Ripper*.

In December 1979 firemen answering an emergency call at the Travel Inn Motor Lodge in New York City ran into a gruesome double murder. Room 417 contained the naked, handless and decapitated bodies of two women. Both victims were prostitutes; one was eventually identified as Deedeh Goodarzi but the other would only be known as 'Jane Doe'.

A few months later in May 1980 an 18-year-old prostitute was lured into a room at the Quality Inn Motel at Hasbrouck Heights, New Jersey. Her male companion subjected her to 3 hours of beating, torture and sodomy until finally her screams alerted hotel residents. When the motel manager knocked on the door she assured him that everything was all right, but by then police were on the premises and her assailant was arrested while trying to slip away.

Richard Cottingham, a 34-year-old computer-operator working for the Blue Cross insurance company, was married with 2 children. His fingerprints were found on the handcuffs which he used to keep his teenage prostitute victim captive. The prints also matched those found on handcuffs clamped on the wrists of another teenage prostitute, Valorie Street, who had been found strangled just over 2 weeks before.

Other hitherto unsolved murders and violent attacks were reviewed in the light of Cottingham's arrest. Two young women who had survived being kidnapped, drugged and tortured in 1978 identified the computer-operator as their attacker. Like Jack the Ripper, who declared he was 'down on whores', Cottingham told one of his victims who survived that 'prostitutes needed to be punished'. He worked shifts at his company's computer centre in Manhattan, and bragged to his workmates about his dealings with prostitutes.

Cottingham was tried in June 1981 on 19 charges. He denied attacking the two women who had identified him, but had to admit his assault on the girl at Hasbrouck Heights. He discussed the phenomenon of sado-masochism in an off-hand, almost arrogant manner and won few friends in court. The judge described him as highly intellectual but totally amoral. Cottingham was found guilty of 15 charges of murder, kidnapping, rape and sodomy, and was given prison sentences totalling 197 years. [567]

COTTON, Mary Ann. Thrice married 40-year-old former nurse who is regarded as Britain's greatest mass murderer.

Mary Cotton went to West Auckland in County Durham in 1871 with her bigamous husband, Frederick, his two stepsons and her own 6-month-old baby. Within two months Frederick died at the age of 39 of gastric fever, and a short while later one of Mary's lovers, Joseph Natrass, moved in as a lodger.

Meanwhile Mary had become pregnant by a local excise officer called Quick-Manning. Between 10 March and 1 April 1872 there were 3 more deaths in Mary's house—Natrass, her own young baby and her late husband's elder boy, aged 10.

On 12 July the other Cotton stepson died, and a suspicious neighbour went to the police. The doctor, who had seen the child the previous day, refused to give a death certificate. A post-mortem

Cottingham: New York prostitute murders

was carried out, and analysis of the stomach contents proved positive for arsenic. Exhumations of two of the other deaths in the Cotton home also showed that arsenic was responsible.

Mary Cotton was charged with the murder of her stepson and taken to Durham Prison, where her child by Quick-Manning was born. She pleaded not guilty at her trial at Durham Assizes in March 1873. The defence line was that the dead boy had been poisoned accidentally by arsenic contained in green floral wallpaper used in his home. But Mary's purchase of soft soap and arsenic (ostensibly for cleaning bedsteads and destroying bedbugs) proved ominous. She was found guilty, and sentenced to death.

The Home Secretary refused to commute the

14314

County Gaol. Durham

7th March 1873

Sir,

I beg to inform you that at the Assizes holden in Durham on Friday the 7th day of March 1873. Mary Ann Cotton was convicted of Wilful Murder and sentenced to be hanged. Consequently in accordance with the Rules laid down in your Order dated 13th August 1868. Mary Ann Cotton will be executed on Monday the 24th Inst. at 8 o'clock A.m.

I have the honor to be,

Sir.

The Right Hon. H.A. Bruce
Secretary of State
Home Department
Whitehall
London

Your Most Obedt. Servant

Armstrong
Lt Colonel
Governor

Cotton: Letter re execution

sentence, despite a mounting wave of sympathy. Mary's baby was taken from her 5 days before she was hanged in Durham prison on 24 March 1873. The hangman did his work badly, and it was 3 minutes before the body stopped convulsing at the rope's end.

Mary Ann Cotton, whose life consisted of a trail of deaths—21 persons close to her died within 20 years—was suspected of 14 or 15 murders. Her motive was either to gain insurance money or to pave the way for a new marriage.

[28, 551, 1001]

COURVOISIER, François Benjamin. Young Swiss valet who murdered and robbed his employer, 73-year-old Lord William Russell, in his bed on 5 May 1840.

Courvoisier, a smooth, deceitful character, came to London from Geneva and worked in various menial jobs before securing the post of manservant to Lord William Russell. The aged peer, whose nephew was Secretary of State for the Colonies, lived comfortably in a London house with 2 maids and a single manservant.

Courvoiser, who was effective head of household below stairs, had been in his post 5 weeks when he annoyed his master by not carrying out his instructions. The following morning the maid found several rooms of the house in disarray, suggesting a burglary. She called Courvoisier, and together they went up to the master's bedroom. The old man was lying dead on the bed, with a wound in his throat.

There was evidence of forced entry at the rear of the house, and some items of jewellery were missing, but many obviously valuable articles had been left untouched. Courvoisier seemed more distressed on his own account than for the tragedy that had occurred. He kept repeating, 'What shall I do? I shall never get another position.'

The valet was arrested when some of the missing items were found in his pantry and bloodstained clothing in his room. Courvoisier's trial was at the Old Bailey in June 1840.

He was identified as having deposited a parcel containing some of Lord William Russell's missing silver with the manageress of a hotel near Leicester Square. The jury found him guilty, and he was sentenced to death. Two days after his conviction he made the first of 3 written confessions.

On 6 July 1840 the 23-year-old Courvoisier was executed at Newgate.

[124, 183, 554, 806, 947]

CRAIG, Christopher. See BENTLEY, Derek

CREAM, Dr Thomas Neill. The Lambeth Poisoner, born in Glasgow in 1850, who graduated in medicine from Canada's McGill University in 1876. He practised as a physician in Chicago, but developed a life of crime involving arson, blackmail, abortion and murder.

In 1881 he was given a life sentence in the States for murdering with strychnine a man called Stott, the husband of his current mistress. He attracted attention to himself by writing to the District Attorney, advising that Stott's body be exhumed. Thus he showed a form of exhibitionism that eventually hanged him. He was released from Joliet Prison in July 1891.

He arrived in London in October, and took lodgings at 103 Lambeth Palace Road. During the next few months Dr Cream glided cross-eyed and silk-hatted through South London, preying on prostitutes to whom he gave pills containing strychnine. This compulsive poisoner murdered Ellen Donworth, Matilda Clover, Emma Shrivell and Alice Marsh, became engaged to a respectable young dressmaker and made a trip to North America.

As he had done in Chicago, Cream indulged in various forms of self-advertisement which led to his arrest. He made an offer to name the 'Lambeth Poisoner' for the modest reward of £300,000, and complained to Scotland Yard about being followed. He was arrested on 3 June 1892 and charged with acting under false pretences. He told officers, 'You have got the wrong man; fire away.'

A murder charge followed, and Louisa Harvey, also a prostitute, related how she picked up the doctor one night in the previous October, and he spent the night with her. In his solicitous way he offered to give her some pills to clear up some facial spots. They met later in a public house, when he made her a gift of some roses. The pills followed, and his insistence that the girl swallow the 'long pills' whole had a sinister ring about it which put her on guard. She feigned swallowing them, and dropped them.

Cream was tried in October. The evidence against him was overwhelming. Harvey's testimony, and a chemist's evidence of his buying nux vomica and gelatin capsules, together with the discovery of 7 bottles of strychnine at his lodgings, spoke eloquently of the poisoner's trade. It took the jury 12 minutes to find him guilty, and he was hanged on 15 November 1892.

In a letter to *The Times*, Cream's optician

Cream: Bogus letter sent by Cream
Cream: Medicine case containing strychnine phial

suggested that the condemned man's moral degeneracy might have been attributable to the fact that his eye defect had not been corrected when he was a child. Cream did not confess to the murders, but on the scaffold was alleged to have declared, 'I am Jack the . . .' (*Jack the Ripper?*), just as the bolt was drawn.

[*1, 21, 110, 120, 152, 231, 232, 244, 332, 399, 442, 500, 577, 584, 606, 724, 729, 907, 947*]

CREIGHTON and APPELGATE. Mary Frances Creighton, with her 36-year-old husband John and their 2 children, were a typical lower middle class American family during the years of the Great Depression. In the 1920s John and Mary had been tried for murder—the poisoning by arsenic of Mary's younger brother. Both were acquitted. Later Mary Creighton alone was tried for another murder by arsenic poisoning. The victim was her mother-in-law, but again she was acquitted.

The Creightons moved to Long Island, and there met Everett and Ada Appelgate. The families became very friendly, and during 1935 the Appelgate moved in with the Creightons. Within

a few months Ada Appelgate was dead, supposedly from a heart attack. Suspicion created by gossip about the Creightons' past history caused inquiry into Ada's death.

An autopsy showed that she had died from arsenical poisoning. Inquiries into the relationship between the 2 families revealed that Everett Appelgate had been having sexual intercourse with the Creightons' 15-year-old daughter. He was held on a rape charge, and Mary Creighton, after intense questioning, made 3 confessions concerning Ada's death in which she accused Appelgate of her murder.

Mary Creighton and Everett Appelgate were charged with first-degree murder and tried in January 1936. Evidence showed that they had been living together, and that Mary was dominated by Appelgate, who threatened her with his knowledge of her past. Mary Creighton convicted herself in the witness-box by agreeing that she gave arsenic-laden milk to Ada.

On 16 July 1936 both died in the electric chair at Sing Sing Prison.

[*443, 529*]

CRIMMINS, Alice. Glamorous 28-year-old New York housewife twice tried for child-murder.

Four-year-old Alice Marie Crimmins and her 5-year-old brother Eddie were reported missing from their home on 14 July 1965 by their father, who was living apart from his wife. The little girl was found dead later the same day—she had been strangled. Eddie was found several days later—he too had been strangled.

Mrs Crimmins told detectives that a hook-and-eye fastener on the outside of the children's room was to prevent them leaving their room to raid the refrigerator. The officers thought that Mrs Crimmins's promiscuous relationships provided the real reason and that the children were victims of a custody dispute between the parents.

Twenty-three months after the crime Mrs Crimmins was charged with her daughter's murder. At her trial in May 1968 a witness testified that she saw Mrs Crimmins on the night of the children's disappearance in the company of a man. Mrs Crimmins was alleged to have been holding one child by the hand and carrying an ominous bundle under her free arm. She was found guilty of manslaughter, and sentenced to a maximum of 20 years in prison.

Almost a year later Mrs Crimmins was sent for retrial after an appeal. In March 1971 she was tried for the murder of her son and the manslaughter of her daughter. An outburst from the prisoner occurred when a former man friend stated that Mrs Crimmins had confessed to him that she had killed her daughter.

The implication was that the mother took the children's lives because she feared her husband would win the suit for their custody.

Alice Crimmins was found guilty of first-degree murder, and also of first-degree manslaughter. She was sentenced to life imprisonment. In 1976 she was transferred to a residential work release establishment.

[168, 391, 431, 503, 870]

CRIMMINS, Craig. A stage-hand convicted of the 'Murder at the Met' in New York City.

On 23 July 1980 Helen Hagnes Mintiks, a gifted Canadian-born violinist, went missing during an interval of a concert at the prestigious Metropolitan Opera House in Lincoln Center. She was last seen at 9.45 p.m. approaching the back stage elevator with a man. She did not rejoin the orchestra, and was reported as a missing person.

The following day, detectives combing the back stage areas of the Opera House found her naked body lying at the bottom of a ventilator shaft. She was bound and gagged, and appeared to have fallen three floors to her death. Her clothes had been cut fom her body with scissors or a knife, and attempted rape seemed to be the motive. Suspicion fell on the back-stage staff, all of whom were questioned, photographed and fingerprinted.

A palm-print found on pipework on the roof of the building matched that of 21-year-old Craig Crimmins, who also appeared agitated by questioning. Crimmins, a quiet personality, at first claimed not to have missed any of his stage cues but then said he had been drunk and was sleeping it off during the critical time that Helen Mintiks was murdered. After dogged interrogation by detectives, and in the knowledge that his alibi was not supportable, Crimmins finally confessed.

He said he encountered the violinist at the elevator and propositioned her. After she slapped him he made her captive and took her up to the higher reaches of the building where he unsuccessfully attempted rape. He cut off her clothes, he claimed, so that she would not readily follow him. He also bound the girl's wrists and tethered her; when she made strenuous efforts to free herself he kicked her off the roof to a crushing death three floors below.

Crimmins was tried for murder in April 1982. In a strong prosecution case, witnesses' testimony destroyed his alibi. He was shown to be missing from work at the crucial time, he was seen at the elevator with the victim, his palm-print was discovered close to the crime scene, and he had confessed. The behind-the-scenes world of the Met was shown as a dark environment where malingering, drunkenness and drug-taking were rife. There was also evidence of resentment of performers and musicians by the stage crews. Defence claims that detectives had brought psychological pressure to bear on Crimmins in order to extract his confession were taken up by newspapers, which depicted him as an innocent hounded by police. When the trial jury found Craig Crimmins guilty of felony murder, press headlines that had been declaring his innocence now called him a 'Baby-faced killer'.

While awaiting sentence Crimmins shared the accommodation of the Prison Infirmary at Riker's Island with *Mark Chapman*, John Lennon's killer. The two were not amenable companions—Crimmins was reported as saying Chapman was 'a nut case'. The Met murderer was sentenced to 20 years to life.

[92]

CRIPPEN, Dr Hawley Harvey. American, born Michigan 1862, hanged at Pentonville 23 November 1910 for the murder of his wife. Crippen qualified as a doctor in 1885, and worked for a patent medicine company. His second marriage was to teenage Cora Turner (real name

Crippen: Suicide note written on ship

Crippen: The cellar grave

Kunigunde Mackamotzki), whose stage name was Belle Elmore.

In 1900 Dr Crippen came to England, where his American qualifications were insufficient to allow him to practise medicine. He took various jobs connected with selling patent medicines. He moved to 39 Hilldrop Crescent, where his wife took in paying-guests. Belle dominated her husband, and the little mild-mannered doctor did much of the housework.

Early in 1910 Belle disappeared. Crippen told inquirers that she had returned to the United States because of a relative's illness. Meanwhile Crippen moved his mistress and secretary Ethel le Neve into Hilldrop Crescent. By this time she was openly wearing Belle's furs and jewellery. Mrs Crippen's disappearance was reported to Scotland Yard, and Chief Inspector Walter Dew visited the house—a search revealed nothing of note.

Alarmed, Crippen and Ethel le Neve fled to Antwerp, where they boarded the SS *Montrose*, bound for Canada. Their disappearance led to a further search at 39 Hilldrop Crescent, where human remains were found in the cellar. Dr (later Sir) Bernard Spilsbury was called in to advise in this, his first major case. Examination (the head, skeleton and limbs were never found) revealed the presence of hyoscine, and a piece of abdominal scar tissue identified the victim as Mrs Crippen.

To avoid identification, Crippen had Ethel le Neve dress as a boy during their transatlantic

Crippen: Crippen and le Neve at Bow Street police court

voyage. Captain Kendall, suspicious of the couple's affectionate behaviour and the ill-fitting disguise worn by le Neve, radioed to London. Wireless was thus used for the first time in a murder hunt. Dew boarded a faster ship, and eventually confronted the runaway pair on 31 July 1910.

Crippen was tried for murder at the Old Bailey on 18 October and found guilty. Ethel le Neve was tried separately as an accessory after the fact and acquitted. Crippen is perhaps the only murderer's name to pass into the language as an expletive.

It was reported in the newspapers in 1981 that Sir Hugh Rhys Rankin, former vice-president of the World Buddhist Federation, met Ethel le Neve in Australia in 1930. She allegedly told him that Crippen killed his wife because she had syphilis. [*1, 88, 110, 133, 191, 209, 230, 231, 259, 266, 275, 296, 323, 328, 346, 409, 438, 463, 464, 606, 642, 677, 687, 705, 722, 724, 729, 757, 795, 846, 873, 907, 915, 921, 928, 947, 960*]

CROSS, Dr Philip. A 62-year-old retired army surgeon tried in Ireland for wife-murder.

Dr Cross retired from military service and settled down in County Cork with his wife Laura and 6 children. Apart from a little hunting and fishing, he kept himself to himself.

Laura Cross employed attractive 21-year-old Mary Skinner as governess to her children. Dr Cross, normally rather shy with the opposite sex, became utterly infatuated with the girl, and a relationship grew up which caused Mrs Cross to dismiss her.

Dr Cross would not abandon his liaison, and maintained a secret relationship.

Mrs Cross soon became ill with stomach pains, for which she received treatment from her husband. On 2 June 1887 she died, allegedly of typhoid fever, and Dr Cross signed the death certificate. She was buried with indecent haste, and 15 days later the doctor married Mary Skinner.

Deep suspicion was aroused about the circumstances of the death. These proved well-founded, for when her body was exhumed it was found to contain arsenic. Dr Cross was arrested and tried at Munster Assizes.

Motive was not difficult to prove, and a

Croydon Poisonings: Duff's exhumed body on its way to the post-mortem

purchase of arsenic was traced to the doctor. Together with his hasty remarriage, this was sufficient to convince the jury of his guilt.

Dr Cross, rejected by his new wife, was hanged in January 1888.

[*34, 252, 531, 554, 724, 816*]

CROYDON POISONINGS. Between April 1928 and March 1929, 3 members of the same family in Croydon died of arsenical poisoning. Verdicts of wilful administration of poison by some person or persons unknown were recorded at the inquests.

Edmund Creighton Duff, a 59-year-old retired colonial civil servant, died at his Croydon home in South Park Hill Road after a brief illness on 27 April 1928. Death was considered to have been caused by degeneration of the heart muscle. On 15 February 1929 Vera Sidney, Duff's sister-in-law, died after a few days' illness. Vera, a 40-year-old unmarried woman with strong ideas about health and fitness, lived with her mother, Violet Emilia Sidney, in near-by Birdhurst Rise. Her death was attributed to natural causes.

On 5 March 1929 old Mrs Violet Sidney, widowed mother of Vera, died after a sudden illness. The family doctor did not feel he could issue a death certificate. Arsenic was found in the old lady's medicine.

The bodies of all 3 victims were exhumed, and all were found to contain arsenic. Three inquests were held over a 5-month period. This was a mistake, for the Coroner failed to take the advice given him by the Director of Public Prosecutions to hold all 3 inquests together. He took them separately, which led to confusion. The inquest on Edmund Duff uncovered another mistake. During the original post-mortem organs from the body required for analysis were confused with those from another body. Consequently, the opportunity to have confirmed poisoning at an early stage was missed.

It was thought that in all 3 cases poison had been administered in food or medicine, which suggested either a member of the family or at least someone close. A good deal of suspicion centred around Grace Duff, widow of Edmund, but there was insufficient evidence to bring a charge.

Officially the case remains unsolved, but in 1975 a re-examination of the evidence by Richard Whittington-Egan made out a case against Grace Duff as the murderess, suggesting that Grace (who died in 1973 aged 87) had a love affair with a Croydon doctor and poisoned her husband out of hatred and a desire to be rid of him. Vera and Violet Sidney were murdered for gain.

[*237, 486, 676, 791, 906, 908, 974*]

CUMMINS, Gordon Frederick. This 28-year-old wartime airman murdered 4 women in London in February 1942. Cummins is frequently compared with *Jack the Ripper* on account of the mutilations he inflicted on his victims.

A handsome man, and married, Cummins was known to his fellow-airmen as 'The Count', because of his pretensions to a noble heritage. He strangled his victims, and in 3 cases carried out crude mutilations.

The police knew after the first murder that the man they were looking for was left-handed, and fingerprints were found on a tin-opener used in the mutilations. Overcome by his lust, Cummins finally gave himself away. He attacked a woman in a street doorway, but her cries attracted a passer-by to her aid and her attacker ran off leaving behind his service respirator bearing his name, rank and number. Shortly after this he attacked another woman, this time running away and leaving his Service belt behind.

Cummins was quickly found, and his fingerprints matched those found at two of the murder scenes. A search of his billet turned up several items belonging to his victims.

His trial for murder at the Old Bailey (which had to be restarted since the wrong exhibits were shown) was short. The jury took 35 minutes to find him guilty, and he was hanged on 25 June 1942.
[*133, 175, 296, 361, 383, 440, 601, 643, 812, 928*]

D

D'AUTREMENT BROTHERS. Celebrated case in which 3 brothers who committed a train robbery and murder were traced by Dr Edward Heinrich's interpretation of scene-of-crime evidence. (See also *Charles Henry Schwartz.*)

On 11 October 1923 a Southern Pacific express bound for San Francisco was held up by gunmen in the Siskiyou Mountains. The mail coach was dynamited, setting the whole coach ablaze. The gunmen ordered the brakeman and fireman to uncouple the coach. During this operation, and in an atmosphere of mounting panic, the raiders killed both men and made good their escape.

Police officers found the detonating equipment together with a revolver and a pair of overalls. In the ensuing manhunt a garage mechanic was suspected on the grounds that grease on his overalls was the same as on the garment found by the wrecked train. At this point Dr Heinrich was brought in, and his examination of the overalls soon cleared the mechanic.

The overalls provided Heinrich with sufficient information to build up a virtual Identikit picture of the man who wore them. He told police they were looking for a left-handed lumberjack working with fir-trees. He was aged between 21 and 25, was not more than 5 feet 10 inches tall and weighed about 165 pounds. Furthermore, he had medium light hair, a fair complexion, light-brown eyebrows and neat personal habits. This description was made possible by a detailed microscopic examination of hairs, fibres and wood dust on the overalls.

Armed with this information, and evidence obtained by detectives, the police visited the home of the D'Autrement brothers—Hugh, and twins Roy and Ray. The brothers were not at home, but corroborating identification was obtained, and they were found after a search lasting 4 years. Hugh was captured in the Philippines, and the twins in Ohio.

The D'Autrement brothers were tried for murder, and the twins confessed, no doubt hoping for leniency. All were found guilty, and sentenced to life imprisonment. Dr Heinrich's role established him as a major criminologist, and highlighted the value of forensic science in crime detection.
[95]

DAVIES, Michael John. A 20-year-old labourer sentenced to death in 1953 for murder.

On the evening of 2 July 1953 4 youths were attacked on Clapham Common by 8 to 10 members of a gang known as 'The Plough Boys'. There was a running fight, and in the twilight 17-year-old John Beckley was left dying of knife-wounds near a bus stop.

Six young men were charged with murder, 4 were acquitted and a fifth found not guilty at the judge's direction. The five received sentences in prison ranging from 6 to 9 months on a second charge of common assault. Michael Davies, alone of the six, was tried for the murder of John Beckley in October 1953 at the Old Bailey. Davies was identified as Beckley's assailant by a bus passenger who had witnessed the last stage of the fight. None of the other youths attacked identified Davies, and none of the other bus passengers recognized him. Nevertheless, he was found guilty.

Davies spent 92 days in the condemned cell before he was reprieved, and his sentence commuted to one of life imprisonment. He was released after 7 years, and has steadfastly protested his innocence. His case has been used in arguments against conviction based on uncorroborated identification evidence.
[*306, 719*]

DEAN, Minnie. Murderess who holds the distinction of being the only woman to have been hanged in New Zealand. She emigrated from Scotland in 1868 and in due course married and settled down at East Winton, some 19 miles from Invercargill. The Deans had an unpretentious house called The Larches with a small well-tended garden in which Minnie grew dahlias and chrysanthemums.

In order to supplement their meagre income, Minnie decided to take up baby-farming. She appeared to be less than successful at her chosen occupation, for 2 of the babies in her care died. Doctors decided in both instances that the deaths had been due to natural causes, although there was some consternation about the lack of proper accommodation at The Larches.

Because of the bad publicity her baby-farming services had attracted, Minnie decided to advertise under a variety of names. In April 1895 the New

Zealand *Times Herald* carried a notice asking for an 'infant to adopt'; replies to 'Mater'. The following month a woman answering Minnie Dean's description was implicated in an incident involving a missing child. A month-old baby had been handed over to Minnie by the child's mother, and £4 changed hands as the minding fee.

Minnie denied having taken the child, but when some of the infant's clothing was found at The Larches she was arrested together with her husband. While detectives were at the house an observant officer spotted an unusually wet area in an otherwise dry flower-bed and, pulling up the blooms, uncovered a shallow grave containing 2 bodies. The skeleton of a third child was found elsewhere in the garden, and one of the 3 corpses proved to be that of the missing child for whom the police were searching.

Morphia traces were found in one of the bodies, and bottles containing laudanum and chloroform were discovered at The Larches. It was well known locally that the garden was Minnie's hobby, and her husband was not allowed to touch the flower-beds. He was considered to have known nothing of her murderous activities, and was released from custody.

Minnie Dean was tried for murder at Invercargill and found guilty. On 12 August 1895 New Zealand's Baby Farmer (who preceded *Amelia Dyer* by a year) was hanged. She declared her innocence on the scaffold and begged the hangman, 'Oh God, let me not suffer.'

[*258*]

DE BOCARMÉ, Hippolyte. The Comte de Bocarmé, a Belgian nobleman, who lived in a château in Tournai, and who murdered a relative out of greed.

De Bocarmé was known as an ill-behaved youth, and regarded as a womanizer and swindler. His business enterprises collapsed, and after his father died he succeeded to the title at the age of 24. In 1843 he married Lydie Fougnies, daughter of an ostensibly rich grocer in Mons.

The Comte and Comtesse de Bocarmé shared a greedy ambition, and when the grocer died they found that the estate amounted to a few thousand francs, and that most of that went to the dead man's son Gustave. Nevertheless, Gustave was invited to the Bocarmé château, and while there he suffered a fall from which he died. A servant saw him stretched out on the floor of the dining-room—several chairs were overturned, and the Comte, who had blood on his face, said the visitor

had died of an apoplectic fit. However, Gustave's body was examined, and poison was suspected. The Comte's valet told the police that his master had a laboratory in the cellar, where he carried out experiments with perfumes and also cultivated poisonous plants. A bottle containing nicotine was found, and the presence of nicotine in the dead man's body was confirmed. The apparatus used to prepare the nicotine had been hidden under the cellar floor.

The Comte and Comtesse de Bocarmé were tried at the Palais de Justice in Mons on 27 May 1851. Each blamed the other. Referring to the Comte's demeanour, a court reporter wrote, 'His air of assurance is prodigious.' De Bocarmé obviously thought his rank would protect him, and his counsel, having painted the Comtesse as a designing woman, pointed out that the Comte had suffered a disturbed upbringing. It was an argument which presaged modern attitudes, but which won no sympathy with the jury at Mons. They found Comte de Bocarmé guilty, but acquitted his wife.

De Bocarmé petitioned the King, but with no success. He was guillotined in July 1851, remarking as he was being prepared that he hoped the blade was sharp.

[*1014*]

DEEMING, Frederick Bayley. A 38-year-old murderer who cemented his victims under hearthstones in England and Australia. Born in Lancashire, Deeming was arrested in Australia after police had been attracted to his house in Melbourne by a disagreeable smell. His wife's corpse was found cemented under the hearthstone, the skull obviously fractured by a heavy instrument.

Using the alias Albert O. Williams, Deeming had worked as a plumber and gas-fitter in Sydney since his arrival from Liverpool in 1891. He had already featured in a larceny charge, and was now wanted for murder. The Melbourne press ran lead stories about Deeming, and put their London correspondents on to the task of finding out more about him. He was traced to a house he had rented at Rainhill, Liverpool, which he vacated in October 1891.

With the exchange of information between the British and Australian police authorities, a picture was built up of Deeming's bigamy and fraud. The Liverpool police found at Rainhill the bodies of Maria Deeming and her 4 children. They had been cemented underneath the floor of the kitchen fireplace.

He was arrested in Southern Cross on 11 March 1892, and at his trial in May was defended by Alfred Deakin, a future Prime Minister of Australia. Despite a strong plea of insanity, the jury found Deeming guilty, and he was executed while a crowd of over 10,000 stood outside the prison on 23 May 1892.

Even after death Deeming continued to excite interest, and part of his skeleton was used to try to prove he had greater affinity with the anthropoid apes than with modern man. It was also suggested that he was an epileptic, a syphilitic and even *Jack the Ripper*. The strangest aspect of Frederick Deeming's crimes were that they brought him no profit.

[69, *180, 234, 244, 284, 577, 591, 715*]

DE FEO. The house at Amityville, Long Island, where Ronald De Feo killed his family acquired international fame through the film *The Amityville Horror*.

On the morning of 13 November 1974 De Feo, who was 22, told a friend that someone had shot his father and mother. When police arrived at the house, which was called High Hopes, they found that De Feo senior and his wife, their two daughters and their two sons were all dead, shot in the back of the head from close range. Ronald De Feo said that his father had dealings with the underworld, and claimed that the killings had been carried out by 2 hit-men, using his rifle in order to implicate him in the murders.

He changed his story several times, but gradually the hatred which he bore for his family came out and he admitted that he was the murderer. De Feo's childhood had been an unhappy period of arguments at home and at school. He was first examined by a psychiatrist when he was 15 years old, and later took to drugs as a means of escape from his unhappy existence. He told his family on one occasion that he would end up killing them all if he stayed at home.

Eventually he did just that. He systematically shot and killed the 6 members of his family as they lay asleep. He fired 8 times, and reloaded his rifle in order to dispatch the last victim. He carefully collected the spent cartridge cases and disposed of them and his bloodstained clothes in a sewer; the rifle he threw into the sea. He told the police, 'Once I got started, I just couldn't stop. I went so fast.'

De Feo was charged with 6 counts of second-degree murder. His defence put forward an argument for insanity which was difficult to sustain in view of his obvious premeditation and concealment of evidence. He was shown a photograph of his father in court and asked, 'Did you kill your father?' He answered, 'Did I kill him? I killed them all. Yes, sir. I killed them all in self-defence.' At a later stage in the proceedings he said, 'When I get a gun in my hand, there's no doubt in my mind who I am. I am God.'

Ronald De Feo was found guilty and given sentences of 25 years to life on each of 6 counts of murder. The house in which he murdered his family was sold for a low price in 1975 but the new owners abandoned it after a month's occupation following disturbing experiences. It was alleged that the house was full of evil phenomena which became the basis for a number of books and films.

[*26, 448, 891*]

DE KAPLANY, Dr Geza. A 36-year-old Hungarian refugee doctor charged in the US with wife-murder.

Dr de Kaplany worked as an anaesthetist at a San José, California, hospital. In August 1962 he moved into an apartment block in the town with his new bride, Hajna, a 20-year-old model.

On the morning of 28 August residents in the area were disturbed by loud music coming from the de Kaplany apartment. Despite the music, a wailing sound could also be heard. The police were called, and they took away Hajna, whose body was in an appalling condition with third-degree corrosive burns. Ambulance men burned their hands on her acid-soaked body. She lingered in agony in hospital for 36 days before dying.

The apartment's bedroom was a virtual torture chamber. The bedclothes were a disintegrating mess of acid-soaked rags, and there was a large hole in the carpet, A leather case contained bottles of hydrochloric, sulphuric and nitric acids. Also lying about were a pair of rubber gloves and a roll of adhesive tape. There was a note on a medical prescription form. It read; 'If you want to live—do not shout; do what I tell you; or else you will die.'

De Kaplany was charged with murder. He pleaded both 'not guilty' and 'not guilty by reason of insanity'. His trial began on 7 January 1963. He was calm, but when photographic evidence was brought before the court he became hysterical and had to be restrained. De Kaplany then changed his plea to guilty, telling Judge Raymond G. Callaghan, 'I am a doctor. I loved her. If I did this—and I must have done this—then I'm guilty.' The defence called psychiatric evidence indicating that de Kaplany's love for his wife had been rejected.

On 1 March, the thirty-fifth day of the trial, the jury reached a guilty verdict, and de Kaplany was sentenced to imprisonment for life. He was released on parole in 1976.

[27, 959]

DE LA POMMERAIS, Dr Edmond. Son of a French country doctor with pretensions to the title of Count who murdered for money.

In 1859 de la Pommerais had a medical practice in Paris too modest to support his grand social ambitions. He ran into debt, and became involved in various frauds.

The doctor married Mlle Dubisy in 1861. Her substantial dowry helped him out of his financial troubles for a time, and also enabled him to maintain a mistress, Séraphine de Pawr. De la Pommerais's newly acquired mother-in-law was also wealthy: when she died suddenly with her son-in-law in attendance the young doctor became rich.

In less than 2 years de la Pommerais recklessly lost the whole of this fortune, and he turned to other money-making schemes. In collaboration with Madame de Pawr he worked out a plan to insure her life for half a million francs. The idea was that she would feign illness and scare the insurance company into paying an annuity as the price for cancelling the policy.

Madame de Pawr became ill according to plan, but died of cholera after being attended by her doctor lover. Far from paying out a sum to cancel the policy, the insurance company began an investigation into its client's death, and Madame de Pawr's body was exhumed. She had been given a massive dose of digitalis.

De la Pommerais was arrested and tried for double murder—his mother-in-law and Madame de Pawr. Popular sympathy was with the young doctor, and it was expected that the Emperor would intervene on his behalf. De la Pommerais was found not guilty of poisoning his mother-in-law but guilty of murdering Madame de Pawr.

Napoleon III failed to respond to pleas that the doctor had been convicted on circumstantial evidence, and, protesting that he was 'the victim of a judicial error', de la Pommerais was guillotined in 1864.

[109, 211, 917]

DE LEEUW, Huibrecht Jacob. Young town clerk at Dewetsdorp in the Orange Free State, South Africa, who staged a fatal explosion in 1927 in an attempt to cover up another crime.

De Leeuw lived beyond his means, and quickly ran into financial difficulties. When he had exhausted the goodwill of his friends by borrowing from them he started to dip into the town's exchequer, of which he was the custodian. He took money from the safe and kept the books in arrears to conceal the deficit. In due course the Mayor, P. J. von Maltitz, decided to cast his eye over the books, and found them to be in a mess. He accused de Leeuw of negligence and set a deadline by which the books must be brought up to date.

The town clerk tried hard to borrow sufficient funds to set the books straight, but failed. When the deadline arrived it was clear that the position had not improved, and he was given a week to sort out the matter or face dismissal. On 8 April 1927 Mayor von Maltitz and 2 members of the finance committee descended on de Leeuw for the showdown over the books. At about 3.0 p.m. a tremendous explosion rent the town hall, blowing the roof off the building and causing a severe fire. Von Maltitz died instantly, and his 2 colleagues who were badly burnt died in hospital, but not before making a dying declaration accusing de Leeuw of misappropriating the town's funds.

The town clerk was arrested and charged with murder. He appeared on trial at Bloemfontein in August 1927. Damning evidence was given by a shopkeeper who said that just before the explosion de Leeuw had rushed into his shop for some matches. It appeared that having set up a petrol and dynamite device he was thwarted for lack of a means of ignition. De Leeuw opted for trial by judge and 2 assessors rather than a jury, and sought unsuccessfully to persuade them that the evidence against him was circumstantial. After being convicted he said simply, 'I am prepared to go to meet my Creator.' He was hanged on 30 September 1927.

[72]

DE MELKER, Daisy Louisa. A shrewd poisoner and a trained nurse who murdered 2 of her 3 husbands and her son, relying on the average doctor not suspecting poison.

Her first husband, William Cowle, made a will in his wife's favour. The Cowles had 5 children, of whom 4 died in infancy, leaving Rhodes Cecil Cowle as the survivor. In 1923, after 14 years of marriage, William Cowle became ill and died an agonizing death which doctors attributed to cerebral haemorrhage.

His widow collected £1700 insurance, and

within 3 years took her second husband, Robert Sproat, who reputedly had savings of £4000. Sproat's will was in favour of his mother, but Daisy got him to change it, leaving everything to her. Sproat died of cerebral haemorrhage in October 1927, and Daisy collected over £4500. Sproat's relatives were suspicious, but beyond severing family ties with her took no action.

Daisy's son by her first marriage, Rhodes, now a teenager, was moody and unreliable. Meanwhile Daisy married her third husband, Sydney Clarence de Melker, a noted rugby football player, in January 1931. They settled down near Johannesburg, but Rhodes was still out of work, and made heavy demands on his mother. He boasted to friends that when he was 21 he would be entitled to an inheritance.

On 3 March 1932 Rhodes was taken ill with what doctors thought was malaria. Within 4 days he was dead. Concern was expressed to the police, and it was found that a Mrs Sproat had bought arsenic from a pharmacy in the city, ostensibly to poison cats. Inquiries about Daisy's background led to a series of exhumations. Arsenic was found in Rhodes and strychnine in Cowle and Sproat.

She was tried on 3 charges of murder in Johannesburg in October 1932. The expert evidence was overwhelming, and the illnesses of her 2 husbands showed classic signs of strychnine poisoning in the form of opisthotonus (arched back). She was found guilty, and hanged on 30 December 1932; she did not confess.
[67, 68, 73, 682]

DE SALVO, Albert. See BOSTON STRANGLER

DEMETER, Peter. Wealthy property-dealer convicted of the non-capital murder of his wife in Canada's longest criminal trial. Peter Demeter, Hungarian by birth, arrived in Toronto in 1956 with eight dollars to his name. He took any work he could find, and by 1962 had registered his own property development company. In 1967 he married an Austrian model, Christine, and by the early 1970s the couple were enjoying all the trappings of success. They owned a luxury home at Mississauga, Ontario, drove Mercedes and Cadillacs and took their holidays in Acapulco.

Outwardly the Demeters' life looked enviable, but friends knew that the couple's personal relationship had become fraught. Demeter was planning an affair with a girl he had met on a trip to Austria, and it was noticeable that he was aggressive towards his wife. Christine told friends that her marriage was sheer hell, and voiced fears that her life was in danger on account of what she knew about her husband's business dealings.

On 18 July 1973 the Demeters were entertaining house guests, and Peter drove them into Toronto to do some shopping, leaving Christine at home with their 3-year-old daughter. When he returned in the evening at 9.45 p.m. he found Christine dead in the garage, where she had been savagely bludgeoned. There was no evidence of sexual attack or of robbery—indeed, the Demeters' daughter, completely unperturbed, was watching TV when her father made his discovery.

Peter Demeter was not immediately under suspicion—after all, he had a perfectly good alibi—but police began to take note as information reached them of the fears for her life which Christine had expressed. Then, in a sensational development, one of Demeter's Hungarian associates came forward to report that Peter had talked to him about getting rid of Christine, and had discussed various methods. This informant agreed to a police suggestion that he be wired up with a transmitter and microphone so that a conversation planned with Demeter could be recorded. Reacting to the news that his associate had been asked by the police to take a lie-detector test, Demeter was recorded as saying '. . . you are the only one who knows . . .'

Demeter was arrested and charged with non-capital murder. His trial began in October 1974, and a bewildering assortment of testimony was given by a variety of Hungarian underworld characters, including a self-confessed murderer, an alleged contract killer and a number of fixers. The tape-recording made by the police had the disadvantage of being entirely in Hungarian, and there were arguments about the quality of its translation.

Evidence was given by a convicted arsonist with a reputation as a contract killer : Christine had approached him with a request to get rid of her husband for a fee of $10,000. He turned down the offer, but a Hungarian go-between by the name of Laszlo Eper was alleged to have had an argument with Christine over money, and had attacked her. Unfortunately, Eper was unable to speak for himself as he had been killed by a police officer in a car chase through Toronto's streets in 1973.

The jury found Peter Demeter guilty as charged, and he was given a 10-year prison sentence. In 1982 he was released on parole and the Demeter house in Mississauga—valued at $132,000—was gutted by fire. He appeared in court in October 1983 charged with arson, and, in another sensational development, was also charged with 2 counts of counselling to commit murder. These charges had resulted from a 2-month police investigation which alleged that Demeter plotted murder against his 19-year-old cousin, whose father was legal guardian of Demeter's daughter.

[502]

DESCHAMPS, Dr Etienne. French-born 55-year-old dentist who created a sensation in New Orleans by killing a 12-year-old girl after sexually assaulting her.

The dentist claimed to possess occult powers, and persuaded a respectable New Orleans carpenter, Jules Deitsch, to help him discover the lost treasure of Jean Lafitte the pirate by the use of hypnotic powers. All he required, he told Deitsch, was a pure young girl as a medium. Innocently, the carpenter surrendered his 12-year-old daughter Juliette into the clutches of the lustful dentist.

Deschamps used the girl's services for 6 months before tragedy struck. The alarm was given by Juliette's 9-year-old sister who frequently witnessed the dentist's occult practices. She fetched her father to Deschamps's lodgings, where they found Juliette lying naked and dead on the bed—with Deschamps covered in blood from self-inflicted stab wounds.

Deschamps recovered from his injuries, and the story of Juliette's death shocked New Orleans. Although he claimed that the girl had agreed to sex, it appeared that he chloroformed her first. This he had done many times, but on 30 January 1889 he went too far and accidentally killed the girl. The authorities thought differently, contending that Deschamps had killed her in order to ensure her silence. He was tried in May 1889, and found guilty. After 2 temporary reprieves and protesting his innocence, Dr Etienne Deschamps was hanged on 12 May 1892.

[898]

DEVEREUX, Arthur. A 24-year-old chemist's assistant and trunk murderer.

Devereux met his future wife, Beatrice, at Hastings in 1896. They married, but life was difficult, because a son was born to them, and it was hard to live on Arthur's low wages. When Beatrice produced twins they were reduced to a virtually impoverished state. Beatrice was undernourished, and Arthur was emotionally ill equipped to deal with the situation.

In January 1905 Devereux obtained a large trunk and a bottle of chloroform and morphine. He

persuaded his wife to drink the drug and give it to the twins on the pretence that it was cough medicine. Devereux put all 3 bodies in the trunk, coated the top with an airtight cover of glue mixed with boric acid, and had it taken to a warehouse at Harrow. He then moved with his son to a new address.

Beatrice's mother, disturbed at her daughter's disappearance, would not be put off by her son-in-law's excuses. She discovered that a Harrow company's furniture van had called at the couple's house. She located the warehouse and found the trunk, which she ordered to be opened. Her worst fears were justified when the bodies of Beatrice and the twins were discovered.

Devereux was arrested in Coventry and sent for trial at the Old Bailey. He contended that his wife had killed herself and the twins, and in a panic he had concealed the bodies in the trunk. It was pointed out by the prosecution that Devereux, before his wife's death, applied for a job describing himself as a widower. His intentions were obvious, and his guilt complete. On 15 August 1905 Arthur Devereux was hanged at Pentonville Prison.

[133, 265, 406, 532, 575, 816, 885, 907]

DIBLANC, Marguerite. Belgian cook in a Mayfair household who murdered her employer, Marie Riel, out of resentment. In November 1871 Diblanc was hired to join the small domestic staff at Mme Riel's house in Park Lane, London. She and her mistress frequently quarrelled, and after four months she was dismissed. There were further quarrels while she was working out her month's notice, but the matters contested were a mystery to the other staff as the arguments were always in French.

On 7 April Mme Riel left the house at midday to walk her dog in Green Park. She failed to return by 4.00 p.m., when she was expected to receive a visitor, but it was not until the following day that inquiries were made about the missing woman. After it was confirmed that she had not gone to stay with any of her friends in London, a search was made of the house. The pantry was inexplicably locked, and when it was opened Mme Riel's body was found crumpled on the floor. Bruises on the dead woman's face and neck attested to the attack she had suffered. Money was missing from the house, as was the cook, Marguerite Diblanc. Diblanc, who was urgently wanted for questioning by the police, was found in lodgings in Paris where she was arrested. She admitted killing Mme Riel out of resentment at not being properly paid.

Diblanc was extradited to England to face a charge of murder. She was tried at the Old Bailey, where an attempt was made to reduce the charge to manslaughter on the grounds of provocation. The servant's story was that when she had been given notice she had demanded to be paid. Her employer abused her, and this led to an exchange of blows. Mme Riel was felled by Diblanc, who was described as a 'coarse, muscular type' of woman with the hands of a man. She dragged the body first down to the cellar and then to the pantry, where she attempted to conceal it.

The trial judge ruled that words alone were insufficient to constitute provocation, and Diblanc was accordingly found guilty of murder. Sentence of death was passed, but she won a reprieve in June 1872.
[867]

DICK CASE. Unusual Canadian case in which a woman was tried twice for the murder of her husband.

On 16 March 1946 a male torso, minus limbs and head, was found by children in a mountain area near Hamilton, Ontario. The remains were identified as 39-year-old John Dick, a Hamilton bus conductor.

He had recently married 24-year-old Evelyn MacLean White, an attractive widow. It was a strange marriage, for Evelyn, known to be promiscuous, refused to allow her husband to live with her. She lived with her mother and daughter, and entertained a lover, Bill Bohozuk, a steel-worker. Eventually Evelyn moved to a new apartment, but her marriage to Dick did not improve, owing to the interference of her mother, Mrs MacLean, who was separated from her husband, Donald. Donald MacLean also worked for the Hamilton bus company. He was an aggressive man, and took an immediate dislike to his son-in-law, John Dick.

Evelyn Dick made 3 statements to the police about the torso, implicating herself and naming Bohozuk as her husband's murderer. Meanwhile at the Dick home police found a basket of ashes in the cellar which yielded fragments of human limb bones and in a suitcase the body of an infant.

On 23 September 1946 Evelyn Dick, her father, Donald MacLean, and her lover, Bill Bohozuk, were charged with the murder of John Dick. Mrs Dick told police that Bohozuk had strangled her baby boy Peter and covered the body with cement.

Evelyn Dick was found guilty, and sentenced to death. The case of Bohozuk and MacLean was referred to a second trial due to lack of evidence. Evelyn appealed, and was granted a new trial. This took place in 1947, when she again faced a jury with Bohozuk and MacLean. Her defence was that she was merely an accessory, and that MacLean, who was known to have hated the dead man, murdered him. This time she was found not guilty. It was an unpopular verdict, but within 4 days she was on

Dick: The torso in the morgue

trial for the murder of her child. On this charge she was found guilty of manslaughter and given life imprisonment. Further legal proceedings followed in which Bohozuk was discharged and MacLean, who pleaded guilty to being an accessory after the fact of murder, was sentenced to 5 years.
[154, 399]

DICKMAN, John Alexander. English railway murderer whose conviction aroused a strong public outcry about circumstantial evidence.

When the 10.27 a.m. slow train from Newcastle arrived at Alnmouth Station in Northumberland on 18 March 1910 a railway porter noticed blood running across the floor of a compartment. Under the seat lay the body of 44-year-old John Innes Nisbet, a colliery wages clerk. He had been shot through the head, and his wages satchel containing £370 was missing.

Witnesses had seen Nisbet, a regular traveller on that train, in the company of another man at Newcastle Station. Statements enabled the police to build up a picture of his travelling companion. This man left the train at Morpeth, where he had paid an excess fare. He was 43-year-old John Dickman, who worked on a commission basis with bookmakers.

When Dickman was interviewed by police he admitted being on the train, and had ready answers about his movements. As his replies did not correspond with witnesses' statements, he was arrested. A search of his home produced a pair of bloodstained trousers and a canvas bag containing £17 in gold sovereigns. Again, Dickman had answers—the blood had resulted from a nose-bleed, and the coins were part of a bookie's trade.

Inquiries showed that Dickman had lost money betting, and was badly in debt. He was picked out as Nisbet's travelling companion at an identity parade, and the missing money satchel was found down a mine-shaft which Dickman was known to have visited. He was sent for trial at Newcastle Assizes in July 1910.

The dead man had been killed by 5 shots of 2 different calibres. This suggested 2 weapons and, the defence contended, 2 murderers. This plea did not save Dickman. Despite his protest in court, 'I declare to all men, I am innocent,' he was found guilty and sentenced to death. A public outcry ensued, and the Home Secretary was petitioned. Still protesting his innocence, John Dickman was hanged at Newcastle Prison on 10 August 1910 with a crowd of 1500 gathered outside the gates.

Years later his name was to be linked to the *Luard* mystery of 1908 as the possible murderer there.
[87, 118, 347, 590, 607, 846]

DOBKIN, Harry. A 49-year-old wartime fire-watcher in London brought to trial for wife-murder.

In July 1942 workmen clearing a bombed chapel in South Lambeth, London, unearthed a female mummified body which had been dismembered and partially burned. The fact that the remains had been buried in limed soil lent weight to the mounting suspicion of murder. Further pathological evidence after examination by Professor Keith Simpson bore this out. The head had been severed from the body and the limbs had been hacked off. Bruised cartilages in the throat suggested death had taken place some 12 to 18 months earlier.

A brilliant feat of forensic detection was completed when the victim was identified as Mrs

Dobkin: Where the body of Mrs Dobkin was found
Dobkin: The body itself

Rachel Dobkin. Her dental history matched that of the victim, and superimposition of her portrait photograph on a photograph of the skull unearthed from the bombsite proved identity beyond doubt. (See *Ruxton.*)

Harry Dobkin was located, and told that his wife's body had been found. He behaved arrogantly in the Coroner's Court until the forensic evidence was produced. He was tried at the Old Bailey in November 1942. It was brought out in court that he had failed to comply with a maintenance order for his separated wife, and that she had repeatedly pestered him for payment. But for the chance hit of a German bomb and the discovery of her handbag at Guildford the crime might never have been detected. He was hanged at Wandsworth Prison on 27 January 1943.

[*3, 365, 451, 489, 496, 564, 598, 679, 759, 851*]

DOMINICI, Gaston. Elderly French farmer convicted of the murder of the Drummond family.

In the summer of 1952 Sir Jack Drummond, a 61-year-old distinguished biochemist, with his wife and 11-year-old daughter, were holidaying in Southern France in their Hillman station wagon. On the night of 4 August the family camped by a river near the Provence village of Lurs. The nearest house was Grand'Terre, a farm owned by 75-year-old Gaston Dominici, a patriarchal figure, and worked by his sons.

Early next morning Gaston's son Gustave raised the alarm on finding the murdered body of a girl near the river bank. When police arrived they found the bodies of Sir Jack and Lady Drummond—both had been shot.

Gustave made a statement saying he heard shots about 1.00 a.m. but was too frightened to investigate. He found the girl's body when he went out at 5.30. Grand'Terre was searched, but the police made little progress until several weeks later when a railway worker told detectives that Gustave had told him that the Drummond girl was still alive when he found her. Gustave confirmed this, and was arrested for failing to give aid to a person in danger of dying. He was imprisoned for 2 months.

The police strongly suspected that the occupants of Grand'Terre knew more about the murders. After persistent questioning over many months Gustave admitted that his father was guilty. His accusation, bitterly contested by Gaston Dominici, was supported by his brother. The old man's obstinacy gradually broke down, and he confessed. He said that he had watched

Lady Drummond undressing, and when he made advances to her Sir Jack intervened and was shot in a struggle. Gaston then shot Lady Drummond and killed her daughter.

Gaston Dominici was tried at Digne Assize Court in November 1954 after he had made several confessions, retractions and counter-accusations, and had attempted suicide. The trial lasted 11 days, and he was found guilty on a majority decision. Sentence of death was subsequently commuted to life imprisonment. He was released in 1960, and died 5 years later.

[*307, 330, 361, 475, 549, 605, 790, 814, 826, 1022*]

DONALD, Jeannie. Convicted murderess whose complete silence when she appeared on the charge of child-murder has led to considerable theory and speculation.

On 21 April 1934 the body of 8-year-old Helen Priestly was found in a sack under the stairs of the Aberdeen tenement where she lived. The girl had been sent on an errand the previous afternoon to buy bread for her mother. She failed to return home, and was reported missing. The sack containing her body was quite dry despite heavy rain a few hours previously. Cause of death was asphyxiation, and there were also signs of rape which later proved incorrect.

The dead girl's neighbours were suspected and in particular the Donald family. Mrs Donald was not on speaking terms with Mrs Priestly, as there had been dissension following an incident when Mrs Donald struck Helen for a misdemeanour. It was known that Helen disliked Mrs Donald, whom she disparagingly called 'Coconut'.

Stains on the floor of the Donald home—said at the time to be blood, though this was later disproved—led to the arrest of Mr and Mrs Donald. Mr Donald was soon released, as he had been at work at the time the murder was committed, but local feeling against Mrs Donald was hostile.

In July 38-year-old Jeannie Donald was tried for murder in Edinburgh. A complex chain of evidence was produced to link the accused to the murder—human hairs found in the sack were claimed to be Mrs Donald's hair. The strongest evidence came from Mrs Donald's own daughter, the dead girl's playmate, who did not recognize part of a loaf found in her home—it was a Cooperative Bakery loaf of the kind that Helen Priestly had been sent by her mother to buy. There were arguments about the injuries to the dead girl.

Donald: The sack containing Helen Priestly's body

The defence claimed they amounted to rape, which exonerated Mrs Donald.

Jeannie Donald did not give evidence, and was found guilty and sentenced to death, although this was later commuted to penal servitude for life. She was released in 1944. It has been suggested that Mrs Donald decided to teach Helen Priestly a lesson for the childish prank of ringing her doorbell and running away. Seeing the child go out on her errand, she hid under the stairs and jumped out on her when she returned and caused her to vomit in terror, choking to death. In the shock of realizing what she had done she simulated rape. [1, 782, 786, 915]

DONNELLY MURDERS. In 1880, 5 members of the Donnelly family were murdered in their homes in a vendetta killing at Lucan in Ontario, Canada. In the early hours of 4 February, James Donnelly, aged 69, and Johannah, Thomas and Bridget were aroused from their sleep and brutally killed with clubs, spades and guns. Their home was then set on fire. Later that same night John, a relative, was shot and killed in his brother's house 3 miles away. The murdering gang (about 20) left prints in the snow.

There was a witness. 11-year-old Johnny O'Connor, who sometimes helped the Donnellys with their livestock, was in James Donnelly's house, and survived by hiding under a bed. He identified one of the attackers as James Carroll, the local constable. The murders were the result of a feud which had its origins in Ireland. Canada received many Irish immigrants in the early 1840s, fleeing the potato-famine ravages and hoping to start new lives. Among the immigrants was James Donnelly, a hard-working Catholic who advocated co-operation with the Protestants. This did not endear him to the extremists known as 'Whiteboys', and passions smouldered in the immigrant community.

Donnelly and those who shared his outlook were called 'Blackfeet', and their opponents made trouble for them. A group of Vigilantes was formed by the 'Whiteboys'. They disputed the worth of English law, and carried out acts of arson and intimidation which won them the title 'Northern Ku Klux Klan'.

It was the Vigilantes who decided to eliminate the Donnellys, but they were so powerful locally that few dared to raise a voice against them. Young Johnny O'Connor was the exception, despite the mysterious destruction by fire of his father's house. He unequivocally identified James Carroll as one of the leaders of the gang.

Carroll and 5 others were brought to trial in October 1880, but the timid jury could not agree a verdict. At a second trial in January 1881 the 6 men were found not guilty. Thus the Donnelly murders went unpunished, despite the well-known identity of the perpetrators.

[515, 668]

DOT KING CASE. Unsolved New York murder of a model, with theft as a motive and overtones of blackmail.

Anna Marie Keenan married a chauffeur when she was 18. They separated after 2 years, and she changed her name to Dot King to match her growing image as a model. Success came in the early 1920s when she met a wealthy businessman by the name of Marshall. Dot's night-club companions envied her successful capture of a 'Sugar-daddy'. Marshall showered her with money and gifts: within a year she had acquired $10 000 in cash and some $20 000 in clothes and jewellery.

On 15 March 1923 Dot King was found dead in her apartment. She was lying on her bed, having apparently committed suicide—an empty bottle of chloroform lay close by. Her arm was twisted behind her back as if she had been held in a hammer-lock, and the telephone—normally at the bedside—was placed as far from the bed as its cord would permit. All Dot's jewellery was missing, and a letter to 'Darling Dottie' promised, ' . . . Only two more days before I will be in your arms.' Hidden under a couch was a pair of men's pyjamas which the maid said belonged to Mr Marshall.

Marshall presented himself to the police and revealed his true identity. He was J. Kearsley Mitchell, the Philadelphia millionaire, who spoke of his friendship with Dot King and entirely cleared himself of suspicion. The newspapers had a field day, and a theory which gained currency was that Dot King was involved in a blackmail plot. It was concluded that she might simply have been the victim of a thief who had been prepared to render her unconscious with chloroform while he ransacked the apartment. But he overdid the anaesthetic and killed the girl in error.

[207, 562]

DOUGAL, Samuel Herbert. A virile ex-soldier who sired children at every posting, and was convicted of the Moat Farm Murder.

Dougal served in the Royal Engineers, and soon gained a reputation as a womanizer. In 1869 he met and married his first wife. Despite his illegitimate children, his marriage lasted until 1885, when his wife died in Canada. Dougal was sent home on compassionate leave, and returned with a new wife

Dougal: Camille Holland's body

who brought a useful dowry with her. Within a few weeks she died after severe vomiting.

Dougal left the Army and forfeited his pension in 1896, when he was imprisoned for forgery. In 1898 he met Camille Holland, a 55-year-old spinster of charm and education, but lacking in worldly wisdom. She also had £7000, and Dougal set about winning her affection.

In 1899 they moved into a lonely farmhouse near Saffron Waldon which Dougal named Moat Farm. Very soon Dougal was found trying to seduce a maid. Although he and Camille were not married, she told him she would not tolerate such behaviour, and ordered him to get out.

Shortly after this Camille disappeared, and Dougal scandalized the neighbourhood by entertaining a succession of women at Moat Farm. For 4 years Camille's disappearance remained a mystery, but the police, dissatisfied with Dougal's explanations, began to delve into his bank transactions. They quickly learned that he had been forging Camille's signature on cheques long after she disappeared. Dougal promptly went to ground, but was identified in London and detained for questioning.

On 19 March 1903 he was arrested for forgery. A thorough search of Moat Farm led to the discovery of Camille's body in an old drainage ditch. She had been shot in the head.

Dougal was tried at Chelmsford Assizes in June 1903, and was sentenced to death. In a last bid to save himself he wrote to the Home Secretary explaining how the gun went off accidentally, killing Camille. He was hanged on 14 July 1903, having confessed his guilt to the chaplain on the scaffold.

[*1, 21, 32, 420, 449, 699, 722, 846, 1006*]

DREW CASE. Case of murder in which no charge was made but in which a suspect suffered 'trial by Coroner'.

On 22 June 1929 a Reading tobacconist was brutally attacked in his shop—dying from his injuries next day—and the contents of his cash register stolen. A man seen by several witnesses near the shop at the time the murder was committed was identified as Philip Yale Drew, an American-born actor performing at Reading's County Theatre with a touring company.

Drew was questioned about his movements, and admitted being a 'bit erratic'. A Coroner's Inquiry into the tobacconist's death was instituted which was virtually a trial of Drew, who had not even been charged with committing a crime. After

hearing some 60 witnesses, the jury returned a verdict of wilful murder against some person or persons unknown, and Drew's ordeal was ended. The result was greeted with acclamation by the people of Reading, who gave the actor a hero's welcome.

The case is significant, as the trial by inquest resulted in widespread criticism, and helped to prompt revision of the Coroners Act. While Drew was not accused of murder, however, a stigma attached to him, and his stage career faded. He died in 1940 at the age of 60.

[*81, 973*]

DUBUISSON, Pauline. A 26-year-old medical student who featured in a celebrated *crime passionel* in Paris.

On 17 March 1951 she shot and killed Félix Bailly in his flat and then attempted to gas herself. She was revived, and was arrested for murder.

Her trial was deferred by another suicide attempt, but in November she was charged. Her background gained her little sympathy. At the age of 17 she had been the mistress of a German colonel, and she kept a notebook in which were recorded details of her lovers' performances. She was listed by the Resistance Movement as a collaborator, and suffered public humiliation.

In 1946 she enrolled as a medical student at the University of Lille. There she met Félix Bailley, a handsome young man and an accomplished athlete. They had a stormy affair, and in 1949 Félix decided to part from her. He returned to Paris to continue his studies there.

Eighteen months later Pauline heard that Félix was to marry. She went to Paris, and after a fruitless attempt to regain Félix's affection she decided to kill him and commit suicide.

The court had some difficulty in entertaining the idea of a *crime passionel*, since such a long period had elapsed between the end of the affair and the fatal shooting. There was also the question of Pauline's obvious promiscuity. The jury found her guilty of murder without premeditation, so she escaped the death sentence but went to penal servitude for life.

[*437*]

DUFF CASE. See CROYDON POISON-INGS

DUMOLLARD, Martin. For 12 years Dumollard and his wife lured young women to their cottage near Lyons on the pretext of engaging them as servants. Once a girl had been ensnared Dumollard murdered her, while his wife stripped off the clothing. This she sold, or, if she fancied a particular garment, wore herself.

In May 1861 Dumollard spoke to a likely victim in Lyons, saying that he had been sent by his employer, who owned a château at Montluel, to look for a housemaid and to offer a good salary. Marie Pichon went with Dumollard to Montluel. They were headed for the cottage, but while they were walking the country lanes Marie became suspicious. Dumollard attempted to strangle her, but she escaped.

Dumollard and his wife were arrested next day. Clothes of at least 10 victims were found in their cottage. Three corpses were discovered, and after his wife had denounced him to save her own skin, Dumollard confessed. He identified some graves, and admitted throwing corpses into the river Rhône.

The couple were tried at Bourg in January 1862 amid great public hostility. Both were found guilty, and Martin Dumollard, psychopathic killer of young women, was guillotined, while his wife was sentenced to the galleys for life.

[290, 388, 554]

DURRANT, William Henry Theodore. This 24-year-old San Francisco medical student and Sunday school superintendent, a brother of Maud Allen the dancer, murdered 2 girls in a church.

On 3 April 1895 Durrant took 21-year-old Blanche Lamont to San Francisco's Emanuel Baptist Church. He strangled her, stripped off her clothes and dragged the body by its hair up to the belfry tower. There the girl's naked body, with hands crossed on her breast, lay undiscovered for 9 days.

Durrant was seen on 12 April with 20-year-old Minnie Williams entering the Emanuel Baptist Church. Durrant killed the girl in a frenzy, strangling her and mutilating the body. Less than 2 hours later he attended a Christian Endeavour meeting.

Minnie Williams's body was found the following day, and Blanche Lamont's body was found in the belfry. His apprehension gave the papers a field day, and 'The Demon in the Belfry' made news across America and in Europe as well.

Durrant was tried and found guilty, but 2 years passed before execution. He was hanged on 7 January 1898, after which there was a stream of confession to the crimes. The suggestion was made that Durrant was not the real killer, but that

the pastor of the Baptist Church was the guilty party. There was a dispute about the funeral, since no crematorium would accept the body, but 6 days after the execution the Pasadena Crematorium agreed to take it.

[383, 483, 777, 816]

DÜSSELDORF DOUBLES KILLER. See BOOST, Werner

'DÜSSELDORF MONSTER'. See KÜRTEN, Peter

DYER, Amelia Elizabeth. A 57-year-old murderess known as the Reading Baby Farmer.

Onetime member of the Salvation Army, Mrs Dyer, who was separated from her husband, took in children at her home in Bristol. In 1895 she moved to Reading, and advertised that she would board and adopt children. In March a bargeman on the river Thames fished out of the water a child's corpse with a tape around its neck, wrapped in a parcel bearing a Reading address. But Mrs Dyer, who used several aliases, had already moved to another house in Reading. Meanwhile 2 more dead infants were found in the river.

She was arrested in April 1896, and tried to commit suicide. By the end of that month bodies of 7 children had been found; all had been strangled with a tape and wrapped in parcels. Charged together with her son-in-law, Mrs Dyer made a brief statement absolving her alleged accomplice and accepting full blame.

At Mrs Dyer's trial in May 1896 the defence sought to prove that she was insane. It was not known how many babies she had killed, but as she had been farming children for 15 years it was likely that the total was more than the 7 known victims. She herself said, 'You'll know all mine by the tape around their necks.' Mrs Dyer's motive was one of greed; she accumulated fictitious boarding fees by quickly disposing of the infants placed in her care. She was executed on 10 June 1896 at Newgate, where her ghost was said to have haunted the Chief Warder.

[322, 1006]

DYER, Ernest. A strange case in which the dream of a dead man's mother led the police to his murderer, who shot himself before he could be questioned.

At the end of the First World War two ex-officers in their twenties, Eric Gordon Tombe and Ernest Dyer, went into business together. After 2

Durrant: Blanche´s body is carried to the belfry

failures they bought a stud farm called The Welcomes at Kenley in Surrey. Tombe put up most of the money, and Dyer moved in with his family. In April 1921 The Welcomes was destroyed by fire, but Dyer's swiftly lodged claim was rejected by the insurance company.

That same month Eric Tombe disappeared after a quarrel with Dyer over money. The Rev. Tombe, the missing man's father, learned for the first time of his son's close association with Dyer, and traced them to The Welcomes. He then went to his son's bank, where he was reassured by the manager, who told him that he had received letters from Eric Tombe, one of which gave power of attorney to Ernest Dyer. The clergyman denounced the signature as a forgery and found his son's bank account, once healthy, had been whittled away in a matter of months.

Many months later in November 1922 a man calling himself Fitzsimmons was staying in a Scarborough hotel. He had been working a confidence trick in a local newspaper, and an alert police department sent a detective to question him. Fitzsimmons, fearful of arrest, put his hand in his pocket, but was seized by the detective and shot with his own gun during the ensuing struggle. Fitzsimmons turned out to be Ernest Dyer, whose room at the hotel contained a passport and cheques belonging to Eric Tombe.

The mystery of Tombe's disappearance was solved when his mother had nightmares in which she saw her son's body lying dead at the bottom of a well. Ten months after Dyer's death detectives were persuaded by Tombe's parents to search The Welcomes. There, in one of the wells on the farm, they found the body of Eric Tombe—shot through the head. Thus the victim was found after the murderer himself was dead.

[*167, 373, 816, 873*]

E

EDMUNDS, Christiana. Remarkable case of a 42-year-old spinster who left a trail of poison in an effort to avert suspicion of attempted murder.

Miss Edmunds, who lived in Brighton with her widowed mother, was a patient of Dr Beard. She was also in love with the married doctor, and he had asked Miss Edmunds to stop writing to him.

On 10 August 1871 Mrs Beard received through the post a parcel of cakes with a note saying, 'Those done up are flavoured on purpose for you to enjoy.' The Beard servants were ill after eating the cakes. Dr Beard saw through this clumsy plan and accused Miss Edmunds of trying to poison his wife.

She was arrested and charged with murder. As the case developed, she was linked with the death several months earlier of a 4½-year-old boy. The boy died of strychnine poisoning after eating chocolates. Now it was considered that 3 anonymous letters sent to the dead boy's father were in Christiana Edmunds's handwriting.

It was found that Miss Edmunds had made several purchases of strychnine from a local chemist for the purpose of destroying cats. It appeared too that she would send children on errands to buy sweets for her, and that she left these lying around where others were likely to pick them up and eat them. Several children became ill as a result.

The accused declared that she had been driven to her action as a result of her intimacy with Dr Beard. She also claimed to be pregnant, a statement disproved by medical examination. The jury found Christiana Edmunds guilty, but did not consider her insane. She had tried to divert suspicion by showing that several others, including herself, had also been poisoned. She was reprieved.
[*111, 380, 399, 725, 947, 989*]

EDWARDS, Edgar. Gentleman charmer with an urge to acquire property by murder.

Edwards was apprehended in London in 1902 while assaulting a man with a lead window-sash weight. When arrested he was found to have on him business cards in the name of John W. Darby, a Camberwell greengrocer. The Darby family were not to be found and most of the contents of their shop had been removed. Police did find a 5-pound sash-weight with blood on it.

Inquiries now focused on Edwards's recently acquired house at Leyton, where neighbours had observed him digging in the garden to a considerable depth. Police found the dismembered corpses of John Darby and his wife, both in their twenties, and of their 10-week-old child. Husband and wife had been battered to death—the infant had been strangled.

Edwards was tried at the Old Bailey in February 1903. The evidence was circumstantial—no witness had seen him with any of the murder victims. It was contended that he killed the Darby family in their shop, wanting the premises for himself, dismembered their bodies and transported them in packing-cases about 6 miles to Leyton, where he buried them. His defence was based on insanity, for which there were ample precedents in his family background. He took an arrogant line in the dock, and occasionally laughed loudly during the proceedings. When he was found guilty he was asked if he wished to say anything. He replied, 'Let 'em get along with it as quick as they like.' After being sentenced he erupted into gales of laughter, and said to the chaplain on the scaffold 'I've been looking forward to this lot!' He was hanged on 3 March 1903.
[*265, 591*]

ELLIS, Ruth. A 28-year-old night-club manageress who murdered her lover, and was the last woman in Britain to be hanged.

David Blakely, a 24-year-old racing-car driver, was shot dead outside a North London public house on 10 April 1955. As Blakely left the pub and walked to his car a blonde approached him and emptied a Smith and Wesson into his body. The

POST-MORTEM EXAMINATION.

Name	ELLIS, Ruth	**Apparent Age**	28 years
At	H.M. Prison, Holloway	**Date**	July 13 1955

EXTERNAL EXAMINATION

Nourishment ... ...
Marks of Violence,
Identification, etc. ...

Well nourished.
Evidence of proper care and attention.
Height – 5ft. 2ins.   Weight – 103 lbs.

DEEP IMPRESSIONS AROUND NECK of noose with suspension point
about 1 inch in front of the angle of the L.lower jaw.
Vital changes locally and in the tissues beneath as a
consequence of sudden constriction.
No ecchymoses in the face – or, indeed, elsewhere.
No marks of restraint.

How long dead

1 hour.

INTERNAL EXAMINATION

Skull ... ...
Brain Meninges ... ...

Fracture-dislocation of the spine at C.2 with a 2 inch gap
and transverse separation of the spinal cord at the same level.

Mouth, Tongue,
Oesophagus ... ...
Larynx, Trachea, Lungs ...

Fractures of both wings of the hyoid and the R.wing of the
thyroid cartilage. Larynx also fractured.
Air passages clear and lungs quite free from disease or other
change. No engorgement. No asphyxial changes.

Pericardium, Heart and
Blood Vessels ... ...

No organic disease.   No petechiae or other evidence of
asphyxial change.

Stomach and Contents ...

Small food residue, and odour of brandy.   No disease.

Peritoneum,
Intestines, Etc. ... ...

Normal.

Liver and Gall Bladder ...

Terminal congestion only.

Spleen ... ...

Normal.

Kidneys and Ureters... ...

Slight terminal congestion only.

Bladder, Etc. ... ...
Generative Organs ... ...

Lower abdominal operation scar for ectopic pregnancy operation
in L.tube, now healed.   No pregnancy.

Other Remarks ... ...

Deceased was a healthy subject at the time of death.
Mark of suspension normally situated and injuries from
judicial hanging – to the spinal column and cord – such as
must have caused instant death.

CAUSE OF DEATH ...

Injuries to the central nervous system
consequent upon judicial hanging.

Signed

M.D. Lond.
146, Harley St., W 1, and Guy's Hospital (Pathologist)
Reader in Forensic Medicine, London University.

Ellis: Post-mortem report

119

woman, who was immediately apprehended, gave her name as Ruth Ellis, and her occupation as modelling.

Formerly a waitress and factory worker, she had a chequered career. In 1944 she had a child by a French-Canadian serviceman, and in 1950 she married George Ellis, a dentist. They soon parted, and she then became a club-manageress and call-girl.

She met David Blakely, and succumbed to his charm and glamorous occupation. In 1953 she had an abortion, and Blakely offered to marry her. Ruth tried to shake him off, but he became highly emotional. In 1955 they lived together, but Ruth continued to see her other lovers. Their affair developed into sordid quarrels, and Blakely took to heavy drinking.

In this highly charged situation, the relationship altered from one of Blakely's dependence on Ruth to one of her reliance on him. When he in his turn tried to extricate himself from their messy affair Ruth became jealous. After Blakely attempted to conceal his whereabouts from her she traced him to the pub, and in a deeply embittered mood after a miscarriage shot him dead.

At her trial in June 1955 Ruth Ellis was asked what she intended when she fired the revolver. She replied, 'I intended to kill him.' The jury found her guilty in 14 minutes. While in Holloway prison strong petitions were organized but on 13 July 1955 Ruth Ellis was hanged.

It was suggested that no reprieve was granted because a passer-by was wounded by one of the shots fired at Blakely.

The case was revived in 1985 by the film *Dance With a Stranger*. Ruth Ellis was portrayed at the time of the shooting as a woman acting almost as if in a trance under the influence of anti-depressant drugs following a miscarriage provoked by her lover's ill-treatment.

The day before she was hanged, Ruth Ellis made a written statement implicating a person who had provided her with a gun and driven her to the scene of the fatal shooting. This statement remained secret for 25 years before the information was finally given to the police. The individual named denied any involvement and the matter was not pursued. [4, 308, 318, 322, 407, 649, 963, 1001]

ELLSOME CASE. A 22-year-old labourer whose conviction for murder in 1911 was set aside in a unique decision by the Court of Criminal Appeal.

On 21 August 1911 a Clerkenwell man on his way back to work in the early morning heard screams and a girl shouting 'Don't, Charles, don't!' Later that morning a girl's body, stabbed in the heart, was found on the pavement. Her name was Rose Render, a 19-year-old waitress, with whom Charles Ellsome lived.

Ellsome was arrested, and his trial before Avory lasted less than a day. A friend of the accused man said Ellsome told him that he had killed Rose. 'She drove me to do it,' he said. Ellsome denied this, but it was proved that he had bought a long-bladed knife the day before the murder. The victim's father stated that Ellsome had driven his daughter on to the streets to earn money to keep him. The jury took less than half an hour to find Ellsome guilty, and he was sentenced to death.

The case went to the Court of Criminal Appeal, and in the first ruling of its kind in a capital case, Ellsome's conviction was set aside on grounds of the trial judge's misdirection of the jury. Charles Ellsome was thus set free, although the Appeal Court judge pointed out that in quashing the verdict no view was expressed as to his guilt. [131, 492, 709, 712]

ELWELL CASE. New York *cause célèbre* of 1920. The murder of Joseph Browne Elwell, bridge and whist expert and a man of considerable standing in the city, remains unsolved.

On 11 June 1920, Elwell's housekeeper arrived at the house as usual about 8.00 a.m. She found her employer slumped in a chair. He had a bullet wound in his forehead. He was rushed to hospital, where he died a few hours later.

Elwell had died from a single shot fired from a .45 calibre army revolver. He had been wearing pyjamas, and was sitting down to read the morning's mail. There was a letter in his lap, and several others lay unopened at his feet.

A search of the house ruled out theft, for $400 in notes and various items of jewellery lay untouched. The bedroom itself attracted attention—its oriental style of furnishing and other trappings suggested a woman's taste.

Elwell had married in 1904, but at the time of his death he was separated from his wife. Stories of his fame and wealth had attracted many women, and their names were listed in a book on his desk. The last woman seen with him was Viola Kraus, recently divorced, who was with him on his last evening. They dined together at the Ritz-Carlton and later went to a show. The party broke up about 2.00 a.m. and Elwell returned home alone.

The letters which Elwell received on the

morning of his death offered no clues. There were only two keys to the house; he had one and his housekeeper had the other. He did not have a firearm; so the murderer had brought his own weapon, but a .45 service revolver hardly seemed a woman's choice of gun.

Police questioned all of Elwell's acquaintances, male and female, but nothing concrete emerged. There were stories of jealous lovers and husbands, of mysterious spies and fashionable matrons mad with passion, but no suspects.

In 1987, in his book on the case, crime writer Jonathan Goodman named Walter Lewisohn as Elwell's murderer, or at least procurer of his death. Lewisohn, a wealthy banker and member of the Manhattan set, was mentally unstable. He was afraid that Elwell, a well-known philanderer, had his eyes on the two women he idolized, his girl-friend, Leonora, and his sister-in-law Viola Kraus.

Fearful that he would lose them, he plotted murder by hiring an assassin. Lewisohn was placed in an asylum in 1922 and two years later, was judged incurably insane. He died in 1938.

[207, 352, 508, 562, 896, 990]

EMMETT-DUNNE, Frederick. A 33-year-old Regular sergeant serving with the British occupation forces in Germany, and convicted of murdering a fellow-sergeant with a karate blow.

Sergeants Emmett-Dunne and Reginald Watters were stationed at Duisberg. Despite their dissimilar characters, the two men were friends— Emmett-Dunne was regarded as a 'hard case' and untrustworthy, while Watters was easy-going and popular with the men.

On 30 November 1953 Watters was reported missing. A search of the camp found him hanging from the stairs in one of the barrack blocks. He appeared to have committed suicide. Emmett-Dunne said Watters had quarrelled with him, alleging that he had been going out with his wife. He had produced a gun, and in self-defence Emmett-Dunne struck him a blow which killed him. Frightened at the outcome, Emmett-Dunne sought the counsel of his half-brother (also stationed at Duisberg), telling him that Watters had been killed accidentally. They decided to make the death look like suicide and an Army court accepted this.

Persistent rumour among Watters's friends that his death was not suicidal led to the case being re-investigated by the army's Special Investigation Branch. Meanwhile Emmett-Dunne had been posted back to England, where he met Mrs

Watters, and married her. Watters's body was exhumed and examined by pathologist Dr Francis Camps, who concluded that the dead man had been killed by a blow to the throat.

Emmett-Dunne was arrested and sent for trial at Düsseldorf in June 1955. The medical evidence was overwhelming, and he was found guilty of murder. He was sentenced to life imprisonment, since the crime had been committed in Germany where there was no capital punishment.

[157, 308, 487, 489, 792, 981]

ERROLL CASE. A suggested *crime passionel* involving members of the British aristocracy in Kenya resulted in an unsolved murder.

Sir Henry John Delves Broughton, a 59-year-old racehorse owner and big-game hunter, married Diana Caldwell in 1940. They honey-mooned in Kenya and there met Lord Erroll, a farmer and Hereditary High Constable of Scotland. Erroll, aged 39, was a man of considerable influence in the colony, and was regarded as a ladies' man.

The trio became very friendly, and it was quickly apparent that Erroll had fallen in love with Broughton's wife. In January 1941 they agreed that Broughton must be told, and Diana broke the news to him. He reacted calmly, suggesting that he and Diana should go away for 3 months to think the matter over. Erroll did not agree, and Broughton gave in, to honour a promise he had made to Diana that if either fell in love with anyone else the other would not stand in the way. Lawyers were contacted, and Broughton settled £5000 on Diana.

On the night of 23 January the trio dined together at the Muthaiga Country Club. Erroll wanted to take Diana to a dance. Broughton raised no objection, provided his wife was home before 3.00 a.m. Broughton left the Club in a drunken state at about 1.30, and was driven to Karen, his rented home. At 2.25 a.m. Erroll brought Diana back.

The following morning Erroll was found dead with a bullet in his head behind the wheel of his car, which had gone off the road less than 3 miles from Karen. Broughton was questioned, and he said that 2 revolvers had been stolen from his house 3 days before the murder. It was also established that one of these weapons had fired the shot which killed Erroll. Broughton was arrested.

Broughton certainly had a motive for killing Erroll, but the prosecution was unable to show how a man of 59 who suffered night blindness might have committed the murder in the time and

Erroll Case: The body in the car

circumstances prevailing. The jury found Broughton not guilty, and he committed suicide in a Liverpool hotel from an overdose of barbiturates on 2 December 1942.

In 1969 journalists Cyril Connolly and James Fox published an article in the *Sunday Times*. This led to a book by Fox entitled *White Mischief*, published in 1982, which proved controversial by virtue of exposing the phoney lifestyle of the British expatriates in Kenya during the early years of the Second World War. The book revealed that on the day after Erroll was found dead, Broughton confessed to a friend's daughter that he had committed the murder.

[*66, 67, 292, 316*]

EVANS, Timothy John. A 24-year-old illiterate van-driver accused of the murder of his wife and baby daughter. Evans occupied the top floor of 10 Rillington Place, a residence made notorious by *John Reginald Halliday Christie*.

Evans told the police in Wales that he had found his wife dead after Christie had tried to perform an abortion on her when he returned home on 8 November 1949, and that he had put her down a drain. The strangled bodies of his wife and child were later found in the washhouse at No. 10. Evans made a statement in which he accused Christie of having caused his wife's death. Later he confessed to the killings himself, and was tried at the Old Bailey in January 1950. Subsequently he retracted this confession, and again blamed Christie, who countered, 'That is a lie'. Evans was found guilty and hanged on 9 March 1950.

Some 3 years later Christie was arraigned at the Old Bailey for murdering his wife. He was also shown to be responsible for the deaths of 5 other women, and, by his own admission, for the death of Mrs Evans, although he denied killing the child.

This revelation resulted in an inquiry into the question of whether a miscarriage of justice had occurred. It was said that Christie believed it would help his defence if he confessed to the murder of Mrs Evans, or, as he put it, 'The more the merrier.' An official inquiry into the matter concluded that the case against Evans was found proven. But in the light of what happened later it seems unlikely he was guilty.

[*1, 175, 260, 300, 317, 402, 851*]

EYRAUD and BOMPARD. Murderous French pair brought to justice by a distinguished piece of forensic detection.

On 13 August 1889 police were led to a riverside spot some 10 miles from Lyons, where a decaying body was found in a sack. The badly decomposed corpse was that of a man who had been strangled. Some distance from the body several rotten pieces of wood were found which, pieced together, formed a trunk bearing railway labels indicating that it had been sent from Paris to Lyons on 27 July 1888.

It was thought that the dead man might be Toussaint-Augssent Gouffé, a court bailiff missing from Paris since 27 July 1888. Gouffé's brother-in-law could not positively identify the corpse. He admitted that Gouffé, a widower, was something of a ladies' man, and he was seen in Paris 2 days before his disappearance in the company of a man and a woman. They were Michel Eyraud, an army deserter and shady business-man, and his young mistress, Gabrielle Bompard. Both had since left the city.

Gouffe was identified beyond doubt by Professor Alexandre Lacassagne, who saw that the dead man had a tubercular infection of the ankle, and estimated his age as 50. Gouffé was known to have limped, and he was aged 59. Dental comparisons finally confirmed the identification.

Eyraud and Bompard were now sought throughout Europe and America. In January 1890 the Chief of the Sûreté received a letter from Eyraud posted in New York. In it he laid the blame for the crime on his partner. Bompard then appeared in Paris, claiming that she had been used by Eyraud. She was arrested, and admitted how she had lured Gouffé to her flat to be killed by Eyraud. Gouffé was officially involved in Eyraud's examination for bankruptcy. After robbing their victim, the pair sewed his body into a sack and disposed of it in the trunk.

Eyraud was arrested in Havana and returned to France for trial. He was guillotined on 3 February 1891, while Bompard was sentenced to 20 years' penal servitude.

[*366, 378, 545, 581, 594, 677, 792, 915, 933*]

F

FAHMY CASE. Marguerite Laurent Fahmy was a 23-year-old Parisian beauty tried for the murder of her playboy husband, Prince Ali Kamel Fahmy Bey.

Mme Fahmy shot her wealthy Egyptian husband in their luxury suite at London's Savoy Hotel on 10 July 1923. That evening they had quarrelled publicly in the hotel restaurant, and Mme Fahmy told the band-leader who invited her to choose a piece of music, 'My husband is going to kill me in twenty-four hours, and I am not very anxious for music.' The argument continued after they retired, and at 2.00 a.m. 3 shots were heard. Prince Fahmy was found lying wounded on the floor of his suite—he died later of gunshot wounds in the head. Mme Fahmy was taken into custody.

The trial of Mme Fahmy in September 1923 aroused great public interest, and she was represented in court by two giants of the English Bar, Sir Edward Marshall Hall and Sir Henry Curtis-Bennett. Prince Fahmy's secretary told the court that his master abused and humiliated his wife, and they quarrelled constantly. Marshall Hall put Mme Fahmy in the witness-box with good effect. She told of her husband's perverted sexual practices, and described the fatal night in the hotel. They had argued, and he seized her by the throat, threatening to kill her—in her terror she shot him.

With dramatic gestures, holding the pistol in his hand, Marshall Hall acted out Prince Fahmy's part in court as he advanced menacingly on his wife, 'As he crouched . . . like an animal . . . she turned the pistol and put it to his face, and to her horror the thing went off.'

The jury took less than an hour to acquit Mme Fahmy. Cheering greeted a popular verdict, and a free woman once again, Mme Fahmy said, 'It is terrible to have killed Ali, but I spoke the truth.'
[*33, 113, 318, 322, 378, 433, 649, 709, 960*]

FEIN, Mark. A 32-year-old New York millionaire businessman who killed his bookie.

Rubin Markowitz, a grocery-store clerk and bookmaker with some wealthy clients, disappeared on 10 October 1963. His body, shot 4 times in the head and chest with a .22 calibre weapon, was found in the Harlem river a month later. On it was a telephone list which was central to his bookmaking activities.

Police checked out the numbers in this list, including one for a Gloria Kendall, a redhead in her mid-thirties who claimed to be girl-friend of Mark Fein, an up-and-coming businessman, and known to be one of Markowitz's clients.

Fein owed Markowitz $7200 on a wager, and was due to repay the debt on 10 October. He evaded police questions, explaining that to answer them would jeopardize his marriage. Gloria Kendall, a prostitute with a criminal record and 30 aliases, went to ground, but emerged later to tell detectives the 'whole truth', that Fein had telephoned her on 10 October and she went to his apartment. There was a cabin trunk which he said contained the body of his bookmaker, and he asked her to dispose of it. With the aid of two friends she took the trunk away and dumped it into the Harlem river.

Fein was arrested and charged with the murder of Rubin Markowitz. The star witness at his trial in New York in October 1964 was Gloria Kendall, who said she had seen the body in the trunk. Fein did not give evidence and his counsel asked the jury: 'Can you pronounce Mark Fein guilty of murder in the first degree on the testimony of Gloria?'

Why so wealthy a man as Fein should have murdered for a small bet is unexplained. However, on 25 November 1964 he was found guilty of murder in the second degree, and sentenced to 30 years to life—the maximum which could be imposed.
[*764*]

Fein: Police report on victim

UNIFORMED FORCES NO. 61 REPORT

DATE: November 8, 1963

NAME: RUBIN MARKOWITZ

SEX: M

COLOR: W

AGE: 40

TIME: 7:00 A.M.

PLACE OF OCCURRENCE: Junction of Hudson and Harlem
Rivers, 225 Street, N.Y. Central Railroad Bridge.

NATURE OF ILLNESS OR INJURY: D.O.A.

COMMENTS: M,W, 5'10", 180 lbs, wearing gray pants,
dark socks, black low shoes, black belt, black tie.
Body badly decomposed. The legs of the body were tied
with a clothesline rope. The legs were tied together
at the ankles, knotted behind with clothesline, which
in turn was tied to pilings.

(s)   William Dwyer

FIELD, Frederick Herbert Charles. Royal Air Force deserter aged 32 who confessed to 2 murders on different occasions.

On 2 October 1931 the strangled body of Norah Upchurch, a 20-year-old prostitute, was found by some workmen in an empty building in London's Shaftesbury Avenue. One of them, Frederick Field, came under suspicion because of a statement he made about a key to the premises which he said he lost. The Coroner's Inquest returned an open verdict.

Eighteen months later Field, now serving in the Royal Air Force, approached a newspaper and made an arrangement whereby his defence costs would be guaranteed should he be charged with murder after divulging his exclusive story. Field made a statement, and was arrested, having confessed to the murder of Norah Upchurch. His account of how he had killed the girl was not consistent with the facts, and it became clear that his confession was a ploy to obtain money from the newspaper. He was tried at the Old Bailey, having previously retracted his confession. The judge directed the jury to acquit him.

In 1936 Field was arrested as a deserter from the armed services. He immediately made a confession to murder, this time claiming to have killed Beatrice Vilna Sutton, a middle-aged widow who had been found dead from suffocation in her Clapham flat on 4 April 1936. Field employed the same technique as before—withdrawing his confession when he came up for trial. But on this occasion he did not escape and he was hanged on 30 June 1936. If he had not confessed to the murders it is unlikely he would ever have been convicted.

[29, 91, 133, 253]

FIELD and GRAY. Jack Alfred Field and William Thomas Gray, both ex-Servicemen in their twenties, murdered a young woman at the Crumbles near Eastbourne.

At mid-afternoon on 19 August 1920 Irene Munro, an attractive 17-year-old typist on holiday from London, left her lodgings at Eastbourne. She was seen in the company of 2 men walking in the direction of the Crumbles, a lonely part of the coast. When she failed to return the alarm was raised by her landlady. The discovery of her body had already been reported—having been found fully dressed in a shallow grave in the shingle. She had been brutally beaten about the head.

Some men working on a near-by railway line recalled seeing the girl, apparently in a happy mood, with 2 men. Other witnesses had also seen the trio, and the police were able to build up descriptions of the 2 men. They were identified as local residents Jack Field and Thomas Gray. Both were out of work, and Gray in particular was regarded as an unsavoury character.

Field and Gray were charged with the murder, and tried at Lewes Assizes in December 1920. Both pleaded not guilty, but they had been seen together with the girl by too many witnesses to contest identification. Gray's attempts while in custody to fake an alibi with the help of a fellow-prisoner did not help, despite his defence by Sir Edward Marshall Hall. Marshall Hall suggested that it would have been unlikely for a girl of Irene Munro's education and refinement to have fallen in with such down-and-out characters as the accused. But it came out that Irene Munro was not above enticing older men, and though she had not been raped it was suggested that her refusal of the two men's sexual advances roused them to fury, and they savagely killed her.

Field and Gray were found guilty, and they were hanged at Wandsworth Prison on 4 February 1921. Neither man made a confession, but each accused the other of the murder.

[1, 133, 541, 555, 649, 873, 960]

FINCH and TREGOFF. California doctor and his mistress who conspired to murder Mrs Finch, and whose case went before 3 trial juries before a verdict was given.

Raymond Bernard Finch, 42, owned part of the West Corina Medical Center. He married for the second time in 1951, and he and his wife Barbara were popular members of the Los Angeles Tennis Club. By 1957 Finch was complaining that his wife was cold towards him, and the couple decided to part.

Using the name George Evans, Finch rented an apartment where he regularly met 20-year-old married ex-model Carole Tregoff. In 1958 'Mr and Mrs Evans' moved to another apartment, and when Carole was divorced the following year conversation turned on Finch's own divorce. However, while Barbara Finch was happy about the separation arrangements, she did not take kindly to the idea of divorce.

Under Californian law an equal division of property is usual, but where the grounds are adultery, cruelty or desertion courts have discretion to grant the innocent party the major share of the property. Barbara Finch decided to claim the whole of her husband's interest in the Medical Center, and also heavy alimony

payments. As a result Dr Finch would be left virtually penniless.

Finch and Tregoff evolved a plan whereby they would hire the services of a man who would obtain compromising evidence against Mrs Finch. This developed into a more violent plot when John Cody, an ex-Marine with a criminal record, was asked to kill her. The murder was fixed for 4 July, but never took place.

On 18 July Finch and Tregoff drove to West Corina to discuss the divorce problem with Barbara. There was a shot, and Mrs Finch was found dead on the driveway with a .38 bullet in her back.

Dr Finch was arrested, and Tregoff also for aiding and abetting. The pair were tried for murder at Los Angeles. John Cody testified that he had been hired to murder for money, but admitted not fulfilling the commission. Dr Finch admitted all kinds of chicanery, but not murder. He said he had been trying to obtain evidence to use against his wife, and alleged that she had produced the gun during their final confrontation. He struggled with her in the garage and again on the driveway—at that point he wrenched the gun from her grasp and threw it into some bushes, where it discharged the shot which killed her. The jury after 8 days were unable to reach a verdict. A second trial jury failed to agree, and a third trial produced a verdict—in January 1961 Dr Finch was found guilty of first-degree murder and Carole Tregoff of second-degree murder. Both were guilty of conspiracy, and received sentences of life imprisonment.

[23]

FISH, Albert Howard. A 66-year-old father of 6, house-painter and sex murderer with extraordinary perversions, including sado-masochism and cannibalism.

Fish was arrested in New York City in 1934, 6 years after he had abducted 12-year-old Grace Budd from her family on the pretence of taking her to a party. Instead he took her by train to an empty cottage in Westchester County where he strangled her and dismembered her body. Over a period of 9 days he ate strips of the girl's flesh, which he cooked with vegetables. This act kept him in a state of continuous sexual fervour.

When arrested Fish had a collection of newspaper cuttings referring to *Fritz Haarmann*, the German mass murderer of the 1920s. Doctors were startled to find 29 needles in Fish's body, most of them near the genitals, which he himself had inserted over many years. By his own admission

Fish: The 'gentle' cannibal

Fish preyed on children, using them for his perverted lusts—he acknowledged at least 100 incidents, including an act of cannibalism. He carried with him his 'implements of hell'—a parcel of knives, a saw and a cleaver with which he carved up his victims.

Fish was indicted for first-degree murder in the case of Grace Budd, and he became the subject of considerable psychiatric examination. He was interested in religion, and especially in the need for purging and physical suffering. 'I am not insane,' he said, 'I am just queer. I don't understand myself.' During his travels through 23 states Fish had been arrested 8 times on various charges, including larceny and the sending of obscene letters.

In March 1934 Fish was tried at White Plains, Westchester County. His confessions were read in court, and his children spoke of his preoccupation with religion. Psychiatric evidence suggested that he was basically a homosexual for whom women were merely a substitute—his real prey was children. The defence argued that Fish was insane, but the jury did not agree. Albert Fish was electrocuted at Sing Sing Prison on 16 January 1936. The first electrical charge failed, allegedly short-circuited by the needles in his body.

[25, 232, 430, 693, 742, 826, 847, 965]

FORSYTH, Francis 'Flossie'. An 18-year-old youth who with 3 others (Norman James Harris, 23; Christopher Louis Darby, 23; and Terence Lutt, 17) attacked and killed Alan Jee in a secluded alley in Hounslow, Middlesex.

In June 1960 the 4 attackers jumped their victim and robbed him. While he was struggling on the ground Forsyth kicked him savagely in the head 'to shut him up'. He died 2 days later, and his blood was still on the toes of Forsyth's shoes, when the police rounded up the latter with the other youths.

Of the 4 youths, Chris Darby was sentenced to life imprisonment for non-capital murder, and the rest were convicted of capital murder in the course or furtherance of theft. Terence Lutt was detained during Her Majesty's pleasure, and Forsyth and Norman Harris sentenced to death and hanged on 10 November 1960.

[*117, 719*]

FOSTER CASE. 28-year-old Evelyn Foster was the victim of a mysterious car fire.

Late in the evening of 6 January 1931 a bus driver travelling from Newcastle to Otterburn saw a blazing car on the moor. He stopped to investigate, and found that the vehicle involved was his own firm' new Hudson taxi. Nearby lay his employer's daughter Evelyn Foster, who was severely burned.

Although in great pain, Miss Foster related what happened. She picked up a fare near her home in Otterburn who said he had been given a lift in a car travelling from Jedburgh, but going on to Hexham. The man said he wanted to go to Ponteland, about 20 miles on, where he would get a Newcastle bus.

When she got to within 6 miles of Ponteland the man became threatening. He told the girl to turn back and on the return journey he assaulted her. She said he poured fluid over her from a bottle he had in his pocket, and having set fire to the car he set the vehicle in motion so that it ran off the road on to the moor, where it came to rest. Evelyn Foster did not survive her severe injuries, and her last words to her mother were, 'I have been murdered.'

Doubts began to appear regarding Evelyn's story when it was established that the car had been carefully driven off the road and set on fire only when it had stopped. Moreover, a pathologist gave it as his opinion that the girl had not been raped.

A Coroner's Inquest returned a verdict of wilful murder, and while the case remains officially unsolved it has been suggested that the girl accidentally immolated herself in the process of setting fire to the car for insurance purposes. The police issued a statement after the inquest, saying they were satisfied that the mystery car did not exist, and were also satisfied that the man did not exist either. (See *Ernest Brown*.)

[*9, 344, 382, 897*]

FOX, Sidney Harry. Rare case in Britain of a son murdering his mother for gain. Fox, 31, was a homosexual and a plausible rogue who moved from place to place, leaving behind a trail of unpaid bills. He posed as an Old Etonian or Royal Air Force officer. He invariably travelled with his elderly mother.

In April 1929 the 63-year-old Mrs Fox made a will, leaving her few possessions to her son. Several days later Sidney insured his mother's life against accidental death. In October the couple moved into the Hotel Metropole at Margate, and Sidney raised his mother's insurance to £3000.

At 11.40 p.m. on 23 October the fire alarm was raised by Sidney Fox. His mother's room was full

Fox: Where Mrs Fox died

of smoke. A resident rushed in and dragged out the old lady, who died shortly afterwards. A verdict of death by misadventure was recorded and Fox began immediately clamouring for the insurance. Suspicion was aroused, and he was arrested. Meanwhile his mother's body was exhumed, and Sir Bernard Spilsbury carried out a post-mortem. His conclusion was that Mrs Fox had been strangled before the fire started.

Fox was charged with murder at Lewes Assizes on 12 March 1930. The trial was marked by a disagreement between Spilsbury and Dr Robert Brontë regarding the evidence for strangulation. Spilsbury claimed to have seen a bruise the size of a half-crown on the dead woman's larynx. Brontë denied that it existed.

Evidence suggested that Fox got his mother drowsy with port and then strangled or suffocated her. The source of the fire in the old lady's room was under the chair in which she had been seated—it had been started with petrol and newspaper.

The jury found Fox guilty. He made no appeal, and was hanged at Maidstone Prison on 8 April 1930.

[1, 13, 133, 205, 282, 323, 350, 386, 406, 451, 510, 541, 559, 607, 618, 757, 846, 863, 921, 1009]

FRANK, Leo. A 29-year-old American-born Jew who held the office of Superintendent of the National Pencil Company at Atlanta, Georgia. A shy, nervous college graduate, Frank was convicted of murder in 1913 and lynched by a mob incensed by the commuting of his death sentence on 17 August 1915.

Mary Phagan, a 14-year-old white girl and a factory employee of the National Pencil Company, was found strangled and beaten about the head in the basement of the Company's premises on 27 April 1913, but she had not been raped. Pencilled notes found by the body were supposed to have been written by the girl. One of them read, 'Mam, that negro hire doun here did this i went to make water and he push me doun that hole a long tall negro black that hoo it was long sleam tall negro i wright while play with me.'

Newt Lee, the Negro nightwatchman who had found the body, was promptly arrested. Leo Frank, standing in for the regular paymaster, had paid the staff, including the dead girl, on that day. He was questioned by the police, and his clothes were examined for bloodstains, with negative results.

Frank: The lynching

The inquest on Mary Phagan recommended that Leo Frank and Newt Lee be held on murder charges. James Conley, a semi-literate Negro employed by the National Pencil Company, made several statements including some startling accusations against Frank. He alleged that Frank asked him to write the pencilled notes and to help him carry the dead girl to the basement.

At Frank's trial in July Conley repeated these accusations, and added that he had also seen the accused committing acts of sexual perversion. The laws of Georgia did not permit Frank to testify under oath, but he was allowed to make a statement. He said that Conley's accusations were lies, and that he had no part in Mary Phagan's death. The defence confidently expected an acquittal, as no white man had previously been convicted on the testimony of a black man, but Frank was found guilty and sentenced to death.

Despite threats to his life, Governor John M. Slaton commuted Frank's sentence to life imprisonment. This was regarded as a betrayal, and a prejudiced band calling themselves the Knights of Mary Phagan abducted Leo Frank from prison and drove 175 miles to Mary Phagan's birthplace, where they hanged him. Photographs of Frank's body were displayed in Georgia's shops.

Mary Phagan came to be honoured as a symbol of Southern womanhood and the victim of a society which exploited girls for pitifully low wages. Strenuous efforts by Jewish organizations to clear Leo Frank's name have failed. The Georgia Board of Pardons continued to refuse appeals even in face of new evidence. In 1982 an elderly man who had worked in the factory at the time of the killing told *The Tennessean* newspaper the identity of the real murderer. He claimed that he saw Jim Conley holding the victim's body and was threatened with death if he told anyone; 'Leo Frank did not kill Mary Phagan,' he said.

[*143, 240, 338, 385, 896, 903*]

FREEDMAN, Maurice. Ex-policeman who lived by borrowing money and by pawning his clothes to raise betting money, and finally resorted to murder.

Freedman, 36, and a married man, was friendly with Annette Friedson, a young typist. Her parents regarded him as undesirable, and accordingly Annette told him they must part. Fearing that he might molest her, Annette's brother took her each day to the City of London office where she worked.

On the morning of 26 January 1932 Freedman waited inside the building and cut her throat.

The murder weapon, a bloodstained razor-blade in a patent holder, was found in a London bus. The blood on it was of a rare type to which Annette Friedson belonged, and the weapon also bore hairs matching those in a fur collar worn by Annette.

When arrested Freedman said that he had decided to kill himself with a cut-throat razor if Annette had truly broken off with him. In the ensuing struggle the girl drew the open razor across her own throat. Freedman denied all knowledge of the safety razor found on the bus, which could hardly have been used in the manner he described. He stated that he had thrown the cut-throat razor into a canal.

Freedman was identified by the conductor of the bus on which the razor was found. At the Old

Bailey he was found guilty, and hanged at Pentonville Prison on 4 May 1932.
[*699*]

FRIEDGOOD, Charles. Dr Friedgood shared with *Dr William Palmer* the distinction of having a piece of legislation named after him as a result of a criminal act. In Friedgood's case it was a New York State law passed in 1978 which prohibited a doctor signing the death certificate of a relative.

The doctor was seated aboard an aircraft on the runway at Kennedy Airport in August 1975, about to take off for London, when the plane was dramatically ordered to return to the terminal. Friedgood was taken off by detectives and charged with the murder of his wife, Sophie, who had died—apparently from a stroke—two months previously.

Friedgood was a successful surgeon in his mid-fifties. He and Sophie had been married 28 years, and their children were grown up. They lived in a large house on Long Island, and to all intents and purposes enjoyed a most satisfactory life. But beneath the surface all was not well, and the Friedgoods were at loggerheads most of the time. Charles had been leading a secret life for several years, and was having an affair with his nurse, an attractive Danish girl. In 1972 this relationship produced a child, and Friedgood made a home for them at a cost of $1,000 a month. Soon another child arrived, and the doctor was under pressure on the one hand to divorce his wife and on the other to keep his second family a secret.

In due course Sophie came to know of her husband's infidelity and she confronted him. On the morning of 18 June 1975 in their Long Island home, her body was found by the maid. Dr Friedgood, who was not at home, was informed of his wife's death and quickly returned. He told friends that Sophie had suffered a fatal stroke. He signed a death certificate to that effect, and instructions were given for her burial. Although it was not against the law for a medical practitioner to sign a death certificate in these circumstances, it was unusual and prudent doctors always called in a colleague on such occasions. Suspicion grew in the minds of the local police, and the burial was halted pending an autopsy.

The medical examiner found several injection marks on the body, and toxicological analysis showed that the agent injected was demerol. A

Furnace: Police 'Wanted' Notice

METROPOLITAN POLICE.

MURDER

WANTED

For the wilful murder of **Walter Spatchett**, whose dead body was found on the 3rd January, 1933, in a shed at the rear of 30, Hawley Crescent, Camden Town, London, occupied as an office by the wanted man.

SAMUEL JAMES FURNACE, born 1890, about 6 feet, well built and set up, complexion fair, hair fair (thin in front), eyes hazel, full face, square jaw, gunshot wounds on left leg and both arms, long scar on right bicep shewing marks of 13 stitches, 1 tooth missing in front upper jaw which may be replaced by false tooth. When last seen on the 7th January, 1933, was wearing a brown suit, black shoes, light trench coat with sliding belt, brown and red check lining edged with brown leatherette binding. He has also a brown overcoat, a grey soft felt hat and a bluish coloured cap. Possesses a fair sum of money. In possession of a revolver. He has passed in the name of Raymond Rogers but might assume any other name.

He might seek employment in the building and decorating trade as a foreman or workman, or in the mercantile marine as a steward or seaman and may take lodgings at a boarding house, apartment house, coffee house, cottage, or any place taking male lodgers.

A warrant for his arrest has been issued and extradition will be applied for.

Any person having knowledge of his whereabouts is requested to inform the nearest Police Station at once.

Metropolitan Police Office
New Scotland Yard S.W.1.
11th January, 1933.

TRENCHARD,

The Commissioner of Police of the Metropolis.

Printed by the Receiver for the Metropolitan Police District, New Scotland Yard, London, S.W.1.

search of Friedgood's house was thwarted because a bottle containing the drug and a hypodermic syringe were misplaced. In the meantime the doctor had forged his late wife's signature on documents giving him access to her safe-deposit boxes. With $600,000 worth of cash, jewellery and bonds in his hand luggage, he made for Kennedy airport and his escape to Europe, where he planned to join his mistress.

Dr Friedgood was tried for murder by a New York court in January 1977. His family testified against him, and, on being convicted, he was sentenced to 25 years to life imprisonment—the maximum penalty. In 1978 New York State passed a law known as the 'Friedgood Bill' which made it illegal for a doctor to sign a death certificate in respect of a relative.

[*401, 571*]

FURNACE, Samuel James. Small-time builder in financial difficulties who shot another man and attempted to burn the body beyond recognition.

On 3 January 1933 the owner of 30 Hawley Crescent in London's Camden Town noticed that the garden shed which he rented to a Mr Furnace was burning. He could not get into the building, as it was locked. He called the fire service. In the meantime a neighbour had broken into the shed, only to find that an inner room was also locked. The door was broken down, and inside was found the badly burned corpse of a man.

The dead man was provisionally identified as Samuel Furnace. A note left in the shed, which he used as an office, read, 'Good-bye to all. No work. No money. Sam J. Furnace.' Talk of suicide, complicated by the fact that the shed had been locked, was further dispelled when the dead man was found to have a bullet-wound in the shoulder. Evidence showed he was dead before the fire started.

Detectives found a wallet with a savings book in the name of Walter Spatchett, and a local doctor confirmed that the body was that of Spatchett.

A search for Furnace, who collected rents for the same firm that employed Spatchett, began. He was eventually found at Southend, and was charged with Spatchett's murder. He told the police that he owned a Webley revolver, and while he was talking to Spatchett the weapon went off accidentally. Thinking he had killed the man, he set fire to the shed, left the 'suicide note' and threw the revolver into the Regent's Canal.

Furnace took his own life. While in custody he drank some hydrochloric acid from a bottle he had concealed in his coat. A revolver was recovered from the canal, and proved to be the murder weapon. The fact that when arrested Furnace had Spatchett's watch on him, and a large sum of money, suggested robbery as a motive. At the inquest on Spatchett a murder verdict was returned against Furnace.

[*133, 196, 281, 369, 975*]

G

GACY, John Wayne. Murderer of 33 boys whose genial socializing disguised his perverted personality. His background was known to the police when they began inquiries in December 1978 after a 15-year-old boy was reported missing in Des Plaines, Illinois. The teenager had gone to a shop to see the renovation contractor about a holiday job.

The contractor was John Gacy, whose case history included a 10-year spell in a correctional institution for committing acts of sexual perversion, including bondage and sodomy. He had served only 18 months before being released, and eventually established himself as a building contractor in Chicago. He was a member of the Junior Chamber of Commerce, and aspired to public recognition. He was regarded as an affable man who liked children, and he entertained them at the local hospitals by dressing up as a clown. He also put on children's parties at his ranch-style house at Norwood near Chicago.

In 1978 Gacy achieved recognition on two counts. He was photographed with President Carter's wife, Rosalynn, and it was to his house that police directed their inquiries over the missing teenager. There, in the crawl space beneath the house, they found the remains of 7 bodies, and when the search was extended to the garden 8 more corpses were discovered. Gacy admitted killing 32 youths, and said he disposed of 27 corpses either in or around the house. In due course his house was pulled down in order to recover all the murder victims' corpses.

Gacy first murdered in 1972, and, during the next 6 years killed 32 times. His victims had all been procured for sexual purposes, and when he had satisfied his lusts he strangled them and, like *Dennis Nilsen*, disposed of the bodies close to hand. Psychiatrists portrayed Gacy as psychologically inadequate, but his practice of posing as a police officer with a red light on his car when prowling for

Gacy: Murder verdict (reprinted from the Baltimore Sun, © 1980, The Baltimore Sun Co)

Gacy guilty of killing 33 in Ill.

From Wire Services

Chicago—John Wayne Gacy yesterday was found guilty of 33 murders, more than any other mass killer in U.S. history.

The jury of seven men and five women reached the verdict after less than two hours of deliberation, indicating that it was unswayed by defense assertions that the 37-year-old building contractor was mentally ill and not responsible for the crimes.

The jurors are to hear arguments today whether he should be sentenced to die in the electric chair.

The verdict followed 28 days of emotionally charged testimony in the trial, which began more than a year after a young man's body was found in a crawl space under Mr. Gacy's home in suburban Northwood township.

More bodies were found, and eventually Mr. Gacy was charged with murdering 33 young men and boys between 1972 and 1978. He also was convicted of deviate sexual assault and of taking victims suggested he knew what he was doing. His black Oldsmobile car was regularly seen cruising the streets of Chicago's gay district where he picked up his victims. He made 3 confessions, but refused to give evidence at his trial. On 12 March 1980, having rejected the defence plea of insanity, the jury convicted him of murder and demanded the death sentence. 'I hope he burns in hell,' the mother of one of his victims was reported as saying.

While in Menard Correctional Center, Illinois, Gacy was attacked by another prisoner. In 1984 the Supreme Court rejected his appeal and confirmed the death sentence. The former Junior Chamber of Commerce 'Man of the Year' and 'Pogo the Clown' children's entertainer prayed for his victims' families while awaiting death by lethal injection. He also planned his funeral service, specifying the hymns to be sung and the type of coffin to be used.
[151, 894]

GARCES, Manuel. Young Chilean male prostitute who murdered an elderly lawyer in Valparaiso in an act of revenge.

On 7 May 1962 the body of Enrique Mercier was discovered in his office at the Consorcio Italiano building in Valparaiso's business quarter. The victim, clad only in his shirt and wearing shoes and socks, had suffered severe head wounds and was barely conscious. He died before he could be moved to a hospital. The office safe was open and the dead man's wallet was missing. The murder weapon, a heavy stone wrapped in a bloodstained piece of brown paper, lay near the body.

Although Mercier was a respected member of his profession, it emerged that he had engaged in homosexual practices with male prostitutes whom he entertained in his office after business hours. The duty lift man on the night of the murder gave the police a detailed description of a young man who ascended to the fourth floor in the company of the lawyer at about 6.45 p.m. The search for this youth was helped when a stolen cheque was presented for payment at a bank.

Seventeen-year-old Manuel Garces was arrested at his lodgings, where the murdered man's wallet and cheque book were found among his effects. He immediately confessed and explained that the lawyer had made him promises about money and a job. Garces, a product of the slums, had led the life of a delinquent and drifted into committing homosexual acts in order to earn a living. He said that the whole idea disgusted him but he acted as a prostitute in the hope that wealthy clients would provide an escape from his impoverished existence.

But he was misused once too often and decided to exact his revenge.

There was a suggestion that Garces had been the scapegoat for a group of homosexuals who had plotted a revenge killing. In the light of this, he claimed that he was covering up for others, but later retracted and reverted to his earlier full confession. A Chilean court sentenced him to ten years' imprisonment for murder and five for robbery. The jury had little option in reaching a guilty verdict in view of his admission that he had picked up a large stone on the sea-shore at San Mateo which he intended to use as the murder weapon. When he was alone with the lawyer in his office he took the stone in both hands and, in his own words, 'hit him twice with it on the back of the head'.
[481]

GARDINER CASE. William Gardiner was foreman carpenter at a small factory in the Suffolk village of Peasenhall. He was in his mid-thirties, married with 6 children and an Elder of the Methodist Church. He was regarded as rather pious and had the nickname of 'Holy Willie'. In 1902 gossip linked Gardiner with 23-year-old Rose Harsent, a member of the church choir and maid in the household of Deacon Crisp, a Baptist Elder. Gardiner appeared before the church elders on what amounted to a charge of immorality. Having admitted nothing more than a minor indiscretion, he promised to put himself beyond criticism.

On the morning of 1 June 1902, following a severe thunderstorm, Rose Harsent was found dead on the kitchen floor of her employer's house, with her throat cut and her body partly burned. The fire had been fuelled with paraffin from a lamp which lay near the body. There was also a broken medicine bottle containing traces of paraffin, and bearing a chemist's label with the names of Mrs Gardiner's children. In Rose's bedroom were two letters and an unsigned note of assignation addressed to D.R., 'I will try to see you tonight at 12 o'clock at your place . . . I will come round to the back.'

The dead girl was 6 months pregnant, so the motive for her death seemed apparent. Gardiner was arrested and charged with murder.

He was tried at Ipswich Assizes in November 1902. Mrs Gardiner said that her husband had been with her all night, apart from a half-hour period at about 11.30 p.m. Gardiner denied writing the note and proclaimed his innocence.

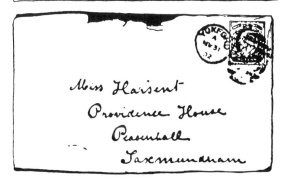

Gardiner Case: The note of assignation

The medicine bottle, with its incriminating possibilities, was explained by Mrs Gardiner, who said it contained camphorated oil and she had lent it to Rose Harsent, who was suffering from a cold. The broken glass, it was suggested, could have caused the injuries, by the girl falling down the stairs. The jury failed to agree, and the judge ordered a new trial.

Gardiner was tried a second time at Ipswich in January 1903. The previous evidence was repeated and again the jury could not agree. The Crown decided not to pursue a third trial, and Gardiner was released, to vanish into obscurity.
[*1, 8, 93, 298, 347, 590, 717, 796, 866, 942*]

GARLICK, Ted Donald. A 25-year-old sex murderer, acquitted of one murder, and later found guilty of another.

A 16-year-old girl, Carol Ann White, phoned her boy-friend from a telephone box at West Drayton on the evening of 11 October 1962, and did not return home. Her father found her purse in the box.

The following day the Garlick family were walking with a dog near their rented home in Hayes. The dog ran into a field, Ted Garlick gave chase and stumbled over the stabbed body of Carol Ann White. He told the police.

Garlick was later questioned once more when the police knew of the death of his wife. They made a suicide pact: she was gassed, and he survived. He was charged with her murder, but acquitted. At the time his wife's mother had said 'God forgive you. He'll kill again.' Carol Ann White had been murdered about 9.00 to 9.30 p.m., and Garlick was seen walking home at about 10.00 p.m.

Further questioning trapped Garlick into lying, and he confessed, producing the murder weapon. He said he saw Carol standing by the call box, and they talked about sex. The girl teased him about his inexperience. 'I don't know how many times I stabbed her' he said.

Garlick was tried at the Old Bailey in February 1963, found guilty and given life imprisonment.
[*643*]

GARTSIDE, John Edward. A 24-year-old double murderer in Yorkshire.

In May 1947 Mrs Doughty visited Percy and Alice Baker, in a lonely part of the Pennines, but found her friends were not at home, and their furniture being loaded on to a removal van. The driver said the couple had parted after a quarrel, and sold up. Mrs Doughty did not believe this, and got in touch with the man's firm, which had a receipt from Mr Baker. Mrs Doughty saw the signature was a forgery and told the police. There were 8 suitcases to go to a shop at Saddleworth which was rented by John Gartside. He was arrested driving Baker's car.

Gartside said he bought the car and furniture from Baker for £450, and used Baker's name at his request, but finally he took detectives to the moors, where the bodies of the Bakers, bearing gunshot wounds, were recovered.

Gartside explained he had called at the Baker home with two loaded guns, and on arrival realized a quarrel was going on. Mrs Baker grabbed a poker and Baker seized one of the guns and shot her. Gartside struggled with Baker for the gun, which went off accidentally, shooting Baker in the head.

Gartside was tried at Leeds Assizes in July. His statements ran counter to forensic evidence, his claims to have acted in self-defence were not substantiated, and he was found guilty and hanged.

[*417*]

GARVIE and TEVENDALE. Sensational Scottish case in which a man was murdered by his wife and her lover.

Maxwell Robert Garvie lived with his wife Sheila and their three children at West Cairnbeg Farm in east Scotland. The Garvies seemed a devoted couple, but in the 1960s their marriage began to break up. Max Garvie developed an interest in nudism and pornography, and his wife told friends that he made abnormal sexual demands on her.

In 1967 Sheila Garvie met 22-year-old Brian Tevendale. They were attracted to each other, and when Tevendale introduced Trudy Birse, his married sister, to Sheila's husband, they made an apparently happy foursome.

On 14 May 1968 Max Garvie left by car to attend a meeting at Stonehaven—he was not seen alive again. Tongues began to wag as Sheila and Tevendale were increasingly seen together. On 16 August the couple were arrested. The following day Max Garvie's body was found in an underground tunnel at St Cyrus—bludgeoned, and shot through the neck. Sheila Garvie and Brian Tevendale, together with Alan Peters, one of Tevendale's friends, were charged with murder.

They were tried at Aberdeen in November. The dead man was shown as having perverted interests, obsessed by pornography and nudism. Trudy Birse admitted being his mistress, and Sheila confessed her intimacy with Tevendale. Alan Peters related how Tevendale shot Garvie in bed, and helped dispose of the body. Sheila denied complicity, but said she felt morally responsible because of her love for Tevendale.

The jury found the case against Peters Not Proven, and brought in guilty verdicts against Sheila and Tevendale, who were sentenced to life imprisonment.

[*321, 413*]

GEIN, Edward. Middle-aged farmer denied an interest in women by an overbearing mother turned into a murdering ghoul.

Gein worked the family farm at Plainfield, Wisconsin, with his mother and brother. His mother exerted influence over her sons, and made them work, and keep away from women. When they both died within one year, Gein turned in

Gein: Ghoulish murderer

upon himself. He sealed off his mother's room, lived in a small part of the farmhouse and neglected the farm itself. He took to reading books on the human body, and developed a morbid interest in female anatomy, which he studied at close quarters by digging up corpses from isolated graves.

His practices were ghoulish in the extreme. He skinned some of the corpses and draped them over his own body in order to experience some bizarre sense of gratification. It was but a short step from grave-robbing to procuring fresh bodies by murder. Gein's first victim was a 51-year-old woman whom he shot dead in 1954 and took to his farm for examination. In 1957 he killed another victim, but was suspected by the woman's son.

A search of Gein's farm revealed the gruesome ornaments of this man's perverted pastime. There were bracelets made of human skin, a tom-tom covered with skin, a sawn-up skull converted into a soup bowl and a refrigerator stacked with human organs. These grim relics were estimated to have come from 15 bodies.

Gein admitted grave-robbing, and was both a necrophile and a cannibal. He was committed for life in December 1957 to an institution for the criminally insane. The Gein farm at Plainfield was burned down by local people, who regarded it as a place of evil.

The film *Psycho*, based on the novel by Robert Bloch and generally regarded as one of the finest film thrillers, was based on the story of Gein. In 1974 he sought a sanity hearing and petitioned for his freedom. His petition was turned down by Judge Gollmar, who subsequently wrote a book about Gein. After spending 30 years in mental institutions working as a carpenter and being a model inmate, Gein died in 1984.

[*108, 339, 400, 693*]

GERAGHTY, Christopher James. See ANTI-QUIS MURDER

GIFFARD, Miles. A 27-year-old ex public school boy who killed his parents in Cornwall.

Giffard had been an irresponsible youth, who failed to secure a steady job, but scrounged off his parents. In 1952 he met a girl he liked, and a serious relationship developed, but it was dashed when his father made him give her up. Giffard wrote to her about his father, 'Short of doing him in, I see no future in the world at all.' A few days later, on 7 November, he battered his parents to death and threw their bodies into the sea from their cliff-top home. He then drove to London in his father's car to see his girl-friend, leaving bloodstained clothing on the back seat.

He did nothing to cover his tracks, using his own name when selling his mother's jewellery. When arrested he told the police, 'I can only say I have had a brain storm.'

The defence at his trial at Bodmin Assizes, in February 1953, was insanity. At the age of 14 he had been seen by a psychiatrist, who was concerned at his mental deterioration. It was also clear that he had been oppressed by his strict father. He was found guilty, however, and hanged in Bristol on 24 February 1953.

[*117, 306, 697, 993*]

GILLETTE, Chester. American factory worker from humble family background who wanted to join high society. He worked in his uncle's garment factory, made steady progress, but had grandiose ideas.

The 22-year-old Gillette's liaison with an 18-year-old secretary, Billie Brown, at the factory resulted in her pregnancy and she begged Chester to marry her.

After unsuccessful pleading she threatened to tell Chester's uncle. Panic-stricken, Chester took her on a hastily arranged holiday, and on 11 July 1906 he rented a boat for a picnic on Big Moose Lake in New York State. Later Chester was seen drying his clothes by a lakeside bonfire at Eagle Bay. Billie Brown's body, with the face battered, was washed up the following day. Chester Gillette, who had inquired at a local hotel whether there had 'been a drowning reported in Big Moose Lake', was arrested.

His trial lasted 22 days, and created considerable public interest. He said the girl had committed suicide. Then that the boat had capsized and Billie was drowned accidentally. From his cell Gillette sold autographed pictures of himself in order to earn money to buy special meals in prison. Found guilty of murder, he was sentenced to death, and appeals lasted for a year. Finally he was electrocuted at Auburn prison on 30 March 1908. Theodore Dreiser based his novel *An American Tragedy* on this case.

[*528, 693, 808*]

GILMORE, Mark Gary. American double-murderer convicted and sentenced to death in 1977 who created controversy by demanding that his execution be carried out.

Gilmore spent half of his adult life in prison, and when he was released on parole in April 1976 he found it difficult to cope with the world outside. He drank heavily, rejected offers from his family to help his rehabilitation and committed theft as if it were second nature.

In July 1976 in the town of Oren, Utah, he brutally murdered 2 men in meaningless acts of violence. The first was a vacation student working at a filling station whom he robbed at gunpoint. He instructed the young man to lie face down on the floor, and then shot him twice in the head. The following night he drove to nearby Provo and walked into the City Centre Motel. He ordered the manager to lie face down on the floor and shot him twice through the head before raiding the cash-box and escaping.

Gilmore's acts of violence were committed with no attempt to cover his tracks, with the result that he was quickly rounded up by the police. That he should have resorted to killing in so casual a manner probably came as no surprise to the psychiatrist who had examined him at an earlier stage in his criminal career and reported, 'He has a high hostility component towards the establishment.'

A Utah court convicted Gilmore of murder and

sentenced him to death. His reaction was to insist that the state carried out its duty to execute him as decided by the court, and he elected to die by firing squad. His lawyer bought the rights to Gilmore's story and contracted Norman Mailer to write it. The resultant book, *The Executioner's Song* (written with Gilmore's full co-operation), won the author the Pulitzer Prize. In the course of answering an interview question about when he formed the intention to kill his first victim, Gilmore said, 'That night I knew I had to open the valve and let something out.'

He gave a farewell party on the eve of his execution and instructed his lawyer to reject a last-minute effort by the state to stay the end. He insisted that the court's decision be carried out, and on 17 January 1977 he was strapped into an old office chair with a mattress placed behind it to arrest the flying bullets. Asked if he had anything further to say, Gilmore replied, 'Let's do it.' Accordingly the 4-man firing squad discharged their guns and their responsibility.

[*644*]

GILMOUR. Christina. An 18-year-old girl who rejected John Anderson in favour of John Gilmour, whom she married on 27 November 1842. They lived at Gilmour's farm at Town of Inchinnan, near Paisley.

The marriage lasted 6 weeks. Outwardly, the couple appeared happy, but Christina was said not to have undressed during the whole period, or consummated the marriage. She said that her heart lay with Anderson.

John Gilmour became ill on 29 December 1842 with stomach pains and vomiting. The sick man's uncle visited them and noticed Christina's preoccupation was with her own unhappiness rather than her husband's illness. A doctor asked for specimens of Gilmour's vomit to be saved for examination—this was not done. He died on 11 January 1843.

After the funeral Christina returned to the farm, but there was talk of arsenical poisoning. She suggested that her husband's body be exhumed, and this was done on 22 April 1843, while Christina was on her way to Liverpool. She sailed to New York on 28 April, informed, it was alleged, that her late husband had died of arsenical poisoning.

The police found that on 26 December 1842 she had instructed a servant to buy arsenic for killing rats, and 12 days later bought arsenic herself from a Renfrew chemist, using a false name.

Police with a warrant sailed to New York on a fast ship (see also *Crippen*). Extradition proceedings were initiated, and Christina was escorted back to Scotland on 16 August. She made a declaration at Paisley on 14 September in which she admitted buying arsenic for the purpose of taking her own life, but not that of her husband.

In January 1844 she was tried at Edinburgh for murder. The prosecution ruled out suicide and accident as possibilities, and maintained that circumstantial evidence was sufficient to show that she poisoned him with repeated doses of arsenic.

The defence conceded that John Gilmour had died of arsenical poisoning, but maintained that possession of poison was to take her own life because of unhappiness—'a broken heart may lead to suicide but not to murder'. The verdict was Not Proven. The bride of 6 weeks lived out her span of 87 years, for 62 of them as a widow.

[*781, 998*]

GIRARD, Henri. So-called first scientific murderer who poisoned for gain and thwarted justice by suicide after swallowing a germ culture.

By virtue of family windfalls and by financial manipulation 46-year-old Girard entertained his friends lavishly. He said he was a bookmaker, but actually made money from a complex maze of dealings based on insurance.

Girard's elaborate money deals did not maintain his life-style, so he included murder as a means of making money. Like *Dr Waite*, he set himself up with various test tubes and pieces of apparatus, and then selected a victim.

A doting admirer was Louis Pernotte, a Paris insurance broker of modest means. In 1910 he entrusted his finances to Girard, giving him power of attorney. Soon Pernotte was insured for a total of 300 000 francs. At the same time Girard, who was nearly broke, was obtaining cultures of typhoid bacteria from Parisian scientific suppliers.

In August 1912 Pernotte with his wife and 2 children travelled to Royan. All four were ill with what appeared to be typhoid. Pernotte returned to Paris to convalesce, and was visited daily by Girard, and treated with injections of camphorated camomile. Wielding the syringe, Girard said to Mme Pernotte, 'Notice, madame, that it is quite definitely your own syringe. You observe that I have nothing in my hands.' Louis Pernotte died on 1 December from a cardiac embolism after being stricken with paralysis. Deeply grieved, Girard informed the widow that her husband owed him 200 000 francs! He decided next to experiment with the poisonous mushroom *Amanita phalloides*,

Girard: The scientific murderer

which he tried on two pre-insured victims. These proved too tough; though ill, they managed to survive, but without suspecting their narrow escape.

In April 1918 Girard picked a war widow, Mme Monin, for poisoning. She was duly set up with insurance policies and then invited to Girard's apartment and given a poisoned apéritif. She collapsed in the Métro station and died. The lady's demise, occurring so soon after the purchase of insurance, caused the companies to inquire further. Girard was arrested on 21 August. He declared, 'Yes, I have always been unhappy, no one has ever tried to understand me: I will always be misunderstood—abnormal, as I have been called—and for all that I am good, with a very warm heart.' Before he could be sent to trial, Girard killed himself in May 1921.

[*525, 933*]

GLASSON, Herbert Edwin. A 25-year-old butcher from Carcoar in New South Wales who fell on hard times and ran amok, robbing a bank and killing 2 people.

On 24 September 1893 the wife of the manager of the City Bank of Sydney in Carcoar heard the sounds of an intruder in the premises. The living accommodation was on the first floor and the only servant slept in the basement. Anne Phillips woke her husband, who armed himself with the bank's revolver and cautiously went downstairs. As he approached the lower level a masked intruder came into view. He was carrying an axe which he used to fell John Phillips.

Anne Phillips doubled back upstairs, intent on protecting her children, shouting out 'Murder' as she ran in order to alert her house guests who were sleeping in a bedroom on the first floor. Awakened by the noise, the 2 guests rushed to the defence of the children; one of them was struck down by the axeman, who told Anne Phillips, 'Money I want. And money I must have.' She gave him the keys to the safe and he retreated downstairs to the bank. The keys did not fit, for they belonged to another bank for which Phillips, now dying on the stairs, was the manager-designate. Thwarted in his robbery attempt and with events completely beyond control, the axeman fled from the house.

The alarm was raised and, incensed at the double murder, angry townsfolk began an immediate search for the masked intruder. House-to-house inquiries in the nearby township of Cowra revealed a stranger holed up in the barber shop. His blood-stained clothing betrayed him and he was arrested. He said, 'I did not do it . . . I am mad.' Herbert Glasson had a letter in his pocket addressed to his wife in which he spoke of anxiety about his mental state. 'I came to myself today', he wrote, 'I had on a black suit of clothes all covered in blood. What I have done I have no idea . . .'

Apart from his mental state, there was no doubt about his financial affairs. He had not paid his assistant at his butcher's shop for 3 months, and had been asked by the bank to reduce his overdraft. A great deal of the proceedings at his trial were taken up with arguments about his psychological state. There were indications of insanity in his family background, and his wife testified that he had suffered a severe bout of sunstroke and believed he was going mad. Nevertheless, the trial jury, advised by the judge not to let 'the subleties of the law of mania affect them', returned a guilty verdict. Glasson in due course fulfilled his assignment with the hangman.

[*838*]

GLATMAN, Harvey Murray. A 31-year-old sadistic killer who photographed his victims before murdering them. Glatman was an intelligent child, but his parents recognized morbidity as he approached adolescence. He was imprisoned for robbery in 1945, and given psychiatric treatment.

After release from prison in 1951, Glatman opened a TV repair shop in Los Angeles, and for a few years led a quiet life. He took up photography as a hobby, but this new-found interest merely kindled his perverted lust. In August 1957 he hired a 19-year-old model on the pretext of being a professional photographer. He raped her, and took photographs while she was helplessly tied up. Then he strangled the girl and buried her in the desert.

Glatman met his next victim through the medium of a Lonely Hearts Club (see *Beck and Fernandez*). This time he took a 24-year-old divorcée out to the desert, where he went through the same rape, photograph and strangulation routine. A third victim met a similar death in July 1958, and then Glatman met a model, Joanne Arena, through a newspaper advertisement. During Glatman's advances to her there was a struggle, and his gun went off, wounding her in the leg. The car stopped, and despite her injury she won possession of the gun and kept it trained on her attacker until a police mobile patrol arrived.

Glatman was found guilty, and refused to appeal, saying, 'It's better this way. I knew this is the way it would be.' He was executed in San Quentin's gas chamber on 18 August 1959.

[*693*]

GOLDSBOROUGH, Fitzhugh Coyle. Indolent son of a wealthy Philadelphia family who murdered a promising writer for an imagined slight and then took his own life.

On 23 January 1911 popular novelist David Graham Phillips left his apartment in Manhattan to walk in Gramercy Park. There he was accosted by Goldsborough, who levelled a pistol at him and shouted, 'Here you go.' He fired 5 shots at the writer, who fell to the ground mortally injured and then, as passers-by gathered at the scene, put the gun to his head and shouting, 'Here I go', pulled the trigger. Phillips lingered for several hours, telling those around him, 'I can fight one bullet, but not five.'

Goldsborough, a neurotic, spoiled young man of 21 from a wealthy background, idolized his sister, who aspired to the role of socialite. He was an idle individual, and spent much of his time reading popular novels, including the work of David Graham Phillips. Among the books he read was Phil-

lips's *The Fashionable Adventures of Joshua Craig*, whose chief character was a selfish girl who moved in high social circles. Goldsborough—who was jealously protective of his sister to the point of being angry with his father if he dared to criticize her—reacted strongly. He believed the author's portrayal of the character in his book amounted to a slur against his sister and decided to take a bitter revenge. Sadly, there was no evidence that Phillips was even aware of the existence of Goldborough's sister.

[*848*]

GOLDENBERG, Jack. An 18-year-old soldier who boasted to reporters that his evidence would lead to the detection of the murderer of a bank official.

In April 1924 William Hall, 28-year-old manager of the small bank near Bordon Camp, was found dead with gunshot wounds behind the bank counter. Over £1000 in notes and coins had been stolen. Police believed that Hall had admitted someone known to him.

At near-by Bordon Camp the roll was called of the 6000 soldiers based there. No absentees were reported, and there were no weapons missing. A signaller told police he had called at the bank about 1.50 p.m. when he spoke with the manager. He returned at 2.15 with information which the manager had asked for, only to find the bank closed.

Lance-Corporal Goldenberg had cashed a cheque that day. He was in the bank at 1.45 p.m. when he noticed a car outside—he described the occupants to the police. Two days after the murder some of the missing bank-notes turned up in local circulation, and Goldenberg began to expound his theories about the murder to reporters. 'I am convinced', he said, 'that my evidence will be very important, and that it will be through me that the murderer or murderers will eventually be arrested.'

An alert warrant officer at Bordon Camp observed his acting furtively; he noticed footmarks on a window-sill of a hut from which the lance-corporal had just emerged. Placing his feet on the marks, the W.O. found that he was looking into the roof beams, among which he could see a parcel. He found £500 in notes from the bank robbery.

When arrested, Goldenberg admitted killing the bank manager. He was found guilty, and although he appealed on the grounds of insanity, was duly executed.

[*452, 1005*]

GOOLD, Maria Vere. Self-styled 30-year-old Lady Vere Goold, twice widowed, was married to an alcoholic Irishman. They sponged off his family and lost the money in gambling in Monte Carlo. They were deprived of further funds until they met Mme Emma Levin, a wealthy widow, in 1907, and managed to borrow from her.

When Mme Levin wanted the money back Maria hit her with a poker and then stabbed and dismembered her body, packing the pieces into a trunk.

Taking the trunk with them, the Goolds went to Marseilles, where the box was labelled for dispatch to London. The luggage clerk complained of the smell (see *Winnie Judd* case), and thought he saw blood dripping from it. Maria told him the box contained poultry. Not satisfied, the clerk sent for the police, and the Goolds were held until the trunk was opened.

The couple were arrested, and Maria declared that while she was talking to Mme Levin a stranger rushed into the room, proclaiming himself the latter's lover. He stabbed her and made off. Maria said they cut the body up, intending to send it to London to avoid trouble with the police.

The couple were taken back to Monaco, where they were tried for murder. Maria indulged in court-room histrionics which earned her the description *une grande comédienne*. She was sentenced to death, subsequently commuted to life imprisonment in the French penal settlement at Cayenne, where she died of typhoid within the year. Her husband, sentenced to life, committed suicide a year after his wife's death.
[*237, 534, 575, 803*]

GORDON, Iain Hay. Maladjusted 21-year-old airman who killed a young woman.

Patricia Curran, 19-year-old daughter of a Northern Ireland judge, left her parents' home at Whiteabbey near Belfast as usual on the morning of 12 November 1952 to attend lectures at Queen's University. She did not return home when expected, and her mother notified the Royal Ulster Constabulary. A search of the grounds was made, and Miss Curran was found severely wounded, in the face and chest, apparently by a shotgun. She died soon afterwards.

A post-mortem showed that the victim had not been shot but had received 37 multiple stab wounds, inflicted with a fine-bladed knife. Her clothes were torn, indicating an intention to rape.

It was Patricia Curran's habit to telephone home for a car when she reached the bus stop. She had

not done so that evening, yet she was found close to the house. An 11-year-old girl had seen her with a man. At near-by Edenmore Royal Air Force Station every airman and civilian employee was checked. All gave a satisfactory account of their movements except Leading Aircraftsman Iain Hay Gordon. Fellow-airmen said that Gordon had asked them to provide him with an alibi. It also transpired that Gordon had contacted the dead girl's brother, asking him whether he (Gordon) was mentioned in her diaries.

Gordon denied the murder at first, and then said he committed it while in a blackout caused by worry and over-study. He was tried at Belfast Assizes in March 1953, where he was found guilty but insane.
[*163, 283*]

GORSE HALL MURDER. Unsolved murder case in which George Harry Storrs, a prosperous building contractor, was killed in his Yorkshire home, Gorse Hall. His attacker—clearly seen by several people, including Mrs Storrs—got clean away.

An intruder entered the grounds of Gorse Hall, near Stalybridge, on 10 September 1909. Standing outside a curtained window, he threatened to shoot. There was noise of a shot and breaking glass, and Storrs rushed forward to tackle the man, who promptly made off. As a result Storrs had an alarm bell fitted at the house which could be heard in Stalybridge.

On 1 November a man with a revolver entered the kitchen at Gorse Hall and forced his way into the living-room. Storrs grappled with him, and Mrs Storrs managed to snatch his revolver and run upstairs to ring the alarm bell; the servants scattered to fetch help. It is thought the man then broke out through the scullery window but re-entered the house by the kitchen, where he attacked Storrs with a knife. When help arrived Storrs lay mortally wounded, and his assailant had fled. Asked if he could identify the man, Storrs with his dying breath replied, 'No.'

A few days later, John Worrall, Storrs's coachman, committed suicide out of grief for his master. Two weeks after the tragedy, a man with a record for burglary, Cornelius Howard, was arrested at Oldham and charged with killing Storrs. Howard was put on an identity parade and picked out by Mrs Storrs—it also became known that Howard was Storrs's cousin.

Howard was sent for trial, but acquitted, the jury reasoning, perhaps, that the dying man would not have denied the identity of his attacker if he was his cousin. Five months later another man, Mark Wilde, was tried for the murder. Wilde had attacked a man in the street with a knife thought to be similar to that used on Storrs. It was also alleged that he had at one time owned the revolver which Mrs Storrs had taken from the assailant, and which was found to be jammed and useless. But Wilde too was acquitted, for while the ladies at Gorse Hall had been certain of Howard, they were hesitant about Wilde.

The murder remains unsolved, and among the many theories—most of which hint at skeletons in the family cupboard—one suggestion is that Howard was Storrs's bastard son in search of recognition.

[8, 118, 252, 267, 351, 590, 846, 897, 942]

GRAHAM, Barbara. Product of an unhappy childhood and a broken marriage, 32-year-old Barbara Graham embarked on a criminal career.

When Barbara was 2 her mother was sent to a reformatory as a wayward girl, and the child was brought up by neighbours. She ran away from home when she was 9, and ended up in the same reformatory. She married in 1941, and went steadily downhill through vagrancy, disorderly conduct and prostitution.

She was 3 times married and divorced, and drew closer to organized crime circles in Chicago and San Francisco. Her fourth marriage was to Henry Graham, who introduced her to drugs. Barbara's decline was completed when she joined up with 3 established criminals in Los Angeles.

On 9 March 1953, Barbara Graham and 3 others broke into the Burbank home of an elderly woman. Barbara hit the woman with her pistol butt. There was no jewellery, and the old lady died of her injuries.

Barbara Graham was arrested, and while in prison she was tricked into accepting the offer of an alibi from a police officer posing as an underworld agent. Why else would she need an alibi for the night of the murder if she were not guilty, argued the prosecution at her trial. She was convicted, and executed in San Quentin's gas chamber on 3 June 1955.

[216, 224, 760]

GRAHAM, Eric Stanley George. Killer of 6 people who featured in New Zealand's most sensational manhunt.

Graham, a dairy farmer, tried to be a breeder of pedigree Ayrshire cattle at his Koiterangi farm. He was a first-rate shot, and was an expert deer-stalker with a wide knowledge of the semi-bush terrain. His stock-breeding proved a failure, and he started to lose money.

He became withdrawn and sullen, blaming his failure on his neighbours. He was quarrelsome, with a violent temper. On 7 October 1941 he clashed with a neighbour, whom he menaced with a rifle. Another neighbour intervened, and the police were informed.

Next day Constable Edward Best went to Graham's farm to warn him, and was met with an aggressive outburst. Best sent for help, and a sergeant and two other constables arrived. The sergeant and Best approached Graham's front door. Graham appeared bearing his guns, which he was told to give up. An argument ensued, and shooting broke out—within minutes 3 police officers lay dead and one, Best, was mortally wounded. Mrs Graham ran out of the house to fetch a doctor and bumped into two men. One of these approached Graham, who shot him (he died later of his injuries).

Graham escaped into the bush, returning to his house later the same night to find it occupied by Home Guardsmen. Shots were exchanged, and 2 men were killed and Graham wounded in the shoulder. He made for the bush again, and it was the night of 12 October before he was found and wounded in the hand. A massive search of military proportions was mounted to catch the twice-wounded killer.

On 15 October his lair was found in a farm outbuilding, and 5 days later he was surprised by a police officer who shot him without warning, inflicting a mortal wound—he died the following day in hospital. At the inquest on the 6 victims the Coroner commended the policeman who 'had removed a great danger before there had been any further loss of life'.

[335, 517]

GRAHAM, John Gilbert. All 44 passengers on a United Airlines inter-city flight were killed on 1 November 1955 when a bomb planted in a piece of luggage exploded in mid-air. Flight 629 had been airborne for 10 minutes after take-off from Denver, Colorado, when the explosion occurred, killing all on board and scattering wreckage over a wide area.

Crash investigators established that the bomb had detonated in the luggage compartment containing baggage loaded at Denver. One of the passengers who boarded the aircraft at this stop was Daisy King, who was travelling to Alaska to see her daughter following a visit to her son and daughter-in-law in Denver. John Graham insured his mother for $37,000 and told his wife that he had put a 'Christmas package' in her suitcase. The seasonal gift turned out to be a bomb comprising 14 lb of dynamite and a timing mechanism.

When Mrs King had lost her first husband she put her son into an orphanage, where he stayed until he was 8 years old. When she married a wealthy rancher in 1940 Mrs King retrieved her boy and showered him with all the things she supposed he had missed in his young life. Far from expressing his gratitude at being plucked from the orphanage, Graham nurtured an abiding hatred of his mother. This first emerged as simple truancy, but then developed into acts of petty crime. As he grew into adulthood Graham started to forge cheques and perpetrate insurance frauds. He escaped the weight of the law because his mother came forward to repay the money.

Graham readily confessed to the crime at first, showing remorse for neither his mother nor the other victims. His main concern seemed to be to remind people that he had been neglected as a child. He subsequently withdrew his confession, but the jury found no difficulty in declaring him guilty. He was sent to the gas chamber in January 1957 when he made another confession. He told prison officers of the load which was lifted from his shoulders when he watched his mother depart on her fateful journey. 'I felt freer than I have ever felt before in my life', he said. He revelled in the vision of his mother's death. Referring to the shotgun cartridges she was carrying in her hand luggage (she intended to use them on a hunting trip while in Alaska), he asked gleefully, 'Can't you just see Mother when all those shells began to go off in the plane?'
[629]

GRAVES, Dr Thomas Thatcher. Medical practitioner convicted of murdering by means of poison sent to his victim through the US Mail. One of Dr Graves's patients in Providence, Rhode Island, was Josephine Burnaby, the rich and elderly estranged wife of a store-owner. When Mrs Burnaby's husband died her doctor persuaded her to give him power of attorney, and prescribed a long recuperative visit to California.

At the end of 1892 Mrs Burnaby announced her intention to return home via Denver, Colorado, where she planned to visit a friend. When she arrived at her friend's house she found that the postman had called with a package addressed to her. She opened the parcel to find a bottle of whiskey

with a handwritten note attached; the words read, 'Wish you a Happy New Year's. Please accept this fine old whiskey from your friend in the woods.' Her friend joined her in drinking some of the liquor, which they concluded was 'vile stuff'. They both fell ill, and within six days were dead.

A private autopsy arranged by one of Mrs Burnaby's daughters revealed that the cause of death was poisoning, and the bottle of whiskey was suspected as being the most likely source. Because of his attempts to profit from Mrs Burnaby's wealth, Dr Graves came under suspicion, although he strongly denied the allegation of murder by post.

The doctor was nevertheless charged with murder, and his claim to innocence seemed well founded in the face of rather tenuous circumstantial evidence. There was nothing to link him with sending the bottle of whiskey through the post—at least, not until the prosecution produced a surprise witness. This was a young man who claimed that Dr Graves had approached him at Boston Railway Station and requested his help to write a note. The doctor gave the excuse that he could not write, and the witness penned the message which accompanied the whiskey bottle from words dictated to him. Evidence of planning was implicit in this act, because it took place several months before the package was dispatched to Mrs Burnaby.

Dr Graves, roundly condemned by the press although supported by his patients, was found guilty and sentenced to death. In April 1893, while awaiting retrial after winning his appeal, he committed suicide by taking poison in his cell.
[190]

GREEN, Leslie. A 29-year-old ex-Borstal boy convicted for the brutal murder of a woman in Staffordshire.

On 16 July 1952 the body of 62-year-old Alice Wiltshaw was found by her husband lying in a pool of blood in the kitchen of their 14-room house at Barlaston. A bloodstained poker lay near.

Rings had been taken from the victim's fingers, and jewellery worth £3000 was missing. The absence of house-breaking signs, and the fact that the murder had occurred when the servants were off duty, suggested that the murderer knew the domestic routine. Traces left by the killer included a footprint and a pair of bloodstained gloves.

Descriptions of a man seen near the house at the time of the murder pointed to the Wiltshaws' former chauffeur-gardener, Leslie Green, who had been dismissed several weeks previously for disobeying his employer.

Green Bicycle Case: The bicycle

Green was traced when he gave the rings stolen from his murder victim to his girl-friend. The former chauffeur tried to brazen it out under police questioning, but among the damning evidence was a bloodstained left-hand glove with a tear in the thumb which corresponded with a recently healed cut on Green's thumb.

Green denied that he had murdered Mrs Wiltshaw, but he was found guilty and hanged at Winson Green Prison, Birmingham, on 23 December 1952.

[*24, 451, 666*]

GREEN BICYCLE CASE. Ronald Vivian Light, 34, an ex-officer and a teacher at Cheltenham School, featured in this famous unsolved case.

On the morning of 5 July 1919 the body of 21-year-old Bella Wright, a factory-worker, was found beside her bicycle in a lane near Long Stretton, Leicestershire, with a bullet-wound in the head—a spent bullet lay near by.

Early that morning Bella had left her uncle's house, 2½ miles away, with a man on a green bicycle. Later this man was seen near the spot where the body was found. The following February, a canal barge brought up the frame of a green bicycle. The usual identification marks on the machine had been removed, but its serial number 103648 was still legible, and it was traced to Ronald Light. A revolver holster and ammunition were also fished up. When arrested Light told the police that he had never owned such a machine. The ammunition found in the canal was thought to be the same type as the murder bullet.

Light was tried at Leicester Assizes in June 1920, with Sir Edward Marshall Hall defending him. Strong evidence was presented of Light's ownership of the bicycle and the holster and ammunition. But Marshall Hall contested the validity of the crime bullet, arguing that a .45 calibre bullet fired at close range would have made a much larger exit-hole. He also gained an admission from a firearms expert that the bullet could as easily have been fired from a rifle as a revolver. The advocate suggested that the girl was killed accidentally by a stray rifle bullet fired at a target. He pointed out lack of motive, and the fact that there were no signs of assault.

When Light went into the witness-box he

admitted his error in denying ownership of the green bicycle, explaining how he 'had drifted into a policy of concealment' on account of his invalid mother. The ex-officer made a good impression and the jury returned a verdict of not guilty.

[*44, 112, 113, 347, 377, 472, 488, 649, 793, 946*]

GREENWOOD, David. Medically discharged Serviceman, aged 21, convicted of the 'Button and Badge' murder at Eltham Common.

On the night of 9 February 1918 a Mr Trew reported that his 16-year-old daughter Nellie was

Greenwood, D.: Incriminating button and badge

ELTHAM COMMON CRIME.

BUTTON AND MILITARY BADGE CLUES.

Mystery still surrounds the death of Nellie Trew, Arsenal clerk, aged 16, who was found dead at Eltham Common, near Woolwich, early on Sunday morning. No more tangible clues have yet been discovered than a large overcoat button and an

FRONT VIEW OF BADGE.

BACK VIEW OF BADGE.

imitation military badge, which were found at the scene of the girl's first struggle with her assailant.

The badge is of white metal, fastened with a shank of copper wire, and is believed to be the full dress collar badge of the Gordon Highlanders. It is not worn at the present time, but it may be an imitation of an actual badge of that regiment. The police are anxious to know if any member of the public can recognize the badge or button as having been worn by any person known to them. It is possible that persons who let lodgings may have seen a lodger wearing such articles.

The button is a black bone overcoat button. It was, apparently, fastened to the garment by part of a pin of iron or mild steel, about 1¼in. long, pointed at

BACK VIEW OF BUTTON.

missing from home. She had left that evening to go to the library, and had not returned.

Next morning her raped and strangled body was found on Eltham Common. Close by were a cheaply produced badge in the shape of a tiger and a bone overcoat button with a piece of wire threaded through it. Photographs of both these articles were given wide coverage, and the tiger motif was recognized as a copy of a badge formerly used by the Leicestershire Regiment.

A man told the police that a fellow-machinist had been in the habit of wearing such a badge. He was David Greenwood, who lived in Eltham, less than 100 yards from the murder scene. Questioned by workmates about the resemblance between the newspaper photographs and his own badge, Greenwood said that he had sold it. Nevertheless, he was persuaded to go to the police, who were quick to notice that Greenwood was wearing an overcoat which had no buttons. He said that they had been missing for some time, but his workmates refuted this. Moreover, the wire attached to the button picked up at the murder scene was of a type manufactured by the firm for which Greenwood worked.

Greenwood was tried for murder in April 1918. His war record showed that he had served in the trenches during the First World War, and it was suggested that he was not now physically capable of overcoming a young girl. The evidence, though circumstantial, indicated she could have torn the button and badge from her assailant's coat. Greenwood was found guilty and sentenced to death, which was commuted to life imprisonment.

[*118, 133, 167, 370, 449, 462, 463, 474, 716*]

GREENWOOD CASE. A 45-year-old solicitor from Llanelly, in Wales, Harold Greenwood was acquitted on a charge of poisoning his wife.

Greenwood had a modest legal practice in Llanelly, and helped by his wife's private income, lived comfortably in near-by Kidwelly. Mabel Greenwood had a religious disposition and was well regarded, whereas her husband was disliked.

Mrs Greenwood had been unwell on and off since the beginning of 1919. On 15 June after Sunday lunch she complained of feeling ill, and by early evening retired to bed with heart pains. The doctor prescribed a stomach mixture. Late that night she was vomiting and suffering diarrhoea. The doctor was sent for again, and soon after 3.00 a.m. Mrs Greenwood died. Death was certified as due to valvular heart disease.

Shortly after the funeral rumours suggested that

the death was not a natural one, helped still further when 4 months after Mabel's death Harold Greenwood remarried. In April 1920 Mabel Greenwood's body was exhumed. The post-mortem showed no evidence of valvular disease of the heart, but did reveal the presence of arsenic in several organs.

A Coroner's Inquest recorded that Mrs Greenwood's death had been caused by acute arsenical poisoning, the poison being administered by her husband. The public present at the inquest broke into applause on hearing its verdict.

Greenwood was tried at Carmarthen, where he was brilliantly defended by Sir Edward Marshall Hall. The prosecution argued that the fatal arsenic had been administered in the bottle of Burgundy from which Mrs Greenwood had drunk a glass of wine at lunch. Marshall Hall smashed this contention by putting Greenwood's daughter Irene into the witness-box, who testified that she drank wine from the same bottle. Greenwood was acquitted, and left the court a free man.

At the time of the trial of *Herbert Rowse Armstrong* Greenwood wrote an article for *John Bull* magazine, telling the world what it felt like to be accused of murder. He died, aged 55, a broken man, 9 years after his acquittal.

[*1, 133, 252, 332, 347, 624, 649, 794, 908, 960, 982*]

GRIFFITHS, Peter. A 22-year-old ex-Service-man convicted of the brutal murder of a child. The case is notable for the fingerprinting of a whole town.

In the early hours of 14 May 1948 the duty nurse in the Children's Ward of Blackburn's Queen's Park Hospital noticed a cot was empty. The body of the missing child, June Anne Devaney, nearly 4 years old, was found lying some 300 feet away in the grounds, sexually assaulted and brutally battered to death.

Prints made by stockinged feet were found on the polished floor beside the child's cot, and a bottle moved by the murderer carried numerous fingerprints. The intruder's fingerprints were isolated from those of the nursing staff.

Armed with the prints, the police decided on an unprecedented step—to fingerprint the entire adult male population of Blackburn. There were over 46,000 sets taken, and on 12 August set No 46253 was found to match the prints on the bottle. Peter Griffiths, a flour-mill packer, was apprehended the same day.

Griffiths said that he removed his shoes outside

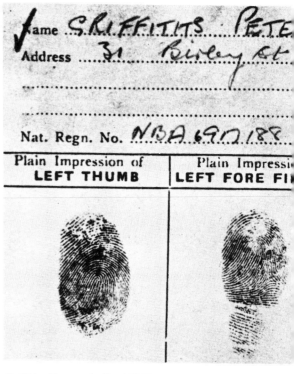

Griffiths: Fingerprint No. 46253

the ward, abducted the child and then silenced her cries by hitting her head against a wall, and added, 'I hope I get what I deserve.' Griffiths was tried at Lancashire Assizes, and in his defence it was suggested that he might have inherited mental disease from his father which made him not responsible for his actions. The jury after retiring for 23 minutes found Griffiths guilty, and he was hanged at Walton Prison on 19 November 1948.

[*1, 132, 417, 424, 552, 599, 605, 643, 666, 916*]

GRIGGS CASE. Ronald Geeves Griggs, a 28-year-old Wesleyan clergyman, acquitted of wife-murder.

Born in Tasmania, Griggs graduated from a Melbourne theological college in 1926 and married a 20-year-old Tasmanian girl, Ethel White. They moved to Omeo, a small farming town in Victoria, where Griggs became Methodist minister.

The new clergyman used both horse and motor-cycle to visit the outlying parts of his parish. He gave forcible sermons, but he seemed lacking in warmth and social sense.

It became apparent that all was not well between Griggs and his young wife—she was left alone a great deal and her husband seemed cold to her. Then in spring 1926 Griggs appeared to change. He began a liaison with Lottie Condon, 19-year-old daughter of John Condon, a staunch Methodist and farmer who lived some 10 miles from the parsonage. Ethel, pregnant with her first child, protested strongly at her husband's affection for Lottie. This had little effect, and Griggs and Lottie became lovers in December 1926.

Griggs made frequent visits to the Condons' house, where the couple slept together. In July 1927 Ethel left for a visit to Tasmania. When she returned to Omeo on the last day of the year she fell ill almost immediately from 'heat and excitement', and the doctor arrived too late to save her.

Rumours spread quickly about Ethel's sudden death, and an exhumation showed arsenic in her body. At the Coroner's Inquiry in March 1928 Ronald Griggs was sent for trial for murder at the Supreme Court at Sale. The prosecution's case was strong motive, and medical testimony showed more than one dose of arsenic. It was also shown that Griggs had access to various sources of the poison kept in abundance by John Condon in his farm workshop. Griggs readily admitted his

Groesbeek: The poison bottles

infatuation with Lottie Condon. The defence contended simply that Ethel Griggs, lonely and despairing, took her own life. The jury was unable to reach agreement, and the judge ordered a retrial.

Griggs faced a second trial at Melbourne in April 1928 and in the interval public opinion swung in his favour. This time he was found not guilty.

[*137*, *179*]

GROESBEEK, Maria. A 33-year-old South African poisoner whose murder of her husband has been compared with *Daisy de Melker's* crimes.

Maria married Christiaan Buys in 1953 after a whirlwind courtship, and they went home to live with his mother and her 6 sons. The 2 women soon quarrelled, and Maria and her husband left. In the next 17 years they had 14 different homes. Their marriage gradually deteriorated, with accusations of flirting directed at Maria, and followed by beatings.

Then 20-year-old Gerhard Groesbeek, a railway shunter friend of Christiaan, came into Maria's life. She declared her love for him and demanded a divorce. It was refused.

In February 1969 Maria started to buy ant poison, a brand containing arsenic. On 14 February, Christiaan Buys became ill with continual vomiting, and was admitted to hospital, where he died on 28 March. An analysis of the viscera showed arsenic.

On 11 June 1969 the widow married Groesbeek. Maria and Gerhard Groesbeek were arrested on a charge of murder. Maria said, 'I just wanted to avenge myself on Chris. I wanted to make him thoroughly sick so that he would give me permission to divorce him.' She accepted responsibility for her husband's death, 'I poisoned him with arsenic.'

Maria Groesbeek was tried at Bloemfontein in November 1969. Maria was found guilty, and the judge said, 'This was a planned murder.' Gerhard Groesbeek was tried 7 months later, found not guilty and acquitted. Maria was hanged on Friday 13 November 1970.

[*74*]

GRUPEN, Peter. A Svengali-like figure who used his family and servants to satisfy his sexual needs and was convicted of murder after a sensational trial in Germany in 1921.

Grupen had fought for his country at the battle of Verdun, and when he returned home to post-war Germany he joined the army of speculators who made a living by exploiting deficiencies in the economy. He joined his 12-year-old step-daughter Ursula, who was staying with her cousin, Dorothea. The latter had at the age of 14 inherited Kleppelsdorf Castle in Silesia following the death of her parents. Dorothea was looked after by her grandmother and governess.

On 21 February 1921, while the family was assembling for lunch, screams announced the discovery by one of the maids of the bodies of the two girls. Dorothea and Ursula (who were known not to be the best of friends) were dead from gunshot wounds. Beneath Dorothea's body was a note to her grandmother which read, 'I shot Dörte first and then myself. Now you won't have to worry about Dörte any more . . .' It was signed, 'Your unhappy Ursel.'

The police questioned the idea of murder followed by suicide because the wounds had not been inflicted at close range and, most telling of all, the revolver which was found at the scene of the shooting had its safety-catch on. Grupen immediately came under suspicion on account of rumours that he had made his step-daughter his love slave and controlled her by hypnosis. He had also made a play for the under-age heiress, Dorothea, who had earned his displeasure by spurning him. He was charged with double murder and sent for trial at Hirschberg in December 1921.

A sordid picture emerged at the trial of a man obsessed with sex who had been intimate with both servants and members of his own family, having in all probability infected his step-daughter with venereal disease. Witnesses testified that he had tried to kill Dorothea during a boating trip, and the circumstances of his wife's mysterious disappearance in 1920 were regarded as suspicious. An expert on hypnosis testified that Grupen was unquestionably a dominant personality who had subjected both his wife and step-daughter to sexual bondage. The subject of hypnosis came up again and again in court, no doubt reflecting current public interest in the power of hypnotic suggestion. The implication was that Grupen used hypnosis to instruct others to carry out his wishes.

On the basis of a great deal of circumstantial evidence and no small amount of prejudice, Peter Grupen was found guilty. He maintained his conviction was a miscarriage of justice, but despite his appeals he was executed in January 1922.
[396]

GUAY, Albert. Three persons headed by Guay placed a bomb on an aircraft, killing its total complement of 23 passengers and crew, including Mrs Guay.

A Quebec Airways DC-3 on a flight from Montreal to Seven Islands exploded in mid-air over Cap Tourmente on 9 September 1949. Airline investigators concluded that a bomb had exploded in the plane's forward baggage compartment.

Life insurance policies covering the passengers were checked. Meanwhile one of the baggage-handlers at Quebec said he had put on board a 28-lb parcel sent by Delphis Bouchard to Alfred Plouffe at St Baie Comeau. It was found that no such persons existed. The freight-loader remembered that the parcel was given to him by a fat, middle-aged woman who arrived in a taxi. Patient checking of cab-drivers produced the cabbie who drove such a woman to the airport on that day.

She was eventually identified from an entirely different quarter. In the course of checking the names on the passenger list, police came to the name of Rita Guay. Her husband Albert, a jeweller in Seven Islands, had been involved in an affray at a local restaurant. Officers investigating this incident learned that one of Albert Guay's regular companions was a fat, middle-aged woman named Marguérite Pitre.

Marguérite Pitre was Guay's mistress, and she was identified by the cab-driver. She owed money to Guay, who treated her as a slave to do his bidding, which included obtaining dynamite. On 23 September Guay was arrested, protesting his innocence. It was discovered that the workshop run by Pitre's crippled brother, Généreux Ruest, had been used to make a timing device, allegedly for dynamiting tree-stumps.

Albert Guay was tried for murder in February 1950, and convicted. Later he made a full confession implicating his 2 accomplices in his plan to collect his wife's insurance.

Guay was hanged on 12 January 1951. Pitre and Ruest were subsequently tried and found guilty; they too were hanged.
[385, 400, 752]

GUNNESS, Belle. Mass murderess notorious in American criminal history for slaying 14 men enticed to her farm by thoughts of marriage. Belle drugged them in their sleep, relieved them of their wallets and butchered their bodies which she later buried on her farm. After faking her own death Belle disappeared in 1908.

Belle was widowed when her husband died from an accident, leaving her with 3 children and a farm at Laporte, Indiana. The widow settled down to work the farm with assistance from handyman Ray Lamphere who soon became her lover.

Belle took to advertising in the Chicago newspapers for suitors, adding the punch-line that 'Triflers need not apply.' Several men replied to her advertisement and in 1908 Andrew Helgelien travelled to Laporte in anticipation of Belle's warm embraces. He also had a pocketful of money as she had primed him as to her need of funds to pay off the mortgage on the farm. On arrival Helgelien was surprised to be introduced to Ray Lamphere whom Belle described as her next husband. Helgelien disappeared and on 28 April 1908 the Gunness farm was destroyed by a fire.

A badly burned female body was found in the ruins and Belle was thought to have perished with her 3 children. Identification was not certain as the corpse was headless—it appeared that the woman had been murdered and the building fired in the hope of destroying evidence of the crime. Lamphere was immediately arrested, and he boasted of his affair with Belle.

Digging in the burned-out farm produced Andrew Helgelien's body, which had been dissected and wrapped up in oil cloth. Thirteen other bodies were also dug up. The police were satisfied that the corpse was Belle when her denture was retrieved from the ashes. Ray Lamphere was charged with murder and arson. He was acquitted of murder but convicted of arson, and sentenced to 2 to 21 years imprisonment. He died in Indiana State Penitentiary.

Lamphere told a cell-mate that the body was not that of Belle but a woman she lured to the farm for the purpose of providing a corpse, after she herself had burned the place down. She threw her denture into the blaze for good measure and escaped with a small fortune which she had taken off the suitors she had butchered like the pigs on her farm. In any event, Belle Gunness was never seen again.

[29, 225, 380, 400, 903, 932]

H

HAARMANN, Fritz. Hawker of smuggled meat in post First World War Germany who became a mass murderer.

Haarmann was a native of Hanover, and he returned there after being discharged from the army. He suffered from epileptic fits, and these may have accounted for his degenerate behaviour. He served sentences for petty thieving, picking pockets and indecent behaviour with small children. Haarmann lived in Hanover's thieves' quarter, where he existed by stealing food and ingratiating himself with the police through informing.

In 1918 Haarmann pretended to be a policeman, and preyed on the young refugees at the railway station, offering them food and shelter. In September he was joined by a 24-year-old criminal, Hans Grans, and together they preyed on the human flotsam of the War. They lured teenage boys from the station to Haarmann's den in Neuestrasse, where they killed them and sold their clothes, after disposing of their bodies for meat. It was estimated that they claimed 2 victims a week over a 16-month period of murder.

On 22 July 1924 the meat trader was accused of indecent behaviour. His lodgings were searched, and articles belonging to the missing boys were found. Meanwhile human bones, the relics of 23 bodies, were discovered on the foreshore of a river. Haarmann confessed to the murders, and implicated Grans, who was promptly arrested.

Haarmann was tried at Hanover Assizes in 1924. He made a second confession giving expression to his sexual perversion, and admitting his surprise that he had only been charged with 27 murders, when he thought the total was nearer to 40. Haarmann, who was 45, was found guilty and beheaded. Grans was sentenced to 12 years' imprisonment.

[*100, 221, 232, 605, 792*]

HAIGH, John George. A 39-year-old self-styled engineer, who committed the Acid Bath Murders.

Like *Neville Heath*, Haigh was regarded as a charmer, by the residents of the Kensington hotel where he was living in 1949. He became friendly with a 69-year-old widow, wealthy Olive Durand-Deacon, who told him her ideas to market cosmetics. Haigh invited her to visit his factory, which was in reality no more than a store-room at Crawley in Sussex. On 18 February 1949 he drove her down.

Haigh had made plans, and among the experimental materials he had ready were a large quantity of sulphuric acid, rubber gloves and an apron and an empty 40-gallon drum. With Mrs Durand-Deacon safely on his premises, Haigh shot the elderly widow through the neck, stripped the body of all valuables and tipped the corpse into the empty drum, which he then filled with sulphuric acid.

Haigh made several trips to his factory to ensure that his victim's body was being satisfactorily eaten up by acid. With another hotel resident, he went to Chelsea Police Station to report that Mrs Durand-Deacon was missing. The police suspected Haigh's glib manner, and when they found he had a record visited his Crawley factory.

Detectives found fragments of Mrs Durand-Deacon, as well as traces of blood. There was also a recently fired .38 Webley revolver. Haigh was apprehended, and told police, 'Mrs Durand-Deacon no longer exists. I've destroyed her with acid. You can't prove murder without a body.' He made a statement and admitted 8 other murders, each involving disposal of the body with acid. They were 3 members of the McSwan family, Dr and Mrs Henderson and 3 unknown people who were no doubt invented by Haigh.

The drum of acid had reduced his victim's body virtually to sludge, but an acrylic plastic denture was identified as belonging to Mrs Durand-Deacon by her dentist.

Tried at Lewes Assizes in July 1949, Haigh's defence was based on a plea of insanity. Despite his claim of vampirish habits in drinking his victim's

UNION GROUP ENGINEERING

THIS NUMBER MUST BE QUOTED

CRAWLEY   CROYDON
PUTNEY   WIMBLEDON
GENERAL ENGINEERING. SMALL REPETITION.
GAUGE MAKERS TO M.O.S. and I.G.A.

ORDER

FROM THE TECHNICAL LIAISON OFFICER
ONSLOW COURT HOTEL
LONDON, S.W.7.
TELEPHONE: KENSINGTON 6300

To _Alfred White Son Ltd,_ __16 Feby.__ _194 9_
28 Dallington St
Goswell Road. E.C.1.

Please supply, Carriage Paid, to the address given below, the undermentioned goods:

1 Carboy Com H_2SO_4.

18.6 lbs

Confirmation of telephonic
order to Mr Brown today

UNION GROUP ENGINEERING.
T.L.O.

INSPECTION ✗
DELIVERY Collect
TERMS Cash.

Haigh: Order for sulphuric acid

blood, the plea failed. He was found guilty, and executed at Wandsworth Prison on 10 August 1949.
[*1, 37, 131, 149, 232, 270, 490, 493, 541, 547, 609, 616, 677, 768, 851, 869, 961*]

HALL, Archibald Thompson. A professional butler who counted an impressive number of titled employers in his curriculum vitae before he turned to murder. Hall was a confidence trickster with a smooth and plausible manner who easily fooled the gullible. He served periodic spells in prison for theft and housebreaking and worked as a butler in between.

In November 1977 he secured a position with Walter Scott-Elliot, a former Member of Parliament, who lived in a Knightsbridge apartment with his wife, who was incapacitated by arthritis. The Scott-Elliots were extremely wealthy, with houses in France and Italy in addition to their London home, which was filled with valuable paintings and antiques. Hall inveigled his way into the elderly couple's confidence and became their trusted servant.

Within weeks Hall had enlisted the help of Mary Coggle, his former mistress, and Michael Kitto, a fellow-thief, in a plan to rob his new employers. On 8 December 1977 Kitto entered the apartment and was being taken on a reconnaissance tour by Hall which included Mrs Scott-Elliot's bedroom in the belief that the elderly lady had retired to a nursing-home for a few days. To their surprise they found her in bed and not amused to find intruders in her room. Hall moved quickly to silence any outcry by smothering her with a pillow. Walter Scott-Elliot called out from his room, asking what the commotion was. He was told that his wife had been having a nightmare but was now sleeping.

The next day Hall bundled the trusting old man off to his club while he and his accomplices devised a new plan. They hired a car, dressed up Mary Coggle in some of the dead woman's clothes and when Scott-Elliot returned home, drugged him and put him in the car next to Coggle. They hoped the bemused man would believe Coggle to be his wife. Mrs Scott-Elliot's body had been loaded into the car boot, and part of the plan was to drive up to Cumbria to dispose of her.

At this point the plan was changed. Hall argued that it would be better to dispose of the body in Scotland, where there was a chance of obtaining a Not Proven verdict if things went wrong. Once again they drugged Scott-Elliot and put him in the car for the drive to Scotland. They stopped at a

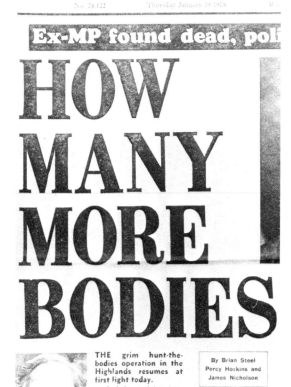

No. 24,122   Thursday January 19 1978

Ex-MP found dead, poli

HOW MANY MORE BODIES

THE grim hunt-the-bodies operation in the Highlands resumes at first light today.

By Brian Steel
Percy Hoskins and
James Nicholson

Hall: Murder headlines

remote area near Loch Earn and pitched his wife's body into a stream. Relieved of their murder victim, they drove back to Cumbria with Scott-Elliot asleep in the back of the car. 'The old man didn't know which day of the week it was,' Hall remarked later.

Leaving the old man in their Cumbrian hide-out with Coggle, Hall and Kitto drove to London and ransacked the Knightsbridge apartment. This accomplished, they returned north and, picking up Coggle and the old man, drove once more to Scotland. At a bleak spot in Inverness-shire they partially strangled Walter Scott-Elliot and battered him to death with a spade. His corpse was put into a shallow grave.

Thieves and murderers frequently fall out, and Archibald Hall and his accomplices were no exceptions. Mary Coggle insisted on keeping Mrs Scott-Elliot's mink coat, which the men wanted to burn as it was too identifiable. To settle the quarrel, Mary was asphyxiated with a plastic bag and her body thrown into a stream by the Glasgow to Carlisle Road.

Hall and Kitto sold some of their booty and spent Christmas with Hall's brother. To satisfy Donald

Hall's curiosity as to the source of their wealth, they took him to their hideout in Cumbria. Then, murder being their answer to every situation, they chloroformed him and loaded his body into the car for another trip to their disposal grounds in Scotland. Their downfall came when they decided to stay overnight at a hotel in North Berwick. Wondering if his guests (who had no luggage with them) would be able to pay the bill, the hotel proprietor telephoned the police, quoting their car registration number. Hall had changed the number-plates following the ransacking of the London flat, and it soon became apparent that the registration number did not match the make of car. Police officers arrived at the hotel to question the car-owner and the game was up when Donald Hall's body was found in the boot.

Archibald Hall made a full confession, including admission of another murder which brought the tally of his victims to 5. While in custody he tried to take his own life, but survived to stand trial in Edinburgh alongside Michael Kitto. They were sentenced to life imprisonment, and received additional sentences on further charges of murder and manslaughter in London. The 'Monster Butler', as Hall was dubbed by the newspapers, faced imprisonment for the rest of his natural life.
[197, 596]

HALL-MILLS CASE. Unsolved double murder in which a New Brunswick (N.J.) church minister and his choir-singer lover were found dead under a crab-apple tree.

On 16 September 1922 a young couple walking in Lovers Lane, New Brunswick, found the bodies of a man and a woman lying on their backs with arms outstretched and letters and cards scattered around them. The Rev. Edward Wheeler Hall, Rector of St Johns Episcopal church, had been shot through the head with a single bullet. His companion, Mrs Eleanor Mills, had been shot in the head 3 times, and her throat cut.

It was well known that the minister was enamoured of the choir-singer. The letters strewn around the bodies were love-letters written by Mrs Mills to the minister. 'I have the greatest of all blessings', read one, 'a noble man, deep, true and eternal love.' Mr Hall's wife seemed immune to the gossip and Mr Mills, elevated to church sexton by the minister, was flattered by his wife's relationship.

Several people came forward as witnesses. A 54-year-old widow, Mrs Gibson, who raised hogs, achieved fame in the case as the 'Pig Woman'. She said that on the night of 14 September she saw 4 shadowy figures in Lovers Lane and heard shots and screams. There were shouts of 'Don't, don't, don't', and the name 'Henry' was mentioned. A Grand Jury was convened in November, but refused to indict anyone.

Four years later, a statement by a former maid in the Hall household created a sensation. She had

Hall-Mills Case: The scene of the crime

been a confidante of the minister, and knew, she said, that he intended to elope with Mrs Mills. Mrs Hall, together with two of her brothers, William and Henry Stevens, was charged with murder.

The trio were tried at Somerville, New Jersey, in November 1926. It was asserted that Mrs Hall had been trying to catch her husband in a compromising situation with Mrs Mills. The star witness was the 'Pig Woman'. She said she had recognized Mrs Hall and her brother Henry in the group of 4 figures under the crab-apple tree. Expert witnesses identified William Stevens's fingerprints on one of the dead man's visiting cards found at the scene of the crime. All three were acquitted and Mrs Hall went into seclusion, dying in 1942.
[57, 144, 378, 544, 683, 727, 896]

HAMBLIN, Louie. A 16-year-old found guilty of rape and murder in Vermont in 1982 and sentenced to 45 years to life imprisonment. On 15 May 1981 two 12-year-old girls on their way home from school in the small town of Essex Junction decided to take a short cut through the woods because of bad weather. They were viciously assaulted by 2 youths, being raped, tortured and stabbed. One of the girls managed to escape, and although injured, reached nearby railway tracks, where she encountered a railwayman who raised the alarm. Her companion's brutally abused body was later found in the woods.

The survivor gave descriptions to the police, and after an artist's impression of the two attackers had appeared in the newspapers a school-teacher came forward with information. From the sketches, he identified two youths who had been students at his school. They were arrested, and the news elated a community which had been stunned by these brutal attacks.

The public mood changed to frustration when it became known that one of the attackers was aged 15, and therefore came under the protection of the juvenile law. The 2 suspects had been picked out from a series of photographs by the surviving victim, and she also identified them in a line-up. The younger of the two teenagers made a confession to the assault, the details of which he changed several times. He said the attacks had been 'just for the fun'.

Within three weeks of the murder, local citizens had collected over 27,000 signatures on a petition to the state governor demanding changes in the juvenile law. The state legislature passed a law in July 1981 which made it possible where a serious crime had been committed to try individuals aged between

10 and 16 as though they were adults. An attempt to make the law retroactive in order to try the 15-year-old accused in the Essex Junction murder was rejected as unconstitutional.

Louie Hamblin was tried for murder in 1982, and the girl who survived the attack gave evidence in court. Her vivid testimony shattered the defence, whose only argument was that Hamblin's juvenile companion committed the murder in order to eliminate her as a witness. He was sent out of the state for rehabilitation, in the knowledge that he would be released into society again when he reached the age of 18 and his previous record would be destroyed. In 1983 he was reported to have changed his name and to have moved to Arizona.

Hamblin, who became a born-again Christian, received several death threats while in prison. He maintained his innocence, and told his psychiatrist that society had no right to prosecute him. He wrote poetry while in prison which reminded some observers of the sentiments in *Jack Abbott*'s book *In The Belly of The Beast*. Hamblin—described as pathologically anti-social—said he thought he should be released into the woods where the girl had been killed, and that her father should be given the opportunity to hunt him down.
[664]

HAMMERSMITH NUDES MURDERS.
A series of 6 murders in London between February 1964 and February 1965 had the common characteristics that all the victims were prostitutes, and all were found nude. This earned the killer the name 'Jack the Stripper', after *Jack the Ripper* whose anonymity he shared.

The pattern was of prostitutes being strangled or suffocated and their bodies, stripped of clothing, being dumped in various places.

In the last 4 murders the nude victims had flakes of paint on them. Analysis showed these to be multicoloured lead acetate paints of the type used in car sprays. Garages and factories using such paint were checked, and samples taken for matching purposes.

The police theory was that after they had been killed the victims were stripped, and their nude bodies left for a time in areas where paint spray equipment was used. They were then moved to the places where they were discovered. The women disappeared between the hours of 11.00 p.m. and 1.00 a.m. and were abandoned between 5.00 and 6.00 a.m. The police deduced from this that the likely occupation of the killer involved him in night work.

The murders stopped suddenly in 1965, a fact which was later associated with a suicide of a 45-year-old man in South London who left a note saying he was 'unable to stand the strain any longer'.

This particular man worked for a security firm, and on every occasion that a murder victim disappeared he had a paint spray shop on his 10.00 p.m. to 6.00 a.m. round, which he patrolled in a van. The man was never named.

[257, 620]

HANRATTY, James. The conviction and execution of 25-year-old Hanratty for the A6 Murder has been the subject of continuing controversy.

On the evening of 22 August 1961 a car containing lovers Michael Gregsten, a married man, and Valerie Storie, was parked by a field near Slough in Buckinghamshire. A man tapped on the window and threatened the couple with a gun. He told them he was on the run and, getting into the back seat, ordered Gregsten to drive off. They travelled about 30 miles before the unwelcome passenger instructed Gregsten to pull in to a lay-by on the A6 road.

When the gunman asked for a duffle bag to be passed to him Gregsten moved, and was killed instantly by 2 shots. The man then raped the girl, and having dragged her dead lover on to the lay-by, fired several shots at her and made off in the car.

Valerie Storie survived, though paralysed, and described the attacker. The car was abandoned at Ilford, and a loaded revolver found on a London bus was the murder weapon. An Identikit picture was made up from Valerie Storie's description, but as this differed from that of a man seen driving Gregsten's car after the murder, 2 pictures were published. Gregsten's widow saw a man in the street whom she said was her husband's murderer. The man was James Hanratty, a petty criminal, who did not resemble either of the Identikit pictures.

Valerie Storie recalled fuller details, such as icy-blue eyes, a singular characteristic of Hanratty. In the meantime, two .38 cartridge cases from the murder weapon were found in a London hotel room occupied on the night before the murder by Mr J. Ryan, an alias used by Hanratty. But on the night after the murder the same room was occupied by Peter Louis Alphon, who was put on an identity parade, but who Valerie Storie did not recognize.

Hanratty was arrested in Blackpool on 9 October, picked out in an identity parade and sent for trial. The issue of identification plagued the whole proceedings. There were grave doubts that Hanratty was the man featured in the Identikit pictures, but the trial hinged on his alibi, which placed him in Liverpool and beyond the possibility of committing murder on the A6. But Hanratty refused to name his friends because he believed that would have broken their trust. He then inexplicably changed his alibi, saying that he had stayed not at Liverpool but in Rhyl. There were no witnesses to substantiate this either.

The jury spent 9½ hours before they found him guilty. He simply told the court, 'I am innocent.' After he was hanged at Bedford on 4 April 1962 witnesses were found who thought they had seen him at Rhyl. There was considerable public disquiet that Hanratty's guilt had not been proved beyond reasonable doubt, and this was heightened by the suggestion made by Peter Alphon that Hanratty's guilt had been contrived, but there is little doubt that the verdict was the correct one.

[23, 129, 288, 297, 312, 512, 661, 805, 851]

HARRIES, Thomas Ronald Lewis. A 24-year-old farm-worker who murdered his adopted aunt and uncle.

John Harries, aged 63, and his ailing wife Phoebe, aged 54, disappeared from their Carmarthenshire farm on 16 October 1953. Neighbours noticed that Harries's cows were unmilked—an unusual occurrence for so good a farmer. Ronald Harries, a distant relative adopted as his nephew by John Harries, said his aunt and uncle had gone to London for a holiday, leaving him in charge of the farm.

Local police called in Scotland Yard, and it was felt that Ronald Harries knew more than he was saying. His story had been contradicted, and he was in financial difficulty.

He cashed a cheque for £909 which he said had been made out to him by his uncle, and which on examination proved to have been altered from £9.

Suspecting that the missing couple had been killed and buried locally by Harries, detectives tied cotton threads across the gaps in the hedges around Cadno farm where Harries lived. They deliberately made a great deal of noise to alarm Harries, who, anxious to learn if his secret had been discovered, inspected the fields. At dawn detectives found where the thread was broken, and it led them to the grave of John and Phoebe Harries.

Harris, when told the news, said, 'I am sorry to

hear that Uncle and Auntie are dead. I was their favourite.' He was charged with double murder. The circumstantial evidence was strong, and it was clear from the testimony that Ronald had taken over his uncle's farm, as he had been seen searching drawers and cupboards.

Harries was tried at Carmarthen Assizes in March 1954, found guilty and hanged at Swansea Prison.

[163, 307, 451, 791, 814, 962]

HARRIS, Carlyle. A 23-year-old medical student executed for wife-murder. The trial resulted in the first conviction for morphine poisoning in New York.

Nineteen-year-old Helen Potts was a student at a New York boarding school. She died there on 1 February 1891 after Carlyle Harris had prescribed medicine for her. He gave her some capsules containing one-sixth of a grain of morphine to relieve her insomnia. The grief-stricken mother said that Helen had a heart condition, a fact which Harris chose to ignore. He offered one of the capsules to the coroner for analysis, confident that it had been properly dispensed.

The *New York World* published unsavoury facts about Harris. He was a gambler and a womanizer, and had secretly married Helen Potts on 8 February 1890. The dead girl's uncle, a doctor, who had performed an abortion on his niece, claimed to have been told by Harris that he too had performed a similar operation. Mrs Potts now accused Harris of murdering her daughter, and on 30 March a Grand Jury indicted him.

At his trial in New York in January 1892 Harris was alleged by the prosecution to have substituted morphine for quinine in one of the capsules, and to have administered it to his wife, of whom he had grown tired. A battle of the experts ensued, involving the American toxicologist Dr Rudolph Witthaus. The prosecution contended that morphine had been found in the body, and this was borne out by the doctor who had examined Helen and observed her pin-pointed pupils—the universal sign of morphine poisoning. The defence contested this, arguing that it was not possible to base an accusation of morphine poisoning on the known symptoms of the case.

An acquittal was fully expected, despite the fact that Harris did not testify. The verdict of guilty of first-degree murder therefore came as a surprise. Harris was executed at Sing Sing prison and his mother had fixed on her son's coffin a plate bearing the inscription: 'CARLYLE HARRIS, Mur-

dered May 8th 1893. Aged 23 yrs, 7 mos, 15 days, We would not if we had known.'

[105, 383, 862, 917]

HARRIS, Jean. On 10 March 1980 the 57-year-old headmistress of a respected private school for girls in Virginia set out on a 5-hour drive to New York state. When she reached her destination she shot dead her lover, Dr Herman Tarnower, a renowned cardiologist, and created an overnight sensation.

Herman Tarnower, aged 69, who had achieved international recognition for his *Scarsdale Diet*, had had a relationship with Harris for 14 years, but he was growing tired of her in favour of a younger woman who worked with him in his medical practice. Knowing that their relationship was on the verge of breaking up, and that her teaching career was also in decline, Jean Harris became suicidally depressed. She therefore decided to take decisive action. When she began her long drive to see Tarnower at his home in Westchester she had made out her will, and put a .32 revolver in her handbag.

It was late evening by the time Harris arrived at her destination. Four shots were fired, and the housekeeper who rushed to the scene found Tarnower lying wounded on the floor in her arms. The doctor died later, and Harris was arrested as she was about to drive away from the house. She told the police simply, 'I did it.' She did not deny firing the gun but claimed that the killing was accidental. Her account of the incident was that Tarnower was asleep when she arrived and that after she woke him up they talked, and in her wretched state of mind she produced a gun and invited him to kill her. In the ensuing tussle to possess the gun Tarnower was fatally wounded in the chest.

Jean Harris's trial for murder lasted nearly four months. Her defence was based on an accidental killing but a number of factors worked to her disadvantage. Over 30 live rounds of ammunition were found in her car—rather a lot to ensure a suicide, it was pointed out. Moreover, on the day before the shooting she had written a long letter to Tarnower which spoke of her wretchedness and humiliation. She also bitterly attacked him and his 'psychotic whore' (as she described a woman who had replaced her in his affections). The letter was a devastating catalogue of bitterness and resentment—fit prelude to a jealous rage. When Harris turned up at Tarnower's house on the fatal night, having nurtured her resentment during the long drive, she was enraged to see articles belonging to her rival lying around his bedroom. She stormed about, ripping up clothes and throwing things around, until he tried to calm her—with the result that the gun was produced.

It came out during the trial that Tarnower had prescribed amphetamine and barbiturate drugs for Harris to help her through her professional crises at school. She had for ten years been taking meth-amphetamine, a powerful stimulant, which can produce mind-altering side-effects if administered over a long period. It was argued that Harris had been without the drug for three days prior to the shooting, with the result that she was suffering withdrawal feelings of fatigue, depression and in-ability to cope with life. It was while she was in this disturbed state that she unintentionally shot her former lover.

The jury took 8 days to reach a decision on Jean Harris's guilt but finally convicted her of second-degree murder, and she was gaoled for 15 years. The case has fascinated a number of writers, and several books have been published, including Jean Harris's own account written while in prison. The essentials of her story were consistent with the evidence she gave in court, in as much as her intention was to kill herself and the resultant tragedy was an accident. She has shown extraordinary strength of character in prison, in particular by using her skills to coach inmates to better educational standards.

[18, 215, 411, 701, 874, 927]

HAUPTFLEISCH, Petrus Stephanus François. South African matricide involving fire and asphyxia, reminiscent of the *Sidney Fox* case.

Hauptfleisch, 40, drank so heavily that his wife and child left him. He worked in Richmond, in Cape Province, as a slaughterer. He lived with his 67-year-old widowed mother, who had to bear with his heavy drinking habits.

At one period Hauptfleisch improved but then relapsed, and on 7 December 1924 came home roaring drunk, saying he would stone his mother to death. On 13 January he ran out of the house screaming that his mother had been 'burned in the kitchen fire'. A neighbour found Mrs Haupt-fleisch dead, lying on her side on a brick-built kitchen stove with her face and chest badly burned.

Hauptfleisch moved his mother's body before the doctor came. He told the doctor that against his advice his mother had decided to clean the chimney by burning it out with petrol. The doctor found post-mortem lividity on the back of the body, which indicated that Mrs Hauptfleisch had died lying on her back and not on her side. There was also evidence of suffocation and post-mortem blisters.

Hauptfleisch was arrested and tried in Cape Town in September 1926. He drew on his inheritance from his dead mother to pay for his defence—an act which heightened public anger against him. The prosecution suggested that Hauptfleisch asphyxiated his mother while she was lying on her bed, carried her to the stove, poured petrol over her body and set fire to it. Despite continued protestations of innocence, he was found guilty and was hanged on 23 December 1926.

[65, 76, 679]

HAUPTMANN, Bruno Richard. German-born 36-year-old immigrant to the United States responsible for the kidnapping and murder of the Lindbergh child.

On 1 March 1932 the 20-month-old baby boy of famous aviator Charles A. Lindbergh was kidnapped from his luxurious home in New Jersey. Footprints were found near the house, together with a broken wooden ladder and a ransom note demanding $50 000. The note contained several simple spelling errors, of a nature suggesting the writer might be German. The signature was formed of two interlocking circles.

A nationwide hunt for the kidnapper began, and the first lead came as the result of a letter from a Dr Condon in a New York newspaper appealing to the kidnapper's humanity. He received a letter signed with two interlocking circles. At a meeting the kidnapper gave his name as John. Later 'John' sent the missing child's night clothes to prove his authenticity, at the same time increasing the ransom to $70 000.

At a second meeting Colonel Lindbergh was present with the money. John said he would reveal the whereabouts of the child when the cash was handed over, and the anxious father was directed to the Massachusetts coast where his son was supposed to be in a boat. Lindbergh rushed there, but there was no boat and no child.

On 12 May the baby's body was found in a shallow grave only a few miles from the Lindbergh house. A US Forestry Service scientist identified the lumber yard which had machined the wood used to make the kidnapper's ladder. But it was the ransom money which eventually trapped him, when a filling-station attendant took a note in payment which had come from the ransom. The driver was traced through his car registration number—his name was Bruno Hauptmann, a 36-

year-old former German soldier who had entered the USA illegally in 1923.

Hauptmann was arrested on 19 September, and over $11 000 of the ransom money was found in his garage. His trial for the murder of Charles Lindbergh Jr began in January 1935—he was found guilty. Hauptmann went to the electric chair at Trenton State Prison, New Jersey, on 3 April 1936. It is still contended that he was not the kidnapper.

Hauptmann's widow tried on two occasions to clear her husband's name, claiming that he had been wrongfully convicted. Both attempts were rejected by the US Court of Appeals. In 1985 it was claimed by Ludovic Kennedy in a new book on the case that Hauptmann had been deliberately framed by the police who faked evidence and intimidated witnesses. In 1987 a stage play at Chicago's Stormfield Theatre portrayed Hauptmann in a sympathetic light as the outsider cast against Lindbergh, the American hero.

[*143, 189, 214, 264, 304, 372, 476, 523, 528, 605, 679, 792, 820, 826, 843, 951, 967, 968*]

HAY, Gordon. A historic case in which dental evidence played a central role in convicting the murderer.

On 7 August 1967 a 15-year-old girl, Linda Peacock, who had been reported missing from her home the previous day, was found dead in the cemetery near the village of Biggar in Scotland. She had been raped and strangled; of special significance to the crime investigators were bite-marks on her right breast made by her assailant.

Photographs of the bite-marks were sent to a specialist in forensic dentistry, who thought it would be possible to identify the girl's attacker by means of dental evidence. Local police inquiries focused on a school for problem teenage boys. Detectives learned that one of the boys was covering up for his room-mate, Gordon Hay, who had been absent from school at the time Linda Peacock was attacked. Hay denied being absent, but agreed to have a dental impression taken.

In order to ensure that the matching of dental characteristics was fair and objective, impressions were taken from 28 boys, including Hay. After comparison with the bite-marks left on the victim, attention was directed to 5 suspects and then, by a process of careful elimination, to Hay. His teeth showed a rare characteristic in the form of small pits in the canine teeth, and he also had a missing filling. The bite-marks made on the victim's body corresponded exactly with these features.

Gordon Hay was tried in 1968, and his defence attempted unsuccessfully to have the dental evidence ruled inadmissible on a technicality. The evidence matching the bite-marks on the victim with dental impressions provided by Hay proved conclusively to the jury that he had attacked the girl, and they found him guilty. As he was under 18 at the time the crime was committed, he was ordered to be detained during Her Majesty's pleasure. A subsequent appeal was dismissed and the conviction brought about by a new forensic technique was upheld.

[*688*]

HEARN CASE. Middle-aged widow charged with murder by arsenical poisoning.

Mrs Sarah Ann Hearn lived in Lewannick in Cornwall with her invalid sister, who died in 1930. Mrs Hearn's neighbours were a farmer and his wife, William and Annie Thomas. They were concerned for her, now living on her own, and went out of their way to be friendly.

On 18 October 1930, the Thomases offered to drive Mrs Hearn to Bude. She made some sandwiches with tinned salmon, which they ate during the afternoon's outing. On the way home Annie Thomas was taken ill, and later went to Plymouth Hospital, where she died on 4 November. A post-mortem showed that the dead woman had arsenic in her body. At the funeral pointed remarks were made by relatives about Mrs Hearn's connection with Annie's death.

Mrs Hearn then went through the pretence of committing suicide, leaving a note for William Thomas and clothing on a near-by cliff-top. But she went to Torquay, and became a housekeeper under an assumed name. A Coroner's Inquest decided that Annie Thomas had died of arsenical poisoning. The body of Mrs Hearn's sister was exhumed, together with that of an aunt who had lived with them, and found to contain arsenic. She was arrested at Torquay for murder.

She was tried at Bodmin Assizes in June 1931 for the murder of Annie Thomas. She was defended by Sir Norman Birkett, who contended that Mrs Thomas became ill from food poisoning and subsequently received arsenic, though this was not administered by the accused. Mrs Hearn in the witness-box denied that she had poisoned anyone, or that she had contrived Mrs Thomas's death in order to marry her husband. She was acquitted.

[*44, 252, 255, 710, 791, 908, 977*]

HEATH, Neville George Clevely. A 28-year-

Heath: Whip marks on a victim's body

old sadistic Royal Air Force officer who murdered 2 young women.

On 21 June 1946 the body of a 32-year-old film extra, Margery Gardner, was found savagely mutilated and beaten in a London hotel room. The hotel room had been booked the previous week in the names of Lt Colonel and Mrs Heath. Neville Heath was known to the police, for he had a criminal and Borstal record and had been court-martialled twice, as well as fined for unlawfully wearing uniform and decorations.

Posing as Group Captain Rupert Brooke, Heath met 21-year-old Doreen Marshall at a Bournemouth hotel on 3 July. They dined together and sat in the hotel lounge until after midnight. When they left together Miss Marshall did not return. Two days passed, and the hotel manager reported a missing resident to the police.

Like *John George Haigh*, Heath had an extraordinary compulsion to go to the police. He asked them if they had a photograph of the missing girl, and, still posing as Rupert Brooke, he went to the police station to see it. He was immediately recognized and detained. Among his belongings (left in Bournemouth West Station) were a bloodstained scarf and a metal-tipped whip.

Doreen Marshall's body was found on 8 July in Branksome Chine lying in some bushes. Her throat had been cut, and she had been sexually and savagely mutilated. Heath was charged with the murder of Margery Gardner, and tried at the Old Bailey in September 1946.

The suave former officer had sexual lusts which his fellow-Servicemen had recognized as abnormal. A defence plea of insanity did not dissuade the jury from finding him guilty, and he was hanged on 16 October 1946.

[*1, 13, 78, 148, 171, 323, 441, 451, 497, 601, 609, 677, 678, 697, 737, 743*]

HEIRENS, William. Brought up to regard sexual relations as unclean, 17-year-old Heirens found gratification in burglary and murder.

At the age of 13, he was arrested for possessing a loaded pistol. He had already committed 11 burglaries and set fire to 6 houses. At his parents' Chicago home officers found an arsenal of weapons hidden. Heirens was sent to a private home for correction, and then enrolled as a student at Chicago University.

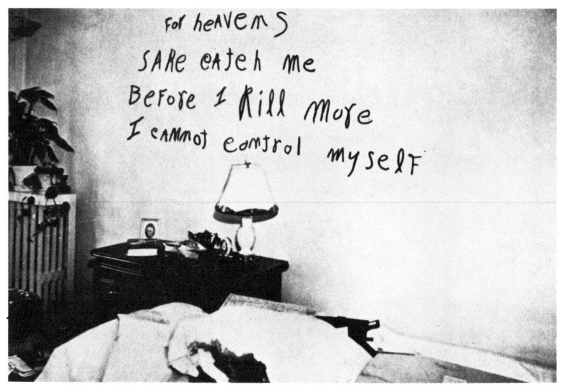

Heirens: The writing on the wall!

An above-average student, Heirens was also a clever burglar, and during his student days regularly robbed apartment houses. In March 1945 he disturbed a sleeping woman, and slashed her throat and stabbed her several times. In June he was again found entering an apartment. This time he knocked out the owner. But in another incident in October he killed a woman with 2 shots, and stabbed her. He scrawled a message in lipstick on a wall, 'For heavens sake catch me before I kill more I cannot control myself.'

In January 1946 Heirens kidnapped a 6-year-old girl from her bed. He left a note demanding $20 000, and took the girl to a near-by basement where he killed her and cut the body into pieces, dropping them down sewer gratings in the street.

On 26 June an intruder was seen in a Chicago apartment block, and police arrived to find the caretaker and a tenant grappling with Heirens, who was overpowered and taken into custody. He denied being involved with the killings. He said the murders were committed by 'George', attributing the savage side of his personality to his *alter ego*, which he called George Murman.

Heirens, who confessed to reaching sexual climax during his bouts of murderous housebreaking, was judged insane. He was sentenced to 3 consecutive life terms, and was never to be released.
[*224, 299, 693, 826*]

HEPPER, William Sanchez de Pina. Onetime BBC translator and American spy in Spain, who raped and murdered an 11-year-old girl.

Hepper, who was 62, earned a living as a painter of flowers and portraits. He had a flat in Chelsea and a studio at Brighton. His daughter had a friend, 11-year-old Margaret Spevick, who had broken her arm in an accident. Hepper wrote to Mrs Spevick suggesting that the girl could have a holiday at Brighton where she could convalesce and sit as his portrait model.

On 3 February 1954 Hepper took Margaret to Brighton. Mrs Spevick went down to visit her daughter. But when she arrived on 7 February she could get no answer from the flat, and the caretaker let her in. On the bed lay Margaret's raped and strangled body, and her unfinished portrait stood on an easel near by.

Three days after the discovery, Hepper was

arrested in Spain. He was extradited to Britain, and stood trial at Lewes Assizes in July 1954.

The defence argued that Hepper was suffering from paranoia, and to demonstrate this the accused collapsed in the witness-box, and later claimed loss of memory and sexual impotence. He said that he was haunted by dreams of his wife's infidelity, and had gone to Spain to see his dying brother. Hepper was found guilty and hanged at Wandsworth Prison on 11 August 1954.

[*367, 541, 599*]

HEYS, Arthur. A Leading Aircraftsman, and a family man, convicted of the brutal murder of a WAAF in wartime Britain.

Heys was based at an RAF station near Beccles in Suffolk. On the evening of 8 November 1944, he went out with some fellow-airmen to a dance. When the time came to return to their camp Heys was missing.

He turned up just after midnight, at the women's quarters. The duty corporal told him to return to his own billet. On the way he accosted 27-year-old Winifred Mary Evans, a radio operator. He raped her and savagely suffocated her, leaving the body in a ditch where it was found the following morning.

At the next pay parade the police asked the duty corporal to identify the man she had seen. She picked out Heys, who had tried to disguise himself by lining up with the R's instead of the H's.

Heys told the police that he was back in quarters by 12.30. His hut-mates denied this, saying it was nearer 1.00 or 1.30 a.m. He had spent a good deal of time cleaning his clothes early the next morning, even to the extent of missing breakfast. There were scratches on his hands, and a hair on his overcoat was of the same type as the victim's.

He was charged with the murder, and while in custody he contrived to smuggle out a letter to the Commanding Officer of the RAF Base which stated that an airman stood wrongly accused of a murder committed by the anonymous letter-writer. As the letter gave away details known only to the police and to the murderer, it was virtually a confession. At his trial in January 1945 at Bury St Edmunds Heys was found guilty, and hanged.

[*175, 361, 495*]

HICKMAN, Edward. A 23-year-old college student who used kidnapping and murder as a means of raising money for tuition fees.

He prowled about a wealthy Los Angeles suburb on 15 December 1927 before selecting 12-

Hickman: Pathetic ransom letter

year-old Marion Parker, kidnapping her and demanding a ransom of $7500 in a note which he signed 'The Fox'. Hickman sent several notes elaborately headed 'DEATH', one of which advised, 'If you want aid against me, ask God, not man,' and a tragic letter from Marion.

Hickman met Perry Parker by arrangement on the outskirts of Los Angeles on the 17th to hand over the girl and collect the ransom. Holding a blanket-wrapped bundle in the car, the kidnapper said he would leave the child further up the road after he had the money. Having secured the ransom, Hickman drove off, and Parker went to recover his daughter. The girl was dead from strangulation, and her limbs had been cut off.

Hickman was arrested in Seattle, where he was holidaying on the ransom money. He made 2 attempts to commit suicide in furtherance of a trial defence based on insanity. His efforts failed to convince a jury, and he was found guilty of a horrible crime and hanged at San Quentin Prison on 19 October 1928.

[*160, 619, 638*]

HILL, Harold. A serving soldier of 26 who committed double murder.

Doreen Hearne, aged 8, and Kathleen Trendle,

aged 6, went missing from their homes on 19 November 1941. They were seen walking home from school at Penn, Buckinghamshire, and asking the driver of an army vehicle for a ride. Three days later their bodies were found lying in Rough Wood about 4 miles from the village.

The girls had been stabbed in the throat and chest, but there was no sexual assault. Tyre impressions had been made in the soft earth near by, and there was also a patch of oil-stained soil. Other items included a khaki handkerchief with the laundry mark RA 1019 and Doreen Hearne's gas-mask container.

Children who saw the 2 girls asking for a lift gave a description of both the vehicle and driver. A 12-year-old boy included the military identification marks on the vehicle in his account, and the authorities were able to trace the lorry to Yoxford in Suffolk. Oil was leaking from the rear axle, and its identification marks were the same. In addition, its tyre impressions matched those found near the wood. The driver was Harold Hill, and he was also the owner of laundry mark RA 1019.

Blood spots were found on his spare uniform, and his presence in Rough Wood was confirmed by his fingerprints on the gas-mask container. He had 2 previous convictions for indecent assault on girls.

He was tried in January 1942. A plea of schizophrenia was insufficient against circumstantial evidence, and he was found guilty. He was executed in April 1942.

[*133, 326, 424*]

HILLEY, Marie Audrey. Gentle-looking only daughter of a mill worker in Anniston, Alabama, who poisoned her husband and attempted to poison her daughter. Frank Hilley died in 1975, aged 45, following a short illness; cause of death was given as infectious hepatitis. Marie claimed life insurance to the value of $31,140 and indulged in a modest spending spree.

Marie's colleagues at the local foundry where she worked as a secretary thought that she consistently spent beyond her means. She also developed something of a persecution complex, claiming that she received anonymous telephone calls of a harassing nature and that her house was regularly burgled. Over a period of 2 years she complained to the police about these occurrences on an almost daily basis. Not surprisingly, there was a widely held belief that she had orchestrated the whole thing.

In July 1978 Marie Hilley insured the life of her 18-year-old daughter Carol for $25,000. In 1979 Carol became ill with a wasting disease of myste-

Hill: The murderer's truck showing military identification marks

rious origin and spent a great deal of time in hospitals undergoing tests and coming very close to death. Her mother was very solicitous, visiting her regularly and bringing her special dishes to eat. After 5 months of agonizing illness, and having reached the point where she could hardly walk, Carol mentioned casually to a friend that her mother had given her injections. Added to the knowledge that Marie had also given injections to both her husband and her mother, this information gave rise to suspicions of poisoning.

A urine sample was found to contain arsenic, and Carol's hair contained a hundred times more than the normal level of arsenic. On 17 September 1979 petite, soft-spoken and innocent-looking Marie was arrested on a charge of passing worthless cheques, and was questioned about her daughter's illness. Meanwhile her husband's body was exhumed and was found to be riddled with arsenic. High levels of the poison were also found in the corpse of her mother, Lucille Frazier, who had died of cancer. Most significantly, a pill bottle containing arsenic was found among the contents of Marie's jewellery box.

Marie Hilley was charged with the attempted murder of her daughter, but before proceedings against her could begin she jumped bail and in November 1979 disappeared for three years. She was indicted in her absence for the murder of her husband, and when she was finally apprehended in January 1983 an extraordinary double-life was exposed. In 1980 she had married a boat-builder from Florida and the couple settled down to live in New Hampshire, where Marie took a job as a secretary.

During the time that a nationwide search was in progress to locate her, Marie went alone to Houston, telling her new husband that she had to attend to the affairs of a relative who had recently died. At this point she embarked on an elaborate plan whereby she feigned her own death. Her obituary was published, and it was announced that she had donated her body to medical science. Marie then reappeared masquerading as her twin sister Teri Martin, and in an eerie incident returned to console her grieving husband. It was as Teri Martin that she was arrested in 1983.

At her trial, which shared many similarities with that of *Herbert Rowse Armstrong*—an arsenic poisoner in a different age—she pleaded her innocence and her sanity. It soon became clear that her lawyers were not entirely familiar with all the intricacies of the web she had woven. For example, when she was originally arrested she had made a statement to the police in which she admitted giving her sick daughter 2 injections without the knowledge or consent of her doctors.

Defence attempts to put the blame for harassment which Marie had experienced on her daughter by seeking to show she was the author of various handwritten notes proved disastrous. The handwriting expert called by the defence was shown to be inexperienced, and acknowledged that he had never before testified in court on handwriting analysis. Attempts to discredit Carol Hilley by implying that she was mentally unstable, a drug-user and sexually deviant also failed. Vital testimony was provided by Carol's brother, who had written to the Coroner in 1979 saying that he thought it probable his mother had injected both his father and his sister with arsenic.

Marie Hilley was found guilty of first-degree murder in respect of the death of her husband and of attempted murder in the case of her daughter. She was sentenced to life imprisonment and 20 years for the respective crimes—the maximum punishment allowed. 'I maintain my innocence,' she said. In February 1987 Marie disappeared while out of a prison on a weekend furlough. She was found 4 days later suffering from exposure, and died in hospital. She was buried in a grave next to her murdered husband.

[*631*]

HINDLEY, Myra. See MOORS MURDERS.

HINKS, Reginald Ivor. A 33-year-old petty criminal and ne'er-do-well who graduated from snatching women's handbags to murder for greed.

In 1933 Hinks was a Hoover salesman in Bath. He met Constance Anne Pullen, a divorcée with one child, who lived with her elderly father. After a whirlwind courtship they married, Hinks being attracted to the inheritance she would have after her father's death.

James Pullen was 85 and lived in Bath, looked after by a male nurse. Hinks moved in with his wife, and immediately took over. He forced the nurse to leave, and inflicted a strict diet on Pullen.

With £900 that he obtained from his father-in-law, Hinks bought himself a house in Bath. He tried to obtain more of the old man's money, but was baulked by Pullen's solicitor, who out-manoeuvred him by legal safeguards.

Senile though James Pullen was, Hinks started taking him for long, tiring walks, and often left him in busy streets. His hopes that the old man would die under the strain did not materialize, so he planned murder made to look like suicide.

On 1 December 1953 Hinks telephoned the fire brigade to say Pullen was dead, with his head in the gas oven, and added that any bruise found on the back of the old man's head 'happened when I pulled him out of the gas oven'. Pullen had undoubtedly died of gas poisoning, and there was certainly a bruise on the back of his head which medical examination proved had been caused *before* death.

Hinks was arrested and committed for trial at the Old Bailey. He even wore a black arm-band out of respect for his dead father-in-law. He was found guilty, and hanged at Bristol on 4 May 1934.

[*499, 710, 791*]

HIRASAWA, Sadamichi. Probably Japan's best-known murderer, who ranked with Rudolf Hess as a long-serving prisoner; both men lived into their nineties and died in prison in 1987. Hirasawa was convicted of murder in Tokyo in 1948 and spent almost the next 40 years of his life behind bars at the centre of continuing controversy.

The Shiinamachi branch of the Imperial Bank of Tokyo was the unlikely location for mass murder on 26 January 1948. Just before the bank closed a man wearing an official armband identifying him as a representative of the Tokyo Metropolitan Disinfectant Corps came in. He presented a business card naming himself as Dr Jiro Yamaguchi, and he explained that he had instructions to administer medical treatment on account of an outbreak of dysentery in the area. Japan at that time was under the rule of the American occupying forces.

Dr Yamaguchi gave each of the employees a pill

and then dispensed a small quantity of liquid into a number of small cups using a dropper bottle. Within seconds of drinking the medicine the assembled bank staff dropped where they stood; 10 died immediately, 2 died later and 4 eventually recovered after hospital treatment. Picking his way through the bodies, Dr Yamaguchi seized over 180,000 yen in cash and cheques and walked away from a scene of mass murder that had been quickly achieved through the use of cyanide.

Police inquiries soon revealed that Dr Yamaguchi had carried out a dummy run for his method a few days before at the Mitsubishi Bank without fatal consequences to the staff. It also became known that the staff of the Yasuda Bank had been 'immunized' a few months before by Dr Shigeru Matsui, again with no undesirable results.

It was the Japanese custom of exchanging business cards which provided the police with a lead. Yamaguchi is such a common name in Japan that there was little hope of tracing the murderer by the usual checking procedures. The breakthrough came when Dr Shigeru Matsui called the police to offer assistance. He had read descriptions of 'Dr Yamaguchi' and thought it possible that he might have met the murderer at some time and exchanged business cards. Matsui's reasoning was that the murderer subsequently presented his card by mistake at the Yasuda Bank. If that was the case, it followed that Dr Matsui possessed the murderer's business card. Among the cards given to the police by the doctor was that of Sadamichi Hirasawa, a middle-aged artist, identified by a process of elimination as 'Dr Yamaguchi'.

Hirasawa matched survivors' descriptions of the murderer, and a search of his living-quarters produced a medical bag and clothing and rubber boots similar to those worn by 'Dr Yamaguchi'. Hirasawa made a confession and was put on trial for murder in December 1948. He pleaded partial insanity due to an anti-rabies injection in 1925 which he claimed also led to a deterioration of his skills as a painter. In the course of the trial he withdrew his confession, alleging it had been made under duress. He was nevertheless found guilty and sentenced to be hanged. His lawyers successfully appealed against hanging, which they claimed violated a Japanese law protecting citizens from contributing to their own destruction—it was after all the condemned person's body weight which made hanging effective. The Supreme Court rejected an appeal against conviction in 1955 and Hirasawa saw out the rest of his life in prison.

He painted pictures in Sendai Prison and wrote

Hirasawa: Murder at the Tokyo bank

his autobiography. He also became a controversial figure, as campaigners for his freedom contended that he was the victim of a cover-up. Collusion between the Japanese and American governments to hide wartime crimes was alleged. The real murderer was said to have been an ex-Japanese officer who served in the Imperial Army in a secret biological warfare unit whose purpose was to penetrate enemy lines with assassination squads trained to kill by means of special poisons, including cyanide. At the end of the war the agents involved in these squads were allowed to return home by the occupation forces in exchange for documents relating to their activities, and especially on research into untraceable toxins. When the Tokyo bank murders occurred the police were inclined to search for an individual with a military medical service background. Fears that this would bring to light matters which they preferred should remain secret led the occupation forces to initiate a cover-up and Hirasawa became the scapegoat.

When Hirasawa's death was recorded in 1987 his adopted son declared he would devote his life to proving his father's innocence. Japan's Prime Minister offered his condolences to the family and prayed that Hirasawa might rest in peace. The dead

man's lawyer swore revenge, and the newspapers reprinted details of one of the most mysterious cases in modern Japan.
[675, 868]

HOCH, Johann. Middle-aged Chicago packing-house employee whose exploits earned him the title 'The Stockyard Bluebeard'. This unprepossessing man married 2 or 3 times a year during his heyday, freeing himself by poisoning his wives, or by simply absconding.

Hoch advertised in a Chicago newspaper in December 1904: 'Wishes acquaintance of widow . . . object matrimony'. A 46-year-old candy-store owner, Julia Walker, replied—she became Mrs Hoch within a few days. Hoch talked of his investments and inheritance, but in the meantime he was short of funds and his wife withdrew all her savings.

Mrs Hoch was suddenly taken ill and died a month after her wedding. Hoch appeared grief-stricken, but 4 days later married his dead wife's sister, Amelia. He remarked, 'The dead are for the dead and the living for the living.'

A familiar pattern emerged, for Amelia withdrew her savings and made them over to her husband. She was lucky when Hoch simply disappeared. He was reported missing, and inquiries showed that he had similarly treated dozens of women, using various aliases.

In January 1905, after Hoch's picture had appeared in several newspapers, a New York boarding-house keeper told police that a man answering his description was lodging with her, and had offered marriage. Hoch was arrested, and when searched was found to be carrying a unique fountain pen. The device contained a white powder which Hoch at first alleged was tooth powder but later admitted, 'It's arsenic. I bought it intending to commit suicide.' Julia Walker's exhumed body was found to contain traces of arsenic.

A fantastic account of Hoch's philanderings was pieced together. He married 24 women between 1892 and 1905, and of these half had died suddenly with symptoms of acute illness, after making over their savings to their husband. Hoch admitted multiple bigamy, commenting, 'Marriage was purely a business proposition to me. When I found they had money I went after that.'

He was found guilty of murder at Chicago in May 1905 and was hanged on 23 February 1906.
[862]

HOFRICHTER, Adolph. Austrian army officer who took his revenge for not being promoted by sending poisoned nerve tonic to some of his fellow-officers.

In December 1912 several Austrian Army staff officers based in Vienna received unexpected gifts through the mail. The gifts were in the form of a box of capsules with an accompanying letter explaining they were a 'nerve strengthening remedy'. Most of the recipients threw this concoction which promised 'startling results' into the waste bin, except

Hofrichter: Officer, gentleman and murderer

Captain Richard Mader, who decided to give the remedy a try. Within seconds of swallowing one of the capsules he collapsed and died.

Analysis of the remaining capsules shopwed that they contained lethal quantities of potassium cyanide. Inquiries established that 12 officers had been sent boxes of capsules, and the one distinction that all these men shared was that they had recently been promoted. Thus the theory quickly developed that the sender of the capsules might be an officer who had failed to gain promotion, and who consequently bore a grudge. By a process of elimination, suspicion came to rest on 28-year-old Lieutenant Hofrichter, an infantry officer based at Linz, who had failed to gain the staff appointment it was known he desired. A search of his quarters produced a number of capsules and pillboxes which proved sufficient evidence to warrant his arrest.

There was public disquiet when it was learned that Hofrichter would be tried not by the civil courts but by court-martial and in secret. The lieutenant professed his innocence and, despite other circumstantial evidence, he could not be linked to any purchase of poison. What began to tell against him was the revelation that he led a secret life of debauchery, drugging young women as a preliminary to forcing his attentions on them. Under pretence of being a doctor, his ploy was to advertise for a governess in order to attract his victims.

The public sympathy and support he had enjoyed fell away at this unsavoury news and Hofrichter made a full written confession. The court-martial convicted him of murder and he was sentenced to death. On consideration that he was 'morally abnormal', his sentence was commuted to imprisonment and, on instructions from the Emperor of Austria, he served 20 years.
[*1014*]

HOLMES, H. H. Holmes, properly known as Herman Webster Mudgett, was America's first mass murderer, and admitted killing 27 people at his house in Chicago. He was a handsome man whose appearance made him a favourite with the ladies.

He first married in 1878 while still a student, and in 1886 contracted a bigamous marriage with Myrta Belknap. He took to fraud as a means of livelihood, and in 1888 worked in Chicago as a chemist in a drugstore. The proprietress disappeared in 1890, leaving Holmes in command of a business which thrived on sales of patent medicine.

Holmes lived in the flat above the store, sharing the premises with Icilius Conner, a jeweller, whose attractive wife Julia acted as Holmes's secretary. Opposite the drugstore was a large vacant plot which Holmes purchased with the intention of building a hotel. The design of the Gothic-style hotel with its 100 rooms and numerous turrets and battlements was supervised by a shifty character called Benjamin F. Pitzel. Completed in 1891, the hotel, regarded locally as a monstrosity, was christened 'Holmes's Castle'. Hundreds of guests stayed at Holmes's hotel, and many disappeared, including Julia Conner and her daughter.

An insurance fraud which resulted in the death of Pitzel took the police to the hotel, but Holmes had fled. He was finally caught in Philadelphia and charged with embezzlement and later with murder.

When police searched Holmes's hotel they found a veritable death house. There were air-tight

Holmes: Record of the arrest

rooms with gas inlets and in the basement, along with the bones of several female skeletons, were vats of acid, asbestos and steel-lined, windowless rooms containing trays of surgical instruments and instruments of torture. Some of the rooms had chutes connected to upper rooms which carried human cargoes to a gruesome death below.

At Holmes's trial in 1895, in which he conducted his own defence, a car mechanic told how he had worked for Holmes stripping flesh from bodies which he thought had come from the city mortuary. Holmes was found guilty of murder, and while awaiting execution confessed to 27 killings. He was hanged at Philadelphia's Moyamensing Prison on 7 May 1896.

[107, 108, 295, 383, 400, 693, 771, 903]

HOLT, Frederick Rothwell. Young British officer, invalided out of the army after suffering amnesia and depression in the First World War, who murdered his girl-friend.

In 1918 Holt returned to Lancashire, where he met Kitty Breaks. They fell in love, and despite her married status they lived together for nearly 2 years. On 24 December 1919 Kitty's body with bullet wounds was found on sandhills at St Annes, near Blackpool. Near by were a revolver and a pair of gloves belonging to Holt. There was also a clear set of footprints which matched the impressions of Holt's shoes. He was arrested and sent for trial at Manchester Assizes.

Sir Edward Marshall Hall, who defended Holt, suggested the accused was unfit to plead. He had a persecution mania, and complained that the police had sent dogs and germ-laden flies to his cell. The prosecution's case was that he had killed Kitty Breaks for her life insurance of £5000, and because he was tired of the girl.

Marshall Hall contested this view, reading from letters written by the accused to the girl, and clearly expressing tender feelings. The advocate made a powerful plea for Holt as a man who had suffered for his country, and who killed the woman he adored in a moment of uncontrollable impulse because he thought he would lose her.

Holt was found guilty and was sentenced to death. His case went to the Court of Criminal Appeal, and was accorded the distinction of being heard with additional evidence, but was dismissed, and Holt was executed on 13 April 1920.

[32, 488, 605, 649, 960]

HOOLHOUSE, Robert. Unusual case in which a man was convicted of murder and executed on slender evidence. Testimony which supported his innocence went unheeded, and no defence witnesses were called at his trial.

Margaret Jane Dobson and her husband had farmed at High Grange, near Wolviston in County Durham, for over 30 years. In 1933 they had an unpleasant dispute with the tenant of a labourer's cottage on their farm. As a result the Dobsons evicted the family, who moved to a village 4 miles away.

On 18 January 1938 the body of 67-year-old Mrs Dobson, stabbed and sexually assaulted, was found on a farm track. Among local persons questioned was 21-year-old Robert Hoolhouse who, with his parents, had been turned out of their cottage. Hoolhouse became a victim of circumstantial evidence—he had motive, there were scratches on his face, blood and hair on his clothes and he broadly fitted the description of a man seen near the farm. Within 36 hours he was arrested.

He was tried at Leeds Assizes in March 1938 and, although his defence contended that the prosecution had no case to go before a jury, it offered no evidence. The prosecution agreed that a footprint found by the body was not made by the accused, and an acquittal was widely expected. Nevertheless, the jury found him guilty, an appeal was dismissed, and a petition for a reprieve containing over 14 000 signatures was rejected. Robert Hoolhouse was hanged at Durham Gaol on 26 May 1938.

[314]

HOSEIN BROTHERS. Arthur, aged 34, and Nizamodeen, aged 22, convicted of murder, kidnapping and blackmail at the Old Bailey in 1970 in the McKay case, which failed to produce a body.

The two brothers, Indian Moslems born in Trinidad, bought Rooks Farm at Stocking Pelham in Hertfordshire in 1968. They kept calves, pigs and chickens. Arthur Hosein was known locally as 'King Hosein'. The brothers planned a kidnap of the apparently prosperous owner of a Rolls-Royce, which belonged to the *News of the World*, and was allocated to the newspaper's chairman, Australian millionaire Rupert Murdoch. The Hoseins followed the car to a house in Wimbledon which belonged not to Murdoch but to Alick McKay, deputy chairman of the newspaper.

On 29 December 1969 the brothers broke into the house and abducted Mrs Muriel McKay, thinking she was Mrs Murdoch. That evening Alick McKay received a phone call demanding £1 million within two days or 'we kill her'. During the next few weeks 18 phone calls were received from the kidnappers and 3 letters from Mrs McKay. On 9 January 1970, the editor of the *News of the World* was sent a letter demanding £1 million. There was then a letter directing McKay to a telephone box on the London–Cambridge Road where he was to leave the money in a suitcase. The instructions were carried out, but the case was not collected. Further phone calls alleged a double-cross, and issued more instructions. The kidnappers were seen in a car near where the ransom money had been left.

The car was traced to Arthur Hosein but there was no trace of Mrs McKay, though an exercise book used to write one of the ransom notes was found.

The brothers were arrested and sent for trial. They denied all knowledge of the charges, but fingerprint evidence tied them in with the threatening kidnap notes. Nizamodeen was clearly dominated by his elder brother, and admitted making inquiries about the Rolls-Royce. Sentences of life imprisonment for murder and various other terms for kidnapping and blackmail were passed. Mrs McKay's body was never found, and it was presumed to have been fed to the pigs at Rooks Farm.

[*101, 195, 223, 600, 713, 857*]

HUME, Brian Donald. A 39-year-old racketeer and murderer acquitted of a murder to which he later confessed.

A farm labourer in the Essex mud flats at Tillingham on 21 October 1949 found a water-sodden bundle. When he examined his find he uncovered a headless torso clad in a silk shirt and underpants. The head and legs had been severed from a male body with a sharp instrument; stab wounds in the chest showing the probable cause of death. Fingerprints showed the dead man to be 46-year-old Stanley Setty, known as a receiver of stolen cars and a dealer on the black market.

Setty was last seen alive on 4 October, when he had taken over £1000 in car deals. One of Setty's friends was Donald Hume, an ex RAF airman who had been involved in various rackets. Police traced Hume's movements to 5 October, when it was learned he had hired a light aircraft at Elstree and flown off carrying two parcels.

Hume admitted hiring an aircraft, but said the parcels contained parts of a printing press used to print food-ration coupons. He elaborated his story, claiming that he was forced to dump the parcels at sea by 3 men. As he moved one of the parcels he said

it made a gurgling noise and it crossed his mind 'that it might be Setty's body', as he had read about the missing man in the papers. Hume was arrested and charged with murder.

The prosecution evidence at Hume's trial in January 1950 was insufficient to convict him. The jury failed to reach a verdict, and a new jury was sworn in. The judge instructed them to return a not guilty verdict, and Hume pleaded guilty to being an accessory and was sentenced to 12 years.

On his release in 1958 Hume, knowing he could not be charged again with murder, promptly confessed to Setty's murder in the *Sunday Pictorial*. He went to Switzerland, and on 30 January 1959 he robbed a bank in Zürich and while escaping shot and killed a taxi-driver. A Swiss court sentenced him to life imprisonment, and in August 1976 he was returned to Britain as insane and sent to Broadmoor.

[*4, 29, 83, 298, 311, 417, 451, 475, 487, 920, 961, 966, 986*]

HYDE, Dr Bennett Clarke. A 40-year-old doctor who married a niece of Thomas Swope, the Kansas City millionaire, and became his medical adviser.

Octogenarian Swope appointed an old friend, James Hunton, to administer his estate, which was to be divided up on his death among his nephews and nieces. He made a provision that if any of them died their share would be divided equally among the survivors. In September 1909 James Hunton fell ill, and was attended by Dr Hyde. Hunton died, and was followed shortly afterwards by Thomas Swope, who, according to the death certificate issued by Hyde, succumbed to apoplexy. Hyde immediately tried to be appointed administrator of the estate, but was rejected.

Swope's will was enacted and his estate divided, with Hyde's wife as one of the beneficiaries. Within a few weeks, 5 of the inheritors were struck down by typhoid. One of the nephews died, and the rest recovered. The family called in independent medical experts, who could not trace the source of the typhoid. Exhumation orders were granted in respect of Hyde's 2 patients, Hunton and Thomas Swope, and traces of strychnine were found.

On 9 February 1910 a Coroner's Jury returned a verdict of murder, and Hyde was sent for trial. The prosecution alleged that he had used both strychnine and cyanide to poison Hunton and Swope. This was a cunning plan, as the opposite effects of the two poisons would confuse the real nature of the symptoms. In murdering Swope's nephew, Hyde had infected him from a culture of typhoid germs which he had said was for bacteriological studies.

Hyde was found guilty of first-degree murder, and sentenced to life imprisonment. But after numerous appeals he was granted a second trial.

This ended as a mistrial, and a third trial jury failed to agree. As 3 trial juries had failed to secure a verdict, the defence asked for dismissal of the charges, and no further action was taken.

[*29, 315, 862*]

I

INGENITO, Ernest. Ingenito drifted into criminal company as a teenager, and was convicted of burglary. In 1950, aged 24, he joined the r. ks of mass murderers.

In 1947 he married Theresa Mazzoli, and they had 2 sons. The couple lived with the Mazzoli family in Gloucester County, and while Ernie got on well with his father-in-law, Theresa's mother nagged him continuously.

Ernie took to drink, and also had several mistresses. When Mike Mazzoli found out he turned him out. Ingenito made several attempts to see his children, but was refused.

On 17 November 1950 Ernie took two pistols and a carbine from his arsenal and walked to the Mazzoli home. Theresa answered his knock. He demanded to see the children, but she refused. Mike Mazzoli appeared, and Ernie gunned him down. Next he turned his gun on Theresa and wounded her, then went in search of Mrs Mazzoli, who, hearing shots, fled to her parents, who lived nearby. Ernie followed her. At the Poppi home he shot down 4 of the family, including a 9-year-old child, before finding Mrs Mazzoli, who had taken refuge in a closet. He killed her too.

Ingenito drove to Mintola, New Jersey, to the home of Frank Mazzoli, where he claimed 2 more victims. The reign of terror ended at midnight, when, surrounded by police, Ingenito attempted suicide. From hospital Theresa expressed a hope, 'I wish they would hang Ernie.'

In January 1951 Ingenito was tried for the murder of Mrs Mazzoli and sentenced to life imprisonment, which he served in the New Jersey State Hospital for the Insane at Trenton. In 1956 he was tried on 4 further murder counts, and given a life sentence for each. In all, Ernie Ingenito's night of vengeance cost the lives of 7 people.
[*693*]

ISSACS, Carl and Billy. Two brothers with their half-brother and a friend killed five members of a family in Georgia, USA, earning the newspaper headline 'Too evil to be called animals.'

The four men—recently escaped from prison—roamed the back roads of Georgia in a stolen car looking for opportunities to steal. On 14 May 1973 they spotted a mobile home parked in a clearing among cornfields near Donalsonville. They found the trailer unoccupied, but were disturbed by the approach of a jeep carrying the owner, Jerry Alday, and his father. The Aldays were held up at gunpoint and robbed before being pushed into one of the bedrooms where they were shot in the back of the head. Two other members of the family turned up at the trailer, each arriving separately and each being robbed and shot dead. Finally, Mary Alday was abducted by the killers and raped in nearby woods before being shot dead.

The 4 killers were captured a week later and news of the killings in the trailer inflamed public reaction. Billy Issacs, aged 16, testified for the prosecution to avoid a death sentence, and his account of what had taken place decisively proved the guilt of all who had taken part. His brother was sentenced to death and the other two, tried separately, also received death sentences.
[*457*]

J

JACK THE RIPPER. Celebrated series of 5 unsolved murders in Victorian London in 1888. The anonymous killer gained his nickname from the unparalleled ferocity of his crimes—his prostitute victims had their throats cut and their bodies ripped open in sexually motivated killings. The down-at-heel victims were lured into secluded corners of London's East End after nightfall and butchered without sign of struggle. The murderer's clean escape after each killing suggested he was familiar with the intricate maze of East End streets.

The murders occurred within a 3-month period, and ended as abruptly as they began. They inspired comment from Queen Victoria, stirred England's social conscience about poverty in the East End of London, caused a furore in the Government and frustrated the Metropolitan Police Commissioner to the point of resignation. Many incidents added to the sensation of the murders—persons suspected of being the murderer were hounded in the streets, bloodhounds were used with farcical results and letters purporting to have been sent by Jack the Ripper were received by a London news agency. A prominent citizen of the East End, George Lusk, received a letter 'From Hell' accompanied by a piece of kidney which the writer explained, 'I send you half the kidne I took from one woman . . . tother piece I fried and ate . . .'

Probably more has been written about Jack the Ripper than about any other murderer; theories of

Jack the Ripper: The remains of Marie Kelly

Jack the Ripper: Is this the Ripper's grave at Wimborne, Dorset?

identity are legion. The murders have been dramatized in plays, films, books, ballet and television. Jack the Ripper has become a standard by which other murderers, such as *Peter Kürten*, are judged.

Many identities have been suggested for the Ripper, including *Neill Cream*, *George Chapman* and *Frederick Deeming* from the ranks of known criminals, and also Dr Alexander Pedachenko, the Duke of Clarence, Dr Stanley, J. K. Stephen, M. J. Druitt and Sir William Gull from the realm of speculation. Theories concentrating on the Ripper's background have centred on doctors, midwives, slaughtermen, Black Magicians and Freemasons.

After the double murder on 30 September 1888, a message, presumed to have been written by the Ripper, was found chalked on a building near the murder scene: 'The Juwes are the men that will not be blamed for nothing.' The Police Commissioner ordered this to be wiped clean before it could be properly recorded, and thereby instigated lasting controversy. A recent theory suggests that this message was part of a Masonic plot involving Lord Salisbury and Sir William Gull in which ritual killings were carried out as a cover-up to the scandal of the Duke of Clarence and his bastard child.

Another theory arose from Sir Melville Macnaghten's contention that Jack the Ripper committed suicide on or about 10 November 1888. The suicide angle is one of the main planks in a story naming a barrister (later schoolmaster), Montague John Druitt, who was known to have drowned in the Thames, as the mysterious killer.

The centenary of the Ripper murders in 1988 stimulated a number of new books but little in the way of new evidence. Dr Roslyn D'Onston, a dabbler in black magic first suggested as a Ripper suspect in 1930, emerged as a fully fledged candidate. Saturation press coverage of the subject turned up a hitherto unknown snippet in the form of a note scribbled in a book of memoirs by Chief Inspector Donald Swanson, a serving police officer at the time of the murders. He noted for posterity that the man suspected by the police was called Kosminski.

[*50, 164, 208, 230, 242, 271, 277, 412, 416, 459, 506, 516, 540, 563, 626, 654, 655, 706, 800, 835, 876, 886, 934, 972, 994, 1003, 1008*]

JACKAL PIT MURDER. See VAN WYK, Stephanus

JACOBSON, Howard Buddy. Millionaire horse-trainer and property dealer convicted of murder in a New York penthouse in 1980. Jacobson led a somewhat bizarre life which came to light when his girl-friend Melanie Cain, a leading model, decided to escape from his obsessive behaviour. She moved from his apartment in the fashionable penthouse which he owned in Manhattan, across the hall to live with Jack Tupper, a charming if unsuccessful man.

The love triangle thus established was to have a disastrous outcome. Jacobson continuously harassed his ex girl-friend as a means of persuading her to return to him. He also offered money to Tupper if he would withdraw from his relationship with Melanie and leave town. The tension-filled *ménage à trois* continued for several months, and was brought to a head on 6 August 1978, when Tupper was found dead.

Melanie left Tupper asleep in their apartment when she went out for a business meeting. She returned at midday to find Tupper missing, but every indication that he had left against his will; there was blood on the elevator door and wet patches on the carpet. At about 4.30 p.m. that afternoon firemen attending a call at a piece of wasteland in the Bronx found a charred wooden crate from which protruded a human leg. Jack Tupper's body, bludgeoned, knifed and shot, had been padlocked into the crate, which had been soaked with gasoline and set alight. The bus driver, who had reported the fire, saw 2 men at the scene who immediately ran off towards a yellow Cadillac, the registration number of which he gave the police. A call was put out for the car which was stopped on the Bruckner Expressway; Buddy Jacobson and his companion, Sal Prainito, were arrested.

Jacobson told police that Tupper dealt in drugs and was killed in a fight between rival gangs. He claimed that Tupper was attacked in the hallway of the apartment house and that Melanie sought his help. As he did not think it sensible to harbour the body of a known drug-dealer, he enlisted Prainito's help to dispose of the corpse.

Jacobson and his accomplice were charged with second-degree murder and appeared on trial in January 1980. The case was accorded large head-lines in the New York newspapers, and sensation piled on sensation when Jacobson managed to escape from custody between verdict and sentence. Prainito was found not guilty but Jacobson was convicted, although he slipped his captors a second time and escaped from the Brooklyn House of Detention. In June 1980 he was sentenced in his absence to a minimum of 25 years' imprisonment.

Jacobson took a new identity in Des Moines, Iowa, and spent a great deal of time on the telephone trying unsuccessfully to persuade his friends to send him money. Otherwise he drove about more or less aimlessly from state to state and was finally arrested in California, 6 weeks after his great escape. He continued to thwart the authorities with his eccentric behaviour, making long telephone calls to *The New York Times* which printed some of the details. He made a further attempt to gain his freedom in 1981 from the prison in which he started to serve his 25-year sentence at Clinton, near the Canadian border.

[*397, 628, 701*]

JACOBY, Henry Julius. Youth hanged for the murder of Lady White in a case compared with that of *Ronald True*. An argument ensued on the question of whether there were 2 kinds of justice, depending on the wealth and status of the accused and their victims.

Lady White, 65-year-old widow of a former London County Council Chairman, was found dying from head wounds in her London hotel bed on 14 March 1922.

There was no sign of robbery or a struggle, and no traces of anyone having forced an entry—there was every sign of someone inside the hotel having made the attack. An 18-year-old pantry boy, Henry Jacoby, offered various theories regarding the murder. He gave false details about his background, and when he was searched detectives found two blood-stained handkerchiefs. In a statement he described his intention to steal from

guests' bedrooms, when he had taken a hammer with him to 'use if necessary'. He found an unlocked door and entered the room—the woman in bed woke up, and in a panic he hit her with the hammer and fled downstairs, later washing the tool and wiping it dry with his handkerchiefs.

Jacoby was charged with Lady White's murder, and tried at the Old Bailey in April 1922. He gave evidence that he thought the person inside the hotel bedroom was an intruder. When he found out what he had done he made false statements.

The judge advised the jury that if the blows were struck to inflict grievous bodily harm, and the victim died as a result, then the assailant would be guilty in law of murder.

Jacoby was found guilty, and a recommendation to mercy was made on account of his youth. Nevertheless, he was hanged at Pentonville Prison on 5 June 1922. Jacoby's hanging was made the more poignant in the public eye as it came 3 days before murderer Ronald True was found to be insane.

[*133, 695, 716, 745, 798*]

JEGADO, Hélène. Illiterate Breton peasant woman in her late thirties who affected an air of piety in the wake of 23 murders by arsenical poisoning.

Jegado worked as a maid in the homes of various clergymen. She was dismissed from several jobs for stealing, and although involved in a number of deaths always showed such profound grief that she was never suspected.

In 1850 she took a job with Théophile Bidard, a university teacher at Rennes. A junior servant fell ill and died, after being nursed by Jegado. The dead girl meant so much to her, said Jegado, that rather than let her employer replace her she would do the extra work herself.

In due course another girl, Rosalie Sarrazin, joined Professor Bidard's household. He warned her against being dominated by Jegado, but the two women were on very good terms. Soon this amicable relationship broke down, and the split grew when Rosalie was given the task of maintaining the household accounts, Jegado's illiteracy only allowed her to look on with envy. In the summer of 1851 Rosalie was taken ill with stomach pains and vomiting, and died in July.

Magistrates and the police called on Bidard in connection with the girl's death, and were admitted by Hélène Jegado, who declared 'I am innocent', to which one of the magistrates replied, 'Of what? Nobody has accused you.'

Jegado was arrested and tried at Rennes in December 1851. She was accused of 3 murders and 3 attempted murders. Her possession of arsenic was not proved, and no clear motive was established apart from theft and possible jealousy. But her long association with suspicious illness, which included 23 fatalities, was enough. She was found guilty, and guillotined.

[*388, 436, 1011*]

JENKINS, Charles Henry. See
ANTIQUIS MURDER

JONES, Arthur Albert. Child murderer, like *Frederick Nodder*, tried first for a lesser offence and, with fresh evidence brought to bear, sent for trial a second time, but on a charge of murder.

A 12-year-old girl, Brenda Nash, was returning home with a friend at about 10.00 p.m. on 28 October 1960. They parted company about a quarter of a mile from her home at Heston, Middlesex. She was not seen alive again except by her abductor, who strangled her and left her body in a Hampshire copse, to be found on 11 December.

An assault on a girl had taken place in September in the same area, but the assailant had released her, and she gave information which led police to think that this man might also have murdered Brenda Nash. The man drove a black Vauxhall car, and had a liking for peppermints.

The police interviewed all owners of black Vauxhalls—some 5000—registered in Surrey and Middlesex between 1951 and 1954. These included Arthur Albert Jones, whose description matched that given by the girl—he also kept peppermints in his car. On the day after Brenda Nash's body was discovered, a young woman hairdresser in London's West End told police that a fellow-employee had told her that her uncle fitted the description of the wanted man, and he had asked her to provide an alibi for 28 October. Jones was taken in for questioning on 28 December. He told police that on the occasions in question he had been with prostitutes.

Jones was tried in March 1961 for assaulting a girl in September of the previous year, and was sentenced to 14 years' imprisonment. While Jones was serving the sentence for assault, a convict told a prison officer that he had said that he had killed the girl, and this, coupled with new evidence identifying Jones as the man seen with Brenda Nash on the night she went missing, was sufficient to reopen the case. Now the charge was murder, and it took

the jury only 7 minutes to find Jones guilty. He received a life sentence.

[*312, 484, 509, 599*]

JONES, Harold. A 15-year-old boy twice tried for murder.

On 5 February 1921 the 8-year-old Freda Burnell, who lived in Abertillery, was sent to a local seed merchant. She was served by the young assistant, Harold Jones, and was not seen again until her body was found next day near the shop. She had died of shock and partial strangulation. An attempt at rape had also been made.

During the police inquiry a handkerchief belonging to the dead girl was found in the shed at the back of the seed shop. Harold Jones was arrested and tried at Monmouth. He was found not guilty. There were cries of public jubilation.

Fourteen days after his acquittal, the body of 11-year-old Florence Irene Little was found in the attic of Jones's home. He confessed to murdering the girl on 8 July, 'the reason being a desire to kill'. He cut her throat with a kitchen knife and hid the body, leaving tell-tale smears of blood around the trap-door. The girl's clothes were torn, and she had been sexually assaulted.

Tried at Monmouth Assizes in November 1921, self-confessed murderer Harold Jones was sentenced to be detained during His Majesty's Pleasure. He was tried before his sixteenth birthday, and therefore was not eligible for the death penalty. Jones made a statement in which he confessed to the earlier murder of Freda Burnell, of which he had been so gloriously acquitted.

[*1000*]

JONES and HULTEN. An 18-year-old strip-tease artiste, Elizabeth Marina Jones, met American GI Gustav Hulten in London, and they committed the Cleft Chin murder.

A 34-year-old cab-driver, George Edward Heath, was found shot at Staines, on 7 October 1944. Tyre-tracks on a grass verge near the body were made by his private-hire Ford V8 car. Two days later a police officer spotted the car parked in London's Fulham Palace Road. An American army officer eventually emerged from a near-by house and got in. He was apprehended, and found to be armed. At first he gave his name as Richard John Allen, but after being interviewed by the American Army Criminal Investigation Department he corrected it to Private Karl Gustav Hulten, absent without leave and in possession of a stolen pistol. Hulten said he had spent the night of

Judd: 'The Tiger Woman

Judd: The trunk and
its contents

the murder with a girl-friend, Georgina Grayson.

'Georgina Grayson' (the stage name used by Elizabeth Jones) said she had met Ricky on 3 October and on subsequent days. Hulten continued to deny the shooting, but the girl told an acquaintance that she had been questioned, adding, 'If you had seen somebody do what I have seen done, you wouldn't be able to sleep at night.' This was reported, and in a further statement Jones revealed that Hulten shot the cab-driver and told her to go through the dying man's pockets. Hulten had told her he was a Chicago gangster. After admitting the killing he said he was incited by the girl who wanted 'to do something exciting'.

The US Government waived its rights under the Visiting Forces Acts and requested the British Government to try Hulten in a British court. Jones and Hulten were committed for trial at the Old Bailey, where in January 1945 both were found guilty, in Jones's case with a recommendation to mercy. Two days before the date fixed for execution Jones was reprieved, but Hulten, aged 22, was hanged on 8 March 1945.

[*3, 171, 611, 691*]

JUDD, Winnie Ruth. Dubbed 'The Tiger Woman' by the press, 26-year-old Winnie Judd was convicted of the sensational Phoenix Trunk Murders.

Winnie, married to Dr William Judd, worked in a Phoenix medical clinic. She was friendly with a colleague, 27-year-old Agnes LeRoi, and another girl, Hedvig Samuelson, with whom she shared an apartment.

Gunshots and screams were heard coming from the apartment on 16 October 1931. The next morning Mrs LeRoi did not arrive for work, and Winnie Judd was late. That night Winnie called a delivery company to the apartment, and a heavy trunk was moved out.

On 18 October Winnie went by train to Los Angeles with two trunks. On arrival station staff noticed that a dark fluid was dripping from one of them (See *Maria Vere Goold*). Mrs Judd was asked to open it, and promptly disappeared. When an offensive odour became evident, the baggage was opened. The large trunk contained the body of Mrs LeRoi, and the smaller one held dismembered parts of Miss Samuelson's body.

On 23 October, following a plea from her husband, Winnie gave herself up to the police at a Los Angeles funeral parlour. A letter written to her husband was found, and this was a virtual confession.

'The Tiger Woman' was put on trial. Her account of what happened was that during an argument with the two girls Miss Samuelson pulled a gun and shot Winnie in the hand. In the ensuing struggle Winnie shot both girls. Winnie was said to have had an accomplice, and she named him as Carl Harris, a Phoenix businessman. She claimed to have killed in self-defence and to have enlisted Harris's help. He was alleged to have cut up the body of Miss Samuelson.

Winnie was found guilty and sentenced to death. Harris was charged with being an accessory, and Winnie gave hysterical evidence at the hearing. The charge was dismissed, and 10 days before execution, Winnie was granted a retrial. Again she behaved hysterically, but this time the jury found her insane and she was committed to the Arizona State Hospital for the Insane. During her detainment Winnie absconded 7 times, including one escape which lasted 6 years. She was constantly in the news until her parole in 1971.

[*241, 400, 775*]

K

KALLINGER, Joseph. Philadelphia shoemaker whose degeneration from simple eccentricity to violently psychotic behaviour was catalogued by Flora Rheta Schreiber in a memorable book called *The Shoemaker*. Kallinger was a collector of junk on the theory that such discarded articles as old washing machines and vacuum cleaners would come in handy one day.

He entertained some weird ideas about controlling his behaviour by fitting wedges inside his shoes which would harmonize the angle of his feet to his brain function. By achieving this state of harmonization, he believed he could solve any problem, and claimed that he received commands from both God and the Devil. He also developed a persecution complex and turned his house into a fortress, which he called 'Joe Kallinger's Castle', so that he could evade those who spied on him. With the help of his children, he dug a 20-feet-deep hole in the basement and created a cavern which he used as a retreat.

During the early 1970s he regularly hallucinated and came to believe that God had ordered him to destroy mankind. He enrolled his 12-year-old son into his scheme and during 1973 and 1974 father and son committed several robberies. On 7 July 1974 he abducted a boy from a recreation centre in Philadelphia and murdered him after carrying out acts of sexual mutilation. On 28 July he drowned one of his sons after taking out life insurance worth $69,000. These acts of violence were followed by several burglaries which culminated on 8 January 1975 with the murder of a young woman whom he had taken hostage. He fled the scene of the crime, leaving the remaining hostages unharmed, and was easily captured.

Kallinger and his son (now aged 14), who had been present during all these acts of violence, were charged with kidnapping, robbery and assault. The boy was treated as a delinquent, while murder was added to the charges faced by his father. Kallinger was tried on the lesser charges in 1975, and was convicted despite psychiatric evidence diagnosing him as schizophrenic and paranoid.

In 1976 he was tried for murder, and by this time he was claiming to communicate directly with God. When he appeared in court he foamed at the mouth and spoke in an incomprehensible language. His own counsel described him as 'totally crazy', while the prosecution, although believing him to be psychotic, nevertheless thought he was not mentally ill in that he could distinguish right from wrong. The jury found him guilty, and he was sentenced to a minimum of 42 years in prison.

While awaiting trial Kallinger had turned completely to 'religion' and it was at this time that he was visited by Professor Schreiber, who researched his background in preparation for her outstanding study of the man. He was an adopted child who had been subjected to sexual abuse by his parents. They tormented him with the belief that he had been castrated so that he would be able to avoid the wickedness of sex. This sad upbringing was argued as a major cause for his later mental degeneration and hostility towards society.

[*823*]

KEMPER, Edmund Emil. The 25-year-old 'Co-ed killer' who terrorized Santa Cruz County, California. With an IQ of 136, signifying 'superior intelligence', this 6 foot 9 giant perpetrated horrific perversions on his 8 victims before finally giving himself up.

Kemper displayed sadistic tendencies at an early age, and fantasized about death. At the age of 10 he developed a liking for torturing animals and despite his size, was psychologically unable to stand up to other children's jibes and games. (See also *Patrick Mackay*.)

At the age of 15 he was sent to stay on a farm with his grandparents. His mother had warned against this, by saying that the boy was 'a real weirdo' and likely to kill someone. On 27 August 1964 he took a .22 rifle, raised it to his grandmother's head and pulled the trigger. He said aftewards, 'I just wondered how it would feel to shoot grandma.' He then shot his grandfather, and telephoned his mother telling her that both were dead.

Kemper was sent to Atascadero State Hospital for treatment in December 1964, having been judged insane. He was released into the care of the California Youth Authority in 1969, and, against the advice of the hospital, was sent to live with his mother at Santa Cruz. He took labouring jobs, bought a car and began a collection of knives and guns. He also took an interest in the girl student population, the so-called co-eds, at the Santa Cruz campus of the University of California.

He roamed the highways, stopping to give girl hitch-hikers lifts in his car. During 1970–1 he claimed to have given lifts to some 150 girls. It was all part of a plan which he began to put into operation in 1972, when co-eds began to disappear. There was panic when the mutilated remains of an 18-year-old girl were found, and murder was added to the list of disappearances, assaults and rapes.

In April 1973 Edmund Kemper calmly phoned the police and told them who he was. He related a horrifying catalogue of sadism, murder, mutilation, necrophilia and cannibalism. He admitted killing 6 co-eds, graphically relating details of dissection, decapitation and burial. He attempted sexual intercourse in some instances on the dead bodies, and admitted sexual excitement at the act of decapitation. Kemper had just killed his mother with blows from a hammer and had choked her friend, later decapitating her body. He was arraigned at Santa Cruz in April 1973 on 8 counts of first-degree murder. Kemper, who had said of his victims, 'They were dead and I was alive. That was the victory in my case', asked for the death penalty, but the court sentenced him to imprisonment for life.

[*174*]

KENNEDY, William Henry. See BROWNE and KENNEDY

KENT, Constance. A 21-year-old girl who confessed to the murder of her half-brother 5 years before.

During the night of 29 June 1860 4-year-old Francis Savile Kent was taken from his cot in his parents' home at Road, Wiltshire. His body was found the next day in the outside privy with his throat cut, but death was perhaps caused by suffocation. The Kent family consisted of three girls and two boys, all over 15 years of age, by Mr Kent's first wife, and two girls and a boy, all under

5, by the second Mrs Kent, who was pregnant at the time. All the family and 3 servants were in the house but the noiseless nature of the abduction and no housebreaking signs suggested that the murderer was one of the household.

There was no obvious motive, and a vital piece of evidence, a blood-stained nightdress, was lost by the police. This garment, hidden in the boiler flue, was probably not Constance's, but suspicion fell upon her. The girl was arrested and charged with murder, but on 27 July was released by the magistrates on her father's bond of £200. Two months later Elizabeth Gough, the Kents' nurse, was arrested and despite 'grave suspicion against her' she too was released.

Constance did not get on well with her stepmother, and entered a convent at Dinan in France where she stayed for 2½ years. She returned in August 1863 and went to St Mary's Convent at Brighton. Due to her now deep religious beliefs, she confessed her guilt to the Rev. Arthur Wagner during Easter 1865.

Constance was sent for trial at Salisbury Assizes. She pleaded guilty, and was sentenced to death in a brief hearing on 21 July without a single witness being called.

Her sentence was commuted to life imprisonment and she was released in 1885, dying in 1944. [*2, 29, 35, 87, 120, 123, 128, 141, 181, 347, 374, 419, 500, 660, 722, 780, 783, 850, 879, 900, 933, 989*]

KING, Dr William Henry. Amorous doctor whose fraternization with his female patients caused him to poison his wife.

King married in 1855 and graduated at Philadelphia with a medical degree in March 1858. He set up in practice in Brighton, Ontario, and soon became a successful and popular physician, especially with his female patients, of whom one in particular, 20-year-old Melinda Vandervoort (called by him a 'sweet little sugar lump of good nature'), fell for his charm.

It was said that King ill-treated his wife, Sarah, and now he cruelly told her that she was suffering from an incurable illness. Sarah was taken ill with severe abdominal pains in October 1858, which his prescriptions only seemed to make worse. Sarah's father called in a second doctor, whom King fobbed off by saying his wife was pregnant. After 3 weeks of distressing illness Sarah died, and Dr King was apparently grief-stricken.

Sarah's mother, while attending her daughter's sick-bed, discovered a love letter written to King by Melinda Vandervoort. When it became known that King had bought arsenic 2 days before his wife's illness, the Coroner was notified. An exhumation order was granted, and 11 grains of arsenic were found in the stomach.

An inquest found King guilty of murder, but he promptly absconded, and was quickly arrested.

The trial of Dr King in April 1859 at Cobourg Assizes was dominated by the medical profession. Twelve doctors gave expert testimony, and numerous others attended as observers. The scientific details of arsenical poisoning were argued, the defence suggesting that the arsenic found in Mrs King's stomach might have been introduced there while the body was being handled for the post-mortem. King maintained he had not poisoned his wife, but he was found guilty and sentenced to death. His confession was published in 2 Toronto newspapers, and he was hanged on 9 June 1859.

[153]

BUTCHER OF KINGSBURY RUN. 'The Mad Butcher of Kingsbury Run' terrorized the city of Cleveland in Ohio, USA in the 1930s with 10 brutal murders which remain unsolved.

Kingsbury Run was a tract of wasteland through which ran the railway line linking Cleveland and Pittsburgh. The area was strewn with refuse and old junk and was uninviting except for children seeking an adventure playground and adults bent on criminal pursuits. It was there on 23 September 1935 that some children found the bodies of two men who had been beheaded and castrated. The severed heads and missing organs were later found nearby.

One of the bodies was identified as that of Edward Andrassy, a petty criminal with a record of perverted behaviour. Four months later another mutilated body was found in the neighbourhood of Kingsbury Run, that of a local prostitute. During the summer of 1936 a body with the head severed was found in the Run, and public disquiet reached the point where people would not venture out at night. The police seemed powerless, and all that was known was that the killer's victims tended to be drawn from the poorer sections of the community, that both sexes were at risk and that the clean knife-cuts suggested the work of a butcher.

During the next 20 or so months another 6 victims fell to the 'Butcher of Kingsbury Run' before, like the murders of *Jack the Ripper*, the killings suddenly stopped for no apparent reason. The last in the series occurred on 8 April 1938, but speculation continued as to the likely identity of the perpetrator. Some thought he was a hobo who rode the railway tracks looking for his prey, others thought the killer was a woman. Any murder involving a headless corpse was laid at his door, as were 13 unsolved murders which had occurred earlier in Pennsylvania and another 5 unsolved killings in Pittsburgh in the early 1940s. Speculating about the identity of the 'Butcher' remained a favourite pastime, but the cloak of anonymity could not be removed.

[750, 772]

KISS, Bela. Tinsmith from the Hungarian village of Czinkota who disappeared in 1914 leaving 24 murder victims in his wake and a mystery that has never been solved. Bela Kiss was called up to serve in his country's armed forces at the beginning of the First World War. The tinsmith had an air of mystery about him and was believed to practise witchcraft; what was known for certain was that he was a ladies' man. Answering the call to war, he locked up his house, using iron bars and padlocks to secure the windows and doors, and left Czinkota never to return again.

Two years later, in May 1916, police searching the district for supplies of hoarded petrol came across the locked house in Czinkota. Suspecting that the heavy security was to protect black-market supplies of some kind, the police forced an entry and searched the house. In the attic they thought they had found what they sought in the form of seven large metal casks supported on trestles. The close-fitting lid of one of the casks was prised off to reveal not the smell of petrol but the odour of death. Underneath some old clothes was the naked body of a woman with the marks of a strangler's rope on her neck. Each of the metal casks contained a corpse, and 17 more bodies were found buried in the garden and in nearby woodland.

Detailed searches of the house and its contents produced hundreds of pawn tickets for items of female clothing and jewellery. It became apparent that the owner of the house, like *Henri Landru*, had lured girls into his trap by means of newspaper advertisements offering his services as a matrimonial agent and fortune-teller. A picture was constructed of Bela Kiss, a man well known in Budapest on account of his promiscuous habits. He was identified by photographs found in his house, and the War Department confirmed the details of his call-up. But where was he?

According to military records, Kiss had died of fever while serving in Serbia. When the circumstances of his alleged death were closely examined it was shown that the man who died and was believed to be Kiss was too young, and did not answer his known description. The explanation appeared to be that Kiss had indeed been in hospital, and while there had exchanged identity discs with a fatally wounded comrade. Kiss continued his service using the dead man's name, and was thought to have been killed in battle. After the war he was said to have been spotted in Budapest, and in 1924 there was a report that he had joined the French Foreign Legion. In 1932 he was reported to have been seen in New York City, but the man from Czinkota who kept bodies in the attic was never traced and never brought to trial.

[94, 97, 296, 508, 595]

KIRWAN, William Burke. The Ireland's Eye tragedy resulted in a conviction and punishment for murder, but subsequent medical opinion has suggested that the victim died of natural causes.

In June 1852 Kirwan and his wife, Maria, took lodgings at Howth. He was a professional artist doing some local sketching, and his wife, a strong swimmer, enjoyed the sea bathing. On several occasions the couple visited the near-by island Ireland's Eye to pursue their respective interests.

On 6 September they set out on a trip to the island, being rowed there by a Howth boatman, who was to return at 8.00 p.m. Another couple visited the otherwise uninhabited island during the day, but left about 4.00 p.m. They offered Mrs Kirwan a seat on their boat but she declined, saying she would wait for her own boat.

Several people heard cries coming from Ireland's Eye at a point known as Long Hole. When the boat arrived at the island Kirwan was found alone. He said he had not seen his wife since about 6.00 p.m. A search was organized, and a boatman saw Mrs Kirwan on a rock at Long Hole. She was dressed in her bathing costume, and lying dead on a wet sheet.

Blood was issuing from a cut on her breast, and also from the ears. A verdict of 'found drowned' was reached, and she was buried. Doubts were heightened by the knowledge that Kirwan had been giving a great deal of his time and devotion to another woman, Miss Mary Kenny, who had borne him 7 children.

He was arrested and charged with murdering his wife. His trial was dominated by medical evidence. The doctor who examined the exhumed corpse concluded that death was due to asphyxia rather than drowning. The defence argued that the tragic death might have resulted from a fit induced by

entering the water with a full stomach. This would explain the cries which were heard, and was supported by the contention that Mrs Kirwan had suffered from such attacks. Against this was evidence showing that Kirwan had quarrelled with his wife and, on one occasion, threatened her with the words, 'I'll finish you.'

The prosecution's argument that Kirwan simulated drowning by asphyxiating his wife with a wet sheet resulted in a guilty verdict. Kirwan, who proclaimed his innocence throughout, was sentenced to penal servitude for life, and was released in 1879.

[120, 350, 469, 551, 558, 623, 748, 781, 783, 801]

KNOWLES CASE. Noteworthy case in which a man was tried and convicted of murder without the benefit of a jury.

Benjamin Knowles was Medical Officer of the Bekwai District of the Gold Coast territory of Ashanti in the 1920s. He and his wife Harriet lived a typical colonial life in a close-knit white community. Harriet Knowles, an ex music hall performer, was known as a scold, and she often violently berated her husband.

On 20 October 1928 the Knowleses held a lunch party in their bungalow. Among those present was Thorlief Mangin, the local District Commissioner. The party broke up about 2.30, and two hours later the Knowles's house-boy, Sampson, rushed over to Mangin's bungalow, saying he had heard a shot. Mangin went to see Knowles and asked if everything was all right—the doctor said it was.

The following day, Mangin with Dr Howard Gush visited the Knowles's bungalow. Knowles appeared, saying there had been a quarrel and his wife had beaten him with an Indian club. Dr Gush saw Harriet, who had an abdominal gunshot wound. She was taken to hospital, where she made a dying deposition, having been cautioned by her husband to 'tell the real truth'. She had put her husband's revolver on a chair and later, forgetting it was there, sat down on it. The weapon discharged accidentally as she was pulling it out from under her. The next day she died.

The story was not believed, and Dr Knowles was charged with murder, and in November was tried at Kumasi. The law of Ashanti allowed no counsel to act—the prosecution was carried out by the Commissioner of Police, and Knowles defended himself. There was no jury, and the proceedings were conducted by the Acting Circuit Judge of Ashanti. The judge decided that the evidence against Knowles was overwhelming, and he was accordingly convicted and sentenced to death.

This was later commuted to life imprisonment by the Governor of the Gold Coast, and Knowles wa. returned to England pending an Appeal to the King. This was heard in November 1929, and his sentence was quashed on the grounds that the trial judge had not considered the possibility of manslaughter.

[1, 9, 318, 379]

KNOWLES, Paul John. Multiple killer and rapist shot dead by an FBI agent in an attempt to escape from custody in November 1974. During the course of 4 months he had killed 18 times and had an extraordinary encounter with a London journalist who wrote about the insights she gained into his personality in a book called *Killing Time*.

Knowles was a teenage delinquent who turned into a small-time crook, and spent nearly half his life in prison. While he was serving a long term of imprisonment in Florida his case was championed by a woman whom he had befriended through correspondence, and he was released on parole in May 1974. He intended to marry the lady in question, but perhaps sensing a sinister trait in Knowles's character, she turned him down.

Two months later Knowles killed an elderly woman in Jacksonville in the course of robbery and followed this by murdering 2 young girls. His murderous rampage was now in top gear. In August he killed 3 times, and in September added another 5 victims to his tally. One of these was a man whom he encountered in a bar. After strangling him, he stole his car and made full use of his credit cards. Knowles kept on the move, driving from state to state in his stolen car, and in October he raped and strangled a mother and daughter in Marlboro, Connecticut. His technique was to drive up to a house picked at random and ring the door-bell. When the door was opened he gained entry at gun-point. He repeated this *modus operandi* in Woodford, Virginia, and then drove down to Florida.

Constantly on the move and still driving a stolen vehicle, Knowles appeared in Macon, Georgia, at the beginning of November. There he met a man in a bar and was invited back to his acquaintance's house for drinks. Knowles expressed his thanks by killing the man and his teenage daughter. Other victims followed, the complete number never being satisfactorily established, until he met Sandy Fawkes, an English journalist on a visit to the USA, on 8 November. He called himself Daryl Golden,

Knowles, Paul John: Multiple murderer and rapist

and in a hotel bar in Atlanta the man who had murdered twice on the previous day exercised a compelling charm over his new acquaintance.

Knowles and Fawkes spent 6 days and nights together, during which he hinted at being a murderer and spoke of tapes that he had recorded which could form the basis of a book about him. Despite his charm and fascination, Fawkes detected an evil streak in Knowles's personality, and they parted company after he pulled a gun on her. A few days later, and after committing 2 further murders, Knowles was arrested. He enjoyed a spell of short-lived publicity before being shot dead by an FBI agent after shedding his handcuffs and attempting to escape from police custody. He had told Sandy Fawkes during their brief acquaintance, 'I am going to be killed . . . within a year I shall be dead.' His forecast proved to be correct, and the 'Casanova Killer' (as some of the newspapers called him) died the same kind of violent death which he had meted out to at least 18 innocent people. Knowles was something of a personality stereotype for the 'serial murderer'; he had experienced an unhappy childhood, spending his formative years in foster homes. He lacked sexual accomplishment, dreamed of fame and fortune, but lapsed into petty crime and eventually found satisfaction in taking a terrible revenge on society.

[273, 583, 651, 996]

KRAY TWINS. Reginald and Ronald Kray, born on 24 October 1933, were twins. They established a Capone-style grip on London's criminal underworld in the 1960s. The Kray 'firm', as it was known, indulged in rackets, protection and violence which eventually led to murder.

The twins became professional boxers at the age of 17, and a year later were called up for National Service. They spent much of their time in military prisons, and were dishonourably discharged in 1954. They established themselves in an East End billiard hall which became a centre for their criminal enterprises. Ronnie, a self-confessed homosexual, was the dominant twin, and earned the nickname 'Colonel'. He studied Al Capone and the Chicago gangsters, and indulged in fantasies of violence and power. By 1956, with Reggie providing the business flair, the 'firm' became the supreme criminal set-up in London's East End.

In 1965 Reggie married, but it ended with the suicide of his wife in 1967. In an atmosphere of increasing violence the twins became involved in freeing Frank Mitchell, the 'mad axe man', from Dartmoor. His subsequent disappearance is still a mystery. The Krays were tried at the Old Bailey when a man, claiming to know that they had ordered Mitchell's killing, turned Queen's Evidence, but the twins were not convicted.

The Krays turned to gun-play, and in the feud with the rival Richardson gang Ronnie shot George Cornell dead in the saloon bar of the Blind Beggar public house. Then Reggie, consumed with bitterness after his wife's death, fatally stabbed Jack McVitie ('Jack the Hat') because he had threatened his brother.

A full-blooded but discreet police effort was mounted to secure charges against the Krays. The twins were arrested while in bed following a tip-off about a proposed gang killing. They were tried at the Old Bailey in 1969 for the double murder of Cornell and McVitie. At the age of 35, each was found guilty of murder and sentenced to life imprisonment of not less than 30 years.

In 1987 Charles Kray launched a campaign to free the twins after they had served 20 years of their sentences. At the time Ronnie was detained in Broadmoor Hospital and Reggie at Gartree Prison, Leicester.

[101, 233, 605, 620, 621, 733, 851, 928]

KÜRTEN, Peter. A 47-year-old German factory worker and mass murderer who expressed admiration for *Jack the Ripper*. Kürten was caught after a trail of murder which terrorized the town and earned him the title 'Monster of Düsseldorf'.

Kürten's reign of terror began in 1929, when he killed a 9-year-old girl and partially burned her body. There followed a series of sadistic sexual killings of children and young women. He used different methods—stabbing, strangulation and bludgeoning—and some victims survived and were able to describe their assailant.

The wave of attacks caused public hysteria in Düsseldorf reminiscent of that which shook London during the Ripper murders. In May 1930 Kürten was caught by chance. He accosted at Düsseldorf railway station a young woman who had travelled from Cologne to take up a new job. He took her to his lodgings, where he attempted to rape her. The girl resisted, and Kürten let her go when she assured him that she did not know the city well enough to know where he had taken her. She did not report the incident except to a friend in a letter which was incorrectly addressed and undeliverable. The letter arrived in the Post Office dead-letter file, where it was officially opened to return to sender. An alert official realized its significance and immediately notified the police. The girl directed them to the Mettmännerstrasse, home of the 'Düsseldorf Monster'.

Kürten, a mild-looking man, was described as vain by his wife, who had no idea that her husband was leading a double life. She said he loved children, attended church and was a keen trade unionist. Kürten confessed crimes to the police which were an orgy of sadism and perversion.

He was charged with 9 murders, and tried at Düsseldorf in April 1931. Kürten's life of sexual sadism was pieced together by professor Karl Berg, a noted psychiatrist, who stated that Kürten (who was sexually aware at a very young age) found fulfilment in acts of mutilation, stimulation at the sight of blood, humiliation of his victims and a sense of achievement in killing.

A defence plea of insanity was rejected, and Kürten was sentenced to death on all 9 counts of murder. He was guillotined at Cologne's Klingelpütz Prison on 2 July 1931, after eating a substantial meal and asking for second helpings. He expressed a hope that he might hear his blood gurgle when his head was cut off.

[80, 159, 232, 334, 383, 398, 601, 654, 944]

Kürten: The skulls of two of his victims

Kürten: The murderer's victim-location map

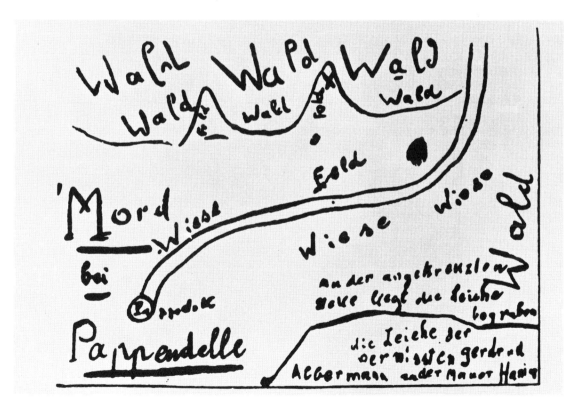

L

LABBÉ, Denise. Unusual case in which a 20-year-old mother at Blois, France, murdered her 2½-year-old daughter as a ritual sacrifice for her lover.

Denise Labbé took a job as a secretary at the National Institute of Statistics at Rennes and became socially involved with student life. She had numerous affairs, and had a child, Catherine, by a young doctor. She was devoted to her daughter, but continued her life much as before.

In May 1954 she met 24-year-old Jacques Algarron, a philanderer and an officer cadet at the Saint-Cyr military school. She quickly fell for him. He was considered a brilliant mathematician, but his mind was steeped in a kind of black philosophy which owed much to Nietzsche.

Denise came entirely under Algarron's domination. He considered himself an example of Nietzsche's Superman, and regarded women as subject to his will. He insisted that Denise sleep with other men, so that she could ask forgiveness from him. It was merely a prelude to a more sinister demand—he asked Denise to prove her love for him by murdering her daughter Cathy.

Denise, despite her love for her daughter, was so completely under Algarron's spell that she had to obey him. Twice she unsuccessfully tried to drown the little girl and finally, on 8 November, she carried out her evil task successfully. She drowned Cathy by holding her head down in a wash-basin filled with water, alleging that the child had drowned accidentally.

Friends were suspicious and the police questioned Denise. Finally, she admitted the murder: 'Yes, I killed my daughter but it was a ritual murder.' She implicated Algarron, who was promptly arrested.

The couple were tried in May 1955. Algarron was arrogant and cold-hearted; Labbé expressed her love for him and her sorrow over the child. Powerful speeches were made by counsel in what became a contest of ideas and oratory. The jury were out nearly 3 hours. They found Denise Labbé guilty with extenuating circumstances, and

Algarron guilty of having provoked a crime. Labbé was sentenced to penal servitude for life and Algarron to 20 years' hard labour.

[*341, 437*]

LACENAIRE, Pierre François. Intellectually minded murderer whose scholarly outlook has led to comparisons with *Thomas Griffiths Wainewright*, although his own crimes were poorly conceived.

Lacenaire was a gifted child, but also a compulsive liar and a cheat. He dabbled in poetry, but never fulfilled his early promise. He deserted from the army, was imprisoned for theft, took a job as a legal copyist and in 1834, at the age of 32, became a commercial traveller in wines and spirits.

In December 1834 a widow and her son were found stabbed and mutilated in their home in Paris. Two weeks later a bank messenger carrying a large sum of money was attacked by 2 men. The police inquiries led to a man called Martin François who admitted murdering the widow and her son, naming a man called Gaillard as his accomplice. Gaillard was in fact Lacenaire, whose whereabouts were divulged by Victor Avril, another accomplice already in police custody. Lacenaire readily confessed his part in the murders, and implicated François and Avril. His main intention seemed to be to revenge himself on them for their betrayal.

Tried at the Seine Assizes in November 1835, Lacenaire and Avril were sentenced to death, and François to penal servitude for life. Lacenaire's trial stimulated public interest, and his poetry was widely read and his opinions quoted. While in prison awaiting execution he wrote his memoirs, in which he bared his soul. He wrote of his sense of injustice, resulting from the favouritism shown to his elder brother. This frustration inspired his hatred of society, and he wrote, 'Society will have my blood, but I in my turn shall have the blood of Society.' A stream of intellectuals visited him in prison, and he readily admitted being urged to kill anyone who outshone him.

At the height of his fame Lacenaire met his death on the guillotine on 10 January 1836. A malfunction of the apparatus caused the descending blade to stick in its grooves; it was wound back again, and the head fell at the second attempt.

[*109, 239, 479, 535, 591, 722, 882*]

LACROIX, George. French escaped convict aged 35 who murdered an underworld character known as Red Max in a Soho flat.

On the morning of 24 January 1936 a man's body was found near the Hertfordshire town of St Albans. He was dead from 6 gunshot wounds in the chest and back, and he had been beaten about the face. His flashy clothing suggested a possible metropolitan origin. He was soon identified as Max Kassell, a Latvian in his late fifties, who was known as Red Max. Kassell operated in the international underground trading in drugs and women from a base in London's Soho.

Police inquiries led to information about a shooting incident at a flat in Soho on the night before Kassell's body was found. It appeared that Kassell owed £25 to a Suzanne Bertron who lived in the flat, and was the mistress of George Lacroix (also known as Roger Marcel Vernon), one of Red Max's former cronies. Lacroix offered to collect the debt for the girl. Kassell was lured to the flat, where, after an argument about money, he was shot several times by Lacroix. Badly wounded, he managed to break a window in a desperate bid to summon help.

After completing the murder, Lacroix dumped the body, and escaped with Suzanne Bertron to Paris. The couple were quickly rounded up by the French police, and a controversy ensued regarding a British request for Lacroix's extradition. The French authorities refused to give up either of the accused, and Lacroix was tried for murder and the girl for being an accessory after the fact in April 1937 at the Assize de la Seine.

British police officers gave evidence at the trial, and Lacroix was found guilty and sentenced to 10 years hard labour, followed by 20 years' expulsion from France. Suzanne Bertron was acquitted.

[*133, 384, 839, 928*]

LAFARGE, Marie. Young Frenchwoman who mixed in aristocratic circles and became entangled in a web of theft and murder.

In May 1839 the Vicomtesse de Léautaud reported the theft of a diamond necklace from her château at Busagny. Suspicion fell on a house guest, 23-year-old Marie-Fortunée Cappelle, a friend of the Vicomtesse, but to prevent embarrassment the Vicomte withdrew the charge.

Marie Cappelle had been at school with the Vicomtesse, but while her friend married a Vicomte from one of France's foremost aristocratic families, Marie had to be content to marry Charles Lafarge, a minor industrialist. What was more, Charles Lafarge was not what he seemed. His business was bankrupt, and he wanted a wife with a reasonable dowry. Marie lived unhappily with a surly mother-in-law in a rat-infested house at Le Glandier.

In December 1839 Marie bought some arsenic to kill the rats. Later she made some cakes to send to her husband, in Paris. He was unwell for a time, and returned to Le Glandier on 3 January 1840. He became ill again, and died on 14 January. Marie was suspected of poisoning her husband, and when arsenic was found in his stomach she was arrested.

When the Léautauds heard about this they pressed their accusation of theft. A search of Le Glandier produced the missing necklace, and Marie was tried for robbery in July 1840. Marie claimed that her possession of the necklace resulted from an agreement with the Vicomtesse. Despite this defence, Marie was given a 2-year suspended sentence.

In September 1840 Marie Lafarge's trial for murder took place at Tulle. Defence lawyers brought in leading Parisian toxicologist Professor Orfila, but unfortunately he found that Charles Lafarge had died as the result of criminally administered arsenic. Marie was sentenced to hard labour for life, but King Louis-Philippe reduced this to simple imprisonment, of which she served 10 years at Montpellier. She maintained her innocence, and wrote her memoirs. Released from prison in 1850, she died the following year.

[*211, 374, 375, 419, 818, 907, 932*]

LAMSON, Dr George Henry. English doctor who used his knowledge of a little-known poison to murder a relative for gain.

After serving as a surgeon in the Russo-Turkish war, Lamson returned to England, and in 1876 married a young woman who with her brothers had inherited a share of her parents' estate. Lamson had the use of his wife's money, and in 1880 bought a medical practice at Bournemouth. The previous year one of his brothers-in-law died and his inheritance passed into Lamson's hands by way of his wife.

Dr Lamson made two trips to America, after which he became so hard up that he pawned his watch and surgical instruments. He also set about money-raising in earnest, and his efforts centred on his 18-year-old brother-in-law, Percy Malcolm John, a cripple who lived at Blenheim House School at Wimbledon.

On 3 December 1881 Lamson visited Percy and they took refreshment with the school's principal. Lamson produced some ready-cut pieces of Dundee cake which he offered round. He also had some capsules, one of which he ostentatiously filled with sugar and gave to Percy as medicine. Lamson then left, saying he had to catch a train to Paris. Within ten minutes of his departure Percy was taken ill, and died later that night.

The police were called and Dr Lamson was sought for questioning. On 8 December he returned from Paris and appeared at Scotland Yard, where he was subsequently charged with murder.

Lamson, who was 29, was tried at the Old Bailey in March 1882. He was accused of administering aconitine, at that time a little-known vegetable poison. It was shown that Lamson had bought a quantity of the poison from a manufacturing chemist on 24 November. His administration of the poison was particularly brazen; in front of a witness he had given his brother-in-law a perfectly harmless capsule of sugar while the aconitine was conveyed on the pre-cut piece of Dundee cake in a method used in the following century by *Herbert Rowse Armstrong*.

Lamson was found guilty and executed at Wandsworth Prison on 28 April 1882 after confessing to the chaplain.

[*1, 87, 134, 141, 152, 231, 259, 332, 409, 414, 642, 722, 725, 795, 880, 917*]

LANCASTER CASE. A love triangle involving an airman ended in a murder trial and his disappearance on a long flight which remained a mystery for 29 years.

William Newton Lancaster had an undistinguished career as a First World War pilot. He married in 1919 and left the Royal Air Force in 1926. The following year he made a record-breaking 13 000-mile flight from London to Australia with 'Chubbie' Miller, Australia's top woman flyer. Although both were married, Lancaster and 'Chubbie' became lovers and flying

partners, spending the next 4 years together, mostly in America.

While Lancaster was in Mexico 'Chubbie', who had remained in Miami, fell in love with American writer Charles Haden Clarke and they wrote to Lancaster telling him of their marriage plans. In April 1932 Lancaster bought a revolver, returned to Miami and confronted Clarke. A quarrel ensued, and eventually all three participants retired to bed. Later Lancaster awakened 'Chubbie', telling her, 'Haden has shot himself.' Clarke died later of a head wound—a pistol was found lying on his bed, leaving suicide notes typed on Lancaster's machine.

Lancaster was arrested and tried for murder in Miami in August 1932. 'Chubbie' stood by him when she testified that Haden had said Lancaster was 'one of the finest men he knew'. Experts argued over the question of Clarke's wound being suicidal. Lancaster, who had denied the killing, was found not guilty. He and 'Chubbie' returned to England but their relationship had changed. In April 1933 Lancaster set off alone on an attempted record-breaking flight from London to South Africa. After a stop in North Africa he was reported missing.

In February 1962, 29 years later, a French patrol in the Sahara found Lancaster's body beside his wrecked plane. His log-book diary contained a record as he waited to die in the desert. He wrote of his love for 'Chubbie' and the last entry was made on the eighth day after he crashed, and exactly 12 months since Clarke's death.

[*49*]

LANDRU, Henri Désiré. France's infamous 'Bluebeard', family man, lover of roses, philanderer and murderer of 10 women and a boy.

Landru was a dealer in second-hand articles, furniture, toys and cars. He also perpetrated swindles, for which he received prison sentences. During the First World War he enticed widows by the prospect of matrimony, stripped them of any assets and then killed them.

He placed advertisements in the newspapers such as, 'Widower . . . with comfortable income, affectionate, serious . . . desires to meet widow with a view to matrimony.' He received nearly 300 replies to 7 such advertisements, and he carefully recorded the applicants' prospects in a note-book, with special reference to their financial status. Between May 1915 and January 1919, Landru murdered at least 10 women. He moved into the Villa Ermitage at Gambais—and quickly installed

Landru, Henri Désiré

a stove. The clouds of smoke and offensive smell produced by this apparatus caused little concern in a country district.

In 1919 a Mlle Lacoste asked the Mayor of Gambais to help trace a middle-aged widow who had disappeared after a visit to Gambais with a bearded man. The Mayor made inquiries when he had a similar request about another widow who had disappeared also with a bearded man, and the Villa Ermitage was mentioned. The owner of the house (known locally as M. Dupont) was no longer there, but the police hunted Landru.

When Landru was apprehended his notebook was found, with its damning implications. Among the meticulous details of his day-to-day spending were a list of 10 of the missing women, and notes of one-way train tickets to Gambais. At the Villa Ermitage ashes from the stove were sifted, and revealed bone fragments and teeth from human bodies.

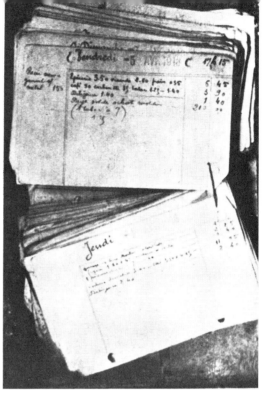

Landru: Trial exhibits including notebook

Landru: The stove from his villa

Landru was tried at the Court of Assize of the Seine-et-Oise in November 1921, charged with 11 murders. He denied everything, and completely calm in court, he thanked the experts, commenting, 'In acknowledging that I am sane they are thus proclaiming my innocence.' He was nevertheless found guilty and sentenced to death. He provoked extreme public reactions—reviled by many but swooned over by some. The 52-year-old bald-headed, red-bearded, unprepossessing Casanova had corresponded with 169 women, and was alleged to have associated in all with 283. He was guillotined on 25 February 1922.

Forty-six years later a newspaper announced his alleged confession. The words, 'I did it. I burned their bodies in my kitchen oven' were found scribbled on the back of a framed drawing which he was said to have given one of his lawyers before execution.

[*2, 45, 60, 100, 232, 244, 296, 298, 347, 368, 387, 435, 470, 504, 558, 609, 639, 669, 722, 850, 945*]

LANG, Donald. Illiterate, deaf-mute, black American whose involvement with 2 murders (separated by an interval of 6 years) taxed the legal system's capacity for fairness.

On 12 November 1965 the body of Ernestine Williams, a 38-year-old prostitute, was found in an alley in Chicago. She had been beaten and stabbed. It was soon established that the last person seen with her was 25-year-old Donald Lang, a deaf-mute who worked as a labourer for a freight-haulage company. Lang was questioned—with difficulty, due to his disability—and a competency hearing found him mentally unfit to stand trial. He was committed to a hospital for the criminally insane in January 1966.

In 1970 a second competency hearing was held and the case against Lang was dismissed. A free man, he returned to his family in Chicago. On 26 July 1971 the body of a murdered prostitute was found in a room at the Viceroy Hotel, Chicago. Earline Brown had been asphyxiated, and the person last seen in her company on the night of her death was Donald Lang. He was arrested and identified by two witnesses as the man seen at the hotel with Brown. Bloodstains on his clothes proved to match the blood group of the victim. The arraignment proved to be a repeat of what had happened in 1966; Lang was judged incompetent to stand trial. This opinion was overruled by an earlier Illinois Supreme Court decision in the intervening years that despite his disability, Lang had the right to a trial and could not simply be shut away in a mental institution.

Consequently, Lang was tried for murder in January 1972 and justice was seen to be done. The forensic evidence told against him and he was found guilty. The trial judge sentenced him to a minimum of 14 and a maximum of 25 years' detention in a special treatment facility.
[*719*]

LAURIE, John Watson. A 25-year-old pattern-maker from Glasgow who carried out robbery and murder on Goatfell, the high peak on the Isle of Arran.

On 12 July 1889 Laurie met Edwin Rose, a London clerk on holiday in Scotland, and they travelled together on the steamer from Rothesay to the Isle of Arran. Using the name John Annandale, Laurie invited the Englishman to share his lodgings on the island. They became friendly with two other young men, and walked and boated together. One of the men took Rose quietly to one side and advised him to be cautious of Laurie; he particularly warned him against going through with a climb of Goatfell which Laurie had proposed.

Rose decided to ignore the advice he had been given and the day after his two friends returned to the mainland, he and Laurie left their lodgings without saying where they were going. Their land-lady assumed they had simply absconded to avoid paying her. But when Rose did not return home as planned after his holiday his brother became alarmed, and on 27 July he arrived on the Isle of Arran. It was ascertained that Rose had set out to climb Goatfell on 15 July in the company of Laurie, whose lone departure from the island the following morning had been witnessed.

A search of the 2866-ft peak involving 200 islanders led to the discovery of Edwin Rose's body. He had been bludgeoned to death and robbed; his body was concealed by a mass of rocks piled over it. Laurie's movements were pieced together from information provided by local people. A shepherd had seen him coming down in an exhausted condition from Goatfell, unaccompanied, on the evening of 15 July. Earlier in the day, several fell-walkers had seen him with another man. When news broke of the murder on Goatfell, Laurie left his employment in Glasgow and moved to Liverpool. A large-scale hunt was mounted, and newspapers in Scotland and the North of England were filled with accounts of the murder. Laurie gloried in the publicity and wrote to the newspapers to tell them, 'I smile when I read that my arrest is expected hourly.' While he gloated the police stuck doggedly

admitted to Perth Criminal Asylum, where he died in 1930.
[*343, 454, 725, 787*]

LEE, Jean. The 32-year-old ring-leader of a trio in Australia who tortured and murdered an old man for gain.

Jean Lee was an attractive, red-headed girl who took up the life of a call-girl after marrying young. The Second World War brought Servicemen of several nations to Australia—and Jean Lee was a sought-after prostitute.

Like many of her kind, she teamed up with a man who protected her and shared in the profits. Jean's partner was a petty criminal named Robert David Clayton. After the War, the couple embarked on a blackmail technique whereby Jean enticed men into compromising situations only to be discovered by Clayton, 'her husband', who demanded compensation, usually an immediate cash settlement. In this they were joined in 1949 by Norman Andrews, who contributed violence.

On 7 November 1949 Jean Lee and her companions met a 73-year-old bookmaker, William George Kent, in a Carlton (NSW) hotel bar. The trio persuaded him to retire to his hotel room with Jean. She got him drunk, and tried to pick his pockets. But the old man, befuddled as he was, kept a tight hold on his money. In desperation, Jean hit him over the head with a bottle and tied him up. Clayton and Andrews rushed in to help.

They ripped out the trouser pocket where he had his bank roll and ransacked the room. They found nothing, so they tied his thumbs together with a bootlace, jabbed him repeatedly with a broken bottle and kicked him.

Police later found the terribly bruised and battered body of William Kent, still trussed up, in his room. The hotel supplied descriptions of two men and a woman, who the police had no difficulty in naming. The trio were arrested in Sydney after celebrating their triumph at a night club.

They were tried in March 1950 and were found guilty. An appeal against sentence of death was heard, and a retrial was granted on the grounds that a statement from one prisoner had been used to extract confessions from the others. The High Court confirmed the death sentences and they were hanged on 19 February 1951 at Pentridge Jail.
[*519*]

LEE, John. A 19-year-old servant who became a

Laurie: The Goatfell murderer writes to the newspapers

to their task and on 3 September an alert police officer spotted Laurie about to board a train at Ferniegair. He took to his heels, but was eventually cornered in a nearby wooded area where as the net closed he tried unsuccessfully to cut his throat.

John Laurie was tried for murder at Edinburgh in 1889. He admitted being with Rose on the Isle of Arran and confessed to robbing him although he denied committing murder. His defence counsel contended that the dead man sustained his injuries by a fall. Laurie's possession of some of Rose's belongings, his use of an alias and general evasion told against him, and he was found guilty on a majority verdict of the jury. Sentence of death was commuted to life imprisonment after he was assessed as being of unsound mind. He escaped from Peterhead Prison in 1893 but was recaptured and legend after surviving 3 attempts to hang him following a conviction for murder.

Lee was footman to Emma Keyse, an elderly and wealthy spinster who had been a maid to Queen Victoria. Miss Keyse ran an abstemious household and required her servants to attend daily prayers. On 15 November 1884 she was found dead, with her throat cut and her head battered, in the dining-room, which was on fire.

Circumstantial evidence pointed to Lee, who had served a sentence for theft, and it was thought that he had been angered by his employer's meanness in reducing his already poor wage because of some trivial offence.

Lee was tried and convicted for murder and received the death sentence. Preparations for the execution were made, and Berry the hangman placed the hood and then the noose over the condemned man's head and pulled the lever— nothing happened. The executioner furiously worked the lever to and fro but the trap refused to open. He even stamped on the doors of the drop without success.

Lee was removed and the apparatus was checked and tested with weights—it worked perfectly. Lee was replaced, the lever was pulled, but again the drop would not open. The humiliated executioner made further checks to his apparatus, and repeated the satisfactory test drop. The condemned man once more was stood on the scaffold and the lever was pulled—to the horror of all present, save Lee (who had dreamed that he would not hang), the trap still refused to budge. It was thought that heavy rains had so swollen the wood that when a weight was placed upon it the edges of the trap became firmly fixed.

John Lee was returned to his cell and reprieved within hours. He said, 'It was the Lord's hand which would not let the law take away my life. . . .' He spent twenty-two years in prison, and was released on 17 December 1907, then married and emigrated to America. 'The man they could not hang' died in the USA in 1933.

[32, 740, 993]

LEFROY, Percy. An unsuccessful 22-year-old journalist whose real name was Percy Mapleton. He murdered an elderly man for gain, and achieved the minor distinction of being Britain's second railway murderer after *Franz Müller*.

Isaac Frederick Gold, a 64-year-old Brighton retired merchant and dealer in coins, boarded a train to go home to Brighton on 27 June 1881 at London Bridge station. As the train entered

Lee, J.: 'The man they could not hang'

Merstham Tunnel passengers heard shots, and Mr Gold's body was later found lying near the entrance to Balcombe Tunnel. He had been shot in the neck and there were knife wounds in his body.

When the train arrived at Preston Park, a stop on the outskirts of Brighton, the ticket collector noticed a passenger alighting whose clothing was bloodstained, and with a watch-chain hanging from his shoe. The man was questioned. He said his name was Lefroy, and explained that there were 3 passengers in his compartment of the train. When the train entered Merstham Tunnel he

MURDER.
£200 REWARD.

WHEREAS, on Monday, June 27th, ISAAC FREDERICK GOULD was murdered on the London Brighton and South Coast Railway, between Three Bridges and Balcombe, in East Sussex.

AND WHEREAS a Verdict of WILFUL MURDER has been returned by a Coroner's Jury against

PERCY LEFROY MAPLETON,
whose Portrait and Handwriting are given hereon,—

and who is described as being 22 years of age, height 5 ft 8 or 9 in., very thin, hair (cut short) dark, small dark whiskers ; dress, dark frock coat, and shoes, and supposed low black hat (worn at back of head), had scratches from fingers on throat, several wounds on head, the dressing of which involved the cutting of hair, recently lodged at 4, Cathcart Road, Wallington, was seen at 9.30 a.m. 28th ult., with his head bandaged, at the Fever Hospital, Liverpool Road, Islington. Had a gold open-faced watch (which he is likely to pledge), " Maker. Griffiths, Mile End Road, No 16261."

One Half of the above Reward will be paid by Her Majesty's Government, and One Half by the Directors of the London Brighton and South Coast Railway to any person (other than a person belonging to a Police Force in the United Kingdom) who shall give such information as shall lead to the discovery and apprehension of the said PERCY LEFROY MAPLETON, or others, the Murderer, or Murderers, upon his or their conviction ; and the Secretary of State for the Home Department will advise the grant of Her Majesty's gracious PARDON to any accomplice, not being the person who actually committed the Murder, who shall give such evidence as shall lead to a like result.

Information to be given to the Chief Constable of East Sussex, Lewes, at any Police Station, or to

The Director of Criminal Investigations, Gt. Scotland Yard.

JULY 4th, 1881.

(4313)   Harrison and Sons, Printers in Ordinary to Her Majesty, St. Martin's Lane.

Lefroy: Police 'Wanted' Notice

heard a shot, and he was knocked out by a blow to the head. On recovering consciousness he found that he was alone.

Lefroy was searched and was found to be carrying some German coins of a type which it was later found Mr Gold dealt in. Lefroy was arrested but allowed to return to his Croydon lodgings with a police officer. He entered his lodgings by the front door, leaving his escort on the doorstep while he escaped through the rear. While in hiding he sent a telegram to a Mr Seal asking for wages, and he was traced and taken into custody.

Lefroy was tried at Maidstone Assizes in November 1881 and ably defended by Montagu Williams, but he was convicted and sentenced to death. He made a full confession the day before he was hanged on 29 November 1881.

[*349, 379, 554, 589, 933, 947, 969, 988, 1003*]

LEHNBERG, Marlene. Nineteen-year-old aspiring model who persuaded a coloured cripple to kill her lover's wife in what South African newspapers called the 'Scissors Murder'.

Marlene, a vivacious girl with a taste for glamour, worked as a hospital receptionist near Cape Town. There she met Chris van der Linde, a happily married man twice her age, and fell in love with him. He enjoyed her attentions, but did not want to break up his marriage. Marlene made it plain that she wanted to marry him, and in September 1974 she told Susanna van der Linde about the affair. When this failed to get a divorce Marlene said she was pregnant.

In order to break the stalemate, Marlene decided to kill Susanna, and enlisted the aid of 33-year-old Marthinus Choegoe, an impoverished coloured cripple. She promised him her car and a radio, and also, sex, if he would act as assassin. Choegoe struggled with an offer he could not refuse, and Marlene prompted him in a letter: 'If you think it will be better or quicker, then use a knife but the job must be done.'

After several abortive attempts to carry out his mission, Choegoe entered the van der Linde home on 4 November 1974 and stabbed Susanna repeatedly with a pair of scissors. Police inquiries soon led to Choegoe, who, with his distinctive limp, had been seen in the murder area. He readily confessed to the killing, and implicated Marlene Lehnberg.

They were tried for murder at Cape Town in March 1975, when argument centred round the question of whether Marlene had taken part in the actual killing—she said no, Choegoe said yes. The

girl's letter to Choegoe was cited as clear premeditation, and it was not believed that a one-legged man acting alone could have overpowered the victim. Both were found guilty with no extenuating circumstances, and sentence of death was passed on them. This was later commuted to terms of imprisonment.

[77]

LEONSKI, Edward Joseph. American GI based in Australia and dubbed 'The Singing Strangler' for murdering 3 women to 'to get their voices'.

In May 1942 Melbourne was shocked by 3 murders in 16 days—a holocaust which inspired reference to *Jack the Ripper* in the newspapers. On 2 May, Ivy McLeod was strangled on her way home. A week later, Pauline Thompson was found strangled in the street. On 28 May the killer claimed his third victim, Gladys Hosking, whose strangled body was also found in the street.

On the night of the last killing an American serviceman was challenged by a sentry at his camp guard-room. The GI was dishevelled and out of breath and his uniform was soiled. When he explained that he had fallen down in the park he was allowed to pass. When news of the Hosking murder broke the sentry told police of the incident. Detectives linked this to another incident reported by a woman who had been entertaining a GI in her flat some days previously. The man threatened to strangle her, but calmed down when she said she would call the police.

All US troops at the camp in question were paraded, and the Australian sentry picked out the soldier he had noticed on the night of the murder. He was a burly Texan, Edward Joseph Leonski. Leonski's tent mate told police that the Texan exhibited extremes of emotion and had told him, 'I'm a Dr Jekyll and Mr Hyde. I killed! I killed!' He also knew that Leonski kept press cuttings of the Melbourne murders in his wallet.

Leonski readily confessed to all 3 murders. He explained that he liked women with soft voices; 'That's why I choked these ladies. It was to get their voices.' He related how he met Pauline Thompson and escorted her home. She sang as they walked along: 'Her voice was sweet and soft and I could feel myself going mad about it.' He admitted attacking the girl, but when he returned to his billet thought he had experienced a nightmare.

Leonski was court-martialled, and a defence plea of insanity was rejected despite a family history of mental instability. Found guilty and sentenced to death, Leonski sang in his cell prior to execution on 9 November 1942.

[*246, 335, 519, 645*]

LEOPOLD and LOEB. The trial for murder of two teenage youths from prominent Chicago families is one of America's outstanding criminal cases.

On 22 May 1924, in a culvert on some waste ground near Chicago, workmen found the naked strangled body of 14-year-old Bobby Franks, son of millionaire businessman Jacob Franks. Near by lay a pair of spectacles.

Jacob Franks had already received a typewritten ransom note for $10 000 from a 'George Johnson', but before he could deal with it his son's body was found. All Johnsons were checked, and the sons of wealthy Chicago families interviewed. Among those who readily offered to help was 18-year-old Richard Loeb, son of the Vice-President of Sears, Roebuck and Co. He was an able student and proved very talkative.

The police were checking their only real clue—the spectacles found at the scene. These were traced to an oculist whose records showed that they had been sold to a Nathan Leopold.

Leopold and Loeb: Where the body was found

Leopold, who was 19, another son of a wealthy family and a friend of Richard Loeb, was a brilliant student. Shown the spectacles, he said, 'If I were not positive that my glasses were at home, I would say these are mine.' Asked to produce his own spectacles, he was unable to find them.

The other main aim was to find the Underwood machine on which the ransom note had been typed. Questioned about this, Leopold denied that the machine he used was an Underwood. But his fellow-students had borrowed his typewriter, and their typed sheets came from the same machine as

Leopold and Loeb: Leopold's spectacles

the ransom note. Meanwhile Richard Loeb broke down under questioning and made a full confession. He said that he and Leopold had killed Bobby Franks for the excitement of committing a perfect murder that would be incapable of detection.

Leopold and Loeb were tried in Chicago in July 1924 with famous lawyer and humanitarian Clarence Darrow appearing for the defence. He faced fierce public demands for the deaths of the killers. Darrow pleaded mitigation based on reduced responsibility and mental illness. His appeal, however, was only against capital punishment, and he argued the case passionately enough to save the two youths. They were imprisoned for life on the murder charge, and sentenced to 99 years for kidnapping. Richard Loeb was killed in a prison homosexual brawl in 1936, while Nathan Leopold served 33 years and won his freedom in 1958. He married in 1961, and died 10 years later.

[*143, 170, 213, 214, 216, 224, 305, 373, 439, 528, 568, 605, 639, 640, 890, 932*]

LEWINGDON BROTHERS. Gary and Charles Lewingdon were convicted at separate trials in 1979 of 9 serial killings in Columbus, Ohio. The .22 Calibre Murders, as they became known, were distinguished by a confession made by a woman who had seen the dead victims and mistakenly believed she was implicated.

On 13 February 1978 Mickey McCann, a club-owner, was found dead in his house from gunshot wounds, together with his mother and girl-friend. The victims had been shot in the head with a .22 calibre weapon in an execution style which led investigators to think the killings might have been ordered by an organized crime syndicate. The following month detectives working on the case were approached by Claudia Yasko, a 26-year-old waitress, who confessed to the murders and recounted graphic details of the crime scene.

While Yasko was in custody a number of other murders occurred in the Columbus area in which the killing was carried out with a .22-calibre gun. On 26 May firearms tests proved that the same weapon had been used in the later killings as in the McCann murders, thereby ruling out Claudia Yasco as a suspect. She was found to be suffering from a form of schizophrenia, and after a lie-detection test gave results in her favour the charges against her were dropped. Her detailed knowledge of the crimes continued to be a mystery.

In December 1978 the ninth victim fell to the .22

Calibre Murderer when James Annick was shot dead at his home. He was also robbed, and when a man attempted to obtain goods in a Columbus store using a stolen credit card an alert check-out assistant raised the alarm. Gary James Lewingdon was arrested, and under questioning admitted killing Annick. His brother, Charles Thaddeus Lewingdon, was also implicated, and the trail of .22-calibre murders was traced back to a double killing at Newark, Ohio, in December 1977. In all 9 murders had been committed using the same weapon.

Charles Lewingdon was arrested on 10 December 1978, and after 3½ hours' questioning confessed to the nine murders. He was tried on 3 charges in February 1979, and on conviction was given 3 life sentences with further charges to be heard. The charges against his brother Gary were combined and he was found guilty of committing 8 murders. His request to the judge that he be provided with a dose of sodium pentothal so that he could end his life was refused. He was sentenced to serve 8 consecutive life terms of imprisonment. He later became psychotic, and was transferred to a hospital for the criminally insane.

While the serial killers had been found, and the .22 calibre murders solved, there remained the mystery of Claudia Yasco's confession. This was finally resolved by Daniel Keyes, who interviewed Claudia at length and published the outcome in 1986. It appeared that she had overheard her boy-friend and Gary Lewingdon discussing the McCann murders a week before they occurred. She tried unsuccessfully to warn McCann of the impending disaster, and on the night of the triple shooting was inveigled by her boy-friend into accompanying one of his associates to the murder scene. Their purpose was to search for drugs. Claudia, her mind distorted by mental illness and the prescribed drugs she was taking, was so overwhelmed by her vivid recollection of the murder scene that she mistakenly confessed to being involved.

[*526*]

LEY, Thomas John. See CHALKPIT MURDER

LIGHTBOURNE, Wendell Willis. Teenaged golf caddie whose violent exploits terrorized Bermuda and resulted in 3 murders.

A 72-year-old woman living alone in a cottage at Southlands beach was found raped and murdered on 7 March 1959. Two months later another woman living alone in the same area was found raped and beaten to death in her house. These savage attacks followed a series of assaults on women in the previous 12 months.

Scotland Yard officers were called in, but large-scale fingerprinting of males between the ages of 18 and 50 produced no firm leads. In July a man broke into a flat in the Southlands beach area and attacked a middle-aged woman.

On 28 September the killer struck again. A 29-year-old secretary, Dorothy Rawlinson, a keen swimmer, had cycled to a Southlands beach and was reported missing. A search of the beach produced her bloodstained clothes, partially buried under the sand. Soon after the girl's body was found on a coral reef about 2 miles away, badly eaten by sharks. Had it not been for the clothes it might have been thought she drowned accidentally.

Witnesses had seen a young Negro on the beach on the day of the girl's disappearance—he was described as being in an agitated state. He was identified as Wendell Lightbourne, a 19-year-old golf caddie, who was arrested. He broke down and admitted killing the girl on the beach: 'I want to get it off my mind, I can't go to heaven now.' Questioned about the other murders, Lightbourne said he knew where the women lived, and showing detectives scars on his fists admitted, 'I get nasty.'

Lightbourne was sexually aggressive, and suffered from feelings of inferiority. He decided to take it out on the wealthy, leisured classes which Bermuda attracted. He told police, 'I don't like blood . . . it makes me feel funny.' Tried at Hamilton for the murder of Miss Rawlinson in December 1959, he was found guilty and sentenced to death. He was reprieved, and in January 1960, after being examined by three psychiatrists, had his sentence commuted to a term of life imprisonment to be served in Britain.
[*335, 643*]

LIPSKI, Israel. A curious Victorian case in which a young Jewish immigrant was executed for a murder of which many thought he was innocent.

The 3-storey lodging house at 16 Batty Street in London's East End housed 15 persons. On 28 June 1887 a relative called to see Miriam Angel, who occupied a room on the second floor. The visitor found the girl—who was six months pregnant—lying dead in her bed, with yellow froth around her mouth.

A doctor was called; he examined the body

FIFTH EDITION.

Lipski: He confessed to murder

(noting especially the yellow substance around the mouth) and suspected corrosive poisoning. A search was then made of the room to find the poison-container, and in the course of this a man was found hiding under the bed. Israel Lipski, 22, whose room was in the attic, was dragged out in a semi-conscious state. He too had yellow staining around his mouth.

When he was revived Lipski said that two workmen had attacked the girl and then assaulted him. The corrosive poison was nitric acid, an unusual agent for procuring murder. The position of the victim's body suggested a sexual motive for the attack, and there were indications of necrophilia. Lipski's story was not believed, and he was charged with murder.

Lipski was tried in July 1887 before Mr Justice James Fitzjames Stephen, who summed up heavily against him. The imputation was that the young man had seen the victim in her room through a window situated on the stairs leading up to his attic, and had been overcome by temptation. Whether out

Lipski: Murder in the bedroom

of fright or guilt, Lipski made a full confession to murder the day before he was hanged at Newgate. [*277, 301*]

LOCK AH TAM. Respected and influential member of England's Chinese community who went berserk after a family party at their Birkenhead home and shot dead his wife and 2 daughters.

Tam was born in Canton in 1872, and came to England as a ship's steward. He rose to a prominent position as organizer of Chinese dock labour in European ports and looked after the welfare of Chinese seamen. He founded the Chinese Progress Club in Liverpool in 1918, and his job frequently involved him in fights with violent seamen. In one in 1918 his head was severely injured.

In 1924 Lock Ah Tam lost money and his normally pleasant disposition was replaced by erratic and often violent behaviour. He was declared a bankrupt, and took to heavy drinking.

His wife loyally stood by him, despite being threatened by his violent behaviour.

On 1 December 1925 Lock Ah Tam held a family dinner party to celebrate his son's coming of age. When the guests left, Tam shot his wife and 2 daughters. He telephoned the police and told them what he had done.

Lock Ah Tam was defended at his trial by Sir Edward Marshall Hall, who argued passionately that though the accused was guilty of the act, he was insane at the moment he committed it. Marshall Hall suggested Tam was in a state of unconscious automatism brought on by an epileptic fit from the head injury he had received 8 years earlier, and had killed his family as if walking in his sleep.

The jury deliberated for only 12 minutes before finding him guilty and he was hanged. [*113, 649, 958*]

LONELY HEARTS KILLERS. See BECK AND FERNANDEZ

LONERGAN, Wayne. Royal Canadian Air Force serviceman, aged 27, who was the central figure in a sensational New York murder case.

A 22-year-old brewery heiress, Patricia Burton Lonergan, was found dead in her New York apartment on 24 October 1943. Her naked body lay sprawled on the bed—she had been strangled and bludgeoned after returning from a late-night party.

Patricia, a wealthy socialite, had separated from her husband, Wayne Lonergan, 2 months previously when he had gone to Canada to join the RCAF. On the weekend of the murder Wayne had been in New York staying at a friend's apartment and returning to Toronto on the eve of his wife's murder.

Lonergan was arrested in Canada and returned to New York. After 84 hours of police questioning he made a statement which was leaked to the press, and led to headlines saying he had confessed, and admitted taking part in sex orgies. Thus labelled a sex deviant and a wife murderer, Lonergan was charged and sent for trial.

The arraignment in New York in February 1944 resulted in a mistrial. Tried again in March, it came out in court that Lonergan's confession had not been signed or authenticated by him, but the defence failed to exploit the weaknesses in the prosecution's case. Apart from the irregularities regarding the confession, it was not shown that Lonergan had definitely visited the murder scene, or that he had handled the alleged murder weapon—a candlestick.

Despite these inconsistencies and lack of motive, the jury found Lonergan guilty of second-degree murder. He was sentenced to '30 years to life' and after serving 22 years in Sing Sing was paroled in 1965.

[735, 754]

LOUGHANS, Harold. Mrs Rose Ada Robinson was a 63-year-old widow who managed the John Barleycorn public house at Portsmouth. She had been in business there for 40 years, since her husband died. Mrs Robinson kept large sums of money on the premises.

On the night of Sunday 28 November 1943, Welch the barman closed the bar as usual. Mrs Robinson took the cash out of the till and put it in her handbags. Welch left at about 10.35 p.m., and heard his employer bolt the door behind him. Next morning Mrs Robinson was found strangled in her bedroom. The room had been ransacked, and her handbags were empty. A small black button was found beneath a window which had been forced at the rear of the public house.

About a month after the murder, two policemen on the lookout for thieves disposing of their catch saw a shabbily dressed, furtive man in Waterloo Road, London. They followed him into a café, where he tried to sell a pair of new shoes. The policemen took him in for questioning, and he told them, 'I'm wanted for things more serious than this. The Yard wants me. It's the trap door for me now.' He was Harold Loughans, who readily admitted to a dozen house burglaries, adding, 'I want to say I done a murder job.' He made a statement in which he confessed to breaking into the John Barleycorn public house and assaulting Mrs Robinson. When the police took his coat from him he said that after the job he found a button was missing, 'I got the wind up . . . I pulled them all off.' Forensic examination of Loughans's clothes produced various fibres linking him with the Portsmouth murder.

During the preliminary hearings Loughans declared his innocence and claimed that the police had put words into his mouth. He was tried at Winchester in March 1944, and his counsel produced 3 witnesses who swore they had seen Loughans on the night of the murder sheltering from a bombing raid in a London underground station. The jury failed to agree, and a retrial was ordered. This took place 2 weeks later at the Old Bailey, when Loughans's alibi and Sir Bernard Spilsbury's evidence on his mutilated right hand won him a not guilty verdict.

In December 1960 *The People* newspaper published the memoirs of J. D. Casswell, who prosecuted Loughans. Loughans reacted by starting libel proceedings from prison against the paper, and the case was heard in 1963. The jury found for the paper and against Loughans. He was effectively proved guilty of a murder charge after being found not guilty—perhaps the only case on record of a jury in a law case disagreeing with a criminal verdict. Loughans could not, of course, be tried again. Three months after the libel action was heard, *The People* published Loughans's signed confession of murder. He died aged 69 shortly after release in 1965.

[13, 29, 37, 171, 851, 953]

LUARD CASE. On the afternoon of 24 August 1908, Major-General Charles Edward Luard, a 69-year-old retired officer, left his home at Ightham, near Sevenoaks, Kent, with his 58-year-old wife. The General intended making the hour's walk to the golf club at Godden Green, and after accompanying her husband part of the way, Mrs Caroline Luard was going to a summerhouse called La Casa in near-by Fish Pond Woods. The couple parted at the village of Crown Point and went their separate ways.

General Luard returned to Ightham at 4.30 p.m., expecting to find his wife at home. She was not there, which surprised him, as they had invited a friend to tea. After entertaining the visitor the General walked to La Casa, where he found his wife lying dead from gunshot wounds in the head. Her purse was missing, and her rings removed from her fingers. The police suspected that she had been killed by a tramp or itinerant worker.

The precise time of death was 3.15 p.m., for independent witnesses heard shots at that time. A man, later dismissed as a crank, confessed to the murder at London's Bow Street police station, and a note was found beside an abandoned coat and pair of boots on the banks of Regents Park Lake. Signed 'Jack Storm', and written to his father, the letter purported to be a confession of the 'Ightham affair'. The lake was dragged, but no suicide was found.

Meanwhile a most unfair campaign had begun against the General, but his movements on the day of the murder unquestionably placed him half a mile away from La Casa at the time of the shooting. This was brought out at the inquest, and the Coroner said that the General could not have committed the terrible act.

Distressed by these insinuations, and by his grief, the General ended his own life by jumping in front of a train, after leaving a note saying, 'I care for nothing but to join her again'. Thus the tragedy at Ightham was doubled, and Mrs Luard's murder remains a mystery, although later the name of *John Alexander Dickman* was linked with the crime.
[*382, 420, 496, 872, 901, 942, 1009, 1013*]

LUCAN, Lord. The Earl of Lucan (known to his friends as 'Lucky') disappeared on the night of 7 November 1974, leaving murder, assault and a storm of controversy behind. That night Lady Veronica Lucan, in a highly distressed state and with blood streaming down her face, stumbled into The Plumbers' Arms in Lower Belgrave Street. 'I've just escaped from a murderer,' she exclaimed.

Police were quickly on the scene at the Lucan home in 46 Lower Belgrave Street where Lady Lucan, separated from her husband, lived with their 3 children and nanny. Officers found blood-

Lucan: The missing Earl

stains on a stairway leading down to the basement, and on a half-landing found a pool of blood and bloody footprints. At the bottom was a canvas mail-bag which contained the body of Sandra Rivett, the Lucan children's 29-year-old nanny. She had been bludgeoned to death. On the top floor of the house the 2 younger children were asleep and the 10-year-old was awake but looking bewildered.

Lady Lucan had been watching television with her eldest child in the main bedroom when at about 9.0 p.m. Sandra Rivett offered to make tea. After she had been gone for about 20 minutes Lady Lucan decided to go downstairs to find out what was causing the delay. When she reached the kitchen on the half-landing leading to the basement a man leapt out and attacked her with a heavy weapon. She fought him off, and then realized that the assailant was her husband. Lucan told his wife he had killed the nanny in mistake for her. In a calmer frame of mind, the couple went upstairs to talk, and dismissed their wide-eyed 10-year-old to her room. While

Lucan was in the bathroom fetching towels to clean up his wife's injuries she fled from the house and raised the alarm at The Plumbers' Arms.

By the time the police reached the house Lucan had disappeared, and a check on his other London houses failed to locate him. In the meantime he had telephoned his mother telling her there had been a 'terrible catastrophe'. He explained that he had been passing the house when he saw someone attacking his wife. When he entered the house he found his wife hysterical. At about midnight Lucan telephoned again, asking his mother if the children were safe. She told him the police wanted to talk to him; he said he would call them in the morning.

Luckless Sandra Rivett had worked for the Lucans for 5 weeks. She was the same height as Lady Lucan, although she had a fuller figure. Her usual night off was Thursday—the night of the murder—but on that particular week she had taken Wednesday off instead. Thus it was conceivable that she had been killed in mistake for Lady Lucan, the intended victim.

Lord Lucan inherited the title in 1964 and enjoyed a high society life-style. One of his passions was gambling—hence his nickname of 'Lucky'—and he regularly won or lost £5,000 a day. In the early 1970s the Lucans' marriage was under strain and, following their separation in 1973, Lucan had fought and lost an action for custody of his children. During the weeks before the murder he was in a bitter mood, and tried to convince people that his wife was mentally unstable. He was also losing heavily at the gaming tables and was deeply in debt.

On 9 November 1974 police learned that Lucan had written two letters to a friend, postmarked Uckfield, Sussex. One of these referred to the fight which he interrupted at Lower Belgrave Street and said that he proposed to 'lie doggo for a while'. Another friend who lived in East Sussex was visited by Lucan late on the night of the murder. Lucan described his 'unbelievable nightmare experience' and said that his wife had accused him of hiring a man to kill her. Despite his friend's appeals for him to stay the night, the Earl drove off at about 1.15 a.m. His car was found abandoned the following day at Newhaven. Bloodstains were detectable on the inside of the driver's door, and a length of lead pipe was found in the boot.

Police frogmen searched the docks at Newhaven for Lucan's body, and later made an aerial search of the South Downs looking for a grave. Lucan had simply disappeared and, despite numerous alleged sightings from all round the world, his whereabouts (if he is indeed alive) are unknown. At the inquest into the death of Sandra Rivett held in June 1975 the coroner's jury brought in a verdict of murder by Lord Lucan. He was the last person in Britain to be accused in this way, and one of the results of the ensuing controversy was legislation passed in 1977 which made it impossible in future for coroners to charge a person with murder. Despite appeals by his family to apply the legislation retrospectively, the charge of murder against Lord Lucan still stands.

Speculation about Lord Lucan's guilt has continued over the years, with all the fascination that an unsolved crime creates. In 1987 two books were published that offered different interpretations of the events that had occurred thirteen years previously. In *Trail of Havoc* Patrick Marnham argued that Lucan, motivated by his desire to obtain custody of his children, hired someone to kill his wife. The plan went badly wrong when his bungling accomplice killed Sandra Rivett by mistake. The implication is that the real killer, who is not Lord Lucan, is still free.

Another theory was put forward in *Lucan: Not Guilty* by Sally Moore and this also involved a third person. The book speculated that the suspect was a policeman to whom Lady Lucan in a moment of indiscretion had shown her jewellery. The thesis was that this man decided to steal the jewellery but was disturbed by Sandra Rivett, who recognized him. The intruder therefore had to silence Rivett, and would have murdered Lady Lucan too but for the intervention of her husband. The implication here is of an official cover-up.

[*303, 353, 597, 647, 673*]

LUETGERT, Adolph Louis. German immigrant to the United States in the 1870s who settled in Chicago and established a sausage-making business. He was distinguished for his weight (240 pounds) and for his sexual appetite.

Forty-nine-year-old Luetgert maintained a string of mistresses and even had a bed installed in his factory for their visits. His wife, Louisa, grew tired of his behaviour and was worried by the downward trend of the business.

On 1 May 1897, Louisa disappeared, and Luetgert told the family he had hired private detectives to find her. The police eventually searched the factory, including its steam vats. When one of them was drained off some pieces of bone, some teeth and two gold rings, one of which was engraved L.L., were found.

Luetgert was tried for the murder of his wife but he maintained that the bone fragments were animal. His past caught up with him when his mistresses testified against him. One said he had remarked of his wife, 'I could take her and crush her', and another referred to a bloodstained knife which he had asked her to look after.

Luetgert was found guilty and sentenced to life imprisonment. He died in Joliet State Penitentiary in 1911. He never confessed.
[*405, 693, 959*]

MACDONALD, Dr Jeffrey. The archetypal all-American boy whose professional skill and talent turned to ashes when he was convicted of murdering his pregnant wife and children in 1970. The story was told in the best-selling book *Fatal Vision*, and was later screened as a television documentary.

In the early hours of 17 February 1970 at Fort Bragg, North Carolina, military police received a call from Captain Jeffrey MacDonald saying, 'Stabbing . . . Hurry!' They found Colette MacDonald dead on the floor of the main bedroom, and her two young children dead in their bedrooms. Mrs Mac-Donald had been stabbed many times and savagely clubbed, breaking both her arms; the children had been bludgeoned to death. Captain MacDonald had also been wounded, though not gravely.

Dr MacDonald told MPs that 'acid heads' wearing hippie clothing had attacked him and his family. One of them had said, 'Acid is groovy—kill the pigs' and, with echoes of the *Charles Manson* killings in California, the word PIG had been daubed in blood on the bedhead. MacDonald had a first-class background as a scholar, doctor and army officer. As the survivor of a family attacked by drug-crazed intruders he first attracted sympathy and then suspicion.

The lack of disorder in the house seemed incompatible with the presence of 4 intruders, and the idea began to take hold that MacDonald might have killed his family and simulated a Mansonesque attack. After 4 months of investigation in which important crime-scene evidence was lost or inadvertently destroyed, the charges against MacDonald were dropped. He took an honourable discharge from the Green Berets and set up in private medical practice. He also seemed to enjoy the publicity he attracted, and made several appearances on television.

One of those who had grown increasingly suspicious of MacDonald's behaviour was his father-in-law, whose determination to pursue the case led eventually to a trial for murder. But it took time. In 1972 army investigators reported to the Justice Department that the evidence pointed to MacDonald's guilt, and in 1974 the papers were sent back to the military asking for further inquiries to be made. In 1975 MacDonald was called before a Grand Jury and was indicted on 3 counts of murder. He appealed, and on the grounds that his rights had been violated, the indictment was dismissed. Finally, in 1979, 9½ years after the murders, Jeffrey MacDonald was put on trial at Raleigh, North Carolina.

He denied the charges and wept while giving evidence, yet under cross-examination he proved hostile. One of the key aspects of the forensic evidence was that every member of the MacDonald family had a different blood group. This meant that the type and location of every bloodstain could be precisely recorded. It was shown that some of the victims had been attacked in locations other than those in which they were found, in contradiction of MacDonald's account. The jury believed that Mac-Donald, a perfectionist described as 'an individual constantly striving to be superman', had worked himself into a rage which spilled over into uncontrollable violence.

He was found guilty of second-degree murder in respect of his wife and eldest child and of first-degree murder of his youngest child, who it was believed had been calculatedly killed in order to maintain the hippie attack story. MacDonald was sentenced to 3 terms of life imprisonment.

Jeffrey MacDonald continued to maintain his innocence from prison in Texas, and in a long interview with *Playboy* magazine in 1985 said that 'truth is on our side', although his latest attempt to overturn the verdict was turned down by the Court of Appeals. After *Fatal Vision* was shown to American television audiences, Karl Malden, the actor who played the part of MacDonald's father-in-law, received hate mail condemning him for portraying the person who allegedly put an innocent man in prison.
[*636, 701*]

BLOOD TYPE

Colette MacDonald	A	Kimberly MacDonald	AB
Jeffrey MacDonald	B	Kristen MacDonald	O

McDonald, Jeffrey: Scene of the murders

McDONALD, William. The so-called 'Sydney Mutilator' convicted of murder in Australia in 1963. Between June 1961 and November 1962 the mutilated bodies of four male vagrants were found in various parts of Sydney. Multiple knife wounds and genital mutilation were common features of the murders; homosexual motivation was suspected by the police.

One of the victims was mistakenly identified as Allan Brennan, a post-office sorter at the YMCA in Sydney. His workmates expressed their condolences by collecting money to send a wreath to his funeral. A few months later Brennan was spotted, alive and well, walking down a Sydney street. One of the city's newspapers carried a report under the headline 'The Case of the Walking Corpse'. Following a police alert, Brennan (also known as William McDonald) was arrested in Melbourne. In a statement reminiscent of that made by *William Heirens*, the American murderer, he said, 'I cannot help myself, I had the impulse to kill.' McDonald was born in England in 1926, and joined the army in 1944. As a youth he had suffered from severe headaches, and had a fear of becoming mentally ill. During his military service he was subjected to a homosexual attack by an NCO, an experience which permanently bruised his already delicately balanced personality. He was treated by army psychiatrists and diagnosed as schizoid. Following his discharge in 1948, he spent some time in mental institutions before emigrating first to Canada and then to Australia.

His history was one of mental aberration if not of progressive decline, and by 1960 he was inspired by voices which urged him to kill. The rationale for his violent attacks was that they were revenge killings for the homosexual assault he had suffered many years earlier.

McDonald was tried in September 1963 on 1 count of murder. The court was told about the serious psychological injury he had suffered in 1944, which had created feelings of extreme hatred. Mutilation of his victims was a symbolic expression of the sadism to which he had been converted. Against the balance of evidence showing the defendant to be legally insane, the jury found him guilty as charged. He was accordingly sentenced to life imprisonment. While in Long Bay Penitentiary, McDonald attacked a fellow-prisoner and nearly killed him. He was later certified as insane and moved to a mental hospital.

[*821*]

MACKAY, Patrick. Teenage psychopath whose childhood sadism ended in murder.

Mackay's father, who died in 1962 at 42, was an alcoholic who was violent towards his wife and children. Patrick Mackay's behaviour deteriorated afterwards. He had a reputation as a bully at school, and developed a liking for torturing animals, including his pet tortoise. (See also *Edmund Kemper*.) He was in and out of various mental hospitals and approved schools. In 1968 a Home Office psychiatrist described the 15-year-old boy as 'a cold psychopathic killer'. He was twice released from institutions against medical advice.

Mackay adopted the name 'Franklin Bollvolt the First', a fantasy figure based on Hitler, whom he visualized dominating the world. He was obsessed with Fascism, and surrounded himself with books on the Nazis and various emblems, including a crude uniform which he made himself. He committed numerous burglaries and continued to exhibit violent rages, while he also took to regular, heavy drinking.

On 14 February 1974 he stabbed to death 84-year-old Isabella Griffiths in her Chelsea home. On 10 March 1975 he entered the flat of elderly widow Adele Price on the pretext of needing a glass of water. Once inside he strangled her, and later he said, 'I felt hellish and very peculiar inside.'

On 21 March 1975 Mackay attacked and killed Father Anthony Crean, a kindly priest who had tried to prevent his prosecution for theft 2 years earlier. He stabbed the priest several times, and slashed his head with an axe. 'I must have gone out of my mind. It was something in me that exploded,' he said. Local police knew of Father Crean's association with Mackay, and he was arrested 48 hours later. He was charged with 5 murders, and questioned about 6 others.

Patrick Mackay appeared at the Old Bailey in November 1975, charged with the 3 murders to which he confessed. He was judged sane and fit to plead. The 23-year-old psychopath, whose short, murderous career raised so many social questions, was sentenced to life imprisonment.
[*177*]

MAGNUSON, John. On 27 December 1922 James Chapman, a 65-year-old farmer who lived near Marshfield, Wisconsin, received what he thought was a belated Christmas gift. His wife looked on with curiosity as he untied the parcel. There was a tremendous explosion, and both the farmer and his wife were severely injured. Chapman

lost a hand but survived, while Clementine Chapman died of internal injuries.

Police inquiries concentrated on tracing any known enemies of the Chapmans, and Swedish farmer John Magnuson was questioned. He was known to have threatened Chapman over the building of a drainage ditch which was routed over his land. He told neighbours who were seeking signatures on a petition that he had other means of stopping the project.

The wrapping of the bomb parcel had survived the blast, and the misspelling of Chapman's address using the word 'Marshfilld' was adjudged circumstantial evidence pointing at the Swede. Magnuson was arrested, but strongly protested his innocence. At his trial for murder scientific evidence played a major role and there were some star performers in court. Arthur Koehler (who later distinguished himself in the *Hauptmann* trial) testified that wood splinters found in Magnuson's workshop matched wood fragments of the bomb packaging. Albert S. Osborne, an expert witness in the *Molineux* case, said that Magnuson's handwriting and the writing on the bomb wrapping were the same.

Magnuson was found guilty of murder in the first degree, a verdict which he greeted with, 'My God, it is a mistake.' Judge Park, who sentenced him to life imprisonment, told the court that the presentation of the prosecution evidence was the finest he had ever seen.
[*227, 848*]

MAHON, Patrick Herbert. Handsome philanderer with winning ways who committed what an Appeal Court judge described as a 'most cruel, repulsive and carefully planned murder'.

Mahon led an exemplary life until he married at the age of 20 in 1910. There followed a succession of charges for fraud, embezzlement and robbery with violence. In 1922, through his wife's influence, he was made sales manager of a firm at Sunbury. He became attracted to 37-year-old typist Emily Beilby Kaye, and they decided to engage in a 'love experiment' by living together in a bungalow rented for the purpose on a lonely part of the Sussex coast between Eastbourne and Pevensey Bay known as the Crumbles.

On 12 April 1924 Mahon bought a saw and a knife before travelling down to Eastbourne to meet Miss Kaye. His firm and his wife thought he was travelling on company business, while Miss Kaye, completely infatuated with Mahon, told friends she was engaged and planned to visit South Africa. When Mahon failed to obtain a passport as he had promised, there was an argument in the 'love bungalow' during which Mahon claimed Emily attacked him and, falling down in the process, struck her head on a coal bucket. She allegedly died from this blow.

Mrs Mahon, concerned by her husband's pursuit of other women, went through the pockets of one of his suits. There she found a cloakroom ticket which, when presented at Waterloo railway station, produced a Gladstone bag containing bloodstained female clothing. Mahon was stopped by the police when he turned up to collect the bag. His excuse that he had carried dog meat failed, it having been established that the bloodstains were human.

Detectives visited the bungalow at the Crumbles. They found pieces of boiled flesh in a saucepan; sawn-up chunks of a corpse in a hat box, a trunk and a biscuit tin; and ashes in the fire containing bone fragments. Sir Bernard Spilsbury pieced together the body of the pregnant Emily Kaye, but no head was ever found.

Patrick Mahon was tried at Lewes Assizes in July 1924. He maintained that Miss Kaye died accidentally by hitting her head on the coal bucket. But the purchase of a knife and saw, together with the information that he had been fleecing Kaye of

her savings, went against him. He was found guilty and told the judge that he was 'too conscious of the bitterness and unfairness of the summing up' to say anything except that he was not guilty. Avory passed the death sentence and unfair or not, he was hanged at Wandsworth Prison on 2 September 1924.

[2, 32, 133, 159, 202, 220, 349, 384, 386, 485, 541, 555, 575, 618, 661, 757, 819, 846, 928, 964]

MAJOR, Ethel Lillie. A 43-year-old Lincoln-shire gamekeeper's daughter who murdered her husband with strychnine.

At the age of 24 Ethel Major had an illegitimate daughter. To avoid stigma, Ethel's parents treated the baby girl as Ethel's sister. In 1918 Ethel married Arthur Major, and the couple lived with Ethel's parents. In 1919 they had their first child. The first few years of marriage went well, and then in 1929 the Majors moved into their own house at Kirkby-on-Bain.

Soon the gossips were at work, and Arthur Major learned the truth about his wife's 'sister', Auriel. He was furious when Ethel refused to tell him the father of her illegitimate child. The marriage began to break up, from constant quarrels and Arthur's violent behaviour.

Mahon: The murderer goes back to the bungalow

In 1934 Ethel found her husband was receiving letters from another woman. She remonstrated, often in writing, with her neighbours, the doctor, a solicitor and even the Chief Constable, about her husband's behaviour. Arthur retaliated by publicly declaring that he would not be responsible for his wife's debts.

On 22 May 1934 Arthur Major was taken ill with severe pain. Ethel blamed some corned beef he had eaten. After 2 days of agonizing suffering he died of what the death certificate described as status epilepticus. The police received an anonymous letter stating that a neighbour's dog had died after eating food scraps put out by Ethel. The dog's body was exhumed, and found to contain strychnine. Arthur's funeral was halted, and post-mortem examination showed that he too had died of strychnine poisoning. Ethel had access to a box in which her gamekeeper father kept a small quantity. When interviewed by the police she said, 'I did not know that my husband died of strychnine poisoning.' Told that strychnine had never been mentioned, she added, 'Oh, I'm sorry. I must have made a mistake.'

Ethel Major was tried at Lincoln Assizes in November 1934, and defended by Norman Birkett. No defence witnesses were called, and she herself did not give evidence, so her counsel had the last word. She was found guilty, and despite the jury's recommendation to mercy was executed on 19 December in Hull Prison.

[44, 113, 367, 460, 598, 795, 1023]

MALENO and SOLI. John S. Knight III, grandson of John S. Knight, an American newspaper-owner, was found murdered in his penthouse suite in Philadelphia on 7 December 1975. He had been stabbed and strangled.

Knight had dined with friends that evening, 2 of whom stayed overnight in his apartment. In the early hours of the morning they were disturbed by 3 armed intruders who were ransacking the apartment. Knight was lying dead amid the wreckage. Although the murder victim was a wealthy man with a taste for Savile Row suits and art treasures, he kept little money in his apartment. He had been murdered, it seemed, for $190 stolen by his assailants.

In the intensive inquiries which followed it was discovered that Knight led a double life. The scion of the famous newspaper family who moved in high social circles also liked the low life. He had a propensity for picking up young homosexuals and taking them back to his penthouse suite. Photo-graphs depicting homosexual activities were found among his possessions, together with a diary listing addresses of prostitutes of both sexes.

By a process of elimination police narrowed their search to three men, Felix Melendez, Steven Male-no and Salvatore Soli, who were known to have menaced rich homosexuals. Maleno gave himself up, and Melendez was found dead four days after the penthouse murder; Soli was picked up in Miami. Melendez, who had been Knight's lover, was executed by Maleno on Soli's instructions. Both men blamed their dead companion for killing Knight.

In due course Maleno confessed to taking part in the killings of Knight and Melendez, but Soli contested the charges. He was put on trial for murder in May 1976 and found guilty of first-degree murder, robbery, burglary and criminal conspiracy. With an air of defiance, he told the judge, 'If it's death, give it to me now.' One of the jurors later said they came close to 'giving him the chair'. In the event, 38-year-old Soli was sentenced to life imprisonment.

[61]

MALIK, Abdul (also known as Michael X). Born in Trinidad as Michael de Freitas, he adopted the Muslim faith in 1963 and changed his name to Abdul Malik. He was greatly influenced by Malcolm X, the American Black Power leader who visited England in 1965, when Malik was active in London's immigrant communities.

Malik founded the Racial Advancement and Action Society (RAAS) in London, and acquired a certain charisma which enabled him to wield influence and become a media figure. In due course his preaching of extreme racialism brought him into conflict with the law, and in 1967 he was imprisoned for 12 months. In one of his speeches he spoke of dealing with 'the white monkeys', and talked of killing with a clear conscience. In 1970 he was convicted on a robbery charge, and with all his activities under close surveillance, decided to leave England. When Jamaica refused him permission to become a resident he settled in Port of Spain, Trinidad.

Malik gathered together a small band of followers at his house, called La Chance, which formed the basis of his commune. His attempts to influence religious and political groups on the island did not succeed, and 'the best known black man in the world', as he liked to think of himself, was left in an organizational vacuum.

On 19 February 1972 the fire brigade was called

out to La Chance, which despite their efforts was completely destroyed. When the police arrived on the scene an observant officer noticed that a bed of lettuce in the garden had unusually tall and yellow-coloured plants in it. The bed was probed, and a grave discovered containing a man's body. Further digging in the garden resulted in the discovery of another grave, this time containing a female corpse. Professor Keith Simpson, the British pathologist, was called in to examine the two bodies, which were identified by dental and fingerprint evidence.

Both the corpses had been subjected to murderous violence. The man had been slashed and battered to death and the woman had been slashed, stabbed and buried alive. Both had been followers of Abdul Malik who had disappeared leaving 3 members of his commune to face the music. He was eventually traced to Guyana, where he was arrested and deported to Trinidad to face murder charges.

Malik's strange influence over the members of his group emerged during his trial. He ordered the killing of Gail Benson in January 1972 because she was causing mental distress to another of his followers. She was hacked almost to death with a cutlass and buried alive in a pit dug by two of the others. Joe Skerrit, the group's handyman and Malik's cousin, was killed because he refused to fall in with a plan to carry out a armed robbery. He was bludgeoned to death and buried in the garden.

Malik was tried in August 1972 for the murder of Skerrit. He was convicted, and one of his accomplices was found guilty of manslaughter. The following year 2 other members of Malik's commune were convicted of the murder of Gail Benson and sentenced to death. Malik's appeal was turned down, and he was executed on 16 May 1975. Admission of Abdul Malik's exclusive commune brought only disaster for its members, 2 of whom were murdered, 1 died accidentally and 2 were hanged.
[836]

MALTBY, Cecil. London tailor, 47, who shot and killed his mistress and lived in the flat above his shop for several months with her decomposing body lying in the bath.

Alice Hilda Middleton, whose Merchant Navy husband was on a long tour of duty in the Far East, went to live with Maltby in the summer of 1922. The tailor drank heavily, and neglected his business, spending a great deal of time with Mrs Middleton at race meetings.

Alice Middleton disappeared in August, and when her husband returned on leave in December

he reported her missing. The police made inquiries of Maltby, but he refused them entry to his shop, and would only say that she had left him on 15 August. A watch was kept on his shop but Maltby did not emerge.

On 10 January 1923 a health order was issued enabling the authorities to break in. Two parties of police officers made separate entries through the front and rear of the shop, and having gained access to the first floor heard a single shot. They found Maltby dying in the bedroom, shot through the mouth. The decomposing remains of Mrs Middleton were wrapped in a sheet in the bath in the kitchen. Attached to the sheet was a note, 'In memory of darling Pat, who committed suicide on 24 August 1922, 8.30 a.m.' Nailed to the door was another In Memoriam note asking, 'Why did you do it? Everyone loved you. I cannot live without you. When I can brace up my courage I shall soon be with you.'

Various letters left by Maltby suggested that on 24 August he had struggled with Mrs Middleton for a gun when she was threatening to kill herself. The implication was that the gun went off during the struggle, killing her accidentally, but this was at variance with 3 wounds in her back, which had been fired at her when she was in a sitting or lying position.

A Coroner's Jury returned a verdict of murder and *felo de se*, adding he was in a sound state of health and mind and took his life to avoid the consequences of his own act.
[196, 695]

MAMIE STUART CASE. Mamie Stuart was a 26-year-old ex-chorus girl whose body was found 40 years after she disappeared. She was murdered by her bigamous husband, who had since died.

Mamie met Edward George Shotton, a marine engineer, in 1917. They married and lived in rented rooms at Swansea. In 1919 they moved to a house called Ty-Llanwydd near Swansea.

A week later Mamie wrote to her parents at Sunderland, who were alarmed when their reply was returned marked 'House Closed'. Just before Christmas they received a telegram from Swansea apparently from their daughter, sending them greetings.

Nothing further happened until March 1920, when the manager of the Grosvenor Hotel, Swansea, reported that an unclaimed portmanteau left by a man two months previously contained torn female clothing. Two weeks later a cleaning woman at Ty-Llanwydd found Mamie Stuart's handbag, containing her ration card and £2, behind the washstand.

Scotland Yard was called in. It was found that George Shotton was already married, and living with his wife and child a few miles from Swansea. When questioned Shotton admitted living with Mamie Stuart, but denied they were married. He said they parted company about 5 or 6 December 1919 after quarrelling. It was known that Shotton could be violent, and Mamie's Swansea landlady recalled her referring to Shotton as being 'not all there'.

Ty-Llanwydd was searched and the garden dug up, but nothing was found. Shotton was charged with bigamy and tried at Glamorgan Assizes. He admitted leaving the portmanteau at the Swansea Hotel, but maintained that someone impersonating him had married Mamie Stuart. He received a sentence of 18 months' hard labour for bigamy.

There the case rested until 40 years later, when on 5 November 1961, 3 men pot-holing on the Welsh coast found a human female skeleton cut into 3 pieces at the bottom of a deep, disused lead-mine air-shaft. The age and height matched Mamie Stuart's description, the pieces of clothing were identified as hers. Identification was confirmed by means of the photo-imposition technique developed in the *Ruxton* case.

A Coroner's Inquest was held in December 1961, and an elderly ex-postman recalled that 40 years earlier he had seen Shotton with a heavy sack outside Ty-Llanwydd. Shotton was shocked, but then recovered and said 'Oh, God, for a minute I thought you were a policeman.' A verdict of murder was reached, but George Shotton had died, aged 78, 3 years earlier at Bristol.

[*738*]

MANNING, Maria and Frederick. Husband and wife murder team whose trial created considerable public interest.

Maria de Roux was born in Switzerland and served as a lady's maid. In the course of her travels she met 50-year-old Patrick O'Connor, an Irishman working in London's docks. He and Maria were well acquainted even after Maria (aged 28) married Frederick Manning, who was the same age, in May 1847.

The Mannings lived at Minver Place, Bermondsey, and O'Connor frequently visited them. The Mannings were in financial difficulties, while O'Connor made a considerable fortune out of money-lending.

Maria Manning sent O'Connor a note on 8 August inviting him 'to dine with us today at half past five o'clock'. O'Connor's subsequent absence from work was noted, and inquiries were made of his acquaintances. Maria answered politely but negatively, but when the police returned they found the house empty. It was searched, and flagstones in the kitchen were prised up to reveal the quicklimed body of Patrick O'Connor shot in the head, with numerous other head wounds caused by a blunt instrument.

Frederick Manning had bought a crowbar several months previously, 'to lift heavy things up, such as stones'. He had also asked a medical student what drug would result in stupefaction such as to 'cause a person to put his hand to paper', and he wanted to know the weakest part of the skull.

A search for the Mannings located Maria in Edinburgh and Frederick in the Channel Islands. They were brought to trial at the Old Bailey in October, man and wife being separately defended. Frederick's defence was that his wife had been the instigator of the crime, while Maria's counsel regarded it as contemptible that a man could try to fix such a crime on his wife. The jury found them both guilty. Maria exclaimed, 'There is no justice and no right for a foreign subject in this country.' Frederick later made a confession in which he said that Maria shot O'Connor and he finished him off with the crowbar. On 13 November 1847 the Mannings were hanged before a crowd of 50,000 in front of Horsemongers Lane Gaol with Maria wearing black satin. The material immediately became unfashionable!

[*103, 554, 593, 660, 921, 1017*]

MANSON, Charles. Highly publicized leader of the 'Family', whose brutal killings in California resulted in an extraordinary trial lasting 9 months.

Manson was born the son of a prostitute. He spent his early life in and out of reform schools, and later served prison sentences for forgery and procuring. On release from a 10-year gaol term in 1954 he set up a commune-based cult, drawing in hippies, drifters and the unemployed at Spahn Ranch near Los Angeles.

Manson had grandiose ideas, and his followers, or family, regarded him as a Christ-like figure. They indulged in free-love practices, pseudo-religious ceremonies and experimentation with drugs. Manson developed a bitter hatred for the Establishment which exploded on 9 August 1969. A group of his followers broke into the Hollywo

Manson: One of his doodles

home of film director Roman Polanski and murdered his pregnant wife, the actress Sharon Tate, and four others. They were shot, stabbed and clubbed, and slogans such as 'War' and 'Pig' were daubed on the walls in the victims' blood. The following night the same group repeated their act at the home of Leno and Rosemary La Bianca, killing them both.

Manson, aged 33, was the leader of this group, and together with three of his girl followers was tried for the 6 murders. The prosecution, led by Vincent Bugliosi, referred to Manson's grudge against society, and contended that he masterminded the murders though he did not participate in them.

The defence was extraordinary. The three girl defendants wanted to testify to their guilt and Manson's innocence, but their lawyers refused to question them. When the judge ruled that they were entitled to testify but that he would first remove the jury, they refused to speak. At this point Manson intervened. He said the members of his family were those persons discarded by society, and his deep hatred came to the surface in several remarkable statements. 'I have done my best to get along in your world,' he said, 'and now you want to kill me. I say to myself "Ha, I'm already dead, have

been all my life . . . I don't care anything about any of you. . . ."'

The prosecutor referred to Manson as 'one of the most evil, satanic men who ever walked the face of the earth'. All four accused were found guilty and subsequently sentenced to death, which in practice meant life imprisonment.

[*89, 138, 504, 528, 569, 702, 804, 817, 1025*]

MANTON, Horace William. 'Bertie' Manton, a driver in the Fire Service, who murdered his wife in what became known as the 'Luton Sack Murder'.

On 19 November 1943 some men on their way to work at Luton saw a sack in the river Lea. The sodden bundle contained the naked body of a woman who had been severely beaten about the face. Death had been caused by strangulation, and the facial injuries suggested an attempt to conceal her identity. She was aged about 35, and had been dead for 18 hours.

A description of the dead woman was broadcast by the BBC and photographs were shown at cinemas in the Luton area. After a number of false identifications police found evidence in February 1944 after a meticulous investigation which included a search of house refuse on a municipal tip for traces of clothing that yielded the tattered pieces of a woman's coat bearing a dry-cleaning tag. The tag was traced to a Luton shop, where records showed that the coat was handed in for dyeing the previous November by Mrs Caroline Manton.

The Manton home was visited, and police officers were told by Bertie that his wife had left him to go to her brother. He denied that the woman in the police photographs was his wife. He produced letters posted in north London between December 1943 and February 1944, and purportedly written by his wife. A characteristic of them was that the word Hampstead was spelled without the letter 'p'. Manton unwittingly gave himself away in a specimen of his writing in which he repeated the spelling error. Only one fingerprint of Mrs Manton was found in the house: her husband had forgotten to clean a pickle bottle in the cupboard.

Manton was arrested, and made a full confession. He and his wife had quarrelled, and he struck her with a heavy wooden stool. He wrapped her body in sacks and wheeled it on his bicycle to the river, where he pushed it into the water. He repeated this story at his trial at Bedford Assizes and said that he had taken his wife by the throat—an admission not previously made, and

one which sealed his fate as a murderer. Manton was found guilty and sentenced to death, which was commuted to life imprisonment. He served only 3 years before dying in prison in 1947.
[*175, 496, 552, 564, 851*]

MANUEL, Peter Thomas Anthony. This was a 31-year-old Glasgow multiple murderer whose eagerness to give evidence led him to the gallows.

Manuel, a single man living with his parents, was a habitual criminal with a record for theft and assault. He had also been imprisoned for rape.

In January 1958 a triple murder occurred in Glasgow. Doris and Peter Smart and their 11-year-old son were found dead in bed, shot through the head at close range. The family had also been robbed. In September 1956 another triple shooting had occurred—Mrs Watt, her 16-year-old daughter Vivienne and Mrs Watt's sister Mrs Brown. Mr Watt was arrested for these killings.

The police had Peter Manuel under routine surveillance—he lived in the area in which the murders occurred—and his home was searched. He was noticed passing some £1 notes printed in a new blue colour. He was known to be hard up at the time, and Peter Smart had drawn some of these new notes from his bank.

Manuel's home was searched again, but the only discovery was of some housebreaking tools. Nevertheless, the police detained him for questioning and also apprehended his father for burglary. Manuel said he would give information on condition that his father was released. He subsequently gave details of the two triple murders and also admitted killing 17-year-old Anne Kneilands in September 1956 and Isabelle Cooke, a girl of the same age, who had gone missing in January 1958. The police were impressed by Manuel's cold-heartedness—when leading them to the place where Isabelle Cooke was buried, he said, 'This is the place. In fact, I think I'm standing on her now.'

He was tried in Glasgow in May 1958 on 8 charges of murder. In the middle of his trial he dismissed his counsel and conducted his own defence. On the question of Manuel's mental condition the judge averred, 'A man may be very bad without being mad.' Acquitted of the charge of murdering Anne Kneilands due to lack of evidence, Manuel was convicted on each of the other 7 counts and sentenced to death. The man who was so keen to give evidence was hanged at Glasgow's Barlinnie Prison on 11 July 1958. There

is little doubt that he committed several other murders, which included that of a Newcastle taxi-driver.
[*85, 245, 310, 542, 601, 609, 679, 688, 999*]

MAREK, Martha. A 34-year-old Austrian murderess whose career included an incredible attempt at fraud, followed by three deaths by poisoning.

Martha Löwenstein was an orphan who was adopted by a poor Viennese family. In 1919 a wealthy storeowner saw her in a dress shop where she worked, and made her his ward. The 15-year-old was sent to finishing schools in England and France and left a large sum of money.

Martha was married in 1924 to Emil Marek, an engineering student. Between them they quickly ran through her inheritance, and to get more money worked out a fraud. They insured Emil against accident for £10000 and in no time at all he had an accident. While he was cutting down a tree the axe slipped, and almost severed his leg. The limb had to be amputated below the knee, and the surgeon concluded that the wound had been inflicted deliberately. It consisted of 3 separate cuts, and the angle was inconsistent with the story of an accidental blow. The police were notified, and the Mareks were charged with fraud. Martha made matters worse by bribing a hospital orderly to say that he had seen the surgeon tampering with the wound. The Mareks were cleared of the fraud charge but were imprisoned for 4 months for bribery.

During the next few years the couple were broke, and in 1932 Emil died of tuberculosis, and was followed within a month by the death of Martha's baby daughter. Martha became companion to an elderly relative, Susanne Löwenstein, who soon died, leaving her possessions to her young companion. For the second time in her life Martha's extravagant tastes ran away with her, and she was driven to renting out rooms.

A female boarder died mysteriously and Martha was suspected of poisoning her. When it was found that the dead woman's body contained thallium (see *Graham Young*), the bodies of Emil Marek, baby Marek and Susanne Löwenstein were exhumed. All contained thallium, a compound which Martha bought at a chemist's shop. Martha Marek was beheaded on 6 December 1938.
[*852, 854, 855*]

MARWOOD, Ronald Henry. Scaffolder, aged

25, whose first wedding anniversary celebration ended in the murder of a London policeman.

Following visits to various pubs where he consumed 10 pints of brown ale on 14 December 1958, Marwood was in Seven Sisters Road, Holloway. There he became involved in a gang fight in which knives, bottles and knuckledusters were used. A 23-year-old police constable, Raymond Henry Summers, tried to break up the fight, during which he was stabbed to death with a 10-inch knife.

Eleven youths were charged for brawling, and Marwood, who denied any involvement, was released. But on 27 January 1959 he walked into a police station and admitted, 'I did stab the copper that night.'

Marwood was tried at the Old Bailey in March 1959, when he pleaded not guilty. He stated that he heard the police constable telling the brawling youths to break it up and struck out at the officer, intending to push him away. He did not know that he had his knife in his hand. He went to the police station of his own accord because he had lied when first questioned. But he maintained that the police 'put down things' he did not say, including the alleged statement that he had stabbed the dead policeman.

The defence said that there was no evidence connecting the accused man with the fatal blow, and that if in the excitement of the fight and with his brain clouded with drink, he did strike the policeman, the verdict should be one of manslaughter. The jury found Marwood guilty of the capital murder of a police officer, and he was hanged at Pentonville Prison on 8 May 1959.
[311, 487]

MARYMONT, Marcus. A 37-year-old Master Sergeant serving with the US Air Force based at Sculthorpe, Norfolk, who murdered his wife.

In June 1958 Marymont's wife, 43-year-old Mary Helen, died at the base hospital after being admitted in a critical condition. When told that his wife was dying Marymont seemed more concerned to discuss his marital problems with the doctor. He also mentioned that his wife had been ill with similar symptoms several times during the past year. Doctors suspected poison, and Marymont, having first agreed to an autopsy, then withdrew his consent.

The US military authorities learned that the Master Sergeant had been having relations with 23-year-old Cynthia Taylor, a married woman living apart from her husband. Marymont said, 'I

felt my wife was very cold to me and my feelings were directed more towards Cynthia.' He had tried to buy arsenic from a shop at Maidenhead and 2 cleaners at the USAF base identified Marymont as having asked them where he could get arsenic.

Marymont was tried by a US General Court Martial at Denham in December 1958. The prosecution claimed he poisoned his wife because he loved another woman. Pathological evidence indicated that the dead woman had received a dose of arsenic 24 hours before her death. Marymont said that he was sure he had not given his wife anything.

The defence argued that all the evidence was circumstantial, and that in the accused's favour it should be mentioned that he had a good Service record. The court, sitting in closed session, found Marymont guilty of murdering his wife with arsenic, and guilty of misconduct with Mrs Taylor. He was sentenced to life imprisonment, to be served at Fort Leavenworth Prison, Kansas.
[311, 487]

MASON, Alexander Campbell. Nicknamed 'Scottie', 22-year-old Mason, a deserter from the Canadian armed forces in the First World War, came to Britain where robbery led to murder.

On the evening of 9 May 1923 two figures were seen struggling near a taxi-cab in a south-west London suburb. Shots were fired; a man ran away, leaving cab-driver Jacob Dickey dying in the street.

At the scene police found a revolver, a jemmy and a distinctive gold-mounted walking-stick. A photograph of the stick was published and information led the police to 'Eddie' Vivian, a convicted criminal living in a Pimlico flat with his prostitute girl-friend. Vivian made a statement admitting ownership of the walking-stick and implicating 'Scottie' Mason.

Mason was tried for murder at the Old Bailey in July 1923, and Vivian was principal prosecution witness. He said that he and Mason had been planning house robbery, and claimed that Mason had obtained a revolver, mentioning that he wanted to hold up a taxi-driver. Vivian contended that on the fatal night he was ill with food poisoning, and unable to accompany Mason. Mason took his friend's walking-stick and left the flat on his own. He returned late that evening in an excited and dishevelled state, saying that he had shot a taxi-driver.

Mason denied all this, maintaining that Vivian's illness was a ruse to quieten his girl-friend's

Mason, Alexander Campbell

apprehension about their plan. When the girl left the house Vivian abandoned his bed, and they went out together. Mason said that Vivian struggled with the taxi-driver and shot him, after which they fled their separate ways and later met at Vivian's flat.

The jury found Mason guilty, and he was sentenced to death. Sentence was commuted to life imprisonment, and he was released in 1937 after serving 14 years, later to die in the Second World War in the Merchant Navy.

[2, 47, 81, 118, 167]

MASSET, Louise. Cultured 36-year-old woman of mixed French and English parentage who murdered her child.

On 27 October 1899, naked and still warm, the body of a 3-year-old boy was found wrapped in a shawl, in a woman's lavatory at a London railway station. A doctor thought the child had first been stunned and then suffocated.

He was identified as Manfred Louis Masset by Miss Helen Gentle, who had been paid to look after the child since he was a few weeks old. Manfred was the illegitimate son of Louise Masset, a children's governess. Miss Gentle believed the father was French and regularly sent money to support the boy.

On 16 October Miss Gentle received a letter from Louise Masset saying that Manfred's father wanted the boy to be sent to France. On 27 October, Helen Gentle took him to Stamford Hill, where she left him with his mother.

Later that day Louise Masset arrived at her sister's home in an hysterical state. She blurted out, 'I'm hunted for murder, but I didn't do it.' Her account of what happened involved her 19-year-old lover Eudore Lucas, a French clerk, whom she had agreed to meet secretly at Brighton on 27 October. Lucas knew about her child, and it was decided to place the boy in the care of a Mrs Browning and her assistant who were starting a children's home. After collecting Manfred, Louise Masset took him to London Bridge Station where she handed him over with £12 to the two women.

Louise Masset was identified as a woman seen with a child, and clothes found at Brighton were identified as Manfred's by Miss Gentle. Louise Masset could not produce a receipt for the £12, and the baby-minders could not be traced. She was found guilty and hanged at Newgate on 9 January 1900.

[592, 607, 885, 1001]

Maybrick: Exhibits at the trial

MAYBRICK, Florence Elizabeth. A 36-year-old Southern belle born in Alabama and tried in Liverpool for the murder of her husband.

Florie married James Maybrick, an Englishman who ran a trading firm in Liverpool, in 1881. Maybrick's family did not approve, not liking Florie's mother, thrice-married Baroness von Roques. Maybrick was 23 years older than Florie and a hypochondriac. He was always dosing himself, and had told friends that he regularly took arsenic as an aphrodisiac.

After spending the first 3 years of their married life in America, the Maybricks settled down in Liverpool. They moved into Battlecrease House, had 2 children and seemed happy enough. There were 5 servants including a nanny, Alice Yapp.

In 1887 Florie learned that her husband kept a mistress; she also discovered that they were in financial difficulty. She was forced to reduce her spending but ran up embarrassing debts. She found comfort in the arms of Alfred Brierley, a friend of her husband. In March 1889 the couple spent a week-end together in London. Maybrick was furious when he found out, and a quarrel ensued in which he beat Florie.

Shortly after this Florie bought a dozen arsenic-based flypapers from a local chemist. Five days later she purchased a further two dozen papers from another shop. In the meantime, James Maybrick drew up a new will excluding his wife. On 28 April 1889 James was taken ill. Florie mentioned to the doctor that he had been taking a 'white powder'. He seemed to improve, but died on 11 May. During his illness Florie had written to

Brierley saying that James 'is sick unto death'. The letter was never sent. Alice Yapp found an excuse for opening it and immediately handed it over to Maybrick's brother Edwin. Hostility mounted against Florie; she was kept a prisoner in the house while her husband's brothers searched the residence. In Florie's room they found a packet labelled 'Arsenic: Poison for Cats'.

Florie was arrested after traces of arsenic were found in her husband's body, and a Coroner's Jury returned a verdict of murder against her. She was tried at Liverpool in July 1889. The evidence against her appeared damning, particularly the flypapers which Florie said she used to make an arsenical cosmetic preparation (see *Madeleine Smith*.) Most devastating was the prejudice shown towards the unfaithful wife. The defence suggested that Maybrick died a natural death; that traces of strychnine, hyoscine and morphine found in his stomach were the remnants of hypochondriac dosing. The judge (who later was committed to an asylum) summed up heavily against her.

Florence Maybrick was found guilty, and received the death sentence, but the sentence was commuted to life imprisonment, of which she served 15 years, being released in 1904. She died in the United States in 1941, aged 76.

[*1, 21, 106, 108, 176, 234, 254, 332, 356, 364, 419, 572, 606, 613, 632, 633, 659, 670, 676, 681, 792, 807, 872, 907, 989, 1003*]

MERRETT, John Donald. Acquitted of murdering his mother, Merrett went on to an extraordinary criminal career of forgery, blackmail, fraud and homicide before taking his own life.

Born in New Zealand in 1908, he was a bright youth with a flair for languages and a passion for girls. His mother placed him at Edinburgh University, hoping that she could keep a watchful eye on him. Donald, however, exchanged his lectures for female company.

On 17 March 1926 Merrett breakfasted with his mother. The daily help was attending to her duties when she heard a shot and Donald cried out, 'My mother has shot herself.' Mrs Merrett lay on the floor bleeding from a head wound—she was taken to hospital where she was regarded as an attempted suicide. She recovered consciousness and gave a rambling account that she had told Donald to go away and not to annoy her. Merrett maintained she had money problems. She died on 1 April from meningitis and was accorded a suicide's burial.

In November Donald Merrett was charged with both murder and forging his mother's cheques. He was tried at Edinburgh in February 1927. The prosecution believed that the nature of the shooting and the wound ruled out suicide, while Sir Bernard Spilsbury and Robert Churchill the gunsmith maintained the opposite view for the defence. The jury returned a Not Proven verdict on the murder charge but found Merrett guilty of forgery. He received a year's imprisonment.

Soon after his release Merrett inherited £50 000, and married 17-year-old Vera Bonnar. He changed his name to Ronald Chesney, and having quickly spent the money embarked on a career of blackmail and fraud. He served with the Royal Naval Volunteer Reserve during the Second World War, and then immersed himself in the black market of post-war Germany.

In 1954 Merrett decided to rob his wife, who with her mother (calling herself Lady Menzies) was running an old people's home at Ealing. In February he slipped back into England, made his wife drunk on gin and drowned her in the bath. Lady Menzies saw him, and he had to kill her too.

Her battered and strangled body was found in the house, and what was planned as an 'accident' became a double murder.

An international alert was put out for Merrett alias Chesney and on 16 February his body, with a bullet-wound in the head, was found near Cologne. On his clothing were found fibres and hair linking him to Lady Menzies's death. An inquest in London decided that Merrett had killed his wife and mother-in-law.

[1, 8, 29, 306, 318, 331, 420, 423, 424, 641, 652, 678, 780, 865, 897, 915, 930, 962, 998]

MERRIFIELD, Louisa May. Middle-aged woman who poisoned an elderly woman for gain.

Louisa Merrifield at the age of 46 had been married 3 times and served a prison sentence for ration book frauds. With her third husband, 71-year-old Alfred, she had had 20 domestic jobs in 3 years.

On 12 March 1953 the Merrifields took up an appointment as living-in housekeepers and companions to Mrs Sarah Ann Ricketts, an elderly woman who owned a modern bungalow in Blackpool. Friction soon developed, with Mrs Ricketts complaining that she did not get enough to eat and Louisa Merrifield boasting to various people that she had worked for an old woman who had died and left her a bungalow worth £3000. When asked who had died, she replied, 'She's not dead yet, but she soon will be.'

On 9 April Louisa called a doctor, asking him to certify that Mrs Ricketts was fit enough to make a new will. On 14 April she died. An autopsy showed death due to phosphorus poisoning. The bungalow and garden were searched with the Merrifields still in residence, and Louisa requesting the Salvation Army band to play *Abide with Me* outside. (See *Mary Pearcey*.)

The Merrifields were tried for murder at Manchester in July 1953. The prosecution contended that Mrs Ricketts had died of phosphorus poisoning, taken in the form of rat poison. Witnesses related Louisa's ill-advised remarks about her prospective inheritance. There was little doubt as to the identity of the murderer but no poison was found at the bungalow.

Louisa was found guilty, but the jury were unable to reach a verdict on Alfred. She was hanged at Manchester's Strangeways Prison, on 18 September 1953. Alfred Merrifield was eventually released to inherit a half-share in Mrs Ricketts's bungalow and to appear in Blackpool's

side-shows before dying, aged 80, in 1962.

[283, 306, 460, 598, 712, 1001]

MESRINE, Jacques. French master criminal designated Public Enemy No.1 by the police. He grew up in occupied France and joined the army when he reached military age. He served in Algeria during the civil war in that country, and was decorated for bravery. When he left the army he found civilian life unexciting, and he quickly graduated via petty crime to robbery and, in due course, to murder.

From 1962 onward Mesrine led the life of a criminal. He robbed banks and kept on the move to avoid capture, crossing international borders if he thought the opportunity for crime was attractive. In 1968 he went to Canada and tried his hand at kidnapping. With the help of an accomplice he abducted a Montreal millionaire and demanded a ransom of $200,000. This plan backfired when their hostage escaped but they quickly moved to another town where they befriended a wealthy widow who was later found strangled. Mesrine and his girl-friend were arrested in the USA and taken back to Canada to stand trial for murder. They were acquitted of this charge but received prison sentences for the crime of kidnapping.

After serving 1 year of his 10-year term, Mesrine led a number of prisoners in a sensational gaol escape. While on the run he reverted to bank robbery, and in woods near Montreal narrowly avoided recapture by shooting two forest rangers. Leaving a trail of bank robberies behind him, Mesrine travelled to the USA and then to Venezuela. There he lived on the proceeds of his robberies, and relished the press reports which called him an international criminal.

In 1973 Mesrine returned to France, committing numerous robberies and acquiring millions of francs while the police hunted high and low for him. The manhunt eventually met with success, and the arch-criminal—France's Public Enemy No. One—was put behind bars. While in La Santé prison he wrote a book called *The Death Instinct* which contained detailed descriptions of murders he claimed to have committed. In May 1977 he was put on trial and received a prison sentence of 20 years.

After serving 12 months of his sentence, Mesrine contrived a spectacular escape and once again embarked on a series of robberies and daring confrontations with the authorities. In Normandy he walked into a police station posing as a Gaming Squad inspector, apparently for the pleasure of taunting the police. He moved to London for a few weeks in 1978, where he quietly plotted to kidnap the judge who had sentenced him at his recent trial. In November, back in Paris, he put the plan into action but his scheme went wrong and he only narrowly escaped capture.

Mesrine's violent life came to a characteristically violent end in November 1979 in a Paris street. The police had traced him to an apartment block, and decided to employ maximum force. When Mesrine walked from the apartment towards his car parked in the street he was cut down by a hail of bullets. The man who had tantalized the police for so long lay dead in the gutter, and it was reported that the officers at the scene danced with joy.

[*822, 996*]

MILLER, James William. Convicted of the Truro Murders in Adelaide, South Australia, in 1980. A number of young women went missing in the area during 1977, and 2 years later their bodies began turning up at Truro, in the Adelaide hills. A reward of $A30,000 for information flushed out Miller, who was said to have been implicated with another man in picking up girls and killing them.

Miller had spent most of his life in prison for theft or housebreaking, but had no record of violence. Under questioning he denied any part in killing the girls, but admitted knowing where the bodies were because he had helped to bury them. He claimed that a close friend with whom he had a homosexual relationship, 23-year-old Chris Worrell, killed the girls, and that he had tried to persuade his friend—who he knew needed help—to see a doctor.

The first killing occurred on 24 December 1976 when they picked up a girl in Adelaide and drove out into the hills. Miller left the couple together in the car, as he believed they intended to have sex. When he returned the girl was dead. 'I killed her,' said Worrell. Miller helped him bury the corpse. The pattern was repeated 6 times when Worrell was overcome by one of the violent moods to which he was subject. How long the murder spree would have lasted if fate had not intervened can only be guessed at, for on 19 February 1977 Worrell and a girl-friend were killed in a car crash. Miller, a passenger in the same car, survived.

At Miller's trial the prosecution alleged that the killings were a joint enterprise of the two men. The judge described for the jury the meaning of 'acting in concert'. He said that for people to be acting in concert in the commission of a crime, their assent to the understanding or the arrangement between them need not be expressed in words. Miller, who readily admitted a close relationship with Worrell,

was found guilty on 6 counts of murder and sentenced to life imprisonment.

In 1984 Miller wrote his account of the Truro murders from his cell at Yatala Labor Prison. He proclaimed his innocence of murder, and was bitter that his appeal had been turned down. The appeal was based on an alleged misdirection of the jury by the trial judge and the discovery of new evidence which showed that Worrell had received psychiatric treatment while serving in the Royal Australian Air Force. Regrettably for Miller, none of this altered his conviction, although his case was widely aired in Australia's national press.

[*667*]

MILLS, Herbert Leonard. A 19-year-old literary poseur who tried to commit the perfect murder.

Mills, who lived in Nottingham, phoned the *News of the World* newspaper on 9 August 1951, saying that he had discovered the body of a woman, and adding, 'It looks like a murder.' He had not informed the police, which the newspaper promptly did.

Mills took the officers to a lonely spot in Sherwood Vale where lay the body of 48-year-old Mabel Tattershaw, a Nottingham housewife. Mills described himself as an artist and poet and, when interviewed by a *News of the World* reporter, said he went to Sherwood Vale to relax. When he saw the body he read a poem before deciding what to do. He wanted payment, and wrote his own handwritten account which was a murder confession. The newspaper handed this to the police, and Mills was arrested. When charged he replied simply, 'Yes.'

Mills had thought about the perfect murder, and he decided on an experiment. He met Mrs Tattershaw by chance at a cinema and arranged a meeting next day. They decided to meet on the following day. The poor woman was flattered. Mills described the murder in an entirely cold-blooded way, 'The strangling itself was quite easily accomplished,' he said.

He was tried in November 1951, but although his counsel tried to construct a defence based on Mills finding the body of the woman and then trying to gain notoriety by informing the press rather than the police, forensic evidence clearly linked Mills to the dead woman by means of fibres from his suit found under her finger-nails. Mills was found guilty and condemned to death. His reaction was to smile at both judge and jury. He was executed in December.

[*373, 418, 598, 791*]

MILSOM and FOWLER. Victorian murder in which a child's lantern played a significant part.

Henry Smith, an elderly retired engineer, was found dead with head wounds in the kitchen of his North London house on 14 February 1896. The old man had been bound with strips of cloth, cut with penknives, and these and a child's toy lantern were found by the body. Entry had been forced, and the safe burgled.

The day before the murder 2 men were seen around the house. They were Albert Milsom and Henry Fowler, men with criminal records and now missing from their Kentish Town homes.

When the child's lantern found at the murder scene was recognized by 15-year-old Henry Miller, Milsom's brother-in-law, as belonging to him, the missing pair were linked with the murder, and a £10 banknote stolen from Mr Smith's safe was traced to Fowler.

It was several weeks before they were apprehended at Bath. Fowler denied all knowledge of the crime, but Milsom, the weaker of the pair, admitted the theft, although he attributed the violence to his partner.

The pair were tried at the Old Bailey, when the judge said that the evidence of the two penknives showed both men were involved in tying up their victim. Fowler attempted to strangle Milsom in the dock and was torn away by warders.

Both men were found guilty and sentenced to death. They were hanged, with a man called Seaman between them, and it is alleged that his last words were, 'This is the first time I've ever been a bloody peacemaker.' The date was 9 June 1896.

[10, 234, 239, 438, 553, 873, 932]

M'LACHLAN, Jessie. Celebrated case in which a 28-year-old domestic servant was found guilty of a murder which she may only have witnessed.

Glasgow accountant John Fleming would go straight from his office at week-ends to his villa at Dunoon, leaving his town home at Sandyford Place occupied by his aged father, James Fleming, and a 25-year-old servant girl Jessie M'Pherson.

Returning from Dunoon on 7 July 1862, John was told by his father that Jessie M'Pherson had not been seen since the Friday. The door to the servants' quarters was locked. On gaining entrance they found the semi-nude body of the girl dead in the bloodstained sheets of her bed. There were several bloody footprints on the floor.

The girl had been hacked with a cleaver. Her box had been rifled, and some of her best clothes, together with some of the family silver, were missing. It was found that two of old Mr Fleming's shirts kept in a basement chest were spotted with blood. This, coupled with the fact that he failed to report the girl's disappearance, led to his arrest.

On 9 July a pawnbroker reported that the missing silver had been pledged in his shop. The police arrested Jessie M'Lachlan, a former servant at Sandyford Place, who admitted pawning the silver at the request of old Mr Fleming, who wanted money. The bloody footprints found in the dead girl's room were matched to those of M'Lachlan, and some discarded bloodstained clothing was also proved to belong to her. She was accused of murder, and old Mr Fleming was released.

Jessie M'Lachlan's trial at Glasgow in September 1862 excited great public interest. Old James Fleming gave evidence, and despite several witnesses' statements about his randy disposition, the judge tried to preserve his reputation. The circumstantial evidence told against the accused, and the jury returned a unanimous guilty verdict. Before sentence was passed, Jessie M'Lachlan made a statement in which she admitted tending Jessie M'Pherson, who she found lying insensible with head injuries. She learned from the dying girl that old Mr Fleming had tried to force himself on her. Remarking that such statements were rarely more than falsehoods, the judge passed sentence.

It was alleged that Jessie M'Lachlan had not been given a fair trial. After numerous petitions her sentence was commuted to penal servitude for life. It was felt that she might only have been a witness to murder. Jessie served 15 years in prison before being released on 5 October 1877 and going to America, where she died on 1 January 1899.

[1, 21, 29, 114, 442, 452, 532, 780]

MOLINEUX, Roland B. Born in 1868, Molineux moved in New York's high society in the 1890s. He was a factory manager, and belonged to the exclusive Knickerbocker Athletic club. He had delusions of grandeur, which he bolstered with the aid of murder.

A fellow-member, Henry C. Barnet, was courting a young girl on whom Molineux had designs. In November 1898 Barnet died mysteriously, and within weeks Molineux had married her. This caused a great deal of rumour, and it was whispered that Barnet had taken poison sent to him by post.

Later Molineux had a row with another club member, Harry Cornish, who had bested him at weight-lifting. When the Club refused his demand to disbar Cornish, Molineux resigned. Then, on 23 December 1898, Cornish received by post a bottle of Bromo Seltzer anonymously. He gave a dose to his landlady, Mrs Katherine J. Adams, for a headache—she complained of its bitter taste, had convulsions and died. (See *Jean-Pierre Vaquier*.)

The Bromo Seltzer contained mercury cyanide, and when the writing on the postal wrapper was checked with Knickerbocker Club members, the writing conformed with that of Roland Molineux.

Molineux was sent for trial. His claims of innocence, and a defence backed by his father's wealth, could not persuade 14 handwriting experts that the writing was other than his. He had ordered a consignment of mercury cyanide, ostensibly for use in his factory. He was found guilty and sentenced to death, but it took 18 months for an appeal for a retrial to be considered. During this time he joined the ranks of literary murderers (see *Lacenaire*) by writing a book entitled *The Room With the Little Door*.

A second trial was granted in 1902, and the delay was to his advantage. He posed as the victim of prejudice, won the verdict and was set free. Molineux wrote for several newspapers, but lost heart after his wife divorced him. He entered an asylum in 1913, and died there 4 years later.

[*470, 538, 562, 729, 734, 887, 896*]

MONSON, Alfred John. Monson coached boys for entrance examinations. He became involved in complex financial dealings which ended with a murder charge.

In 1890 Major Hambrough, a retired officer and near-bankrupt landowner, placed his 17-year-old son Cecil under Monson's tuition. Monson took a hand in the Major's affairs. Hambrough's estates were so organized that he received an assured annual income, and when his son reached the age of 18 they could be sold by mutual consent. Hambrough had mortgaged his life interest in the estates for £37 000, which he spent. He borrowed from a moneylender named Tottenham, and he was trying to buy back the life interest and mortgage it elsewhere.

Monson, with Cecil firmly under his influence, decided to purchase Major Hambrough's interest in the estate by manipulation at both the Major's and Tottenham's expense. Disagreement followed, and Monson moved from Yorkshire to Ardlamont in Argyllshire, with his wife, children and Cecil Hambrough. The house was taken on a lease, although Monson had told a friend that Cecil

had bought it for £48 000. His next step was to take out life insurance on Cecil for £20 000. The premium was paid by Monson out of money gained by false pretences. Next, Cecil was persuaded to advise the insurance company that in the event of his death the payments should be assigned to Monson's wife.

On 10 August 1893 Monson (having already tried to drown Cecil the previous day while they were fishing from a boat), went out rabbit-shooting with him and a man named Scott. Monson returned to the house and announced, 'Mr Cecil has shot himself.' The doctor who examined the dead youth asked if he had taken out any insurance. Monson said no. The insurance company sent 2 investigators, and Monson was arrested and charged with attempted murder and murder.

Monson was tried at Edinburgh in December 1893. The prosecution contended that Cecil was shot in a manner which ruled out suicide. It was shown that Monson had lied on matters relating to the guns and ammunition used for the shoot. The defence maintained that Monson would not have benefited from Cecil's death. The judge summed up in favour of the accused, remarking in a famous statement, 'It is the business of the Crown to prove the case, and not for the defence to prove innocence.' The verdict was one of Not Proven.

[*1, 355, 554, 722, 780, 784, 786, 998, 1013, 1015*]

MOORE, Alfred. Yorkshire farmer in his late thirties who supplemented his low earnings by burglary. Petty crime led to a shooting at his remote farm near Huddersfield.

The police were catching up with Moore, and on 14 July 1951 set a trap for him. They surrounded his farmhouse late at night, intending to catch him red-handed when he returned home. In the early hours of the morning 5 shots rang out, and the police found two of their number, an inspector and a constable, lying on the ground with gunshot wounds. The inspector died on his way to hospital, and the other officer died later.

It was ascertained that Moore was back in his farmhouse, and he was promptly arrested on a shooting charge. He claimed that he had been in bed since midnight, and that the only weapon he owned was a shotgun—the fatal shots had been fired from a revolver. An identity parade was staged in the hospital where the dying constable lay—he picked out Moore, who was duly charged with murder. A search of the farm produced a quantity of stolen property but no murder weapon, nor could mine-detectors locate one.

The farmer was tried at Leeds Assizes in December 1951. He denied involvement in the shootings, repeating that he was indoors at the time, but the police constable's death-bed identification of Moore was sufficient to condemn the accused. He was found guilty, sentenced to death and hanged at Armley Prison, Leeds, on 6 February 1952.

[*118*]

MOORS MURDERS. Ian Brady, aged 28, and Myra Hindley, aged 24, were tried at Chester Assizes for multiple murder.

Brady and Hindley worked in the same office. After hours they developed a violent appetite for sadism, Nazism and pornography. In September 1964 the couple went to live with Hindley's grandmother in Hattersley. They were friendly with Hindley's sister Maureen and her husband 17-year-old David Smith. Brady sought to impress Smith with his books on sadism and his handguns. They talked of robbing banks and of murder.

To prove to Smith that he was no idle boaster, Brady picked up 17-year-old Edward Evans, a homosexual, in Manchester on the evening of 6 October 1965 and took him home. At 11.30 that night Hindley went to Smith's house and asked him home. There Smith watched a murder. On the sofa in the living-room was a young man. He was still alive, but Brady, wielding an axe, proceeded to smash his head in. He said, 'It's done. It's the messiest yet. It normally only takes one blow.'

Terrified by what he had seen, Smith telephoned the police early next morning. At the house police found the body of the dead youth in a bedroom. A search produced two left luggage

Moors Murders: Brady and Hindley

tickets which corresponded with two suitcases at Manchester Central Station. The cases contained coshes, wigs, papers, photographs and two tape recordings.

Some of the photographs were of a little girl. She was 10-year-old Lesley Ann Downey, who had been missing from her home since December 1964. The child's voice was identified on a tape recording pleading to be allowed to go home. Her body was found buried on the moors north of Manchester.

Another child, 12-year-old John Kilbride, missing from home since November 1963, featured in some of Brady's notes—notes which were a plan of murder. From photographs showing Brady and Hindley on the moors, police were able to identify search areas. John Kilbride's moorland grave was found a few hundred yards from that of Lesley Ann Downey.

The trial of the Moors Murderers lasted 15 days. Brady and Hindley were convicted on 6 May 1966 and sentenced to life imprisonment.

The Moors Murderers continued to excite interest, first with suggestions that Hindley had become a socially reformed character fit to be paroled and, secondly, by persistent rumours that there were more bodies to be found on the moors. Despite a campaign on her behalf by Lord Longford, Hindley remained in prison; Brady, who is detained in Park Lane High Security Hospital, Liverpool, has said that he never wants to be released.

In 1986 Hindley made a private confession to two more killings which led to searches on Saddleworth Moor for further graves. In April 1987 her confession was made public and it became known that she and Brady had killed Keith Bennett, aged 12, and Pauline Reade, aged 16. The girl's body was found in August 1987, 24 years after she had disappeared. At different times both Hindley and Brady assisted the police in their searches. In January 1988 the Director of Public Prosecutions announced that no further charges would be brought against the Moors Murderers.

[*4, 343, 408, 415, 599, 646, 747, 766, 857, 871, 984, 1002*]

MOREAU, Pierre-Désiré. A 32-year-old Parisian pharmacist who poisoned his wife.

Moreau, ambitious, with a herbalist shop in Paris, married a woman of scanty means. After 3 years of marriage Mme Moreau died after a brief illness during which she was treated by her husband.

Moreau married again, this time for money. His second wife, like his first, became ill with persistent vomiting which would not respond to treatment. Before she died the second Mme Moreau confided her fear that her husband was poisoning her. Her body was exhumed, and contained large amounts of copper. The first Mme Moreau's body was also exhumed and also contained copper.

At Moreau's trial a book in his pharmacy marked at the passage on copper sulphate was produced. On his second marriage he only received half of his wife's dowry—her death was therefore necessary for him to obtain the rest.

Pierre-Désiré Moreau was guillotined in Paris on 14 October 1874 before a large crowd.

[736]

MOREY, Edward Henry. Celebrated Australian murder known as the 'Hand in Glove Case', and as notable as the *Shark Arm Case*.

On Christmas Day 1933 fishermen found a body caught on a tree in the Murrumbidgee, near Wagga Wagga. The corpse, which had been in the water about 5 weeks, was male, aged between 45 and 50. Identification was impossible, as the face was unrecognizable and the skin was missing from both hands. Severe injuries to the back of the head indicated murder.

Detectives searching the banks of the river retrieved what they thought was a glove in the water, but the object turned out to be a human glove—the decomposing, water-bloated skin from a man's hand and wrist. The human glove—presumed to have come from the dead man—was worn by a detective, thus enabling a fingerprint to be made. The print belonged to a vagabond, Percy Smith.

The dead man's movements were traced, and he had been seen in his wagonette with a trapper named Edward Morey. Morey was arrested and charged with murder after bloodstains were found on his clothing and an axe in his possession. He was tried for murder at Wagga Wagga, when the proceedings were interrupted by the shooting of Moncrieff Anderson, one of the prosecution witnesses. Mrs Anderson claimed that her husband had been shot by intruders, but police noticed that the handwriting on Lillian Anderson's statement was the same as that on two love letters from 'Thelma Smith' found on Morey.

Meanwhile, Morey was found guilty of murdering Percy Smith, and was sentenced to death. When Lillian Anderson appeared in court she said that her husband and not Morey had killed

Smith. She said her husband's death was accidental. Morey gave evidence, and denied knowing Mrs Anderson.

The jury disagreed twice, but finally Lillian Anderson was convicted of manslaughter. She had been judged sane, but with a mental age of 14. Her extraordiny intervention was put down to an attraction for Morey, whom she tried to protect by killing her own husband and naming him as the real murderer.

Mrs Anderson served 10 years of a 20-year prison sentence, and although Morey's appeal was dismissed he was later reprieved.

[426, 853]

MORGAN, Samuel. Soldier found guilty of murder in wartime Britain.

The body of 15-year-old Mary Hagan, sexually assaulted and strangled, was found on 2 November 1940 in a concrete blockhouse in Liverpool, after she had been reported missing.

Among the various items near the body was a small piece of fabric which proved to be a piece of bandage made of materials used in military dressings, and impregnated with acriflavine. It had been used to dress a cut on a finger or thumb.

A few days later a 28-year-old soldier, Samuel Morgan, stationed at Seaforth Barracks, was detained. He had a cut on his thumb which he said was caused by barbed wire, and he had used his own field dressing.

Forensic evidence showed that the bandage found matched in every way, even down to the precise stitching on the selvedge, the type of field dressing issued to Morgan's unit, and samples of soil from the blockhouse floor compared with dirt on Morgan's uniform. It was also established that on the night of the murder Morgan had visited a Liverpool hotel, arriving as a witness described it, 'out of breath' with his thumb bleeding.

Samuel Morgan was found guilty of Mary Hagan's murder and hanged at Walton Gaol on 4 April 1941.

[283]

MORRIS, Raymond Leslie. The A34 child murderer who boasted to his first wife, 'I've never made a mistake in my life' eluded police for over a year before being brought to justice.

Christine Ann Darby, 7, was kidnapped in broad daylight in Coronation Street, Walsall, on 19 August 1967 by a man driving a grey car. The grey car and the local accent of the man which had been overheard by some children were the two most positive clues. Christine's suffocated and sexually assaulted body was found 3 days later 14 miles away on lonely Cannock Chase. Car-tyre tracks were near by.

Two people who had been on Cannock Chase reported seeing a man with a grey car, an Austin A55 or A60, on the day of the murder. A wide-scale manhunt ensued, and Identikit pictures were published nation-wide. Some 1375000 vehicle registrations were examined, out of which 23097 were grey Austins, the owners of which were interviewed. House-to-house inquiries were also made in and around Walsall.

On 4 November 1968 in Walsall, a man tried to entice a 10-year-old girl into his car. The child resisted, and when the man realized he was being watched by a woman, he drove off. She noted the registration number and informed the police.

The vehicle was traced to 29-year-old foreman engineer Raymond Morris, who lived with his second wife in Walsall. It was ascertained that Morris's previous car had been a grey Austin A55,

and that in 1966 he had been reported for allegedly interfering with small girls.

Mrs Morris confirmed her husband's claim to have been out shopping with her on the day Christine Darby was missing. Nevertheless, the police arrested him on 15 November. His wife now shattered his alibi by saying she had been mistaken. Morris was also positively identified by the 2 witnesses who had seen him on Cannock Chase.

Detectives found photographs at Morris's home depicting a small girl in indecent postures. His work-mates liked him, though they thought him a little unsociable, and he was highly respected by his parents as a man who never swore and who loved children. But his first wife, whom he had divorced, spoke of her exhausting sex-life with him. Morris was sent for trial at Staffordshire Assizes in February 1969. He went into the witness-box and professed disgust at the photographs he had taken, but claimed the police had tried to extort a confession from him. Morris was found guilty and sentenced to life imprison-

Morris: The destruction of the murder car

ment. The murder of two other little girls also found on Cannock Chase earlier remained unsolved.

[*289, 428, 599*]

MORRISON, Stinie. Russian Jew, alias Morris Stein, convicted in 1911 of a murder which he may not have committed.

Leon Beron was 48, and a Russian Jew known in London's East End as a property-owner. He usually carried large sums of money. On 1 January 1911 his body was found in some bushes on Clapham Common. His skull had been fractured, and he had been stabbed. A crude letter 'S' had been slashed on each side of his face. Two weeks previously 3 police officers had been killed by anarchists, led by the mysterious Peter the Painter, in the Houndsditch Murders. It was thought that Beron's death might have been a revenge killing, and that the significance of the letter 'S' lay in the Russian word *spic*, which meant a double agent.

Beron had frequented the kosher Warsaw Restaurant. The proprietor told police that Beron had been there on the night of the murder and had left with another man—handsome, well-dressed 30-year-old Stinie Morrison. Several people said they had seen Beron and Morrison together.

A cab driver said that he had picked up 2 men speaking in a foreign tongue and taken them to Finsbury Park Station—Morrison fitted the description of one of them. Two more cabbies claimed to have had Morrison as a fare on that night.

Morrison was not at his lodgings, but returned on 8 January, when waiting policemen trailed him to a restaurant where he was arrested at breakfast. He replied when charged with Beron's murder, 'All I can say is that it's a lie.'

Morrison's counsel at his trial at the Old Bailey in March 1911 was later criticized for trying to discredit the prosecution witnesses. This left the way open when Morrison was in the witness box for the prosecutor to bring out a detailed and damaging account of the accused man's criminal background. Although the judge summed up for an acquittal, the verdict was guilty. In passing sentence the judge used the familiar words, 'May God have mercy on your soul', to which Morrison replied, 'I decline such mercy. I do not believe there is a God in Heaven either.'

Morrison was reprieved, but died at Parkhurst Prison, on 24 January 1921, aged 41, starving himself and still protesting his innocence, after refusing food.

Morrison: The body of Leon Beron

[*1, 5, 32, 87, 118, 261, 345, 357, 384, 438, 442, 447, 563, 579, 594, 606, 611, 613, 618, 639, 670, 705, 720, 884, 896, 949, 958, 964, 1007*]

MORSHEAD CASE. The murder of Lieutenant Colonel Henry Morshead in Burma in 1931 remains officially unsolved, but his son—who carried out his own investigation nearly 50 years later—found a possible solution.

Morshead, a distinguished soldier, surveyor and explorer, was appointed Director of the Burmese section of the Survey of India in 1929. He lived at Maymyo, some 40 miles from Mandalay, and at the time of his death his wife and children were on leave in England.

On the morning of 17 May 1931 Morshead's horse, riderless and with blood on its saddle, was found at Maymyo. An immediate search was mounted for the missing officer, and a whole battalion of the Burmese Rifles was called out to assist. The following day Morshead's body was found in the jungle near Inyla village. He had been shot in the chest at close range, while his body also gave evidence of a gunshot wound inflicted from farther afield.

A reward was offered for information, and rumours were rife that Colonel Morshead had been killed by rebels, whose activities were on the increase. Another allegation was that he had been killed accidentally by a man out shooting jungle fowl. A former Gurkha was questioned, but no charge was made.

The British Government's version of the official police report was to the effect that Morshead's death defied explanation, and a veil was drawn over the incident. The dead man's widow was given only a meagre pension on the grounds that her husband had not been killed while on active service.

In 1980 Morshead's son travelled to Burma to visit the scene of his father's death. He discovered that there had been a misunderstanding between Morshead and a local businessman, Syed Ali, over a lady related to the Colonel whom Syed Ali had taken out riding. One of the rumours current after the shooting was that Syed Ali was implicated in some way; he left the district shortly afterwards. One suggestion made was that he hired an assassin to kill Morshead, and had ensured secrecy through his influence as Master of the local Freemasonry lodge. [686]

MULLENDORE CASE. E. C. Mullendore III,
32-year-old heir to the Cross Bell ranch, was shot dead on 26 September 1970 in a gunfight at this Oklahoma ranch.

E. C., as he was known, lived at the ranch with his wife Linda and their 2 children. His father, 69-year-old irascible Gene Mullendore, lived with them and dominated its management. E. C. was heavily in debt, and Linda was accused of over-spending by Mullendore senior.

E. C. started to borrow money from dubious financiers and also took out $16 million worth of life insurance, employing 'Chub' Anderson as his servant and bodyguard.

On 26 September Anderson and E. C. drove down the ranch road to E. C.'s house for an evening meal. While Anderson was in the house he heard shots, and pursued 2 intruders who shot him in the back. E. C. lay dying from a .38 head wound.

Linda Mullendore's claim on her husband's insurance was the largest single life claim in American insurance history. It heightened her alienation from the Mullendore family, whose grieving members (now bankrupt) raised a thirty-foot monument over E.C.'s grave.

The police investigation of E.C.'s murder was inconclusive; it remains unsolved. It was known that the dead man had been threatened, and he himself had said some of the people he dealt with were 'pretty tough . . . connected with the Mafia'. [546]

MÜLLER, Franz.
A 25-year-old German tailor who committed Britain's first train murder. (See also *John Dickman* and *Percy Lefroy*.) He killed and robbed for a mere 30 shillings, which helped him buy a sea passage to America.

On 9 July 1864 70-year-old Thomas Briggs, chief clerk of a London bank, was found on the railway line between Hackney Wick and Bow. He died later from the severe blows struck with his own walking-stick. He had been attacked in a first-class compartment of a North London railway train and, having been robbed of his gold watch and other possessions, was thrown out. A silk hat, not belonging to the victim, was found in the compartment.

Checks on jewellers' shops located the chain from the dead man's watch which had been exchanged for a new one in a Cheapside shop. The jeweller described a man with a foreign accent who called on 11 July. A description of the hat found at the scene of the crime brought forward a man who recognized it as one belonging to Franz Müller, a German tailor working in London.

Müller's lodgings were traced, but the tailor had already sailed to America as an immigrant on board S.S. *Victoria*. Police officers took passage on a faster liner, and were waiting at New York when the *Victoria* berthed. Müller was found with the missing gold watch and a cut-down hat which had been altered to disguise its appearance. In his haste Müller had taken his victim's hat, leaving his own behind.

During his trial at the Old Bailey in October 1864 Müller's mix-up over the hats was a prominent feature. Hatmakers and jewellers gave evidence, and the jury took only 15 minutes to convict him.

Various petitions were raised, including a personal message to Queen Victoria from the King of Prussia. Despite the protests, Müller was hanged on 14 November 1864 before a large crowd, confessing, 'Ich habe es gethan' ('I did it'). Müller achieved a minor claim to fame by lending his

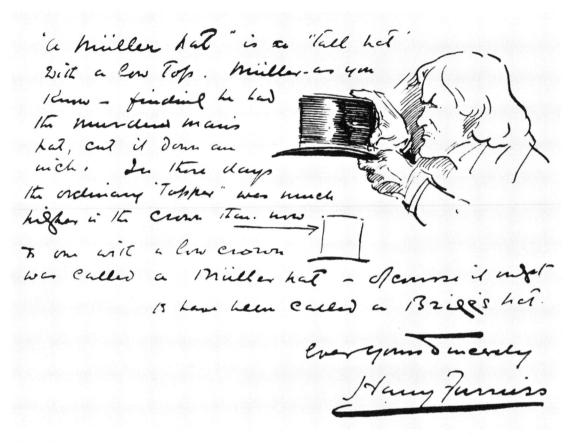

Müller: Cartoonist's comment on Müller's hat

name to a cut-down hat worn by fashion-conscious young men.

[*1, 21, 87, 349, 376, 475, 584, 593, 606, 660, 830, 969*]

MÜLLER, Dr Richard. German dentist convicted of a blazing-car murder in which his wife was the victim.

Müller and his wife Gertrud were returning to their home in Otterbach late on the evening of 18 February 1954 when their car headlights picked up a hedgehog in the road ahead. Frau Müller thought it would be fun to take the hedgehog home to show their sons. Her husband stopped the car and walked back along the road to pick up the animal. As he did so he heard a roar and, looking back, saw his car enveloped in flames. He raced to the blazing vehicle, but the intense heat prevented him from saving his wife. She was consumed in the flames, and Müller returned home late that night with his burned hands bandaged to tell his sons that their

mother was dead. That, at any rate, was the account he gave to the police.

There was dissatisfaction with the dentist's story for several reasons, not least of which was the practice he had adopted of carrying four full cans of petrol in the boot of his car. It also appeared that when he stopped the car—ostensibly to retrieve the hedgehog—he parked so close to roadside trees that it was impossible to open the door on the passenger's side. Inquiries quickly produced a possible motive, for it seemed that Müller was involved in an affair with another woman who had broken off the association after being warned by Frau Müller.

Dr Müller was tried for murder at Kaiserslautern in November 1955, when he pleaded not guilty. The defence maintained that the evidence brought against him was largely circumstantial. Nevertheless, the matter of the petrol cans (one of which was found next to the charred remains of the victim and another on the back seat of the car) provided adequate testimony for the jury to convict him. Unlike *Alfred Rouse*, who was hanged for perpetrat-

ing a blazing-car murder, Richard Müller received a prison sentence of 6 years, widely regarded as a remarkably light punishment.
[*678*]

MULLIN, Herbert. American mass murderer of the early 1970s whose behaviour was influenced by schizophrenia and drug-taking. He committed at least 10 murders in the belief that his action would avert impending natural disasters.

Mullin appeared to have had a normal boyhood, but in his late teens decided he wanted to be a conscientious objector and study religion in India. By the time he had reached the age of 21 those close to him noted he was undergoing personality changes, and persuaded him to seek psychiatric advice. He was suffering from paranoid schizophrenia, and began hearing voices which commanded his actions. Mullin received treatment in hospital and was discharged early in 1970. He was in hospital again in the summer of that year in Hawaii, and when he returned home to California was in a disturbed state.

On 13 October 1972 he began his murderous spree after hearing voices commanding him to kill. His first victim was a tramp whom he butchered on a lonely mountain road. Eleven days later he picked up a college student and stabbed her to death in his car. He bought a gun and began to kill indiscriminately, shooting 5 people on a single day in January 1973. Further killings followed until he was arrested on 13 February 1973.

Mullin confessed in detail to 13 killings which he claimed resulted from voices commanding him to take human sacrifices in order to save California from an imminent earthquake. He had confessed to a minister with whom he had discussed his problem that 'Satan gets into people and makes them do things they don't want to'. At his trial Mullin pleaded not guilty by reason of insanity, but despite the strength of the evidence to support this the jury found him responsible for his actions and he was convicted of 2 counts of first-degree murder and 9 of second-degree murder. He was given 2 life sentences and other terms of imprisonment, to keep him inside until the year 2025.

The case was used to emphasize the folly of state legislation in California at that time, which had closed a number of mental hospitals on grounds of economy. Mullin had been in and out of hospital, and had been diagnosed and treated for paranoid schizophrenia. It was argued in some quarters that had there been continuous supervision of his prob-

lems a tragedy might have been averted, and 13 lives saved.
[*602, 603*]

MURRELL CASE. Unsolved and controversial murder of a 78-year-old spinster who was a noted rose-grower and anti-nuclear campaigner. On 21 March 1984 she was abducted from her home at Shrewsbury and taken to Moat Copse 7 miles away, where she was repeatedly stabbed and left to die. Her body was found 3 days later at a point some 500 yards from her ditched car.

The immediate interpretation of events was that the elderly woman, who had been out shopping, returned home and disturbed an intruder. There was evidence of a struggle having taken place in the house, and also that it had been systematically searched; the telephone connection had been ripped away from the wall socket. As information emerged that was relevant to the police inquiry, surprise was expressed that such little progress was made.

It appeared that Miss Murrell's assailant had driven her car, with her slumped in the passenger seat, through the centre of Shrewsbury and past West Mercia Police HQ. The car was driven erratically, and no less than 69 witnesses came forward with information. It was ditched at Hunkington, and it was believed that Hilda Murrell was pulled or dragged across fields to the copse where she was stabbed and abandoned. The knife was discarded in a nearby hedge, and the victim died of hypothermia. A possible suspect was later seen running towards Shrewsbury town centre. He was wearing running shoes, and his trousers were mud-stained. Over 48 witnesses saw him, and the police issued a photo-fit picture based on their descriptions of the running man.

Because of Hilda Murrell's strongly held anti-nuclear views, a theory emerged that she had been silenced because she knew too much. At the time of her death she was preparing a paper which she intended to present to the public inquiry looking into the construction of Sizewell B nuclear-power station. A parallel was drawn with the death of Karen Silkwood in a car accident 10 years previously in the USA. Silkwood was planning to meet a journalist to tell him about nuclear contamination incidents; Murrell planned to make public anti-nuclear views which her friends thought would prove to be powerful opposition to the Sizewell B project. Significantly, the only item said to be missing from Hilda Murrell's home was the final draft of her paper. The idea that the elderly rose-grower was eliminated because she was a nuisance to the nuclear industry was dismissed by the police.

Hard on the heels of the nuclear connection came the suggestion that Hilda Murrell had become caught up in the aftermath of the sinking of the Argentinian cruiser *General Belgrano* during the Falklands War in 1982. In a statement to the House of Commons made in December 1984 Tom Dalyell MP referred to the possible connection. Murrell's nephew, a retired naval officer who had served with naval intelligence during the Falklands War, was said to have had knowledge regarding the background to the sinking which if divulged might have proved embarrassing to the government.

Despite the theories and allegations of a conspiracy and police cover-up, Hilda Murrell's death remains as much a mystery today as it was in 1984. Certainly the police had a wealth of evidence but a massive investigation (which involved questioning a fifth of the population in Shrewsbury) produced no results. Among the many curious angles to the affair was the statement by a farmer who walked through Moat Copse the day after Hilda Murrell was abducted—he was convinced there was no body there at that time. With its security connotations, the case has parallels with the *Bogle-Chandler* affair. [*193, 864*]

N

NAN PATTERSON CASE. New York chorus girl who faced 3 trials for the murder of her lover, Caesar Young.

On the morning of 4 June 1904 Francis Thomas Young, known as Caesar by his friends, a gambler and racehorse-owner, drove along Broadway in a hansom cab. He was accompanied by Nan Randolph Patterson, 22-year-old girl from the popular musical *Floradora*. A shot rang out inside the cab and the woman told the driver to make first for a drugstore and then to near-by Hudson Street Hospital. Caesar Young was dead on arrival, lying across his companion's lap with a bullet wound in the chest—a still warm gun was in his coat. Nan Patterson was arrested for murder.

Caesar Young was married but ignored his wife. His affair with Nan Patterson was notorious, and he had paid for her divorce. An elopement was foiled by Mrs Young and reconciliation followed. Caesar tried to persuade Nan to go to Europe. She refused, claiming that she was pregnant. Trying to force the pair apart, Mrs Young persuaded Caesar to take a holiday in England, and she booked their passages for 4 June.

The day before sailing, Caesar Young spent a long time in Nan Patterson's company—he drank heavily, and they quarrelled. Early the next morning they met again and during a cab drive Nan claimed Young shot himself. A bystander heard the shot and a voice in the cab exclaim, 'Look at me, Frank. Why did you do it?'

Nan Patterson was charged with murder and tried in November 1904, but the judge announced a mistrial when a juror died suddenly. In the second trial in December Nan gave evidence, passionately protesting her innocence, but the jury were deadlocked. The third trial was in April 1905. Again the jury were deadlocked, and waves of sympathy (including several offers of marriage) reached Nan in prison.

Ten days later the judge granted a motion that she be discharged. Two thousand people cheered her to freedom and children sang:

'Nan is free, Nan is free,
She escaped the electric chair,
Now she's out in the open air'

[573]

NEILSON, Donald. Kidnapper and murderer known as the 'Black Panther' on account of the black hood which he wore to disguise his appearance and terrorize his victims.

Neilson, aged 39, a married joiner with a 16-year-old daughter, lived at Bradford. He was arrested by chance on 11 December 1975 after he committed countless robberies, kidnapped and murdered a teenage girl and killed 3 sub post-office officials.

Neilson, who changed his name from Nappey, was a juvenile delinquent who was morose and difficult. After completing his National Service he had a number of jobs—house repairs, plumbing and taxi-work—all of which were unsuccessful. His reaction to his own failure was to develop a hatred against society.

Neilson decided on a plan to kidnap 17-year-old Lesley Whittle after reading about her family's fortune. He made meticulous plans, reconnoitring the system of underground drainage shafts near Kidsgrove where he planned to hide his victim.

On 13 January 1975 Neilson took Lesley from her home near Kidderminster and kept her confined in one of the drainage shafts while he demanded a £50 000 ransom from her relatives. The girl's naked body was found on 7 March 1975, hanging from a wire about the neck.

Neilson defied capture for 9 months. When his house at Bradford was searched police found a variety of knives, guns, ammunition, hoods and military clothing in the attic. He was charged with the kidnapping and murder of Lesley Whittle, and with the murders of 3 post-office officials during armed raids between 1971 and 1975.

Neilson was tried at Oxford in June 1976 for the murder of Lesley Whittle, and in July for the other 3 murders. His defence was based on his proneness to accident—according to his account Lesley Whittle fell from the ledge on which she was perched in the drainage shaft and was hanged accidentally by the wire used to tether her. In the cases of the post-office killings, he claimed his gun went off by accident.

Convicted on 4 counts of murder, Neilson was sentenced to 21 years in the Whittle case, and to life for each of the other counts.

[*287, 427, 651, 928, 936*]

NELSON, Dale Merle. Canadian mass murderer who butchered horribly members of 2 families, in crimes allegedly caused by LSD.

Nelson was known to the inhabitants of West Creston, British Columbia, as a normally friendly person, but given to periods of depression when he drank heavily, hoping that this would overcome his feelings of sexual impotence.

After spending a large part of the day drinking, Nelson went on the rampage on the night of 5 September 1970. He entered the home of Mrs Shirley Wasyk, who was alone with her 3 daughters. There he battered her to death, then choked 7-year-old Tracey and mutilated her body with a knife slash to the abdomen. He attacked 8-year-old Sharlene before a terrified 12-year-old Debbie escaped and went for help.

The killer transferred his attentions a short distance away to the Phipps family. Ray Phipps was at home with his common law wife Isabelle St Amand and their 4 children. Nelson shot him dead at the front door and then systematically shot his wife and children. Eight-year-old Cathy St Amand was missing—she was presumed to have been taken by Nelson, who had managed to slip back to the Wasyk house after the police had been there and remove Tracey's body.

Nelson's abandoned car was found in woods near West Creston, and some 40 feet away the dismembered remains of Tracey Wasyk lay scattered about. Some of the child's organs were missing, and never found. Thirty-six hours after the killings, Nelson, armed with a rifle, gave himself up without violence. He told the police where to find the body of Cathy St Amand.

Nelson told a police officer, 'It must have been the LSD.' He was tried at Cranbrook Assizes in March 1971 for the murders of Tracey Wasyk and Cathy St Amand. The defence admitted virtually all the facts in the hope of showing that Nelson was insane. The two surviving girls of the Wasyk family gave vivid evidence of what Dale Nelson, their cousin, had done. The defence psychiatrist

contended that Nelson was suffering from a disease of the mind which prevented him distinguishing between right and wrong. The jury found Nelson guilty, and by implication, sane. The evidence regarding LSD was not substantiated. He was sentenced to life imprisonment.

[*605, 888*]

NELSON, Earle Leonard. American sex killer known as the 'Gorilla Murderer'. Over a period of less than 2 years this Bible-loving killer raped and strangled 22 landladies in the USA and Canada.

Nelson was born in 1892 and suffered a childhood accident resulting in a head injury which caused him intense pain. In 1918 he was put in a home for mental defectives for assaulting a child. He escaped 3 times, and was judged insane by a California court.

In San Francisco on 20 February 1926 Nelson raped and strangled a 63-year-old woman in the attic of her rooming house. During the following months Nelson went across America, preying on women offering rooms or houses for rent. From San Francisco to Philadelphia he raped and strangled 20 women—at the peak of his activity, murdering once every 3 weeks.

In June 1927 he crossed into Canada and made for Winnipeg. There he took a room under a false name, telling the landlady that he was 'a very religious man of high ideals'. Within days there were 2 murders in the city. A 14-year-old girl living in the same house as Nelson was found dead; elsewhere in the city the raped and strangled body of Mrs Emily Paterson was discovered by her husband.

The police interviewed a second-hand clothing dealer who had sold some garments to a man changing his clothes in the store's stock-room. He left behind some articles, including a fountain pen, which had been taken by the killer from the Paterson home. A description was circulated, Nelson was recognized by a Wakopa storekeeper and arrested 4 miles from the US border.

He was tried at Winnipeg in November 1927 for the murder of Emily Paterson. His wife's testimony did him little good, showing him to be a jealous man who believed he had a Christ-like appearance. The defence plea was based on insanity. The judge dwelled on this and asked whether Nelson's cunning in changing his clothes, keeping on the move and altering his name were the acts of an insane man or a man trying to escape the consequences of his actions. The jury found Nelson guilty, and he was sentenced to death on 14

November 1927. He said 'I have never committed murder; never, never, never.' He was hanged at Winnipeg on 13 January 1928.

[*244, 372, 592, 693*]

NESSET, Arnfinn. Manager of an old people's home in Orkdal, Norway, convicted of murdering 21 of his patients. Between 1977 and 1980, while Nesset ran the nursing-home, 30 elderly patients—an unusually high number—passed away. Another unusual occurrence was the large amount of curacit, a muscle-relaxing drug, which Nesset kept in his office. It was the discovery of the curacit during routine police inquiries that first created suspicion.

Nesset's claim that he had intended to use the curacit in order to put down his dog did not withstand scrutiny. For one thing, he did not own a dog, and for another, the quantity of the drug in his possession was sufficient to kill 200 people. He was arrested in March 1981, and admitted killing 27 patients. He subsequently withdrew this admission, but his defence counsel at his trial for murder in Trondheim in October 1982 maintained that Nesset had been carrying out mercy killings.

Curacit is normally administered to patients undergoing surgery to relax their muscles. In lethal doses it kills slowly and painfully, and was hardly a satisfactory agent for carrying out euthanasia. Witnesses testified that they saw Nesset giving injections to patients in the nursing-home but no one was sure which drugs he was administering. As curacit, a derivative of curare, breaks down rapidly after entering the body, there was little to be learned by performing post mortem examinations on the victims.

Apart from his confession—later withdrawn—in which he said, 'I've killed so many, I'm unable to remember them,' the evidence against Nesset was circumstantial. He pleaded not guilty to the charges at his trial, which was the most striking case of mass murder ever heard in Scandinavia. His motive was thought to be gain, and he was proved to have embezzled small sums of money from his patients. The psychiatrists who examined Nesset had found him sane and fit to appear on trial. He was born illegitimate and brought up in a remote, rural community. As an adult, he suffered from an inferiority complex and feelings of rejection. His position in a home looking after elderly people gave him a sense of power, and perhaps he really was practising mercy killing according to his own twisted definition. At any rate, it seemed that the money he gained by fraudulent means was not intended for his own use but was destined for missionary and charitable work.

The trial jury found little in Nesset's actions to warrant mercy on their part, and found him guilty on 21 counts of murder. He was sentenced to the maximum term of imprisonment permissible under Norwegian law—21 years; a year for every life he took.

[*94, 996*]

NEU, Kenneth. Aspiring 25-year-old night club singer with a background of mental illness who murdered twice for gain.

Neu, broke and jobless, roamed the streets of New York in September 1933. In Times Square he met Lawrence Shead, a theatre-owner, who invited him into a bar, and offered him a job. They retired to Shead's apartment, where the older man made sexual advances. Neu hit Shead with an electric iron, smashing his skull. He then put on one of Shead's suits and made off with his watch and wallet.

Two weeks later, still wearing Shead's suit, Neu appeared in New Orleans. He met a young waitress who wanted to see New York. He promised to take her, but had to raise some cash. He went to a hotel and spoke to Sheffield Clark, a store owner from Nashville. After the initial encounter, Neu followed Clark up to his room, and there demanded money. Clark threatened to call the police. Neu hit the old man and throttled him.

He ransacked Clark's room, and found $300 which he stole along with the dead man's car keys. He picked up his waitress, and removed the car's licence plates, putting up a crudely lettered sign which declared, 'New car in transit.' They reached New Jersey before being stopped by a police patrol asking about the notice. Not satisfied with Neu's explanation, they found he could be the man wanted for the murder of Lawrence Shead.

Asked if he knew Shead, Neu replied, 'Sure . . . I killed him. This is his suit I'm wearing now.' He also admitted killing Clark in New Orleans: 'He seemed like a nice old man. But I was desperate for money.'

Neu was tried in New Orleans in December 1933 for the murder of Sheffield Clark. In court he wore Clark's shoes and Shead's suit, and based his defence on insanity. Defence doctors stated that he had neuro-syphilis, and had suffered brain deterioration. Nevertheless, the jury found him guilty—he flippantly tossed a coin in the air when being sentenced, wishing the judge 'Good luck.' While in prison under sentence of death, he sang in his cell and composed a verse, 'I'm fit as a fiddle and ready to hang.' He continued in this vein, and was hanged on 1 February 1935.

[898]

NEWELL, Susan. Murderess distinguished for her lack of motive in killing a youth and wheeling his body through the streets of Glasgow.

On a June morning in 1923 a woman with a little girl was seen pushing a hand-cart with a bundle on it through the Glasgow suburbs. A lorry-driver stopped and offered to give them a lift. She accepted, the driver lifted her cart up and they drove off. When they neared the centre of the city the woman said she would continue on foot. The driver helped lift the cart down, the bundle fell off, and was hastily retrieved by the woman, who moved off quickly, trailing the little girl behind her.

This scene was witnessed by a housewife, whose keen eyes observed a foot and a head protruding from the bundle. Shocked, she called her sister, and together they followed the woman, who grabbed up the bundle and fled down a side street, where she met a policeman. The bundle contained the strangled body of a 13-year-old boy. The woman was 30-year-old Susan Newell, and the body John Johnston, a newspaper-seller.

She explained that she was protecting her husband by hiding the body of the boy, whom he had killed the previous evening. John Newell gave himself up and denied all knowledge of murder, but both were sent for trial.

The Newells, a quarrelsome pair, rented a room in a Glasgow suburb. Their landlady had given them notice to quit. John Newell's claim to have been assaulted by his wife and to have told the police was substantiated, and he was acquitted. Janet Newell, who was 8, told the court that she had helped her mother put the body in a bag.

The defence's attempt to prove Mrs Newell insane failed, and she was found guilty on a majority verdict and recommended unanimously for mercy. She made no confession, and was hanged at Glasgow's Duke Street Prison on 10 October 1923.

[460, 1001]

NICHOLSON, William Lawrence Warren. The 31-year-old ex-police officer who murdered his wife and tried to cast blame on a mysterious coloured assailant.

Nicholson lived at Fish Hoek, a South African resort town. On 1 September 1956

passers-by heard terrified screams rising above the radio music coming from his house. Two pedestrians saw Nicholson, covered in blood, come rushing out. 'My wife!' he shouted. 'I think she's been murdered.'

Police arrived to find Sylvia Nicholson lying in front of the fireplace, her head smashed by multiple hammer blows. Nicholson was calm, and he did not seem too upset when she died later in hospital.

He claimed that the family returned home about 10.25 p.m. He went in and out a few times to get things from the car and saw a coloured man bending over his wife, so he grabbed a hammer, and rushed at the intruder, who struck him with an iron bar. Nicholson tried to chase him, but he disappeared in the darkness. There was no sign of forced entry, and police searched the house except, at Nicholson's request, the room in which his daughter lay asleep.

The police were suspicious of Nicholson, and took him into custody. He told a visiting priest that he had foolishly picked up an object thrown away by his wife's assailant which was his own hammer. In his confused state of mind, he cleaned the hammer and hid it. The priest advised him to tell the police. Nicholson freely admitted that in fear he cleaned his fingerprints, and those of the alleged murderer, from the hammer, and wiped it clean of his wife's blood.

He was tried for murder in Cape Town in February 1957. He claimed he was devoted to his wife, who was in poor health and whose treatment was a strain on the family budget. His story about the coloured intruder was torn apart by the prosecution, and Nicholson was reduced to fumbling replies. It was emphasized as almost inconceivable that an ex-police officer should destroy evidence vital to the search for a murderer. The jury found him guilty. He maintained his innocence, and was hanged on 12 August 1957.

[75]

NILSEN, Dennis. A mild-mannered civil servant, aged 37, who murdered 15 young down-and-outs over a 5-year period in London. All the victims were male students or drifters whom he picked up in bars and took home with promises of providing accommodation.

Nilsen's activities were discovered by accident in February 1983 when a drain-cleaning company was called to Cranley Gardens in North London to unblock the street drains. Pieces of rotting flesh were found clogging up the pipe outside No.23. At first it was thought that the offending material was dog meat or the discarded contents of a deep-freeze but further inquiries determined that the flesh was of human origin.

When police officers knocked at the door of 23 Cranley Gardens Dennis Nilsen seemed almost eager to tell his horror story using the most matter-of-fact language. He admitted to killing and dismembering 15 people, although he excused his uncertainty about the precise number by saying, 'I didn't keep a body count.' Plastic bags containing 3 severed heads were found in a wardrobe at his house, together with a tea chest containing other portions of bodies. He mentioned that in addition to the 3 bodies at Cranley Gardens there were 13 others buried in the back garden of a house he previously occupied in Cricklewood.

Dennis Nilsen served in the Army as a cook in Aden, Cyprus and Germany, and when he was discharged in 1972 joined the Metropolitan Police for a while. He later took employment with a security firm, and in 1974 became a civil servant working in a London Job Centre. His employment gave him contact with society's less advantaged members and his otherwise lonely private life became peopled with drop-outs whom he took home. He spent a great deal of his time in bars and clubs where he readily befriended other lonely souls and commiserated with them during heavy drinking bouts.

In December 1978, after his flat-mate of 3 years left him, Nilsen's mind gave way to the destructive elements that lurked beneath the surface. He took his victims home and, often so insensible with drink that he could not recall their identities, strangled them and dismembered their corpses. He was faced with a tremendous problem when it came to disposing of their bodies. At times there were as many as 4 or 5 sets of remains stowed under the floorboards of his flat in Cricklewood and suitcases crammed with human organs reposing in the garden shed. He had periodic bonfires to dispose of some of the remains, but when he resorted to flushing the results of his carnage down the WC he succeeded only in blocking the drains and attracting suspicion.

Dubbed 'The Murderer of the Century', Nilsen was tried at the Old Bailey in October 1983. His cold, remote and remorseless nature was debated in court by psychiatric experts. The man who had once described himself as a 'creative psychopath' was defended on the grounds of diminished responsibility. The jury decided on the evidence that he was responsible for his actions and found him guilty. He was sentenced to life imprisonment.

Nilsen: The 'creative psychopath'

In 1985 Brian Masters published a book about Nilsen called *Killing for Company* which had the distinction of being based on personal access to the gaoled murderer. The author painted a picture of an unloved child who grew into an isolated adult obsessed with the sexuality of death. One of the objectives of this unique study was to show how an ordinary individual could degenerate to such a point. Masters commented that Nilsen's victims were really props in his world of fantasy, not real people.

The subject of this study wrote an account in prison in which he tried to analyse himself. His presence among other criminals was not welcomed, for while he was in Wormwood Scrubs a fellow-prisoner slashed him across the face with a razor. The house where Nilsen committed his last 3 murders was put up for sale in November 1983. Although it attracted a great many morbid sightseers, it did not sell quickly. Some of the original furniture found its way to Scotland Yard's Black Museum and, once curiosity had died, Nilsen's house of horror was sold in 1984 for a sum reported to be well below the asking price.

[*580, 622, 653*]

NODDER, Frederick. Man in his forties found guilty of abducting a child whose body was not found until he was in prison.

A 10-year-old girl, Mona Lilian Tinsley, failed to return to her Newark, Nottinghamshire, home after school on 5 January 1937. Her parents notified the police, and an 11-year-old boy said he had seen Mona with a man with staring eyes at a bus stop. A passenger on a Newark-Retford bus had seen the man and child and a bus company official saw them together at Retford.

The man was identified as Fred Hudson, a lorry driver who had lodged with the Tinsley family. He was known as Uncle Fred to the children and as Frederick Nodder, father of an illegitimate child, to the police. He was interviewed and said he knew Mona, but had nothing to do with her disappearance. Nevertheless, a number of witnesses picked him out as the man seen with the girl on the bus.

Nodder on 6 January made a statement that Mona had asked him to take her to see an aunt in Sheffield. He said they went by bus to Worksop and he left her there with money and instructions on how to get to Sheffield, which was 18 miles away. He then returned to Retford. Mrs Grimes, Mona's aunt at Sheffield, said that Mona never arrived. Nodder was charged with abduction.

Widespread searches were made for Mona, including dragging of rivers, canals, ditches, drains and dumps, but to no avail. At Birmingham Assizes in March 1937 Nodder was sentenced to 7 years' imprisonment for abduction. The judge remarked, 'What you did with that little girl, what became of her, only you know. It may be that time will reveal the dreadful secret which you carry in your breast.'

In June Mona Tinsley's body was found by a family boating party in the river Idle. Her strangled corpse was floating at a point over 20 miles from Newark. Nodder was now tried for murder at Nottingham Assizes in November. He was found guilty, and the judge on this occasion told him, 'Justice has slowly but surely overtaken you.' Nodder was hanged at Lincoln Prison on 30 December 1937.

[*1, 133, 142, 472, 489, 599, 607*]

O

OAKES CASE. Sir Harry Oakes, a 69-year-old American-born gold prospector, became a multi-millionaire and a Canadian citizen. He was created a Baronet in 1939 in recognition of his services to the British Empire and on 8 July 1943 was found burned and battered to death in his house at Nassau, in the Bahamas.

This unsolved murder occurred during the Duke of Windsor's Governorship. The island's own police force was ignored by the Duke, who called in two American detectives from the Miami Police Department. As a result of their investigations, Oakes's son-in-law Alfred de Marigny was charged with murder.

At de Marigny's trial the prosecution produced fingerprint evidence which was successfully repudiated on the grounds of incompetent police procedure. De Marigny was acquitted, the jury adding a rider that he should be deported.

The case has many strange and unexplained aspects. The precise nature of the weapon which caused the fatal wounds was never established; mysterious bloody hand-prints in the murder room were never explained; and the reason for scattering feathers over the partly burned corpse has never been explained.

Ray Schindler, the famous private detective, was called in by de Marigny's wife, Nancy, to assist in her husband's defence. Schindler claimed to have been obstructed by the authorities, and in 1944 he wrote to the Duke of Windsor, seeking to reopen the case. This, and similar attempts by others hoping to shed light on this unsolved murder, was refused.

[*98, 226, 456, 461, 470, 476, 508, 560, 581, 694, 897*]

ONUFREJCZYK, Michael. An ex-Polish soldier with a distinguished service record who became a farmer in Wales. His trial for the murder of his partner was significant because there was no body.

In December 1953 routine police checks on aliens in Britain were made at Cefn Hendre, a farm at Llandilo in Carmarthenshire. According to the records, Stanislaw Sykut ran the farm in partnership with Michael Onufrejczyk, but the former was missing. Onufrejczyk said Sykut had left to return to Poland, and had sold him his share in the farm.

Further inquiries showed that none of his friends knew about it, and, he had neglected to take £450 which he had saved with the Post Office Savings Bank. Onufrejczyk said that he had been lent money by a Mrs Pokora to buy out Sykut but she denied this. Onufrejczyk told other lies, and on 19 August 1954 was charged with Sykut's murder.

Onufrejczyk was tried at Swansea in November 1954. The prosecution case was that the 59-year-old Pole had murdered his partner out of greed. It was known that they had quarrelled, and that the accused had threatened Sykut. Bloodstains were found in the farmhouse kitchen, and it was suggested that when Onufrejczyk learned that his partner had taken legal steps to dissolve the partnership, he attacked him. Onufrejczyk in evidence claimed that Sykut was still alive, and that there was no evidence proving he was dead. Defence counsel said he could find no case in English criminal history for the last 300 years where there had been a conviction of murder without identification of the body or part of a body, or an admission by the accused indicating the victim was dead.

The jury found Onufrejczyk guilty, and he was sentenced to death. An appeal was dismissed when the Lord Chief Justice observed that the Court thought it was clear that the fact of death could be proved, like any other fact, by circumstantial evidence. On 24 January 1955 Onufrejczyk's sentence was commuted to life imprisonment. (See also *Edward Ball, Hosein Brothers* and *Shark Arm Case*)

[*307, 371, 905*]

Oakes Case: Sir Harry's body on the bed

ORROCK, Thomas Henry. Orrock was the son of a respectable chapel-going Dalston family, but he drifted into the criminal fringe, and bought a revolver in order to show off.

On a foggy London night in December 1882, Orrock set out on a self-imposed initiation ceremony. He was equipped with house-breaking tools, and armed himself with his revolver. He was caught in the act of breaking into a chapel at Dalston through a window by Police Constable George Cole, and was being taken to the police station when he fired 4 shots at PC Cole, who fell dying. Orrock made off under cover of the fog.

Two women had seen the shooting, and they ran to the police station. They were unable to give a description, but said he was wearing a wide-brimmed hat. Sergeant Cobb knew most of the local young men, and recalled seeing Orrock in

such a hat earlier that same evening. He was brought in and put on an identity parade, but both women witnesses failed to pick him out. He was released, and promptly disappeared.

More than a year later, Sergeant Cobb learned that a group of local youths had gone with Orrock to Tottenham marshes to observe his practice shooting. Shown the tree used as a target, Cobb prised out bullets embedded in it, and it was found that these were fired from the weapon which killed PC Cole.

Orrock was located at Coldbath Fields Prison, where he was serving a term for burglary. He was tried for murder, found guilty on 19 September 1884 and executed, having first confessed to the crime.

[*181, 182, 388, 553, 885, 933*]

P

PALLIKO, Alan. He predicted that he would make his first million by the age of 35. Millionaire status in fact eluded the former police officer, but he acquired notoriety as a murderer.

Palliko married Katherine Drummond in 1964, but their relationship deteriorated quickly due to his preoccupation with guns and body-building and his tendency to infidelity. He met Sandra Stockton, whose husband was mysteriously shot dead in their Los Angeles home in December 1966. Three bullets had been fired into his head while he sat in his living-room watching television. The police investigation established that Sandra Stockton had bought a gun earlier in the year, and her liaison with Palliko was also discovered.

Aware of her husband's adultery, Katherine decided to demand a divorce. She had already suffered 2 attempts on her life. In August 1965 she sustained a broken pelvis as the result of a hit-and-run incident, and a few months later she was attacked by Palliko. He lay in wait for her one night when she was attending a meeting, and assaulted her when she returned to her car. Striking her with his fists and gripping her around the throat, he said simply, 'I'm going to kill you.' She struggled free and Palliko was arrested for assault. Against the advice of the police, Katherine dropped the charge.

In October 1967 Palliko became the owner of a bar in Burbank, California, and moved into a luxury apartment close by. He also found a new companion, an attractive swimming-pool instructor whom he married in March 1968. Judy Palliko managed a second bar which her husband had acquired but as in previous relationships, this new marriage quickly became tension-filled.

On 18 April 1968 Palliko hired a distinctive yellow Jaguar car for Judy's use and two days later she was found dying at the wheel of the vehicle. She had been shot twice, and beaten about the head with a gun-butt. After she died in hospital Palliko confided to a friend that he had committed murder, and he also admitted killing Sandra Stockton's husband. A search of Palliko's apartment revealed an arsenal of guns including a .38 pistol which he kept under his pillow. He was arrested and charged with murdering his wife and also Henry Stockton. Palliko and Sandra Stockton were tried together for conspiring to commit the 2 murders. Sandra had taken out a large insurance on her husband and when he was killed the pay-out of $75,000 funded Palliko's high living style.

Palliko had also insured his wife, and the prosecution argued that the reason for leasing the distinctive yellow Jaguar for Judy to drive was to mark her for easy assassination in the car-park near their apartment. Vincent Bugliosi, the prosecutor who achieved recognition at the trial of *Charles Manson*, argued a powerful case against Palliko and Stockton. They were convicted of murder; she received a life sentence and he was condemned to death, although in 1972 this was commuted to life imprisonment.

[*139*]

PALMER, Dr William. Notorious 32-year-old English poisoner of possibly 14 people whose trial in 1856 made legal history.

Palmer took to crime at an early age. But he was not without intelligence, and in 1846, having qualified as a doctor at St Bartholomew's Hospital, set up in practice at Rugeley, Staffordshire.

He married, and built up a modest business. But behind the scenes his domestic life was far from blissful—he had an illegitimate child by a servant girl, and was in constant financial difficulty through betting. He disposed of his mother-in-law so that her fortune would pass to his wife, and thence to him, and later indulged his fancy in horse-racing by setting up his own racing stable.

Four of Palmer's children died as infants. As his gambling interests increased, so the trail of death in his wake became greater. His wife and brother died after Palmer had insured them for large sums, and his creditors and illegitimate children went the same way.

In 1855, hard-pressed as always for money and in the hands of moneylenders, Palmer attended Shrewsbury Races in the company of John Parsons Cook who won his bets while Palmer lost. To celebrate his winning, Cook arranged a supper party at which he became ill. The racegoers returned to Rugeley, where Cook stayed at the Talbot Arms Hotel opposite Palmer's house. Palmer kindly volunteered to collect Cook's winnings for him, and promptly used them to pay off his own debts. Meanwhile Cook deteriorated and, following Palmer's ministrations, died on 21 November.

The dead man's stepfather was suspicious, and an autopsy showed small traces of antimony. The inquest returned a verdict of wilful murder against Palmer even before he was arrested. A great wave of hostility arose against him, and the 'Palmer Act' was passed by Parliament making it possible for an accused person to be tried in London if he was unlikely to get a fair trial in his own county.

Palmer was tried at the Old Bailey in May 1856, and despite an 8-hour plea by his counsel, was found guilty of murder and sentenced to death.

He was hanged outside Stafford Gaol on 14 June 1856. He made no confession, and the large crowd which witnessed his execution hissed 'Poisoner!' at him as he mounted the scaffold.

[1, 21, 48, 87, 110, 111, 120, 134, 141, 152, 231, 244, 259, 286, 332, 358, 500, 606, 724, 795, 872, 880, 907]

PAMELA COVENTRY CASE. The body of 11-year-old Pamela Coventry was found in fields near Hornchurch, Essex, on 19 January 1939. She had been strangled and sexually assaulted.

Most of the girl's clothing was missing. Her legs had been trussed up with electric cable, and a cigarette end, presumed to have been dropped by the murderer, was found lying on the body.

Extensive police searches in the district turned up various items of the missing clothing. It was thought that the wanted man was still living locally. Part of the house-to-house questioning was based on information gleaned from the cigarette end, which was hand-rolled from used tobacco. This line of inquiry quickly produced a suspect, 28-year-old Leonard Richardson.

Richardson was co-operative. Police learned that he had been home from work on the day of the murder. He rolled his own cigarettes, often from used tobacco, and electric cable of the unusual type used to tie up the dead girl was found in his home.

Richardson was tried for murder at the Old Bailey in March 1939. On the fifth day the jury informed the judge that they would be unable to convict him, and a formal verdict of 'Not guilty' was given. The case remains unsolved.

[157, 914, 920]

PANZRAM, Carl. Cynical murderer and incorrigible hard-case. Thirty-year-old Panzram declared, 'I don't believe in Man, God nor Devil. I hate the whole damned human race including myself.'

Much of his early life was spent in corrective institutions where he was brutalized by punishments. Of his term in Fort Leavenworth Prison, completed in 1910, he said, 'All the good that may have been in me had been kicked and beaten out of me long before.'

His adult life consisted of robberies interspersed with terms of imprisonment and gaol breaks. He also indulged in arson to get his revenge on the

Palmer: Words on Cook's gravestone

"His own iniquities shall take the wicked himself, and he shall be holden with the cords of sin."

"Enter not into the path of the wicked, and go not into the way of evil men; avoid it, pass not by it, turn from it and pass away; for they eat the bread of wickedness and drink the wine of violence."

SACRED TO THE MEMORY
OF
John Parsons Cook,
LATE OF CALTHORPE LODGE,
IN THE COUNTY OF LEICESTER,
Whose Life was taken away
at Rugeley,
On the Night of the 22nd Nov., 1855,
IN
THE 29th YEAR OF HIS AGE.

AMIABLE AND AFFECTIONATE IN HIS DISPOSITION, KIND AND GENEROUS IN HIS CONDUCT.

He was sincerely beloved, and will long be lamented by his kindred and friends.

"Keep thy heart with all diligence; ponder the path of thy feet; lest thou give thine honour unto others and thy life unto the cruel; lest thou mourn at the last, when thy flesh and thy substance are consumed."

"Whoso hearkeneth unto Me shall dwell safely, and shall be quiet from fear of evil."

system, and he practised sodomy on his victims whom he variously assaulted, robbed and killed.

In 1920, Panzram carried out robberies which netted him over $45000, and by his own admission killed 10 men in the process. He kept on the move, sailing to Europe and working in Africa.

In August 1928 while in Washington awaiting trial for burglary and murder he wrote his memoirs. On receiving a sentence of 25 years to be served at Fort Leavenworth he said, 'I'll kill the first man who bothers me.' On 20 June 1929, Panzram killed the prison laundry foreman.

For this murder he was tried and convicted. He objected when a reform group sought to prevent his hanging; he said (perhaps unconsciously quoting!) 'I wish you all had one neck, and I had my hands on it. . . . I believe the only way to reform people is to kill them.' He wrote to President Hoover demanding his 'constitutional rights' in the form of a prompt hanging. This self-confessed killer of 21 persons and sodomizer (on his own admission) of a thousand more was hanged on 5 September 1930 at Fort Leavenworth. His autobiography was published 40 years later, edited by one of his gaolers.

[320, 693]

PARKER and HULME. Pauline Parker, aged 16, and her friend Juliet Hulme, aged 15, stood accused of murder in a sensational New Zealand trial in 1954.

The 2 girls developed a close relationship with lesbian overtones and aspects of fantasy which Mrs Honora Mary Parker was at pains to break up. Early in 1954 Juliet Hulme's father decided to take his daughter to South Africa. Juliet was determined not to be separated from Pauline, who made plans to go there too.

The girls knew that Mrs Parker would oppose their plan, so they killed her. Pauline's diary referred to their intentions: 'We decided to use a brick in a stocking rather than a sandbag.' On 22 June the girls reported finding Mrs Parker's badly battered body. Their claim that Pauline's mother had slipped and fallen was difficult to square with the 45 separate injuries to the dead woman's head which the girls said were caused by her head bumping on the ground as they carried the body.

Pauline readily admitted killing her mother with a half-brick inside a stocking. Hulme said they intended to frighten Mrs Parker into consenting to Pauline travelling to South Africa. The pair were tried for murder at Christchurch. It was clearly shown that the teenage girls were precocious, self-

centred and had engaged in various sexual practices—the prosecution referred to them as 'dirty minded little girls'. The defence pleaded paranoia and insanity. The jury found them guilty, and as they were under 18, they were sentenced to be detained during Her Majesty's Pleasure. They have since been released.

[307, 372, 393, 792, 1000]

PATRICK, Albert T. American attorney tried for murder of a millionaire business-man in a sensational case.

The 84-year-old William Marsh Rice had made a fortune in Texas oil, hotels, property and land. He had married twice, but had no children. In 1896 he took on 23-year-old Charles F. Jones as a general factotum, who became his secretary and confidant, by 1900 having full charge of the old man's banking arrangements.

Albert Patrick, a Texan lawyer, handled a legal action regarding Mrs Rice's will, in which under Texas law she laid claim to half her husband's estate for her relatives. When she died Rice disputed this, as he wished to leave all his funds to establish 'The Rice Institute', a non-profit-making organization to further art and science. Patrick was engaged to represent the late Mrs Rice's interests.

On 24 September 1900 a cheque was presented for $25,000 at Rice's bank. The cheque was in Jones's writing, and payable to 'Abert T. Patrick', being endorsed 'Albert T Patrick' on the back. The signature appeared to be that of William Rice, but the clerk refused it because of the faulty endorsement. The man left and returned with a correct endorsement. The bank telephoned Jones, who said that the signature was that of Rice. Still not satisfied, a bank official later telephoned, insisting on speaking to Mr Rice, only to be told that the millionaire was dead.

Patrick told bank officials that he had another of Rice's cheques for $65 000, and also an assignment for all his bonds and securities. A post-mortem on Rice revealed traces of mercury in his organs, and congestion of the lungs due to 'some gas or vapour'.

On 4 October Patrick and Jones were arrested on charges of forgery. Jones made a confession in which he accused Patrick of administering chloroform to Rice, and said he had later committed the murder following Patrick's instructions.

Patrick was tried for murder in January 1902. Bank officials and document experts declared that Rice's signature on various of the papers and

cheques was forged. Doctors testified that the millionaire had died by inhaling a gaseous irritant, probably chloroform. (See also *Adelaide Bartlett*.) Jones admitted obtaining chloroform and mercury tablets. The latter were given to Rice, and finally Jones chloroformed him in his sleep.

Patrick was found guilty of first-degree murder, which under New York law meant the electric chair, but the death sentence was commuted to life imprisonment. Jones, because he turned state evidence, was discharged. In November 1912 Governor John A. Dix granted Patrick a full and unconditional pardon. In 1940 Patrick died.

[*144, 165, 169, 562, 726, 887, 922*]

PAYNE, Arthur D. Successful Texas lawyer who killed his wife and injured his son in a car-bomb explosion and was brought to justice through the campaigning efforts of a newspaperman.

On 27 June 1930 Payne decided to walk to his office, leaving the family car free for his wife's use. Later that morning Mrs Payne set off in the car with her 9-year-old son to do some shopping. She had driven only a short distance when the car began to emit clouds of smoke and then disintegrated in a huge explosion. Mrs Payne was killed by the blast but her son, although badly injured, survived.

The cause of the blast was a quantity of high-explosive detonated by a time fuse. While the police seemed reluctant to class the incident as murder, no such hesitation curbed the editor of the *Amarillo News*, who declared that Mrs Payne had been murdered and that he would head an investigation. This he did by hiring a crime reporter to probe into Arthur D. Payne's background.

Apart from the fact that a majority of Amarillo citizens thought him guilty, it appeared that Payne had fallen in love with his secretary and had promised to marry her. This provided a possible motive, added to which he had heavily insured his wife and children, naming himself as beneficiary. Payne was evasive when questioned about these matters, but his mistress was more forthcoming. She reported that he had told her he would get rid of his wife if necessary.

He was arrogant when arrested but broke down under questioning and made a full confession—almost a novel—running to 60,000 words. He admitted trying various methods to kill his wife before using the car bomb. A trial jury lost little time in finding him guilty, but he cheated his

executioners by blowing himself up in his cell. His method of self-destruction was sufficiently powerful to destroy part of his cell but no one else was harmed.

[*340*]

PEACE, Charles Frederick. Probably England's most notorious criminal. A scourge of the police for 20 years, committing countless thefts and burglaries, and 2 murders.

Born in 1832, Peace has been described as 'a monkey of a man'. He was small, agile and enormously strong. He was the archetype of the cat-burglar, moving swiftly and silently about the roof-tops, plundering the upper rooms as he went. His ability to contort his rubber-like features enabled him to disguise his appearance, and an interest in theatricals, music and versifying made him a versatile and elusive character.

He played the violin, and used an old instrument case to carry his house-breaking tools.

Charlie Peace liked his neighbour's wife. Mrs Katherine Dyson at first responded, but then rejected him. Peace would have none of this, and persecuted the woman with letters and threats. Soon an incident occurred in Manchester in which Police Constable Nicholas Cock was shot and killed while arresting an intruder. The murderer was Peace, but three Irishmen, the Habron brothers, were tried for the murder, and William was sentenced to death—fortunately commuted to life imprisonment.

Peace returned to the Dysons, and after a drinking bout attempted to waylay Mrs Dyson. He was intercepted by her husband, whom he shot dead. Peace now had a reward on his head, and moved to London, where he continued his burglary. While burgling a house at Blackheath on 10 October 1878 he was challenged by PC Edward Robinson. He fired 3 shots at him, but missed, and was finally overpowered and arrested.

Tried in November at the Old Bailey for attempted murder, he was found guilty and sentenced to life imprisonment. While travelling under escort by train to Sheffield he threw himself out, but was recaptured. Tried at Sheffield Assizes for the murder of Dyson, he was found guilty. While awaiting execution he made a full confession of his crimes, including the shooting of PC Cock (William Habron was subsequently released from prison). Peace was hanged at Armley Jail, Leeds, on 25 February 1879. He wrote his own memorial card: 'In memory of Charles Peace who was executed in Armley Prison Tuesday February

Parker and Hulme: Juliet and Pauline

Peace: An example of his handwriting

25th 1879. Aged 47. For that I don but never intended.'
[*1, 21, 29, 290, 388, 478, 746, 826, 957, 985*]

PEARCEY, Mary Eleanor. Cited as a classic example of jealousy leading to murder, Mrs Pearcey killed her rival and murdered the woman's baby as well.

A police constable in Hampstead noticed, lying in Crossfield Road, a woman's body with the head almost severed. Another police officer near by found an abandoned perambulator with blood-stained cushions. Next day, 25 October 1890, the corpse of an 18-month-old baby was found on waste ground.

It was found that a Mrs Phoebe Hogg had taken her baby out on 24 October, and had not returned. Frank Hogg, her husband, seemed unworried, but his sister Clara Hogg discussed her anxiety with Mrs Pearcey, a family friend. The two women went to the mortuary to see the body found in Crossfield Road. Clara recognized her sister-in-law on the slab; Mrs Pearcey reacted hysterically and drew the attention of the police to her. They found that Frank Hogg had a key to Mrs Pearcey's house. It was obvious the couple were having an affair. A search of Mrs Pearcey's kitchen showed signs of violence—there was broken glass and furniture lying around the house, and bloodstains. Mrs Pearcey played the piano during the search, and attributed the bloodstains to her killing of mice, but could not explain other articles, such as bloody clothing, two knives and a chopper, in the same way.

She was searched and her underclothes were bloodstained. She was tried at the Old Bailey in December 1890, when it became clear from her love-letters that she was infatuated with Frank Hogg, and murdered his wife out of jealousy. A neighbour stated that she heard a woman screaming in Mrs Pearcey's house on 24 October. Another witness saw the accused wheeling a perambulator on that day. Mrs Pearcey had obviously lured the unsuspecting woman to her house and then proceeded to hack mother and child to death in blind fury.

Mary Pearcey maintained her innocence, but she was hanged on 23 December 1890.
[*322, 378, 449, 500, 554, 558, 592, 711*]

PEEL CASE. The sudden disappearance of a respected judge and his wife from their Florida home led to a young judge being tried for complicity in their murder 5 years later.

Judge Curtis Chillingworth and his wife had a beach house at Manalapan, near Palm Beach, Florida. The judge did not appear for his court sitting on 15 June 1955. That same day 2 carpenters went to the house, but there was no reply. The car was in the garage, and on the steps to the beach were bloodstains; on the beach itself were footprints and signs of a scuffle. Two years later, no bodies having been found, the Florida authorities declared the couple dead.

Among persons who might have borne the Chillingworths a grudge was Judge Joseph A. Peel, aged 31, who was a glamorous figure and not too highly regarded. Peel had twice been guilty of professional negligence, and Judge Chillingworth had been obliged to issue a public reprimand. Terrified that he would be disbarred, Peel may have decided to kidnap and murder Chillingworth.

Two underworld figures, Floyd Holzapfel and Bobby Lincoln, carried out Peel's instructions. They held the judge and his wife at gun-point, took them out to sea and drowned their weighted bodies.

Holzapfel was not paid—due to Peel's financial difficulties—and sought to implicate Peel in the disappearance. Peel was arrested, and in the trial in 1961 Holzapfel admitted abducting the elderly judge and his wife. Asked why, he replied, 'To save him,' pointing at Peel. Holzapfel was sentenced to the electric chair and later reprieved.

Peel, protesting that it was a plot to ruin his political career, was found guilty of being an accessory before the fact. The jury added a recommendation to mercy, and Judge Peel was sentenced to life imprisonment.

[90, 108, 1012]

PELTZER BROTHERS. Léon and James Peltzer, born in Germany and naturalized Belgians, ran a flourishing export business in Antwerp until 1873, when they met financial difficulties. A lawyer friend, Guillaume Bernays, saved them from bankruptcy with the help of their elder brother Armand, a successful businessman in South America.

The brothers dispersed after the bankruptcy hearing, but Armand stayed in Antwerp and struck up a close friendship with Bernays. He also became friendly with Mme Julie Bernays, who was separated from her husband. Rumour soon started about an affair, and Bernays was angered. On 17 September 1881 he had a stormy confrontation with Armand.

Following reports from his wife's maid-servant, Bernays wrote to Armand breaking off their friendship. Armand attempted reconciliation, but his letter was returned unopened.

On 1 November Léon Peltzer returned to Belgium to help his brother. Using the name Henry Vaughan, he sought legal advice from Guillaume Bernays, whom he persuaded to visit him in Brussels on 7 January 1882. Bernays was reported missing, and on 19 January his body was found at 159 rue de la Loi following a letter addressed to the 'Coroner of Antwerp' and signed by Henry Vaughan, who claimed to have met Bernays in Brussels and to have been present when the lawyer accidentally shot himself with his revolver.

Rumour had it that Vaughan was Léon Peltzer, who had decided to help his brother Armand out of a sense of brotherly indebtedness. Public feeling against the brothers was strong, and when they were brought to trial in November 1882 Léon confessed to the killing but declared Armand was innocent. Both brothers were found guilty and

sentenced to death. Armand died in prison in 1885 and Léon, after serving 30 years imprisonment, drowned himself in 1922.

By an incredible coincidence, Léon Peltzer's body when recovered from the sea was placed on the carpet which had been in the room at 159 rue de la Loi where he had shot and killed Bernays. By a series of different purchases over the years this carpet ended up as a wagon-cover used by a farmer at Clemskerke, who offered it as a winding-sheet when Peltzer's body was washed up.

[2, 211, 221, 366]

PERRY, Arthur. New York's Perry-Palm case was a triumph for the use of forensic evidence.

A woman's body with the head battered in was found lying near some warehouses in Queens County, New York, on 2 July 1937. Her 2-year-old child lay uninjured next to her. A nightwatchman at a near-by junk-yard heard screams the previous evening and notified the police. He was drunk at the time, and the police doubted his story.

The body was identified as 20-year-old Mrs Phennie Perry. Close by were a man's black left shoe with a hole in the sole and blood-soaked papers—letters and bills addressed to Ulysses Palm—and a receipt book.

Police immediately called on Palm, but he was out. A man's right black shoe, the fellow of the one found, was discovered. Palm was a Baptist deacon, and worked in a chain store. He was highly regarded by his landlord, who said that Palm sublet a room to the Perrys.

Palm admitted that the receipt book belonged to his church, but said the shoes belonged to Perry, who said that Palm had written to his wife, threatening to kill her if she were not more friendly. Perry claimed to have confronted Palm, and the police found that at the time stated Palm was 8 miles away. Forensic examination of Perry's socks linked him conclusively to the crime. On one sock a soiled patch was found corresponding to the hole in the shoe. The area was analysed, and contained traces of human blood and earth of the same type as that where the body was found.

Perry was tried in November 1937, found guilty and sentenced to death. A second trial was ordered on the grounds that the judge had admitted hearsay evidence. This took place in November 1938, and proved even more conclusive than the first. A prosecution witness claimed that Perry had confessed to him in prison, saying, 'I don't know

why I did it.' Arthur Perry was electrocuted in August 1939.
[776]

PETIOT, Dr Marcel. A 49-year-old physician and member of the Resistance who was charged with murdering 27 people at his Paris house.

Attention was drawn to the doctor's activities in March 1944 by the foul-smelling smoke emitted from the chimney at 21 rue Lesueur. In the basement of the house police found a furnace fuelled with the dismembered remains of 27 bodies.

Dr Petiot had fled, but the police caught up with him 9 months later. He freely admitted to killing 63 persons, alleging that they were traitorous Nazi collaborators.

No. Twenty-one, rue Lesueur, was a death-house which, in addition to the basement furnace, contained a sound-proofed room with a spy-hole. (See *H. H. Holmes.*) The purpose of this, claimed the prosecution at Petiot's trial, was to obtain money. It was alleged that he promised to arrange escape routes out of German-occupied France for wealthy Jews. Among the exhibits in court were 47 suitcases which contained over 1500 items of clothing—most with identification marks removed.

The doctor's attitude in court was to bluster. His extraordinary career and background were brought out by the prosecution. Against this shady past, however, had to be set his achievements in setting up a wealthy Paris medical practice and of becoming a small-town Mayor.

Petiot's profits from his wartime escape route were estimated at over a million pounds, but the doctor insisted that he had only killed members of the Gestapo. The jury, bearing in mind the facilities in the death house at rue Lesueur and the ominous contents of the 47 suitcases, did not believe him. He was found guilty, and sentenced to death. Flippant to the last, he is said to have asked to relieve himself before execution and when refused, added that when one went on a voyage one took all one's luggage. He was guillotined on 26 May 1946.
[*231, 232, 298, 373, 390, 525, 635, 790, 792, 832*]

PHOENIX TRUNK MURDERS. See JUDD, Winnie Ruth

PIERRE, Dale Selby. US airman aided by fellow-serviceman William Andrews, who committed the Hi-Fi shop murders in Ogden, Utah, on 22 April

Petiot: The knife has fallen!

1974. During the course of robbery, the intruders held captive the two proprietors of the shop and 3 friends who had called by. The victims were herded into the basement, tied up and forced to lie on the floor. Their wallets, purses and jewellery were taken and then the robbers subjected them to appalling violence.

A bottle of Drano, a caustic compound to unblock drains, was produced and the victims were forced to drink the thick liquid, having been told, 'We're going to have a cocktail party.' Next each victim was shot in the back of the head while they lay on the floor; the teenage shop assistant was raped first. This resulted in three immediate deaths and one badly wounded youth. The fifth victim, who was only superficially injured, was subjected to further assault by an attempt at strangulation and a ballpoint pen was forced down into his ear.

Doctors saved the lives of the two survivors, one of whom was able to give the police descriptions of the murderers. Suspicion quickly focused on Dale Pierre, an airman at the nearby USAF base Hill Field. He had been interviewed during a previous murder investigation and had been heard discussing a prospective crime to which any witnesses would be eliminated. He had also talked specifically of his intention to rob a Hi-Fi shop, declaring 'If anybody gets in my way I'm going to kill 'em.'

Police investigators found some of the personal possessions stolen from the Hi-Fi shop victims in a garbage dump close to Pierre's quarters at the air force base. A search of the airman's quarters turned up a rental agreement for a garage store which, on inspection, proved to contain $24,000 worth of stolen hi-fi equipment. Of particular significance to the detectives was a half-used bottle of Drano found in the garage. Pierre and Andrews were arrested, together with a third airman who was eventually convicted of aggravated robbery.

Dale Pierre and William Andrews were tried for murder and found guilty on all counts. Sentence of death was passed by the judge at the trial held in Farmington, Utah. They remained in the maximum security wing of Utah State Prison and on five occasions won reprieves from death by firing-squad. Pierre was finally executed by lethal injection on 28 August 1987, 13 years after committing the crimes for which he was sentenced to death. He was the first person to be executed in Utah since the sensational case of *Gary Gilmore*. Newspapers reported that relatives of some of Pierre's victims held parties in restaurants near the State Prison while opponents of capital punishment carried out protests.

[*530*]

PODMORE, William Henry. Motor mechanic and petty criminal who brutally murdered a man who had uncovered his false dealings.

The body of 58-year-old Vivian Messiter, an oil company agent, was found behind some boxes in a locked garage at Southampton on 10 January 1929. A puncture wound over the left eye led the police to think the man had been shot. But the real cause of death was multiple fractures of the skull—Messiter had been battered to death. Sir Bernard Spilsbury examined the body, and concluded that the murder weapon was a heavy hammer.

In the dead man's lodgings police found a reply from a William F. Thomas to an advertisement for local agents. He was already wanted for a wages robbery. Thomas's lodgings were located, but their quarry had flown. He had gone hurriedly,

leaving valuable clues which established his real name was William Henry Podmore.

Podmore was found in London and questioned. He said he had worked in Southampton as Messiter's assistant. There was insufficient evidence to charge him with murder. He was imprisoned for 6 months for fraud.

Meanwhile an oil sales receipt book was found which contained entries recording sales to fictitious persons giving commissions to W. F. Thomas. The top copies of these entries had been torn out, but the pencil used to write them had left indentations on the pages beneath. These were made legible by special photography, and provided proof that Podmore was operating a swindle against Messiter's company.

Podmore was charged with murder in December 1929, and was tried at Winchester Assizes. The case made against him suggested that he was found out and accused by Messiter. Knowing that he was already wanted for fraud, he killed him. Podmore's guilt was confirmed by Spilsbury's evidence; a hammer found in the garage was unquestionably the murder weapon. An eyebrow hair on it was identified with the hair of the dead man.

Podmore was found guilty, and was hanged in Winchester Prison on 22 April 1930.

[*2, 133, 302, 488, 742, 798, 846, 921, 1010, 1023*]

PODOLA, Guenther Fritz Erwin. A 30-year-old barber's son born in Berlin whose career of housebreaking and blackmail ended in the murder of a London policeman and a trial which made legal history.

Podola emigrated to Canada, but was deported in 1958 after conviction for theft and burglary. He worked in Germany, and then came to England. He frequented London's Soho clubs, calling himself Mike Colato. He obtained money by housebreaking and blackmail.

In July 1959 he burgled the South Kensington flat of Mrs Verne Schiffman, stealing jewellery and furs worth £2000. A few days later he tried to blackmail her, claiming to be a private detective with photos and tape recordings. She had nothing to fear, and told the police—her phone was tapped and when the blackmailer rang his call was traced.

Within minutes 2 detectives were at the South Kensington call box; he was still there. He broke free, and was caught near a block of flats. One policeman went to fetch the patrol car, leaving Detective Sergeant Raymond Purdy with their quarry. The man pulled out a gun, shot Purdy dead and escaped.

He was identified as Podola by his palm prints, and on 16 July police burst into a South Kensington hotel where Podola was and broke down the door of his room, knocking him over. Podola was taken to hospital apparently suffering partial loss of consciousness. When he recovered he said he could not remember anything.

Before his trial Podola was examined by 6 doctors, 4 of whom thought he was suffering amnesia, with 2 in favour of malingering. He was tried at the Old Bailey in September 1959, the judge ruling that the question of the accused man's amnesia would have to be settled first. It was proved that Podola had given himself away in a letter written while he was in custody. The murder trial itself lasted only 1½ days. The prosecution case was conclusive, and Podola—still claiming loss of memory—was found guilty.

In dismissing Podola's appeal, the judge said, 'Even if the loss of memory had been a genuine loss of memory, that did not of itself render the appellant insane.' The gunman was hanged at Wandsworth Prison on 5 November 1959.
[*311, 312, 381, 513*]

POMMERENCKE, Heinrich. A 23-year-old multiple sex killer known as 'The Beast of the Black Forest.'

At 15 Pommerencke had a reputation for molesting girls outside a Mecklenburg dance hall. He committed several rapes during 1955–7 when in Hamburg, and in 1958 attacked 2 girls in Austria.

His violent sexual desires led to murder in 1959. After leaving a cinema he saw 18-year-old Hilda Knothe. He followed her into a park, where he raped her and cut her throat.

In the summer of 1959 he murdered again. He

Podola: Where Purdy was shot

knew that trains were good places to pick up girls. He boarded a train bound for Italy and among the sleeping passengers he saw a young student, Dagmar Klimek. He molested her, and when she tried to escape he pushed her out of the train. Pulling the communication cord, he jumped out, raped and stabbed her to death.

Within a month Pommerencke claimed 2 more victims, but was arrested in 1960 in Freiberg. It was obvious that he matched the descriptions of a man wanted for rape in the Black Forest area.

Pommerencke made a full confession. He admitted becoming 'tensed up' after watching sex films. He was tried at Freiberg in October 1960, charged with 10 murders with rape, 20 cases of rape alone and 35 assaults and burglaries—he was sentenced to a total of 140 years in prison.

[601]

PRITCHARD, Dr Edward William. Glasgow physician who poisoned his wife and mother-in-law.

Pritchard was admitted to the Royal College of Surgeons and gazetted as naval assistant surgeon in 1846. He married Mary Jane Taylor in 1850 and resigned his commission the following year to take up private practice in Yorkshire.

In 1860 he moved to Glasgow, to a fresh practice, but was disliked by the medical fraternity for his boastful ways. He gave popular travel lectures, became a Freemason and handed out photographs of himself. Pritchard's house in Berkeley Terrace was badly damaged by fire in 1863, and a servant girl died in the blaze.

The doctor made a 15-year-old servant girl pregnant and aborted her with a promise that he would marry her should his wife die. Mary Pritchard became ill on 1 February 1865 with violent sickness. Her husband suggested irritation of the stomach, and a second doctor thought gastric fever. Mrs Pritchard's elderly mother, Mrs Taylor, came to nurse her daughter. The day before, Pritchard bought aconite.

Mrs Pritchard's condition gradually deteriorated, and Mrs Taylor was also taken ill. The old lady used an opium mixture to relieve neuralgia—and to a Dr Paterson, who had been called in, Pritchard suggested that she had overdosed herself by taking 'a good swig of it'. She died on 25 February, Mrs Pritchard on 18 March. In the presence of relatives Pritchard had the coffin lid removed and ostentatiously kissed his wife's corpse.

Suspicion of Pritchard came in an anonymous letter sent to the Procurator-Fiscal. The doctor was arrested and both his wife and mother-in-law were found to have been poisoned with antimony. He was tried at Edinburgh in July 1865, and the circumstantial evidence weighed heavily against him. Dr Paterson was extremely hostile towards Pritchard, and was rebuked by the judge.

Pritchard was found guilty and made 3 confessions. He was hanged in Glasgow on 28 July 1865 before a crowd of 100 000—the last person to be publicly hanged in Scotland. Years later, when the prison was replaced by a High Court, his body was disinterred and his boots found to be in an excellent state. Somebody stole them!
[1, 21, 35, 134, 231, 259, 290, 332, 409, 455, 482, 724, 741, 780, 781, 789, 795, 907, 947]

PUTT, George Howard. Caught literally red-handed, the Memphis murderer had claimed 5 lives and terrorized citizens for a month.

On 14 August 1969 Roy and Bernalyn Dumas, both middle aged, were found strangled in their apartment. Mrs Dumas had been sexually mutilated with knife cuts.

Eleven days later an elderly widow, Leila Jackson, a landlady, was also found strangled and mutilated. On 29 August a third killing occurred which put the city into a new state of panic. A 21-year-old girl, Glenda Sue Harden, was found stabbed 14 times in a public park. Housewives locked themselves in.

On 11 September screams in an apartment block brought people to the aid of the fifth victim, but 59-year-old widow Mary Christine Pickens lay dead from multiple stab wounds. Her assailant, bloody knife in hand, was pursued. Police squad cars were alerted, and the man was apprehended by 2 officers—he was shirtless, out of breath and covered with blood. He said he had injured himself jumping over a fence, but the Memphis killer, 23-year-old Buster Putt, had been caught. His early denials were followed by the admission 'I killed them all'.

Putt related how he had picked out the Dumas apartment for robbery at random, a robbery which turned into sadistic violence. He made an improvised mask to terrorize Mrs Dumas, and claimed to have raped her. This was never substantiated, but the mutilations, clearly demonstrated by pathologists, were denied by Putt.

In between killings, Putt sold his blood to a Memphis company for $5 a pint, and returned home to his pregnant wife—the night before the final killing his nightmare woke her up.

Putt was tried for the murder of Mary Pickens in October 1970. The defence plea was one of insanity, but psychiatrists disagreed. He was found guilty and sentenced to death. Appeals and renewed attempts to prove insanity lasted until the US Supreme Court ruling which set aside the death penalty. In April 1973 Putt was tried for the Dumas murders and found guilty. He was sentenced to imprisonment totalling 497 years.
[663]

PYJAMA GIRL CASE. Antonio Agostini, an Italian immigrant working in Sydney, Australia, was found guilty of the manslaughter of his wife. The case took 10 years to solve.

On 1 September 1934 the partly burned body of a young woman dressed in pyjamas was found in a culvert near Albury, New South Wales. Death had been caused by blows to the skull, but there was also a gunshot wound in the head. Identification proved a problem. The girl appeared to be English, and the only distinctive feature about her was her ears, which were lacking lobes. A full description, together with photographs and fingerprints, was widely circulated.

The Pyjama Girl's body was placed in a tank of formalin at Sydney University, where it was viewed by a number of people helping the police. The peculiar feature of the ears led to her tentative identification as Linda Agostini, wife of an Italian restaurant worker.

Agostini was interviewed by the police in July 1935. He said that he had married an English girl named Linda Platt, but they had separated. Shown photographs of the dead woman, he denied that she was his wife. Interest in the case waned. Agostini was interned for part of the War. The Pyjama Girl stayed in her bath of formalin.

In 1944 the newly appointed Commissioner of Police for New South Wales, W. J. Mackay, looked at the case, and tried again to identify the victim, who was taken out of the bath, had her face made up and her hair dressed. Photographs quickly led to an identification—7 people said this was Linda Agostini.

Agostini was contacted, and stated that his wife had begun to drink heavily, and that their marriage was breaking up. He claimed that she threatened him in bed with a revolver, and in the subsequent struggle the gun went off and killed her. He then took her pyjama-clad body in his car to the culvert, poured petrol over it and set it on fire.

He was sent for trial on 19 June 1944. His account of the firing of the gun did not convince the court, for it was known that it was the blows to the head which killed his wife. The jury brought in a verdict of manslaughter. Agostini served 6 years' hard labour before being deported to Italy.
[179, 519]

Pyjama Girl Case: Agostini under police escort
Pyjama Girl Case: Searching for clues

Q

QUEEN, Peter. Unusual case in which the son of a Glasgow bookmaker was convicted of murder despite strong expert testimony that the victim had strangled herself.

Queen married young, but separated when his wife became an alcoholic. His father engaged a young woman, Chrissie Gall, as a nursemaid, and she and Peter became jointly attracted.

Chrissie Gall developed heavy drinking habits, and when her father turned her out she moved in with James Burns and his wife, friends of Peter

Queen. In 1930 Queen and Chrissie lived as man and wife in the same house.

The Burnses tried to cure Chrissie of alcoholism, but she threatened suicide. 'Some day some of you will come in and find me strung up,' she said. In the summer of 1931 Queen and Chrissie set up on their own. Chrissie continued to drink, and was tormented by the fact they were 'living in sin'.

On 20 November a friend, Mrs Johnston, called and found Chrissie drunk. Queen came home, and Mr and Mrs Johnston returned later to find

Queen: The body of Chrissie Gall

Chrissie asleep. They left at about 11.00 p.m. Four hours later, Queen, highly agitated, rushed to a police station and said, 'I think you will find my wife dead.' He was alleged to have added, 'I think I have killed her.'

Chrissie was in bed, strangled with a clothes-line. Queen was charged with murder. Two pathologists considered the case a homicide, but both Sir Sydney Smith and Sir Bernard Spilsbury regarded it as suicide. Their reasons included the apparent lack of a struggle.

Queen was tried at Glasgow in January 1932. He denied telling the police he had killed Chrissie, maintaining he had said, 'Don't think I have killed her.' There was no record of this conversation at the police station. The jury returned a majority verdict of guilty with a recommendation to mercy. Sentence of death was passed on Queen, and commuted to life imprisonment. He was later released, and died in 1958. Commenting on the case, Sir Sydney Smith remarked, 'So, in the only case where Spilsbury and I were in pretty complete agreement, the jury believed neither of us.'
[*133, 487, 542, 865*]

QUERIPEL, Michael. Teenage clerk who commited a brutal murder and was detected by a palm-print left at the scene of the crime.

On the night of 29 April 1955 a Mr Currell reported that his wife was missing after taking her dog for a walk on Potter's Bar golf course. The dog had returned alone.

At dawn next day her body was found near the seventeenth tee. She had been battered to death with a heavy iron tee marker which lay near by with a bloody handprint on it. A stocking was around her throat.

The palm-print was not in the criminal records. House-to-house checks were made in the area, and palm-prints were taken from local employees—

Queripel: The murder weapon

nine thousand of them—and checked with the print on the tee marker. (See *Peter Griffiths.*)

On 19 August a matching print was found, belonging to 17-year-old Michael Queripel, a local-government employee. Queripel told police that he had found the body, but then he admitted, 'I hit her . . . I tried to strangle her.' He said he had a migraine, and walked on the course to clear it. He saw the woman and hit out at her, and finally battered her to death after tearing at her clothing.

He pleaded guilty to murder at the Old Bailey on 12 October, and the judge ordered that he be detained during Her Majesty's Pleasure.
[*369, 370, 656, 759*]

R

RABLEN, Eva. Fun-loving wife who poisoned her deaf husband with strychnine in Tuttletown, California.

Carroll Rablen was deaf through a First World War injury. His attractive second wife Eva liked dancing, and they went to dances where she took the floor while he watched, since he did not dance.

On 26 April 1929 the Rablens were at the weekly dance at Tuttletown. Carroll stayed in his car while Eva enjoyed herself inside. About midnight Eva took a cup of coffee and some refreshments to her husband and returned to the hall.

Seconds later Carroll Rablen was writhing in the car. His cries brought his father and others to his aid. Before he died he complained of the bitter taste of the coffee.

The contents of his stomach were analysed, but no poison was found, though Rablen's father said he thought Eva had poisoned his son for the insurance.

The police searched the dance-hall without success. A second search, however, turned up a bottle marked 'Strychnine' with the address of a local pharmacist. The drug store had made such a sale on 26 April to Eva Rablen, and she was arrested.

The contents of the dead man's stomach were again analysed, and this time traces of strychnine were found. Vestiges of the poison were also found in the coffee cup.

Eva Rablen's trial was held outdoors in view of the great public interest in the case. Confronted with the damning evidence, she changed her plea to guilty. The sentence was life imprisonment. [95]

RATTEN, Leith. Controversial murder case in which the convicted man is widely believed to be innocent, and a victim of a miscarriage of justice.

On 7 May 1970 police were called to a house in Echuca, a small town on the river Murray in Victoria, Australia. Leith Ratten told the officers

Rablen: The trial is held in an open-air dance pavilion

that he had been cleaning his guns in the kitchen when the shotgun accidentally discharged and killed his wife. Beverly Ratten, 8½ months pregnant, lay dead on the floor, a shotgun wound under her left armpit having penetrated her heart.

Ratten said that both he and his wife had been standing when the weapon discharged. The pathologist's finding that the angle of the shot was at 45° to the vertical was later to prove contentious. When inquiries showed that Ratten had been engaging in an extra-marital affair a motive seemed to be apparent. He was tried for murder in August 1970 and convicted on largely circumstantial evidence. He was sentenced to death, although this was commuted to life imprisonment in September 1971.

Ratten's supporters exhausted the appeal system in their efforts to have his case re-examined. His appeal was turned down at every stage, despite the emergence of powerful new evidence. Doubt was cast on the official reconstruction of the shooting. If the fatal shot entered the victim's body at an angle of 45° while she was in a standing position, the butt of the shotgun would have been at a height from the floor of 9 feet 10 inches—an unlikely feat for a man of Ratten's height of 5 feet 7½ inches. An alternative interpretation, supported by independent experts, was that the shot in Mrs Ratten's body had

had a horizontal flight, which would have been consistent with her husband's explanation of an accidental discharge.

[*671*]

RATTENBURY-STONER CASE. Sen-
sational case with similar ingredients to the *Thompson-Bywaters* affair, in which an elderly husband was murdered after the wife had taken a young lover.

Francis Rattenbury, a 67-year-old architect, married Alma in 1928. She had already had two husbands, and lived at the Villa Madeira in Bournemouth. The disparity in age and outlook soon became apparent. Alma, 31, was lively and unconventional, whereas her husband was retiring and dull.

In 1934 Alma advertised for a chauffeur-handyman, and 18-year-old George Stoner was given the job. Stoner, illiterate and lacking all distinction save youth, soon became Alma's lover. She doted on him, and took him to a London hotel, buying him silk shirts and a fashionable suit.

On their return to Bournemouth, Stoner felt he had gained a new independence. He refused Mrs Rattenbury's instructions to drive her and her husband to Bridport, being jealous of Alma in her husband's company for a night.

Late on the night of 24 March 1935 Alma found her husband with blood streaming from his head. Francis Rattenbury had a fractured skull, and died in hospital. Alma was questioned by the police, but she was incoherent through drink, flirting with the officers and claiming that she 'did it with a mallet'. A bloodstained mallet was found, but with no fingerprints.

Stoner, who had meanwhile confessed that he had killed Rattenbury, and Alma were both arrested. The lovers were loyal to each other—Alma declined to withdraw her confession, and Stoner denied that she had influenced his behaviour.

They were tried for murder in May 1935 at the Old Bailey, both pleading not guilty. Alma claimed that she could not recall anything that happened after her husband's body was found. Stoner's claim that he was under the influence of drugs was shown to be unfounded. He was found guilty and sentenced to death. Alma was acquitted. Three days later she committed suicide. Stoner's sentence was commuted to life imprisonment.

[*1, 58, 91, 131, 171, 425, 493, 607, 612, 676, 687, 691, 977*]

RAVEN, Daniel. Curious case in which a young advertising agent was convicted of murdering his parents-in-law.

On the night of 10 October 1949 Leopold and Esther Goodman were found dead in their Edgware home, battered to death with part of a television aerial. The couple had visited their daughter earlier that evening at a Muswell Hill nursing home, where she had recently given birth to a son. The Goodmans were accompanied by their son-in-law, 23-year-old Daniel Raven, who had driven them home and then gone on to his own house.

Police were impressed by Raven's immaculate appearance so late at night, and a check showed he had changed his suit. A partly burned suit was found in the gas boiler. The trousers were bloodstained, and his shoes had blood-spots. He was charged with double murder.

Raven said he had returned to the Goodman house later that night and found his parents-in-law dead. He knelt down, getting blood on his trousers in the process. He then ran away in panic.

He was tried at the Old Bailey, where he pleaded not guilty. His wife gave evidence for him, but he admitted that he did not get on with his in-laws. He was sentenced to death and hanged at Pentonville on 6 July 1950.

[*83, 656, 961*]

RAYNER, Horace George. The 75-year-old founder of Britain's first departmental store was William Whiteley, murdered by his alleged natural son. He was an astute businessman, but he also had a strong streak of righteousness. His motto was, 'Add conscience to your capital', and he styled himself as the 'Universal Provider'.

On 24 January 1907 a young man walked into Whiteley's office, and staff heard raised voices. 'Is that your final word?' asked the stranger. 'Yes.' 'Then you are a dead man.' The stranger fired two shots at point-blank range into Whiteley's head, and then ineffectively turned the gun on himself. Whiteley was dead, and the man (identified as 27-year-old Horace Rayner) had written in his notebook, 'To all whom it may concern; William Whiteley is my father. . . .'

Rayner was tried for murder at the Old Bailey in March, and pleaded not guilty, maintaining he had acted while temporarily insane. The trial centred less on his sanity than on his illegitimacy. His alleged father, George Rayner, repudiated paternity of his son, stating that his mistress, Emily Turner, now dead, had improperly registered the birth, although he had agreed to act as foster-father.

Louisa Turner, Emily's sister, produced the sensation of the trial. She had been Whiteley's mistress for many years, and together with George Rayner and sister Emily they frequently made a foursome for weekends at Brighton. Both girls had illegitimate children—Emily had two by Rayner and Louisa one by Whiteley.

In 1881, when Mrs Whiteley learned of the Universal Provider's behaviour, she sued him for divorce.

Rayner was found guilty and sentenced to death. Within a week nearly 200 000 signatures were collected on a petition for reprieve, and the Home Secretary responded by commuting sentence to life imprisonment. Rayner twice tried to commit suicide, and was released in 1919 after serving 12 years.

[265, 275, 550]

READ, James Canham. A middle-aged Victorian lady-killer who murdered his pregnant mistress.

Read earned £3 a week as a book-keeper at London's Royal Albert Docks. He was married with 8 children, but had a number of love affairs on the side.

One mistress was a Mrs Ayriss, and in 1892 he met her sister, 18-year-old Florence Dennis, and was instantly attracted to her. He had an affair with her while continuing to meet both Mrs Ayriss and another woman in Mitcham.

Early in 1894 Florence became pregnant and told her parents, naming Read as the father. She wrote to him, asking him 'What arrangements have you made'. Read asked her to meet him near Southend late in June. Florence Dennis did so, and was not seen alive again.

When her sister failed to return Mrs Ayriss grew anxious, and sent Read a telegram. He replied that he had not seen her for 18 months. He then stole money from his office and went to his mistress at Mitcham. He gave himself away by writing to his brother from that address, and was arrested after Florence Dennis's body was found with a bullet wound in the head.

Read was tried for murder at Chelmsford Assizes in November 1894. His affair with Florence was proved by letters, and she had told her parents that Read was the father. He insisted that he had met Mrs Ayriss that evening near Southend because she wanted money for Florence, pregnant by a soldier. No evidence was

called for the defence, and Read was found guilty and hanged at Chelmsford on 4 December 1894.
[11, 141, 219, 532, 932, 1006]

REES, Melvin David. A 28-year-old professional musician whose 9 murders accompanied by sexual assault earned him the name of 'Sex Beast'.

On 26 June 1957 an army sergeant and his girl, Margaret Harold, stopped on the roadside near Annapolis, Maryland. After driving off they were overtaken by another car which forced them to stop. A man jumped out and threatened them with a revolver. He attempted to caress Margaret, but she pushed him away and he shot her. The sergeant bolted. He reached a farmhouse after running a mile, and raised the alarm.

The car was still there, but the assailant had vanished. In a near-by derelict cinder block building the walls were plastered with pornographic photographs.

Margaret Harold's killer was not caught, and in January 1959 truck-driver Carroll Jackson, driving his wife and 2 children home after a visit to relatives, was overtaken by a car and forced to stop. The driver leapt out holding a gun, and forced the family to get into the trunk of their car. He then drove off. Next day the Jacksons' car was found abandoned with the keys still in the ignition. There were no signs of the family.

Two months later some men near Fredericksburg, Virginia, found the body of Carroll Jackson with a bullet-hole in the head, and underneath him the suffocated body of his 18-month child. A few weeks later some boys playing near the scene of Margaret Harold's death found the rest of the Jackson family. Mrs Jackson had been repeatedly raped and then strangled—the 4-year-old girl died of a fractured skull.

A manhunt ensued, with the police looking for the man described by the army sergeant. Widespread publicity for the case produced a letter from a man in Norfolk, Virginia, in which a young musician named David Melvin Rees was accused of the murders. He was found in West Memphis, Arkansas, working as a piano salesman.

Rees was picked out as Margaret Harold's murderer by the army sergeant. His parents' home near Washington was searched, and his gun and notes recalling his sadistic crimes in detail were found. Rees was tried first in Baltimore (where he received a life sentence) and next for the Jackson murders at Spotsylvania, Virginia, where he was convicted and executed in 1961.

[693, 883]

ROBERTS, Harry Maurice. Leader of a gang of 3 car thieves who panicked when questioned by a plain-clothes police patrol and shot dead 3 officers in what became known as the 'Braybrook Street Massacre'. The killings provoked a public outcry, and demands for the reintroduction of capital punishment.

The driver of a police patrol Q car known as Foxtrot Eleven was in Hammersmith on 12 August 1966 and stopped his vehicle in Braybrook Street, near Wormwood Scrubs Prison. In addition to the driver, the patrol consisted of Detective Sergeant Christopher Head and Detective Constable David Wombwell—all were in plain clothes. The patrol questioned 3 men in a blue estate car. Head and Wombwell walked over to the car and were immediately gunned down, one of the men rushing over to the patrol car to shoot the driver through a side window. With the 3 policemen lying dead, the gunmen made off.

A man driving into Braybrook Street was suddenly confronted with a blue car reversing towards him. Thinking there might have been a break from the prison, he noted the vehicle's licence number, PGT726. The police quickly traced a blue Vanguard estate car with this registration to John Edward Witney at a Paddington address where he was found with his wife. He said he had sold his car the previous day to a stranger for £15.

A man reported seeing a blue Vanguard in Lambeth, where it was found in a railway arch garage rented to Witney. In the vehicle were some spent .38 cartridges and car theft equipment. Witney was arrested and charged 'with others' with murder. His companions were named as John Duddy and Harry Roberts, both with criminal records.

Duddy was picked up quickly in Glasgow, but Roberts successfully eluded police for 3 months. He was known to have served in the army in Malaya, and to be skilled at living outdoors. A wide-scale search was mounted in Epping Forest. In November, Roberts' secret lair was found in woods at Hertfordshire and he was rounded up in a near-by barn.

Roberts joined Witney and Duddy, who had already been sent for trial at the Old Bailey. Only Witney gave evidence and he said that Roberts terrorized him. In December 1966 all 3 men were found guilty, and in passing life sentences the judge said, 'My recommendation is that you should not be released on licence, any of the three of you, for a period of 30 years. . . .'

[101, 222, 666, 691, 858, 928, 929, 985]

ROBERTSON, James Roland. Serving police officer who was convicted of murdering a woman by running her over in a Glasgow street in 1950.

A taxi-driver in Prospecthill Road in the early house of 28 July 1950 stopped his cab to investigate an obstruction in the road. To his horror he found himself looking at a badly mangled body. The initial police reaction was that the dead woman had been the victim of a hit-and-run incident. This view changed when it became apparent that there was none of the debris normally associated with the impact of a vehicle on the human frame. Moreover, the post-mortem identified a bruise on the victim's head which could have occurred before death. It looked as if the woman had been knocked unconscious and then been repeatedly run over by a driver carrying out several figure-of-eight manoeuvres.

The car involved in the incident was located where it had been abandoned in a side street. Its last known owner was James Robertson, a serving police officer, who was arrested and charged with the murder of the woman, Catherine McCluskey. Robertson did not deny ownership of the car but said he had found it abandoned, and on checking police records had confirmed that it was stolen. Instead of reporting the matter, he decided to take the car for his own use. He admitted knowing Mrs McCluskey, and had fathered her second child. Regarding the night of 27 July, Robertson said that he absented himself from duty between 11.00 p.m. and 1.00 a.m. in order to sort out his car, which was giving him trouble. In his log he recorded an incident at 12.50 a.m. when a woman was knocked down and fatally injured by a hit-and-run driver.

After he had been accused of murder, Robertson gave a different account of events. He said that while driving down Prospecthill Road he saw Mrs McCluskey and stopped to speak to her. She wanted a lift, but he refused because officially he was on duty. He drove on but then relented and reversed, intending to pick her up after all. It was then that he realized he had knocked her down and her body had become jammed beneath the car. He drove backward and forward until the obstruction was freed.

Police Constable Robertson was tried for murder in Glasgow in 1950. He elected to give evidence, and was destroyed under cross-questioning which led to his conviction and a sentence of death. He was hanged on 16 December 1950.

[*598, 845*]

ROBINSON HILL CASE. The mysterious death of a wealthy doctor's wife in Texas led to accusations against her husband and to his death at the hands of a hired killer before he could be tried for 'murder by omission'.

Joan Robinson was the adopted daughter of oil tycoon Ash Robinson. She married John Hill, an up and coming plastic surgeon in Houston. The couple lived in style at exclusive River Oaks, but by 1968 their marriage was breaking up. Hill pursued other women, and his wife spent more time at her horse farm.

In March 1969 Joan Hill fell ill and her husband took her to Sharpstown Hospital, where she died on 19 March. After a hurried post-mortem the body was made ready for burial before cause of death had been properly certified. The authority of the Medical Examiner was thus bypassed, although slides made of tissues at the post-mortem suggested death had been caused by a liver infection.

Ash Robinson refused to accept the account given of his daughter's death, and began openly to accuse Dr Hill of allowing his wife to die. When Hill remarried three months after the funeral these accusations were renewed. Hill responded with a slander and libel lawsuit for 5 000 000 dollars. In November Joan Robinson Hill's body was exhumed and a second post-mortem carried out. The Sharpstown Hospital pathologist produced a jar containing a preserved brain which he said had been extracted at the first post-mortem, but it was suggested that the brain was not that of Mrs Robinson Hill. The medical evidence was controversial, for while the preserved brain showed signs of meningitis, the brain stem in the body did not.

Three Grand Juries considered the case in little over a year. The third, convened in April 1970, was based on a Texas law whereby John Hill was indicted with causing the death of his wife by 'murder by omission', the implication being that he killed his wife by deliberately withholding treatment. Hill was tried in February 1971 and his second wife, since divorced from him, testified that he kept bacteria culture dishes in the bathroom. Her claim that Hill tried to kill her led to a declaration of a mistrial.

Before a new trial could be held John Hill was shot dead in his house by a hired gunman, who, having jumped bail, was killed by a police officer.

Ash Robinson (who had made it known publicly that he held Dr Hill responsible for the death of his daughter) died in 1985. In the continuing controversy over the case, Dr Hill's family sued Robinson on the grounds that he had hired the gunman who killed the Houston doctor. A civil court jury cleared Robinson of this charge, and he moved away from Houston to avoid further publicity. The case was turned into a best-selling book, *Blood and Money*, by Thomas Thompson and a successful television film called *Murder in Texas*.

[*431, 909*]

ROBINSON, John. The Charing Cross Trunk Murderer.

The left-luggage attendant at Charing Cross railway station noticed an offensive smell coming from a large black trunk deposited 5 days earlier, on 6 May 1927. When opened, the trunk contained several parcels wrapped with paper and string— they held the dismembered portions of a female body and several items of clothing. Sir Bernard Spilsbury examined the corpse, which had been dead about a week. The cause of death was asphyxia. The left-luggage attendant said the man who had left the trunk had a military appearance. He gave instructions that his property be handled

Robinson: A vital clue

Robinson: Charing Cross left-luggage office in 1927

Robinson: The trunk

with care, and then drove away in a taxi. A published photograph of the trunk brought forward a dealer who had sold it on 4 May.

An undergarment found in the trunk bore the laundry mark P. HOLT, which was traced to a Chelsea family who used the mark. They had employed a 'Mrs Rolls', who was Minnie Bonati, the estranged wife of an Italian waiter. Mr Bonati identified the remains as those of his wife, and he himself was cleared.

A taxi-driver said that on 6 May he had taken a fare with a heavy trunk from 86 Rochester Row to Charing Cross Station. Police found a John Robinson had not been seen for several days. Robinson was eventually found in Kennington.

At first he denied any knowledge of Mrs Bonati and the trunk, but then confessed. He claimed that Mrs Bonati had asked him for money, and visited his office on 4 May. She was abusive and attacked him. He pushed her away, she fell and to his horror he realized she was dead (see *Patrick Mahon*). He cut up the corpse (with a knife bought from the same shop that Patrick Mahon used) in his office overlooking Rochester Row police station.

Robinson was tried at the Old Bailey in July 1927, and was found guilty, and executed at Pentonville Prison on 12 August 1927.

[*133, 142, 196, 220, 238, 274, 349, 545, 705, 710, 757, 964*]

ROBLES, Richard. Convicted of the Wylie Murders in New York, being the second man to have confessed to the crimes.

Janice Wylie, 21-year-old daughter of author Max Wylie (and niece of writer Philip Wylie), shared a Manhattan apartment with 2 other girls, Emily Hoffert, a 23-year-old teacher, and 21-year-old Pat Toller, a researcher for *Time* magazine. On 28 August 1963 Janice had the day off from *Newsweek*, and Emily was home. Pat left the apartment to work a normal day, and on her return found the bodies of her flat-mates on the bedroom floor. Both had been killed with multiple stab wounds, and Janice had been eviscerated—the killer had bound the two bodies together with strips torn from the bed sheets.

Death occurred about midday and 3 blood-stained knives from the kitchen had been used to commit the murders. There was no evidence that either girl had been raped, or of burglary or missing articles. It became known that for several weeks Janice had been receiving obscene phone calls which she reported to her father.

There were numerous theories about the sexual and ritualistic aspects of the crime. Eight months later a semi-literate 19-year-old Negro, George Whitmore, was charged with attempted rape and confessed to the murders, but within weeks he stated the confession had been beaten out of him. He was charged with the assault, found guilty of attempted rape, and sentenced to from 5 to 10 years.

In the autumn of 1964 two drug addicts, Nathan and Marjorie Delaney, said they might be hiding the murderer. Richard Robles, a 22-year-old heroin addict with a police record for burglary, who frequented the Delaneys' apartment for fixes, spoke about girls in a violent way and they believed he had been out on a burglary on the day of the murders.

Robles was arrested on 26 January 1965 and confessed to the Wylie murders. He claimed to have performed various sexual acts with Janice with her consent, and then to have been overcome by an uncontrollable urge to violence. He was put on trial in October 1965. The legality of his confession was challenged, but its inconsistencies and omissions were put down to his drug addiction. He was found guilty on 1 December of first-degree murder and sentenced to life im-

Robles: The victims' bodies are removed by the police

prisonment. Whitmore was exonerated completely.
[*136, 431, 528, 566, 834*]

ROSS, Colin. Perpetrator of the Gun Alley Murder in Melbourne, Australia, in 1921. On 31 December the naked body of a 13-year-old girl was found by a police patrolman in a cul-de-sac near Gun Alley in the city's Eastern Arcades, a bustling market area. The girl had been strangled, and it was thought that she had been murdered elsewhere and placed where she was found.

Police inquiries in the district led to Colin Ross, a wine-bar owner, who admitted entertaining the girl in his bar. Ross was anxious to help the police, and in his eagerness said more than was good for him when he divulged details of the crime not yet known to the public. Moreover, a witness came forward who claimed to have seen Ross in Gun Street manoeuvring an awkward bundle. A search of Ross's home in another part of Melbourne produced a blanket on which were found several long strands of red hair. The dead girl had long, flowing tresses of red hair, samples of which matched the hairs on the blanket.

A reconstruction of the crime placed the girl in Ross's wine bar, where he assaulted and strangled her. In order to remove (as he thought) all traces of evidence, he stripped the body and carefully washed and dried it. Then, with the body concealed in a blanket, he emerged into the street after dark and made off for Gun Alley, where he intended to hide it under a street drain grating. This plan was foiled by a policeman routinely walking his beat, causing Ross to panic and simply dump the body in the street and disappear quickly into the darkness.

Ross was charged with murder, and the tell-tale evidence of the matching hair proved to be decisive. The forensic analysis was carried out by the renowned Australian scientist Dr Charles Taylor, who clearly demonstrated the individual characteristics of hair. This was put to a severe test when Ross's defence produced a fair-haired woman who had visited the bar and challenged the prosecution to distinguish between samples of her hair and that of the murder victim. Dr Taylor was equal to the test and proved beyond reasonable doubt that the young murder victim had been in contact with the blanket found at Ross's home. Despite his denials and claims of being framed by the police, Colin Ross was found guilty of murder. Sentence of death was carried out at Melbourne Gaol on 24 April 1922. After he was executed, an acquaintance was reported to have said that Ross explained his prefer-

ence for young girls over women of experience by his comment, 'I prefer them without feathers'.
[*115, 363, 392*]

ROTTMAN, Arthur. A 21-year-old German sailor on board a New Zealand vessel, interned in 1914. He was allowed to work on a farm, where he later committed the Ruahine Axe Murders.

Rottman worked at the Ruahine farm of Joseph and Mary McCann. He was liked by local folk, and a regular job was to take the morning's milk to the near-by dairy factory. On 27 December 1914, he arrived at the factory early, explaining that McCann was going away on a fleecing trip. Rottman later that morning boarded a train for Wellington.

Next day neither Rottman nor McCann appeared with the daily milk-yield. The factory manager anxiously walked up to the farm where he found Joe McCann in a cowshed lying in a pool of blood, his head split open. In the farmhouse he saw Lucy McCann and her baby boy, both dead from head blows. Bloody axes were found near the cowshed and under the window of Rottman's room.

By this time Rottman was at Cape Terawhiti near Wellington. He turned up at a construction camp, asking for work. William Kelly was alone, as the other men were on Christmas holiday. Rottman stayed the night with Kelly, and the following morning read the news about the Ruahine Axe Murders. Kelly wanted to talk about the crimes, but his visitor ignored the subject. Rottman pleaded with him not to tell the police of his whereabouts.

As soon as his visitor left Kelly informed the police, who apprehended Rottman. He immediately volunteered his guilt: 'I am guilty, I know I'm done.'

Defence counsel pleaded the accused man's insanity at his trial at Wanganni. Rottman admitted that McCann had been angry with him for missing his milking shift, and that he had been drinking heavily. He claimed while under the influence to have taken an axe and swung it around his head. He could not remember what happened after that. Medical experts debated homicidal mania, frenzy and mad drunkenness, but Rottman was found guilty, and hanged at Terrace Gaol, Wellington, on 8 March 1915.
[*925*]

ROUSE, Alfred Arthur. The Blazing Car Murder is one of the celebrated cases. The identity

Rouse: Remains of the Morris Minor

of the victim was never established, but Rouse talked too much, and so convicted himself.

In the early hours of 6 November 1930 two young men walking home to Hardingstone, Northants, were passed by a respectably dressed man carrying a small case. They noticed a blaze in the distance, and asked him what it was. He replied, 'It looks as though someone is having a bonfire up there.' They hurried towards it, and found a Morris Minor ablaze. The heat was too intense to approach.

When the blaze was extinguished the car was found to contain an unrecognizably incinerated corpse. The car owner was traced by the vehicle's registration number plate MU1468, which was still intact. He was 37-year-old Alfred Arthur Rouse, a commercial traveller living in North London. After the fire he went to Wales (via his London home) in order to see his latest pregnant girl-friend, but newspaper reports of the case frightened him.

Rouse returned to London on 7 November, and was seen by police. He said, 'I am responsible. I am glad it is over.' He said that on a journey to Leicester he had given a man a lift. He stopped the car near Hardingstone to relieve himself, and asked his passenger to fill the tank from a spare tin of fuel. Before leaving the car the man asked him, 'What about a smoke?' Rouse, a non-smoker, produced a cigar and walked off down the lane. He had hardly got his trousers down when he 'saw a light' and, rushing back to the car, saw it was a mass of flames. He could not open the door, then he panicked and ran away. 'I lost my head,' he said, 'and did not know what to do.' He was arrested and charged with the murder of an unknown man. He then said 'My harem takes me to several places.'

Rouse's job as a salesman enabled him to womanize, and he seduced as many as 80 women during the course of his travels. He had children by several of the women, and had also committed bigamy.

He was tried at Northampton Assizes in January 1931. Evidence showing that the car's carburettor had been tampered with confirmed his guilt, and he was sentenced to death and hanged at Bedford on 10 March 1931. His confession was later published in the *Daily Sketch*.
[*1, 2, 43, 44, 113, 133, 158, 410, 423, 442, 472, 607, 618, 710, 720, 757, 791, 977*]

ROWLAND, Walter Graham. Twice convicted of murder, reprieved in the first and nearly in the second through another man's confession.

The body of 40-year-old Olive Balchin, killed by hammer blows to the head, was found on a bomb-site in Manchester on 20 October 1946. A blood-stained leather-beater's hammer lay near by.

She had been seen with a man that night, whose description, added to that provided by the shopkeeper who had sold the hammer, led the police to interview a man in a hostel in the city. He was a 39-year-old labourer, Walter Graham Rowland, who asked 'You don't want me for the murder of that woman, do you?'

At police headquarters Rowland admitted knowing Olive Balchin, but denied killing her. He had previously been convicted for child-murder, but was reprieved. Forensic examination of his clothes provided evidence of hair and dust, and blood on one of his shoes was of the same group as Balchin's.

Rowland's trial was at Manchester Assizes in December 1946. He protested innocence, but was found guilty. While he was in the condemned cell, David John Ware, a prisoner at Liverpool, stated that he had killed Olive Balchin.

Rowland's appeal was heard in February 1947, but application to introduce fresh evidence, including Ware's statement, was refused, and the appeal was dismissed. A Home Office inquiry followed, and after Ware admitted his earlier statements were false, it was decided that there had been no miscarriage of justice. Rowland was hanged at Strangeways Prison on 27 February 1947, still maintaining his innocence.

In November 1951, when Ware was charged with attempted murder at Bristol Assizes, he admitted to the police, 'I have killed a woman. I keep having an urge to hit women on the head.' He was found guilty but insane.
[*4, 402*]

RUAHINE AXE MURDERS. See ROTT-MAN, Arthur

RUSH, James Blomfield. The 49-year-old 'Killer in the Fog' who committed double murder in East Anglia.

Rush was an auctioneer and surveyor who rented Potash Farm on an estate near Wymond-ham in Norfolk. He was on bad terms with his landlord, Isaac Jermy, who lived at near-by Stanfield Hall. Rush took as his mistress Emily Sandford, the Jermy family's governess, and he also borrowed £5000 from Jermy. Rush was taken to court by Jermy on a charge of bad farm-management, and later threatened him.

In May 1848 Emily Sandford was pregnant by him. He was bankrupt and had to repay his debt to Jermy by the end of November.

On the evening of 28 November a man wearing an Inverness cloak emerged from the swirling fog at Stanfield Hall, shot Jermy and his son dead and wounded his wife and maid before disappearing. Two servants at the Hall said the intruder was Rush. Police arrested him at Potash Farm, where a search produced a deed, apparently signed by Jermy, cancelling his mortgage.

Rush was tried for murder at Norwich in March 1849, when he defended himself by bullying and abusing all present. Jermy's maid, crippled by her injuries, identified Rush as the intruder, and the

Rush: The death mask

jury took only 6 minutes to find him guilty.

Full of bravado at the end, Rush told the Governor of Norwich Gaol that he would like 'roast pig and plenty of plum sauce' for dinner, and instructed the hangman to put the noose 'a little higher' and to take his time when he was executed on 21 April 1849.

[1, 21, 290, 367, 577, 588, 678]

RUSSELL, George. Small-time house-breaker who murdered an old woman during a robbery. The case is notable for the crucial part played by fingerprint evidence.

On 1 June 1948 a Maidenhead milkman noticed an untouched supply of milk on the step of Mrs Freeman Lee's house. Mrs Lee, aged 94, was an eccentric recluse who lived alone. The milkman peered through the letter-box and saw a discarded woman's shoe and some keys lying on the floor near a large black trunk.

The police were called, and broke into the house. Failing immediately to find the old lady, they focused their interest on the trunk. Mrs Lee's body was found inside. Her arms had been tied behind her back, and she had head injuries. Cause of death was asphyxiation, probably in the trunk.

The victim was popularly believed to be wealthy, and robbery was assumed as the motive for the murder. The house had long been neglected, and its contents were dust-laden and festooned with cobwebs. Amid this dust Chief Superintendent Fred Cherrill found on the lid of a cardboard box the partial fingerprints of a possible intruder—prints which were traced to George Russell, a convicted thief and housebreaker, at whose trial in Oxford 15 years previously Cherrill had given evidence.

Russell was located at St Albans. He gave a rambling account of his movements, and despite his denials, a scarf found among his possessions proved to have belonged to Mrs Lee. When confronted by the fingerprint evidence he broke down and wept. He admitted approaching Mrs Lee about a job as a gardener, and in seeking to clear himself made a damaging remark: 'I was told she had a lot of money by another man. Did I murder this poor woman for something she was supposed to have, and had not?' A reasonable answer was that he knew Mrs Lee had no money because he had ransacked the house.

At his trial at Berkshire Assizes Russell was found guilty and sentenced to death. He was hanged at Oxford Prison on 2 December 1948.

[175, 417, 851]

RUXTON, Dr Buck. A 37-year-old Parsee doctor qualified in Bombay who anglicized his name from Bukhtyar Rustomji Ratanji Hakim. In 1928 he took Isabella Van Ess into his home; although they were not married she called herself Mrs Ruxton. In 1930 they settled in Lancaster, where Dr Ruxton had a practice.

The Ruxtons quarrelled and had a highly emotional relationship. He accused his 'wife' of infidelity, and she twice sought police protection. In 1935 Mrs Ruxton and her 20-year-old maid Mary Rogerson disappeared. Ruxton reported that his wife had left him for another man.

On 29 September 1935 a woman on a bridge over the river Annan on the Carlisle to Edinburgh road, saw a human leg lying below. The police made a thorough search, and discovered pieces of 2 human bodies. Parts of them, both female, had been wrapped in a 15 September copy of the *Sunday Graphic*. This was a 'slip' edition sold only in Morecambe and Lancaster. Dr Ruxton was questioned, but he denied that the two bodies were Isabella and Mary, and he wanted a statement issued to that effect.

A woman patient whom he asked to help tidy his house found two bloodstained carpets and a heap of bloodied clothing. He offered the woman a

Top: Sequence showing photographic imposition of Ruxton's portrait on an X-ray of the skull

Bottom: His confession

Lancaster.
14 . 10   35.

I killed Mrs Ruxton in a fit of temper because I thought she had been with a man. I was Mad at the time. Mary Rogerson was present at the time. I had to Kill her.

B Ruxton.

bloodstained suit, and later asked her to burn it. Callers at the house mentioned an offensive smell and the doctor did some spraying with eau-de-Cologne. On 13 October Ruxton was charged with murder.

The 2 bodies had yet to be properly identified, but a team of pathologists and anatomists from Edinburgh and Glasgow Universities examined them. The age, height and general size matched the missing women, but all distinguishing characteristics had been removed or mutilated; Mrs Ruxton had prominent teeth—the teeth had been extracted; Miss Rogerson had a squint in one eye—the eyes had been removed. Body I was identified by fingerprints, and a photographic superimposition of Mrs Ruxton's portrait on an X-ray of the head of Body II matched perfectly.

Dr Ruxton was tried at Manchester Assizes in March 1936 for the murder of Isabella Ruxton. He made a poor showing in the witness-box. To the suggestion that having murdered his wife he then killed the only witness, he replied, 'That is absolute bunkum, with a capital B.' He was found guilty and hanged at Strangeways Prison on 12 May 1936. On the following Sunday his confession was published.

[1, 43, 44, 113, 132, 231, 236, 333, 409, 607, 677, 791, 816]

S

SACCO and VANZETTI. Both Nicola Sacco and Bartolomeo Vanzetti were Italian immigrants to America. Known anarchists, they were convicted of murder in a case which made newspaper headlines around the world.

On 15 April 1920 a payroll robbery occurred in South Braintree, Massachusetts, which ended in a double murder. Two employees of the Slater and Morrill Shoe Company were transferring $16 000 from one of the Company's factories to another. The cashier and guard were shot and killed by two men who made off in a car with the money.

On 5 May two Italians, a shoemaker named Sacco and a fish-seller called Vanzetti, were apprehended by the police as they had been seen in a car similar to that used in the payroll robbery. Both men were charged for possessing firearms without permits. They were questioned about another hold-up in the area, and Sacco, who produced a firm alibi, was absolved of suspicion. But Vanzetti, despite testimony placing him elsewhere at the time, was charged with robbery and sentenced to 15 years' imprisonment. In the meantime both men were charged with the Braintree murders.

Sacco and Vanzetti were tried for murder in May 1921. Their radical leanings, plus the fact they were armed when arrested, were against them. In addition to being described as 'dagos' and 'sons of bitches' the trial judge referred to them as 'anarchistic bastards'. The prosecution proved that Sacco's .32 Colt was the murder weapon, an opinion supported by Major Calvin Goddard, exercising his reputation in the field of forensic ballistics. Both men were found guilty of first-degree murder, and sentenced to death.

The next 6 years were taken up with various legal procedures and stays of execution. Finally, the sentences of death were confirmed on 9 April 1927, when the Supreme Judicial Court of Massachusetts turned down an appeal for a new hearing. Sacco and Vanzetti vainly protested their innocence, but the 2 men were electrocuted on 23 August 1927. The case is significant for the long-delayed execution of sentence and the doubt of their guilt.

In 1977 Sacco and Vanzetti had their names cleared in a special proclamation signed by the Governor of Massachusetts.
[57, 143, 214, 263, 272, 293, 304, 420, 480, 690, 742, 802, 843, 846, 916, 935]

SANGRET, August. A 30-year-old French-Canadian soldier of Red Indian stock who murdered a girl in what became known as the 'Wigwam Murder'.

Two soldiers walking on Hankley Common near Godalming in Surrey on 7 October 1942 saw an arm protruding from a mound of soil, and the badly decomposed body of a fully dressed woman was unearthed.

Pathologist Professor Keith Simpson concluded that the girl had been stabbed with a knife having a hooked tip, and had then been killed with heavy blows struck with a blunt instrument. The attack had occurred at some distance from the grave and there was evidence that the body had been dragged to the ridge where it was buried.

She was identified as Joan Pearl Wolfe, who had left home and was living rough, in the woods near an army camp in a crude shelter made of tree branches and heather, thus earning the name 'Wigwam Girl'

A search of Hankley Common produced the girl's identity card and a letter to a Canadian soldier, named August Sangret, informing him that she was pregnant. Sangret admitted being intimate with the girl and living with her in the wigwam—which, with his Red Indian ancestry, he did not find unusual. His clasp-knife was lost, presumed stolen. Recently washed stains on a battle-dress proved to be blood, and one of the murder weapons, a heavy birch branch with blood and hair on it, was found near the grave. A clasp knife with a hooked tip was found on 27 November blocking a waste pipe.

Sangret: The body of Joan Pearl Wolfe

Sangret was tried for murder at Kingston Assizes in February 1943. A police reconstruction depicted Sangret attacking the girl with his hook-bladed clasp-knife. and then battering her skull with a heavy birch branch. Burial on high ground was suggested as a flash-back to Sangret's Red Indian origins when the bodies of conquered enemies were buried on a hill top. He was found guilty with a recommendation to mercy but was hanged at Wandsworth Prison on 29 April 1943. [*1, 37, 361, 369, 371, 496, 564, 851*]

SATAN MURDER. A 17-year-old youth from Northport, New York State, involved in the death of another teenager in June 1984 in what was described as a 'sacrificial killing'.

Ricky Kasso came from a good family background but began using drugs at the early age of 13. He dropped out of school and isolated himself from his parents. To the contemporaries with whom he traded drugs he was known as the 'Acid King'. He also became obsessed with satanism, and was caught grave-robbing in a search for bones to use in his magical fantasies. In April 1984, on so-called 'Witches Night', he and some friends went to Amityville to see the house made famous by the *De Feo* killings.

In June, after he had fallen asleep at a party, Kasso discovered that several packets of 'angel dust' which he had in his pocket had been stolen. He accused teenager Gary Lauwers, and on several occasions beat up the youngster, demanding that he pay him the value of the drugs. On 16 June Kasso and several of his friends met at Northport; most of them went off to a birthday party but Kasso, Gary Lauwers and two others decided to go into Aztakea Woods where they had secreted some mescaline. During the course of the night Kasso revived the argument about the alleged stolen drugs and violently attacked Lauwers. He repeatedly stabbed the youth, declaring to his drugged companions, 'He's gotta say he loves Satan.' In a frenzy he hacked at the boy's face and cut out his eyes, later announcing that he had made his first sacrifice for Satan.

Residents near Aztakea Woods reported hearing a disturbance at around 2.30 a.m. but the police took no action. On 4 July 1984 Gary Lauwers's body was found partially hidden in some bushes. When reports of the brutal nature of his death reached the newspapers headlines appeared informing the shocked residents of Northport that a ritual killing had occurred in their midst.

Kasso, the 'Acid King', was taken into custody on 4 July 1985. He told his friends that he would take his own life if he was put in gaol. In the early hours of 6 July he was found dead in his cell. The news—sensationalized with such headlines as 'Satanic Cult Murderer Suspect Is Found Hanged in Jail Cell'—was given worldwide coverage. Kasso's 18-year-old friend, who was present at the scene of the killing, was indicted for murder but a trial jury found him not guilty.

[881]

SCHMID, Charles Howard. At school 22-year-old Schmid was good at sport, and he excelled as a gymnast. This was compensation for his lack of height—he was 5 foot 3. He tried to raise his height by wearing cowboy boots with padded soles, and he wore cosmetics to make his appearance so bizarre that people would talk about it.

Fantasy soon turned to violence, and on 31 May 1964, while drinking with 2 friends, Mary French and John Saunders, he said he wanted to kill a girl. With his companions he enticed 15-year-old Alleen Rowe into his car and drove out to the desert, where his audience watched him rape her and then kill her with a rock. They buried the body in a shallow grave near Tucson, Arizona.

In August 1965 a girl-friend of Schmid, 17-year-old Gretchen Fritz, disappeared with her sister. Schmid boasted later, 'You know I killed Gretchen?' He claimed to have strangled both girls and thrown them in a ditch. A friend, Richard Bruns, asked him to prove it. Schmid simply showed him the bodies.

Bruns was thoroughly frightened, and had nightmares which so terrified him that he went to the police and told them about Schmid, who was arrested on 11 November 1965. Mary French and John Saunders were arrested for aiding and abetting him, but they turned States Evidence against their onetime friend.

Full details of Schmid's actions were described at his trial for the murder of the Fritz sisters. The prosecutor said, 'This man must be shown no mercy.' Schmid was condemned to death, French was sentenced to 4 to 5 years imprisonment, and Saunders received a life sentence for their part in the murders.

Schmid was then tried for the earlier murder of Alleen and sentenced to 55 years in prison. Appeals delayed his execution, and he escaped the death penalty under the US Supreme Court ruling abolishing capital punishment. He died later in prison.

[329, 693]

SCHREUDER, Frances Bradshaw. Thwarted heiress convicted of first-degree murder for coaxing her 17-year-old son to murder her father.

On 23 July 1978 Franklin J. Bradshaw, an elderly self-made millionaire who ran an auto-parts business, was found shot in his warehouse in Salt Lake City, Utah. Bradshaw (known as 'Utah's Howard Hughes') was thought to be worth $60 million. A man of regular habits, he lived frugally, and with his self-help philosophy took the view that if members of his family wanted more money 'they can go to work like anybody else'.

This outlook did not appeal to his youngest daughter, Frances. She had contracted two unsuccessful marriages, and in the 1970s was bringing up a family of three. Her two teenage boys, Marc and Lawrence, turned out to be delinquents, and Frances herself was unstable. As early as 1964 a New York psychiatrist she visited reported that 'her need for treatment is urgent . . . her problems are serious'.

Frances Schreuder was frequently bailed out of her financial problems by her mother, with whom she had a love-hate relationship. Mrs Bradshaw gave her daughter money, chiefly to take care of her grandchildren's needs, but without Mr Bradshaw's approval. He was frequently called upon to sort out his daughter's financial affairs, but invariably applied his self-help ethic. This attitude provoked resentment on Frances' part which increasingly led to abusive behaviour. In 1975 she was declaring quite openly, 'This family can't keep going much longer, not unless somebody kills my father.' Franklin Bradshaw—perhaps aware of the antagonism towards him—became more remote from his family and spent long hours at his warehouse.

In the summer of 1977 the two Schreuder boys

Schmid: The murderer uncovering a victim's skull

went to stay with their grandparents. In no time at all they were stealing from the elderly couple, taking money, forging cheques and prying into Bradshaw's private papers. The pair of delinquents stole thousands of dollars—as much as $50,000 according to some sources—and they did it to please their mother. The old man's reaction was to revise his will, leaving his estate to his wife and two eldest daughters and completely omitting Frances. When she suspected her father intended to disinherit her she began looking for a gun. 'Murdering Dad' became a sick joke between her and the two boys. Marc was sent on the lethal errand to New York City where he bought a .357 magnum Smith & Wesson; his mother gave him a rare hug when he returned, mission accomplished.

In July 1978, at his mother's request, Marc killed his grandfather with 2 shots fired at close range. In November, at a time when Frances was ingratiating herself by donating large sums of money to the New York City Ballet, her sister denounced her as a thief and a forger to the FBI. In due course Marc Schreuder was charged with murder. He had confessed the act to his lawyer, saying that his mother threatened to commit suicide because his grandfather planned to disinherit her. At his trial in 1982 Marc's defence counsel admitted that he had killed his grandfather, not for money but to please his mother. The young man refused to testify against her, and she did not attend her son's trial. He was found guilty of murder in the second degree and was sentenced to 5 years to life in prison.

In September 1983 Frances Schreuder was brought to trial after Marc agreed to give evidence. The proceedings lasted only 4 days. To the question, 'Whose idea was it to kill your grandfather?' Marc replied, 'My mother's.' The jury was out for less than 5 hours and found her guilty of first-degree murder; she was sentenced to life imprisonment. [17, 188]

SCHWARTZ, Charles Henry. Remarkable case in which a murderer went to considerable lengths to fake his own death in a fire. Charles Schwartz was 36, married with 3 children, and lived in Berkeley, California, where he carried out chemical research in his own laboratory at Walnut Creek.

On the night of 30 July 1925 a terrific explosion and fire wrecked Schwartz's laboratory. Charred remains were found in the ruins. Berkeley's fire chief had doubts if the fire was a genuine one. His report of finding evidence of arson was rejected until other evidence was found. A man had driven away from the scene in Schwartz's car, and a mysterious break-in occurred at the house, when several photographs of Schwartz had been stolen.

Dr Edward Heinrich, the criminologist in the *D'Autrement* case, was called in. Sufficient of the dead man's right ear lobe remained to enable a comparison to be made with a photograph of Schwartz. The fire victim had a good-sized mole, whereas Schwartz's ear lobes did not. Examination of the teeth showed 2 missing from the upper jaw, as had Schwartz—but Heinrich observed that the empty sockets in the charred mouth were swollen, suggesting the teeth had recently been extracted.

The fingertips of the body had been destroyed with acid, and the eyes gouged out in obvious attempts to foil identification. The fire victim—clearly not Schwartz—had been killed by a blow on the back of the head. The corpse was that of an itinerant preacher, Gilbert Warren Barbe, a friend of Schwartz, and missing from Berkeley's streets.

Schwartz was found at Oakland when an apartment housekeeper reported her boarder to the police. When officers arrived they found Schwartz dead on his bed from a self-inflicted gunshot wound. He had left a note for his wife confessing his guilt and seeking her forgiveness. [95, 366]

SCOTT, Leonard Ewing. Unusual case in which a 61-year-old man was convicted of murder without the discovery of a body. After protesting his innocence for nearly 30 years, he confessed in 1984 that he had murdered his wife and buried her body in the desert near Las Vegas. Scott's wife, 63-year-old Evelyn, was last seen alive on 16 May 1955 at her home in Bel Air, California. She had been a wealthy widow, veteran of 4 marriages, when she encountered Ewing Scott in 1949. He was a stock salesman of modest prospects who rapidly changed Evelyn's life-style after they married. He insisted they moved house away from her circle of friends and he slowly took over the management of her investments, bragging that he knew best how to look after his wife's affairs. He also beat her up occasionally.

In May 1955 he took over Evelyn's bank safe-deposit boxes by virtue of a co-renters' agreement. When friends and family inquired about her, he told them she had been taken ill and had gone away for treatment. Scott also cancelled the insurance premiums on his wife's jewellery and gave away some of her personal effects. He said, 'I'm just going to wait until she is gone seven years and then she'll be declared legally dead.'

In January 1956 Scott proposed marriage to another woman. Evelyn's friends grew increasingly suspicious about her disappearance and asked the police to make inquiries. When questioned Scott maintained that she had simply gone away and left him, as she had done before. Suspicion hardened, though, when Evelyn's denture and spectacles were found in the garden of the neighbouring house. Investigation of Scott's finances turned up irregularities which led to his indictment on charges of theft and forgery. In May 1956 he failed to appear for a scheduled court appearance and dropped out of view for nearly a year.

He was picked up crossing the Canadian border in April 1957, having been posed as a fugitive. He was charged with murder despite the lack of evidence, and especially a victim's body. He was tried at Los Angeles in October 1957, when in the absence of a body, witnesses or a murder weapon, the prosecution relied entirely on circumstantial evidence. The case against him was strong on motive, and it was suggested that he had carried out a preconceived plan to eliminate his wife in order to acquire her wealth. He did not testify on his own behalf, and when the jury found him guilty of first-degree murder he told his lawyers, 'I guess some people like Lincolns and some people like Fords.' He was sentenced to life imprisonment.

Scott continued to protest his innocence from prison, and declined to accept parole on the grounds that it was tantamount to admitting guilt. He was unconditionally discharged in 1978 at the age of 81. He returned to California, and in 1984 admitted to writer Diane Wagner that he had killed Evelyn with a mallet and buried her body in the desert. He claimed she had tried to poison him. (See also *Onufrejczyk*.)
[*943*]

SEADLUND, John Henry. A 28-year-old burglar who graduated to kidnapping and murder, exhibiting a callous indifferences to the fates of his victim and his partner, and utlimately to himself.

Seadlund travelled around the USA, taking odd labouring jobs and indulging in petty crime. In 1937 he met James Atwood Gray, and went into partnership with him.

On 25 September 1937 the pair in Seadlund's car spotted an expensive limousine in Franklin Park, Illinois. They stopped it by swerving in front and producing a gun. The driver was 72-year-old Charles P. Ross, a wealthy Chicago businessman, with his secretary.

Seadlund ordered Ross into his car and drove off, leaving the kidnapped man's passenger to raise the alarm. Ross was driven to Wisconsin, where he was made to write to a friend to produce ransom money. 'I am held for ransom', he wrote. 'Try and raise $50 000.' This note was sent to the FBI, where J. Edgar Hoover took a personal interest. A second note was received giving instructions which Mrs Ross obeyed by inserting an advertisement in a Chicago newspaper.

The FBI checked the ransom notes for fingerprints, and it was evident that the kidnapper had used a new typewriter. A check on typewriter sales in Chicago was made, and a description given of a man who had recently purchased a new portable. He was traced to a rooming-house where he had stayed, and fingerprints found matched those on the ransom notes.

Fifty thousand dollars in marked money was delivered as instructed to the kidnapper, who was now known to be John Henry Seadlund. He had a passion for the race-track, and the trail of marked dollar-bills was pointing west. The authorities surmised that Seadlund might turn up at the Los Angeles' Santa Anita racetrack.

Hoover flew to Los Angeles to take charge, and on 14 January 1938 Seadlund was arrested at the race-track, attempting to place a bet. In custody he admitted his guilt. Of Ross he said, 'Dead, of course. I shot him.' He also said that he had killed Gray and he led the police to a pit at Spooner, Wisconsin, where the two dead men were buried. While in Cook County Jail, Seadlund asked if he would be 'hanged or fried'. In the spring of 1938 he was electrocuted.
[*693*]

SEDDON, Frederick Henry. A 40-year-old cold, calculating poisoner who murdered for sheer greed.

He was a District Superintendent with the London and Manchester Industrial Assurance Company. He lived at 63 Tollington Park, Islington, with his wife, their 5 children and his aged father.

In July 1910 the Seddons took in as a lodger 49-year-old Miss Eliza M. Barrow. She was neither pleasant nor intelligent; but she had money. During the next few months Seddon acquired all Miss Barrow's assets, which she exchanged for an annuity, amounting to £3 a week.

Miss Barrow became ill with vomiting and diarrhoea on 1 September 1911. A doctor was called, but she died 2 weeks later. With typical meanness, Seddon arranged for burial in a

Seddon: In the dock at the Old Bailey

common grave, gaining a commission from the undertaker for introducing the business.

None of Miss Barrow's relatives were told of her death, and her cousin, Frank Vonderahe, learned about it when he called on the Seddons. Vonderahe asked about his late cousin's properties. He got evasive answers, with the assurance that all had been properly made over to Seddon. He went to the authorities, and Miss Barrow's body was exhumed, to reveal that she had been poisoned with arsenic. Seddon was arrested on 4 December, and his wife some weeks later.

The Seddons were tried at the Old Bailey in March 1912. The prosecution amply demonstrated that Seddon had motive, method and opportunity to poison Miss Barrow. He revealed himself a man ravaged with greed.

The jury found Seddon guilty, but his wife was acquitted.

The judge was a Mason, and Seddon (also a Mason) made a Masonic sign, saying, 'I declare before the Great Architect of the Universe I am not guilty.' The judge replied, 'You and I know we both belong to one brotherhood . . . But our brotherhood does not encourage crime.' The death sentence followed. He was hanged at Pentonville on 18 April 1912.

[*1*, *32*, *47*, *58*, *91*, *131*, *133*, *259*, *275*, *323*, *356*, *438*, *449*, *464*, *471*, *532*, *761*, *907*, *921*, *948*, *1006*]

SEYMOUR, Henry Daniel. Onetime vacuum-cleaner salesman convicted of murder, in a case distinguished by careful police work and the part played by circumstantial evidence.

In August 1931 Mrs Anne Louisa Kempson, a 54-year-old widow, was found dead in her Oxford home, with her head battered with a heavy object, and a sharp instrument pushed through the throat. The house had been ransacked.

Sir Bernard Spilsbury examined the body, and confirmed that the weapon could have been a hammer, but no weapon was found. Mrs Andrews told police of dealings she had had with an electric-cleaner salesman named Seymour. He called on her the day before Mrs Kempson was murdered, and said his money had been stolen while he was swimming. Mrs Andrews lent him some and he went away, but later the same night Seymour returned. He had missed the last bus, and Mr and Mrs Andrews gave him a bed for the night.

Next morning Mrs Andrews noticed a brown parcel in the hall-way which belonged to Seymour. The package contained a brand-new chisel and hammer. Seymour left her, taking his parcel with him. Mrs Kempson's house was a mere 10 minutes' walk away.

An ironmonger gave a description of a man who had bought a hammer and chisel from his shop the day before. It was also established that Seymour had sold some vacuum cleaners in the area, including one to Mrs Kempson. Then the manager of an Aylesbury hotel reported the finding of a hammer, well washed and with its brand labels removed, in a suitcase which he had retained in lieu of payment. Seymour was traced to Brighton, where on 15 August he was charged. He was tried for murder at Oxford in October 1931. The prosecution case had been carefully prepared, and was based on meticulous police work—even the washed-off hammer labels were found as tiny scraps of paper in Seymour's bag. Seymour was evasive in the witness-box, and found guilty and hanged at Oxford Prison on 10 December 1931. [133, 274, 282, 369, 449, 598, 806, 813, 928]

SHARK ARM CASE. The identification of a human arm disgorged by a captive shark in an Australian aquarium led to an accusation of murder against Patrick Brady.

On 25 April 1935 a recently caught tiger shark swimming in a Coogee Beach aquarium regurgitated its stomach contents, which included a human arm which bore a tattoo of a pair of boxers.

With the aid of this and fingerprinting, the police identified the limb as belonging to James Smith, a 40-year-old ex-boxer. Smith, who had

Shark Arm Case: The tattooed arm

been missing for two weeks, was employed by Reg Holmes, a Sydney boatbuilder. It was found that Smith had spent a holiday in a rented cottage on the coast with 42-year-old Patrick Brady. Brady, who was known to the police as a forger, was arrested. He denied killing Smith, but implicated Reg Holmes in forgery dealings.

Holmes denied even knowing Brady, but 3 days later he was pursued by a police launch in Sydney Harbour. He was stopped in his speedboat after a chase, and found to have a superficial bullet-wound in the head. Holmes now told a different story. He admitted knowing Brady, and accused him of killing Smith and of disposing of the body.

Brady was charged with Smith's murder on 17 May, and while he was in custody Reg Holmes was shot dead in his car. The murder occurred on the eve of the Coroner's Inquiry into the Shark Arm affair.

Medical evidence stated that the arm had been severed with a sharp knife, though not as part of a surgical operation. Brady's lawyer argued strongly that an arm did not by itself constitute a body, and that there was no conclusive proof that Smith was in fact dead.

Both Smith and Brady had been involved in drug-running and underworld intimidation. Holmes would have been a star witness and 2 men were charged with his murder, but were acquitted.

Patrick Brady was committed for trial, but it took only 2 days for the judge to acquit him after hearing circumstantial evidence. Brady died in hospital during August 1965. He protested his innocence throughout, and suggested that the severed arm bore bullet-wounds. A famous forensic expert examined the arm and concluded that Smith's body was dismembered and put into a tin trunk for disposal at sea. The arm would not go into the trunk, so it was roped to the outside, but it worked loose and was swallowed by a shark.

[*336, 372, 520, 865*]

SHELLEY and NEWMAN. Pair of labourers who went by the nicknames of 'Tiggy' and 'Moosh', convicted of murdering a fellow-navvy.

A man passing a smouldering refuse tip at Scratchwood Sidings, between Mill Hill and Elstree, on 2 June 1931 noticed a smoke-blackened human arm protruding. The badly charred body of a middle-aged man was extricated, and examined by Sir Bernard Spilsbury. The pathologist put death at 2 or 3 days before discovery, and caused by a skull fracture, leaving a rectangular-shaped depression.

He was 45-year-old Herbert Ayres, identified by fragments of clothing still on the body, and also a tattoo on his forearm. Ayres was known as 'Pigsticker'; he was a labourer, and one of a group of casual workers who lived in rough shacks by the railway siding.

A worker told police that on 30 May he had seen 'Pigsticker' attacked by 2 others whom he knew as 'Moosh' and 'Tiggy'. This pair, whose real names were William Shelley, aged 57, and Oliver Newman, aged 61, were rounded up by police, despite 3 fierce dogs guarding their shack. Under the floor of 'Tiggy's' hut was a bloodstained axe, the back of the blade fitting exactly the depression in the dead man's skull.

They were tried at the Old Bailey. They admitted fighting with Ayres, but said only fists were used. He had stolen food from them, so they beat him up to teach him a lesson. When they realized they had killed him they buried his body in the tip.

Shelley and Newman were found guilty, and executed on 5 August 1931.

[*133, 371, 497*]

SHEPPARD, Dr Samuel. A 30-year-old neurosurgeon convicted of murdering his wife, but cleared of the charge 12 years later.

Sheppard worked at Bay View Hospital, Cleveland, and with his wife Marilyn lived in a home overlooking Lake Erie. On the evening of 3 July 1954 the Sheppards entertained some friends to dinner, who were seen out at 12.30 by Mrs Sheppard after her husband had fallen asleep on the couch. She did not disturb him, but went upstairs to bed.

According to Sheppard, he was woken by screams. He rushed upstairs, but was knocked out. When he came to, still dazed, he found his wife lying dead on the bed. Hearing noises downstairs, he investigated and chased an intruder out of the house towards the beach, but again he was knocked unconscious. When he recovered he telephoned a neighbour, saying, 'I think they've got Marilyn.'

The room was bespattered with blood, for Marilyn had been savagely beaten with a blunt weapon. The bedroom had also been ransacked. Sheppard's behaviour was thought suspicious, and soon he was arrested.

His trial began in October 1954 in Cuyhoga Country. Many questions were raised in court. What had happened to the T-shirt worn by Sheppard? Why had morphine been taken from his medical bag? Was it a surgical instrument that made the bloody imprint on Mrs Sheppard's pillow? Speculative solutions pointing to Sheppard's guilt were provided. In addition, the doctor's infidelity—which he had at first denied—was offered as a motive for killing his wife.

Sheppard was found guilty of second-degree murder and sentenced to life imprisonment.

With the help of his lawyer, F. Lee Bailey, Sheppard secured a second trial in October 1966. Bailey dismissed the prosecution's case as 'ten pounds of hogwash in a five pound bag'. The jury declared Sheppard not guilty 12 years after the death of his wife.

Sheppard regained his medical practice, but he was finally forced out of the profession. He married twice more and turned to professional wrestling, but his health declined, and he died in April 1970.

[*36, 152, 445, 528, 744, 789, 841, 842*]

SHOWERY, Allan. Strange case of murder which involved psychic detection in obtaining a conviction.

On 21 February 1977 Teresita Basa, a 48-year-old Filipino woman who had come to work in Chicago from Manila, was found dead in her apartment. She had been stabbed and burned, and her body, wrapped in sheets, was found lying on the floor. She worked as a medical auxiliary in the city's Edgewater Hospital, where she seemed to be well liked and did not appear to have any enemies. Robbery seemed to be the motive for her murder.

The police were making little headway in their

Sheppard: The battered body of Marilyn Sheppard

investigation until they received a tip-off that a doctor and his wife (also from the Philippines) might be able to throw some light on the case. The doctor explained that about 5 months after the murder, his wife had experienced a psychic phenomenon in which the dead woman spoke through her and named the murderer. They thought this occurrence so bizarre that they decided not to report it. But when Teresita Basa spoke twice more through the doctor's wife they viewed the matter more seriously. The person named in these incidents was Allan Showery, a medical orderly who worked at the Edgewater Hospital.

The problem for the police was to judge how seriously to take this information. Their hesitation was overcome when a visit to Showery's apartment followed by a search produced some jewellery stolen from the crime scene. In due course Showery was charged with murder. The *Chicago Tribune* learned of the psychic aspects of the case and ran the story on 5 March 1978 under the headline 'Did Voice From the Grave Name Killer.'

Amid considerable public scepticism Showery was sent for trial in January 1979. The jury could not agree, and a mistrial was declared. A month later, acting contrary to his legal advisers, Showery admitted his guilt. He was sentenced to 14 years imprisonment for murder and 4 years on each of 2 counts of robbery and arson.

[*896*]

SIMPSON, Joe Willie. The Upper West Side of Manhattan, New York City, has one of the highest murder rates in the world. On New Year's Day 1973

Katherine Cleary, a 28-year-old teacher of deaf children, was brutally murdered in her apartment. She had been badly beaten and abused; there were 18 knife-wounds in her neck and abdomen.

The victim had been born with a spinal defect, and corrective surgery had left her with a limp. There were also psychological scars, and it seemed that she hated herself to the point where she invited abuse. She was known to frequent a bar near her apartment where she picked up rough, unrefined men. Neighbours occasionally heard screams from her apartment when her companions gave her a hard time.

Police discovered that on the night she died she picked up a stranger in her usual bar. This man was traced by virtue of painstaking detective work, and identified as Willie Joe Simpson. Described as a hustler, Simpson and his wife lived in New York with a homosexual friend. As a teenager, Simpson had been admitted to a mental hospital for treatment of ill-defined problems. He suffered from headaches, and what was described as psychologically induced paralysis.

By the end of 1972 Simpson was at the end of his mental tether. His wife was pregnant, he had no income to maintain her, and he was consuming up to a quart of whisky a day. In November, he told his friend, 'I can't stand it any more . . . I'm falling apart.' On 1 January 1973 Simpson went to his local bar and met Katherine Cleary. They went up to her apartment, where he brutally murdered her.

Simpson was arrested in Springfield and taken to New York's Tombs prison on 9 January. He confessed to her killing, and 5 months later hanged himself in his prison cell.
[*291*]

SLATER, Oscar. A 37-year-old German Jew, whose real name was Leschziner, was convicted of murder in Glasgow in a case which was proved later to be a miscarriage of justice.

Miss Marion Gilchrist sent her servant, Helen Lambie, out to buy an evening newspaper on 21 December 1908. The girl was gone about 10 minutes. When she returned she found a neighbour, Arthur Adams, standing outside the door—he had been disturbed by a commotion in Miss Gilchrist's flat. As Helen Lambie entered the flat a man appeared from within and calmly walked past her and Adams. On the way he also passed 14-year-old Mary Barrowman.

Miss Gilchrist was found lying dead by the fireplace—she had been savagely beaten. The old lady (she was 82) had been quite well off, and was known to have jewellery worth several thousands of pounds hidden about her flat. The only item which appeared to be missing was a diamond crescent-shaped brooch.

On Christmas Day a bicycle dealer told police that Oscar Slater had offered for sale a pawn ticket for a diamond crescent brooch. Detectives went to Slater's lodgings only to find that he had left for Liverpool, sailing for the United States on 26 December.

Slater had pawned the brooch a month before Miss Gilchrist's murder, and in any event it was not her brooch. The police nevertheless asked for Slater's extradition and sent Helen Lambie, Mary Barrowman and Arthur Adams across the Atlantic to give evidence of identification. Slater was returned to Britain to face trial for murder.

At the trial in Edinburgh in May 1909 prosecution counsel made an unprecedented attack on Slater's moral standing which did not even earn a rebuke from the judge. Helen Lambie stuck to her evidence despite discrepancies, but Arthur Adams said that Oscar Slater 'closely resembled' the man he had seen. Most damaging of all was Mary Barrowman's open admission that she had been shown Slater's photograph before she attended the identification parade!

Slater's defence counsel did not put him into the witness-box, and despite the shaky evidence of identification, a majority verdict was guilty, and Slater was sentenced to death. He was later reprieved and sent to Peterhead Prison, where he served 18 years before being released, following growing public disquiet about his conviction.

There were strong accusations against the Glasgow police, and Sir Arthur Conan Doyle and William Roughead campaigned vigorously for the inquiry which led to Slater's release. Helen Lambie, who had gone to live in America, was asked to attend the appeal but refused. Slater was awarded £6000 compensation, and died in 1948. It is likely that a young relative was the guilty person.
[*1, 127, 132, 345, 377, 452, 465, 612, 679, 687, 718, 780*]

SMALL CASE. Ambrose J. Small, 56-year-old Canadian theatrical magnate and millionaire, disappeared in Toronto. Murder was suspected, but although several impostors appeared his body was never found.

On 2 December 1919 Small sold his theatrical holdings for a down payment of a million dollars. The transaction took place in Toronto, and Mrs

Theresa Small banked the money and returned home to await her husband for dinner. Small spoke to his attorney in the afternoon about paying off his staff, but agreed to retain the services of his secretary and booking manager, John Doughty.

Small was never seen again.

His wife thought he might be out with friends, but when he failed to turn up he was reported missing. The police checked the city's hospitals, hotels and stations, and his photograph was widely published. Numerous false sightings were made in Canada, the USA and Mexico, but then the police discovered that John Doughty had also disappeared. He had not been seen since Christmas, and he had taken $100 000 worth of negotiable bonds from Small's bank-deposit boxes.

The Toronto police discovered facts about Small. He had a secret room at the Grand Opera House with a side entrance, furnished in Oriental style, and obviously a love nest. It was clear that Doughty hated Small, and the boilerman at the Opera House spoke of a fight between the two on the night of 2 December.

Bodies found in many parts of Canada and the USA were offered to the Toronto authorities as the missing man. The Toronto municipal refuse tip was turned over, and the ashes from the Grand Opera House boilers were examined—but no vestige of Small was to be found.

Then, in November 1920, John Doughty was found in Oregon, working in a lumber camp. He was brought back to Canada, and admitted taking the missing bonds, which he said he had left with his sister. The full amount was accounted for. Doughty was tried at Toronto in March 1921 for theft, but this turned out to be almost an inquest into Small's disappearance, and Doughty received a 5-year sentence for stealing the bonds.

A campaign of hate now developed against Theresa Small. She was widely regarded as a paragon of virtue and a benefactress of the Catholic Church. She went into seclusion after her husband's disappearance, but this did not stop suggestions she had murdered him to get his wealth for the Church. Obscene pictures of Theresa were published in Toronto tabloids in a scurrilous campaign against her. The floors of her home were taken up in a search for her husband's body.

Ambrose Small was officially declared dead in 1924, and Theresa died in 1935. In May 1944 Toronto's Grand Opera House was pulled down. Police were there to observe the demolition of the basement floors, but no human remains were

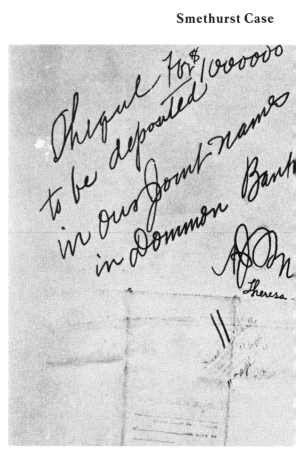

Small Case: Endorsed million dollar cheque

found, and the mystery has remained unsolved. [*617, 863*]

SMETHURST CASE. A 54-year-old doctor who curiously called in extra assistance when his bigamous wife was dying of poison, but who was reprieved through discrepancies in analytical tests.

Dr Thomas Smethurst obtained his medical degree from the University of Erlangen in Bavaria. In 1828 he married a woman 20 years his junior whose money he used to set up a hydropathic clinic. In 1858 the Smethursts took in a lodger, a 43-year-old spinster with property and an assured income, named Isabella Bankes.

Smethurst was immediately attracted to Miss Bankes, and to avoid embarrassment she moved to other lodgings, but at length Smethurst deserted his semi-invalid wife and lived bigamously with Isabella at Richmond.

In March 1859 Miss Bankes was taken ill, and Smethurst called in medical help. Poisoning was suspected, but its cause could not be ascertained.

Another doctor was called in, and a solicitor drew up a will (that left everything to 'my sincere and beloved friend Thomas Smethurst') which Miss Bankes signed. Baffled at the cause of the illness, doctors decided to analyse the patient's vomit, which proved to contain arsenic. Dr Smethurst was arrested on 2 May on a charge of administering poison. Miss Bankes died next day, and Smethurst was again arrested, this time for murder.

At the preliminary hearings Dr Alfred Swaine Taylor, government analyst and distinguished chemist, said that he had found arsenic in the body, and also in a medicine bottle taken from the sickroom. On the basis of this evidence, Smethurst was sent for trial.

Smethurst's trial opened at the Old Bailey in July 1859, and after 2 days stopped through the illness of a juryman. It started again on 15 August. There was a sensational development. Dr Taylor admitted that impurities had been found in the test reagents. Nevertheless, clinical experts maintained that Miss Bankes had been given an irritant poison. The defence replied by saying her bismuth medicine was contaminated by arsenic. The judge summed up against Smethurst, and the jury found him guilty. He was sentenced to death on 19 August, but the evidence was vitiated by the medical fuss (see also the *Stauntons*) particularly in regard to Dr Taylor's tests. The Home Office ordered an inquiry, as a result of which Smethurst was reprieved, and a pardon granted on 15 November. On 1 December he was tried at the Old Bailey for bigamy and given a sentence of a year's imprisonment. Four months later, in April 1862, he brought proceedings to prove Miss Bankes's will, and was successful.

[*1, 21, 41, 110, 134, 184, 231, 232, 409, 533, 678, 720, 723, 724, 725*]

SMITH, Edgar. A 23-year-old ex US Marine convicted of murder on circumstantial evidence, who confessed 19 years afterwards.

On 4 March 1957, 15-year-old Victoria Zielinski disappeared from her home in Mahwah, New Jersey. Her body was found next day buried in a near-by sand-pit—her head smashed, with her brains spattered in the sand. Police interviewed Joe Gilroy, who said that he had noticed bloodstains in his car after lending it to a friend, Edgar Smith.

Smith said he knew the dead girl, and had given her lifts. He had borrowed Gilroy's car because his own had broken down. He explained that he had vomited on his trousers, which he then discarded. Police could not find the soiled garments where

he said he left them, but they found a bloodstained pair near the murder scene. Smith now said he was covering up for a friend. He admitted picking up Victoria Zielinski and taking her to the sand-pit where they argued and she left the car. Later he saw her, bleeding from the head, with her boy-friend, Don Hommell, who explained that she had tripped and injured herself. While looking at the girl's injury Smith had stained his trousers with blood.

Hommell was questioned and had an alibi, so Smith was charged with murder. At his trial in May 1957 the prosecution maintained that he killed the girl after she refused his advances. Smith's lawyer criticized the circumstantial nature of the evidence, and attacked the character of Hommell, whom he claimed was a psychopath. Smith was found guilty of first-degree murder and sentenced to death.

During his confinement in Trenton Prison, Smith made 14 appeals, and was granted 13 stays of execution. He won his freedom in 1971, but within 5 years was in court again charged with kidnapping and attempted murder in San Diego. He was found guilty and imprisoned, and in the course of his trial confessed to the murder of Victoria Zielinski.

[*860, 861*]

SMITH, George Joseph. Rogue, bigamist and harmonium-playing 43-year-old Brides in the Bath murderer.

A petty criminal in his youth, Smith married 19-year-old Beatrice Thornhill in 1898; she was his only legal wife. Like *Landru*, Smith soon realized that the opposite sex were easy prey.

In 1910 Smith met 33-year-old Beatrice Constance Annie ('Bessie') Mundy, well educated and with a bank balance of £2500. He 'married' her at Weymouth under the name of Henry Williams. He left her within a month but met her again and went to live at Herne Bay. Bessie made a will bequeathing all she owned to her husband. In July 1912 Smith bought a bath from an ironmonger, and then told Bessie's doctor that his wife had been having fits. On 13 July the doctor was called to the house, to be told by Smith, 'I am afraid my wife is dead.' Bessie lay naked in the bath with her head below the water. An inquest decided she had died by misadventure. Her assets went to Smith.

He moved to Southsea, where on 4 November 1913 he 'married' 25-year-old Alice Burnham. Alice was insured for £500, and the couple moved to Blackpool, where they found suitable accommodation—with the facility of a bathroom. Next

Smith, G. J.: An exhumed victim returns to the grave

came the visit to the doctor, and on 12 December Mrs Smith was found dead in the bath. A verdict of death from misadventure was given at the inquest, and Smith collected the insurance money, the landlady shouting 'Crippen' after him as he left the house.

A clergyman's daughter, Margaret Elizabeth Lofty, became the next Mrs Smith after she had taken out a life insurance policy for £700. They were 'married' at Bath on 17 December 1914 and found lodgings, suitably with a bath, at Highgate in London. There followed the customary visits to the doctor and lawyer, and on 18 December Mrs Lloyd died in her bath. The verdict was again misadventure.

The account of the 'Bride's Tragic Fate' was given wide coverage, and was read by Alice Burnham's father, who saw striking similarities with the death of his daughter, and also by the Blackpool landlady. The police were alerted, and

on 1 February 1915 Smith was arrested for bigamy and subsequently charged with murder.

He was tried at the Old Bailey in June for the murder of Bessie Mundy, and defended by Sir Edward Marshall Hall, who tried unsuccessfully to exclude evidence of the other 2 deaths. The landlady at Smith's Highgate lodgings stated that she heard noises and splashing from the bathroom, and later heard Smith playing on the harmonium in the sitting-room *Nearer My God to Thee.* Bernard Spilsbury pointed out that the size of the bath would not permit accidental drowning, suggesting that the method used was probably simultaneously lifting up the knees and pressing on the head, so that the body slid along the bath, taking the head under water.

The jury declared Smith guilty. He was sentenced to death, and was hanged at Maidstone Prison on Friday 13 August 1915.

[*1, 32, 38, 47, 58, 100, 110, 133, 201, 220, 232,*

SMITH, Dr Jay. Principal of Upper Merion High School, Pennsylvania, and a former Colonel in the US army reserve, whose secretive habits—which included murder— earned him the title 'Prince of Darkness'. During the 1970s Smith stamped his eccentric presence on the school and there were strong overtones of intense sexual activities among the teaching staff, especially involving Bill Bradfield, a poet and devotee of Ezra Pound.

On 25 June 1979 the nude body of Susan Reinert, a teacher at Upper Merion, was found in her car at the Host Inn in Harrisburg. She had been dead for about 24 hours, and asphyxiation was given as the cause of death. It was apparent from bruises on her body that she had at some time been bound in chains. An immediate worry for the police was that her two children were missing.

It was discovered that the victim had taken out investments of $25,000 and insurance worth $730,000, naming Bill Bradfield as the beneficiary. A comb found in the car with the body bearing the inscription 79th USARCOM—or United States Army Reserve Command—provided a link with Dr Smith. Three months later analysis of blood samples showed that Susan Reinert had been given large amounts of morphine which had arrested her breathing.

The newspapers caught the flavour of scandal and began to link the murder with other phenomena— 'Satan Cult Death' ran one headline. As the investigation of Susan Reinert's death proceeded Dr Smith was gaoled for 5 years on firearms, drugs and theft charges. Chains had been found in the basement of his house whose links matched the contusions on the dead woman's body. Furthermore, a letter came to light from Smith to his wife, urging her to clean up the basement. He wrote, 'I can't stress the importance of this: clean out and then clean up.'

Bill Bradfield was arrested in May 1981 and charged with theft by deception and found guilty. In 1983 he was tried for the murder of Susan Reinert and her two children, whose bodies had still not been found. The prosecution argued that the teacher was killed for her insurance, and the judge indicated that there was an accomplice. Bradfield was found guilty on all counts and was sentenced to life imprisonment. Attention then switched to Dr Jay Smith, who had completed his term of impris-

onment for firearms and drug offences. In June 1985, 6 years to the day that Susan Reinert's body was found, Smith was arrested and charged with murder.

At his trial a former prison inmate testified that Smith had told him in reference to Susan Reinert, 'I killed the bitch.' A green lapel pin habitually worn by Karen Reinert had been found under the passenger seat of Smith's car. His letter directing his wife to clean up the basement of their house had also carried an instruction about the car: 'Clean it up *thoroughly.*' Stephanie Smith had died after a serious illness, and was therfore unable to be questioned about her husband's activities.

The evidence was mainly circumstantial, and motive was uncertain. Susan Reinert's knowledge of Smith's alleged satanic orgies was suggested as a reason for her murder. Letters which Smith had written to his 'love woman' used language which indicated sexual abandon and suggested something rotten in the state of Merion High School. On 30 April 1986 Dr Jay Smith was found guilty on all 3 charges of murder in the first degree, and, after answering questions at a sentencing hearing, the jury unanimously recommended death.
[*825, 956*]

SMITH, Madeleine. The trial of a respected 21-year-old woman for allegedly poisoning her foreign paramour took Glasgow by storm, and shocked England by the frankness of her love-letters.

Eldest daughter of James Smith, an architect and a pillar of Glasgow society in the 1850s, Madeleine was an elegant girl whose days were filled with artistic pursuits but little excitement. In the spring of 1855 she began an affair with 34-year-old Pierre Emile L'Angelier, from Jersey. L'Angelier saw Madeleine in the street, and was so taken with her that he sought to overcome the social barriers which existed between a packing clerk and an architect's daughter. Madeleine did not refuse his entreaties.

The couple exchanged letters secretly, with Madeleine's maid acting as a go-between. Her letters were passionate in the extreme. In June 1856, at the Smiths' country house, the two became lovers, and Madeleine's letters now referred to 'My own, my beloved husband', and were signed Mini L'Angelier.

When the Smiths returned to Glasgow secret meetings were made more difficult than before, although the couple were able to converse, with L'Angelier standing in the street and Madeleine

Smith, M.: Madeleine in 1856

talking through the barred windows of her basement bedroom. Mr Smith had an inkling of what was going on, and forbade it to continue. He had his own plans as to who Madeleine should wed, and introduced a suitor.

L'Angelier became aware of this threat, and was jealous and returned one of her letters. Madeleine promptly called it off, and requested the return of *all* her letters. L'Angelier's reaction was to threaten to send the letters to her father. In desperation Madeleine begged him not to do this, and wrote him love-letters again.

In February 1857 L'Angelier became ill. He was confined to his bed for over a week, and on 23 March, after returning to his lodgings late at night, was convulsed with pain and died. An autopsy showed that his body contained 82 grains of arsenic. On 31 March, after Madeleine's letters to L'Angelier were found, the girl was arrested. She made a Declaration (statement) admitting that she had bought arsenic which, like *Florence Maybrick*, she used as a cosmetic, but she denied administering the poison to L'Angelier, 'And this I declare is the truth.'

She was tried at Edinburgh in June 1857. The prosecution case was that she had secretly met L'Angelier within her father's house, and when he became an obstacle to her marriage plans she poisoned him with arsenic administered in a chocolate drink.

The law at that time did not permit the accused to testify; instead, the court listened to Madeleine's Declaration. Her advocate pointed out that L'Angelier was known to be an arsenic-eater, and to have had a history of stomach ailments. Furthermore, he was depicted as a seducer and a blackmailer. The jury on 9 July returned a verdict of Not Proven on the charge of murder. She eventually married an artist in London and died aged 93 in America on 12 April 1928. The gravestone in Mount Hope Cemetery bears simply Lena Sheehy, the surname of her second husband.

[*1, 21, 35, 87, 96, 134, 145, 211, 254, 290, 322, 332, 419, 452, 466, 507, 553, 612, 660, 680, 687, 729, 785, 792, 998*]

Smith, M.: A letter to her lover

SNIDER, Paul. The victim of the 'Playmate Murder', centrefold model Dorothy Stratten, was on her way to stardom when she was brutally killed by her jealous husband in an act of murder coupled with suicide.

At eighteen, Dorothy Ruth Hoogstraten was working as a waitress in Vancouver, Canada, and had ambitions of becoming a secretary. In 1978 she met Paul Snider, an unprincipled entrepreneur, who saw in Dorothy's beauty a commodity that could be marketed. 'That girl could make me a lot of money,' he confided to a friend. He dazzled her with visits to expensive restaurants and night clubs, and in due course persuaded her to pose for *Playboy* magazine.

Dorothy's natural talent made her an immediate success. She changed her name to Stratten, and began to consider a career in films and TV. In 1979 she married Snider, and the following year she was

chosen as Playmate of the Year and rapidly increased both her prospects and her earning potential. Snider had neither the talent nor the charm of his wife, and he grew resentful of her success and the following she was building up. They argued frequently, and separated when it was clear that their future paths were on divergent courses.

Snider would not divorce her, and proved obstructive to the extent of hiring a private detective to catalogue her movements. When Dorothy returned from a film session in New York he asked her to meet him at their bungalow in Los Angeles. The meeting took place at about midday on 14 August 1980, and when Snider's current girl-friend arrived later in the day she found the bedroom door closed. It was assumed that the couple wanted their privacy, and the room was not entered until several hours later, when their dead bodies were found. Both had suffered shotgun wounds, Dorothy's injury being in the face.

It appeared that 21-year-old Dorothy (who had been hailed as possibly the next Marilyn Monroe) had been murdered by Paul Snider who then turned the gun on himself. It was found that he had recently bought a 12-bore shotgun and had remarked to an acquaintance, 'Sometimes Playmates get killed.' The circumstances of Dorothy's tragic killing have been made into a number of films, including a TV production, *Death of a Centrefold*. [*99, 701*]

Snider: Playmate and husband

SNYDER and GRAY. Ruth May Snyder aged 32 and Henry Judd Gray aged 35 (known as the 'Granite Woman' and 'Lover Boy') were executed for the murder of Albert Edward Snyder after a sensational trial.

Ruth was married to Albert Snyder, 13 years her senior. She was unhappy, and by chance met Gray, a corset salesman, whose marriage was a drab one. The couple met in New York in June 1925. They continued to meet, mostly in hotel bedrooms, and Gray, a weak character with a mother complex, was entranced by the powerful personality of Ruth Snyder; he called her his 'Queen, my Momsie, my Mommie', she responded with 'Lover Boy'.

With Gray firmly under her domination, Ruth told him of various accidents which had befallen her husband. 'What are you trying to do?' asked Gray. 'Kill the poor guy,' replied Snyder. She told Gray she had taken out life insurance on her husband with double indemnity totalling 96 000 dollars. Albert Snyder had several narrow escapes, including two gassings and a poisoning, but survived.

Claiming that her husband had 'turned into a brute—a killer', Ruth decided to make sure next time. In February 1927 she won Gray over. Her plan required the purchase of chloroform, a sash weight and some picture wire. Very early on 20 March Gray entered the Snyder home and hid until the family returned from a bridge party. Albert, the worse for drink, retired to bed.

Ruth fetched Gray from his hiding-place, and together they approached the sleeping Albert. Gray brought the sash weight crashing down on his head. Snyder struggled, and cried out to his wife to help him. Her answer was to hit him with the sash weight, but still he struggled, and he had to be killed with chloroform and the picture wire.

The alarm was raised later that morning, when Ruth Snyder was found bound and gagged with her husband dead. She said she had been attacked by a prowler, but the police were suspicious. They found Gray's name in Ruth's address book, and told her that he had been arrested, and had confessed. Thus tricked, Ruth claimed that she and Gray had plotted to kill her husband, but that she had not struck a single blow. Gray admitted his part in the plot and said, 'She had this power over me. She told me what to do and I just did it.' The pair were tried in April 1927, and

both were found guilty and sentenced to death. Their appeals were dismissed, and while waiting in condemned cells they each wrote their autobiographies—Ruth received over 164 offers of marriage from men who obviously wanted to live dangerously. The 'Granite Woman' and 'Lover Boy' were electrocuted at Sing Sing on 12 January 1928 within 4 minutes of each other. A press photographer had a camera strapped to his ankle and obtained a picture of Ruth at the moment of death.

[*57, 192, 237, 264, 305, 343, 503, 543, 638, 676, 843*]

SOBHRAJ, Charles. Born in Japanese-occupied Vietnam in 1944, Hotchand Bhawanni Gurmukh Sobhraj graduated from robbery to murder. He developed a Nietzschean type of philosophy believing in the supremacy of the strong.

In 1969 Sobhraj acquired French citizenship and married; his father told the bride-to-be that she was marrying 'a destructor'. He had already shown his propensity for gambling, theft and petty crime, which quickly degenerated into full-scale criminal activity. He frequently deserted his wife to travel to India, where he set up a dubious car-import business, leaving a trail of unpaid bills. In 1971 he carried out a jewel robbery in Delhi, evading capture by escaping to Afghanistan.

During the next few years Sobhraj preyed on tourists in Greece and Turkey, stealing their money and documents and leaving his brother to face the consequences. By 1975 he was back in India and Thailand and set himself up as a gem-dealer in Bangkok. He took an apartment in the centre of the city and offered accommodation to young people travelling to see the world, whom he first befriended and then robbed.

In October 1975 a 23-year-old drop-out from California arrived in Bangkok on her way to Nepal. She encountered Charles Sobhraj, who took her back to his apartment; her body was later found at Pattaya, where she appeared to have died by drowning. A number of Sobhraj's visitors fell ill during the time they spent under his roof. He told them they had 'Bangkok Belly' which he could cure with his special medicine. In November a Turkish visitor intending to deal in gems was entertained by Sobhraj, and his body was later found at Pattaya; he had been beaten to death and burnt with petrol.

At the end of 1975 Sobhraj visited Hong Kong, where he persuaded a Dutch couple to visit him in Bangkok. They turned up at his apartment at the same time as a young woman looking for her missing

Snyder and Gray: Ruth dies in the electric chair

Turkish boy-friend. All three were later found dead but by this time Sobhraj had transferred his activities to Katmandu. He made his way using money, credit cards and passports stolen from luckless tourists.

In Nepal he entertained a young American couple whose burnt bodies were later found in a field near Katmandu. The police were quick to question him, but he eluded their continuing inquiries by making a quick exit to India. In Calcutta a young man studying Eastern religion who had been befriended by Sobhraj was found dead in his room, having been drugged and strangled.

And so it went on; wherever Charles Sobhraj travelled, murder seemed to follow. By the beginning of 1976 he was wanted for questioning in connection with 8 murders in several countries. He was traced to Bangkok in March 1976, but managed to escape from custody by bribing officials. His apartment was searched, and several kilos of proprietary drugs were found, along with hypodermic syringes and a mass of personal documents belonging to twenty different people. Sobhraj was now the most wanted man in Asia; warrants were out for his arrest, and Interpol had alerted police forces throughout the world.

Sobhraj next turned up in Delhi where he ingratiated himself with a party of French tourists at the Bikram Hotel. He warned them of the hazards of dysentery, and he offered them his preventive medicine: twenty gullible visitors swallowed the pills he gave them. The pills were designed to induce sleep, and Sobhraj's plan was to enter their rooms while they lay unconscious and rob them. The plan backfired when some of the visitors collapsed in the hotel lounge, and Sobhraj was accused of giving them poison. He was arrested, and this time the authorities managed to hold on to him.

When his record caught up with him, Sobhraj was eventually tried in India on a charge of murder but was convicted only of culpable homicide and sentenced to 7 years' hard labour. In 1982 he was tried for the murder of the young student in Calcutta, and this time was sentenced to life imprisonment. Sobhraj had an uncanny knack of escaping from prison and did so again by slipping out of Tihar gaol after drugging wardens. He was recaptured after several weeks of freedom.
[698, 910]

SODEMAN, Arnold Karl. A child-strangler who smiled his way through a 5-year murder investigation in Australia in the 1930s.

On 9 November 1930, 12-year-old Mena Griffiths

failed to return home after playing with friends in Fawkner Park at South Yarra in Melbourne. Her body was found 2 days later in an empty house; she had been strangled. Friends of the dead girl talked of a tall man who watched them playing and sent them off with money to buy sweets while asking Mena to do a special errand for him.

The police inquiry into the girl's murder lost direction when a man was arrested and charged on the basis of having been seen by 3 witnesses in Fawkner Park. He was sent for trial, but was able to prove a satisfactory alibi. The fact that his arrest was mistaken was adequately proved when a second child was murdered. A 16-year-old, Hazel Wilson, was found dead from strangulation on 10 January 1931 but the murder inquiry quickly lost its impetus.

The murders remained unsolved for 4 years, when in January 1935 interest was reawakened by the killing of a 12-year-old girl in Inverloch in a fashion greatly resembling the earlier deaths. Thousands of holidaymakers at the seaside resort were questioned, including one Arnold Sodeman, but once again an innocent man was charged and then released.

A fourth victim was added to the long-running murder series in December 1936 when a 6-year-old girl was found dead from strangulation at Leongatha. On this occasion the police manhunt achieved the breakthrough for which investigators had been hoping. A man on a bicycle had been seen talking to the victim the day before she was murdered. A few days later, when the news of the murder was at its height, a labourer reported to the police that one of his colleagues on a nearby construction site had been involved in a curious incident. Arnold Sodeman, normally a mild-mannered man, flew into a rage when his workmates pulled his leg to the effect that he was the man with the bicycle.

Sodeman was interviewed, and, after lengthy denials, finally confessed to the killings. 'I can't say why I did this,' he told police. He admitted 4 murders in all, and demonstrated his particular strangling grip in which he locked his thumbs together to increase the pressure. Sodeman's family had a history of mental illness and he was aware that he developed violent urges after he had been drinking. He appeared to have led a normal home life, and was devoted to his wife and daughter. In a written message to his wife he asked her not to make any effort in his defence as he intended to plead guilty. He was duly convicted at his trial and was hanged on 1 June 1936 at Pentridge Prison. It was discovered that he suffered from a form of chronic meningitis which was triggered off by drinking alcohol.

[*246*]

SPECK, Richard Franklyn. Semi-illiterate 24-year-old onetime garbage collector who liked comic magazines, drugs and alcohol. He had the legend 'Born to Raise Hell' tattooed on his forearm, and became a mass murderer.

On the night of 14 July 1966 Speck, reeking of alcohol, arrived outside a Chicago nurses' residence. His knock was answered by 23-year-old Corazon Amurao, who saw he was holding a knife and a gun. 'I'm not going to hurt you', he said. He ordered the girl and two of her friends into an upstairs room, where there were 3 other girls. Three more girls returned to the residence, and they were added to the captive group. Speck made all the girls lie on the floor, and he bound them hand and foot with strips torn from a bed sheet.

Speck asked the girls where they kept their money. He took the cash, and then led one of them to another room, where he stabbed and strangled her. It was later suggested that this act sexually stimulated Speck to the violence which followed, for at roughly 20-minute intervals he stabbed and strangled the remaining girls. Corazon Amurao managed to escape by squirming under a bed, where she remained undetected. When Speck left the house she raised the alarm.

The police soon identified Richard Speck by fingerprints. Meanwhile he had gone to a city bar where he spent the next few days drinking heavily. A Chicago newspaper which said the surviving nurse could identify the killer was published on 16 July 1966. That night Speck slashed his wrist, and when an ambulance was called he told the doctor who he was.

He was identified by Corazon Amurao, and his fingerprints undeniably placed him at the murder scene. He was tried for first-degree murder in April 1967 and found guilty, being sentenced to the electric chair on 6 June 1967. After the US Supreme Court's abolition of capital punishment Speck was re-sentenced to life terms of imprisonment totalling 400 years. He maintained his innocence until 1978 when he was quoted as telling a newspaper, 'Yeh, I killed them. I stabbed them and choked them'.

[*22, 432, 693, 749*]

SPENCER, Henry. A 34-year-old murderer who nearly turned his own execution into an evangelical meeting.

In June 1914 Spencer turned up in Wheaton, Illinois, claiming to be a salesman. He met Allison Rexroat, a woman much older, whom he courted attentively. She said she had a sizeable bank account, and, with marriage suggested, she transferred her savings to Spencer's name.

One summer's day the couple decided to take a picnic on a quiet hillside near Wheaton. Spencer returned to town alone, and went to Miss Rexroat's bank, where he withdrew her entire savings. Before he could board a train the local sheriff appeared asking him about his movements. Suspicion had been aroused by a friend of the Rexroat family who had seen a man withdrawing the savings.

Spencer claimed to know nothing of the woman's whereabouts, but a farmer who had noticed the couple found her body in a hillside grave with the head smashed with a hammer. Spencer protested, but finally broke down and confessed to murder.

At his trial the defence claimed that the confession had been beaten out of him, but he was found guilty. The day before his execution he was interviewed by the press, and claimed to have embraced religion and to have reformed his character. 'I've joined the ranks of God's children . . . I did evil. Evil was in me. Now it's gone.'

A crowd of thousands turned up at Wheaton on execution day in August 1914, and Spencer provided an extraordinary spectacle by declaring, 'This is the happiest moment of my life.' He continued in this sanctimonious vein and recited several psalms. Finally as the trap was sprung he made a declaration of his innocence, shouting out, 'I never harmed a hair on her head. So help me God!'

[*693*]

STARKWEATHER, Charles. Like *Richard Speck*, American garbage man and lover of comic magazines. Known as 'Little Red' on account of his bow-legged, unprepossessing physical appearance and red hair, Starkweather (aged 19) modelled himself on film star James Dean.

Starkweather had already killed while committing a robbery, before he started on the week of killing which made him a mass murderer.

On 21 January 1958 Starkweather visited the home of his girl-friend, 14-year-old Caril Ann Fugate; while waiting for her to return he toyed with the .22 hunting rifle which he had with him.

Starkweather: Caril and Charlie

The girl's mother shouted at him to stop fiddling with it—he shot both her and her husband dead. When Caril Ann arrived home he entered her sister's bedroom and choked the 2-year-old to death.

The couple put a notice on the door, telling the world, 'Every Body is Sick with the Flu.' A relative called, and though apparently fobbed off by Caril Ann, notified the police. Officers went to the house, and they too were sent away by the girl. When they returned the house was empty save for the 3 corpses.

An alert went out for Starkweather and his companion, and in the week of terror which ensued 'Little Red' shot and stabbed 7 people. Twelve hundred police and National Guardsmen were deployed in the hunt for the pair, who were eventually located at Douglas, Wyoming.

When arrested, Starkweather attempted to absolve the girl by saying she had been his hostage, but when the girl called him a killer he changed his tone. In his confession he said, 'The more I looked at people, the more I hated them because I knowed there wasn't any place for me with the kind of people I knowed. . . . A bunch of God-damned sons of bitches looking for somebody to make fun of. . . .'

Caril Ann Fugate maintained her innocence at the couple's trial, but she was found guilty and sentenced to life imprisonment, and Starkweather was condemned to death. He died in the electric chair on 25 June 1959 at Nebraska State Penitentiary. Caril was released on parole in 1977.

[19, 56, 108, 693, 763, 903]

THE STAUNTONS. Louis Staunton, his mistress Alice Rhodes, his brother Patrick and Patrick's wife Elizabeth were charged with murdering Harriet, Louis's 36-year-old wife, by starving her to death.

In 1875 Harriet, a plain and not very bright girl with an endowment of £3000, married Louis Staunton, an auctioneer's clerk. The girl's mother was against the marriage. She called once on the couple at their house in Brixton—she was asked not to return.

Soon after Harriet produced a son, they moved to Kent, where Louis's brother Patrick, an artist, and his wife Elizabeth lived. At this time too Elizabeth's sister, Alice Rhodes, began a relationship with Louis Staunton. Louis sent his wife to live with his brother and, using Harriet's money, lived near by with Alice Rhodes. In October 1876 Harriet went to London with Louis

to sign some legal papers, and was not seen again until April 1877.

On 8 April Patrick and Elizabeth Staunton left Harriet's child at a London hospital, where it died as the result of its starved condition, and on 12 April Louis and Elizabeth booked accommodation for an 'invalid lady' at a house in Penge. Harriet Staunton was installed the next day, and a doctor was called, who found her emaciated and filthy. She died soon after, weighing only 5 stone 4 with not a particle of fat on her. The doctors now concluded that she died of starvation and neglect.

The Stauntons and Alice Rhodes were arrested and tried for murder at the Old Bailey in September 1877. Medical evidence predominated—doctors at the post-mortem said she died of starvation, whereas other expert witnesses maintained it was tuberculosis. The judge in his summing up virtually ignored the medical evidence and was heavily biased against the prisoners. They were all found guilty, and sentenced to death.

The Lancet observed that before murder by starvation was proved it was necessary to prove death by starvation. Some 700 doctors signed a document declaring their lack of conviction in the conclusions from the post-mortem appearances. The Home Secretary reprieved the accused. They were given prison sentences, except Alice Rhodes, who was released.

[1, 110, 141, 178, 442, 611, 612, 911, 950, 988]

STELLA MARIS CASE. Alfonso Francis Austin Smith was educated at Eton and Cambridge, and served with distinction in the First World War in the Dragoon Guards. He was married with 3 children.

John Derham, also an Old Etonian, and Smith became firm friends, but Derham fell in love with Mrs Smith, and her marriage began to crumble. On 12 August 1926, while staying at Whitstable in a villa named Stella Maris, Smith sent a telegram to Derham in his wife's name asking him to come up to Whitstable. The trio met at a hotel and then returned to Stella Maris.

At about 11.00 p.m. a shot was fired in the villa, and Mrs Smith's sister rushed down to the drawing-room, to find Derham holding Smith on the floor and hitting him with the revolver. Mrs Smith was trying to pull Derham off. He then staggered out into the street and collapsed. He died later from a gunshot wound in the abdomen.

Alfonso Smith was charged with murder. He said, 'I intended to shoot myself, but in the struggle for the revolver it went off and shot Derham.' Smith was tried in November 1926 at Maidstone Assizes, where Sir Edward Marshall Hall defended him. The prosecution put in one of Smith's letters to his wife, which read, 'This problem can only be solved in one way, the removal of your lover Derham or myself. . . . May God forgive me for what I am about to do, and may he forgive you. . . .' He had also written to Derham, 'You damned swine, I only wish you had the courage to meet me. . . .'

Marshall Hall maintained that the dead man's wound was consistent with the gun discharging accidently during the struggle in which Derham tried to prevent Smith shooting himself. Smith went into the witness-box. He said he had invited Derham to Stella Maris to talk things over, and he described how the tragedy occurred. He produced a revolver which he had hidden in his hip-pocket, and declared his intention to shoot himself. Derham tried to take the weapon, which went off accidentally.

The jury found Smith not guilty, but Mr Justice Avory sentenced him to 12 months' hard labour for possessing a firearm and ammunition without a licence.

[*159, 378, 420, 492, 897, 960*]

STEPHENSON, David Curtis. Controversial case in which a 34-year-old man was convicted after the person he had criminally assaulted committed suicide.

Stephenson was a member of the Klu Klux Klan who became Grand Dragon of the Realm of Indiana. He was said to have enrolled over 300 000, and to have made a fortune by taking a cut from the enrolment fees. He lived in a large house at Indianapolis, and opposed the Klan's Imperial Wizard, Hiram W. Evans. In 1923 he seceded from the national organization and went into politics. He was influential in electing Indiana's Republican Governor in 1924, and modestly declared, 'I am the law in Indiana.'

Rivalry in the Ku Klux Klan continued, and Stephenson was accused of immoral behaviour. On 15 March 1924 he had 28-year-old Madge Oberholtzer abducted from her parents' home and taken to his mansion. He was drunk. He told her, 'I love you more than any woman I have ever known.' Stephenson, aided by two men named Gentry and Klinck, drove the girl to the railroad station and boarded a train. Once in their berth, Stephenson attacked her, stripped her and savagely assaulted

her. She lost consciousness and they left the train at Hamilton, putting up at a hotel.

The girl, in severe pain from her injuries, persuaded one of the men to take her to a drugstore, where she bought tablets of bichloride of mercury. She swallowed 6 tablets in a suicide attempt. She was extremely ill, and her abductors drove her back to Indianapolis. On 17 March Klinck carried her into her parents' house, saying she had been involved in an automobile accident. Her superficial wounds began to heal, but she died from the poison on 14 April 1925.

Stephenson, together with Gentry and Klinck, was charged with murder, and in October arraigned at Hamilton. They did not take the stand. Of Stephenson's bestial assault there was no doubt, but the defence argued that the girl committed suicide, and therefore homicide did not come into it. The prosecutor replied, 'By those acts D. C. Stephenson and his cohorts became murderers just the same as if they plunged a dagger into her throbbing heart.' The Grand Dragon of Indiana was found guilty of murder in the second degree and sentenced to life imprisonment. Gentry and Klinck were found not guilty.
[*143*]

STRAFFEN, John Thomas. A 22-year-old child-murderer whose escape from Broadmoor permitted him to kill again.

Straffen was a child thief and school truant, and in 1940 was sent to a school for mentally defective children. In 1947, when he was 17, and judged to be mentally about half that age, he assaulted a child and was committed to an institution as feeble-minded. He was released in February 1951, and within 6 months had strangled 2 small girls at Bath. No sexual motive was involved; he hoped it would annoy the police, whom he did not like.

He was arrested, and readily confessed the murders. 'It didn't take long', he said, 'only about two minutes.' He was tried at Taunton Assizes in October, but was found insane and committed to Broadmoor. Six months after being admitted, he escaped.

He was recaptured on the same day, though not before he had murdered again. Late that night Linda Bowyer was reported missing, and her strangled body was found next morning in a near-by field.

Interviewed at Broadmoor, Straffen completely gave himself away, saying 'I did not kill the little girl on the bicycle', even before he was asked. He was arrested, and charged with murder. Tried a second time, on this occasion at Winchester in July 1952, he pleaded 'not guilty', although it had been considered he would be 'unfit to plead'.

Straffen was found guilty, sentenced to death, and later reprieved. It is unlikely he will ever be released from prison.

[1, 13, 261, 514, 599, 697, 767, 798]

STRATTON BROTHERS. Alfred, aged 22, and Albert, aged 20, both petty criminals, represent a landmark in British criminal history by being the first persons convicted of murder by fingerprint evidence.

Thomas Farrow was an elderly man with a paint shop in south-east London, and lived in the flat above with his wife. When his assistant arrived on 27 March 1905 Mr Farrow was found dead in the parlour with his head battered in, and Mrs Farrow lay unconscious in one of the bedrooms. She died of her injuries 4 days later.

A cash-box had been forced open, and its metal tray bore a thumb-print. Fingerprint technique was in its early stages in Britain, but this thumb-print was regarded as a vital clue. All those known to have handled the box were fingerprinted, including the dead couple, but none matched.

Suspicion centred on two young men, Alfred and Albert Stratton, who had records for burglary and house-breaking. Alfred's girl-friend admitted that both brothers had been out all that night, and, when Alfred returned he destroyed his coat and dyed his brown shoes black. A milk roundsman had also seen 2 men hurrying from Farrow's shop early on that morning.

The brothers were arrested, and their fingerprints taken. Alfred's right thumb-print was a perfect match with that on the cash-box. Both brothers were tried at the Old Bailey in May 1905, when the fingerprint evidence was immediately contested by the defence. The battle of the experts was won by the prosecution, led by Sir Richard Muir.

Mr Justice Channell was cautious about the fingerprint evidence, but the jury brought in a guilty verdict, and the two were hanged together, blaming each other.

[132, 449, 552, 624, 916, 933]

STROUD, Robert Franklin. The 'Birdman of Alcatraz' who spent most of his life in prisons, and used his time to make himself an authority on diseases in the canary.

Stroud was convicted of manslaughter in the early 1900s, when he killed a man in a fight over a dance-hall girl. He served 12 years in the

penitentiary on McNeil Island, and later at Fort Leavenworth.

On 26 March 1916, shortly before he was due to be released, for apparently no motive he killed a prison guard in Leavenworth's mess hall before a large assembly of prisoners and prison staff. He was convicted of murder and sentenced to death, though he maintained that the prison officer died as the result of a heart condition.

After his mother pleaded with President Woodrow Wilson to grant a commutation of sentence, presidential commutation was granted on the understanding that Stroud would remain in solitary confinement for life. This did not worry Stroud, who was a loner anyway, and it allowed him to pursue his ornithological studies, a field in which his established reputation had undoubtedly helped to save him from execution.

He won concessions from the prison authorities, enlarging his cell to allow him to carry out experimental work. He was eventually transferred to Alcatraz where he earned his famous nickname. He died in prison in 1963, aged 76.

[319, 693]

STUART, Rupert Max. A 27-year-old Australian aborigine who featured in an historic murder trial.

A 9-year-old girl, Mary Olive Hattam, disappeared on 20 December 1958. She left her home in Ceduna, South Australia, with 2 friends to play on a near-by beach. She stayed while the others went off exploring. When they returned she had gone, and her father called the police.

The missing girl was found in a cave near the beach. She had been sexually assaulted, and her head battered in; a bloodstained stone lay near by. Footprints in the sand were examined by native trackers, who said they were made by an aborigine.

Among itinerant workers living near Ceduna who were questioned was an aborigine named Rupert Max Stuart. He had come to town with the Fun Land Carnival the night before. He had been arrested for drunkenness—a serious offence, for aborigines were forbidden alcohol. Stuart made a statement in which he confessed to raping Mary while drunk, and then to hitting her with a stone.

He was tried for murder at Adelaide, and found guilty. Sentence of death was passed, and there began a remarkable series of appeals and stays of execution. The first appeal, that the verdict was against the weight of evidence, was dismissed. A further appeal based on the argument that Stuart did not know sufficient English, either to make a

Sutcliffe: Yorkshire Ripper on his wedding day

proper statement or to defend himself adequately, was also dismissed. His lawyers took his case to the Judiciary Committee of the Privy Council in London.

The Council rejected Stuart's petition, and the matter was dealt with by a Royal Commission sitting in Adelaide. After 77 days' deliberation, the Commission announced on 3 December 1959 that the original verdict was justified. The last appeal had thus failed, but the sentence of death had already been commuted to life imprisonment. [*172, 477*]

SUTCLIFFE, Peter. The Yorkshire Ripper's 13 killings over a 5-year period between 1975 and 1980 terrorized a number of Yorkshire towns. His victims were mostly—though not exclusively—prostitutes, and that association with *Jack the Ripper* was powerful enough to earn Sutcliffe the name by which he was known until he was arrested.

He roamed the red-light areas of Leeds and Bradford and picked up women whom he killed with a hammer, savagely stabbing and slashing their bodies. Sutcliffe took risks, prowling the streets at night in his car looking for likely victims and then chancing being disturbed when he killed them in alleyways often within yards of busy streets. He also had incredible luck, for he was questioned several times by the police in the course of their inquiries, which eventually inspired such headlines as 'Nine Times Police Let The Ripper Go Free.'

The first victim was Wilma McCann, murdered in Leeds in October 1975 and the last was Jacqueline Hill in November 1980, also murdered in Leeds. In between there were killings in Bradford, Manchester, Huddersfield and Halifax and 4 more murders in Leeds. The police mounted a massive murder investigation, in the course of which 250,000 persons were interviewed, 32,000 statements were taken and 5.2 million car registrations were checked at a cost of £4 million. The police were taunted with letters and tapes purporting to have been sent by the murderer, and a great deal of valuable time was wasted on hoaxes. Especially wasteful of valuable resources was the tape-recording beginning, 'I'm Jack . . .' sent to the police in June 1979 after the eleventh murder. Specialists in dialect pinpointed the voice to Wearside, and the tape was played at pubs and clubs in the area in the hope that a member of the public would be able to identify the voice. The sender was never identified, and on one of the occasions that Sutcliffe was questioned he was dismissed because he did not speak with a Wearside accent.

The 5-year search for the Yorkshire Ripper came to an end on 2 January 1981 in Sheffield. A police patrol car spotted a car parked in a dark driveway and decided to question the occupants. The man gave his name as Peter Williams but was unable to name his female companion, who the police officers thought was a prostitute. Dissatisfied with his answers, one of the officers put a call through to police HQ to have the car's registration number run through the computer. The reply came back within minutes, indicating that the number belonged to a different make of vehicle. At that point the game was up for Peter Sutcliffe, who was taken in for questioning.

Sutcliffe's trial opened on 5 May 1981 and he pleaded not guilty to murder by reason of diminished responsibility. His background was that of an introverted personality but he married in 1967 after courting the same girl for 7 years. They lived in Bradford, where she worked as a teacher and he had a job as a lorry-driver. Neither his wife nor his workmates suspected that Sutcliffe led such a secret life of violence, although a hint of things to come perhaps lay in the wording of a message he placed in the window of his vehicle: 'In this truck is a man whose latent genius if unleashed would rock the nation, whose dynamic energy would overpower those around him. Better let him sleep?'

Sutcliffe's mentality and methods had as much in common with *Peter Kürten* as with Jack the Ripper, even down to the use of a hammer as a murder weapon. He had confessed a hatred of prostitutes, and part of his defence was that he had been given a mission by God to rid the world of them. He had received his divine instructions while standing in a cemetery at Bingley and gazing across the moors. After 3 weeks listening to the evidence, the jury tended to believe he was evil rather than mad, and found him guilty on 13 charges of murder. He was sentenced to life imprisonment.

[*55, 140, 206, 287, 536, 700, 1019*]

T

TAYLOR CASE. William Desmond Taylor was a successful Hollywood director in the days of the silent movies. On 1 February 1922 he was found murdered in his Spanish-style house near Wilshire Boulevard in the film-making city. Sensation marked the subsequent criminal investigation and the case remains officially unsolved although latter-day sleuths believe the identity of the murderer is known.

Taylor graduated to film-making by way of gold-prospecting, antique-dealing and small acting roles in the early movies. He was a man of cultured tastes and, so it was rumoured, a large sexual appetite. When he became chief director for Paramount he directed many of the leading actresses of the day, including Mabel Normand, an established comedienne, and Mary Miles Minter, a rising star just 20 years old.

Mabel Normand visited Taylor at his request on 1 February to pick up some books he had promised her. She declined an invitation to dinner and left in her chauffeur-driven car at about 7.45 p.m. Taylor's butler had already left, having first prepared a cold supper for his employer. At about 8.15 p.m. neighbours heard what they assumed to be a car back-firing, and a man was seen leaving Taylor's house. Some time later Edna Purviance, who lived next door, called on Taylor but received no reply.

The following day when the butler returned at about 7.30 a.m. he found 54-year-old Taylor lying on the floor of the living-room with blood trickling from his mouth. A doctor was called and pronounced Taylor dead, probably from a gastric haemorrhage. As the news broke, so hysteria and chaos set in. Friends, neighbours and colleagues rushed to the house, and their concern was less for the departed Taylor than a desire to destroy clothes, papers and bottles of prohibited liquor—anything that might be found to tarnish their reputations. Vital evidence was also destroyed during this unseemly episode, and when the police were finally called in it was found that Taylor was a murder victim, having been shot twice in the back.

A systematic search of Taylor's house produced hundreds of love letters implicating Mabel Normand and Mary Miles Minter. Some of the young film-star's letters gave Hollywood journalists a field day. 'I'd lie on the couch and wait for you,' she wrote to Taylor, '. . . then I'd wake to find two strong arms around me and two dear lips pressed on mine . . .' Far from keeping a low profile, the starlet turned up the tension when she kissed Taylor's corpse at his funeral and claimed that he spoke to her, confiding, 'I shall love you always, Mary.' In the ensuing scandal her career and that of Mabel Normand were ruined. The aftermath was all negative; the police failed to solve the murder, Taylor's butler went insane, Mabel Normand died, aged 33, from tuberculosis and Mary Miles Minter faded into obscurity.

The unsolved mystery was of such compelling interest that in 1967 King Vidor, the Hollywood director, mounted his own investigation with a view to identifying the murderer and making a film of his conclusions. His findings did not reach the screen in his lifetime, but remained in his personal papers. In due course his biographer, Sidney D. Kirkpatrick, gained access to these. In his book *A Cast of Killers*, published in 1986, Kirkpatrick suggested that Taylor's murderer was Charlotte Shelby, the domineering mother of Mary Miles Minter.

A picture was painted of a mother protective yet jealous of her daughter's success. She also, apparently, wanted Taylor for herself, and tried physically to prevent her daughter from seeing him. The denouement came when Mary Miles Minter escaped from the locked room in which her mother had sought to confine her and fled to Taylor's house. Charlotte Shelby confronted them there, gun in hand, and in her daughter's presence shot Taylor dead.

[*342, 537, 750*]

TESSNOW, Ludwig. Sex murderer who killed 2 girls and 2 boys in separate incidents in Northern Germany.

In July 1901 the bodies of 2 small boys were

Taylor Case: The murder locale

found in a wooded area near Rügen—they had been horribly mutilated in a sexually motivated crime. A woman told police she had seen the boys talking to a journeyman carpenter. This man, Ludwig Tessnow, was questioned. Spots on his clothing were thought to be bloodstains, and he was arrested.

The police found that Tessnow had been suspected 3 years previously regarding the deaths of 2 girls near Osnabrück, and there was an incident in which several sheep in a field near Rügen had been badly mutilated the month before the boys were killed. A shepherd identified Tessnow.

Stains on Tessnow's clothing were found to be human and sheep blood. Ludwig Tessnow was tried and found guilty. He was executed at Griefswald Prison in 1904.
[*915, 918*]

TETZNER, Erich. A 26-year-old German businessman convicted of the murder of an unknown man in a blazing car. Tetzner murdered

for gain, and the case has many similarities with that of *Alfred Arthur Rouse.*

On 27 November 1929 police went to a motor accident near Regensburg. A green Opel had crashed and caught fire. The trapped driver, thought to be Erich Tetzner, a Leipzig businessman, was burned to death.

The police were satisfied that it was an ordinary road accident, and released his body for burial. But the insurance company, from which Frau Tetzner was claiming a large sum on accident policies recently taken out, was not satisfied. An autopsy was carried out: the badly charred, unrecognizable body was that of a small man—Tetzner was big. The age was put at about 23—Tetzner was 26. The air passages did not contain soot particles, and blood samples proved negative for carbon monoxide.

Frau Tetzner was watched, and in December a telephone call from France proved to be from her husband. Tetzner was arrested in Strasbourg.

He immediately confessed. He changed the details of his confession several times, but there seemed little doubt that Tetzner killed a man, probably a hitch-hiker, and then burned his body in the car to defraud the insurance company.

Erich Tetzner was tried in March 1931, found guilty and executed at Regensburg on 2 May 1931. [*915, 918*]

THATCHER, Colin. Millionaire Saskatchewan rancher and politician convicted of murdering his ex-wife in the garage of her home in Regina, Canada.

Jo Ann Wilson, aged 43, was bludgeoned and shot in a brutal assault when she drove home on the evening of 21 January 1983. Her cries were heard by a man walking down the snow-covered street, and the source was pinpointed by the sound of a gunshot. A shadowy figure was seen to emerge from the garage and flee into the night. Jo Ann Wilson lay dead: she had sustained severe blows to the head, and had a bullet in the brain. In his haste the killer left behind in the snow a small yet incriminating piece of paper. It was a credit-card slip for a gasoline purchase dated 18 January 1983 and signed 'Colin Thatcher'.

A previous attempt had been made on Jo Ann's life in 1981, when she was wounded in the shoulder by a shot fired through a window at her home. The assailant was not caught, but the incident followed the Thatchers' bitterly contested divorce and child-custody proceedings in which she won the largest settlement granted by a Canadian court up to that time. She also won custody of the youngest of their 3 children and later married Tony Wilson, a steel-industry executive.

After the divorce Thatcher nursed a smouldering resentment towards his former wife which emerged in truculent behaviour over access to the children. He expressed his hatred on numerous occasions to his American girl-friend, who lived in Palm Springs, California. At the same time he was successful politically, and became Minister of Energy and Mines in the state legislature. But even in debates on political matters he was known as a hard man, and some called him the 'J. R. Ewing of Saskatchewan'.

Eventually his hatred took a more tangible form and he told his girl-friend several times that he wanted to kill his ex-wife, or arrange for someone to kill her. In January 1982 he bought a .357 magnum Ruger, ostensibly to protect his property, and drove out into the desert to practise his shooting skill. In due course his girl-friend broke off their relationship on account of the brutal treatment she received from him. Her evidence was to prove vital in due course when she recalled Thatcher telling her, 'It's a strange feeling to blow away your wife.'

Following a meeting with a man whom he had approached at one time to arrange a contract killing, Thatcher was arrested and charged with Jo Ann's murder. His meeting was monitored by the police, and the incriminating conversation which took place was tape-recorded. Despite bitterly cold weather and a snowstorm, crowds of people turned out to attend the trial for murder of Colin Thatcher in October 1984.

He went into the witness box to testify, and adopted the arrogant, blustering tone which characterized his performances in the State Legislature. This did him little good, and his outbursts of temper served only to confirm the evidence of those who had depicted him as a man who could barely rein in his anger. At one point he invited prosecuting counsel to 'step outside', presumably to settle their differences in a stand-up fight. He had the politician's answer for everything, and claimed that the tell-tale credit slip found at the murder scene had been planted in order to frame him. Thatcher was convicted of first-degree murder and given a life sentence. He appealed in May 1985, but his conviction was upheld.

[*86*]

THAW-WHITE CASE. The roof garden at New York's Madison Square Garden was the scene of a fatal shooting on 25 June 1906. Stanford White, aged 52, a distinguished architect, was shot 3 times by Harry Kendall Thaw. White, a bullet in his brain, lay dead on the floor and Thaw stood over him, a smoking pistol in his hand.

The case made immediate news because of the dead man's professional standing, and his murder by the playboy son of a Pittsburg railroad magnate. White was well known as a womanizer.

Thaw, aged 34, was equally well known for his gambling and spending. His wife was a beautiful model, Evelyn Nesbit, an ex-*Floradora* chorus girl. (See also *Nan Patterson*.) The reason for the murder seemed to be that Stanford White had seduced Thaw's wife, the teenage Evelyn, 4 years before her marriage. Thaw's motive was revenge, and he was convinced of his moral right to kill the man. His mother supported him, saying, 'I am prepared to pay a million dollars to save his life.' Some unsavoury stories came out concerning the chivalrous avenger, who it was alleged ill-treated his women, including his wife, with brutal whippings.

Thaw was tried for murder in January 1907 but

NO FRIEND

Comes Forward To Take the Part Of Murdered Stanford White.

New York, June 27.—Throughout all the developments since the tragedy with the amassing of so much favorable evidence on the part of Thaw's friends one thing stands out prominently. Not one friend of White has come forward to defend his name from the ignominous remarks which have been made about him, and the attacks which have been made upon his reputation. If he has friends who believe that Thaw's malice toward him was unjustified they have not come forward to assert themselves or defend the character of the dead man.

Just how soon, the real facts in the case will be brought out in an official way, is uncertain. It probably will not be until the trial of Thaw begins. The coroner's inquest tomorrow will not develop the details which are so eagerly awaited. Acting District Attorney

Thaw-White Case: The victim finds no friends

the jury could not reach a verdict. A second trial took place a year later, when Thaw was found not guilty by reason of insanity. He escaped from an asylum in 1913 and went to Canada. The Canadian authorities returned him to the USA, and with the aid of family money he won a retrial in 1915 which declared him sane and not guilty. Eighteen months later he was indicted for kidnapping and whipping a 19-year-old youth. Once again he was declared insane, only to have the decision subsequently reversed. He died, aged 76, in February 1947.

[*57, 108, 170, 304, 377, 378, 556, 562, 605, 672, 696, 809, 904*]

THOMAS, Arthur Alan. New Zealand double murderer.

Jeanette and Harvey Crewe, who had a farm at Pukekwa, were visited by Jeanette's father on 22 June 1970. No one was there except the Crewes' 18-month-old child, but blood-stains were found.

The police were joined by army personnel in a search, and on 16 August Jeanette's body was found in the Waikato river, wrapped in bed sheets, and bound up with wire. She had been shot in the head with a .22 bullet. All .22 weapons owned locally were collected for investigation.

Harvey Crewe was found on 16 September, floating in the Waikato river, also killed by a .22 bullet. A car axle was found in the river; it had been used to weight the body.

Test firing of the .22 rifles led the police to Arthur Thomas, who farmed land some 8 miles from the Crewes. His rifle was one of 2 which could have fired the .22 No. 8 murder bullets.

In November 1970 Thomas was charged with double murder. He was tried in Auckland Supreme Court in February 1971. Evidence was given regarding Thomas's relationship with Jeanette Crewe, whom he had courted at one time. the prosecution claimed that a .22 cartridge found at the scene linked Thomas and his rifle to the killings. But the defence pointed out that the cartridge case had been found over 4 months afterwards, and after several previous police searches.

Other evidence showed Thomas was in possession of wire similar to that used to bind the bodies, and in his farm were stubs which could have come from the axle used to weight Harvey Crewe's body. Despite the inconclusive evidence, Thomas was found guilty and imprisoned for life.

In 1980, after serving 9 years' imprisonment, Arthur Thomas was pardoned following a Royal Commission Inquiry. Evidence which had proved incriminating at his trial was shown to have been planted. The New Zealand Government awarded him compensation of over NZ$1 million.
[62, 1020]

THOMAS, Donald George. A 23-year-old petty criminal and army deserter convicted of murdering a police officer.

A man was stopped in a London street on 13 February 1948 by plain-clothes policeman Nathaniel Edgar and questioned in connection with burglaries in the district. The man fired 3 shots and fled. The dying officer told colleagues that his assailant's name and address were written in his notebook—Donald Thomas, 247 Cambridge Road, Enfield.

Donald George Thomas had been on the wanted list of the military police since the previous October. He was not at the Enfield address, but was traced to lodgings at Clapham. He spotted police officers coming to his room and tried to get a gun hidden under the pillow. He was quickly

overpowered, and remarked, 'You were lucky. I might just as well be hung for a sheep as a lamb.'

In Thomas's room were found 17 rounds of ammunition, a rubber truncheon and a book entitled *Shooting to Live with the One-hand Gun.* Bullets fired from Thomas's Luger pistol matched those in Edgar's body, and his landlady said that he had confessed the murder to her.

Thomas was tried for murder in April 1948. He had started his crime record at the age of 16, when he was sent to an approved school. He was called up for military service in 1945, and deserted immediately. Thomas was convicted of the murder of Police Constable Edgar and sentenced to death, but owing to the suspension of the death penalty for a trial period, this was commuted to life imprisonment.
[83, 417, 827]

THOMPSON and BYWATERS. Edith Thompson, aged 28, and her young lover Frederick Bywaters, aged 20, provided a murder drama which has inspired many books and plays, and showed how unwise it is to keep love letters.

Edith worked as manageress and book-keeper for a City of London millinery firm. She was married to Percy Thompson, 4 years her senior, who was a shipping clerk. They lived an uneventful life in Ilford, Essex.

In the summer of 1921 Edith and Percy Thompson went on holiday to the Isle of Wight together with Edith's unmarried sister and her young man, Frederick Bywaters. Edith and Bywaters were attracted to each other, and after the holiday the young man lived with the Thompsons, but Percy quarrelled with him and Bywaters left.

Bywaters was a ship's writer with the P. and O. line, and in September he sailed for the Far East. During the separations which followed, Edith wrote long and frank letters to him. Bywaters returned to England in September 1922, and immediately met Edith. On 3 October, as the Thompsons were returning home together from a London theatre, Bywaters stabbed Percy Thompson and disappeared. Edith called for help for her dying husband; on the following day she named her lover, and both were charged with murder.

Thompson and Bywaters were tried at the Old Bailey in December 1922. Edith was accused of inciting Bywaters to murder, a charge which the

Thompson and Bywaters: Freddie, Percy and Edith

prosecution supported with her letters to her lover. Her endearments were mixed with hints about taking her husband's life. She had, she wrote, put pieces of glass from a light bulb into his food, 'big pieces too—not powdered'. She discussed various poisons, and wrote to Bywaters, 'Yes, darlint you are jealous of him—but I want you to be—he has the right by law, to all that you have the right to by nature and love—yes darlint be jealous, so much that you will do something desperate.'

Against the advice of her counsel Edith Thompson gave evidence, but she was severely dealt with in cross-examination. The judge reminded the jury that they were 'trying a vulgar, common crime', and dismissed the letters as 'full of the outpourings of a silly but at the same time wicked affection'.

Bywaters denied that there was anything in the letters which incited him to violence. Both accused were found guilty and sentenced to death. At the same hour on 9 January 1923 Bywaters was hanged at Pentonville Prison and Edith Thompson was hanged at Holloway Prison.

[1, 110, 125, 131, 133, 201, 203, 219, 249, 323, 386, 402, 463, 611, 612, 677, 711, 720, 757, 921, 964, 971]

THORN, Fred. New York's so-called 'jig-saw murder' in which pieces of a corpse scattered in the harbour were found.

Two boys swimming in New York Harbour in June 1897 found a parcel wrapped in red oilcloth. This contained the upper trunk of a male corpse. The following day the lower trunk, wrapped in similar oilcloth, was found in the Harlem river, and, later still, the legs.

The parts of the 'jig-saw murder' were pieced together, and were complete, save for the head. The well-developed torso and smooth, well-cared-for hands belonged to Willie Guldensuppe, a Turkish bath masseur. Confirmation of identity lay in a piece of skin missing from below the left breast. Guldensuppe was known to have been tattooed in that area, and it was suggested that a piece of skin had been removed to render the corpse unidentifiable.

Guldensuppe lived with a midwife named Augusta Nack who was separated from her husband and had several lovers. One of these was Fred Thorn. He, jealous of the masseur, had shot him. He cut his throat and let him bleed in a full bath-tub, finally cutting the body into pieces and dumping the oilcloth-wrapped parcels into the harbour. Suspicion was aroused by bloodstained

water which drained into the street from the soakaway system of the house. Augusta Nack turned State's Evidence, revealing that the head of the unfortunate masseur had been embedded in plaster of Paris and sunk. Augusta was identified by a shopkeeper on account of her purchases of red oilcloth. She received 15 years and Thorn was electrocuted at Sing Sing in August 1898.

[400, 788]

THORNE, John Norman Holmes. Unsuccessful chicken farmer aged 24, and onetime Sunday school teacher who murdered his fiancée.

Thorne lived in a hut on his chicken farm at Crowborough, Sussex in a squalid manner. In 1921 he met 23-year-old London typist Elsie Cameron. Elsie was a rather plain girl; despite Thorne's lack of prospects, she decided he would make a suitable husband. They became engaged.

In November 1924 Elsie informed him (untruthfully) that she was pregnant. She told him that he had promised to marry her, and packed a travel bag, arriving at Thorne's farm on 5 December. Thorne was already interested in a local girl.

Five days after Elsie's departure from London, her father sent a telegram to Thorne, asking if he knew what had happened to his daughter. Thorne replied saying she had not arrived. Mr Cameron contacted the police. Officers visited the farm and seemed satisfied.

The police, hearing that Elsie had been seen going to the farm, paid another visit armed with shovels. On 15 January 1925 Elsie's travel bag was unearthed, and Thorne was invited to make a statement. He informed the police that Elsie was dead but that he had not killed her; he claimed to have found her body dangling from a beam. He decided to dispose of it by cutting it into pieces which he wrapped in parcels—placing the head in a biscuit tin—and burying the lot under his chicken run. Thorne was charged with murder. He was tried at Lewes Assizes in March 1925, and the outcome very much depended on the opposing experts' views as to how Elsie Cameron met her death. Creases in her neck might have been made by a rope or been merely natural folds in the skin. Since there were no marks on the wooden beam in the hut, the latter view seemed the obvious one.

Thorne was found guilty. He was executed at Wandsworth on 22 April 1925.

[2, 32, 133, 159, 220, 386, 398, 451, 485, 510, 541, 593, 611, 613, 757, 921, 932, 964]

Thorne, N.: Inside the chicken-farmer's hut

TOAL, Gerard. Father James McKeown, Irish village priest, had 2 servants. His housekeeper was 36-year-old Mary Callan, and his chauffeur and odd-job man was 18-year-old Gerard Toal. When he returned home on 16 May 1927 the priest found that Mary Callan was not there. Toal said he knew nothing, and as her bicycle was missing it was assumed that Mary had gone home.

She did not appear next day, and McKeown questioned Toal further. The lad simply said that Mary gave him his dinner at midday and then went away. It was known that he did not like the housekeeper, but no significance was attached to that. The missing woman's mother had not seen her, and knew nothing of her whereabouts.

Months went by, and then Peggy Galagher, who was now Father McKeown's housekeeper, found hidden in Toal's room parts of a woman's bicycle. Confronted with this discovery, Toal insisted that he had stolen them. Police made a search of Toal's room, and questioned him. McKeown was dissatisfied with the whole affair, and told Toal to go. In April 1928 he left, saying he was going to Canada, but 10 days later he was under arrest for stealing in Dundalk. The police then made a thorough search of Father McKeown's house and garden. Female clothing and more bicycle parts were found in the ash-pit. Toal admitted that he and Mary Callan had quarrelled. When her badly decomposed body was found in a water-filled quarry several hundred yards from the house Toal was arrested and charged with murder.

His trial took place in Dublin in July 1928. The judge advised against a verdict of manslaughter, and Toal was found guilty and hanged on 29 August 1928.

[*217*]

TREVOR, Harold Dorian. Jailbird aged 62 who murdered a woman from whom he was stealing.

A 65-year-old widow, Mrs Theodora Greenhill, was visited by her daughter at her Kensington flat on 14 October 1941. Getting no answer, she let herself in. On the floor of the drawing-room she found her mother lying dead.

Mrs Greenhill had been sitting at her writing bureau, on which was a sheet of notepaper on which she was writing a receipt for rent: 'Received from Dr H. D. Trevor the s . . .'. The old lady had been hit on the head with a beer-bottle and then strangled. The bureau had been ransacked, and in the bedroom was a metal money-box which had been emptied.

Pieces of glass from the broken bottle carried

fingerprints, and there were also thumb-prints on the dressing table and money-box. Mrs Greenhill wanted to let her flat, and her assailant had posed as a likely tenant. The name 'Trevor' struck a chord in the memory of Scotland Yard fingerprint expert Fred Cherrill, and he checked the records for prints. He found that the prints of Harold Dorian Trevor matched.

Trevor was well known to the police as 'The Monocle Man' through using one, and for calling himself such names as Sir Charles Warren and Commander Crichton. He was a petty thief, who had been in and out of prison for 40 years. Trevor, who was arrested at Rhyl in North Wales, also liked passionate oratory.

At the Old Bailey in January 1942 he declared, 'No fear touches my heart. My heart is dead. It died when my mother left me . . . My life to the age of sixty-two has been all winter', and referring to the relatives of the murdered woman who were in court, he said, 'If my life can be of any satisfaction to them, take it'. He was found guilty and hanged at Wandsworth Prison.

[*133, 175*]

TROPPMANN, Jean-Baptiste. This 28-year-old mass murderer had been cossetted by his mother but ill-treated by his father. He had aspirations to wealth.

A labourer working in fields outside Paris noticed freshly dug earth, and he uncovered a human head. The bodies of a woman and 5 children were disinterred. They had been strangled or beaten to death, and then brutally mutilated with a pick-axe. The woman was Hortense Kinck, who with her children had called at a near-by hotel on 19 September 1869, looking for her husband. The family was traced to Roubaix near the Belgian border, but the husband, Jean Kinck, and the elder son, Gustave, were not found.

A Paris cab-driver was hired by a young man and woman with 5 children late at night on 19 September and told to drive beyond the Flanders Gate. They stopped about a mile outside the gate, and the man took the woman and 2 children, saying they were looking for the family's father. The 3 children left with the cabbie told him that M. Troppmann had brought them to meet their father. Then, 25 minutes later, Troppmann reappeared alone and dismissed the driver, who left him with the 3 remaining children.

Troppmann was found at Le Havre, where he was hoping to get a passage to America. His pockets were found to be stuffed with Jean Kinck's personal property. He told the police that Jean Kinck, having learned of his wife's adultery, killed her and the children with the aid of Gustave, his 16-year-old son. This account was shown to be false by the discovery of Gustave's body near the spot where his mother had been hastily buried. Then on 25 November Jean Kinck's body was found buried at Herrenfluch in Alsace, poisoned with prussic acid.

Troppmann had met Jean Kinck while he was in Alsace selling weaving machinery. Both men were Alsatians, and this common bond drew them together. Kinck was a successful businessman, manufacturing brushes, and Troppmann, envious of the other's achievements, decided to obtain Kinck's money. He proposed a scheme for printing counterfeit banknotes in an abandoned château at Herrenfluch, lured Kinck there and killed him. He then wrote to Mme Kinck on behalf of her husband, asking her to obtain 5500 francs, and requesting her to go with the family to Paris. There they were met by Troppmann, who killed them and took the papers and money. Troppmann lied to try and explain the 8 deaths, but he was found guilty and guillotined on 19 January 1870. [100, 244, 479, 591, 722]

TRUE, Ronald. A 30-year-old Walter Mitty character given to bouts of extreme anger, who was found guilty of the murder of a prostitute.

Olive Young, who was 25, had a flat in Finborough Road, Fulham. Her cleaning woman, Miss Steel, arrived on the morning of 6 March 1922, and suddenly a man whom she recognized as Major True appeared from Olive Young's bedroom. He told her not to wake her mistress, gave her a tip and left in a taxi.

When Miss Steel entered the bedroom she found the bed empty but containing 2 blood-stained pillows and the dressing-table ransacked. In the bathroom Miss Young's savagely bludgeoned body lay with a dressing-gown cord tight around the neck.

Major True, whose visiting card lay on Miss Young's sideboard, was arrested at the Hammersmith Palace of Varieties. He denied any knowledge of the murder.

On the day Olive Young's body was found he bought a new suit, which he changed into at the shop. The assistant noticed a large patch of blood on his trousers. True explained that this had occurred in a flying accident that morning. He also pawned 2 of the woman's rings.

True lived partly in a world of fantasy; he told friends that a man was impersonating him, and forging his cheques. To defend himself against this double he carried a gun with a plentiful supply of dum-dum ammunition. He had served in the Royal Flying Corps in 1914, but was invalided out after a serious crash. It was while recovering in hospital that he had first alluded to this other 'self', and made extravagant claims about his rank and record as a fighter ace.

He was tried for murder at the Old Bailey in May 1922, and his counsel, Sir Henry Curtis-Bennett, tried to establish his insanity, but he was found guilty, and sentenced to death. While in Pentonville Prison, True learned that the Home Secretary had reprieved him on the grounds of insanity, and he was committed to Broadmoor, where he died aged 60 in 1951.
[1, 110, 261, 323, 386, 442, 449, 497, 554, 605, 687, 716, 745, 798]

TRUSCOTT, Steven Murray. Youth who was convicted of raping and murdering a 12-year-old girl at Goderich, Ontario, and, at the age of 14, sentenced to death.

Steven went for a bicycle ride on the evening of 9 June 1959 and was told by his parents to return by 8.30 p.m. He was seen to stop near the school and speak to 12-year-old Lynne Harper, whose father was an officer at the RCAF air-base. The girl sat on the cross-bar of his bicycle and they pedalled off together. Steven arrived home on time, but Lynne did not.

Her parents made inquiries of her school friends, including Steven, who immediately said that they had been out together on his bicycle. He added that he left her at Highway No. 8, and she was picked up by the driver of a grey Chevrolet. A search was launched, and the girl's body was found in Lawson's Wood near the air-base. She had been raped and strangled, and an analysis of her stomach contents put the time of death at between 7.00 and 7.45 p.m. Steven was medically examined, and found to have sore genitals. He said he had had this condition for 4 or 5 weeks; he also had some scratches. He was charged with murder.

At his trial in September 1959 Steven's defence counsel argued that there was no direct evidence linking the boy with the incident in Lawson's Wood. On the other hand, the prosecution contended that Steven was the last person seen with Lynne Harper, and that the soreness was consistent with raping an immature girl.

The jury found Steven guilty, with a plea for mercy. The Canadian Prime Minister commuted

Truscott: The body of Lynne Harper

Truscott: Steven, aged thirteen

the sentence to life imprisonment, and an appeal was heard in January 1960, which upheld the guilty verdict. Forensic experts were later called in to try to reopen the case by appointing a Royal Commission, but without success. Too young to be placed in an adult penitentiary, Steven went to the Ontario Training School for Boys. He has since been released.

[*561, 851, 926, 1000*]

Udderzook: The execution

U

UDDERZOOK, William E. Perpetrator of an insurance fraud which led to murder.

In February 1873 a cottage burned down near Baltimore. Among the onlookers was the owner, and William Udderzook, a tool-maker from Baltimore, who approached him and said, 'I think Mr Goss is in the house.'

The body of a man burned beyond recognition was removed from the ruined cottage. The dead man was presumed to be Winfield Scott Goss, an inventor, who had recently rented the cottage. It was thought strange that 37-year-old Goss, an active man, failed to escape before the fire took a firm hold. Goss had $25 000 insurance.

Udderzook, his brother-in-law, had visited the inventor at his cottage to see his experiments. He took a gallon of kerosene, a bottle of whiskey and an axe. The lamp gave trouble, and Udderzook went to a near-by cottage to fetch another. When he returned the cottage was ablaze. The coroner found that an explosion of the lamp was the cause of death.

The insurance company refused to pay out, for there was doubt that the dead man was Winfield Goss. After an examination of the teeth, it was thought that it might be a cadaver stolen from a medical school.

In June 1873 Udderzook was in a hotel in Jennerville, Pennsylvania, where he was seen in the company of another man who disappeared. Blood was found on the floor of a carriage used by Udderzook, and later a farmer found a shallow grave in near-by woods which contained a body later identified as Winfield Goss.

Udderzook was tried for murder at West Chester in October 1873. Goss had been persuaded to take out heavy insurance and then to have his death faked so he and Udderzook could share the proceeds.

The plot went well, but Goss, who was drinking heavily, threatened to expose the scheme. Udderzook made his 'death' permanent. He was executed in November 1874, having asked to be buried near Goss so that 'our spirits may mingle together'.
[*729*]

UNRUH, Howard. Insane killer who in a small American town shot dead 13 people in as many minutes because he hated his neighbours.

Unruh had a conventional childhood in Camden, New Jersey. He was called up for military service in the Second World War and became a sharp-shooter. He was very withdrawn, very fond of his rifle and of Bible-reading, and not interested in girls.

He served with distinction as a tank machine-gunner in Italy and France. After the War he studied pharmacy, and was enrolled at Temple University, Philadelphia.

Unruh became increasingly withdrawn, and would not even talk to his parents. He imagined the neighbours insulted him, and he kept a notebook in which he entered details of all the imagined grievances. He took his relaxation by practising his marksmanship in the basement. He decided to shut out the world by building a high wall round the yard of his father's house. On 5 September 1949 he found that someone had stolen the massive gate which was the seal of his achievement.

Later that morning, Unruh emerged armed with two pistols. He visited a neighbour who ran a shoe-repair shop and shot him dead. The barber was next, then the drugstore and tailor's shop, with pedestrians and car drivers caught up in 12 minutes of carnage which resulted in 13 dead.

Armed police surrounded Unruh and he gave himself up. He said, 'I'm no psycho. I have a good mind.' Medical experts disagreed, and 28-year-old Unruh was declared incurably insane and committed to an institution without trial. He told a psychiatrist, 'I'd have killed a thousand if I'd had bullets enough.'
[*693*]

V

VACHER, Joseph. A 29-year-old tramp who roamed the French countryside, begging food from farms and killing 11 people in a manner which earned him comparison with *Jack the Ripper*.

Vacher was one of 15 children in a peasant family. After a period of army service; in 1893 he wounded a girl with a gun and then tried to commit suicide. The bullet lodged in an ear duct, and caused facial paralysis. He was found mentally unstable, and committed to an asylum at Saint-Robert, which discharged him as cured in April 1894.

The next month saw a series of murders. In a period of 3½ years Vacher murdered 7 women and 4 youths, who were variously strangled, knifed, disembowelled, raped and sexually mutilated.

Vacher eluded the authorities until 4 August 1897, when he attacked a woman in woods near Tournon. Her husband arrived, and between them they overpowered him. Vacher was charged with offending against public decency, and sentenced to 3 months. There was suspicion that he had committed the recent series of murders, but witnesses failed to identify him. At first Vacher denied involvement, but then he wrote to the examining judge, 'Yes, it is I who committed all the crimes with which I am charged— and I committed them all in moments of frenzy.' He said he had been bitten by a mad dog as a child, and believed that his blood was infected.

He was examined over a period of 5 months by a team of doctors headed by Professor A. Lacassagne, the famous criminologist. He was pronounced sane, and was tried in October 1898 at the Assizes of Ain, charged with the murder of a shepherd in 1895. He tried to convince the court of his madness, and the judge was obliged to ask 'all decent women to withdraw'.

He was found guilty, and carried semi-conscious to the guillotine on 31 December 1898. His severed head was later examined by experts. [*525, 577*]

VAN BUUREN, Clarence Gordon. A 33-year-old South African sex murderer.

Myrna Joy Aken, 18, disappeared from her Durban home on 2 October 1956. She had been seen in the company of a man who also called at her office.

After a search failed her family approached a medium for help. He said the girl would be found 60 miles away, lying in a culvert. He accompanied a search party, and Joy Aken's body was found as predicted at Umtwalumi. She had been shot several times with a .22 calibre weapon; raped, and her body mutilated.

Police searching ground near Joy's home apprehended Clarence van Buuren, who lived opposite. He had a record for theft and forgery, and had had an unhappy domestic life.

Van Buuren said he had met Joy, who was also unhappy at home, and suggested they had a talk and a drink. She declined, so he left her in his car while he went into a bar. He returned an hour later to find that both car and girl had disappeared. Later he found the car parked about 50 yards away, and on opening the door he saw the girl with blood on her face.

Van Buuren said he panicked and got rid of the body by driving to Umtwalumi and throwing it into the culvert. He was sent for trial in February 1957. The fact that he had in his possession a quantity of .22 ammunition of the type which killed Joy weighed heavily against him. He was found guilty, and hanged at Pretoria Central Prison on 10 June 1957. [*521*]

VAN NIEKERK and MARKUS. Murderous pair of ex-convicts who repaid the kindness shown them by South African farmers with death and arson.

Waterval Farm in South Africa's Transvaal was managed by 60-year-old Bill Nelson, whose companion was Tom Denton, a 55-year-old ex-soldier who ran a general store for the native labourers.

Two strangers, 34-year-old Andries Van Niekerk and 24-year-old Edward Markus, arrived at the farm on 1 December 1925. Both were ex-convicts. They impressed the farmers with their hard-luck stories, and received hospitality and work.

Late the next night shots were heard at the farm, and some of the buildings were on fire. In the ruins were found the bodies of Nelson and Denton—both shot through the head.

Van Niekerk and Markus went on the run, but gradually the police net grew tighter as news of various swindles was pieced together. A vital clue turned up, a receipt made out to A. Van Niekerk which was found on a farm where the pair had committed a robbery. With the police closing in, they split up, but Van Niekerk was arrested after a violent struggle, and then Markus was apprehended and proved altogether more docile. He quickly confessed to the murders.

The pair were tried at Pretoria in February 1926. Markus's confession was read out in court—he claimed to be an unwilling accomplice acting under the influence of Van Niekerk, who was mentally unbalanced. For Van Niekerk it was argued that his sanity was questionable, and that he was not responsible for his actions. Both men were found guilty and hanged on 14 April 1926.
[65]

VAN WYK, Stephanus Louis. Glib South African swindler whose smooth talking won him an acquittal on the Jackal Pit murder charge, but did not prevent his conviction for a second murder.

Van Wyk existed on the proceeds of fraud and swindle. In 1929 he was sentenced to 18 months' hard labour on fraud charges. He was convinced that he had been betrayed by his nephew, 28-year-old John Moller, a clerk in the Supreme Court at Bloemfontein, and developed a hatred of him, threatening, 'I'll deal with him when I get out. He'll be sorry he did it.'

Within days of his release in July 1930, Van Wyk visited Moller, and they went off together in the latter's car. The young man did not return home, and was reported missing; Van Wyk meanwhile had vanished. Requests were published for him to come forward, and he decided to help.

However, the police had already recovered Moller's body. A woman living on a farm near Waterral had reported that Van Wyk had knocked her up on the night Moller went missing, asking for a torch. He said his car had broken down. A search was made, and Moller's body was found buried in a jackal pit—his head had been smashed, and there was an injury at the base of the spine. A pick and shovel were retrieved near by, and also a muddy pair of socks bearing the label 'S van W'.

Van Wyk was confronted with this information, and promptly arrested. His story was that he and Moller had gone out in search of £3000, the buried proceeds of a robbery hidden since 1929. Working in the dark, he had accidentally struck Moller with the pick, and Moller fell into the jackal pit, injuring his head in the process. He panicked, and decided to bury the body there.

Van Wyk was tried for murder in Bloemfontein in October 1930 and acquitted. In January 1931 he approached a farmer who intended to sell up his farm Apeldoorn and go to England. Van Wyk made Cyril Tucker an acceptable offer for his farm, but Tucker was killed in his bed by Van Wyk wielding a hammer, and his body was buried in a ploughed field.

The new 'owner' of Tucker's farm then drew attention to himself by trying to pass off a polished farthing as a half-sovereign. The police questioned him, and he related how he and Tucker had argued over a girl, and when the farmer came at him with a gun he struck out in self-defence. Again he panicked and buried the body. Tried in Pretoria for murder a second time, Van Wyk, despite a plea of insanity, was found guilty, and while in the condemned cell confessed to killing Moller. He was hanged on 12 June 1931.
[72, 73]

VAQUIER, Jean-Pierre. Extremely vain Frenchman aged 45 who clumsily poisoned his mistress's husband. (See also *Roland Molineux*.)

While working at the Victoria Hotel, Biarritz, in January 1924, Vaquier met Mabel Theresa Jones, wife of the landlord of the Blue Anchor Hotel at Byfleet in Surrey, who was on holiday following a business failure. She spoke no French and Vaquier spoke no English, but their friendship grew, and when Mrs Jones left France to return home the following month Vaquier followed, and stayed in London.

Mrs Jones visited him there, and on 14 February Vaquier arrived at the Blue Anchor Hotel. He stayed at the hotel, saying he was awaiting payment for an invention.

On 1 March Vaquier went to London, where he visited a chemist's shop and purchased 20 grammes of perchloride of mercury and ·12 of a

Vaquier: The Blue Anchor in 1924

gramme of strychnine, which he said were for wireless experiments. He signed the poison book in the name of Wanker and returned to the Blue Anchor Hotel.

There was a party at the hotel on 28 March, and Mr Jones as usual drank heavily. Next morning he went to the bar parlour, where a bottle of bromo salts was kept, and poured some into a glass of water, exclaiming after he had drunk it, 'My God! They are bitter.' Mrs Jones took the bottle of salts and put it in a kitchen drawer. Mr Jones became ill, and while the doctor was with him Vaquier ran into the kitchen, saying, 'Medicine, doctor, quick!' and took the bottle.

Mr Jones died in agony, and a post-mortem disclosed strychnine poisoning. The bottle of salts was found in the kitchen, empty and washed out,

but traces of strychnine were detected in it.

A statement was taken from Vaquier, who said he loved Mr Jones 'like a brother', and that his death was caused by a 'coward, jealous of my presence here'; he was inclined to blame the potman. Vaquier also made statements to the newspapers which published his photograph. However, a London chemist identified him as a Mr Wanker who had bought strychnine at his shop.

Vaquier was tried for murder at Guildford Assizes in July 1924. He maintained that Mrs Jones's solicitor had asked him to buy the strychnine, and advised him to sign a false name. He was found guilty, and was hanged at Wandsworth Prison on 12 August 1924.

[*1, 32, 133, 159, 332, 364, 421, 422, 423, 485, 492, 555, 649, 710, 712, 757, 906*]

VERA PAGE CASE.

VERA PAGE CASE. Unsolved murder of 11-year-old Vera Page in which there was strong circumstantial evidence against a police suspect.

Vera Page was reported missing from her Notting Hill home on 14 December 1931. Two days later a milk roundsman found her raped and strangled body lying in some shrubs at an Addison Road house near by. Detectives examining the scene concluded that she had been killed elsewhere and had then been dumped. Sir Bernard Spilsbury examined the body; he found that her face was dirty with coal-dust, and that candle grease had been dropped on her clothes. Most significantly, the pathologist found a finger bandage smelling of ammonia, presumably worn by the assailant, and caught in the child's clothing.

Inquiries about Vera Page's movements led to the discovery of her red beret and torn-up swimming certificates in the basement of a Ladbroke Grove house. Over 1,000 persons were interviewed, and one knew Vera Page and recently had worn a finger bandage—Percy Orlando Rush, a 41-year-old married laundry worker.

Rush was like a man seen in the area on 16 December, wheeling a barrow which bore a bundle wrapped in red cloth. When interviewed, Rush was not wearing a bandage, but he plainly had a sore finger, and when the bandage found at the scene was placed on it, the fit was perfect. He also worked in a place where ammonia was commonly used, and in his pocket was a pyjama cord which would have made a highly effective ligature for strangulation.

Rush gave evidence at the Coroner's Inquest on the death of Vera Page. He agreed that he knew the little girl, and was questioned extensively about his sore finger and its bandage. The bandage, he said, was made by his wife, and he wore it to protect a cut from the ammonia and discarded it 2 days before the body was found. He denied that the bandage found by Vera Page's body had dropped from his finger. Although the coroner questioned Rush fully, the jury returned an open verdict of murder against some person or persons unknown.

It is significant that the house next to that where Vera Page's beret was found had an accessible empty cellar—the floor was dusty with coal, as were Vera's face and clothing. It is likely that after the girl's abduction she was violated and murdered in that cellar, and her dead body dumped in the near-by garden. There is little doubt that Rush (who died some 30 years later) was guilty of the child's murder.

[*133, 196, 382, 705*]

'VERONICA' MUTINEERS.

'VERONICA' MUTINEERS. The *Veronica* was a British-owned sailing barque. In mid-October 1902 the vessel sailed from the Gulf of Mexico bound for Montevideo. The captain, Alexander Shaw, was known as a hard taskmaster, and his crew of 12 was described as the 'dregs of the Gulf waterfront'.

The First Officer, Alexander MacLeod, brutally treated a seaman over some minor misdemeanour, and tempers became further frayed when rations had to be cut because of the slow passage.

Two German crewmen, Gustav Rau and Otto Monsson, had smuggled revolvers aboard. They enlisted the help of a Dutchman, Willem Smith, and a 19-year-old lad, Harry Flohr, to take over the ship. On 8 December First Officer MacLeod was beaten up and thrown overboard. Captain Shaw and the Second Officer, Fred Abrahamson, were shot and wounded and held hostage; 2 other seamen were killed.

Rau had the Captain and Second Officer killed, and 2 of the remaining seamen quickly followed. That left the 4 mutineers and the Negro cook, Moses Thomas, as the sole survivors of the original complement of 12. Rau set fire to the *Veronica*, and the 5 seamen took to the ship's boat, leaving the barque to burn. They were picked up by a tramp steamer, and Rau said they were the survivors from the *Veronica*. It was noticed that the Negro cook, Moses Thomas, kept himself apart from the others. In due course he told the true story of what had happened.

The 5 men were taken to Liverpool, where they were met by police. The youth Harry Flohr turned King's Evidence, and he was supported by Moses Thomas. Rau, Monsson and Smith appeared at Liverpool Assizes in May 1903 charged with murder, conspiracy, arson, piracy and theft. The trial was conducted on a charge of murdering Captain Shaw, and an immediate point of interest was the lack of a *corpus delicti* (see also *Camb* and *Onufrejczyk*); apart from the statements of Flohr and Thomas, there was no direct evidence. Nevertheless, all 3 accused were found guilty, a recommendation to mercy being made in the case of Monsson on account of his youth and previous good record. Otto Monsson was duly reprieved, and Gustav Rau and Willem Smith were hanged at Liverpool's Walton Prison on 2 June 1903.

[*1, 558*]

VOIRBO, Pierre.

VOIRBO, Pierre. The apprehension of a 30-year-old tailor for murder: a triumph of detection for French policeman Gustave Macé.

In January 1869, a Paris restaurant-owner with a business in rue Princesse noticed that his well-water was tasting foul. On investigation he found a parcel containing part of a human leg floating in the well. Gustave Macé, later to become chief of the Paris detective force, soon discovered another leg.

Police questioned a tailoress who had lived above the restaurant. Among her visitors was a tailor called Pierre Voirbo for whom she did jobs. He was always helpful, and often fetched water for her from the well. Inquiries revealed that one of Voirbo's acquaintances was a retired craftsman named Désiré Bodasse who had been missing for several weeks. The legs found in the well had been sewn into calico with stitches which clearly showed a professional touch and one of the legs was encased in an old stocking with the letter B worked into it with red cotton. Bodasse's aunt identified it as belonging to her nephew.

Voirbo was questioned, and admitted anxiety over Bodasse's disappearance, but his glibness did not fool Macé, who searched his rooms and found securities belonging to Bodasse which had been soldered into a tin box and suspended in a cask of wine. Convinced that Voirbo had dismembered Bodasse's body on the table in his room, Macé looked at the floor for areas where blood might have collected. He noticed a marked hollow in one part of the tiled floor, and with Voirbo looking on, tipped a jug of water on to the floor—the water collected in the hollow, and the tiles when lifted up were caked with dried blood on the underside.

Voirbo confessed: apparently Bodasse had refused to lend him money, so he killed him. He committed suicide with a concealed razor while awaiting trial.

[235, 366, 534, 553, 575, 634, 970]

VOISIN, Louis. French butcher working in London who disposed of one of his mistresses. He wrote a note to confuse the police, which provided evidence against him because of spelling mistakes. (See also *Thomas Henry Allaway*.)

A road-sweeper tending the gardens at Regent Square, Bloomsbury, on 2 November 1917 noticed a sacking bundle inside the railings. He opened it and found the trunk and arms of a woman wrapped in a bloodstained sheet. A further search turned up another bundle containing the legs but no head or hands. The sheet bore the laundry mark II H, and there was a scrap of paper with the words 'Blodie

Belgium' scrawled on it. The police surgeon thought the remains had been dissected with some skill, perhaps suggesting a butcher.

The mark was traced to a Frenchwoman living near Regent's Park. She was 32-year-old Emilienne Gerard, who had been missing for 3 days. When police went to her rooms they found bloodstains in the kitchen, and on the table was an IOU for £50 signed by Louis Voisin.

Voisin, who was her lover, lived near by. The police found him entertaining another lady friend, Berthe Roche, in his kitchen, and they were taken in for questioning. Voisin was asked to write the words 'Bloody Belgium'. Laboriously he did, with the same spelling errors as in the note. He and Berthe Roche were charged with murdering Mme Gerard.

Voisin paid Mme Gerard's rent, and in return had a key to her rooms. The kitchen of Voisin's own basement rooms was splashed with blood, and one of Mme Gerard's earrings was found caught up in a towel. In the coal cellar was a cask containing her head and hands.

There was a Zeppelin raid on London on the night of 31 October, and it was believed that Mme Gerard went to Voisin's rooms, only to find him with Berthe Roche. They quarrelled, she was killed and Voisin then disposed of her body. The 'Blodie Belgium' note, thought up by Voisin to confuse the authorities, merely pointed to the murderer.

Voisin and Roche were tried at the Old Bailey, but the judge directed that the woman be remanded to be charged as accessory after the fact. Sentence of death was passed on Voisin, who was hanged at Pentonville Prison on 2 March 1918. Berthe Roche, tried later, was sentenced to 7 years' imprisonment, subsequently being certified insane and dying on 22 May 1919.

[47, 133, 236, 492, 501, 575, 585, 712, 757, 873, 921, 964]

VOLLMAN, John. A 20-year-old American who murdered a Canadian girl and was convicted on forensic evidence.

Gaetane Bouchard, 16, disappeared on 13 May 1958 while out shopping after school in Edmundston, a Canadian border town. No one had seen Gaetane since school, although Mr Bouchard learned that his daughter had been dating John Vollman, an American from Madawaska, across the US–Canadian border. He contacted Vollman, who said that they had broken off their relationship as he planned to marry

Voisin: Cellar showing the cask which contained victim's head and hands

another girl.

The police searched for the missing girl, but it was Mr Bouchard himself who found her. He drove to an out-of-town gravel pit now a lover's retreat. There he found his daughter dead from stab wounds in the chest. Police made a vital discovery—two small chips of green paint.

A farmer recalled that he had seen her and a friend offered a lift by the driver of a green Pontiac with a Maine licence plate. Two other witnesses also saw this car, and they were sure Gaetane was sat next to the driver. Gaetane's friend said John Vollman had a reputation for wanting to 'go too far'. He owned a 1952 green Pontiac, and when

police interviewed him he denied having been in Edmundston, but his Pontiac had lost 2 spots of paint, which the chips matched for fit, type and colour. Hair found in the dead girl's clenched fist matched his hair.

Vollman claimed loss of memory resulting from psychic shock. His trial for murder was in Edmundston in November 1958, when he admitted inviting the girl into his car. She refused his advances and they struggled—after that he could remember nothing. He was found guilty and sentenced to death, subsequently commuted to life imprisonment.

[*914*]

VON SCHAUROTH CASE. The 'Murder-by-request' case in South Africa.

Baron Dieter von Schauroth, 36-year-old farmer and man about town, was found dead near Cape Town on 25 March 1961 with 2 gunshot wounds in the head, and he had been robbed, with diamonds strewn around.

Von Schauroth lived with his young wife at the farm he had inherited from his father in South-West Africa. The couple frequented Cape Town's theatres, races and night clubs, and the Baron spent freely. In 1960 he regularly deposited and withdrew large sums of cash at his bank and was thought to be involved in illegal diamond trading. He also took out heavy life insurance.

In the course of his diamond dealing Von Schauroth met 23-year-old Marthinus Rossouw who acted as a go-between and styled himself the Baron's bodyguard. Rossouw was a film fanatic who affected cowboy dress and liked to be called 'Killer'.

After Von Schauroth's death Rossouw was interviewed by the police. Having failed to establish an alibi, he confessed to killing the Baron. He claimed that Von Schauroth, who was unhappy in his marriage, handed him a revolver and a cheque for Rand 2300, for services rendered, and asked him to kill him.

Tried at Cape Town in September 1961, he was found guilty, and sentenced to death. It had been assumed that Von Schauroth had taken out heavy insurance because he realized the dangers of involvement in illicit diamond trading and wanted to ensure benefit for his family. Now, however, despite the trial verdict, one of the insurance companies refused to pay the widow, a decision which she contested in court.

Rossouw was hanged on 20 June 1962, and after protracted litigation Von Schauroth's widow received an ex gratia payment from the insurance companies.
[70, 658]

VONTSTEEN, Franciscus Wynand. South African real estate agent, convicted of murder in a love triangle. Sonjia Raffanti, aged 23, was divorced in July 1960. Two days later, already pregnant, she married François Swanepoel, a police officer. Sonjia worked in Pretoria, where in 1967 she met Franciscus Vontsteen, who became her lover. Vontsteen was possessive and jealous. Realizing she was becoming deeply involved, Sonjia tried unsuccessfully to break off the relationship.

When Swanepoel was posted to duties on South Africa's northern border, Sonjia and Vontsteen lived together. Sonjia became pregnant, and when the child was born her husband accepted it as his own. This spurred Vontsteen to fresh heights of jealousy.

On 3 July 1971 the Swanepoels returned to find the house had been burgled and a Service pistol stolen. Four days later Sonjia claimed to have been accosted on the street by a Bantu brandishing her husband's pistol and threatening to kill him. On the night of 2 August Sonjia was heard shouting, 'There's a kaffir in the house', and her husband was found dead from gunshot wounds.

Police inquiries pointed to Vontsteen when a man came forward saying that Vontsteen had asked his help to kill Swanepoel. The reason given was that he could not live without Sonjia and if they ran off together he knew her policeman husband would track them down.

Vontsteen simply admitted, 'I shot him' when told that Sonjia had confessed. He admitted theft of the pistol and said he entered the house by prearrangement, when he fired 2 shots into Swanepoel's head with Sonjia lying beside him in bed. Vontsteen spoke of their great love, and of their resolve to do away with the man who stood in their way.

At their trial for murder in Pretoria in 1971, Sonjia was sentenced to 15 years in prison, her guilt being thought less than that of Vontsteen, who was sentenced to death and hanged in October 1971.
[256]

W

WADDINGHAM, Dorothea Nancy. A 36-year-old widow and self-styled 'nurse' who murdered for gain.

Nurse Waddingham had no qualifications, and her only training derived from a period spent as a maid at a workhouse infirmary. After her husband died she decided to set up a 'Nursing Home for Aged and Chronic Cases' at Nottingham. She was aided by 39-year-old Ronald Joseph Sullivan.

In January 1935 Nurse Waddingham took into her care 89-year-old Mrs Baguley and her 50-year-old daughter, Ada, who was bedridden. She quickly realized that they needed a high degree of attention. Then Ada Baguley instructed her solicitor that she wished to leave property to Nurse Waddingham in return for a promise that they both would be looked after for the rest of their lives, and on 6 May 1935 she made a will in favour of Nurse Waddingham with Ronald Sullivan as co-beneficiary.

On 12 May old Mrs Baguley died, to be followed four months later by Ada. Cause of death in Ada's case was given as cerebral haemorrhage, but then the Nursing Home physician received a letter supposedly written by Ada Baguley which stated her desire to be cremated, and requested 'my relatives shall not know of my death'. This note was witnessed by Sullivan. A post-mortem was ordered, and traces of morphine were found. Mrs Baguley's body was exhumed, and morphine was again discovered.

Waddingham and Sullivan were tried at Nottingham Assizes in February 1936, charged jointly with the murder of Ada Baguley. Sullivan was released, as there was no direct evidence against him. In the proceedings against Waddingham, conflict of testimony was soon apparent. She said in court that she had administered morphine in accordance with the doctor's instructions, but Dr Manfield was adamant that he had not prescribed morphia for Ada Baguley. It was alleged that the nurse had complained about the constant attention she had to give Ada, but

inferred that it would not be for long.

Nurse Waddingham was found guilty with a strong recommendation to mercy, but was hanged on 16 April 1936 at Winson Green Prison, Birmingham.

[*116, 332, 385, 460, 711, 795, 859, 1001*]

WAGNER, Louis. A 28-year-old German immigrant to the USA who earned a poor living as a fisherman. One night he rowed to a lonely island and brutally killed 2 women in a robbery which netted him 20 dollars.

On the night of 5 March 1873 Wagner stole a boat in Portsmouth, New Hampshire, and rowed 10 miles to the Isles of Shoals. He landed on the snow-covered rocks of Smutty Nose Island, and made for the Hontvet family house. The men were away fishing, leaving their 3 wives alone.

Wagner knew the house well, as he had lived there when the hospitable Norwegians gave him shelter when his own fishing venture failed. Karen Christensen woke up and mistook the intruder for her brother-in-law. Wagner felled her with a heavy blow when her sister Maren, hearing the commotion, entered the room and struggled with him—she shouted to the third girl, Anethe, to fetch help. The girl was paralysed with fear, and could only shout, 'Louis, Louis, Louis', as she recognized the intruder.

Wielding an axe, Wagner smashed Anethe's head and killed Karen, breaking the axe-handle in the process. Maren meanwhile ran off in the darkness, searching for a boat in the hope of fetching help from a neighbouring island. Wagner ransacked the house for money, and then sat down in the kitchen, calmly eating a meal with the women who had been his friends lying dead around him.

Maren Hontvet endured the cold night and at daybreak raised the alarm. Men arrived from nearby Appledore Island, and the Hontvet brothers returned. Wagner had already rowed back, returning to his lodgings in Portsmouth, and was arrested. Mobs collected shouting vengeance, and Marines with fixed bayonets were needed to protect him.

In June 1873 Wagner was tried for murder at Alfred in New England. The chief witness was Maren Hontvet. Four men testified that Wagner had told them he needed money so badly that he would murder for it. A bloodstained shirt was found hidden at Wagner's lodgings, but the most incriminating evidence was the mass of blisters on his hands caused by his prodigious feat of rowing 20 miles in one night. Louis Wagner was found guilty of first-degree murder and sentenced to death. After various stays of execution he was hanged at Thomaston Penitentiary on 25 June 1875.

[729]

WAINWRIGHT, Henry. Brush-manufacturer with a shop in London's East End who murdered his young mistress.

In 1871 Wainwright, a married man, met Harriet Louisa Lane, a 20-year-old milliner's apprentice, whom he set up as his mistress in a house at Mile End. Harriet bore him 2 children, and styled herself Mrs Percy King.

The strain of running a business and 2 homes began to take its toll on Wainwright's purse. He decided to cut Harriet's weekly allowance. She did not approve of this action. He moved to less expensive accommodation in Sidney Square, but he soon became bankrupt. Next day Harriet left Sidney Square carrying only her night clothes in a parcel—she was not seen alive again.

Harriet's disappearance worried her friends, who were looking after the children. Wainwright explained that she had gone to Brighton. Then came a letter from Edward Frieake, who wrote that he and Harriet were going to live on the Continent.

Meanwhile Wainwright had to give up his shop at 215 Whitechapel Road. Almost a year to the day after Harriet's disappearance he asked a former workman, a man named Stokes, to help him move some parcels at the old shop premises. There were two wrapped in American cloth which Wainwright wanted taken to the Borough. Stokes complained of the weight and the disagreeable smell. After walking a short part of the way Wainwright said he would fetch a cab. While he was away Stokes looked into one of the parcels, and saw a severed arm and a decomposing head. He said nothing when Wainwright returned with a cab and loaded up the two packages. Stokes decided to follow on foot, tracking the cab to a spot near London Bridge. Wainwright was caught in the act of taking the parcels which contained Harriet Lane into a house occupied by his brother Thomas.

Wainwright had taken her into his shop, where he killed her and then buried her beneath the floor. With the help of Thomas, alias Frieake, he returned nearly a year later and having exhumed the body cut it into fragments and made them into parcels for easy disposal. Both brothers were tried at the Old Bailey in November 1875. Thomas was sentenced to 7 years in prison. Henry was executed at Newgate on 21 December 1875, remarking to the spectators assembled at the scaffold, 'Come to see a man die, have you, you curs?' Stokes was awarded £30 for his part in Wainwright's capture, and £1200 was collected for the hanged man's widow and children.

[1, 21, 111, 126, 141, 442, 1006]

WAINEWRIGHT CASE. Thomas Griffiths Wainewright, who turned to murder for gain, became a compulsive poisoner and died a convict, aged 58, in Van Diemen's Land. He has been compared with *Lacenaire*, another man of letters who became a murderer.

Wainewright was brought up by his grandfather, an editor of *The Monthly Review*. At 18, he joined the army and became a dandy. When he tired of this he took up writing and painting, becoming acquainted with De Quincey, Hazlitt and Lamb. He married Eliza Frances Ward in 1821, but was soon in financial difficulties owing to his extravagant life-style. By forging the signatures of the trustees who controlled his stock, he acquired £2000, which did very little to help his difficulties.

In 1829 Wainewright was suspected of poisoning his grandfather with strychnine: the old man died of a fit, and his grandson inherited his wealth, which nearly all went to his creditors. Wainewright could not keep up with his debts, and his mother-in-law, Mrs Abercromby, came to live with him and his wife, bringing her 2 daughters, Madeleine and Helen.

Mrs Abercromby died in 1830, probably poisoned by Wainewright. Then he insured his 20-year-old sister-in-law Helen for £18000. The interest in these policies was held by Madeleine, who assigned it to Wainewright. In December 1830 Helen died and Wainewright asked Madeleine to collect the insurance money. The insurance companies were suspicious, and Wainewright sued them for payment. The case dragged on for 5 years, and the decision went against Wainewright, who fled to France in 1831, where he poisoned the father of a girl he knew, having first insured his life for £3000.

Wainewright returned to England in 1837, but was recognized as 'Wainewright the Poisoner'. He was put on trial, but only for forgery, for which he was sentenced to transportation for life. He died in Tasmania, having said that he had poisoned Helen Abercromby because her thick ankles offended him.

[210, 533, 578, 703, 826, 828]

WAITE, Dr Arthur Warren. A 28-year-old New York dentist convicted of double murder in which he admitted using bacteria. (See *Henri Girard*.)

Waite qualified as a dental surgeon at Glasgow University, and worked in South Africa. In 1915 he married the daughter of John Peck, a millionaire. Dr Waite and his wife had a fashionable house on Riverside Drive. In addition to his dental practice Waite researched on germ culture at Cornell Medical School.

Mrs Peck visited her daughter and son-in-law at Christmas 1915. She was taken ill, and died on 30 January 1916 of alleged kidney disease. Distressed by his wife's sudden death, Mr Peck went to stay with them in February. He died on 12 March, also of alleged kidney disease, leaving his children over 1 000 000 dollars. Waite made arrangements for Mr Peck's body to be cremated, but an autopsy was first carried out, and arsenic was found.

Police found Waite unconscious on 23 March from a drug overdose, and on recovery he was charged with double murder. Despite pleading not guilty, he told the court how he poisoned his mother-in-law by implanting diphtheria and influenza germs in her food. He employed similar methods with his father-in-law, with an added refinement: 'Once I gave him a nasal spray backed with tuberculosis bacteria.' He also used chlorine gas, and tried to induce pneumonia by wetting the old man's bed sheets, the latter finally succumbing to 18 grains of arsenic. Asked why he wanted to kill his in-laws, he replied simply, 'For their money.'

He was found guilty, appeals on the grounds of insanity were rejected, and he was electrocuted on 24 May 1917 at Sing Sing prison.

[558, 722, 862, 887]

Walker: Murderer with many aliases

WALKER, G. Daniel. Man of 90 aliases who murdered an advertising executive at a California ranch and played cat-and-mouse with his victim's girl-friend.

Hope Masters, who lived in Beverly Hills, had separated from her husband and acquired a reputation as a rich socialite. In December 1972 she met Bill Ashlock, an advertising executive, whom she planned to marry. In February 1973 the couple spent the weekend at a ranch-house in Springfield owned by her parents. While there, Ashlock arranged for a photographer to call to take some publicity pictures in connection with his work.

The photographer arrived as expected and said his name was Taylor Wright. During the night of 24 February violence occurred at the ranch. Hope Masters was awakened by an armed intruder, and when she shouted for Ashlock was told that he was dead. The man assaulted her and bound her hand and foot, at which point she identified him as Taylor Wright. She later recalled an extraordinary sequence of events in which he treated her gently but then threatened to kill her. Eventually Taylor Wright took her home to her parents in Beverly Hills and told them how he had arrived at the ranch and discovered Hope tied up and Ashlock dead. 'The man who did this to your daughter has to be insane,' he told them. While Wright was out of the house the police were alerted and Hope Masters recounted what had happened. She was arrested and charged with murder.

Taylor Wright maintained contact by telephone and by sending tape-recorded messages through the mail. The police began to intensify their search for him and he was arrested in a Hollywood motel. His real identity was G. Daniel Walker, and it became apparent he had taken the name Taylor Wright after beating up and robbing a jewellery salesman of that name. A gun in his car proved to be the weapon used to kill Ashlock.

In November Walker and Hope Masters were put on trial, all charges against Mrs Masters being quickly dropped. The trial lasted 2 months, and the court heard details of Walker's fantasy world. The transcript of one of the tape-recordings he sent to Hope Masters ran to 51 pages and declared 'My intent and purposes within the United States are definitely not to be known.' The police were smarter than he believed, for his record of convictions for armed robbery and attempted murder was well known. At the time Ashlock was murdered Walker was on the run from prison. He was convicted of first-degree murder and sentenced to life imprisonment.
[51]

WALTON CASE. Unsolved murder which occurred on St Valentine's Day 1945 when the mutilated body of Charles Walton was found at Lower Quinton in Warwickshire. The elderly recluse had been pinned to the ground with a pitchfork driven through his neck, and the sign of the cross had been crudely scratched across his chest. The suggestion that the murder involved witchcraft soon gained ground.

The victim, aged 74, preferred his own company and was regarded by villagers as an odd sort of person. He worked in the fields, mostly on labouring tasks for local farmers, and liked to talk to the birds. He had lived his entire life in Lower Quinton and was rumoured to have money. On 14 February 1945 he was seen at around midday trimming hedges, and was reported missing by his niece when he did not return home at nightfall. A search-party found Walton's body in a field close to the spot where he had last been seen working.

The combined strength of two policemen was required to release Charles Walton from the pitchfork which stapled him to the ground. Assistance from Scotland Yard was called for, and Detective Superintendent Fabian was despatched to Lower Quinton. One of his first moves was to interview prisoners of war held at nearby Long Marston, but one or two promising leads turned to nothing. Fabian was even less successful in prising any useful

Walton Case: Albert Potter – murder suspect

information from the tight-lipped villagers. 'Silence fell like a physical blow,' when he entered the local pub, he said.

Despite taking 4,000 statements, employing soldiers with metal-detectors to scour the countryside and using the Royal Air Force to take aerial photographs, Fabian failed to establish a breakthrough in his investigation. The tales of witchcraft in the district centred on a phantom black dog which changed into a headless woman, and it appeared there was a precedent for murder by pitchfork. In 1875, in the nearby village of Long Compton, an elderly woman was killed with a pitchfork. The victim was alleged to be a witch, and such ritual killings were rooted in the idea of blood-letting which replenished the fertility of the earth. Indeed, a woman in Birmingham told a newspaper that Walton had been the subject of a blood sacrifice, and claimed that several adherents of an ancient cult lived in the neighbourhood.

Officially, the death of Charles Walton remains unsolved. In his book *Perfect Murder* (published in 1987) Bernard Taylor claimed that Fabian knew the identity of the murderer but was unable to secure strong enough evidence to make an arrest. Walton was allegedly killed by Albert Potter, the farmer who employed him to trim hedges. Potter was in debt, and had borrowed money from Walton who was pressing for repayment. The farmer decided to dispose of his creditor and disguised the killing with hints of witchcraft.
[625, 901]

WALLACE CASE. Celebrated English murder case, in which mild-mannered William Herbert Wallace was convicted of murdering his wife, and had the verdict quashed by the Court of Appeal. Wallace, aged 52, was a Prudential Assurance agent who lived quietly with his wife Julia in Liverpool.

He was due to play chess at the Liverpool Central Chess Club on 19 January 1931. That evening, about 7.30 p.m., before Wallace arrived, a telephone call was made to the café where the club met. The caller, who gave his name as R. M. Qualtrough, asked the club captain to tell Wallace that he wanted 'to see him particularly. Will you ask him to call round to my place tomorrow evening at 7.30?' The address he gave was 25 Menlove Gardens East in Mossley Hill.

Wallace knew neither Qualtrough nor Menlove Gardens East. The next evening he left home in search of the address. He could not find it, and after nearly two hours searching returned home, knowing that the address did not exist.

On reaching home Wallace found his wife dead in the parlour, her head savagely smashed. A poker was missing, and Wallace's mackintosh—heavily stained with blood, and partly burned—lay under the body. Wallace was afterwards criticized for his apparent calm, for he carefully checked the cash-box, and thought that £4 was missing.

The police were called, and established that there was no break-in. When the Qualtrough story emerged it was assumed this was a ruse to get Wallace out, but then the police arrested Wallace on 2 February on a charge of wife-murder.

He was tried at Liverpool Assizes in April 1931. Evidence given about the time of Julia Wallace's death was critical. The pathologist put death at a time before 6.00 p.m. Against this was the testimony of a teenaged milk boy who stated that he had seen Mrs Wallace alive at 6.30 p.m. The prosecution maintained that Wallace had contrived the mysterious Qualtrough 'phone call and, stripping off his clothes, had used the mackintosh as a kind of overall to keep off the blood.

Wallace Case: A note to his counsel at the trial

Despite the judge's summing up in Wallace's favour, the jury found him guilty, and he was sentenced to death. His appeal was heard on 18 May before the Lord Chief Justice, and his counsel's contention that the trial verdict was not supported by the evidence caused the conviction to be quashed, in a decision which made legal history in Britain and confirmed Wallace's innocence.

He returned to work, but was plagued by malicious gossip and ill health. He died of a kidney disorder on 26 February 1933.

In 1981, in a Liverpool Radio City programme devoted to the Wallace case, Richard Gordon Parry was named as the murderer. During the early hours of the morning after the killing, Parry, an insurance agent, took his car to an all-night garage and gave instructions for it to be cleaned inside and out. There were bloodstains in the car and a bloodied glove which Parry seized from the garage attendant, saying, 'If the police found that, it would hang me.'

This incident was reported to the police, who questioned Parry and searched his home. His alibi for the night in question was that he was with his girl friend. Inquiries were not pressed against Parry and he retired to Wales, where he died in the 1970s.
[9, 78, 124, 129, 184, 237, 252, 348, 467, 482, 508, 589, 611, 613, 670, 676, 792, 797, 850, 939, 978, 1018]

WATSON, John Selby. Victorian murder in which a scholarly cleric killed his wife.

Watson studied classics, and was ordained in 1839. After a curacy in Somerset he moved to London, where in 1844 he secured the headship of a grammar school. The following year he married Anne Armstrong. He became a successful scholar, publishing several translations.

By 1870 the numbers of pupils had dropped, and the Governors gave Watson notice. At the age of 66 he had no prospects, and he was a depressed, beaten man.

On 8 October 1871 Ellen Pyne, the Watsons' servant, returned after her day off to be told that her mistress was 'gone out of town'. Watson told Ellen, 'If you find anything wrong with me in the morning, go for Dr Rugg.' Later he was found lying unconscious. He had left a note for Ellen, enclosing her wages, and a letter addressed 'For the Surgeon' in which he stated, 'I have killed my wife in a fit of rage to which she provoked me.'

Mrs Watson's body with head wounds was found in a locked bedroom—Watson himself had swallowed some prussic acid, but he was revived.

In his dressing table was a pistol with a broken, bloodstained butt which had been used to kill his wife.

Watson was tried at the Old Bailey in January 1872. The defence tried to prove he was insane, though he had left detailed letters concerning his literary work before attempting to take his own life.

He was found guilty with a recommendation to mercy, and reprieved. He served 12 years at Parkhurst Prison, where he died aged 80 on 6 July 1884.
[551, 1016]

WEBSTER, John White. Murder involving medical college academics.

Webster was a highly respected Professor of Chemistry and Mineralogy at Massachusetts Medical College in the 1840s. To finance his extravagant life-style he borrowed money from various sources, including miserly Dr George Parkman.

Parkman had given up medicine to engage in real-estate dealings, and had made himself a wealthy man. He lent money to Webster, but grew resentful at not being repaid quickly. He shadowed the Professor, making remarks such as, 'The world does not owe you a living', often in front of other people. When he found that Webster had sold his mineral collection, and had not repaid him, he became furious.

On 23 November 1849 he went to Webster's college rooms and demanded his money. Webster said he did not have it, and Parkman replied, 'I got you your Professorship and I'll get you out of it.' Webster took up a piece of kindling wood and hit Parkman over the head, causing him to collapse. Webster found he was dead, and dragged the body into an adjoining room, where he cut it up and incinerated the pieces in his assay oven.

Parkman's disappearance caused the College authorities to offer $3000 reward to his presumed abductors. A college janitor, Ephraim Littlefield, had seen Parkman enter Webster's rooms. He tried the handle of Professor Webster's private vault—which was locked—and felt the wall behind his assay oven, which was extremely hot.

That night Littlefield took some bricks out of the vault, and saw part of Dr Parkman's leg. Various pieces of a human body were found, but most incriminating were Parkman's teeth, still intact in Webster's oven. Webster tried to commit suicide after arrest, but his trial at Boston opened on 19 March 1850. Sixty thousand people travelled

SPECIAL
NOTICE!

GEO. PARKMAN, M. D.,

A well known, and highly respect- ed citizen of BOSTON, left his House in WALNUT STREET, to meet an engagement of business, on Friday last, November 23d, between 12 and 1 o'clock, P. M., and was seen in the Southerly part of the City, in and near Washington Street, in conversation with some persons, at about 5 o'clock of the afternoon, of the same day.

Any person who can give infor- mation relative to him, that may lead to his discovery, is earnestly requested to communicate the same immediately to the City Marshall, for which he shall be liberally rewarded.

BOSTON, Nov. 25th, 1849.

From the Congress Printing House,(Farwell & Co.) 32 Congress St.

Webster, J. W. 'City Marshall' notice

to see him. He was found guilty, and sentenced to death, being hanged on 30 August 1850.
[2, 57, 102, 478, 575, 594, 661, 724, 729, 893, 912, 933]

WEBSTER, Kate. A 30-year-old Irish woman, alias Catherine Lawler, who progressed from robbing lodging-houses to murdering her employer. She impersonated the dead woman, whose body she had dismembered and part-boiled before disposal.

A man on 5 March 1879 noticed a wooden box lying near the edge of the Thames at Hammersmith. He opened it, and found it packed with bits of boiled human flesh. At first it was thought a practical joke by medical students, but it was found that the remains were those of a Mrs Thomas who lived alone in a cottage at Richmond. On 9 March, a woman saying she was Mrs Thomas was selling the contents of the Richmond house. She was Kate Webster, born in Ireland and twice married, who was Mrs Thomas's servant.

When Kate Webster was sacked she killed her employer with a cleaver. Then she cut up the body and boiled pieces of it in the steam boiler at the cottage. The head was never found, and it was subsequently alleged that Kate Webster kept it in a black bag which she guarded jealously. It was also said that she sold some jars of human dripping to a near-by public house.

She was tried at the Old Bailey in July 1879, found guilty and before being hanged at Wandsworth Prison on 29 July confessed.
[1, 21, 87, 290, 322, 606, 676, 947, 1006]

WEIDMANN, Eugen. Cold-blooded killer born at Frankfurt-on-Main on 5 February 1908 who, with accomplices, robbed and murdered 6 people in and around Paris in as many months. Weidmann had a special aptitude for languages, and easily passed himself off as French or English. After serving 5 years in a German prison for currency offences he went to Paris in the 1930s.

The body of Joseph Couffy, a middle-aged private hire car driver, was found beside the Paris-Orléans road on 8 September 1937, with bullet wounds in the back of the neck.

Five weeks later an abandoned car was found in the Paris suburb of Neuilly-sur-Seine, containing a body. Under a canvas cover was Roger Le Blond, a young businessman. He too had been shot through the back of the neck and robbed. On 20 November Saint-Cloud estate agent Raymond

Lesobre disappeared. He had driven off with an Englishman to view a property. Police found Lesobre dead on the cellar steps, also shot through the back of the neck and robbed.

A man called Siegfried Sauerbrey, who lived near Saint-Cloud, was suspected. On 8 December police called on him and were met by a man calling himself Karrer, who fired his gun, but missed them at point-blank range. He was overpowered. His real name was Eugen Weidmann, alias Sauerbrey, and cars belonging to the the murder victims Couffy and Lesobre were found at his house, La Voulzie.

Weidmann confessed to murder, implicating another criminal, Roger Million, and two others. He said they planned to kidnap wealthy people and demand heavy ransoms. He admitted killing Couffy, Le Blond and Lesobre; also an American girl called Jean de Koven who disappeared in Paris in spring 1937. He also confessed to murdering a woman named Jeannine Keller, whom he strangled in woods near Fontainebleau and buried in a nearby cave. The corpses of both women were found.

Weidmann and his 3 accomplices were tried for murder. He and Million were condemned to death. The other two were acquitted. Million was reprieved, and Weidmann guillotined on 18 May 1939.
[60, 387, 435, 499]

WHITEWAY, Alfred Charles. A 22-year-old building labourer, convicted rapist and murderer.

Teenagers Barbara Songhurst and Christine Reed did not return to their homes in Teddington on 31 May 1953. They had been out together on their bicycles, and had been seen between 11.00 and 11.30 p.m. on the Thames towpath, cycling in a homeward direction.

Next morning Barbara's body was found in the river near Richmond. She had been severely battered about the head, stabbed in the back and raped. Five days later the other girl's body was found in the river—she had been similarly attacked.

At the end of June Alfred Whiteway was detained for assaulting 2 women, one of whom had been raped, on Oxshott Heath in Surrey. Whiteway was married, but owing to housing difficulties the couple lived apart, he with his parents at Teddington and his wife with her parents at Kingston. He claimed that he was with his wife at the time of the murder. An axe which Whiteway had hidden under the seat of the patrol car in which he travelled remained undetected

Weidmann: The cave at Fontainebleau

until an officer cleaning the vehicle found it. When its significance was realized it was matched with the head wounds.

Told that one of his shoes had blood on it, and confronted with the axe, Whiteway signed a statement in which he admitted the towpath killings.

Charged with the murder of Barbara Songhurst, Whiteway was tried at the Old Bailey in October 1953. He pleaded not guilty, denying that he had made a confession. His counsel suggested the statement was a piece of fiction manufactured by the police—an allegation which was hotly denied. He was found guilty and hanged at Wandsworth Prison on 22 December 1953.
[*306, 495, 601, 605, 923, 962*]

WHITMAN, Charles. Mass murderer, 25 years old, who shot 46 people from the 300-foot-high observation tower of the Austin Campus of the University of Texas.

Whitman became unstable when, after years of ill-treatment, his mother left his father in March 1966. He began acting strangely, and this was put down to the strain of intensive studying. He complained of headaches and exhibited sudden bouts of violent temper.

On 31 July Whitman typed a note in which he declared, 'I am prepared to die. After my death, I wish an autopsy on me to be performed to see if there is any mental disorder.'

Late that night Whitman stabbed, then shot, his mother. Then he stabbed his wife, and in a note wrote, '12.00 a.m.—Mother already dead, 3 o'clock—both dead.' There followed further outpourings against his father, and the cryptic finale, 'Life is not worth living.'

On 1 August, armed with several pistols, and ammunition, Whitman climbed the observation tower, taking with him sandwiches, peanuts, toilet paper and a transistor radio. He killed the receptionist on the 27th floor with a crushing blow from his rifle butt, and then barricaded the stairway. Two people climbing up to the observation level were shot down in their tracks.

At 11.40 a.m. Whitman began shooting at students; he was an expert ex-Marine marksman. In the next 96 minutes he shot and killed 16 persons and wounded 30 others. Police failed to dislodge him, as did an attempt from a low-flying aircraft. Eventually, police decided on a charge over the barricaded stairway and in the fusillade, Whitman was shot to pieces.

An autopsy showed Whitman had a tumour in the hypothalamus region of the brain. Doctors doubted whether his behaviour was caused by this. [*693, 883*]

WIGWAM MURDER. See SANGRET, August

WIJEDASA GANG. The Havelock racecourse in Colombo, Ceylon (now Sri Lanka) was the scene for the Ceylon Turf Club's first meeting of the year on 29 January 1949. Large sums of money were taken in the betting offices and stored over the weekend in the club safe. It was the routine practice on Monday mornings to transport the cash to the bank. A hire car was used, and the regular driver was John Silva.

On Monday 31 January the car arrived as usual, but Silva was not at the wheel. A strange driver was in charge of the vehicle but he had an armed police escort in accordance with normal practice. The Turf Club cashier loaded the car with trunks containing £40,000, and satchels of coins were put into the Turf Club's van which was to follow the hire car to the bank.

What should have been an uneventful drive to the bank was distinguished by a fast getaway on the part of the hired car, which left the accompanying van far behind. The car did not take its regular route, and on the way it was ambushed by armed men and hijacked with its valuable cargo. It was later discovered that the regular driver had been abducted before the robbery by 2 men his firm had undertaken to drive to Puttalam, about 80 miles from Colombo.

A search was made for John Silva, who had been seen in Puttalam the day before the Turf Club robbery with 2 men whose aim appeared to be to make him insensible with drink. The police at Puttalam received a postcard from an anonymous sender telling them that Silva had stolen the money and gone into hiding. Silva was found by chance in thick jungle country where he had been taken by his abductors. He had been securely tied to a tree with coils of rope around his hands, legs and body. A gas mask had been placed over his head and the tube through which air was drawn had been blocked off. Silva had in consequence died of suffocation.

What had begun as a robbery ended with murder, the investigation of which achieved a speedy breakthrough when one of the robbers confessed in the hope of obtaining leniency. He made a full statement, implicating seven other men. Three of these were discharged at a preliminary hearing, and five were sent for trial. They claimed that the intention behind sending the postcard was to alert the authorities to Silva's whereabouts.

The trial of the 5 men took place before the Colombo Assizes in January 1950 and lasted for 25 days. The jury found one of the accused not guilty, but Wijedasa, Seneviratne, Premalal and Munasinghe were found guilty of conspiracy to commit robbery and murder. All four were executed at Welikade prison.

[20, 854]

WILKINS, Dr Walter Keene. Elderly doctor who murdered his wife, and then took his own life.

The Wilkinses lived at Long Beach, Long Island. On 27 February 1919 the couple returned home by train from New York City and, the doctor said, surprised a gang of house-breakers who beat and robbed them. When the police arrived Dr Wilkins was found in the driveway tending his wife.

Mrs Wilkins died of her injuries next day—she had been hit on the head 17 times. The doctor's clothes were torn, and his hat was badly dented. A piece of lead piping and a broken hammer repaired with wire were found near by.

Mrs Wilkins's will—dated 1903, when she was previously married—tied up all her assets, leaving practically nothing to the doctor. On 16 March Dr Wilkins disappeared, and afterwards his attorney said that he had been given a document purporting to be Mrs Wilkins's will, dated 1915. The paper, found by Dr Wilkins in the attic, differed from the earlier will in that it left him 2 properties and other bequests, but it was unwitnessed, and therefore invalid.

Blood splashes had been found on the underside of Wilkins's hat-brim, and the wire binding the murder weapon was the same as picture wire used in his house. Mrs Wilkins's velvet hat, her gloves and false teeth were all found undamaged inside the house. On 18 March Dr Wilkins reappeared in Baltimore, and he was promptly charged with his wife's murder.

The 67-year-old doctor was tried in June; his fingerprints had been found on both the piece of lead piping and on the broken hammer, and the tie-pin he alleged had been stolen was in his overcoat pocket. He was found guilty of first-degree murder, but managed to hang himself at Mineola Jail.

[776]

WILLIAMS, John. The 'Hooded Man', whose real name was George MacKay, and who murdered a policeman.

On the evening of 9 October 1912 Countess Sztaray, who lived in South Cliff Avenue, Eastbourne, was driven in a brougham to an appointment. As they left the driver spotted a man crouching on the canopy over the front door. Assuming the house was about to be burgled, the Countess telephoned the police.

Ten minutes later Inspector Arthur Walls arrived and told the man to come down, but there were 2 shots. Walls fell dead, and the intruder made off.

A man named Edgar Power walked into Eastbourne police station the next day and said he knew the murderer, one John Williams, and also his brother and girl-friend, Florence Seymour. He said Williams had sent a postcard to his brother (who lived in London) requesting money urgently and saying, 'If you would save my life, come here at once.'

The police arrested Williams in London. He was charged, and was taken to Eastbourne, where he arrived with his head hooded. None of the witnesses to the shooting of Inspector Walls picked him out in an identity parade.

The arrests of Edgar Power and Florence Seymour followed when they were found searching in the shingle on the beach. A gun was found which could have fired the bullets. Florence Seymour, who was pregnant by Williams, said that on the night of the murder she sat on a sea-front seat while Williams went off, returning later without his hat. After the Inspector's murder on the following day Williams sent off the postcard to his brother and buried his revolver.

Williams was tried at Lewes Assizes in December 1912. Williams, a known burglar, admitted reconnoitring the area. In his favour it was agreed that the gun found was of a common type, and could not be definitely linked to the murder. The jury nevertheless found Williams guilty and he was sentenced to death.

Florence gave birth to her child, and her request to marry Williams was refused. The day before he was executed, 29-year-old Williams saw Florence and the baby. He pressed a piece of prison bread into the baby's hand, saying, 'Now nobody can ever say that your father has never given you anything.'

[88, 118, 420, 421, 422, 423, 1006, 1007]

WILLIAMS, Wayne B. When 23-year-old free-lance photographer Wayne Williams was arrested in May 1981 the series of child murders in Atlanta, which had claimed 28 victims, ceased. The first murder occurred in July 1979, and the toll of young black male victims increased. Atlanta, and especially its South Side, was plunged into fear.

The murder victims had been killed by what was described as gentle asphyxiation. The bodies were otherwise unmarked, and, although they were found either nude or partially clothed, there were no indications of sexual abuse. Ranging in age from between 7 and 28, the victims came from mostly poor families, and could reasonably be termed 'streetwise'. A homosexual motive was the most popular, but theories abounded, including suggestions that a white racist was at work.

The police investigation at the height of the scare was costing the City of Atlanta a quarter of a million dollars a month. The killings became a nationwide scandal, and President Reagan announced a grant of $1.5 million to boost the investigation. In addition, numerous celebrities, including Frank Sinatra, Burt Reynolds and Sammy Davis Jr, contributed to fund-raising events in the effort to trace the killer. The police dealt with thousands of inquiries and interviewed hundreds of people offering information but still the murders continued. 'It's like a disease going around', was one resident's description. Millions of black Americans wore green ribbons as a protest at the lack of progress made in solving the murders.

Finally, in May 1981, Wayne Williams was arrested after he was seen in the early hours near the Chattahoochee river after a loud splash had been heard. Two days later the body of Nathaniel Carter was retrieved from the river, and his murder was added to the list, which included 5 other victims found in the river. From the time Williams was arrested, the murders (which had averaged over 1 a month for 2 years) stopped. For most people in Atlanta, that was sufficiently damning evidence.

Williams was put on trial for 2 murders. He was convicted largely on the strength of forensic evidence, which maintained that carpet fibres and dog hairs found on one of the victims matched fibres and hairs in the suspect's home. Williams maintained his innocence throughout the 9-week trial, but besides the forensic evidence, the most telling factor was that in the 8 weeks since his arrest there had been no more murders. In February 1982 he was found guilty on both counts of murder and sentenced to 2 life terms of imprisonment. Williams appealed against the verdict on the grounds that the evidence was circumstantial.

Since his conviction, considerable disquiet has been expressed about the Williams case. Allegations

have been made about suppressed evidence, particularly a secret file on the child-killings linking them to Ku Klux Klan activities. There have been reports that vital tape-recordings proving the link were destroyed, and that police initiated a cover-up because they feared racial violence if the information became public knowledge. In February 1986 Williams's lawyers won the right to take depositions regarding statements made by Klansmen. A group of opponents to the trial verdict has argued that the case should be reopened because of a different kind of alleged cover-up. This concerned the unpublicized series of 38 murders in Atlanta in which the victims were all female, and which overlapped the series for which Williams was convicted. Williams's continued fight to reopen the investigation gained a strong advocate when a former assistant to the Atlanta police chief joined his campaign, arguing that the original forensic evidence was faulty. [39, 228, 996]

WILSON, Howard. This former policeman turned bank-robber was sentenced to life imprisonment in 1970 for the Glasgow Police Murders. On 30 December 1969 three armed men robbed the Clydesdale Bank in Bridge Street, Linwood. They locked bank staff in the premises and made their escape with over £14,000, part of their haul consisting of coins which were in several canvas bags, a metal box and a suitcase.

The robbers drove to Howard Wilson's flat in Allison Street, Glasgow, which was situated close to Southern Police Division's HQ. While they were struggling to transfer the heavy load of coins from their car the robbers were observed by Inspector Andrew Hyslop. He recognized Wilson as a former policeman, and decided that the incident required further investigation. Having called for assistance, Hyslop, supported by a sergeant and three constables, went up to the flat. They saw a suitcase full of notes and coins, and were unobstructed when requesting a search of the premises.

As the search began Wilson drew a gun and fired at Hyslop, wounding him in the face. He also shot two other officers, killing one instantly and mortally injuring the other. One of the remaining officers managed to overpower the armed man while his accomplices either fled or stood by helpless. In due course Wilson took full responsibility for the shooting, and thereby raised an interesting point of Scots law, that of acting in concert or to a common purpose. The 3 men shared common purpose in robbing the bank, and all knew that one of their number possessed a gun. If the gun had been fired on that occasion each man would have been judged guilty, as they had acted in concert. In the circumstances which led to the fatal shooting of the two policemen at Wilson's flat the common purpose did not apply as the outcome was not part of a plan but a unilateral action on the part of one of the number.

In February 1970, in the High Court at Edinburgh, Wilson—who had served for 10 years in the Glasgow Police—was convicted of murder and sentenced to life imprisonment. His associates were convicted only of robbery and were given appropriate terms of imprisonment.

[*64, 586*]

WOOD, Robert. See CAMDEN TOWN MURDER

WOO DAK SAN. Strange case in which a Chinese convicted of murder called on an omen to save him from hanging. On 25 August 1925 in Silver City, New Mexico, an elderly general-store owner named Yee Fong was found murdered. He had been savagely beaten about the head with an axe which was found in his living-quarters but in a macabre gesture the murderer had driven a butcher's knife through his victim's head, pinning it to the floor. This act had been carried out with such force that it required the strength of two police officers to pull it out. The elderly store-owner was known not to trust banks, and it was thought that robbery was the motive for his murder.

Within a few days, acting on information received from the Chinese community, police interviewed Woo Dak San, a would-be business-man in Silver City. He was picked up en route to El Paso, and found to have money hidden in his shoes. He admitted knowing Yee Fong, who he said sold him drugs, but he denied any knowledge of the murder. Significantly, though, he referred to the Chinese belief that if the victim's optic nerve were cut he would not see who attacked him.

Realizing that Woo Dak San was a drug-addict, the police tried to do a deal with him whereby they would help him satisfy his craving in return for a confession. In due course a doctor gave him a shot of morphine and he confessed to the murder, in which he claimed he had been helped by an accomplice. While he was in custody rumour abounded, and it was alleged that he had called on the tong of which he was a member to eliminate all the Chinese in Silver City.

At his trial for murder Woo Dak San was asked why he had confessed. He answered quite simply, 'I made it for dope.' His defence attorney argued that

the confession had been obtained illegally and had no relevance. When the jury returned to deliver its verdict a bird flew into the courtroom and caused a commotion by fluttering against the windows in its efforts to escape. Woo Dak San appeared to be amused by this incident, and informed his guards that it was an omen which would ensure he would never be hanged.

In the event the jury was hopelessly split and could not reach a verdict. A new trial was called, and on 6 March 1926 Woo Dak San was convicted of murder and sentenced to death by hanging. His appeals were dismissed, but public sentiment prevailed when it was alleged that the Chinese had been offered the alternative punishment of a life sentence if he donated his eyes to medical research. Howls of protest followed, and in March 1932 his death sentence was commuted to life imprisonment. In 1940 Woo Dak San—ostensibly saved from the gallows by the intervention of a bird—was pardoned after serving 14 years in prison.

[*278*]

WOOLDRIDGE, Charles Thomas. A trooper in the Royal Horse Guards whose execution for murder in 1896 led Oscar Wilde to dedicate *The Ballad of Reading Gaol* to his memory.

The 30-year-old soldier was living in barracks at Regent's Park, London, while his wife—whom he had recently married—lived in the village of Clewar, near Windsor. Wooldridge visited her when he could get leave, but in March 1896 their relationship was sufficiently strained for his wife to be using her maiden name. During an argument provoked by Wooldridge's jealous feelings he struck her, and, although he bitterly regretted his action it sowed the seeds of future violence.

On 27 March Ellen Wooldridge gave her husband a document requiring his signature whereby he undertook not to molest her. When she failed to appear at the Regent's Park barracks as arranged, Wooldridge stormed out of his quarters, telling the sentry, 'I have to go to Windsor tonight. I must go. I'm going to do some damage.'

He turned up at the house in Windsor, and screams in the street attracted the attention of neighbours. They saw Wooldridge standing over the body of his wife: he had cut her throat. He told the policeman called to the scene, 'Take me! I have killed my wife.'

Attempts by his counsel to reduce the charge of murder to one of manslaughter on the grounds of his wife's infidelity failed. After an absence of only 2 minutes, the trial jury found him guilty. Three weeks after being sentenced he was hanged at Reading Gaol on 7 July 1896. He was said by an eyewitness to have died like a soldier on parade.

Trooper Wooldridge passed into obscurity, save for the dedication to his memory of Oscar Wilde's famous ballad:

> In Reading gaol by Reading town
>   There is a pit of shame,
> And in it lies a wretched man
>   Eaten by teeth of flame.
> In a burning winding-sheet he lies
>   And his grave has got no name.
>
> And there, till Christ call forth the dead,
>   In silence let him lie:
> No need to waste the foolish tear,
>   Or heave the windy sigh:
> The man had killed the thing he loved,
>   And so he had to die.
>
> And all men kill the thing they love,
>   By all let this be heard,
> Some do it with a bitter look,
>   Some with a flattering word,
> The coward does it with a kiss,
>   The brave man with a sword!

[947]

WREN CASE. Margery Wren, an 82-year-old spinster who kept a sweet-shop at Ramsgate, died as a result of injuries received during an assault.

On 20 September 1930 at about 6.00 p.m. a young girl went to Miss Wren's shop. The door was locked, but after knocking persistently, the child roused the old lady, who let her in and served her. Miss Wren was bleeding profusely from severe injuries to the head and face. The child told her parents—they promptly went to the shop. They asked her what had happened, and she pointed to a pair of fire-tongs lying on the floor in a pool of blood. Later she told the doctor that she had tripped over the tongs.

Miss Wren was taken to hospital, and found to have 7 lacerated wounds on the head and 8 bruises on the face. There was evidence of attempted strangulation, and the head injuries had been inflicted with the fire-tongs.

Questioned by police, Miss Wren made numerous statements of a contradictory nature. She said that a man had attacked her with the tongs. Then she said she had fallen down after becoming giddy, only to return to the assault story, saying she had been seized by the throat. 'Nobody hit me, I have no enemies. . . .' 'There were two of them set about me.' Before dying she said, 'I do not wish him to suffer. He must bear his sins. I do not wish to make a statement.'

In her ramblings the dying woman (who lived for 5 days) mentioned several names which the police investigated. Most were cleared, but one local man in particular lied about his movements. When he was found out—he had passed Miss Wren's shop at about the critical time—he said he had lied, as people might suspect him. The identity of Miss Wren's attacker was a secret which died with the victim.

[9]

WRIGHT, Kenneth Ray. A child-murder in Ocoee, Florida, was traced to a local man who tried to conceal his record from the police.

Camellia Jo Hand, aged 8, disappeared after school on Thursday, 10 April 1969. Her parents reported her missing, and a wide search began.

Witnesses said they had seen a blue car in the district, the occupants of which included a girl and a dog. A surveyor and his crew reported that during their lunch break they heard screams, and on 12 April the body of the missing girl's dog was found, and later a shallow grave containing the child's body. She had been horribly mutilated— the face was disfigured, and she had been stabbed, disembowelled and slashed in the genital region. Some 16 feet away officers found 2 bloodstained razor blades.

Police interviewed known sex deviants within a wide radius, and sifted hundreds of statements. Common factors were a man in a blue car and a licence plate with the figures 19 on it.

On 16 April a deputy-sheriff saw a tan Pontiac with 19 forming part of its registration, parked in Ocoee's shopping centre. Its owner was 29-year-old Kenneth Ray Wright, a painter. He was calm and co-operative, and said he had been in the woods to visit a rubbish dump. He took officers to the spot some 150 feet from the shallow grave. A partial print found on one of the razor blades matched Wright's prints and led to his arrest.

He was tried in 1969. The defence sought to discredit the fingerprint evidence, but there were 11 matching characteristics. Wright simply denied killing the girl, but he was found guilty of first-degree murder.

[778]

WYLIE HOFFERT MURDERS. See ROBLES, Richard

Wooldridge: Subject of the Ballad of Reading Gaol

WYNEKOOP, Dr Alice. Respected Chicago doctor who confessed to murdering her daughter-in-law and then retracted the admission.

Dr Wynekoop, a 62-year-old widow, lived on Monroe Street, Chicago, where she had a basement surgery and rented rooms to several boarders. Her children were grown up and successful, except Earle, who had no steady job and was addicted to women and drink. He met 18-year-old Rheta Gardner in Indianapolis and married her. As he was not earning, he was unable to support his wife, so they moved to his mother's house, where Dr Alice made them welcome. Rheta was unhappy because her husband deserted her for long periods, leaving her with her elderly mother-in-law. She was a neurotic, a hypochondriac—she feared she might contract tuberculosis.

Police were called to the house on 21 November

1933; Dr Alice told them, 'Something terrible has happened.' They went down to the basement surgery where Rheta lay face down on the operating table, covered with a blanket. The girl had been shot through the breast (a revolver lay on the table near her head), and there were chloroform burns in her mouth. The angle of the bullet-wound ruled out suicide.

Earle was away, and when he was contacted he said his marriage was a failure and his wife was mentally deranged. Meanwhile, after prolonged questioning, Dr Alice confessed. She said Rheta had asked to be examined, and because of the tenderness in the girl's side she administered a chloroform anaesthetic, and then found that breathing had stopped. She applied artificial respiration, but to no avail, and decided to shoot the already dead girl.

It was strongly believed that this confession was an attempt to shield Earle or, alternatively, to help rid him of a cumbersome wife. Another theory was that Dr Alice murdered the girl for her insurance. Earle himself confessed to murder, but was undoubtedly miles away at the time.

Dr Alice stood trial at Chicago in February 1934, when the prosecution tried to show that she murdered her daughter-in-law for her insurance. The defence demonstrated the Doctor's good reputation, and said that she had confessed under duress. It was suggested that Rheta Wynekoop had been the victim of a burglar, and that Dr Alice found her body when she went to the surgery. Despite her age and reputation the jury found her guilty, and she was sentenced to 25 years' imprisonment.

[771]

Y

YOUNG, Graham. A compulsive poisoner who was committed to Broadmoor after confessing to murder, only to be released 9 years later, to claim 2 further victims, using thallium as a poison.

Bob Egle, aged 60 and a popular storeman at Hadlands, a photographic instruments firm in Hertfordshire, was suddenly taken ill at work in June 1971. He was treated for peripheral neuritis, but his condition deteriorated and he died in hospital. His funeral was attended by the firm's managing director and one member of staff—23-year-old Graham Young.

Young had spent 9 years in an institution for the criminally insane after confessing to the poisoning of his stepmother and the attempted poisoning of his father, sister and a school-friend. He was eventually released, and he had taken a job with Hadlands. What impressed the Hadlands boss at the funeral was that Young seemed remarkably well versed in medical terminology.

Egle's death came after a spate of strange illness at Hadlands which had affected some 70 employees. No one seemed able to pin down the cause, which they called 'The Bug'. In October 1971 Fred Biggs got the 'Bug', and died after 3 weeks of extreme suffering. Graham Young took a pathological interest in Biggs's illness, and boasted of his medical knowledge. Among Young's duties was that of tea-boy.

Two other workers suffered from stomach pains, loss of hair and numbness in the legs. They also complained that their tea tasted bitter. Chemicals used at the works were suspected, and it was decided to call in a medical team to check the factory. The doctor leading the team called the staff together to answer questions and deal with rumours. The most persistent questioner was Graham Young: Did the doctor think the sufferer's symptoms were consistent with thallium poisoning? The doctor concluded that Young was simply a know-all, and ascertained that thallium was not used in the factory.

Young: His favourite photograph

By now Young had attracted considerable attention to himself, and his firm notified the police of their suspicions. His records were checked, and his background revealed. He was arrested, and in his pocket was found a lethal dose of thallium (see *Herbert Rowse Armstrong*). His diary contained the names of his victims, both actual and intended. Eventually he admitted that he had poisoned the 6 persons mentioned, of whom 2 died. 'I could have killed them if I wished as I did Bob Egle and Fred Biggs, but I allowed them to live,' he boasted. Although Egle had been

325

cremated an analysis of his ashes produced 9 milligrams of thallium.

Young was tried at St Albans in July 1972. He denied killing anyone and claimed that the notes in his diary were for a novel he intended to write. The jury found him guilty, and he was sentenced to life imprisonment.

[*399, 444, 507, 1024*]

YUKL, Charles. Sex killer who served 5 years imprisonment following conviction for manslaughter in 1966, and who killed again 14 months after being paroled.

Yukl's father, an immigrant from Czechoslovakia who worked as a musician in New York, was a severe disciplinarian. He beat his son and treated him as a worthless individual; the boy grew up as a loner with a stutter and a fear of women. In 1952 Yukl joined the US Navy, but was dishonourably discharged in 1954 after being court-martialled 3 times. He married in 1961 and after taking various jobs placed advertisements in the newspapers offering his services as a piano teacher.

In August 1966 Suzanne Reynolds, a 26-year-old secretary who aspired to be an actress, began taking voice lessons from Yukl. One day in October, during his wife's absence, Yukl attacked Suzanne Reynolds in his apartment, strangling her with a necktie. He sodomized his victim and mutilated her with a razor blade, after which he dragged her corpse into a nearby vacant apartment and reported its discovery to the police. Bloodstains on his shoes and clothes gave the game away, and he readily admitted to killing her.

Yukl's confession was used in a plea bargain to reduce the charge to manslaughter. He pleaded guilty and, without going to trial, was sentenced to imprisonment for not less than 7½ years. Psychiatrists reported that he had a character disorder with neurotic features, but regarded him as being without psychosis.

He proved to be an exemplary prisoner, and in 1973 was paroled after serving a little over 5 years of his sentence. He returned to his wife and their apartment in New York. After dabbling with college courses and odd jobs he decided on a plan to entice young women into his power. In July 1974 he advertised interviews for young actresses for parts in a film. Several girls applied, including Karin Schlegel. He took 4 of the applicants to dinner, ordering champagne and telling the staff that they were his stars and he was their producer.

On 19 August 1974 his fantasies turned into a nightmare when he killed Karin Schlegel in a re-run of his 1966 killing. He strangled her with a necktie and dragged her razor-slashed body up to the roof of the apartment building, where it was found next day. Yukl was arrested when police compared the recent killing with the one that had occurred 8 years earlier. He did not confess so readily the second time, but finally admitted his guilt. In order to cover up the crime before his wife returned to their apartment he had bundled his victim's corpse under the bed on which they slept the night.

His guilty plea avoided the necessity of a trial and Yukl was duly convicted of murder. He was sentenced to 15 years to life, and on 21 August 1982 hanged himself in the prison hospital.

[*899*]

Z

ZEBRA KILLINGS. Fifteen men and women were shot dead and 8 others wounded during a six-month period in San Francisco in 1973/4. The episode became known as the Zebra Killings because all the victims were white and the killers black. The shootings occurred in the street, where the victims were gunned down indiscriminately at close range. The night of 28 January 1974 went down in criminal history as the 'Night of the Five', when the killers—identified as black by terrified eye-witnesses—claimed 5 victims.

A Black Muslim connection with the killings was suspected by the San Francisco police, and their investigation made progress when an informant came forward following a reward announcement. Anthony Cornelius Harris confessed to his part in the killings and named his associates. On 1 May 1974 a task force of over 100 police officers stormed the apartment blocks where the suspects lived and made 7 arrests.

Larry Green, J. C. Simon, Jesse Cook and Manuel Moore were sent for trial. The proceedings lasted a year and three days—the longest trial in Californian history. Anthony Harris was on the witness stand for 12 days in all and over 150 witnesses gave testimony.

The Zebra killers-to-be attended meetings of the Black Muslims where they were influenced by the violent hatred expressed against whites, who were described as the enemies of Allah. Because the 'white devils' were judged to be beyond redemption, the action proposed was to eliminate them, on the grounds that evil used to fight evil turned it into good. 'Death Angels' were recruited to carry out the task of elimination by murder. To qualify as a 'Death Angel' a convert had to kill 9 white men, 5 white women or 4 white children. A Black Muslim who killed 4 'white devils' was promised free transportation to the Holy City to meet Brother Mohammed.

This dangerous doctrine made Harris and Simon into marauders on the streets of San Francisco looking for quick kills, selecting victims at random and shooting them in the back. The 'Night of the Five' was the brain-child of Simon after he had watched the heavyweight boxing match on television between Mohammed Ali and Joe Frazier. Public indignation over the series of killings reached a shrill pitch, and members of the black community joined groups of citizens acting as bodyguards on the street at night. The use of San Francisco as a background for such films as *Dirty Harry* and *The Streets of San Francisco* was called into question by those who linked violence in the community with violence portrayed on film and television screens.

The jury brought in unanimous verdicts of guilty against the 4 principal defendants, who each received a life sentence.
[*458*]

ZEIGLER, William Thomas Jr. Convicted of killing 4 people in a Christmas Eve shooting spree in his father's furniture store in Orange County, Florida. At 9.15 p.m. on 24 December 1975 Tommy Zeigler telephoned the home of a local judge where a seasonal party was under way and asked to speak to the police chief who was a guest. He told the police officer—who was also a personal friend—'I think there's trouble . . . I'm at the store. I've been shot.'

The Zeiglers, father and son, ran a furniture store near the Tri-City Shopping Center in Winter Garden, a sleepy Florida town. Following Tommy's telephone call, the police rushed to the store to find Zeigler in a state of collapse with a gunshot wound in the stomach, with 4 other victims of violence lying dead in various parts of the showroom. The victims included his wife Eunice, her mother and father and a man identified as Charlie Mays, a customer. Zeigler said that Mays had shot him after attempting robbery.

By a strange act of chance, one of the 20 bullets fired in the showroom incident went astray and struck the clock, stopping it at 7.24. The timing of the shooting was precisely recorded, and it was strange that Zeigler had not called for help until nearly two hours later. While recovering in hospital, the latter elaborated his story. He said he left the store with Ed Williams, one of his employees, to buy drinks for a party. When they returned, at around 7.00 p.m., he said he was hit on the head and lost his spectacles and so had seen little of what happened. He claimed to have pulled out his .22 gun (which jammed), and said he was attacked by several assailants.

Williams had disappeared, but when he reported voluntarily to the police he had a different story to tell. He alleged that Zeigler pulled a gun on him but it jammed when he fired it and Williams, frightened for his life, ran off as hard as he could. Investigation of Zeigler's background showed that his marriage to Eunice was far from happy and that his wife had asked her parents to take her away with them after the Christmas vacation. It was also revealed that Zeigler had asked one of his workers to buy him two handguns about a year previously, and that he had recently taken out life insurance on his wife worth $520,000. On 29 December he was charged with murder.

Herb MacDonell, the celebrated criminologist and expert on interpreting bloodstains, was called in to examine the evidence at the crime scene. He proved that all the shots fired during the Christmas Eve massacre came from guns owned by Zeigler. Moreover, his reconstruction of events pointed the finger of suspicion at Zeigler himself as guilty of the 4 killings and his own self-inflicted wound.

Tommy Zeigler was convicted of 2 counts of first-degree murder and 2 of second-degree murder. The jury recommended life imprisonment but the judge gave sentence of death. From prison, where he remained pending the outcome of various appeals, Zeigler was reported as saying, 'Life in prison is much like life anywhere else. You make of it what you want.'

[574]

ZODIAC MURDERS.

The Zodiac murderer killed 5 people and wounded 2 others during a 9-month period in California in 1969. The murderer was never caught, and earned his name on account of letters sent to 2 San Francisco newspapers signed with a Zodiacal cross surmounting a circle. The letters described the murders in such detail that it was believed only the killer could have written them.

The first murders occurred on 20 December 1968 when the bodies of 2 teenagers dead from gunshot wounds were found in their car in a lovers' lane in the San Francisco area. Further attacks followed,

and on 5 July 1969 a man phoned in to the Vallejo Police Department to report a double murder. Police found the victims in the exact location described by the caller, who also claimed responsibility for the previous murders. The girl in the latest incident was dead, but her escort survived serious wounds.

On 27 September 1969 it was the turn of Napa Police Department to receive a telephoned report of a double murder. Again the victims were discovered as directed by the caller; on this occasion they had been stabbed. Again the male victim survived his injuries. The sign of the Zodiac was found scrawled on the car, and the survivor told police that he and his girl-friend had been attacked by a man wearing a hood with the zodiac sign on it. On 11 October the killer struck again, killing a taxi-driver by shooting him in the back of the head. The following day a letter signed by the Zodiac killer was sent to the *San Francisco Chronicle*; the envelope also contained a bloodstained fragment from the shirt of the latest victim.

On 21 October a caller who claimed to be the Zodiac Killer telephoned the police at Oakland and said that he would give himself up if he could be represented by a famous defence lawyer. The following day, thousands of breakfast-time TV viewers were watching Melvin Belli, a renowned criminal lawyer. Belli had a regular morning show transmitted throughout the San Francisco area, and he answered the telephone to a man purporting to be the Zodiac Killer. A soft-voiced caller complained to Belli, 'I don't want to go to the gas chamber. I have headaches.' The same individual called Belli 15 times on one occasion saying, 'I've got to kill! I've got to kill!' He arranged to meet the lawyer in Daly City, but did not keep the appointment. One of the survivors who had heard the real killer's voice said the man who called in to the TV programme was not the same. Belli received a note at the end of the year wishing him a Happy Christmas, after which contact ceased.

Suddenly, in 1971, the Zodiac Killer appeared to restart his newspaper correspondence with a letter to the *Los Angeles Times* signed with the familiar cross over a circle. The San Francisco Police Department received a Zodiac letter in 1974 in which the writer threatened to 'do something nasty' if he did not gain more publicity in the newspapers. He also claimed to have killed 37 times. With that the Zodiac Killer faded from the scene, and his crimes remain unsolved.

[63, 359, 583]

This is the Zodiac speaking

I have become very upset with
the people of San Fran Bay
Area. They have <u>not</u> complied
with my wishes for them to
wear some nice ⊕ buttons.
I promiced to punish them
if they did not comply, by
anilating a full School Bass.
But now school is out for
the summer, so I punished
them in an another way.
I shot a man sitting in
a parked car with a .38.

⊕-12   SFPD-0

The Map coupled with this
code will tell you who-e the
bomb is set. You have until
next Fall to dig it up. ⊕

C △ J I ■ ⊙ O ⅄ ⅃ A M �ꓒ ▲ Ω O R T G
X ⊙ F D V ⊋ ⊡ H C E L ⊕ P W △

Zodiac Murders: Letter from an uncaught killer

329

Bibliography

1. NOTABLE BRITISH TRIALS (eighty-three titles)
2. FAMOUS TRIALS (sixteen titles)
3. OLD BAILEY TRIALS (seven titles)
4. CELEBRATED TRIALS (six titles)
5. ABINGER, Edward: *Forty Years at the Bar*, London (1930)
6. ABBOTT, Jack Henry: *In the Belly of the Beast*, London (1982)
7. ABRAHAMS, Gerald: *According to the Evidence*, London (1958)
8. ADAM, H.L.: *Murder by Persons Unknown*, London (1931)
9. ——: *Murder Most Mysterious*, London (1932)
10. ——: *Old Days at the Old Bailey*, London (n.d.)
11. ——: *Police Work From Within*, London (1914)
12. ADAMS, N: *Dead and Buried?* Aberdeen (1972)
13. ADAMSON, Iain: *The Great Detective*, London (1966)
14. ADLEMAN, Robert H: *The Bloody Benders*, London (1971)
15. ALAN, A J et al: *Great Unsolved Crimes*, London, (n.d.)
16. ALCORN, Robert Haydn: *The Count of Gramercy Park*, London (1955)
17. ALEXANDER, Shana: *Nutcracker*, New York (1985)
18. ——: *Very Much a Lady*, Boston (1983)
19. ALLEN, William: *Starkweather: The Story of a Mass Murderer*, Boston (1976)
20. ALLES, A C: *Famous Criminal Cases of Sri Lanka* – 9 vols, Colombo (1977–84)
21. ALTICK, Richard T: *Victorian Studies in Scarlet*, London (1970)
22. ALTMAN, Jack *and* ZIPORYN, Marvin: *Born to Raise Hell*, New York (1967)
23. AMBLER, Eric: *The Ability to Kill*, London (1963)
24. ANDREWS, Allen: *Intensive Inquiries*, London (1973)
25. ANGELELLA, Michael: *Trail of Blood*, New York (1979)
26. ANSON, Jay: *The Amityville Horror*, London (1978)
27. ANSPACHER, Carolyn: *The Acid Test*, London (1965)
28. APPLETON, Arthur: *Mary Ann Cotton*, London (1973)
29. ARCHER, Fred: *Killers in the Clear*, London (1971)
30. ARMBRISTER, Trevor: *Act of Vengeance*, London (1976)
31. ARNOLD, Ross: *Maria Marten: Murder in the Red Barn*, (n.d.)
32. ARTHUR, Herbert: *All the Sinners*, London (1931)
33. ASHTON-WOLFE, H: *The Underworld*, London (1926)
34. ATHOLL, Justin: *The Reluctant Hangman*, London (1956)
35. ATLAY, J B: *Famous Trials*, London (1899)
36. BAILEY, F Lee *with* ARONSON, Harvey: *The Defence Never Rests*, London (1972)
37. BAILEY, Guy: *The Fatal Chance*, London (1969)
38. BALCHIN, Nigel: *The Anatomy of Villainy*, London (1950)
39. BALDWIN, James: *The Evidence of Things Not Seen*, New York (1985)
40. BALL, J M: *The Sack-em-up Men*, London (1928)
41. BALLANTINE, Serjeant: *Some Experiences of a Barrister's Life*, London (1883)
42. BANKS, Harold K: *The Strangler!*, New York (1967)
43. BARDENS, Dennis: *Famous Cases of Norman Birkett KC*, London (1963)
44. ——: *Lord Justice Birkett*, London (1962)
45. BARDENS, D: *The Ladykiller; The Life of Landru, the French Bluebeard*, London (1972)
46. BARKAS, J L: *Victims*, New York (1978)
47. BARKER, Dudley: *Lord Darling's Famous Cases*, London (1936)
48. ——: *Palmer; The Rugeley Poisoner*, London (1935)
49. BARKER, Ralph: *Verdict on a Lost Flyer*, London (1969)
50. BARNARD, A: *The Harlot Killer*, London (1953)
51. BARTHEL, Joan: *A Death in California*, New York (1981)
52. BARTON, George: *The True Stories of Celebrated Crimes*, (n.d.)
53. BARZUN, J : *Burke and Hare: The Resurrection Men*, New Jersey (1974)
54. BEAL, E (Ed): *The Trial of Adelaide Bartlett for Murder*, London (1886)
55. BEATTIE, John: *The Yorkshire Ripper Story*, London (1981)
56. BEAVER, Ninette, RIPLEY, B K *and* TRESE, Patrick: *Caril*, Philadelphia (1974)
57. BECCHOFER ROBERTS, C E: *Famous American Trials*, London (1974)
58. ——: *Sir Travers Humphreys: His Career and Cases*, London (1936)

59. BEDFORD, Sybille: *The Best We Can Do*, London (1958)

60. BELIN, Jean: *My Work at the Sûreté*, London (1950)

61. BELL, Arthur: *Kings Don't Mean a Thing*, New York (1978)

62. BELL, Terry: *Bitter Hill*, Manurewa, New Zealand (1972)

63. BELLI, Melvin: *My Life on Trial*, New York (1976)

64. BELTRAMI, Joseph: *The Defender*, Edinburgh (1980)

65. BENNETT, Benjamin: *Famous South African Murders*, London (1938)

66. ——: *Freedom or the Gallows*, Cape Town (1956)

67. ——: *Genius for the Defence*, Cape Town (1967)

68. ——: *Murder is my Business*, Cape Town (1951)

69. ——: *Murder Will Speak*, Cape Town (1972)

70. ——: *The Amazing Case of the Baron von Schauroth*, Cape Town (1966)

71. ——: *The Cohen Case*, Cape Town (1971)

72. ——: *The Evil That Men Do*, Cape Town (1950)

73. ——: *Up for Murder*, London (1974)

74. ——: *The Noose Tightens*, Cape Town (1974)

75. ——: *This Was a Man*, Cape Town (1958)

76. ——: *Too Late for Tears*, Cape Town (1950)

77. ——: *Was Justice Done?*, Cape Town (1975)

78. ——: *Why Did They Do It?*, Cape Town (1953)

79. BENTLEY, W G: *My Son's Execution*, London (1957)

80. BERG, Karl: *The Sadist*, London (1945)

81. BERRETT, James: *When I Was at Scotland Yard*, London (1932)

82. BERRY, James: *My Experiences as an Executioner*, Newton Abbot (1972)

83. BEVERIDGE, Peter: *Inside the CID*, London (1957)

84. BIERSTADT, Edward Hale: *Enter Murderers*, New York (1937)

85. BINGHAM, John: *The Hunting Down of Peter Manuel*, London (1973)

86. BIRD, Heather: *Not Above The Law*, Toronto (1985)

87. BIRMINGHAM, George A: *Murder Most Foul*, London (1939)

88. BISHOP, Cecil: *From Information Received*, London (1932)

89. BISHOP, George: *Witness to Evil*, Los Angeles (1971)

90. BISHOP, Jim: *The Murder Trial of Judge Peel*, New York (1963)

91. BIXLEY, William: *The Guilty and the Innocent*, London (1957)

92. BLACK, David: *Murder at the Met*, New York (1986)

93. BLACKHAM, Robert J: *Sir Ernest Wild KC*, London (1953)

94. BLAND, James: *True Crime Diary*, London (1987)

95. BLOCK, Eugene B: *The Chemist of Crime*, London (1959)

96. BLYTH, H: *Madeleine Smith*, London (1975)

97. BOAR, Roger *and* BLUNDELL, Nigel: *The World's Most Infamous Murders*, London (1983)

98. BOCCA, Geoffrey: *The Life and Death of Sir Harry Oakes*, London (1959)

99. BOGDANOVITCH, Peter: *The Killing of a Unicorn*, London (1985)

100. BOLITHO, William: *Murder for Profit*, London (1926)

101. BORRELL, Clive *and* CASHINELLA, Brian: *Crime in Britain Today*, London (1975)

102. BOROWITZ, Albert: *A Gallery of Sinister Perspectives*, Kent, Ohio, USA (1982)

103. ——: *The Woman Who Murdered Black Satin*, Kent, Ohio, USA (1981)

104. BOSANQUET, Sir Ronald: *The Oxford Circuit*, London (1951)

105. BOSWELL, Charles *and* THOMPSON, Lewis: *The Carlyle Harris Case*, New York (1961)

106. ——: *The Girl with the Scarlet Brand*, London (n.d.)

107. ——: *The Girls in Nightmare House*, New York (1955)

108. BOUCHER, Anthony: *The Quality of Murder*, New York (1962)

109. BOUTET, Frederic: *International Criminals Past and Present*, London (n.d.)

110. BOWEN-ROWLANDS, Ernest: *In the Light of the Law*, London (1931)

111. ——: *Seventy-Two Years at the Bar*, London (1924)

112. BOWKER, A E: *A Lifetime with the Law*, London (1961)

113. ——: *Behind the Bar*, London (1947)

114. BRAND, Christianna: *Heaven Knows Who*, London (1960)

115. BRENNAN, T V: *The Gun Alley Tragedy*, Melbourne (1922)

116. BRESLER, Fenton: *Lord Goddard*, London (1977)

117. ——: *Reprieve*, London (1965)

118. ——: *Scales of Justice*, London (1973)

119. BRETT, Peter: *The Beamish Case*, Melbourne (1966)

120. BRICE A H M: *Look upon The Prisoner*, London (1933)

121. BRIDGES, Yseult: *How Charles Bravo Died*, London (1956)

122. ——: *Poison and Adelaide Bartlett*, London (1962)

123. ——: *Saint With Red Hands*, London (1954)

124. ——: *Two Studies in Crime*, London (1959)

125. BROAD, Lewis: *The Innocence of Edith Thompson*, London (1952)

126. BROCK, Alan: *A Casebook of Crime*, London (1948)

127. BROME, Vincent: *Reverse Your Verdict*, London (1971)

128. BROOKES, Canon J A R: *Murder in Fact and Fiction*, London (1926)

129. BROPHY, John: *The Meaning of Murder*, London (1966)

130. BROWN, Wenzell: *Introduction to Murder*, London (1953)

131. BROWNE, Douglas G: *Sir Travers Humphreys*, London (1953)

132. BROWNE, Douglas G *and* BROCK, Alan A: *Fingerprints: Fifty Years of Scientific Crime Detection*, London (1953)

133. BROWNE, Douglas G *and* TULLETT, E V: *Sir Bernard Spilsbury: His Life and Cases*, London (1951)

134. BROWNE, G Lathom *and* STEWART, C G: *Trials for Murder by Poisoning*, London (1883)

135. BROWNING, Normalee: *The Psychic World of Peter Hurkos*, London (1972)

136. BRUSSEL, James A: *Casebook of a Crime Psychologist*, New York (1968)

137. BUCHANAN, A J (Ed): *The Trial of Ronald Geeves Griggs*, Sydney (1930)

138. BUGLIOSI, Vincent *and* GENTRY, Kurt: *The Manson Murders*, London (1974)

139. BUGLIOSI, Vincent *and* HURWITZ, Ken: *Till Death Us Do Part*, New York (1978)

140. BURN, Gordon: *Somebody's Husband, Somebody's Son*, London (1984)

141. BURNABY, Evelyn: *Memories of Famous Trials*, London (1907)

142. BURT, Leonard: *Commander Burt of Scotland Yard*, London (1959)

143. BUSCH, Francis X: *Guilty or Not Guilty?*, London (1967)

144. ——: *They Escaped the Hangman*, London (1957)

145. BUTLER, Geoffrey L: *Madeleine Smith*, London (1935)

146. BUTLER, Ivan: *Murderers' England*, London (1973)

147. ——: *Murderers' London*, London (1973)

148. BYRNE, Gerald: *Borstal Boy: The Uncensored Story of Neville Heath*, London (n.d.)

149. ——: *John George Haigh: Acid Bath Killer*, London (n.d.)

150. BYRNES, Thomas: *Professional Criminals of America*, New York (1886)

151. CAHILL, Tim: *Buried Dreams*, New York (1986)

152. CAMP, John: *One Hundred Years of Medical Murder*, London (1982)

153. CAMPBELL, Marjorie Freeman: *A Century of Crime*, Toronto (1970)

154. ——: *Torso*, Toronto (1974)

155. CAMPS, Francis E: *Camps on Crime*, Newton Abbot (1973)

156. ——: *Medical and Scientific Investigations in the Christie Case*, London (1953)

157. ——: *The Investigation of Murder*, London (1966)

158. CANNELL, J C: *New Light on the Rouse Case*, London (1932)

159. ——: *When Fleet Street Calls*, London (1932)

160. CANTILLON, Richard H: *In Defence of the Fox*, Atlanta, USA (1972)

161. CAPON, P: *The Great Yarmouth Mystery*, London (1965)

162. CAPOTE, Truman: *In Cold Blood*, London (1966)

163. CAPSTICK, J: *Given in Evidence*, London (1960)

164. CAPUTI, Jane: *The Age of the Sex Crime*, London (1988)

165. CAREY, Arthur A: *On the Track of Murder*, London (1930)

166. CARGILL, David *and* HOLLAND, Julian: *Scenes of Murder – A London Guide*, London (1964)

167. CARLIN, Francis: *Reminiscences of an Ex-Detective*, London (n.d.)

168. CARPOZI, George: *Ordeal by Trial*, New York (1972)

169. CARVALHO, C *and* SPARKS, B: *Crime in Ink*, New York (1929)

170. CASSITY, John Holland: *The Quality of Murder*, New York (1958)

171. CASSWELL, J D: *A Lance for Liberty*, London (1961)

172. CHAMBERLAIN, Sir Roderic: *The Stuart Affair*, London (1973)

173. CHANDLER, Geoffrey: *So You Think I Did It?* Melbourne (1969)

174. CHENEY, Margaret: *The Co-ed Killer*, New York (1967)

175. CHERRILL, Fred: *Cherrill of the Yard*, London (1954)

176. CHRISTIE, Trevor L: *Etched in Arsenic*, London (1968)

177. CLARK, Tim *and* PENYCATE, John: *Psychopath*, London (1976)

178. CLARKE, Sir Edward: *The Story of my Life*, London (1918)

179. CLEGG, Eric: *Return Your Verdict*, Sydney (1965)

180. CLUNE, Frank: *The Demon Killer*, Sydney (1948)

181. COBB, Belton: *Critical Years at the Yard*, London (1956)

182. ——: *Murdered on Duty*, London (1961)

183. ——: *The First Detectives*, London (1957)

184. ——: *Trials and Errors*, London (1962)

185. COHEN, Sam D: *One Hundred True Crime Stories*, Cleveland, USA (1946)

186. COLE, Hubert: *Things for the Surgeon*, London (1964)

187. COLE, Peter *and* PRINGLE, Peter: *Can You Positively Identify This Man?*, London (1974)

188. COLEMAN, Jonathan: *At Mother's Request*, New York (1985)

189. CONDON, John F: *Jafsie Tells All*, New York (1946)

190. CONRAD, Barnaby: *A Revolting Transaction*, New York (1983)

191. CONSTANTINE-QUINN, M: *Doctor Crippen*, London (1935)

192. COOKE, Fred J: *The Girl in the Death Cell*, New York (n.d.)

193. COOK, Judith: *Who Killed Hilda Murrell?*, London (1985)

194. COOPER, C R: *Ten Thousand Public Enemies*, (n.d.)

195. COOPER, William: *Shall We Ever Know?*, London (1971)

196. CORNISH, G W: *Cornish of the Yard*, London (1935)

197. COPELAND, James: *The Butler*, London (1981)

198. COTTRELL, Richard: *Blood on their Hands*, London (1987)

199. COULTER, Jack: *With Malice Aforethought*, Perth, Australia (1982)

Bibliography

200. CRAY, Ed: *Burden of Proof*, New York (1973)
201. CREW, Albert: *The Old Bailey*, London (1933)
202. CRIMINOLOGICAL STUDIES NO 1: *Patrick Mahon*, London (n.d.)
203. —— NO 2: *The Case of Thompson and Bywaters*, London (n.d.)
204. —— NO 3: *The Case of Major Armstrong*, London (n.d.)
205. CROCKER, W C: *Far From Humdrum*, London (1967)
206. CROSS, Roger: *The Yorkshire Ripper*, London (1981)
207. CROUSE, Russel: *Murder Won't Out*, New York (1932)
208. CULLEN, Tom: *Autumn of Terror*, London (1965)
209. ——: *Crippen: The Mild Murderer*, Boston (1977)
210. CURLING, Jonathan: *Janus Weathercock*, London (1938)
211. CURTIN, Philip: *Noted Murder Mysteries*, London (1914)
212. DAMORE, Leo: *In His Garden*, New York (1981)
213. DARROW, Clarence: *The Story of my Life*, New York (1932)
214. DAVID, Andrew: *Famous Criminal Trials*, Minneapolis, USA (1979)
215. DAVID, Jay: *The Scarsdale Murder*, New York (1980)
216. DAVIS, Bernice Freeman *and* HIRSCHBERG, Al: *Assignment San Quentin*, London (1961)
217. DEALE, Kenneth E L: *Beyond Any Reasonable Doubt*, Dublin (1971)
218. ——: *Memorable Irish Trials*, London (1960)
219. DEANS, R Storry: *Notable Trials: Difficult Cases*, London (1932)
220. DEARDEN, Harold: *Death Under the Microscope*, London (1934)
221. ——: *Queer People*, London (1922)
222. DEELEY, Peter: *The Manhunters*, London (1970)
223. DEELEY, Peter *and* WALKER, C: *Murder in the Fourth Estate*, London (1971)
224. DEFORD, Miriam Allen: *Murderers Sane and Mad*, London (1966)
225. DE LA TORRE, Lillian: *The Truth About Belle Gunness*, New York (1955)
226. DE MARIGNY, Alfred: *More Devil Than Saint*, New York (1946)
227. DERLETH, August: *Wisconsin Murders*, Sauk City, USA (1968)
228. DETTLINGER, Chet *with* PRUGH, Jeff: *The List*, Atlanta USA (1983)
229. DEVLIN, Patrick: *Easing the Passing*, London (1985)
230. DEW, Walter: *I Caught Crippen*, London (1938)
231. DEWES, Simon: *Doctors of Murder*, London (1962)
232. DICKSON, Grierson: *Murder by Numbers*, London (1958)
233. DICKSON, John: *Murder Without Conviction*, London (1988)
234. DILNOT, George: *Celebrated Crimes*, London (1925)
235. ——: *Great Detectives*, (n.d.)
236. ——: *Man Hunters*, London (1937)
237. ——: *Rogue's March*, London (1934)
238. ——: *The Real Detective*, London (1933)
239. ——: *Triumphs of Detection*, London (1929)
240. DINNERSTEIN, Leonard: *The Leo Frank Case*, New York (1968)
241. DOBKINS, Dwight J *and* HENDRICKS, J: *Winnie Ruth Judd: The Trunk Murders*, New York (1973)
242. DOUGLAS, Arthur: *Will the Real Jack the Ripper*, Chorley (1979)
243. DOUGLAS, Hugh: *Burke and Hare: The True Story*, London (1973)
244. DOUTHWAITE, L C: *Mass Murder*, London (1928)
245. DOWDALL, Lawrence: *Get Me Dowdall*, London (1979)
246. DOWER, Alan: *Crime Chemist*, London (1965)
247. ——: *Deadline*, Victoria, Australia (1979)
248. DOWNIE, R Angus: *Murder in London*, London (1973)
249. DUDLEY, Ernest: *Bywaters and Mrs Thompson*, (n.d.)
250. DUFFY, C: *88 Men and 2 Women*, New York (1962)
251. DUKE, Thomas S: *Celebrated Criminal Cases of America*, San Francisco (1910)
252. DUKE, Winifred: *Six Trials*, London (1934)
253. ——: *The Stroke of Murder*, London (1937)
254. DUNBAR, Dorothy: *Blood in the Parlour*, New York (1964)
255. DUNCAN, Ronald (Ed): *Facets of Crime*, Cornwall (1975)
256. DU PREEZ, Peter: *The Vontsteen Case*, Cape Town (1972)
257. DU ROSE, John: *Murder Was My Business*, London (1971)
258. DYNE, D G : *Famous New Zealand Murders*, Auckland NZ (1969)
259. EATON, Harold: *Famous Poison Trials*, London (1923)
260. EDDOWES, M: *The Man On Your Conscience*, London (1955)
261. EDDY, J P: *Scarlet and Ermine*, London (1960)
262. EDWARDS, Owen Dudley: *Burke and Hare*, Edinburgh (n.d.)
263. EHRMANN, Herbert R: *The Case That Will Not Die*, London (1970)
264. ELLIOTT, Robert G *with* BEATTY, Albert R: *Agent of Death*, New York (1940)
265. ELLIS, Anthony: *Prisoner At The Bar*, London (1934)
266. ELLIS, J C: *Black Fame*, London (n.d.)
267. ——: *Blackmailers and Co.*, London (1928)
268. ESHELMAN, D: *Death Row Chaplain*, New Jersey (1962)
269. FABIAN, Robert: *Fabian of the Yard*, London (1950)
270. FAIRLIE, Gerard: *The Reluctant Cop*, London (1958)
271. FARSON, Daniel: *Jack the Ripper*, London (1972)
272. FAST, Howard: *The Passion of Sacco and Vanzetti*, London (1954)

273. FAWKES, Sandy: *Killing Time*, London (1977)
274. FAY, E S: *The Life of Mr Justice Swift*, London (1939)
275. FELSTEAD, S T: *Sir Richard Muir*, London (1927)
276. FERGUSSON, Erna: *Murder and Mystery in New Mexico*, New Mexico (1948)
277. FIDO, Martin: *Murder Guide to London*, London (1986)
278. ——: *The Crimes, Detection and Death of Jack the Ripper*, London (1987)
279. FIELDER, Peter *and* STEELE, Peter: *Alibi at Midnight*, London (1974)
280. FINNEY, Jack: *Forgotten News: The Crime of the Century and Other Lost Stories*, New York (1983)
281. FIRMIN, Stanley: *Crime Man*, London (1950)
282. ——: *Murderers in Our Midst*, London (1955)
283. FIRTH, J B: *A Scientist Turns to Crime*, London (1960)
284. FITZGERALD, John D: *Studies in Australian Crime*, Sydney (1924)
285. ——: *Studies in Australian Crime: Second Series*, Sydney (1924)
286. FLETCHER, G: *The Life and Career of Dr William Palmer of Rugeley*, London (1925)
287. FLETCHER, Tony: *Memories of Murder*, London (1986)
288. FOOT, Paul: *Who Killed Hanratty?*, London (1971)
289. FORBES, Ian: *Squad Man*, London (1973)
290. FORSTER, Joseph: *Studies in Black and Red*, London (1896)
291. FOSBURGH, Lacey: *Closing Time*, New York (1975)
292. FOX, James: *White Mischief*, London (1982)
293. FRAENKEL, Osmand: *Sacco-Vanzetti Case*, London (1931)
294. FRANK, Gerold: *The Boston Strangler*, London (1967)
295. FRANKE, David: *Torture Doctor*, New York (1975)
296. FRANKLIN, Charles: *The World's Worst Murderers*, London (1965)
297. ——: *The Woman in the Case*, London (1967)
298. ——: *A Mirror to Murder*, London (1964)
299. FREEMAN, Lucy: *Before I Kill More*, New York (1955)
300. FRENCH, Stanley: *Crime Every Day*, London (1976)
301. FRIEDLAND, Martin L: *The Trials of Israel Lipski*, London (1984)
302. FROST, George: *Flying Squad*, London (1949)
303. FULLER, Graham (Ed): *Unsolved* (part-work), London (1984)
304. FURNEAUX, Rupert: *Courtroom USA 1*, London (1962)
305. ——: *Courtroom USA 2*, London (1963)
306. ——: *Famous Criminal Cases – 1*, London (1954)
307. ——: *Famous Criminal Cases – 2*, London (1955)
308. ——: *Famous Criminal Cases – 3*, London (1956)
309. ——: *Famous Criminal Cases – 4*, London (1957)
310. ——: *Famous Criminal Cases – 5*, London (1958)
311. ——: *Famous Criminal Cases – 6*, London (1960)
312. ——: *Famous Criminal Cases – 7*, London (1962)
313. ——: *Guenther Podola*, London (1960)
314. ——: *Robert Hoolhouse*, London (1960)
315. ——: *The Medical Murderer*, London (1957)
316. ——: *The Murder of Lord Erroll*, London (1961)
317. ——: *The Two Stranglers of Rillington Place*, London (1961)
318. ——: *They Died by the Gun*, London (1962)
319. GADDIS, Thomas E: *Birdman of Alcatraz*, New York (1955)
320. GADDIS, Thomas E *and* LONG, James O: *Killer: A Journal of Murder*, New York (1970)
321. GARVIE, Sheila: *Marriage to Murder*, Edinburgh (1980)
322. GAUTE, J H H *and* ODELL, Robin: *Ladykillers*, London (1980)
323. ——: *Lady Killers 2*, London (1981)
324. ——: *Murder Whatdunit?*, London (1982)
325. ——: *Murder Whereabouts*, London (1986)
326. GERBER, S R *and* SCHROEDER, O: *Criminal Investigation and Interrogation*, Cincinnati, Ohio (1962)
327. GIBBS, Dorothy *and* MALTBY, Herbert: *The True Story of Maria Marten*, London (1949)
328. GILBERT, Michael: *Doctor Crippen*, London (1953)
329. GILMORE, John: *The Tucson Murders*, New York (1970)
330. GIONO, Jean: *The Dominici Affair*, London (1956)
331. GLAISTER, John: *Final Diagnosis*, London (1964)
332. ——: *The Power of Poison*, London (1954)
333. GLAISTER, John *and* BRASH, James Couper: *Medico-Legal Aspects of the Ruxton Case*, London (1937)
334. GODWIN, George: *Peter Kürten – A Study in Sadism*, London (1938)
335. GODWIN, John: *Killers in Paradise*, London (1962)
336. ——: *Killers Unknown*, London (1960)
337. GODWIN, John: *Murder USA*, New York (1978)
338. GOLDEN, Harry: *The Lynching of Leo Frank*, London (1966)
339. GOLLMAR, Robert H: *Edward Gein*, Delavan, Wisconsin, USA (1982)
340. GOLLOMB, Joseph: *Crimes of the Year*, New York (1931)
341. GOODMAN, Derrick: *Crime of Passion*, London (1958)
342. GOODMAN, Jonathan: *Acts of Murder*, London (1986)
343. ——: (Ed) *The Pleasures of Murder*, London (1984)
344. ——: *The Burning of Evelyn Foster*, London (1983)
345. ——: (Ed) *The Christmas Murders*, London (1986)
346. ——: *The Crippen File*, London (1985)
347. ——: *The Country House Murders*, London (1988)
348. ——: *The Killing of Julia Wallace*, London (1969)
349. ——: *The Railway Murders*, London (1984)
350. ——: (Ed) *The Seaside Murders*, London (1985)
351. ——: *The Stabbing of George Harry Storrs*, London (1983)

Bibliography

352. ——: *The Slaying of Joseph Bowne Elwell*, London (1987)

353. ——: *Murder in High Places*, London (1986)

354. ——: *Posts Mortem*, Newton Abbot (1971)

355. GOUGH, W C: *From Kew Observatory to Scotland Yard*, London (1927)

356. GRAHAM, Evelyn: *Fifty Years of Famous Judges*, London (1930)

357. ——: *Lord Darling and his Famous Trials*, London (1929)

358. GRAVES, Robert: *They Hanged My Saintly Billy*, London (1957)

359. GRAYSMITH, Robert: *Zodiac*, New York (1986)

360. GREEN, Jonathan: *The Directory of Infamy*, London (1980)

361. GREENO, Edward: *War on the Underworld*, London (1960)

362. GREENWALL, Harry J: *They Were Murdered in France*, London (1957)

363. GREX, Leo: *Stranger Than Fiction Murder*, London (1985)

364. GRIBBLE, Leonard: *Adventures in Murder*, London (1954)

365. ——: *Clues That Spelled Guilty*, London (1961)

366. ——: *Famous Feats of Detection and Deduction*, London (1933)

367. ——: *Famous Judges and Their Trials*, London (1957)

368. ——: *Famous Manhunts*, London (1930)

369. ——: *Famous Stories of the Murder Squad*, London (1966)

370. ——: *Great Detective Exploits*, London (1958)

371. ——: *Great Manhunters of the Yard*, London (1966)

372. ——: *Hallmark of Horror*, London (1973)

373. ——: *Murders Most Strange*, London (1959)

374. ——: *Queens of Crime*, London (1932)

375. ——: *Sisters of Cain*, London (1972)

376. ——: *Stories of Famous Detectives*, London (1963)

377. ——: *Stories of Famous Modern Trials*, London (1970)

378. ——: *Strange Crimes of Passion*, London (1970)

379. ——: *Such Was Their Guilt*, London (1974)

380. ——: *Such Women are Deadly*, London (1965)

381. ——: *They Challenged Scotland Yard*, London (1963)

382. ——: *They Got Away With Murder*, London (1971)

383. ——: *They Has a Way With Women*, London (1967)

384. ——: *Triumphs of Scotland Yard*, London (1955)

385. ——: *When Killers Err*, London (1962)

386. GRICE, Edward: *Great Cases of Sir Henry Curtis Bennett*, London (1937)

387. GRIERSON, Francis: *Famous French Crimes*, London (1959)

388. GRIFFITHS, Arthur: *Mysteries of Police and Crime*, London (1898)

389. GRIMSHAW, Eric and JONES, Glyn: *Lord Goddard – His Career and Cases*, London (1958)

390. GROMBACH, John V: *The Great Liquidator*, New York (1980)

391. GROSS, Kenneth: *The Alice Crimmins Case*, New York (1975)

392. GURR, T and COX, H H: *Famous Australian Crimes*, London (1957)

393 ——: *Obsession*, London (1958)

394. GURWELL, John K: *Mass Murder in Houston*, London (1974)

395. GWYNN, Gordon: *Did Adelaide Bartlett . . .?*, London (1950)

396. HABE, Hans: *Gentlemen of the Jury*, London (1967)

397. HADEN-GUEST, Anthony: *Bad Dreams*, New York (1981)

398. HAESTIER, Richard: *Dead Men Tell Tales*, London (1934)

399. HAINES, Max: *Crime Flashback*, Toronto (1980)

400. ——: *Bothersome Bodies*, Toronto (1977)

401. ——: *The Murderous Kind*, Toronto (1983)

402. HALE, Leslie: *Hanged in Error*, London (1961)

403. HALL Sir John: *The Bravo Mystery and Other Cases*, London (1923)

404. HALLWORTH, Rodney and WILLIAMS, Mark: *Where There's a Will . . .*, London (1983)

405. HALPER, Albert (Ed): *The Chicago Crime Book*, Cleveland, USA (1967)

406. HAMBROOK, Walter: *Hambrook of the Yard*, London (1937)

407. HANCOCK, Robert: *Ruth Ellis*, London (1963)

408. HANSFORD JOHNSON, P: *On Iniquity*, London (1967)

409. HARDWICK, M: *Doctors on Trial*, London (1961)

410. HARLOW, Alvin F: *Murders Not Quite Solved*, New York (1938)

411. HARRIS, Jean: *Stranger in Two Worlds*, London (1987)

412. HARRIS, Melvin: *Jack the Ripper: The Bloody Truth*, London (1987)

413. HARRIS, Paul: *The Garvie Trial*, Aberdeen (1969)

414. HARRIS, Richard (Ed): *The Reminiscences of Sir Henry Hawkins*, London (1904)

415. HARRISON, Fred: *Brady and Hindley*, London (1987)

416. HARRISON, Michael: *Clarence*, London (1972)

417. HARRISON, Richard: *Criminal Calendar*, London (1951)

418. ——: *Criminal Calendar II*, London (1952)

419. HARTMAN, Mary S: *Victorian Murderesses*, New York (1976)

420. HASTINGS, Macdonald: *The Other Mr Churchill*, London (1963)

421. HASTINGS, Patricia: *The Life of Sir Patrick Hastings*, London (1959)

422. HASTINGS, Sir Patrick: *Autobiography*, London (1948)

423. ——: *Cases in Court*, London (1949)

424. HATHERILL, George: *A Detective's Story*, London (1971)

425. HAVERS, Sir Michael, SHANKLAND, Peter and BARRETT, A: *A Tragedy in Three Voices*, London (1980)

426. HAWKES, George H: *Hand in Glove*, Sydney (n.d.)

427. HAWKES, Harry: *Capture of the Black Panther*, London (1978)

428. ——: *Murder on the A34*, London (1970)

429. HÉBERT, Jacques: *The Coffin Affair*, Quebec (1982)

430. HEIMER, Mel: *The Cannibal*, New York (1971)

431. HELPERN, Milton *with* KNIGHT, Bernard: *Autopsy*, New York (1977)

432. HENDERSON, Bruce *and* SUMMERLIN, Sam: *The Super Sleuths*, London (1976)

433. HENRY, J: *Detective Inspector Henry's Famous Cases*, London (n.d.)

434. HEPPENSTALL, Rayner: *A Little Pattern of French Crime*, London (1969)

435. ——: *Bluebeard and After*, London (1972)

436. ——: *French Crime in the Romantic Age*, London (1970)

437. ——: *The Sex War and Others*, London (1973)

438. HICKS, Seymour: *Not Guilty M'Lord*, London (1939)

439. HIGDON, Hal: *The Crime of the Century*, New York (1975)

440. HIGGINS, Robert: *In The Name of the Law*, London (1958)

441. HILL, Paull: *Portrait of a Sadist*, London (1960)

442. HODGE, Harry: *The Black Maria*, London (1935)

443. HOFFMANN, Richard *and* BISHOP, Jim: *The Girl in Poison Cottage*, London (1958)

444. HOLDEN, Anthony: *The St Albans Poisoner*, London (1974)

445. HOLMES, Paul: *The Sheppard Murder Case*, New York (1961)

446. ——: *The Trials of Dr Coppolino*, New York (1968)

447. HOLROYD, J E: *The Gaslight Murders*, London (1960)

448. HOLZER, Hans: *Murder in Amityville*, London (1980)

449. HONEYCOMBE, Gordon: *The Murders of the Black Museum*, London (1982)

450. HORWELL, John E: *Horwell of the Yard*, London (1947)

451. HOSKINS, Percy: *The Sound of Murder*, London (1973)

452. ——: *They Almost Escaped*, London (1937)

453. ——: *Two Men Were Acquitted*, London (1984)

454. HOUSE, Jack: *Murder Not Proven*, Glasgow (1984)

455. ——: *Square Mile of Murder*, Edinburgh (1961)

456. HOUTS, Marshall: *King's X*, New York (1972)

457. HOWARD, Clark: *Brothers in Blood*, New York (1983)

458. ——: *The Zebra Killings*, New York (1979)

459. HOWELLS, Martin *and* SKINNER, Keith: *The Ripper Legacy*, London (1987)

460. HUGGETT, R *and* BERRY, P: *Daughters of Cain*, London (1956)

461. HUGHES, Rupert: *The Complete Detective*, New York (1950)

462. HUMPHREYS, Christmas: *Seven Murderers*, London (1931)

463, HUMPHREYS, Sir Travers: *A Book of Trials*, London (1953)

464. ——: *Criminal Days*, London (1946)

465. HUNT, Peter: *Oscar Slater: The Great Suspect*, London (1951)

466. ——: *The Madeleine Smith Affair*, London (1950)

467. HUSSEY, R F: *Murderer Scot-Free*, Newton Abbot (1973)

468. HYDE, H Montgomery: *Carson*, London (1935)

469. ——: *Cases That Changed the Law*, London (1951)

470. ——: *Crime Has Its Heroes*, London (1976)

471. ——: *Lord Reading*, London (1967)

472. ——: *Norman Birkett: The Life of Lord Birkett of Ulverston*, London (1964)

473. ——: *Sir Patrick Hastings: His Life and Cases*, London (1960)

474. ——: *United in Crime*, London (1855)

475. HYDE, H Montgomery *and* KISCH, John H: *An International Casebook of Crime*, London (1962)

476. HYND, Alan: *Violence in the Night*, London (1955)

477. INGLIS, K S: *The Stuart Case*, Melbourne (1961)

478. IRVING, H B: *A Book of Remarkable Criminals*, London (1918)

479. ——: *Studies of French Criminals of the Nineteenth Century*, London (1901)

480. JACKSON, Brian: *The Black Flag*, London (1981)

481. JACKSON, Christopher: *Manuel*, London (1965)

482. JACKSON, J H: *Murder Book*, New York (1945)

483. JACKSON, Joseph Henry *and* OFFORD, Lenore Glen: *The Girl in the Belfry*, London (1957)

484. JACKSON, Sir Richard: *Occupied With Crime*, London (1967)

485. JACKSON, Robert: *Case for the Prosecution: A Biography of Sir Archibald Bodkin*, London (1962)

486. ——: *Coroner: The Biography of Sir Bentley Purchase*, London (1963)

487. ——: *Francis Camps*, London (1975)

488. ——: *The Chief: The Biography of Gordon Hewart, Lord Chief Justice of England 1922–40*, London (1959)

489. ——: *The Crime Doctors*, London (1966)

490. JACKSON, Stanley: *John George Haigh*, London (1953)

491. ——: *The Old Bailey*, London (1978)

492. ——: *Mr Justice Avory*, London (1935)

493. ——: *The Life and Cases of Mr Justice Humphreys*, London (1955)

494. JACOBS, Philip A: *Famous Australian Trials and Memories of Law*, Melbourne (1943)

495. JACOBS, T C H: *Aspects of Murder*, London (1955)

496. ——: *Cavalcade of Murder*, London (1955)

497. ——: *Pageant of Murder*, London (1956)

498. JAPAN GAZETTE: *Death of Mr W R H Carew* (1896)

499. JESSE, F Tennyson: *Comments on Cain*, London (1948)

500. ——: *Murder and its Motives*, London (1924)

501. JOHNSON, W Branch: *The Age of Arsenic*, London (1931)

502. JONAS, George *and* AMIEL, Barbara: *By Persons Unknown*, Toronto (1977)

503. JONES, Ann: *Women Who Kill*, New York (1980)

504. JONES, Elwyn: *On Trial*, London (1978)

505. ——: *The Last Two to Hang*, London (1966)

506. JONES, Elwyn *and* LLOYD, John: *The Ripper File*, London (1975)

507. JONES, Richard Glyn (Intro): *Poison!*, London 1987)

508 ——: *Unsolved!*, London (1988)

509. JONES, Walter: *My Own Case*, Maidstone (1966)

510. JOWITT, Earl: *Some were Spies*, London (1954)

511. JOYNER, William B: *Murder Squad*, Johannesburg (1968)

512. JUSTICE, Jean: *Murder v. Murder*, Paris (1964)

513. KARPIS, Alvin: *Public Enemy Number One*, New York (1971)

514. KEETON, G W: *Guilty But Insane*, London (1961)

515. KELLEY, Thomas P: *Vengeance of the Black Donnellys*, Winnipeg (1962)

516. KELLY, Alexander: *Jack the Ripper: A Bibliography of the Literature*, London (1973)

517. KELLY, G G: *The Gun in the Case*, Auckland N Z (1963)

518. KELLY, Tom: *Washington's Most Famous Murder Stories*, Washington (1976)

519. KELLY, Vince: *The Charge is Murder*, London (1965)

520. ——: *The Shark Arm Case*, Sydney (1963)

521. KENNAUGH, Robert Charles: *Contemporary Murder*, Johannesburg (1968)

522 KENNEDY, Ludovic: *Ten Rillington Place*, London (1961)

523. ——: *The Airman and the Carpenter*, London (1985)

524. KENT, Arthur: *The Death Doctors*, London (1974)

525. KERSHAW, Alister: *Murder in France*, London (1955)

526. KEYES, Daniel: *Unveiling Claudia*, New York (1986)

527. KEYES, Edward: *The Michigan Murders*, London (1978)

528. KEYLIN, Aileen and DE MIRJIAN, Arto (Ed): *Crime as Reported in the New York Times*, New York (1976)

529. KILGALLEN, Dorothy: *Murder One*, New York (1967)

530. KINDER, Gary: *Victim*, New York (1982)

531. KINGSTON, Charles: *Dramatic Days at the Old Bailey*, London (1923)

532. ——: *Enemies of Society*, London (1927)

533. ——: *Law-Breakers*, London (1930)

534. ——: *Remarkable Rogues*, London (n.d.)

535 ——: *Rogues and Adventuresses*, London (1928)

536. KINSLEY, Peter and SMYTH, Frank: *I'm Jack*, London (1980)

537. KIRKPATRICK, Sidney D: *A Cast of Killers*, New York (1986)

538. KLAUS, Samuel: *The Molineux Case*, London (1929)

539. KLAUSNER, L D: *Son of Sam*, New York (1981)

540. KNIGHT, Stephen: *Jack the Ripper: The Final Solution*, London (1976)

541 KNOWLES, Leonard: *Court of Drama*, London (1966)

542. KNOX, Bill: *Court of Murder*, London (1968)

543. KOBLER, John: *The Trial of Ruth Snyder and Judd Gray*, New York (1938)

544. KUNSTLER, William A: *The Minister and the Choir Singer*, London (1964)

545. KURTH, Ann: *Prescription: Murder*, New York (1976)

546. KWITNY, Jonathan: *The Mullendore Murder Case*, New York (1974)

547. LA BERN, A: *Haigh: The Mind of a Murderer*, London (1973)

548. ——: *The Life and Death of a Lady Killer*, London (1967)

549. LABORDE, Jean: *The Dominici Affair*, London (1974)

550. LAMBERT, Richard: *The Universal Provider*, London (1938)

551. ——: *When Justice Faltered*, London (1935)

552. LAMBOURNE, Gerald: *The Fingerprint Story*, London (1984)

553. LAMBTON, Arthur: *Echoes of Causes Célèbres*, London (n.d.)

554. ——: *Thou Shalt Do No Murder*, London (n.d.)

555. LANG, Gordon: *Mr Justice Avory*, London (1935)

556. LANGFORD, Gerald: *The Murder of Stanford White*, Indianapolis, USA (1962)

557. LARSEN, Richard W: *Bundy: The Deliberate Stranger*, New York (1980)

558. LAURENCE, J: *Extraordinary Crimes*, London (1931)

559. LEACH, Charles E: *On Top of the Underworld*, London (1933)

560. LEASOR, James: *Who Killed Sir Harry Oakes?*, London (1983)

561. LEBOURDAIS, Isabel: *The Trial of Steven Truscott*, London (1966)

562. LEBRUN, George P and RADIN, Edward: *It's Time to Tell*, New York (1962)

563. LEESON, B: *Lost London*, London (1934)

564. LEFEBURE, Molly: *Evidence for the Crown*, London (1975)

565. ——: *Murder With A Difference*, London (1958)

566. LEFKOWITZ, Bernard and GROSS, Kenneth G: *The Sting of Justice*, London (1970)

567. LEITH, Rod: *The Prostitute Murders*, New Jersey (1985)

568. LEOPOLD, Nathan F Jr: *Life Plus 99 Years*, London (1958)

569. LESBERG, Sandy (Ed): *Picture History of Crime*, New York (1976)

570. LEVINE, Richard M: *Bad Blood*, London (1983)

571. LEVITT, L: *The Healer*, New York (1980)

572. LEVY J H (Ed): *The Necessity for Criminal Appeal*, London (1899)

573. LEVY, Norman: *The Nan Patterson Case*, New York (1959)

574. LEWIS, Alfred Allen and MACDONELL, Herbert Leon: *The Evidence Never Lies*, New York (1984)

575. LEWIS, Leonard: *Trunk Crimes Past and Present*, London (n.d.)

576. LINCOLN, Victoria: *A Private Disgrace: Lizzie Borden by Daylight*, New York (1967)

577. LINDSAY, Philip: *The Mainspring of Murder*, London (1958)

578. LINDSEY, J: *Suburban Gentleman*, London (1942)

579. LINKLATER, Eric: *The Corpse on Clapham Common*, London (1971)

580. LISNERS, John: *House of Horrors*, London (1983)
581. LISTON, Robert: *Great Detectives*, New York (1966)
582. LIVINGSTON, Armstrong *and* STEIN, John G: *The Murdered and the Missing*, New York (1947)
583. LLOYD, Georgina: *One Was Not Enough*, London (1986)
584. LOCK, Joan: *Tales from Bow Street*, London (1982)
585. ——: *Marlborough Street*, London (1980)
586. ——: *Blue Murder!*, London (1986)
587. LOGAN, Andy: *Against the Evidence*, London (1970)
588. LOGAN, Guy H B: *Dramas of the Dock*, London (1930)
589. ——: *Great Murder Mysteries*, London (1928)
590. ——: *Guilty or Not Guilty?*, London (1928)
591. ——: *Masters of Crime*, London (1928)
592. ——: *Rope, Knife and Chair*, London (1930)
593. ——: *Verdict and Sentence*, London (1935)
594. ——: *Wilful Murder*, London (1935)
595. LONGWORTH, Frank: *With Detectives Round the World*, London (1937)
596. LUCAS, Norman: *The Monster Butler*, London (1979)
597. ——: *The Lucan Mystery*, London (1975)
598. ——: *The Laboratory Detectives*, London (1971)
599. ——: *The Child Killers*, London (1970)
600. ——: *The Murder of Muriel McKay*, London (1971)
601. ——: *The Sex Killers*, London (1974)
602. LUNDE, Donald T: *Murder and Madness*, San Francisco (1976)
603. LUNDE, Donald T *and* MORGAN, Jefferson: *The Die Song* New York (1980)
604. LUNDSGAARDE, Henry P: *Murder in Space City*, New York (1977)
605. LUSTGARTEN, Edgar: *The Illustrated Story of Crime*, London (1976)
606. ——: *A Century of Murderers*, London (1978)
607. ——: *The Judges and the Judged*, London (1961)
608. ——: *Defender's Triumph*, London (1951)
609. ——: *The Business of Murder*, London (1968)
610. ——: *The Chalkpit Murder*, London (1974)
611. ——: *The Murder and the Trial*, London (1960)
612. ——: *The Woman in the Case*, London (1955)
613. ——: *Verdict in Dispute*, London (1949)
614. LYNCH, P P : *No Remedy for Death*, London (1970)
615. LYONS, Frederick J: *George Joseph Smith*, London (1935)
616. MCCAFFERTY, John: *Mac, I've Got a Murder*, London (1975)
617. MCCLEMENT, Fred: *The Strange Case of Ambrose Small*, Toronto (1974)
618. MCCLURE, James: *Killers*, London (1976)
619. MCCOMAS, Francis: *Graveside Companion*, New York (1962)
620. MCCONNELL, Brian : *Found Naked and Dead*, London (1974)
621. ——: *The Evil Firm: The Rise and Fall of the Brothers Kray*, London (1969)
622. MCCONNELL, Brian *and* BENCE, Douglas: *The Nilsen File*, London (1983)
623. MCCONNELL BODKIN, M: *Famous Irish Trials*, London (1918)
624. MCCONNELL, Jean: *The Detectives*, Newton Abbot (1976)
625. MCCORMICK, Donald: *Murder by Witchcraft*, London (1968)
626. ——: *The Identity of Jack the Ripper*, London (1968)
627. ——: *The Red Barn Mystery*, London (1967)
628. MCCURTIN, Peter: *Murder in the Penthouse*, New York (1980)
629. MACDONALD, John: *The Murderer and His Victim*, Springfield, Ohio, USA (1961)
630. MACDONALD, John D: *No Deadly Drug*, New York (1968)
631. MCDONALD R Robin: *Black Widow*, New York (1986)
632. MACDOUGALL, A W: *The Maybrick Case: A Treatise*, London (1891)
633. ——: *The Maybrick Case: A Statement of the Case as a Whole*, London (1891)
634. MACÉ, Gustave: *My First Crime*, London (1886)
635. MAEDER, Thomas: *The Unspeakable Crimes of Dr Petiot*, Boston (1980)
636. MCGINNISS, Joe: *Fatal Vision*, New York (1983)
637. MACGREGOR, G: *The History of Burke and Hare*, London (1884)
638. MACKAYE, Milton: *Dramatic Crimes of 1927*, New York (1928)
639. MACKENZIE, F A: *World Famous Crimes*, London (1927)
640. MCKERNAN, M (Ed): *The Crime and Trial of Leopold and Loeb*, New York (1957)
641. MCLEAVE, Hugh: *Chesney – The Fabulous Murderer*, London (n.d.)
642. MCLAUGHLIN, Terence: *The Coward's Weapon*, London (1980)
643. MCKNIGHT, Gerald: *The Murder Squad*, London (1967)
644. MAILER, Norman: *The Executioner's Song*, London (1979)
645. MALLON, Andrew: *Leonski*, Victoria (1979)
646. MARCHBANKS, D: *The Moors Murders*, London (1966)
647. MARHAM, Patrick: *Trail of Havoc*, London (1987)
648. MARJORIBANKS, Edward: *The Life of Lord Carson*, London (1963)
649. ——: *The Life of Sir Edward Marshall Hall*, London (1929)
650. MARKS, L *and* VAN DEN BERGH, T: *Ruth Ellis: A Case of Diminished Responsibility*, London (1977)
651. MARNE, Patricia: *Crime and Sex in Handwriting*, London (1981)
652. MASSIE, Allen: *Ill Met by Moonlight*, London (1980)
653. MASTERS, Brian: *Killing for Company*, London (1985)
654. MASTERS, R E L *and* LEA, Edward: *Sex Crimes in History*, New York (1966)

Bibliography

655. MATTERS, Leonard: *The Mystery of Jack the Ripper*, London (1928)

656. MATTHEWS, David A: *Crime Doctor*, London (1959)

657. MAXWELL, R: *The Christie Case*, London (n.d.)

658. MAY, H J: *Murder by Consent*, London (1968)

659. MAYBRICK, F E: *Mrs Maybrick's Own Story*, London (1904)

660. MAYCOCK, Sir Willoughby: *Celebrated Crimes and Criminals*, London (1890)

661. MEADLEY, Robert (Ed): *Classics in Murder*, London (1984)

662. MEWSHAW, Michael: *Money to Burn*, New York (1987)

663. MEYER, Gerald: *The Memphis Murders*, New York (1974)

664. MEYER, Peter: *The Death of Innocence*, New York (1985)

665. MICHAUD, Stephen G and AYNESWORTH, Hugh: *The Only Living Witness*, New York (1983)

666. MILLEN, Ernest: *Specialist in Crime*, London (1972)

667. MILLER, James William: *Don't Call Me Killer!*, Victoria (1984)

668. MILLER, Orlo: *The Donnellys Must Die*, Toronto (1962)

669. MILLER, Webb: *I Found No Peace*, London (1936)

670. MOISEWITSCH, Maurice: *Five Famous Trials*, London (1962)

671. MOLOMBY, Tom: *Ratten – The Web of Circumstance*, Victoria (1978)

672. MOONEY, M M: *Evelyn Nesbit and Stanford White*, New York (1976)

673. MOORE, Sally: *Lucan: Not Guilty*, London (1987)

674. MORAIN, Alfred: *The Underworld of Paris*, London (1928)

675. MORIKAWA, Tetsuro: *The Truth About the Teigin Incident*, Tokyo (1977)

676. MORLAND, Nigel: *Background to Murder*, London (1955)

677. ——: *Hangman's Clutch*, London (1954)

678. ——: *International Pattern of Murder*, London (1977)

679. ——: *Pattern of Murder*, London (1966)

680. ——: *That Nice Miss Smith*, London (1957)

681. ——: *This Friendless Lady*, London (1957)

682. MORRIS, H H: *The First Forty Years*, Johannesburg (1948)

683. MORRIS, Richard B: *Fair Trial*, New York (1952)

684. MORRIS, Terence and BLOM-COOPER, Louis: *Murder in England and Wales Since 1957*, London (1979)

685. ——: *A Calendar of Murder*, London (1964)

686. MORSHEAD, Ian: *The Life and Murder of Henry Morshead*, Cambridge (1982)

687. MORTIMER, John: *Famous Trials*, London (1984)

688. MUNCIE, William: *Crime Pond*, Edinburgh (1979)

689. MURRAY, John Wilson: *Memoirs of a Great Detective*, London (1904)

690. MUSMANNO, Michael A: *Verdict!*, New York (1958)

691. NAPLEY, Sir David: *Murder at the Villa Madeira*, London (1988)

692. ——: *Not Without Prejudice*, London (1982)

693. NASH, Jay Robert: *Bloodletters and Badmen*, New York (1973)

694. NASSAU DAILY TRIBUNE: *The Murder of Sir Harry Oakes Bt*, Nassau (1959)

695. NEIL, Arthur Fowler: *Forty Years of Manhunting*, London (1932)

696. NESBIT, Evelyn: *The Untold Story*, London (1934)

697. NEUSTATTER, W Lindesay: *The Mind of the Murderer*, London (1957)

698. NEVILLE, Richard and CLARKE, Julie: *The Life and Crimes of Charles Sobhraj*, London (1979)

699. NICHOLLS, Ernest: *Crime Within the Square Mile*, London (1935)

700. NICHOLSON, Michael: *The Yorkshire Ripper*, London (1979)

701. NOGUCHI, Thomas: *Coroner at Large*, New York (1985)

702. NOGUCHI, Thomas with DIMONA, Joseph: *Coroner to the Stars*, London (1984)

703. NORMAN, C: *The Genteel Murderer*, New York (1956)

704. O'BRIEN, Darcy: *Two of a Kind: The Hillside Stranglers*, New York (1985)

705. ODDIE, S Ingleby: *Inquest*, London (1941)

706. ODELL, Robin: *Exhumation of a Murder*, London (1975)

707. ——: *Jack the Ripper in Fact and Fiction*, London (1965)

708. O'DONNELL, Bernard: *The World's Strangest Murders*, London (1957)

709. ——: *Cavalcade of Justice*, London (1951

710. ——: *Crime That Made News*, London (1954)

711. ——: *Should Women Hang?*, London (1956)

712. ——: *The Trials of Mr Justice Avory*, London (1935)

713. O'FLAHERTY, M: *Have You Seen This Woman?* London (1971)

714. OLSEN, Jack: *The Man With the Candy*, New York (1974)

715. O'SULLIVAN, J S O: *A Most Unique Ruffian*, Melbourne (1968)

716. OSWALD, H R: *Memoirs of a London County Coroner*, London (1936)

717. PACKER, Edward: *The Peasenhall Murder*, Oxford (1980)

718. PARK, W: *The Truth About Oscar Slater*, London (1927)

719. PARKER, Tony: *The Plough Boy*, London (1965)

720. PARMITER, Geoffrey de C: *Reasonable Doubt*, London (1928)

721. PARRIS, John: *Most of my Murders*, London (1960)

722. PARRISH J M and CROSSLAND, J R: *The Fifty Most Amazing Crimes of the Last Hundred Years*, London (1936)

723. PARRY, Edward Abbott: *The Drama of the Law*, London (1924)

724. PARRY, Leonard A: *Some Famous Medical Trials*, London (1927)

725. PEARCE, Charles E: *Unsolved Murder Mysteries*, London (1924)
726. PEARSON, Edmund: *Five Murders*, New York (1928)
727. ——: *Instigation of the Devil*, New York (1950)
728. ——: *More Studies in Murder*, London (1953)
729. PEARSON, Edmund: *Murder at Smutty Nose and Other Murders*, London (1927)
730. ——: *Studies in Murder*, New York (1924)
731. ——: *Trial of Lizzie Borden*, London (1939)
732. PEARSON, Francis: *Memories of a KC's Clerk*, London (1935)
733. PEARSON, John: *The Profession of Violence*, London (1972)
734. PEJSA, Jane: *The Molineux Affair*, New York (1983)
735. PERRY, Hamilton Darby: *A Chair for Wayne Lonergan*, London (1972)
736. PESKETT, S John: *Grim, Gruesome and Grisly*, London (1974)
737. PHILLIPS, Conrad: *Murderer's Moon*, London (1956)
738. PICTON, Bernard: *Murder, Accident or Suicide*, London (1971)
739. PIERREPOINT, Albert: *Executioner: Pierrepoint*, London (1974)
740. PITKIN, J: *The Prison Cell and Its Light and Shadows*, London (1918)
741. PLAIDY, Jean: *A Triptych of Poisoners*, London (1958)
742. PLAYFAIR, Giles: *Crime in Our Century*, London (1977)
743. PLAYFAIR, Giles *and* SINGTON, Derrick: *The Offenders*, London (1957)
744. POLLACK, Jack Harrison: *Dr Sam – An American Tragedy*, Chicago (1957)
745. POLLOCK, George: *Mr Justice McCardie*, London (1934)
746. POSTGATE, Raymond: *Murder, Piracy and Treason*, London (1925)
747. POTTER, J D: *The Monster of the Moors*, London (1966)
748. POYNTER, J W: *Forgotten Crimes*, London (1928)
749. PRESLEY, James *and* GETTY, Gerald W: *Public Defender*, New York (1974)
750. PURVIS, James: *Great Unsolved Mysteries*, New York (1978)
751. RADIN, Edward D: *Crimes of Passion*, New York (1953)
752. ——: *Headline Crimes of the Year*, Boston (1952)
753. ——: *Lizzie Borden: The Untold Story*, New York (1961)
754. ——: *Twelve Against the Law*, New York (1953)
755. RAE, George W: *Confessions of the Boston Strangler*, London (1967)
756. RAE, Isobel: *Knox the Anatomist*, Edinburgh (1964)
757. RANDALL, Leslie: *The Famous Cases of Sir Bernard Spilsbury*, London 1936)
758. RAPHAEL, John N: *The Caillaux Drama*, London (1914)
759. RAWLINGS, William: *A Case for the Yard*, London (1961)
760. RAWSON, Tabor: *I Want to Live*, New York (1958)
761. READING, Marquess of: *Rufus Isaacs: First Marquess of Reading*, London (1942)
762. REID, D *and* GURWELL, J: *Eyewitness*, Houston (1973)
763. REINHARDT, James Melvin: *The Murderous Trail of Charles Starkweather*, Springfield, Ohio, USA (1960)
764. REUBEN, William A: *The Mark Fein Case*, New York (1967)
765. RICE, Craig: *Forty-Five Murderers*, New York (1952)
766. RITCHIE, Jean: *Myra Hindley – Inside the Mind of a Murderess*, London :1988)
767. ROBERTS, G D: *Law and Life*, London (1964)
768. ROBEY, Edward: *The Jester and the Court*, London (1976)
769. ROBINSON, Edward: *Just Murder*, London (1947)
770. RODELL, Marie F (Ed): *Charleston Murders*, New York (1947)
771. ——: *Chicago Murders*, New York (1945)
772. ——: *Cleveland Murders*, New York (1947)
773. ——: *Denver Murders*, New York (1946)
774. ——: *Detroit Murders*, New York (1948)
775. ——: *Los Angeles Murders*, New York (1947)
776. ——: *New York Murders*, New York (1944)
777. ——: *San Francisco Murders*, New York (1947)
778. ROEN, Samuel: *Murder of a Little Girl*, New York (1973)
779. ROOT, Jonathan: *The Life and Bad Times of Charlie Becker*, London (1962)
780. ROUGHEAD, William: *Classic Crimes*, London (1951)
781. ——: *Famous Crimes*, London (1935)
782. ——: *Tales of the Criminous*, London (1956)
783. ——: *The Act of Murder*, New York (1943)
784. ——: *Rogues Walk Here*, London (1934)
785. ——: *Mainly Murder*, London (1937)
786. ——: *Murder and More Murder*, New York (1939)
787. ——: *What is Your Verdict?*, London (1931)
788. ROVERE, Richard H: *Howe and Hummel*, New York (1947)
789. ROWAN, David: *Famous American Crimes*, London (1957)
790. ——: *Famous European Crimes*, London (1955)
791. ROWLAND, John: *Criminal Files*, London (1957)
792. ——: *More Criminal Files*, London (1958)
793. ——: *Murder Mistaken*, London (1963)
794. ——: *Murder Revisited*, London (1961)
795. ——: *Poisoner in the Dock*, London (1960)
796. ——: *The Peasenhall Mystery*, London (1962)
797. ——: *The Wallace Case*, London (1949)
798. ——: *Unfit to Plead*, London (1965)
799. RULE, Ann: *The Stranger Beside Me*, New York (1980)
800. RUMBELOW, Donald: *The Complete Jack the Ripper*, London (1987)
801. RUSSELL, Donn: *Best Murder Cases*, London (1958)
802. RUSSELL, Francis: *Tragedy in Dedham*, London (1963)

Bibliography

803. RUSSELL, Guy: *Guilty or Not Guilty?*, London (1931)

804. RUSSELL, J D: *A Chronicle of Death*, Woodbridge, USA (1971)

805. RUSSELL, Lord: *Deadman's Hill: Was Hanratty Guilty?*, London (1965)

806. ——: *Though the Heavens Fall*, London (1956)

807. RYAN, B *with* HAVERS, Sir Michael: *The Poisoned Life of Mrs Maybrick*, London (1977)

808. SAMUELS, Charles: *Death Was the Bridegroom*, New York (1958)

809. ——: *The Girl in the Red Velvet Swing*, New York (1953)

810. SAMUELS, Charles and Louise: *The Girl in the House of Hate*, London (n.d.)

811. SANDERS, Bruce: *Killers Unknown*, London (1960)

812. ——: *Murder Behind the Bright Lights*, London (1958)

813. ——: *Murder in Big Cities*, London (1962)

814. ——: *Murder in Lonely Places*, London (1960)

815. ——: *They Caught These Killers*, London (1968)

816. ——: *They Couldn't Lose the Body*, London (1966)

817. SANDERS, Ed: *The Family*, New York (1970)

818. SAUNDERS, Edith: *The Mystery of Marie Lafarge*, London (1951)

819. SAVAGE, Percy: *Savage of Scotland Yard*, London (1934)

820. SCADUTO, Anthony: *Scapegoat*, London (1976)

821. SCHMALZBACH, Oscar R: *Profiles of Murder*, Sydney (1971)

822. SCHOFIELD, Carey: *Mesrine*, London (1980)

823. SCHREIBER, Flora Rheta: *The Shoemaker*, New York (1983)

824. SCHWARTZ, Ted: *The Hillside Strangler*, New York (1981)

825. SCHWARTZ-NOBEL, Loretta: *Engaged to Murder*, New York (1987)

826. SCOTT, Sir Harold (Ed): *Crime and Criminals*, London (1961)

827. ——: *Scotland Yard*, London (1954)

828. SECCOMBE, Thomas (Ed): *Twelve Bad Men*, London (1894)

829. SEEDMAN, A A: *Chief!*, New York (1974)

830. SELLWOOD, Arthur and Mary: *Victorian Railway Murders*, London (1979)

831. SERENY, Gitta: *The Case of Mary Bell*, London (1972)

832. SETH, Ronald: *Petiot*, London (1962)

833. SHANKLAND, Peter: *Death of an Editor*, London (1981)

834. SHAPIRO, Fred C: *Whitmore*, London (1969)

835. SHARKEY, Terence: *Jack the Ripper: A Hundred Years of Investigation*, London (1987)

836. SHARP, James: *The Life and Death of Michael X*, Trinidad (1981)

837. SHARPE, Alan: *Australian Crimes*, Sydney (1979)

838. ——: *Crimes That Shocked Australia*, Sydney (1982)

839. SHARPE, F D: *Sharpe of the Flying Squad*, London (1938)

840. SHELMAN, Byron E: *Death Row Chaplain*, New York (1962)

841. SHEPPARD, Sam: *Endure and Conquer*, Cleveland, Ohio, USA (1966)

842. SHEPPARD, Stephen: *My Brother's Keeper*, New York (1964)

843. SHERIDAN, Leo W: *I Killed for the Law*, New York (1938)

844. SHEW, E Spencer: *Companion to Murder*, London (1960)

845. ——: *Second Companion to Murder*, London (1961)

846. SHORE, W Teignmouth: *Crime and its Detection*, London (1931)

847. SHULTZ, Gladys Denny: *How Many More Victims?*, Philadelphia (1965)

848. SIFAKIS, Carl: *The Encylopaedia of American Crime*, New York (1982)

849. SILK, Stafford: *The Bogle Mystery*, Sydney (1963)

850. SIMPSON, Helen et al: *The Anatomy of Murder*, New York (1937)

851. SIMPSON, Keith: *Forty Years of Murder*, London (1978)

852. SINGER, Kurt (ed): *Crime Omnibus*, London (1961)

853. ——: *My Greatest Crime Story*, London (1956)

854. ——: *My Strangest Case*, London (1958)

855. SINGER, Kurt *and* SHERROD, Jane: *Great Adventures in Crime*, Minneapolis, USA (1962)

856. SINGULAR, Stephen: *Talked to Death*, New York (1987)

857. SKELHORN, Sir Norman: *Public Prosecutor*, London (1981)

858. SLIPPER, Jack: *Slipper of the Yard*, London (1981)

859. SMITH, Arthur: *Lord Goddard*, London (1959)

860. SMITH, Edgar: *Brief Against Death*, New York (1968)

861. ——: *Getting Out*, New York (1972)

862. SMITH, Edward H: *Famous American Poison Mysteries*, London (1926)

863. ——: *Mysteries of the Missing*, New York (1927)

864. SMITH, Graham: *Death of a Rose Grower*, London (1985)

865. SMITH, Sir Sydney: *Mostly Murder*, London (1959)

866. SMITH-HUGHES, Jack: *Eight Studies in Justice*, London (1953)

867. ——: *Unfair Comment Upon Some Victorian Murder Trials*, London (1951)

868. SMYTH, Frank *and* LUDWIG, Myles: *The Detectives*, London (1978)

869. SOMERFIELD, Stafford: *The Authentic Story of J G Haigh*, Manchester (1950)

870. SPAIN, David M: *Post Mortem*, New York (1974)

871. SPARROW, Gerald: *Satan's Children*, London (1966)

872. ——: *Vintage Victorian and Edwardian Murder*, London (1971)

873. SPEER, W H: *The Secret History of Crimes*, London (1929)

874. SPENCER, Duncan: *Love Gone Wrong*, New York (1981)

875. SPIERING, Frank: *Lizzie*, New York (1984)

876. ——: *Prince Jack*, New York (1978)
877. STACK, Andy: *Lust Killer*, New York (1983)
878. ——: *The Want-Ad Killer*, New York (1983)
879. STAPLETON, J W: *The Great Crime of 1860*, London (1861)
880. ST AUBIN, Giles: *Infamous Victorians*, London (1971)
881. ST CLAIR, David: *Say You Love Satan*, New York (1983)
882. STEAD, Philip John: *The Memoirs of Lacenaire*, London (1952)
883. STEIGER, Brad: *Mass Murderer*, New York (1967)
884. STEVENS, C H McCluer: *Famous Crimes and Criminals*, London (1924)
885. ——: *From Clue to Dock*, London (1927)
886. STEWART, William: *Jack the Ripper*, London (1939)
887. STILL, Charles E: *Styles in Crime*, Philadelphia (1938)
888. STILL, Larry: *The Limits of Sanity*, Toronto (1972)
889. STODDART, Charles: *Bible John*, Edinburgh (1980)
890. STONE, Irving: *Clarence Darrow For the Defence*, London (1949)
891. SULLIVAN, Gerald *and* ARONSON, Harvey: *High Hopes: the Amityville Murders*, New York (1981)
892. SULLIVAN, Robert: *Goodbye Lizzie Borden*, London (1975)
893. ——: *The Disappearance of Dr Parkman*, New York (1971)
894. SULLIVAN, Terry *and* MAIKEN, Peter T: *Killer Clown*, New York (1983)
895. SUSSMAN, Lesley (Contributor): *Murder Most Eerie*, Norfolk, Virginia, USA (1982)
896. SUTHERLAND, Sidney: *Ten Real Murder Mysteries Never Solved*, New York (1929)
897. SYMONS, Julian: *Beyond A Reasonable Doubt*, London (1960)
898. TALLANT, Robert: *Murder in New Orleans*, London (1953)
899. TANENBAUM, Robert K *and* GREENBERG, Peter S: *The Piano Teacher*, New York (1987)
900. TAYLOR, Bernard: *Cruelly Murdered*, London (1929)
901. TAYLOR, Bernard *and* KNIGHT, Stephen: *Perfect Murder*, London (1987)
902. TAYLOR, Lawrence: *Trail of the Fox*, London (1981)
903. TEETERS, Negley *with* HEDBLOM, Jack H: *". . . Hang by the Neck . . ."*, Springfield, Ohio, USA (1967)
904. THAW, Harry K: *The Traitor*, New York (1926)
905. THOMAS, David: *Seek Out The Guilty*, London (1960)
906. THOMPSON, C J S: *Poisons and Poisoners*, London (1931)
907. ——: *Poison Mysteries in History, Romance and Crime*, London (1925)
908. ——: *Poison Mysteries Unsolved*, London (1937)
909. THOMPSON: *Blood and Money*, New York (1976)
910. ——: *Serpentine*, New York (1981)
911. THOMSON, Basil: *The Criminal*, London (1925)
912. THOMSON, Helen: *Murder at Harvard*, Boston (1871)
913. THORP, Arthur: *Calling Scotland Yard*, London (1954)
914. THORWALD, Jurgen: *Crime and Science*, New York (1967)
915. ——: *Dead Men Tell Tales*, London (1966)
916. ——: *Marks of Cain*, London (1965)
917. ——: *Proof of Poison*, London (1966)
918. ——: *The Century of the Detective*, New York (1965)
919. TIDYMAN, Ernest: *Dummy*, Boston, USA (1974)
920. TOTTERDELL, G H: *Country Copper*, London (1956)
921. TOWNSEND, W and L: *Black Cap*, London (1930)
922. TRAIN, Arthur: *True Stories of Crime*, New York (1908)
923. TRAINI, Robert: *Murder for Sex*, London (1960)
924. TRAVERS, Robert: *Murder in the Blue Mountains*, London (1972)
925. TREADWELL, C A L: *Notable New Zealand Trials*, New Plymouth, NZ (1936)
926. TRENT, Bill *with* TRUSCOTT, Steven: *Who Killed Lynn Harper?* Montreal (1979)
927. TRILLING, Diana: *Mrs Harris*, New York (1981)
928. TULLETT, Tom: *Strictly Murder*, London (1979)
929. ——: *No Answer From Foxtrot Eleven*, London (1967)
930. ——: *Portrait of a Badman*, London (1956)
931. TURNER, C H: *The Inhumanists*, London (1932)
932. TWYMAN, H W: *The Best Laid Schemes . . .*, London (1931)
933. TYLER, Froom: *Gallows Parade*, London (1933)
934. UNDERWOOD, Peter: *Jack the Ripper – One Hundred Years of Mystery*, London (1987)
935. VALENTI, Michael: *Question of Guilt*, New York (1966)
936. VALENTINE, Steven: *The Black Panther Story*, London (1976)
937. VAN EVERY, Edward: *Sins of New York*, New York (1930)
938. VANSTONE, Charles: *A Man in Plain Clothes*, London (1961)
939. VEALE, F J P: *The Wallace Case*, Brighton (1950)
940. VON FEUERBACH, Anselm Ritter: *Narratives of Remarkable Criminal Trials*, London (1846)
941. VON SONNENBERG, E L *and* TRETTIN, O: *Continental Crimes*, London (1935)
942. VILLIERS, Elizabeth: *Riddles in Crime*, London (1928)
943. WAGNER, Diane: *Corpus Delicti*, New York (1986)
944. WAGNER, Margaret Seaton: *The Monster of Düsseldorf*, London (1932)
945. WAKEFIELD H Russell: *Landru*, London (1936)
946. ——: *The Green Bicycle Case*, London (1930)
947. WALBROOK, H M: *Murders and Murder Trials 1812–1912*, London (1932)
948. WALKER-SMITH, Derek: *Lord Reading and His Cases*, London (1934)

949. ——: *The Life of Mr Justice Darling*, London (1938)

950. WALKER-SMITH, Derek *and* CLARKE, Edward: *The Life and Famous Cases of Sir Edward Clarke*, London (1939)

951. WALLER, George: *Kidnap*, London (1961)

952. WALLING, George W: *Recollections of a New York Chief of Police*, New York (1887)

953. WALLS, H J: *Expert Witness*, London (1972)

954. WALSH, Sir Cecil: *The Agra Double Murder*, London (1929)

955. WALTON, Mary: *For Love of Money*, New York (1987)

956. WAMBAUGH, Joseph: *Echoes of Darkness*, New York (1987)

957. WARD, D: *King of the Lags*, London (1963)

958. 'WARDEN': *His Majesty's Guests*, London (n.d.)

959. WARDEN, R *and* GROVES, M (Ed): *America's Murder Most Foul*, New York (1980)

960. WARNER HOOKE, Nina *and* THOMAS, Gil: *Marshall Hall*, London (1966)

961. WEBB, Duncan: *Crime is My Business*, London (1953)

962. ——: *Deadline for Crime*, London (1955)

963. ——: *Line-up For Crime*, London (1956)

964. WENSLEY, Frederick Porter: *Detective Days*, London (1931)

965. WERTHAM, Frederick: *The Show of Violence*, New York (1949)

966. WEST, Rebecca: *A Train of Powder*, London (1955)

967. WHIPPLE, Sidney B: *The Lindbergh Crime*, New York (1935)

968. ——: *The Trial of Hauptmann*, London (n.d.)

969. WHITBREAD, J R: *The Railway Policemen*, London (1961)

970. WHITELAW, David: *Corpus Delicti*, London (1936)

971. WHITELEY, Cecil: *Brief Life*, London (1942)

972. WHITTINGTON-EGAN, Richard: *A Casebook on Jack the Ripper*, London (1975)

973. ——: *The Ordeal of Philip Yale Drew*, London (1972)

974. ——: *The Riddle of Birdhurst Rise*, London (1975)

975. WILD, Roland: *Crimes and Cases of 1933*, London (1934)

976. ——: *Crimes and Cases of 1934* (London 1935)

977. ——: *The Jury Retires*, London (1937)

978. WILKES, Roger: *Wallace: The Final Verdict*, London (1984)

979. WILKINS, Philip A: *Dramas of the French Courts*, London (n.d.)

980. ——: *Inside the French Courts*, London (n.d.)

981. WILKINSON, Lawrence: *Behind the Face of Crime*, London (1957)

982. WILLCOX, Philip H: *The Detective-Physician*, London (1970)

983. WILLIAMS, Brad: *Due Process*, London (1961)

984. WILLIAMS, E: *Beyond Belief*, London (1967)

985. WILLIAMS, Guy: *The Black Treasures of Scotland Yard*, London (1973)

986. WILLIAMS, John: *Hume: Portrait of a Double Murderer*, London (1960)

987. WILLIAMS, J: *Suddenly at the Priory*, London (1957)

988. WILLIAMS, Montague: *Leaves of a Life*, London (1891)

989. WILLIAMSON, W H: *Annals of Crime*, London (1930)

990. WILLEMSE, Cornelius W: *A Cop Remembers*

991. WILSON, Colin: *A Casebook of Murder*, London (1959)

992. ——: *Order of Assassins*, London (1972)

993. ——: (Intro) *Murder in the West Country*, Bodmin, Cornwall (1975)

994. WILSON, Colin *and* ODELL, Robin: *Jack the Ripper: Summing-up and Verdict*, London (1987)

995. WILSON, Colin *and* PITMAN, Pat: *Encyclopaedia of Murder*, London (1961)

996. WILSON, Colin *and* SEAMAN, Donald: *Encyclopaedia of Modern Murder*, London (1983)

997. WILSON, H J (Ed): *The Bayly Case*, Wellington NZ (1934)

998. WILSON, John Gray: *Not Proven*, London (1960)

999. WILSON, J G: *The Trial of Peter Manuel*, London (1959)

1000. WILSON, Patrick: *Children Who Kill*, London (1973)

1001. ——: *Murderess*, London (1971)

1002. WILSON, Robert: *Devil's Disciples*, London (1986)

1003. WINSLOW, L Forbes: *Recollections of Forty Years*, London (1910)

1004. WOLFE, Linda: *The Professor and the Prostitute*, New York (1986)

1005. WOOD, Stuart: *Shades in the Prison House*, London (1932)

1006. WOOD, Walter (Ed): *Survivors' Tales of Famous Crimes*, London (1916)

1007. WOODHALL, Edwin T: *Detective and Secret Service Days*, London (n.d.)

1008. ——: *Jack the Ripper: Or When London Walked in Terror*, London (1937)

1009. ——: *Secrets of Scotland Yard*, London (1936)

1010. WOODLAND, W Lloyd: *Assize Pageant*, London (1925)

1011. WRAXALL, Sir Lascelles: *Criminal Celebrities*, London (1863)

1012. WYDEN, Peter: *The Hired Killers*, London (1964)

1013. WYNDHAM, Horace: *Consider Your Verdict*, London (1946)

1014. ——: *Crime on the Continent*, London (1928)

1015. ——: *Dramas of the Law*, London (n.d.)

1016. ——: *Famous Trials Retold*, London (n.d.)

1017. ——: *Feminine Frailty*, London (1929)

1018. WYNDHAM-BROWN, W F: *The Trial of William Herbert Wallace*, London (1933)

1019. YALLOP, David A: *Deliver Us From Evil*, London (1981)

1020. ——: *Beyond Reasonable Doubt*, Auckland NZ (1978)

1021. ——: *To Encourage The Others*, London (1971)

1022. YOUNG, Gordon: *Valley of Silence*, London (1955)

1023. YOUNG, Hugh: *My Forty Years at the Yard*, London (1955)

1024. YOUNG, Winifred: *Obsessive Poisoner*, London (1973)

1025. ZAMORA, William: *Trial By Your Peers*, New York (1973)

Additions to the Bibliography

1026. ANDERSON, Christopher P: *The Serpent's Tooth*, New York (1987)

1027. BEGG, Paul: *Jack the Ripper: The Uncensored Facts*, London (1988)

1028. CANNING, John (Ed): *Unsolved Murders and Mysteries*, London (1987)

1029. LANE, Brian (Ed): *The Murder Club Guides*, London (1988)

1030. MILLS, James: *The Prosecutor*, New York (1988)

1031. MUNN, Michael: *The Hollywood Murder Casebook*, London (1987)

1032. SIGGINS, Maggie: *A Canadian Tragedy*, Toronto (1987)

Specialist Booksellers

(Booksellers specializing in second-hand, non-fiction crime
books)

Rod and Margot Armitage,
16 The Nook, Crookesmoor, Sheffield, S10 1EJ England.

Clifford Elmer,
8 Balmoral Avenue, Cheadle Hulme, Cheadle, Cheshire, SK8 5EQ, England.

W.H. Gillespie,
Tutt's Cottage, Manor Close, The Street, East Preston, Sussex, England.

Grey House Books,
12a Lawrence Street, Chelsea, London, SW3 5NE, England.

J.C.G. Hammond,
Crown Point, 33 Waterside, Ely, Cambridge, CB7 4AU, England.

Patterson Smith,
23 Prospect Terrace, Montclair, New Jersey 07042, USA.

Frank R. Thorold (Pty) Ltd.,
4th Floor, S.A. Fire House, 103 Fox Street, Johannesburg, South Africa.

Wildy & Sons Limited,
Lincoln's Inn Archway, Carey Street, London, WC2, England.

Richard Williams,
Unit C, 24 Dunstall Street, Scunthorpe, South Humberside, England.

Those who have enjoyed reading this book about crimes past and present will also enjoy three monthly magazines: *True Detective*, *Master Detective* and *True Crime*, all of which deal with murder throughout the world. They are published by Argus Consumer Publications Ltd, 12/18 Paul Street, London EC2A, 4JS, England.

Classified Index of Cases

The letter code in brackets following each entry denotes the country in which the death of the victim took place.

(ASH)	Ashanti (Ghana)	(IND)	India
(AUST)	Australia	(IRE)	Ireland
(AUS)	Austria	(JAP)	Japan
(BAH)	Bahamas	(KEN)	Kenya
(BELG)	Belgium	(MON)	Monaco
(BER)	Bermuda	(NOR)	Norway
(CAN)	Canada	(NZ)	New Zealand
(CHIL)	Chile	(SA)	South Africa
(FRA)	France	(SL)	Sri Lanka
(GER)	Germany	(TRI)	Trinidad
(GRE)	Greece	(UK)	United Kingdom
(HUN)	Hungary	(USA)	United States of America

Classified Index